REVIEW of EDUCATIONAL RESEARCH

Volume VI   FEBRUARY, 1936   Number 1

MENTAL AND PHYSICAL DEVELOPMENT

This issue revises and brings down to date the Review of Educational Research for April, 1933, entitled *Mental and Physical Development*.

AMERICAN EDUCATIONAL RESEARCH ASSOCIATION
A Department of the
NATIONAL EDUCATION ASSOCIATION
1201 SIXTEENTH STREET NORTHWEST
WASHINGTON, D. C.

AMERICAN EDUCATIONAL RESEARCH ASSOCIATION

THIS ASSOCIATION is composed of persons who are engaged in technical research in education, including directors of research in school systems, instructors in educational institutions, and research workers connected with private educational agencies. The Association became a department of the National Education Association in July, 1930.

Officers of the Association for 1935-36

President
PHILIP A. BOYER
Philadelphia Public Schools

Vice-President
HOLLIS L. CASWELL
George Peabody College for Teachers

Secretary-Treasurer
WILLIAM G. CARR
Research Division
National Education Association

Executive Committee
The president, vice-president, and secretary, *ex officio*, and the following past presidents:

T. C. HOLY
Ohio State University

PAUL T. RANKIN
Detroit Public Schools

EDITORIAL BOARD, 1935-36
FRANK N. FREEMAN, *Chairman*, University of Chicago
MARGARET A. NORTON, 464 Riverside Drive, New York City
WALTER E. MORGAN, California State Department of Education, Sacramento
The President and Secretary, *ex-officio*

Active Membership—Persons desiring membership may obtain an application form from the office of the Secretary-Treasurer. This form when properly filled in should be submitted to the Secretary-Treasurer for the consideration of the Executive Committee. Upon approval of the application by the Executive Committee the person applying will be invited to become a member of the Association. The Executive Committee has defined the qualifications for membership as follows:

Membership in the Association is restricted to persons of good ability and sound training who are working in the field of educational research, and who can present satisfactory evidence in the form of published or unpublished studies which show ability to arrange, to organize, and to conduct research investigations and experiments. In addition, evidence of an abiding interest in the field of educational research is essential.

Membership in the National Education Association is a prerequisite to active membership in the American Educational Research Association. Any form of N. E. A. membership—annual, five-dollar, or life—satisfies the preliminary requirement.

Active members of the Association pay dues of $5.00 per year. Of this amount $4.00 is for subscription to the REVIEW. See back inside cover page of this Issue. The REVIEW is published in February, April, June, October, and December each year.

Entered as second-class matter April 10, 1931, at the post office at Washington, D. C., under the Act of August 24, 1912.

CHAPTER I
The Development of Intelligence and Motor Control in Infancy

The Neonate

DURING THE LAST THREE YEARS there have been a number of studies published on the activities of the newborn infant during the hospital period, the age range usually being from a few minutes or a few hours after birth to ten or twenty days of age, when the baby leaves the hospital.

Irwin (41, 42, 45) used the stabilimeter-polygraph technic which automatically records all movements made by the infant. The infant was placed on the stabilimeter for three and one-fourth hours in the afternoon between two feedings. The average number of oscillations caused by the movements of the infant was 31.6 per minute and the individual variations were enormous. The standard deviation was 31.8. One two-day-old infant averaged only 0.8 oscillations per minute while another averaged 74.7. One nine-day-old child made 10.7 movements per minute while another of the same age made 175.2 or approximately ninety times as many. The above results corroborate an earlier study in which a continuous record of four infants was kept for twenty-four hours and the average number of oscillations recorded per minute was 31.6. There was a rapid increase in motility between the first and fourth day, the average number of movements before the fourth day being about seventeen and thereafter in the neighborhood of thirty-eight. No relationship between motility and sex (45), body temperature (46), physical measurements (49), nutritional status (46), or sleep (42) was found. Pratt (63) also found no relation between sex or race and bodily activity, or between bodily activity and change in temperature between 74 and 88 degrees or change in humidity between 22 and 90 percent.

When the period of three and one-fourth hours between feedings was divided into fifteen-minute periods, there was a fairly constant increase in the number of movements from an average of seventeen per minute for the first fifteen minutes to fifty in the last fifteen minutes, an increase of approximately 200 percent. Since the hour when the greatest number of babies were asleep was near the middle of the period, Irwin concluded that the increased motility was not due to waking but to hunger contractions. Valentine and Wagner (80) found the motility of the right arm to be slightly greater than the left.

According to Irwin (47), the motility of the newborn is "mass activity" from which more restricted activities are differentiated. Taylor (22:69-81) holds that with the exception of a few structural reflex activities infant behavior is best characterized by general activity. Dennis (19), on the other hand, is of the opinion that there are a number of different mass activities.

Aside from the studies of the spontaneous activities of the neonate there have been a number of studies dealing with responses to specific stimuli. Chaney and McGraw (13) studied the responses made to various stimuli by twenty-five infants under twenty-three minutes of age and a group of 100 infants aged one to ten days. The tendon reflexes were more easily stimulated a few minutes after birth than later, while responses to cutaneous stimuli were much more difficult to arouse in the younger than in the older group. Between one and ten days only a few reflexes appeared to be related to age. When there was a change to greater or less reaction the change occurred between the seventeenth and seventy-fifth hour after birth. It was just after this age that Irwin (41) found a marked increase in motor activity. There were marked individual differences both in the quality and quantity of the reflex responses.

Pratt (62) made elaborate studies of the plantar reflex of infants ranging in age from one to twenty-one days. He obtained 1,581 responses in the homolateral limb from 2,500 stimulations in thirteen different cutaneous areas on the foot and leg. Among these responses 185 different patterns were found. While the number of different responses appears large, according to the author it is only 3 percent of the possible number of patterns. The effects of certain physiological states are also studied.

Beasley (5, 6) stated that he found evidence of fairly accurate visual discrimination by the tenth day in all the 251 infants he studied and earlier in the majority of cases. The curve of development of the pupillary reflex follows that of the learning curves during the first five to eight days. Binocular fixation can be elicited through a significant distance range during this period. Horizontal, vertical, and circular pursuits all develop markedly during the first ten days. Squints or cases of incoordinate binocular fixation during pursuit are infrequent and certainly not typical. A special technic for studying visual ocular and color vision in the newborn infants is described. The data pointed toward the conclusion that in regard to visual fixation and pursuit the negro infants at birth were appreciably more advanced in development than the white infants. The experimental apparatus and conditions appear to have been well standardized and controlled.

Weiss (82, 83, 84, 85) found that auditory and visual stimuli reduced the activity of the newborn infant as measured by the stabilimeter in proportion to the intensity of the stimuli. The immediate reactions were responses to change; the maximum quieting effect of the stimuli was not reached until from two to four minutes. As the light was dimmed activity increased, but crying also increased. Weiss (85) stated that age, sex, and physiological factors all influenced the experimental results. Contrary to the results of Weiss, Pratt (60, 61) found that repeated auditory stimuli increased the gross total activity of newborn infants during the period of stimulation. This increased activity was more marked when other stimuli were absent. The periods of excitation were brief and died down almost immediately when the stimulus was removed. Pratt concluded that they could not be interpreted as evidence of the "emotion of fear." When the sound stimuli were repeated at short intervals, the reactions gradually decreased. Neither change in general activity nor the pattern of activity was produced in appreciable amounts to either single or repeated visual stimuli.

Haller (34) also found that for infants between the ages of three and five weeks, tones more frequently caused discomfort than comfort and that sounds of high intensity were more disturbing to the child than sounds of low intensity. The responses were definitely related to the stimuli and usually ceased as soon as the stimulus was removed. There was no indication that the response was one of fear.

Jensen (50), using well-controlled and standardized procedures, noted the differential sucking reactions to change in temperature of the milk and to the addition to the milk of various substances. Large individual differences were found in the temperature changes which caused differential reactions in sucking, but the threshold for the same infants tended to remain constant over the period tested. No differential responses were found to acid, glucose, or water. Differential reactions were made when sucking air; all but one of the seventeen infants reacted differentially to .9 percent salt solution and all but three to a .45 percent solution.

Dockeray (23) also found wide individual differences in taste threshold. He found a few infants who always expressed aversion to an acidulated formula, a large group that reacted differentially to these formulas at irregular and unpredictable times, and a third group that always reacted as to the regular formula. The superimposed order of the regular formula or of previously avoided foods did not affect the feeding reactions.

Disher (21), in a study of ninety-one infants' reactions to substances of various odors placed in the nose, found large variations in reactions both from one individual to another and from the same individual from day to day. No sex, race, or age differences could be demonstrated.

Other studies of the reactions of infants during the first ten days after birth that have been reported during the last three years deal with the latent time of body startle or the Moro reflex and the infant's response to vertical dropping movements by Irwin (43, 44); smiling and posture during nursing and defecation by Dennis (18, 20); reaction time by Stubbs and Irwin (74).

Dennis (16), after a study of the literature, presented a list of all responses of newborn infants "which are known at the present time together with available information concerning their stimuli." Gilmer (32, 33) developed a much shorter classification of nine spontaneous responses plus a few isolated movements based on moving pictures and one hour observation periods between the ages of one and ten days. He included crying, stretching, sneezing, mouthing, yawning, open mouth, chewing, sucking, smiling, and a few isolated movements. Regarding his classification, Gilmer wrote: "By no means has the above classification been 'selective'; all behavior which occurred has been included."

A more complete review of the literature on the experimental studies of the newborn infant was made by Hurlock (39) and by Richards and Irwin (65). Whether or not such studies as those reported above on the reflexes and spontaneous activities of the newborn infant are dependent upon or are related to the development of intelligence and motor control has not been proved. It is quite possible that if the development of motor activity and intelligence of these infants was followed into later childhood some of the activities of the newborn would be found to be correlated with later development, but as yet no such follow-up study has been made.

General Development

Several investigators have published detailed, running accounts of certain types of behavior development based on observation periods of stated lengths at stated intervals. Bridges (8, 9, 10) was especially interested in the social and motor development between birth and two years of age; Dudley, Duncan, and Sears (25) in motor development between fifty-eight and sixty-seven weeks; and Kelting (53) in eating, sleeping, crying, and social behavior under ten months. Another method of depicting development of behavior at different ages in different situations is the moving pictures that have been put out by Gesell (28), Valentine and Wagner (80), and Kellogg and Kellogg (52).

Shirley (69) presented an intensive study of the mental, motor, and social development of twenty-five infants followed from the day of birth until two years of age. The infants were examined both by a pediatrician and a psychologist every day during the first week in the hospital, every two days during the second week, every week during the first year, and every two weeks during the second year. The psychological examination consisted of a series of test items compiled by the author. Since the tests were given in the homes they were of necessity somewhat less formally presented than is the usual intelligence test. The items were not scored plus and minus during the examination, but a descriptive record was made of the child's responses to each item and of all other behavior of the child during the half-hour examination, whether or not the activity was in connection with a test item.

An analysis of the mass of data which was collected, together with a study of that reported in the literature, led the author to the following conclusions (70:254):

> A consistent sequence of motor items unrolls at varying speeds but in an unvarying order that is little influenced by specific training or by divergent environmental

factors. The unfolding of motor skills proceeds in accordance with biological laws. The chief one is the *law of developmental direction* or the anterior-posterior growth law. A second law is that of *priority of the flexor muscles over the extensors in strength.* A third law of neural and muscular action that may be operating in cases of sudden integration of motor skills is the *all-or-none law.*

The number of cases in Shirley's study is small, but the consistency with which each baby's development follows the sequences described lends weight to her conclusions. Consistent sequences were noted not only in the development of motor control but also in the development of social reactions and speech.

Among others Irwin (48) and Thompson (76) offered additional evidence of the head-downward or anterior-posterior sequence of development.

Shirley (69: Vol. II, 399-400) is of the opinion that in addition to the gradual behavior growth there emerge new types of behavior which are just as truly a phase of development as the improvement of behavior already present. She stated:

When we compare the small number of abilities of the newborn child with his large repertoire of acts at two years, we realize what a vast number of new behavior items have emerged in the interval. It is hardly possible that this great development has been solely the improvement in and reorganization of behavior items already possessed.

The largest volume of work on infants has come from Gesell's laboratory at Yale University. Gesell, Thompson, and Amatruda (30) presented their results based on 524 developmental examinations obtained from 107 infants between the ages of four and fifty-six weeks. A number of the infants were examined at intervals of four weeks throughout the period of the study. The general situations, materials, and procedures used were more strictly standardized, but otherwise similar to those described in Gesell's earlier books (29). Some twenty-five situations and the babies' responses to them are described in detail. Tables are presented which give the percent of babies at each age which made each response. For example, the situation for which the greatest number of responses are listed is one in which the infant is sitting before a platform with a hand bell placed directly before him. Seventy-eight responses are listed and the percent of babies making each response at each age interval is given. There are eight situations for which over fifty responses are recorded. Accompanying this volume is a two-volume atlas (26) which includes 3,200 analytic action photographs. Volume I is arranged to show the normative behavior development in twenty-four different situations. Volume II shows the development of the child in its normal home environment—eating, bathing, playing, sleeping, etc. The value of the cinema records for the study of behavior is described both in the atlas and in a separate article (27).

The Development of Grasping

Several articles and monographs using the above described data have come out from the Yale laboratory. They all appear to have been done under carefully standardized conditions and are mostly reported in great detail.

Halverson (36) described the development of the infant's ability to pick up a one-inch cube. The regard given the cube, the method of approach, and the method of grasping are described for each age level. Two, three, or more pages are given to each of eleven methods of approaching the cube; this is followed by the methods of grasping, of lifting, and of disposing of the cube. Another article (37) followed, describing the methods used by the infant in different stages of development of grasping objects of different shapes, and a third study by Halverson (35) dealt with the reaching and picking up of small objects.

Castner (12) also used the data from Gesell's clincal studies and described the development of fine prehension from transient regard through prolonged regard and occasional attempts at grasping to final success. In progress toward skill the development of the actual grasping in the infant passes through palmar prehension, scissors closure, and finally an overhand pincer-like prehension. During this period reaching progresses from a round semicircular reach with frequent misses to a straight direct reach with no fumbling.

Conditioned Responses in Infancy

The youngest age at which an attempt at conditioning has been reported is that of Ray (64) who attempted to condition the fetal movements produced by a loud sound to a vibration against the mother's abdomen. The results were not reported.

Marquis (58) was successful in conditioning sucking movements to the sound of a buzzer in infants as young as five days. These experiments were performed under carefully standardized conditions and with adequate controls.

Kasatkin and Levikova (51) established sucking movements in response to a light stimulus in six infants at about the age of two months. Though the age at which the experiments were begun with the different infants varied from fourteen days to one month and seventeen days, the conditioned response was established in all the infants at approximately the same age (range seven days). Thus the formation of the conditioned response appeared to depend more on the maturity of the infant than on the amount of training. By the end of the fourth month, sucking movements had been conditioned to a green light and inhibited to a yellow light in five of the six infants.

Wenger (86) conditioned blinking to a light in the newborn infants, to the Hull tactual vibrator, and the responses to an electric shock to a tone. Conditioning first occurred on the seventh day. There were two control groups for each experiment.

Bregman (7) was unsuccessful in her attempt to condition the emotions of infants eight to sixteen months of age to objects that were of little interest to the child. She used wooden forms and colored curtains as conditioned stimuli, a startling electric bell as an unpleasant unconditioned stimulus, and a toy and pleasant tone as pleasing unconditioned stimuli. The experiments do not appear to be sufficiently extensive or well controlled to warrant her rather sweeping conclusions (7:196):

> Changes in emotional behavior, in attitude and interest, are not, as a general rule, at least, readily brought about by joint stimulations in early life, and that conditioning *per se* cannot be accepted as a cover-all explanation of the emotional modification which takes place during that period.

Color Discrimination

Staples (72) mounted a colored and a gray disc of equal brightness on a gray background of the same brightness and saturation as the gray disc and held them before infants who were between three and five months of age for two minutes. How the infants distinguished between the gray disc and the gray background of equal saturation and brightness was not made clear, but Staples reported that the infants fixated on the color for an appreciably longer time than they did on the gray disc. There was no reliable difference in the time of fixation of the four colors used.

The older infants, between six and twenty-four months, were asked to "get the prettiest ball." The percent of infants who reached for the color as distinct from any other response rose from 50 percent at six months to 90 percent at eighteen months. There was no further increase between eighteen and twenty-four months. When two of the colored discs were mounted on the gray background there was evidence to indicate that the children probably distinguished between the colors at twelve months and unquestionably did so by fifteen months. Red was definitely preferred to any other color at all ages, yellow was preferred to blue or green, and blue to green. With the exception of blue there was a definite tendency for the color preference to become less marked with increase in age.

Form Discrimination

Skeels (71) studied form perception in eight children between the ages of eighteen and twenty-four months. He hid a toy under one form of a four-hole form-board and asked the child to find it. All the children learned to go directly to the correct form. At the beginning, the end, and in the middle of the training period, the subjects were asked to place the forms in the form-board. No child succeeded in purposefully placing the forms or appeared to have profited by the period of training.

The form under which the toy had been hidden was not placed any more frequently than the other forms.

Constancy of Mental Development

For the purpose of determining how consistently a baby held his relative position in the group, Shirley (69) converted the scores made on her tests into percentile ranks within the group, into the percent of the median, and into the percent of the highest score. A number of growth curves were plotted. In spite of the markedly consistent sequence of development, there was found a markedly inconsistent rate of development, especially during the first year or year and one-half after birth. Three general characteristics of the growth curves were noted: (a) an irregular rate of growth during the first year; (b) a settling down to a more steady rate the second year; and (c) a slowing down of the rate of growth with age.

Over short intervals of time the correlation coefficients were fairly high, varying from .16 to .96 with only two below .50, but at longer intervals of ten or more weeks the coefficients hover around zero, averaging —.006. Similar figures were obtained when the Gesell schedules or Minnesota preschool tests were correlated with Shirley's tests. The curves of development and the correlation coefficients between motor, vocal, and social development give further evidence of the inconsistency in the rate of development in the various types of behavior.

Bayley (1, 3), using a scale based largely on items from Gesell's schedules but also including some items of her own and some from other sources, reached conclusions similar to those of Shirley in regard to the inconstancy of mental test ratings. She found no significant relationship between the scores made by infants under fifteen months of age and those made at three years. This was true even when the infant test scores for three successive months were averaged. Bayley stated:

> This series of correlations, with remarkably consistent trend, shows that, though the children remain relatively stable in their scores over short periods, their position in the group is liable to great variation over longer age intervals . . . (3:47).
>
> The findings show that the tests are measuring different functions, or groups of functions, at successive age levels, rather than, as has been often supposed, a unit function of intelligence which extends throughout life. . . . A selection of half of the tests, through fifteen months, which seemed to be more truly "mental," gave no greater consistency in scores than did the discarded half (3:84).

The test of Bayley had reliability coefficients for the several months obtained by the split-half method and corrected by the Spearman-Brown formula that ranged from .50 to .95, and between tests given a month apart the correlation coefficients averaged slightly above .80. The number of cases at each age level was approximately fifty.

Shirley (69:Vol. II, 440) offered the following as a tentative explanation of the inconsistencies of mental development during the first year after birth:

> Inconsistencies in first year development may be attributed to the great speed of development, to the catching up of premature babies and the slowing down of postmature babies in developmental rate, and to the difficulties of motivating babies and of reducing unfavorable personality traits to a minimum. Finally it is suggested that it is impossible for the baby to settle down to a consistent rate of development until a sufficient number of traits have emerged to serve as a foundation for future skills. Fixity and consistency apparently are end points rather than starting points in behavior development.

The studies of Gesell (29) and Bühler (11) led them to conclusions opposite from those of Shirley and Bayley, namely, that mental growth proceeds at a regular rate from early infancy and that the trend of development in infancy can be determined with sufficient accuracy to be of value in predicting future mental development.

Cunningham (14), using the Kuhlmann extension of the Binet tests, found considerably greater consistency of results between one age and another after one year. Thirty-seven cases who were tested at the ages of twelve, eighteen, and twenty-four months were also tested at the age of eight years with the Stanford-Binet. The correlation coefficients were .55, .42, and .24 respectively. Driscoll (24), using the same data, found correlation coefficients of .69 between the age of twelve and eighteen months, of .76 between eighteen and twenty-four months, and .58 between twelve and twenty-four months. These coefficients are not high, but are far above the zeros reported by Bayley and Shirley for slightly younger infants.

Symmes (75) also found a considerable amount of consistency. Unfortunately, she grouped the results from the infants with those from older preschool children and also considered such factors as environment and the family background when making the ratings. It is, therefore, difficult to determine the significance of the constancy reported.

When Thurstone's method of absolute scaling was applied to Bayley's data, a mental growth curve was obtained that showed rapid growth with increasing increments up to ten or eleven months. After fifteen months the rate became almost constant. The growth of motor ability showed increments during the first twenty-one months which were larger than the mental growth increments for the same children. The rapid growth was followed by rapidly decreasing increments. The correlation between the adjacent motor tests were fairly high, but over longer periods were only slightly higher than those found between the mental tests.

Steckel (73) plotted the growth curve of infancy by Thurstone's method of absolute scaling, using all the items in Gesell's schedule which were found at two or more age levels. Contrary to Bayley's results, she found the curve to be negatively accelerated as early as the fourth month before birth.

The Effects of Environment and Training on Development

The studies on the relationship of environmental factors to mental development in infancy are unsatisfactory, as are those on older children, on account of the difficulty of separating the effects of environment from those of heredity. Vance and others (81) compared the mental development of small groups of infants in professional homes, labor homes, boarding homes, institutions, and college management homes. The average I.Q.'s ranged from 118 in the professional homes to 88 in the institutions, but no attempt was made to separate the effects of heredity and environment.

Ripin (68) compared the mental development, as measured by test items selected from the works of Gesell and Bühler, of infants in institutions with those in homes of low socio-economic status. The two groups showed no difference up to the sixth month, but from seven months on the private home group made the better ratings. The greatest differences were found in the postural, language, and "mental" items; the smallest differences in the emotional, manipulative, and social items.

Bayley (2, 3) was unable to find any environmental factors which showed any relationship to intelligence during the first eighteen months of infancy; the correlation coefficients were slightly but not significantly negative. The same was true in relation to the education of the parents. After twenty months of age the coefficient between the education of the parents and the intelligence of the child rose to .50; that between intelligence and socio-economic status also rose with age but remained below .30.

McGraw (57) gave special training to one of a pair of twins and kept the other for a control. The twins at birth were thought to be monozygotic, but were not proved to be so. Beginning at the age of twenty days the twins were brought to the laboratory for seven or eight hours a day, five days a week. One twin was stimulated at regular intervals to those activities of which he was capable. As development advanced he was stimulated to more and more advanced activity. The control twin was left quietly in his crib, was allowed no more than two toys, and aside from his routine care received little attention. The purpose was to study the growth of particular behavior patterns and to determine the influence of exercise or use of an activity upon its development.

Both the control and the experimental twin were put through motor activity tests every two weeks to determine their developmental stage. The conclusions reached were that exercise in activities which were necessary for normal development were influenced little if at all by practice. These include the early reflexes such as grasping and the startle reflex, and activities such as crawling, walking, reaching, prehension, etc. (Both twins started walking at approximately the same time.) Other activities that are not necessary for normal development, such as swimming, climbing, skating, jumping, etc., were greatly influenced by practice. Before the end of his twenty-two months of systematic, daily training, the experimental twin showed remarkable skill in these activities.

In the meantime the control twin was left to his own devices in his crib, but at twenty-two months he was given two and one-half months of intensive training. Except in tricycling, the control twin's activities were, at the end of his training period, still inferior to those which the experimental twin had reached after the same amount of training at a younger age.

McGraw explained the differences in ability as the result of the "acquiescent attitude" developed through training in the experimental twin and to the starting of training at just the right stage of development. The control twin could never be made to jump from a pedestal to the floor even from a height as low as $7\frac{1}{2}$ inches, or from a higher pedestal into the waiting arms of the experimenter. This is explained on the ground that before training was begun he had developed the perception of height which had not yet been developed in the experimental twin at the time his training was begun and that he, therefore, was less cautious. On the other hand, the experimental twin's inferiority on the tricycle was explained on the ground that he was put on the tricycle before his ability was sufficiently developed and that as a result he lost interest.

At the age of twenty-four and one-half months both twins were given systematic training in activities that were very different from those in which they had been previously trained, namely, acquiring a lure through the manipulation of sticks and strings. In these activities the experimental twin, except for somewhat greater persistence, showed no superiority over his control brother.

During the month of training in perception and manipulation, the twins did not see any of the gross motor activity apparatus. At the end of the month Jimmie made his best performance in practically every situation wherein he had previously been exercised, while the experimental twin showed an obvious though temporary deterioration in practically every performance. The explanation given was that the control twin had gained in cooperativeness and in acquiescence during the month of training in manipulation, whereas the experimental twin had been completely cooperative before. When the twins were brought in for a check-up a few weeks after the close of the experiment, the control twin had returned to his former uncooperative attitude; the experimental twin had retained the cooperative attitude he had held from the beginning.

McGraw is of the opinion that the greatest effect of the differential training was the development of an attitude of acquiescence in the experimental twin.

A book has been written on growth and child psychology based on these experiments. To the reviewer these experiments are of great interest in showing the remarkable motor skills that may be developed in infancy through appropriate systematic training. Before the age of twenty-two months the experimental twin was able to climb a 70 degree incline and slide down, stack boxes to attain an object beyond his reach, roller skate, coast down an incline of 4.5 degrees on skates and turn a corner, let himself off a stool 63¼ inches in height, and find, as they were called for, eight objects which he had hidden the day before. But it would seem that the results of these experiments might better be used as illustrations rather than a basis for the author's theories, for after all there was only one experimental subject and one main control and whether or not the twins were monozygotic is uncertain. (There is from time to time mention of a control group, but no information regarding it is given.) No mental tests were made on the infants until the end of the twenty-second month. At that time there was no significant difference in the I.Q.'s obtained.

It sounds reasonable to attribute the experimental subject's cooperative attitude to his intensive training, but it would be just as reasonable to attribute the control twin's uncooperative attitude to the so-called "inferiority complex" developed through association (at home) with his much trained brother. The control twin's refusal to jump from a pedestal may have been the result of a well-developed perception of height, but there is no evidence to show that it was not the result of a past bruise and lack of confidence in the experimenter. In other words, it appears that the author was too ready to generalize from one example which may not have been typical. She stated: "While use of the activity will not advance appreciably the day a child begins to walk alone and will not alter the general method of progression, exercise may influence the grade with which he steps, his speed and his mien of progression."

Dennis (17), with a pair of fraternal twins, experimented in the opposite direction. Until eleven months the twins were given no toys; bedclothes when present were arranged so that they could not be played with, there was nothing to reach for, nothing to see except plain walls, plain furniture, sky, and the tops of trees. There were no pictures or other ornaments in the room. The children came from a family of average socio-economic status. The father was a taxi driver, the mother a salesgirl.

Beginning on the 245th day a dangling ring was presented to each infant for thirty seconds every day for forty days. One infant first reached for it on the thirteenth day and the other on the sixteenth day. The first reachings were clumsy but quickly improved. The infants were placed in a sitting position for the first time at nine months. Neither twin made the slightest effort toward balance, but the retardation was temporary; in thirty-six days one of the infants sat alone for twenty seconds.

When first put on their feet on the 264th day, neither supported his weight. One twin pushed momentarily and slightly on each of the ten trials, the other in four of ten trials. During the remainder of the day and the following three days, many trials were given. Approximately eight hours after their first failure both supported their weight momentarily and by the end of the 367th day both had stood continuously for two minutes. One twin walked at seventeen months, the other at twenty-six months. The experimenters did not wait until the infants made attempts to reach, sit, or stand; but as soon as it was clear that a response was delayed, efforts were made to establish it. During the experiment the infants were in the best of health with large firm muscles and no rickets. Muscular weakness was in any case ruled out by the fact that the infants never attempted the responses in question and by the fact that grasping and standing were learned quickly, once the opportunities were given.

It is interesting to note that it is these very activities of reaching, grasping, sitting, and standing that McGraw concluded were unaffected by special exercise.

Development of the Prematurely Born

Inman-Kane (40) studied the amount of prematurity and underweight at birth among the mentally defective and among unselected school children. He found (a) that among school children who were either underweight or premature at birth there was more than the usual amount of feeble-mindedness, and (b) that an appreciably larger proportion of the mental defectives than of the general population had been either underweight at birth or prematurely born. He wrote that the evidence appears conclusive that the condition of prematurity or underweight at birth is an etiological factor in mental deficiency. The mental defect is not attributed to premature birth or underweight, per se, but to damage, usually intercranial hemorrhages, caused by the birth process. Gesell (31) stated that a study of individual cases of prematurely born children leads to the conclusion that development is not appreciably affected by mere precocity of birth.

The most extensive work on the development of prematurely born children has been done by Hess, Mohr, and Bartelme (38). They examined 250 such children both with the Gesell and the Binet tests and compared the results with those obtained by Gesell and by Kuhlmann from their standardization groups. Also 124 prematurely born were compared with their 152 full-term siblings. When the chronological ages were corrected for the amount of prematurity and those cases eliminated in which intercranial hemorrhages had resulted in brain damage, there were no indications that the mental development of the prematurely born was not equal to that of the control groups. A comparison of the behavior of the 124 prematurely born children with their full-term siblings gave some indications that they were somewhat inferior in their habits and social adjustment. However, as the authors point out, the differences found are difficult to evaluate since the siblings were older than the premature group.

Miscellaneous Studies

Marquis (59) studied the movements in sleep from birth to one year of age both by observation and by means of attaching the crib springs to a recorder. The first half-hour of the nap was found to be the quietest period after which the movements gradually increased until waking.

During the night the second hour was quietest. The periods of sleep without movements were nearly twice as long during the daytime nap as during the night sleep. Between the eighth and twentieth weeks the average number of movements began to decrease and the quiet periods to increase. There was also noted a decrease in the frequency of movements of the larger parts of the body with advance in age and a corresponding increase in the frequency of movements of the small parts.

Richardson (66, 67), using Gesell's set-up, described the development of ability in the child to pull a lure to him by means of an attached string; to select the string attached to the lure from among others that are not attached; and to secure a lure by means of a simple horizontal rotating lever. The ability to obtain the toy by pulling in a string increased from zero at twenty-four weeks to 90 percent at forty weeks. Ability to obtain a toy by means of the lever increased from 20 percent at forty weeks to 83 percent at fifty-two weeks. In the multiple-string situation, where the loose strings were offered along with the attached string, there was no consistent increase with age, a result which is attributed to varying interest in the lure and to the emotional adjustment to the examiner.

Dennis (15) tabulated data from Hrdlicka's book to show that children who first learn to run on all fours do not walk later than those who creep, as Hrdlicka claimed. He found that the average age reported was 12.97 months.

All those studying the mental development of the infant have been able to demonstrate measurable increments of growth in behavior over periods of one month. Thompson (77) tested one infant with the one-inch cubes daily between the ages of forty-six and fifty-two weeks. She found that:

> Daily growth in behavior is shown on 60 per cent of the days while at intervals of seven days it was almost invariably evident. Daily growth in weight in the same infant during the same period was indicated on 46 per cent of the days and at intervals of eight days it, too, was almost invariable. That behavior changes are occurring as surely and rapidly as physical growth changes is not an overstatement.

Thompson (78) found that in the course of normal development, some responses to particular situations increase in frequency as development proceeds, others decrease, and still others increase to a certain frequency and then decrease or fluctuate. She is of the opinion (a) that many of the bits of behavior which decrease in frequency with age, or which first increase and then decrease, are as good indicators of development as those which steadily increase in frequency, and (b) that they should be considered when estimating the developmental status of the child.

CHAPTER II
Mental Development from Two to Twelve Years

IN THIS REVIEW the authors have endeavored to bring together the investigations that deal with the mental development of children from two to twelve years of age.[1] The review takes its departure from the summary presented by Cattell (117) in the *Review of Educational Research* in April, 1933, but the scope of the topics under review has been extended somewhat.

Research studies during the past few years have added much to our knowledge of children, but enormous gaps remain to be filled. We can sympathize with the educator who grows impatient with psychology when research findings continue to lag so far behind the practical needs of the day. On the other hand it is sometimes discouraging to find how little available research material has permeated into school practices and how strongly education seems to be fortified against suggestions for critical evaluation or change.

A survey of recent research literature reveals certain constructive trends as well as many continuing weaknesses. An increasing number of studies deal with real aspects of behavior, in a "natural" setting, as distinguished from exhaustive studies of artificial problems by means of superficial technics. However, studies based upon limited cross-sectional snapshots still far outnumber investigations in which an attempt is made to probe the developmental process through continuous study of the same child over an extended period of time. Likewise, many studies continue to deal with isolated aspects of behavior rather than with the relationships between aspects of behavior.

In many areas of study where other more intimate methods are essential for preliminary exploration, the research worker is still a slave to statistics. To upbraid research workers for using statistics is an easy and low form of criticism, but there are times when statistics become the tail that wags the dog. It would be good for educational research if a penetrating and revealing analysis of a few subjects could acquire as much respectability as superficial but "reliable" measurements of large numbers.

In reading a wide variety of studies, one sees many contrasts in the interpretation of data. One writer unhesitatingly jumps from specific findings to universal implications; another is so conservative that he avoids generalizations or applications of any kind. Frequently, the latter is a worker who has been most painstaking in his research, but who shies away from any general ideas when the fatal moment comes for sending his study out into the world. Often it seems that research workers omit illumi-

---
[1] The authors are grateful to Mary D. Fite for bibliographical assistance.

nating data because they may not meet the requirements of scientific objectivity, refrain from reporting insights that cannot be supported by statistical tables, and avoid general conclusions for fear of future refutation.

The problem of child development as seen by L. K. Frank (147) is "the problem of discovering the rate and direction of change in the structures and functions of the child and of revealing the interrelationships existing among the several structures, functions, processes and activities." From this point of view some of the research material presented in this section may mark the beginnings of what may become an integrated science of childhood.

Growth of Intelligence

The study of mental growth from birth through three years of age which was made by Bayley (3) is a significant contribution to our understanding of intelligence. Mental tests, tests of reflexes, physiological and anthropometric measures composed the examinations given monthly to sixty-one infants. Test items were taken from several infant and preschool tests. Growth was found to be accelerated at first, with a deceleration in rate after ten or eleven months, and an almost constant rate after fifteen months. In general, variability increased with age except between six and twelve months. This coincides with other evidence presented which indicates a change in the functions measured before and after this period. The findings show that the tests are measuring different functions or groups of functions at successive age levels, rather than a unit function of intelligence which extends throughout life. These differences are evidenced in the results of item analysis, in the directional change in the standard deviation score, and in the low correlations over long-time intervals.

Another study from the same Institute presents data concerning the growth and decline of intelligence between the ages of ten and sixty. Jones and Conrad (189) examined 1,191 cases from villages in rural New England on the Army Alpha Scale. The chief characteristics of the developmental curve were linear growth to about sixteen years, negative acceleration beyond sixteen to a peak between eighteen and twenty-one, and a gradual decline to fifty-five involving recession to the fourteen-year level. A study of the data of adolescents reveals interesting material. Information and vocabulary tests exhibit no postadolescent decline, the adult deriving much more of his intellectual power from accumulated stocks of information than the ten-year-old. A differential rate of growth during adolescence for bright and dull children was indicated by the increased standard deviations of scores.

Hsiao (176) presented somewhat similar findings in an investigation of 1,131 subjects in the eastern part of the United States using eight tests from Army Alpha. It was found that between the ages of eleven and fifty-four the early part of the mental growth curve was linear and then became negatively accelerated. Mental maturity varied with the functions tested.

His data do not support Jones and Conrad's finding that variability of intelligence increases at puberty.

F. N. Freeman (148) discussed the question of whether the child who develops rapidly also continues to develop longer than the slow-growing child, and drew conclusions on the subject from long-time records of several hundred children in the elementary and high school of the University of Chicago. A group of 100 children, ranging from somewhat below average to bright, was divided into three groups based on scores on the test during the middle years and the average curve drawn for each group. "The children in the bright group begin to advance at an accelerated rate at about ten years of age. Their curve then advances more steeply for two or three years than do the curves of the other two groups. The curves of these bright children, however, begin to slow down sooner than do those of the others. None of the groups reach their complete development by 17, so that it is impossible to say how far apart they will be when their growth reaches its final level. By 17, however, the upper curve is slowing up, whereas the lower group of children is continuing to advance at an undiminished rate."

Constancy of the I.Q.

The validity of using intelligence tests for purposes of prognosis stands or falls on the constancy of the intelligence rating of children as they develop. A variation of about 5 points plus or minus on two Stanford-Binet ratings is generally regarded as a normal degree of fluctuation and is not considered as evidence of lack of constancy. If larger differences occur the question arises as to whether such variations may be ascribed to inadequacy of the test, faulty technic of the tester, or unusual conditions confronting the child at the time of the testing. The great variability of children when retested during the early years has raised certain questions as to the adequacy of tests used at this level as well as to the possibility of securing cooperation from children below six. One of the difficulties in the studies reported is that the interval between tests often has varied as much as several years and yet data have been thrown together. R. L. Thorndike (318) treated the results of various experimenters by the method of least squares and reported that the correlation between Binet test and retest decreases as interval increases. Studies of the influence of environment on I.Q. do not always adequately differentiate between what may be a change in score on a specific test and what may be a fundamental change in the intellectual ability of the subject.

The studies summarized under this topic deal with superior or gifted children, subnormal children, problem children, and preschool children.

Because Terman's data gave evidence of loss of I.Q. points for children with I.Q. of 140 or above during a six-year period, whereas the Harvard Growth Study showed a tendency for the superior child to increase I.Q. as he advanced in age, Cattell (116) studied the changes which took place with age in the I.Q. of 288 boys and 268 girls. Table 1 shows changes in I.Q. points on test and retest for this group:

TABLE 1.—CHANGES IN I.Q. POINTS ON TEST AND RETEST, AFTER CATTELL (116)

I.Q. Level	Boys		Girls	
	Number	Median	Number	Median
Below 80	24	− 2.5	17	−2.5
80 to 89	59	− 4.7	53	−4.3
90 to 99	99	+ 0.9	84	−2.0
100 to 109	69	+ 4.3	70	+2.0
110 to 119	28	+ 6.2	33	+2.7
120 and above	9	+12.0	11	+7.0

The conflict between these results and the Stanford findings may be due to the method of selecting the cases and the difference in the ages of the two groups. A similarity in the two studies is shown regarding sex differences in that the Stanford study showed a greater decrease in the I.Q.'s of the girls than of the boys, while this study shows a smaller gain among the girls than among the boys.

Lincoln (209), testing ninety-two younger children (before entrance to kindergarten or first grade) who scored 119 I.Q. or above on the Stanford-Binet, and reexamining them at intervals ranging from five to eight years, found a range of I.Q. changes from a 36-point loss to a 35-point gain. Slightly more than one-third of the group changed less than 5 points. Comparisons were made of performance on different test items.

One hundred sixteen children who had tested 130 I.Q. or above on Stanford-Binet at the first test were retested ten years later by means of the Army Alpha test by Hollingworth and Kaunitz (173). The median age of children at retest was 18.5 years. Since 82 percent of the children who were in the top centile remained there ten years later and since no individual regressed to or nearly to normal, the authors concluded that the results validate the predictive power of available mental tests and the constancy of intellectual development of gifted children.

Nemzek (250) made computations from data already published by others and concluded that correlations between repeated I.Q. ratings of superior children tend to be lower than for unselected groups and that the direction is toward increased scores on later tests. The author attributes this latter to practice effect. Lämmermann (198) gave batteries of intelligence tests to fifty-three children between nine and ten years of age for six successive weeks. The rank order obtained from the individual tests did not change much and there was no leveling effect due to practice. But the experimental group improved considerably more than a control group, which fact the author attributed to practice effect.

The study of subnormal children by H. T. Parker (259) supports other findings regarding the constancy of the I.Q. in retarded children. The data for the study consisted of 1,462 tests of 552 subnormal children nine to fifteen years of age from the Education Department of Tasmania. The average interval between tests was approximately one to one and one-half years. In three-fourths of the cases a decline in I.Q. was reported after a period of about four years, with an average annual decline of about 1.5 points in I.Q. over the total period from nine to fifteen years of age. The author stated that the decline is practically independent of particular classroom methods.

Two studies were contributed from the Institute of Juvenile Research dealing with problem children. Brown (106) reported on 124 children examined two or more times over periods varying from two to twelve years. The children had a mean chronological age of 8.19 at the first test and 15.86 at the last test; a mean I.Q. of 81.94 at the first test and 78.02 at the last test. There is a correlation of .79 ± .02 between I.Q.'s on first and last test in which the average time interval between test and retest is 7.67 years. In general agreement with Thorndike, correlations between tests and retests were higher for those examined within a two-year interval than those examined after three years. There was a tendency for these individuals to lose in their rating rather than gain after an interval of five to twelve years. The data as presented do not permit exact comparisons with Cattell but indicate that there is not the tendency for lower I.Q.'s to decrease score with age and for higher I.Q.'s to increase score with age.

Gildea and Macoubrey (157) attempted to analyze factors which may have affected the change in I.Q. of 431 children, ages six to sixteen with I.Q.'s ranging from 30 to 120. This was done by matching children who had fluctuated 10 or more points with children whose scores fluctuated less than 6 points. The length of time elapsing between two tests was greater for the children with greatest fluctuation in I.Q. Children who gained in I.Q. more frequently showed improved physical condition and symptomatic behavior and had parents whose attitude became improved.

Driscoll (24) investigated the usefulness of two preschool tests (Merrill-Palmer and Kuhlmann-Binet) for prognosing the future mental ability of children. A total of 254 children, ranging in age from twelve months to forty-eight months at the time of the initial test, was included. Comparisons were made with initial test scores and retests given at intervals of six months, twelve months, eighteen months, and twenty-four months; also between tests given before four years and tests given after five years with the Stanford-Binet. In general the data show that the retests gave positive but not sufficiently high correlations to make confident prediction of a child's exact future status possible on the basis of tests given before four years of age. Line and Kaplan (210) presented data from fifty-four case histories, each having at least five Binet tests, the first of which was given before the age of three. Among other findings the authors stated that the increase in I.Q. is greater for those who originally appear to be less bright. This is in agreement with Wellman's study of preschool children (328) but is not in line with Cattell's study of older children just cited. Kawin (192) reported similarly a great amount of variability on retests of preschool children. Since the tests were given at intervals varying from one to forty months, results are difficult to analyze. No consistent relationship was found with chronological age, level of intelligence, interval between test, or sex. Correlations of .552 were reported by Cunningham (14) between Kuhlmann-Binet tests given to twenty-seven children at twelve months of age and Stanford-Binet tests given seven years later.

That a change in environment may bring about an improvement in the I.Q. of children was proposed by Lithauer and Klineberg (212) on the basis of a study of 120 children who were tested upon entrance to an orphan asylum and again after a period varying from a few months to several years.

Other studies on this topic include W. S. Miller (244) and Nemzek (249) who summarized researches on the constancy of the I.Q.

Factors Related to Intelligence

A large number of studies has been published, the general purpose of which has been to understand factors which may have influenced growth in intelligence or factors which may correlate with ratings of intelligence. F. S. Freeman (150) summarized and interpreted research up to the present time on the nature and causes of variation in intelligence and special abilities.

Among these studies are several which attempt, from different approaches, to discover the relation of heredity and environment in determining the level of intelligence. The accumulating evidence emphasizes the interrelation of factors and the importance not only of heredity but of parent relations, sibling relations, social interaction, school guidance, nutrition, illness, motor skills, and the like on the development of any individual child.

One approach to understanding the factors related to intelligence has been to study the relation of intelligence of children and the socio-economic status of parents. Lawrence (200), studying over 1,700 children eleven and twelve years of age in homes and institutions in England, found a correlation of $.25 \pm .07$ to $.29 \pm .06$ between I.Q. of children and fathers' class, this being greater for children who remained longer in their homes. Hildreth (170), Jordan (190), Engle (137), and Kirihara (194) studied the relation of intelligence of children to occupations and socio-economic status of parents, and found in general that scores increased with the economic level.

Another approach to the same problem has been through studying the correlation of the intelligence of children and parents. A large group of studies has in general found a correlation of about .50 between the intelligence of children and their parents; but just what this correlation means, no one has ever made quite clear beyond the fact that a chance resemblance would give a correlation of zero. Such studies, however, do not tell us whether the correlation is due to the influence of home environment or to the influence of inheritance. Penrose (266), in a British study of 100 families, claimed that likenesses between the intelligence of children and parents can be accounted for by the assumption of alternative, additive Mendelian factors.

Two methods have been used in an attempt to evaluate these factors. One method has been to study children in adopted homes. Studies by Leahy (201, 202) of the influence of the home environment on intelligence offer the most comprehensive and careful inquiries into this question since the investigations by Burks (110) and F. N. Freeman and others (149). In a preliminary study Leahy (202) analyzed the social case histories of the unmarried mothers of 2,287 children who were placed in adoptive homes and 4,213 children who were retained by their own mothers. In general, children who were adopted had true mothers who were higher in educational attainment and true parents who attained higher occupational status, this tendency being greater for true parents of children placed at three months or younger. There was a positive relation between cultural level of adoptive homes and of true homes indicating a resemblance between adoptive parent and child entirely apart from any influence of environment and training. In a later study (201), a comparison was made of the children in foster homes and children living with their own parents. Leahy concluded that variation in I.Q. is accounted for by variation in the home environment to the extent of not more than 4 percent; that the hereditary component in intelligence causes greater variation than does the environment; but that variation in personality traits measured in this study appears to be accounted for less by variation in heredity than by variation in environment.

Another method of attempting to solve the nature-nurture controversy is through the study of twins reared in different environments. Schwesinger (295), after presenting an analysis of present information regarding the influence of heredity and environment, stated that the only direct attempts which can be made to study their effect on intelligence of the individual are those which compare the development of identical twins reared in different environments. The assumption is, of course, that identical twins being identical at birth, any differences that occur are due to environmental influences. Newman (251, 252) has added two more case studies of identical twins reared apart to the four reported by Cattell (117). One pair of twins reported were thirteen and one-half years old. One (Richard) was adopted at the age of one month into a truck farmer's family. He had lived in several different places and in every way had supposedly inferior advantages to the other twin (Raymond). Raymond was adopted at fourteen months by the family of a well-to-do city physician. The twins at the time of the report were physically almost indistinguishable. They were in the same grade in school and both had the reputation of being very alert and interested in studies. They had always had many interests in common. The results of five intelligence tests showed them to be approximately equal, what little difference there was being slightly in favor of Richard. Temperament-emotional tests showed rather decided differences, but the writer believed that the boys were yet too young for these differences to be taken seriously. Richard, however, seemed to be distinctly more aggressive and more positive in his reactions, probably because of the more varied and harder life that he had had.

Case VIII is an account of a pair of identical twins studied at sixteen years who had at three months been adopted into different families. Twin M had in every way had superior cultural and social advantages, while Twin R's home life had been anything but broadening or stimulating. Educational advantages, however, in terms of schools attended had been approximately equal. Scores on intelligence tests showed in every case large differences in favor of M. Performance on temperament-emotional tests showed that M's emotional life was more like that of the average person than R's, though both were highly emotional. "These findings tend to emphasize the educational value of the informal cultural environment of the home superimposed upon the formal discipline of the school."

Previous studies have pointed out that the assumptions underlying the twin studies are open to question. Mason (231) studied three pairs of monozygotic twins and one pair of dizygotic twins who were examined in kindergarten and seven years later in junior high school. She concluded:

In general, in neither physical, mental, or personality traits were these twins "identical." The monozygotic pair III differed markedly in physical appearance and in intelligence. The dizygotic pair IV was much alike in physical and intellectual measurements. Only Twins II were strikingly alike in personality. It would seem best, then—as others have pointed out—to discard the term that implies duplicate or identical characteristics.

Sontag and Nelson (308, 309), in their report on triplets, contributed to this point of view. Other studies of twins include P. A. Parker (262), Orgler (257), Carter (115), and White (329).

Hurst (180) attempted to work out a genetic formula for the inheritance of intelligence. This formula, which is "hexagenic involving one major and five minor pairs of genes" is said to be sufficiently accurate in a qualitative sense to be used as a working hypothesis for families.

In order to determine the nature and extent of environmental influences upon mental test performance, Jones, Conrad, and Blanchard (188) studied the performance on Stanford-Binet tests of over 1,400 children from rural and urban homes. In summary it is inferred that a rural child moving to the city would increase his intelligence test scores merely as a result of changed environmental conditions. His handicap is specific, not general; depending on the test items, it is sometimes transitory but more often cumulative. Nature-nurture inquiries of a fundamental character can in the future be conducted more profitably on the basis of specific tests, rather than on the general composites represented in I.Q. or mental age.

Gandy's interesting comparison of the concepts of urban and rural children (153) throws some additional light on environmental influences. In such areas as nature, recreation, occupations, institutions, and transportation she found thirty-two concepts that seemed to be significantly urban and thirty-three that seemed to be significantly rural. Furfey (152), also interested in rural and urban boys, found a precocity of urban boys over rural fairly evenly divided over the six tests presented.

Schwesinger (295) stated, "In regard to the influence of physical factors, health, disease, injury, etc., on intelligence, the evidence is strikingly and consistently negative, except in those cases of extreme injury, toxic condition, bacterial invasion or other damage to the control nervous system." This is substantiated by Nilson (255) who studied physically disabled children; by Richey (274) who found only a small and statistically unreliable difference between children with diseased tonsils and children with removed or "normal" tonsils and adenoids; by Schell (290) in studying the effect of intestinal protozoa on intelligence and personality traits. On the other hand, Liefmann (208) in Germany found that among ten-year-old girls the healthier child is generally the abler one, in line with other similar studies. In contrast, Maller's statistical study of 100,000 fifth-grade pupils in New York City (223) presented negative correlation of I.Q. with such health measures as visual defects, teeth defects, condition of tonsils, nutritional status. However, by holding economic status constant, a correlation of $.28 \pm .04$ was found between health and intelligence. He also found negative correlations with such neighborhood social data as death rate, infant mortality, juvenile delinquency, and birth rate but a positive correlation of neighborhood rentals (economic status) and intelligence of children.

Studies which specifically aimed toward analyzing sex differences reemphasize the negligible differences which are found between the sexes in general intelligence but indicate differences on specific items within the tests. Armstrong (89) found differences in specific items of the performance scales for boys and girls in grades four to eight, some in favor of boys and some in favor of girls. Heilman (168) reported that the difference in average scores of ten-year-old children in spelling and language was in favor of girls, and in favor of the boys in arithmetic and nature study. Conrad, Jones, and Hsiao (120), in an extensive study in rural Vermont, found similarly that some test items had no sex differences, some only slight, and some in favor of one or the other sex. The impressive fact is the similarity of developmental curves for the two sexes. The authors concluded that the direction and extent of sex differences in a composite mental test are dependent upon the composition of the test and the weighting of its parts. Rosanoff and associates (280) studied the sex distribution of I.Q. in eighty-three pairs of mentally deficient opposite sex twins, 233 pairs of normal or superior opposite sex twins, thirty-four pairs of superior monozygotic twins, and 2,017 siblings—a total of 1,010 boys (average I.Q. 105.6) and 1,007 girls (average I.Q. 107.9). They concluded that there was about one-fifth or one-fourth difference in favor of girls which seems to be due to sex-linked genetic factor or factors. This they believe is due to the greater vulnerability of male fetuses which brings a higher incidence of both relative and absolute mental deficiency in the male than in the female sex. Such pathogenic factors which affect the fetal period are more often at work in multiple than in single births.

Factors influencing scholastic ability have been studied by Engle (137), Farson (141), Monnin (247), H. T. Parker (261), Rogers (279), Levy (205), and Russell (285). Home environment, including maternal overprotection, economic status of family, physical and mental status of the student, and personality traits including perseveration, were among the factors found to be influencing school achievement.

Wellman's investigation (328) of the effect of attendance at nursery school upon the intelligence quotients of 600 children has significant implications. Children were studied at six-month intervals while attending the nursery schools and at approximately one-year intervals up to the age of fourteen years and six months, when they were attending elementary and high school. Significant gains in I.Q. were made while the children attended nursery school, the greatest gain being made by children in the lower levels of I.Q.

Saller (286, 287, 288, 290) in Germany made a series of studies of the relation between intelligence, social stratum, and differential rate of reproduction. His conclusions pointed out the relation of higher intelligence to smaller reproductive rate and of lower intelligence to greater mortality, the effect of environmental factors on intelligence of rural children, and the effect of both hereditary and environmental factors on children's school work.

A negative trend of correlations between basal metabolism and mental speed was reported by Steinberg (312). Intelligence appears to have no particular relation to age interval of siblings according to the study of Finch (144) of 1,023 pairs in 614 families. Pintner and Forlano (271) found no consistent relation between month of birth and intelligence.

Other studies in this general area include those by Vértes (326), Murphy (248), Barke (92), Hildreth (169), Holman (174), Jenkins (184), MacKane (219), and Van Wagenen (325). W. R. Miles (242) has summarized previous studies on the relation of age and human ability.

Mental Retardation

The relation of mental deficiency to heredity has been the concern of psychologists for many years. Woodall (334) studied 119 children over six years of age whose mothers had been patients of the Fernald State

School, an institution for the mentally defective and mentally retarded. Mental levels of the children ranged from imbecility to superiority, with 16 percent of average or superior mentality and 44 percent mentally defective. The study is in agreement with generally accepted principles in that although the average mental level and general physique of the children were superior to their mothers, a high positive correlation was found between the I.Q.'s of mothers and children.

McNeil (221) is convinced that heredity plays a very small part in the production of mental deficiency and that its influence has been greatly exaggerated. His conclusions are based on clinical observations of 1,000 cases of mental deficiency where he found in 85 percent of the cases that the condition was congenital and in 65 percent antenatal in origin.

Since there is considerable evidence that a larger proportion of gifted children come from the higher socio-economic classes, it might logically be assumed that the lower socio-economic classes contribute more than their share of mentally retarded children. Paterson and Rundquist (263) attempted to test this assumption by studying the parental occupations of 823 inmates of the Minnesota School for Feeble-Minded. It was found that 87.4 percent of the fathers came from the three lower occupational levels as compared with 59 percent of the random sample and 12.6 percent from the upper three levels. The authors called attention to the fact that the fathers of "idiots" tend to be representative of the general occupational distribution found in society and state: "These results suggest that pathological and accidental cases of feeble-mindedness occur on all levels of society, whereas cases of simple feeble-mindedness due to biological heredity arise from parents whose low mentality confines them to the semiskilled and unskilled levels of work."

In an effort to determine whether the size of the family in which the mentally deficient is born and subsequently lives has any effect upon his characteristics, Dayton (129) studied 20,473 retarded children in the public schools of Massachusetts. Evidently the statistics were taken from school records, though the author does not state this. The average size of the family of the mentally deficient was not different from that of the general population if correction is made because of the preponderance of foreign element. The author analyzed certain characteristics of children which seemed to be associated with larger and smaller families. Undoubtedly more insight would be obtained if a study were based, not upon analyzing one factor in isolation from the many factors affecting child life, but rather upon the interrelation of various factors on development.

Fairbank (138) reported a study of 122 children, seventeen years after they had been diagnosed as subnormal, and compared them with 100 normal children from the same community. So-called normal sex life (marriage) as well as abnormal sex-life (promiscuity, prostitution, and illegitimate births) were more frequent (though only slightly so) among the subnormals than the normals. The police records were about the same for both groups, though there was a larger percent of juvenile court records for the subnormal. Economically there were differences but not great ones: the subnormals almost equal the normals in self-support (two-thirds earning their living as laborers) though 10 percent were receiving financial aid; their living conditions were not so comfortable as those among the normals. There was a discrepancy in education between the two groups since several of the normals graduated from high school and a few went to college, but most of the subnormals went no further than the fifth grade.

Lithauer (211) reported a follow-up study of twenty-five slow children who were retained in the kindergarten until they had attained a mental age of six years. During the five years, sixteen had made normal progress. Suggestions are given for adapting school work to the needs of these children.

The effect of physical and mental training on mentally deficient, birth lesion children was studied experimentally by Martz and Irvine (229). Special physical training, academic and occupational instruction were given for periods from four to twelve months, to eighteen patients at Letchworth Village. There were gains in I.Q. in all but one case, idiots gaining most on the average and morons least. The effectiveness of the physical training seemed to be a direct function of its duration.

Supervised play as a means for specific as well as general education for mentally retarded children was upheld by Schlotter and Svendsen (293) on the basis of two years' work at the Lincoln State School in Illinois. Daily periods of supervised play brought such results as general improvement in individual behavior, attitudes, and group discipline; actual learning of complex games; improvement in table manners and in dressing; improvement in attitude of employees toward wards. Many practical contributions in the field of play with subnormals are offered.

Other studies include a survey of 500 retarded children in Massachusetts by Lord (213); an analysis of the responses of forty-three abnormal boys ten to fourteen years of age to the Rorschach Test by Ganz and Loosli-Usteri (154); and a discussion by Peters (267) of the "indeterminate" type of abnormal child on the basis of data secured from the application of the Bourdon test of concentration to 129 retarded children.

Language

Researches in the development of language have made material progress in defining sequences in the growth of vocabulary, sentence structure, and ideational content. Several studies give girls an edge over boys in early language development.

Fisher (145) studied the development of language in preschool children through an analysis of stenographic records of the language of seventy-two children, aged two to five years. Each child's language was recorded during a total period of nine hours in the nursery school. The findings showed the rate of decline with age in the amount of non-verbal or incomprehensible speech, in the proportion of exact repetition and incomplete sentences, and in the increase with age in length of sentences and in proportion of complex sentences. Girls were, on the whole, superior to boys. A high degree of egocentricity was revealed at all age levels, with a decreasing amount of talking about things and an increasing amount of talking about people.

Stalnaker (310) traced the development of language as shown by records of the conversations of fourteen children, aged two to four years. The findings include an analysis of the words, parts of speech, sentence structures, and grammatical forms most frequently used. According to the findings, the younger the child the more egocentric the speech will be.

M. E. Smith (303) analyzed grammatical errors in the speech of 220 children aged one and one-half to six years, as revealed by records of the children's spontaneous conversations. The most common error was the omission of an essential word; next in frequency were errors in the use of a verb; the use of articles was found to be learned relatively late; case was the most troublesome feature in the use of pronouns. As early as the age of three, many errors were due to generalization: rules for regular forms were extended to words of irregular inflection. Girls were superior to boys at two years but not consistently thereafter.

In a study of the development of the sentence, M. E. Smith (305) analyzed the spontaneous speech of children, aged one and one-half to six years. Parts of speech and aspects of sentence structure were analyzed in detail. There was a high correlation between sentence length and vocabulary. Girls excelled boys at two years. Smith also dealt with the relationship between language development and the child's social status and his order of birth. The relationship between vocabulary and the child's social status was also touched upon in a brief study by Cuff (124). Nice (254) studied the development of sentence structure through an analysis of complete records of the language of a child who was observed from the age of fourteen months through thirty-one months and then again at the age of three. The results give an interesting picture of the changes that took place from month to month. La Brant (196) studied aspects of language development through an analysis of compositions written by about a thousand children in the fourth through the twelfth grades. Children were compared with psychologists who contributed to "Psychologies of 1930."[1] All clauses were classified according to main and dependent clauses, and changes with age were noted.

Children's questions, their frequency, form, and function were studied by M. E. Smith (304) in a further analysis of records of the language of 219 preschool children. The proportion of questions to total number of sentences was found to increase up to the age of four years and then showed a decline. "What" and "where" were used most frequently by the youngest children; "how," "when," and "why" were not used at all

---

[1] Murchison, Carl, editor. *Psychologies of 1930*. Worcester, Mass.: Clark University Press, 1930. 497 p.

at two years but showed a yearly increase thereafter. Questions as to the whereabouts or the names of persons and things declined with age, while questions concerning fact, time, invention, intention, and causality increased. Boys asked more causal questions than girls, while girls exceeded boys in questions concerning social rules and questions concerning places and names.

The amount and nature of a child's vocalizations in relation to the situation in which he is acting (alone in nursery, in the bath, in the company of other children, etc.) were studied by Ellesor (136).

The development of language in twins was studied by Day (128), whose subjects included twenty pairs of twins at each age level from two to five years. Again in this study boys were found to be somewhat inferior to girls at most age levels and upper occupational groups were superior to the lower occupational groups. Most of the twin groups were below average in I.Q. On the average, the twins began to talk one month later than their older siblings. Identical twins showed higher resemblance in language development than did fraternal twins.

The effect of a bilingual environment was studied in a further investigation by M. E. Smith (306). The subjects were eight children who made frequent moves between America and China. A bilingual environment did not seem to delay the first use of words but operated as a handicap at a later age; change from a monolingual environment to a bilingual one apparently is likely to affect a child's speech more than a change in the opposite direction. The author also concluded that it probably is better for young bilingual children to receive their two languages from quite separate sources rather than to be spoken to in two languages by the same person. Children, aged ten to fourteen years, enrolled in three bilingual schools in South Wales in districts in which children learned Welsh at home before beginning a systematic study of English in school, were compared with children in exclusively English speaking districts in a study by Barke (92). The children in the monoglot schools were superior to the bilingual children in verbal intelligence tests, but on a non-verbal test (Pintner Non-Language Test) the bilingual schools had a slight advantage.

The problem as to whether common emotional expressive reactions are native or acquired is one that has significance from the point of view of language when considered in the broad sense of social communication. Goodenough followed her earlier investigation in this field with a study of a blind-deaf child (159). This child, who had been practically devoid of opportunity to observe the expressions of others, showed in her own expression a strong resemblance to the well-known descriptions of Darwin and Spencer. This observation suggests that the primary forms of expressive behavior are determined by native factors.

Learning

The question of the influence of practice has been investigated not only with infants but with preschool and elementary-school children and adults. Jersild and associates (187) contributed to the discussion of maturation versus training of children by eight experiments, using the equivalent group method. There were 121 practice and 127 control subjects, ranging in age from two to ten years. In all experiments the practiced children showed some advantage over the controls at the end of training but on later tests (several months later) the practiced children maintained this lead only in the case of ability to sing tones and intervals. This is in keeping with the claim that training can help a child to add new items to his repertoire, to extend his knowledge or skill. The gains produced by practice in all experiments were relative to the child's initial capacity, and individual differences between children were not substantially altered by training. Mirenva (246), in studying the influence of psychomotor training on the general development of twins, concluded that the development of more elementary functions such as jumping depends less on training than do the more complex intellectualized psychomotor functions such as hitting a mark by throwing a ball. This is in line with Jersild's findings.

Another study which shows the impotency of training of certain functions was made by Hilgard (171) who studied the effect of early and delayed practice on memory and motor performances in an experiment with a pair of twins. The twins were fifty-four months old at the beginning and sixty-six months old at the end of the experiment. Following initial tests, one twin received practice while the other served as a control; both were then retested; thereafter the second twin was practiced (delayed practice) while the previously practiced twin served as a control. Each practice period was eight weeks in length, and retests were made three months and again six months after the termination of delayed practice. Delayed practice resulted in superiority for the delayed-practice twin in object-memory, digit-memory, ring-toss, and on two of several boards used in a walking board test. At three and again at six months after all practice had ceased, the performances of the children on all tests were as similar to each other as at the beginning of the experiment.

Cox (122) studied the relative effects on learning of adults and boys of elementary-school age who were given no practice, undirected practice, and directed practice or training. Thirty-nine adults (with thirty-one controls) and thirty-nine boys (with thirty-two controls) were included in the experiment. The operations investigated were those involved in assembling and wiring an electric lamp holder and in stripping the same. In the first experiment the practice group was given practice on one of the four operations involved (eleven days' practice for adults and five for children). For both adults and boys this practice resulted in superiority over control group in operations practiced but not in other operations. In the second experiment, where training in one operation was substituted for mere repetitive practice, the practiced group showed marked superiority in all operations. No correlations were found between intelligence and progress during training.

A rolling-ball maze of three levels of complexity was used by Mattson (232) to study the effect of complexity of a task on the learning of fifty children from five to six years of age. Control groups were formed by matching two individuals for sex, chronological age and I.Q., and initial maze ability. The practiced subjects were superior to the unpracticed subjects on the test following practice and less markedly on the retest after sixty days. The superiority was slight upon the simple pattern, marked upon the pattern of intermediate complexity, and still more marked upon the most complex pattern. Individual differences tend to increase as a result of practice on the more complex task whereas they tend to decrease on the more simple task. This is in line with previous studies.

An initial study of the ability of preschool children to generalize methods of solution in a series of similar but different situations was made by K. E. Roberts (276). An ingenious apparatus was devised which made possible nine situations each of which could be solved according to the same general plan. Forty preschool children, between the ages of three years, six months and seven years, ten months with I.Q.'s from 80 to 150, were used as experimental subjects. The data show that these preschool children did apply the learning of the initial situation to later situations. The learning of the initial solution was more closely related to mental age than chronological age but this did not hold for the application of the solution. The author further analyzed data regarding children's verbal responses and concluded that failure to respond verbally should not be taken as inability to respond nor as indicative of inferior ability in learning of the type represented by the experiment.

Investigations concerned with the effect of certain personality manifestations on learning were reported. A study was made by Poyntz (272) who investigated the susceptibility of preschool children (ages twenty-six to sixty-six months) to visual and auditory distractions while performing a relatively simple peg board task. The distractions consisted of sounds from the metronome, music on a toy victrola, electric light which flashed intermittently, a group of toys, and two pictures. The I.Q. range of the children was from 90 to 131 with a median of 106. Some of the distractions (especially the metronome, victrola, and electric light) acted as incentives to the children to hurry and finish. The author concluded that visual distractions have a much more disturbing effect on the performance of a task involving visual attention than auditory distractions. This susceptibility to distraction is a trait independent of sex, chronological age, I.Q., or socio-economic status and varies not only from child to child but from time to time in the same child.

The persistence of eighty-three normal and defective children in six tasks was studied by Crutcher (123). The children ranged in age from seven to sixteen years. Scores of persistence correlated .30 with I.Q.; highest scores were made by children who talked least; the children indicated that they liked best the tests in which highest persistence scores were made.

A study which may have far-reaching effects on the guidance of children in social adjustments was reported by Jack (182). The study dealt with the effect of the learning of certain skills on the child's social adjustments. Five non-ascendant children received training in making block designs, solving a picture puzzle, and telling a story that was illustrated by pictures. The children were then paired with other subjects who initially surpassed them in ascendant behavior. The subjects who had received training showed a decided increase in their ascendance scores.

Carter, Jones, and Shock (114) made an experimental study of the relationship of efficiency in learning lists of words and various measures of affective conditions such as association times, word responses, galvonometer deflections, respiration, and blood pressure. The children studied were fifty-one boys and fifty-one girls in the sixth and seventh grades. The authors concluded that the results indicate a definite relationship between emotional factors and ease of learning. Learning scores of individuals tend to be highest for pleasant words, next for unpleasant, and lowest for indifferent.

The general superiority of the whole method of learning poetry which has been accepted for many years was challenged by McGeoch (217) in a study of 310 children between nine and eleven years of age. In the experiments reported, no reliable differences were found between the whole method and the part method in either learning or retention.

In the field of motor learning, Melcher (235) showed that visual methods in guidance were more effective than manual methods for children three to five years learning a maze. Data from Beebe's study (97) indicate a slight positive relationship between learning on a balance board and nutritional status. Langhorne (199) studied age and sex differences in the acquisition of skill in the operation of a pursuit-meter. The subjects were seventy-eight children, aged seven to seventeen years. In general, it was found that both the limit of improvement and the rate of improvement from practice increased directly with age, with the period of greatest improvement appearing during, or near the beginning of, the adolescent period. The order of the individuation of the movements through practice proceeded from the trunk, shoulder, and arm toward the finger. Beebe (98) also analyzed the eye and hand coordination of eight four- and five-year-old children in aiming and thrusting at a target under conditions of normal vision and under conditions of prismatic deflection.

In investigating motivation in learning, research studies continue to show disagreement regarding the relative effects of reward and punishment, success and failure. The literature indicates the inadequacy of generalizations based upon specific and limited approaches to this problem and shows the importance of taking account not only of the specific nature of the incentive that is used but also of the type of task and the type of child involved in the situation.

Tuckman (321) used the word "wrong," and saying "wrong" plus depriving the child of a fraction of a cent or administering an electric shock, as contrasted with the word "right." The subjects were 100 boys aged eleven to fifteen years; the task was word and nonsense word association. The influence of a mild, spoken "wrong" differed little from an emphatic and substantial pain or deprivation. In every experiment and in every degree, punishment did more harm than good.

In an interesting study by Chase (118), dynamometer tests were given to over 200 children aged two to eight years. Praise or reward (e. g., a gold star) was more effective than knowledge of success; reproof or punishment (e. g., having a button cut off a paper gingerbread boy that had been given to the child) was more effective than mere knowledge of failure. Failure-reproof and failure-punishment were about equal in effectiveness. Failure-repetition was superior to success-repetition. Reproof for failure was more effective than praise for success. According to the findings, the chances are that failure-punishment is more effective than success-reward.

Anderson and R. S. Smith (88) restudied 102 of Chase's subjects after an interval of three years with a slight modification of Chase's methods. Again the subjects performed better when reproved for failure than when praised for success. Failure-punishment was now definitely superior to success-reward. As in the earlier study, success-reward tended to be more effective than success-praise; failure-reproof and failure-punishment continued to be about equally effective. In both studies some motivation was more effective than controlled motivation (no knowledge of results and mere repetition of instructions).

E. L. Thorndike and Forlano (317) found that the learning of a series of lines of English and Spanish words by boys ten and eleven years of age was facilitated by small amounts of money (up to 0.4 cent) but was decreased by an increase to 0.8 cent because of excitement or other factors.

The influence of previous success or failure on a child's interest in returning to a task has been studied by Rosenzweig (282) by means of jigsaw puzzles, one of which the child was allowed to complete and the other of which was removed before completion. Later the child was asked which he preferred to do again. The subjects were thirty-seven children aged five to fourteen years. Thirty-two of thirty-seven children chose the puzzle on which they had succeeded. This tendency was strongest in the youngest children. The results in this study stand in interesting contrast to findings enthusiastically reported by Koffka (195:357) in a review of a study by Ovsiankina. In this investigation, children's reactions to completed tasks as against uncompleted tasks were compared: "For days afterwards children would ask to be allowed to finish the incomplete tasks, while they never asked for the repetition of a completed task."

Marinesco and Kreindler (226) reported experiments on conditioning of the withdrawal response to electrical stimulation in twenty-five children ranging in age from twenty-five days to three and one-half years. The response of the child tended to be general at first; later a specific hand or leg withdrawal occurred. In general the results verify those of Pavlov and his collaborators but certain additional data are reported. The authors urge a revision of educational principles in the light of conditioning.

Whether the ease with which inhibition may be conditioned is constitutional or not was the problem which Cowan and Foulke (121) set out to investigate. There were three experimental series in which the subject was asked to respond to a series of colored lights or a buzz but not to respond to one colored light. This light was always preceded by the same stimulus, this being the "conditioned" color. The subjects included adults, children, and college students, the exact ages, sex, and I.Q. not being given. The results indicate that an inhibition could be conditioned which varied (in delay of response) for different subjects, but the variations were not wide for the same subject at different times. The authors classified the subjects into groups which were termed hyperinhibitive (delayed type), hypoinhibitive (accelerated type), and balanced. A fourth type, the individual who is intermittently subject to domination by the two extreme factors, is suggested. By statistical analysis the authors concluded that the character of variations is not influenced by age or training.

Many technical studies in the field of conditioning and unconditioning of children continue to come from the Russian laboratories but are not included in this review because their immediate significance for education is not apparent.

Among other studies in learning are Davidson (126), Calhoon (111, 112), Bigelow (102), Whiteside (330), Stroud and Maul (314), Düker (133), and Fajans (140).

Memory

Studies of memory may be divided into two groups: studies in the development of memory, and studies of reminiscence and early memories.

Bryan (108) attempted to furnish more definite data concerning the organization of memory as a mental trait by studying 200 children between five and six years of age with an I.Q. range from 60 to 139. The children were given a battery of eleven memory tests and two so-called non-memory tests (a vocabulary test and the Stanford-Binet Intelligence test). The author reported evidence of a central factor through the memory tests and also extending through both the vocabulary and the intelligence test. An analysis of the Stanford-Binet test showed that it is predominantly a memory test on its early levels. The conclusion was drawn that the central factor is probably a memory factor and that it probably indicates a relation between simple retentivity and the more general ability which is termed intelligence in young children.

Another study of preschool children (two-, three-, and four-year-olds) was reported by Mallay (222) who investigated memory span by the use of three types of boxes varying in difficulty for their successful opening. Latent memory spans increased with age, generally following the negatively accelerated curve, but showed variations which might be related to other factors than maturation alone. The methods used by the experimenter greatly affected the length of memory span, two-year-olds evidently being dependent on verbal directions in addition to visual directions. The length of memory span ranged from 0.3 days to 19.8 days depending upon the type of box, the procedure used by the experimenter, and the age group of the children. Certain personality traits of individual children also affected the results.

The development of memory in older children was studied by Hsiao (175) and by Brunswik, Goldscheider, and Pilek (107). Hsiao tested the immediate memory of 639 subjects from eight to nineteen years of age by the use of eighty pairs of stimulus and response words. Exposure was limited to one second for each pair; recall followed immediately upon the presentation of each ten pairs. For memory of physical relationships and for logical-abstract material, the growth curve had a tendency toward positive acceleration before the age of thirteen; but for logical-concrete and concrete-associated-with-abstract materials, the curve was linear between nine and twelve years of age. There was only slight or no growth after the age of fourteen years. Boys were superior to girls.

Substantiation for Karl Bühler's theory of three stages of development (instinct, training, intellect) and Charlotte Bühler's doctrine of phases was found in the study of 800 subjects between six and eighteen years of age by Brunswik, Goldscheider, and Pilek (107).

Holaday and Stoddard (172) studied the ideas remembered by children after having seen a motion picture. Using adult recall as the standard, it was found that very young children remember correctly 50 to 60 percent of what they see; eight- to nine-year-olds remember 60 percent; eleven- to twelve-year-olds, 75 percent; and fifteen- to sixteen-year-olds, 91 percent. It was found, in general, that second- and third-grade children, after six weeks, retained 90 percent of what they could recall the day after they had seen a motion picture.

Other studies in the development of memory include Fedorov's study of children with speech defects (142); Baumgarten's case study of a gifted young orchestra leader (94); Vértes' experiment with deaf-mute children (326); and the investigations of Schiel (291) and Shimidu (300).

In an effort to discover whether age really is a factor in reminiscence, McGeoch (215) tried a learning experiment with 100 preschool children and 100 college students and concluded from the data that reminiscence is not a function of age. In another study McGeoch (216) found no evidence that degree of learning is an influencing factor. One might question whether the author has not simplified the experiment to such an extent that college students would not have equal motivation with preschool children for remembering.

Dudycha and Dudycha (131, 132), through the reports of 129 college students, studied certain factors related to childhood memories. The majority of childhood memories dated back to the third and fourth years of life, the mean age being three years, seven months. Fear, joy, and anger appear the most frequently in childhood memories but wonder and curiosity, sorrow and disappointment, pain, shame, and guilt are also reported. Joy was the most frequent emotion reported by women (one-third reporting memories of joyful experiences); shame and guilt appeared about three times as often in memories reported by women as those reported by men; women also remembered a large percent of experiences that had angered them. Men on the other hand reported a larger percent of remembered fearful experiences. Kamaryt (191), studying the earliest memories of seventh-grade pupils, found that in 80 percent of the 149 answers the recollection was accompanied by a strong emotional tone and half of these were unpleasant, including fear, shame, anger, etc. In the study by Dudycha and Dudycha above, fear was recorded as being associated with 39.5 percent of the memories, anger 8.5 percent, sorrow and disappointment 4 percent. Neither of these studies support the Freudian theory of memory of the pleasant.

Another experimental attempt to explore the validity of certain psychoanalytical theories was the study of memory in relation to successful and unsuccessful activities made by Rosenzweig and Mason (281). Immediately after completion of a series of jigsaw puzzles each child was asked to name all the puzzles and to indicate which ones he liked or did not like, and which ones he felt he had done well. No general tendency was found regarding memory of successful and unsuccessful achievements. The children with highest mental age remembered successes better but so also did the children whom the teachers rated highest for pride. What the relative influence of these two factors might be, the authors do not state.

Imagination

Several studies have dealt with children's fancies and make-believe. The studies have reflected an interest in developmental sequences in the growth of imagination and they have shown a promising trend in breaking away from stereotyped tests that reveal little concerning the child's inner life. They have recognized the significance of a child's imaginary activities as a clew to his social and emotional adjustments and to the educational opportunities that inhere in a child's imaginary tendencies. Although the studies have provided many significant glimpses, research in the field of childhood imagination has barely scratched the surface, and this topic holds alluring possibilities for further study.

Markey (227) studied the development of make-believe through observation of fifty-four preschool children during their free play and by means of experimental situations. Categories were devised for the analysis of various forms of imaginative play and the children were studied from the point of view of their versatility and originality in make-believe activities. This study has more than usual interest for teachers of young children in that sequences in the development of imaginative activities of children from twenty-four to fifty months were described. The observations also revealed many situations in which a teacher might profitably make use of a child's make-believe interests for practical educational purposes. The results of this study showed that a single method of studying imagination is likely to be quite inadequate in giving a picture of any individual child; that the same test of imagination is not equally valid or adequate at all age levels; that sex differences change in relation to the make-up of any particular group of children; that imaginative behavior seems to be related to the methods used in different nursery school groups. In short, this study points definitely to the error of generalizing about the behavior of preschool children from a study based upon any one group of children. It would therefore be interesting to know whether Shallit's findings (299) that five children were responsible for 80 percent of the make-believe play of a group of ten nursery school children would be substantiated in other groups.

The development of creative imagination as expressed in drawings of children between five and seven was studied by Grippen (163) who analyzed children's drawings, evaluated their art exercises, and obtained ratings by teachers and other observers. According to the results, creative imagination as shown in children's drawings rarely functions below the age of five.

That a child's behavior in a make-believe situation may reveal his interests and private feelings has been recognized in psychiatric practice. Levy (206) described behavior of children, all of whom had younger siblings, in a play situation in which dolls representing a mother, a baby, and a younger sister (or brother) were used to bring out the child's reactions of jealousy and sibling rivalry.

The prevalence of imaginary playmates among children is indicated in several studies. Hurlock and Burstein (179) obtained information from 701 high-school and college students from fifteen to forty years of age and found that 31 percent of the females and 23 percent of the males reported having had an imaginary playmate during childhood. Svendsen (315), however, found through interviews that among 119 children over four years of age only 13.4 percent had imaginary companions, while in Jersild and others' interview study (186), one-third of the 400 children reported them. The most frequent time for the appearance of the playmate according to Hurlock and Burstein was between five and seven years for girls but after ten years for boys; but Svendsen reported this first appearance at about two and one-half years. Svendsen stated that the make-believe quality of the companion was recognized at about five to six years. Hurlock and Burstein stated that the phenomena was more frequent and vivid with boys than with girls. Jersild found it more often with brighter than duller children. Hurlock and Burstein stated that in certain aspects of family background and activities of children the people who had imaginary playmates did not differ materially from those who did not have them. Svendsen reported that thirty-five of the forty children showed personality difficulties but seven of them were described as leaders. Friedmann (151) concluded that the creation of an imaginary person coincides generally with an event arousing a feeling of inferiority within the child.

Technics for the study of visual eidetic imagery at the preschool level were developed by Peck and Walling (264). They found eidetic images somewhat more frequently among their preschool subjects than among children of school age. Teasdale (316) found eidetic phenomena more frequently among the younger subjects in a group of 173 ten- to fourteen-year-old boys, and obtained indications that there were two types of eidetic image—one which is very prevalent among young children and decreases with increasing age, and one which is not so rich in detail, which does not show such marked divergence from normal after-images, and which becomes more frequent with increasing age up to fourteen years. Meenes (234) inferred from a study of 100 negro school children that the so-called eidetic image seems to have little relation to imagery and is largely a peripheral phenomenon. Other studies include an investigation of normal children by Marzi (230), an investigation by Bonte (104) of eidetic imagery in relation to suggestibility, and by Rieti (275) of visual eidetic tendencies in children afflicted with mental diseases.

Attention

The amount of time a child will spontaneously devote to a project continues to be a matter of interest to research workers. The findings in this field indicate, in general, that a child's capacity for concentration improves with age; but the span of concentration will be influenced to a large extent by the nature of the situation in which the child is observed. It is, therefore, difficult to derive general educational principles from the data that are at hand. Nevertheless, such findings as are available do offer some suggestions regarding the timing of projects in child training.

K. A. Miles (241) studied sustained visual fixation of preschool children to a delayed stimulus. The child was asked to watch a Jack-in-the-box until it opened, and the experimenter timed the child until he first looked away. The subjects were fifty-eight children aged two to six. The mean fixation time at three and four years was 8 seconds; at five years, 16.8 seconds; at six years, 27.5 seconds. The differences approached statistical significance. The findings also suggest that a brighter child at a given age will be somewhat more capable of sustained attention than a duller child, but this trend was not conclusive.

Van Alstyne, in a study referred to elsewhere (322), recorded the amount of time children at different ages devoted to a given activity during play. There was an average rise of approximately 2 minutes at each age level from two to five years; the means rose from 6.9 minutes at two to 12.6 minutes at five years.

Shacter reported three studies (296, 297, 298) in which measurements were made of the time during which the subject will continue an activity of his own accord under experimental conditions involving both simple and complex tasks. She found that there was little difference in time of sustained attention in the three-, four-, and five-year groups, and that preschool children may be expected to sustain attention within a range of from 8 to 12 minutes, depending on the complexity of the task. Children who were rated as extrovertive by their teachers (Marston Scale) exhibited shorter attention spans than did children rated as introvertive. She found little correlation between intelligence and sustained attention time in simple situations and a higher correlation between intelligence and attention to more complex situations. Bestor (101) studied attention span as distinct from duration of activity. Analysis of overt behavior and of verbal comments indicated that significant variations in behavior do not appear in a score for attention based merely upon the amount of time spent.

Perception and Concepts

The development of perception, and especially visual perception, has received much attention in research studies. These have dealt in considerable detail with the age at which children can discriminate forms and patterns, and to a lesser extent with the developmental sequences that underlie the growth of perception. There has been an increasing number of studies that deal, either implicitly or explicitly, with issues in perception suggested by the principles of Gestalt psychology. Findings have not uniformly conformed to what would be expected in the light of Gestalt principles. The study of perception is still in the process of laying a groundwork of facts, drawn from various angles of approach, which may eventually become integrated into a body of knowledge that will have direct educational implications.

Peckham (265) used a non-verbal adaptation of the Snellen Test in a study of nineteen children aged twenty-one to sixty-two months, and concluded that children of this age group have visual acuity similar in range to that of adults. Gellerman (156) studied form discrimination in two chimpanzees and two two-year-old children. Children learned to discriminate much more rapidly than did the chimpanzees. The author concluded that the children were able to discriminate form per se. Skeels (302) studied form discrimination by means of a conditioning technic in an investigation of forty-one children aged fifteen to forty-six months. A form was presented with a cookie underneath; and subsequently changes were made in the position of this form among other forms which did not have the cookie. In this study children under two years did not show evidence of form discrimination. Genetically, the ability to discriminate form seemed to appear before the ability to see the relationship between two units of the same form.

Abel (87) compared normal children (aged nine years and above), subnormal children, and adults in estimations of extent in horizontal plane. The adults were more accurate when judging by tactual impressions than when judging by visual impressions, while in children the difference between the two sense modalities was not so marked. W. F. Smith (307) studied direction orientation in children (four to eleven years) and adults by means of an instrument, resembling a compass dial, which was placed before the blindfolded subject. Four- and five-year-olds were found to be poorly orientated to the cardinal points of the compass. The greatest gain appeared at the ages of seven and eight. The experiment failed to disclose any evidence in support of a vestigial sense of direction. The author concluded that ". . . (this ability) is learned over a period of years."

Hartmann and Triche (166) compared the responses of adults to eight common laboratory illusions with the responses of first- through sixth-grade children. Individual differences exceeded the influence of chronological age as such. The authors concluded that it was impossible to find characteristic differences such as should be found if children's figural perceptions are really independent of spatial position, as certain authorities maintain. N. E. Miller (243) studied the relative potency of specific as compared with configurational cues in the perceptions of ninety-eight children aged one to thirteen years. The children were asked to find a toy hidden in a varying array of boxes, after a screen had momentarily been interposed. Position was dominant over color and configuration at the youngest levels, but the latter became dominant over position at an earlier age than did color. A series of experiments that compared the potency of a specific color with a configurated cue did not conform to findings that would be deduced from the Gestalt principle that configurational relation is a more primitive cue than absolute relation. It is concluded that if the configurational factor as a cue comes into conflict with a specific color, the latter is dominant with the younger children and more dominant the younger the children. Batalla (93) employed preschool and school age children as subjects in an investigation which used a body-maze to study "insightful" behavior. The children tended to react to the maze pathways as separate units, without a grasp of the total pattern or field relationships, even though the situation was regarded by the author as one that offered opportunities for "insightful" behavior. The observed behavior was only rarely suggestive of insight, ideational response, or "structured" response.

Children's perceptions as revealed by their drawings were studied by Hurlock and Thomson (178); 248 children aged four to eight years drew pictures of a man, a girl, a house, and other objects. It was found that the tendency to perceive the specific rather than the general and the tendency to perceive details, background, and color placement increased with age.

Several studies have provided stray glimpses of the mind of the child as revealed by the development of concepts and modes of thought. Many studies agree in showing that the child is slow in developing general concepts of identity, relationship, and causality. There is not a common agreement, however, on the question as to whether the thought processes of the child are essentially different from the thought processes of adults.

The notion that the child goes through a primitive, animistic stage of thought in the development of reasoning was not supported by findings obtained by Mead (233) who made an investigation of the thought of primitive children with special reference to animism. The methods of study included observations of children, analyses of drawings, interpretations of ink blots, and the use of questions designed to provoke animistic responses. The subjects were children of the Manus tribe. The findings indicated that the children of this tribe not only showed no tendency toward spontaneous animistic thought but they also responded negatively to explanations couched in animistic terms rather than in terms of practical cause and effect.

The development of the preschool child's concepts of relationship of time, space, number, part-whole, discordance, and cause was investigated by Grigsby (162), in a study of eighty-three children aged two to eight years, by means of questions dealing with the various relationships. In the relation of time there was progression with age through the successive steps, "I don't know," being told, recognition of a contiguous incident, a series of incidents, and the telling of time by the clock. Developmental differences were also noted with respect to other relations. Ability to identify relations was found to be influenced by the child's degree of empirical familiarity with the situation. Four stages appeared in the development of concepts of causal relations. Mental age played a noticeable part in the maturity of concepts. The development of abstract concepts of magnitude was studied by Thrum (319) by means of various series of objects similar in form but differing in size. The subjects were thirty-four two- to five-year-old children. Children were found to be more familiar at first with *big* and *little* and had most difficulty with the concept of *middle-sized*; age differences were not marked, nor were judgments significantly influenced by the form or order of presentation. Children who were retested after a summer vacation showed improvement. According to Rostohar (284) such terms as "dog" or "bird" do not mean to the preschool child the general idea but the concrete object, and the idea of common kinds and classifications does not arise through abstraction from a series of concrete objects.

Claparède (119) discussed the consciousness of similarity and dissimilarity in the child. He reiterated the view that the earlier and longer an automatic reaction has operated, the longer will self-consciousness regarding it be delayed. Consciousness of a condition arises when habitual reaction fails. Consciousness of differences comes earlier than consciousness of similarities to which reactions have become automatic.

Lacey (197), with 450 subjects from the first three school grades, studied children's concepts of the social world of people and things by means of questions and 125 concepts as depicted by pictures (e.g., "show me the one that brings letters"). Correct answers increased steadily from grade to grade. Concepts of food, clothing, and shelter were quite clear; concepts of distant lands and earlier times were full of errors; concepts of animals, insects, and plants were not clear. Second and third graders differed less than second and first graders. Personal relationships were not grasped as easily as facts about objects.

Becher (95) probed children's understanding of concepts such as sickness, death, mind, etc., by questioning seventy-six five- to fourteen-year-old children. There was evidence of developmental sequences, the main stages of which ranged from mere statement of conditions and consequences, through religious and magical theories, to realistic notions. Children's concepts as revealed by their wishes and ambitions were studied by Jersild, Markey, and Jersild (186) through private interviews with 400 children aged five to twelve. Younger children tended to wish for specific things, while older children phrased their wishes in more inclusive terms. In answering the question as to what changes they would like in themselves if they could be changed, only a small proportion showed a critical insight into their own powers and limitations.

Restorff (273) studied children's understanding of a pictorial situation by asking five- to eight-year-olds to describe and then to imitate little scenes. The principal types of imitation noted were: (a) the child glances briefly at the picture and then imitates only a part, such as an attitude of the hand or arm; (b) he makes a methodical analysis of details, tries to imitate the model constructively; and (c) he grasps the significance of the picture as a whole and acts it out in an understanding way.

Findings obtained in a study by Dysinger and Ruckmick (135) of the emotional responses of children to motion pictures incidentally throw some light on children's concepts and interests. Psychogalvanic and pulse records were obtained while children watched motion pictures. It was found that younger children did not perceive pictures as wholes but as numerous separate incidents. Adult reactions did not give a valid criterion of the reaction of younger children. Reactions to danger and conflict were greatest in children, and especially in boys, under twelve; whereas at the sixteen-year level love scenes elicited the greatest response.

Studies of the development of perception and of concepts have been reported also by Lichtenberger (207), Rostohar (283), Meyer (240), Luh and others (214), Bognar (103), and Hanfmann (164).

The subject of suggestibility in children, which is of interest in connection with the topic of children's concepts and attitudes, has received attention in three investigations.

Messerschmidt (239) studied the suggestibility of boys and girls between the ages of six and sixteen years by means of eleven suggestion tests including lines, forms, odors, colors, etc. He found the highest suggestibility at seven years with a regular lessening with the older age groups. Girls average slightly higher than boys and exceed boys at eight of the eleven ages. The same author (238) studied the responses of 194 boys between five and sixteen years of age to Hull's Postural Suggestion test, in which the examiner gave suggestions such as, "You are falling forward. You can't help yourself. You are falling forward." In this study the most suggestible ages were six and eight years. Suggestibility increased from five through eight years with a gradual decrease from eight on. Only three of the subjects failed to respond negatively or positively during one of the two suggestion periods, while no one remained completely unaffected. The younger children (five through eight years) were slightly more suggestible in the second period of the test but the older children were more suggestible in the first period.

In an effort to clarify certain ambiguities concerning the nature of suggestion as related to hypnosis, Hull and Forster (177) studied orphanage boys aged ten to eleven years by the Binet tests of progressive weight and progressive lines. There were indications of a decided negative effect on suggestibility with increasing practice. On the other hand, the perseverational or immediate practice effects from trial to trial for each day showed a slight tendency toward greater suggestibility.

Moral Judgments

The degree to which a child at a given age level understands rules of conduct, is able to generalize what he has learned in specific situations, and is able to grasp standards of morality represents a problem that not only is significant for character education but also arises as a practical concern in the daily home guidance of the child. It seems that children are called upon to be "moral" long before they have much insight into the what and why of right and wrong. The problem as to the most effective methods of promoting moral understanding has received less attention than the question as to what the normal child actually does understand.

In a study of the moral judgment of the child, Piaget and others (270) questioned children aged four to fourteen years regarding such matters as rules of the game, adult constraint, ideas of justice. Stages in reaction to rules ranged through simple individual regularity, imitation of seniors, cooperation, codification. Up to seven or eight years a majority of the children subordinated justice to adult authority. From eight to eleven years there was progressive equalitarianism, and from eleven or twelve on, the majority of children believed in a qualitarian justice tempered by consideration of equity.

Harrower (165) reported results which not only are rather challenging to Piaget's conclusions regarding stages of moral development, but which also suggest that a question might be raised with regard to the stages discovered by Piaget in other studies of childhood thought. Harrower repeated Piaget's study of moral concepts with some modifications. Findings obtained with a group of children selected to correspond to the group used by Piaget were similar to Piaget's results. But with another group of children, from well-to-do homes, the results were quite dissimilar. Harrower suggested that either (a) the stages of development which Piaget has been emphasizing possibly are not a universal characteristic of development per se, but are found only within certain select groups, or (b) in certain environments these stages can be so far accelerated that children exhibiting characteristics of the third, and most developed stage, are to be found at the ages of the first.

A practical note was struck by McGrath (218) in a study of moral concepts by means of questions put to 1,218 children aged one and one-half to seven years. Understanding of the act of obedience appeared in isolated cases as early as one and one-half years and the concept of the why of obedience as early as three and one-half years; two-thirds of the children appreciated the necessity of the act of obedience at four years but only about half appreciated the why at seven years. Questions such as "If you broke mama's sugar bowl, what would you do?" "If mama asked you who broke it, what would you do?" were used to probe concepts of courage, honesty, and justice. According to the criteria used in the study, these concepts had appeared in over half of the children at six years. The questions dealt also with concepts of ownership and familial responsibility. It was concluded that all the moral concepts under consideration, with the exception of the why of obedience, are within the grasp of the average preschool child.

Other studies of ethical and moral concepts have been reported by A. Frank (146), Illge (181), Kinter (193), and Schneckenburger (294). A study by Schilder and Wechsler (292) deals with children's ideas about death.

Attitudes of preschool children toward their own bodies and the bodies of others were studied by Dillon (130). Thirty-eight nursery school children were observed. The predominant attitude exhibited by children under three and one-half years toward their bodies, and toward the bodies of children of the opposite sex when undressed, was the same as when dressed. The younger group did not differentiate between sexes. Children aged three to five showed more definite awareness and interest, but exhibited no sense of impropriety. A study by Canivet (113), based upon answers to a questionnaire, has shown ways in which sexual attitudes and adjustments may be influenced by the manner in which enlightenment regarding sex is given to the child.

Minard (245) probed the attitudees held by 1,352 seventh- to twelfth-grade children toward the people of other races. Questions were raised such as, "Would you dance with an Italian girl?" and these were scored on a scale ranging from complete absence of race prejudice ("Yes, certainly!") to the undoubted presence of such prejudice ("No, certainly not!"). Little difference was found between boys and girls; scores in tolerance improved from the seventh to the tenth grade, with little change thereafter. Desirable race attitudes did not show much relationship to socio-economic status but were positively related to intelligence although not to a definitive degree. In an investigation of the development of race consciousness, Lehrer (204) studied forty-three New York Jewish children. Until the fourth year, the children showed no consciousness of belonging to the Jewish group. Between four and five such consciousness took the form of an attachment to a larger sphere in which the family was living; later it became expressed in terms of religion, language, and mores.

That motion pictures may have a pronounced effect on children's social attitudes was found by Peterson and Thurstone (268). Tests of attitudes toward nationalities and races, toward crime, criminals, and prohibition were made before and after the children had seen various films that might be regarded as prejudicial in one direction or the other. Changes in attitudes appeared on tests administered soon after the pictures had been seen and continuing effects could be detected after intervals of from two and one-half to nineteen months.

Esthetic Judgments

Studies of the development of esthetic tastes continue to accumulate and in time the isolated findings in this field will no doubt suggest generalizations that will have significant educational implications. Many of the studies are based on children's choices or preferences with only a few dealing with the products of children's constructive activities.

The influence of familiarity upon children's preference for pictures and forms was studied by Mendenhall and Mendenhall (237). Children were asked to judge pictures and poems as good or poor and some of the materials were then presented many times. In general, pictures and poems that were liked grew in favor when presented many times, while those that were disliked grew in disfavor; there were, however, exceptions to this rule.

Children's choices in poetry were studied by Mackintosh (220) who used 400 poems in an investigation of children in grades three through six. The results indicated that literary merit in the accepted sense is not a criterion of the value of a poem to children; children's choices are determined more by the poem's application to real or vicarious experiences. There were variations from grade to grade but some poems were commonly liked by all grades and some were commonly disliked.

Bailey (91) took photographs of block constructions made by fifty-four two- to five-year-old children and had the constructions rated by adults. The results showed that ability to plan and carry out a design increases with age and that with age the designs tend to become more symmetrical and the blocks placed more carefully.

Investigators are still trying to find out what colors children prefer, but there is lack of agreement still. It may be that the question cannot be answered in terms of color alone but only as color is related to other influencing factors in any situation. In a study by Staples and Walton (311) it was concluded that red and yellow are originally preferred colors in infancy and that blue and green grow in favor with increase in age. In a more extended study by Garth and Porter (155) the color preferences of over a thousand children ranging in age from one to nine years were examined. Yellow was found to be the least popular color; red stood high in all age groups; blue tended to be more esteemed with increasing age.

Children's sensitivity to color harmony was probed by Walton (327). Sensitivity to color harmony was found in a few children as early as the fourth year; there was a relationship between age and scores made by the children; color harmony scores were not appreciably affected by intelligence, time spent on a test, or single color preferences. Children who were rated high by teachers with regard to general artistic ability did not rank significantly higher in sensitivity to color than children ranked as non-artistic, by means of a technic developed by Williams (332) who used varied colored scarfs in conjunction with dolls wearing a dress of a certain color. Over 6,000 drawings by individuals ranging from the preschool level to adult years were examined in a study by Graewe (160). The results were judged and classified in terms of conceptual drawings, spacial arrangement, and other factors. Children's esthetic tastes were tested by Bulley (109) by means of nine pairs of contrasted household articles paired from the point of view of good and bad in esthetic value.

Other studies dealing with the development of esthetic reactions include a study by Whorley (331) of children's sensitivity to compositional unity; by Daniels (125) of discrimination of compositional balance; by Jasper (183) of children's sensitivity to graphic rhythm; by Mellinger (236), and by Olney and Cushing (256) of children's interests in pictorial materials; by Tiebout (320) of psychophysical characteristics of artistically superior as compared with inferior children; and by Rodgers (278) of the relation between artistic ability and the environment.

Children's Interests

Several studies have dealt with children's interests as revealed by play activities and choices of play materials. The topic of interests is obviously important from an educational point of view. On the whole it may be said that research in the field of children's interests, especially at the elementary-school level, has shown a decided lag in proportion to the importance attached to interests in progressive educational theory and the role that interests might play in educational practice. The study of children's interests, with an eye to their utility in guidance and education, offers one of the most promising and timely areas of research in educational psychology.

Investigations of children's toy preferences at the preschool level have revealed certain general trends. It appears that choices are influenced not only by the general class to which a given play object might belong, but also by the characteristics of the specific object. To obtain a definitive picture of the relative appeal and usefulness of various materials would therefore require a more extensive selection of materials and a more careful control of the many variables involved than have been afforded in studies that have been made to date.

Van Alstyne (322) observed the uses made of certain play materials by two- to five-year-old nursery school and kindergarten children. Blocks, clay, and the doll corner were very popular at all age levels; wagons appealed more to three-year-olds than to two-year-olds; crayons had more appeal at the age of five than in earlier years; younger children tended to play more with active than with sedentary materials, but at five years interest was divided about equally between the two types. Boys tended to choose materials that called for active play while the girls' choices tended more toward passive play. The study also showed the degree to which various materials stimulate social as distinguished from non-social play. Benjamin (100) examined the toy preferences of 100 children aged fourteen to seventy-six months by means of tests which utilized six toys which were similar in size, color, and cost. A car was chosen considerably more by boys while dolls were chosen more often by the girls. It was not possible in many instances to predict a child's final choice from the amount of time he spent playing with different toys. Vance and McCall (323) studied preschool children's preferences among play materials by the method of paired comparisons of pictures. Interest in clay and housekeeping material was high at all ages; boys tended to show higher preferences for materials requiring larger muscle activity, while girls tended more in the direction of housekeeping materials and materials for more passive play—a tendency which appeared also in Van Alstyne's study. In a study by Manwell and Mengert (225) boys likewise were observed to exhibit somewhat more physical activity in their play than girls.

Children's play in the home environment was studied by M. P. Roberts (277). The study analyzed uses made of play materials, varying types of parent participation in children's play, and various types of play activities. This study has interesting practical implications for parents.

Children's interests in collecting were studied by Durost (134), who obtained information from 918 ten- to fourteen-year-old children by means of questionnaires and interviews, and by Witty and Lehman (333), who presented checklists containing 190 items to several hundred town and country children in grades two to twelve.

Bright children were found by Boynton and Ford (105) to spend more time per day in play than dull children; dull and bright children spent practically the same amount of time in physical play; but in mental recreations, the bright exceeded the dull to the extent of almost an hour per day.

CHAPTER III
Motor Development from Two Years to Maturity

BAYLEY (336) presented the results of a seriatim study of a group of children retested on the California Infant Scale of Motor Development from birth through thirty-six months of age. The infants originally numbered sixty-one; the number measured at any one month from eighteen to thirty-six months ranged from forty-four to fifty-three. At the latter ages the tests were given at three-month intervals. The scale, presented in the appendix to the monograph, contains seventy-six items ranging from 0.2 months to 50.0 months. The reliabilities, based upon split-halves, ranged from .74 to .86 at ages eighteen to thirty-six months. Correlations between retests were low as between eighteen and twenty-one months and between twenty-one months and twenty-four months (.28 and .26), but were considerably higher thereafter (.61 to .75). The combined sigma scores for ages eighteen, twenty-one, and twenty-four months did not correlate very highly with the combined scores at twenty-seven and thirty months (.43) or at thirty-three and thirty-six months (.37), but the scores of the latter two correlated with each other (.73). There was little relationship with mental ability, body build indexes, and mid-parent education, although an earlier study had shown that mid-parent education was as highly related to mental ability of these children as it is customarily found to be at the school ages. Why mental ability correlates only .14 to .27 with motor ability at ages twenty-one to thirty months and then suddenly rises to .51 at thirty-six months is not explained.

Further light on the question as to whether there is a general motor ability in young children was furnished in a recent study by Goodenough and Smart (343). They presented interrelations of a number of motor abilities of 154 children, divided into four groups, carefully selected so as to give a minimum age range within each group. All children were tested at the period midway between their annual birthdays, that is, at ages two and one-half, three and one-half, four and one-half, and five and one-half years. The maximum variation was one month in either direction. The tests used would seem, on *a priori* grounds, to be quite similar, all involving the element of speed and all but one requiring eye-hand coordinations which appear similar. They were: finger tapping, stylus tapping, three-hole test, needle threading, simple reaction, and a walking path test. The reliability coefficients were, for the most part, "encouragingly high when the short time-allowance for the various tests is taken into account." All but four of the twenty-five reliabilities reported were above .80. Yet the intercorrelations were low, at no point exceeding .54 and for the most part approaching zero. Application of the Thurstone method for factor analysis revealed the existence of at least one common factor running through all of the tests and indicated the probability of one or more group factors entering into several of them. The common factor was thought to be something analogous to general motor maturity. The second factor was thought best described as attentiveness or carefulness. These logical inferences should be accepted with some caution, however. For example, the fact that the three-hole test was difficult and uninteresting, young children therefore being less inclined to put forth their best efforts, was used as an explanation for the low factor loading of the first factor at age three and one-half, but this same test had the highest loading of the second factor (attentiveness or carefulness) of any test at age three and one-half.

The curve of motor development and the motor profile of school age children was discussed by Yarmolenko (354). His conclusions were based on a series of tests given to thirty children of each sex in fourteen groups, ages eight to fifteen years. The tests included speed and exactness of walking, grasping and relaying objects, lying down and getting up, ball throwing, standing jump, strength, and motor endurance. There were three stages in the motor growth curve: (a) a negative acceleration in the ninth and tenth years; (b) a positive acceleration at ages ten to twelve for girls and ten to thirteen for boys; and (c) with the approach of puberty a second period of retarded development more evident for girls than for boys.

Special Abilities

A number of investigators have presented scores on separate motor abilities by age groups. Among them may be mentioned Johnson (344) who presented results for 120 children ages four to ten years on throwing a feathered dart at a target, for 360 children three to eleven years on steadiness of right hand, and for 239 children four to eleven years on speed of tapping; Cowan and Pratt (337) who tested 540 children ages three to twelve on a hurdle jump; and Goodenough (342) who studied the speed of tapping of 240 children two and one-half to five and one-half years of age and of thirty-two kindergarten children.

Influence of Motivation

Chase (118) found that the amount of motor energy expended by young children was affected by external incentives. More energy was expended under praise, reward, punishment, and reproof than under conditions of control motivation. Motor energy was measured by a specially constructed type of motivation dynamometer. The subjects were 259 children ages twenty-four to ninety-six months.

Motor Learning

As an outcome of a study of the relative effectiveness of visual guidance versus manual guidance in the motor learning of young children, Melcher (235) developed the hypothesis that ability to use kinesthetic cues as the sole guidance in learning develops with age instead of retrogressing. Twenty-one children thirty-five to fifty-seven months of age were divided into three groups who learned to trace a maze under three conditions of guidance: visual and manual guidance, vision alone, and manual guidance without vision. The method of training in which manual guidance without vision was employed was much less effective in producing successful learning by these children than were the visual methods.

Beebe (98) contributed tentative evidence on the nature of motor learning of eight children fifty-two to sixty months of age who attempted controlled aiming under conditions of prismatic deflection.

Influence of Practice

Viteles (352) concluded that initial scores on tests of short duration may lead to gross errors in the diagnosis of individual motor ability. His subjects were ninety-six children fifteen to eighteen years of age who were tested on the Stenquist mechanical assembly test, Minnesota paper form-board, O'Connor wiggly block, serial discrimeter, spool packing test from the Stanford motor skills unit, and Roberts' obstacle test. Two hours of practice on the serial discrimeter and spool packing brought about considerable change in the relative positions of individuals. Mattson (232) showed that the effects of practice were a function of the complexity of the task. Negligible differences were obtained on a maze of simple pattern, greater effects on a pattern intermediate in complexity, and still greater effects on the most complex pattern. The effects were retained over a two months' rest period. Subjects were fifty preschool and kindergarten children.

Identical twins were found by McNemar (347) to resemble each other more closely than fraternal twins. Forty-six fraternal twins and forty-seven identical male twins of junior high-school age were tested on pursuit rotor, steadiness, speed drill, spool packing, and card sorting. The author thought that heredity was the most plausible explanation for the greater resemblance of identical twins. Practice on the pursuit rotor and spool packing increased the resemblance of fraternal twins but did not change the resemblance of identical twins.

Relation to Mental Ability

The low relationship usually found between mental and motor ability was further substantiated by Bayley (336), McElwee (346), and Nemzek, Cronin, and Brannom (348). In a group of subnormal children, Attenborough and Farber (90) found a somewhat higher relationship between mental ability and manual dexterity and between mental ability and mechanical ability than that usually obtained within normal groups.

Relation to Physical Condition

A review of the literature on the influence of disease upon motor development during childhood prepared by Abramson (335) appeared in the

Psychological Bulletin in 1934. The net result of this survey seems to be that very little is known about the effect of disease upon motor abilities. Long (345) showed that the motor abilities of deaf children were not greatly different from those of hearing children of the same race, age, and sex. His experimental group was composed of eighty-nine Jewish children eight to eighteen years of age in an institution for deaf mutes. These were compared with a control group taken from an orphan asylum. The tests were spool packing, serial discriminator, pursuit rotor, tapping, motility rotor, dynamometer, and balancing board.

Relation to Personality

Cowan and Pratt (337) claimed considerable clinical value for their hurdle jump test in uncovering slight motor retardations which were affecting the personality and social adjustments of children. Often the motor difficulties had gone unnoticed by parents and teachers but were of very real significance, so the authors thought, in the child's adjustment and personality. In view of the specificity of motor abilities usually found, it is surprising that a single test such as the hurdle jump should reveal motor retardations that seem to be of such fundamental importance.

Westphal (353) found no differences between stutterers and non-stutterers. Twenty-six stuttering boys ages eight to seventeen years, with intelligence quotients 72 to 127, were matched on chronological age, intelligence, and race with a group of non-stutterers. There were no significant differences in strength of grip, bead tossing, Seguin form-board, simultaneous writing of digits, or steadiness.

Racial Differences

Eells (340) found that Eskimo, Aleut, and Indian children in Alaska were inferior in mechanical and motor ability to the norms given for American children. Five hundred and ninety-one children ages ten to twenty were given the MacQuarrie test for mechanical ability and 463 were given the Brace scale of motor ability. There were no sex differences in mechanical ability, but the boys were distinctly superior to the girls in motor ability. The motor scores for the boys closely approximated the norms for American children. There was no increase in the girls' scores with age.

Handedness

Differences in degree of use of the preferred hand by children two to six years of age were found by Updegraff (351). The same investigator, in a later article (350), did not find an invariable correspondence between preferential handedness and eyedness. Right-eyed children were usually right-handed, but right-handed children were not necessarily right-eyed. The correspondence between eyedness and handedness in left-handed children was less. Eyre and Schmeeckle (341) found that 86 percent of 280 junior high-school pupils showed correspondence of eye, hand, and foot preference. The correspondence between hand and foot preference was greater than that between eye and hand or eye and foot. Crider (339) demonstrated that the percent of eye preference varies with the opportunities for sighting. When only one opportunity is given, the subject must be classified as either right-eyed or left-eyed. When forty-five opportunities were given to a large group of elementary-school children, inconsistencies in sighting were found in 50 percent of the subjects.

Trends in Recent Investigations

The investigations on motor development during the years 1932 to 1935 have been much in line with previous investigations. Further material has appeared confirming the specificity of motor abilities, particularly of the finer eye-hand coordinations, but the search is still going on for the elusive common motor ability, aided by the newer developments of the tool of factor analysis. A hopeful trend towards a better understanding of motor abilities is the appearance of seriatim studies and of genetic studies of the same abilities over a fairly wide age range.

During the three years little or no attention has been paid to the effects of systematic training (guidance and instruction on how to improve) at the preschool or school ages, but the effects of repetitive practice have received some consideration.

As previously, almost nothing has appeared that contributes to a better understanding of the significance of motor abilities in the life of the child.

CHAPTER IV
Physical Growth from Birth to Maturity

THE SCOPE of this review of research in physical growth is restricted in three directions. First, only investigations published during the triennium September, 1932, to September, 1935, are reported. A review of research published prior to this period appeared in April, 1933. Secondly, attention is confined to studies made by American investigators. Researches contributed by workers of other countries are considered neither irrelevant nor unimportant, but the international literature is too voluminous for even cursory treatment in a single chapter. Finally, consideration is limited to studies carried out on physically normal human subjects ranging in age, for the most part, between birth and the end of the second postnatal decade.

Research Technic

Selection of sample—Boyd (372) discussed factors in the selection of an adequate sample for determining normal variability at successive ages in the weight of internal organs. She showed that, in order to avoid the error inherent in pathologic data, it was essential that subjects included: (a) had died from an accidental cause; (b) had been ill less than twenty-four hours; (c) had showed no symptoms of disease either before injury or at post-mortem; (d) had not suffered gross hemorrhage prior to death; and (e) had not died as a result of poisons known to influence the weight of organs.

Position of subject, location of landmarks, method of measurement—An experimental approach to the location of the nasion in the living was made by Ashley-Montagu (357). Preliminary study had suggested that this landmark was situated "at the point at which a horizontal tangent to the highest points of the superior palpebral sulci intersects the midsaggital plane" (357:92). This hypothesis was tested on 115 adult cadavers of both sexes and ten adult living males. The procedure with the cadavers was to bore a hole vertically through the soft tissues at the point postulated, to dissect the naso-frontal region of the head, and to observe whether or not the gimlet had penetrated the skeletal nasion. With the living subjects, a piece of wire was passed across the postulated point and lateral roentgenograms taken. The results were striking. The gimlet was found to have exactly pierced the nasion for 112 of the 115 cadavers. For the living subjects, in no instance did the fleshy landmark fail to coincide with the bony landmark. The investigator noted that "in those groups of mankind in which an epicanthic fold is normally present in the palpebral region, or in those individuals in whom the skin droops over the superior palpebral sulci, the method of locating the nasion here described cannot be applied" (357:90). Further, the general finding of a constant relation between the level of the nasion and that of the superior palpebral sulci must be interpreted, pending study at various age levels, as specific for the age group studied.

Bayer and Gray (361) presented a historical critique and experimental evaluation of existing methods of measuring the hand. They considered both the position of the hand and arm during measurement and the manner of taking hand measurements. The dual approach of literature analysis and experimental study of points on which authorities disagreed provided a balanced, comprehensive matrix from which to draw recommendations as to a standard position for the hand, the measurements to be taken on the living hand and the dimensions to be determined on the contour form.

The comparability of stature observations determined by two technics was studied by Whitacre (453). The technic differed only in that one required the subject to stand free on the weighing scales while the other necessitated that his heels, buttocks, shoulders, and head make contact with a vertical measuring board. Application of the two methods, in immediate sequence and by the same observer, was made for 398 school children of San Antonio. On finding that 28 percent of the group measured 1.3 cm. or more shorter when standing free on the scale than when against the board, Whitacre concluded that "little if any confidence could be placed in measurements attempting to follow the course of growth in height by the use of first one and then the other technique."

Gray (400) investigated the comparability of thoracic depth data taken with the large sliding compass (the preferred method of Hrdlicka) and with the spreading calipers (the method employed by Martin). Each method was applied on 246 white males and 131 negro males. Both series of subjects were "convicts between the age of 20 and 60 years, measured at the Illinois State Penitentiary in Joliet from 1927 to 1929." Obtained means, specific for anthropometric instrument and racial group, showed the straight-arm method to exceed the curved caliper method by 2 cm., or 10 percent. Gray considered this systematic error of sufficient size to necessitate correction before comparison or pooling of data obtained by the two instruments was justifiable. In consequence, he presented linear regression equations, treating white and negro males separately, for converting measurement values for one instrument into equivalent values for the other.

Cattell (374) proposed the sum of twelve carpal, metacarpal, and epiphyseal dimensions as an improved method of measuring the ossification of the hand and wrist. Her proposal was based on an analysis of some forty measurements taken on each of fifty-four roentgenograms distributed over the elementary- and high-school age period. The twelve measurements proposed and the criteria used in selecting these measurements were enumerated as follows (374:459-60):

The criteria for the selection of measurements to be included in the final battery were: First, that the measurements could be made objectively; second, that they were little influenced by small changes in the position of the hand; third, that the bones measured showed a prolonged period of growth; and fourth, that the combination of measurements should give an approximately equal weight to the short bones, the long bones, and the epiphysis.

The following combination of twelve measurements appeared best to fulfill the above criteria: (1) the widest diameter of five of the carpal bones, the capitate, the triangulate, lunate, navicular and greater multangular; (2) the length of the first and fifth metacarpals; (3) the broadest width of the epiphysis of the first and fifth metacarpals; (4) the broadest width at the distal end of the first metacarpal and the proximal end of the fifth metacarpal shaft; (5) the widest diameter of the radial epiphysis.

A method of measuring the palate in living newborns was devised by Ashley-Montagu (356). Stone casts were made from the fleshy palate and a series of length, breadth, and height dimensions on these casts were orthographically projected for measurement on an enlarged scale, five times natural size. Bakwin and others (358) described six dimensions of the ulna and radius and six measurements of the thoraco-abdominal cavity which may be determined from infant roentgenograms. The dimensions were length of ulna and radius; diameter of ulna diaphysis, radial diaphysis, ulna metaphysis, and radial metaphysis; length, width, and area of thoracic cavity; length, width, and area of abdominal cavity. Stunz (441) constructed X-ray exposure tables for use in securing roentgenograms of the head and extremities on infants and school children. The twofold aim in construction of the tables was (a) "to use such exposure as will show the maximum amount of detail in bone pattern and density and the earliest nuclei of bone growth," and (b) "to give each child the minimum exposure compatible with good results" (441:694). Brief description was made of the position of the subject in taking roentgenograms of the hand, foot, and head. A more extensive and precise discussion of the position of the subject in securing roentgenographic pictures was given by Todd (455:259-62). He made orientation recommendations for obtaining the following series of roentgenograms: anteroposterior of hand, lateral of hand, anteroposterior of elbow, lateral of elbow, anteroposterior of shoulder, dorsi-ventral of foot, lateral of foot, anteroposterior of knee, lateral of knee, anteroposterior of hip, and lateral of head.

Reliability of measurements—The reliability and objectivity of stature observations taken with the subject in the erect position, with heels, buttocks, shoulders, and back of head in contact with a vertical measuring board, was studied by Whitacre (453). A sampling of 159 school children was used. Each child was initially measured by two independent observers and then remeasured by the same observers after an interval of fifteen to thirty minutes. All measurements were made with shoes and stockings removed. Results were (453:460):

> One of the observers duplicated measurements on individual children to within 0.5 cm. or less, for 97 percent, the other observer, for 99 percent of the 159 cases measured: only one difference was as great as 1.0 cm. As between the two observers, there were 81 percent of the children whose four height measurements (two by each observer) differed by 0.5 cm. or less, and 98.6 percent by 0.8 cm. or less.

Supplementary analysis of the comparative reliability of stature observations taken with the child against the board and standing free on the weighing scales (twenty-five subjects being used) showed that observations at the board were duplicated to within 0.8 cm. for 100 percent of the cases. Observations standing free were duplicated to within this margin for only 68 percent of the cases.

Wheeler (452) reported reliability coefficients, based on 200 cases, of .99 for stature and .87 for weight. Stature was taken with a stadiometer and weight with the Fairbanks portable scales. Both measurements were stated to have been made as accurately as possible, shoes and coats being removed. The age range covered was apparently six through seventeen years. It appears, considering this wide range of ages and the size of coefficient obtained for weight, that the measurements were not repeated at a single examination.

"A test of the reliability of the roentgenologic technic in infancy" was made by Bakwin and others (358). They correlated the measurements of the transverse diameter of the heart in duplicate roentgenograms of thirty-six infants in the age period from thirty-two to thirty-nine weeks and obtained a coefficient of .89. The infants were supported in the sitting position by a device described by Wimberger. Seemingly the two roentgenograms were taken in immediate succession. Such a procedure, obviously, would be expected to yield a higher coefficient than if the infant was removed from standard position after one film was taken and then replaced in position for the taking of the second film. Further, the coefficient obtained must be considered specific for the measurement studied. Reliabilities for length of the thorax or width of the abdomen in infants may be of a distinctly lower order, while reliabilities for diameter of the radial or tibial diaphysis are probably higher.

In lieu of reliability coefficients obtained from repeated measurements taken during one examination period, Bayley and Davis (362:33) estimated reliabilities for nine anthropometric measurements in the following ways:

(1) By a study of the coefficients of correlation obtained when one month's measurements are paired with those taken at the next succeeding examination period; (2) by the measurement of a small group of infants after an interval of one week; and (3) less directly, by a consideration of the consistency of the trends of central tendency for the group.

Self-correlations under method one were obtained between measurings at one and two months, at five and six months, at eleven and twelve months, at eighteen and twenty-four months, and at thirty and thirty-six months. The mean coefficients obtained for weight, body length, and head circumference were between .92 and .95; for stem length, bitrochanteric diameter, and thoracic circumference between .82 and .84; for bideltoid diameter, thoracic width, and thoracic depth between .66 and .70. The subjects were sixty-one infants of both sexes measured repeatedly over the three-year period. While the measurement technic was not constant throughout the entire age range (as the subjects passed from infancy to childhood the position of the subject was changed from reclining to standing or sitting to standing for obtaining a number of measurements), the mean coefficients obtained are considered to rank the measurements and roughly estimate the degree of their respective reliabilities for the age period studied. Bayley and Davis also investigated the objectivity of judges' ratings of photographs by means of a seven-point scale of lateral-linear build or general "chubbiness." The photographs were taken nude and covered the same subjects and approximately the same age intervals. Correlations between the ratings of judges B and D (the experimenters) ranged from .71 to .81, with a mean of .76.

Shuttleworth (436) derived a formula for determining "the reliability with which individual differences in gains or increases or increments can be measured." In discussing the terms of the formula he noted that the reliability of increments was in part a function of the reliability of the original gross scores, in part a function of the length of the interval between initial and second measurement, and in part a function of the extent of individual differences in increments during the interval.

Analysis of data—Hellman (403) analyzed data for a series of facial dimensions with reference to dental stage rather than chronological age. In defense of this procedure he claimed: (a) that chronological age, even in yearly intervals, was too fine a time scale for studying growth in facial dimensions, since the differences between successive means for any given dimension were not three times the probable errors of the differences; and (b) that when the "development of the dentition" time scale was divided into eight to ten tooth eruption stages, a more satisfactory measure of the distance covered by the growing face was obtained.

Courtis (375) proposed that physical growth norms be derived by averaging the constants for series of integral equations of individual growth curves. Application of the method, using equations of the multi-Gompertz type, was made for twenty-five individual records giving stature, weight, and number of permanent teeth at annual intervals over the elementary- and high-school years. The derived "curve of constants" for each measurement was considered superior to the commonly employed "curve of means" on the grounds that it more nearly preserved the form of the individual trends upon which it was based. While the method is interesting, an alternative interpretation of the findings suggests itself. It would appear that the steepness of the adolescent phase of the derived normative trends, the characteristic which makes them resemble the individual curves in form, is evidence that the "curve of constants" is less representative of the group as a whole during the adolescent years (and norms are derived for application to groups) than is the "curve of means."

A method of establishing the probable limits of normal variation in the weight of organs was discussed by Boyd (371). She expressed the variability of spleen-weight data in terms of standard deviation multiples and percentile zones, applied the Chi-square test to each method, and found the percentile method the more valid for defining the probable limits of normal variation. Rosahn (433) pointed out that the bar diagram would be more meaningful if, when used to represent graphically the mean levels of two or more series of observations on the same variate, it carried information as to the significance of the difference between the populations under consideration. Illustrative application of this graphic method of representing the significance of the difference between means was made, using stature in two groups of college men. Palmer (424) called attention to a test for determining the probability that two series of observed differences between comparable means would arise as a result of random sampling. The test is for use in situations where nearly all the averages of one population may be "insignificantly" greater or smaller than those of another (e. g., averages of weights of rural school children of different ages greater or less than similar averages for city school children).

Wallis (448) reported a regression phenomenon which he considered inherent in all indexes derived from two positively correlated dimensions. Using the cephalic index to illustrate the phenomenon, he claimed that if individuals of a local group (of like age, sex, and race) are selected on the basis of head length, head width lags as one proceeds from the lowest to the highest values of head length, that is, head breadth becomes relatively less in terms of length (448:524).

> The converse is the case if we select head width as the independent variable. We then find that head length is relatively less in the widest, and relatively greater in the narrowest heads. With increase in width of head, length of head lags, and conversely.

In explanation of the lag it was suggested (448:538):

> The decreasing lag of index with increasing value of independent variable is probably due to the fact that an absolute unit of increase, such as 1 mm., bears a larger proportion to the mean of the independent variable in the lower values than in the higher and so tends to offset the increments of the dimension which is measured against it in the index which comprises the dependent variable.

Wallis' position with reference to the implications of the phenomenon (which he termed "anatomic lag") was that it must be taken into account in all comparative studies aiming to elucidate age, race, or sex factors. In regard to the latter factor he wrote (448:540-41):

> A weighting of anatomic lag is necessary in order to ascertain sex differences which are properly attributable to the factor of sex. It is, for example, commonly stated that women in a given group have a higher cephalic index than do males. They have, however, absolutely shorter heads. By virtue of the principle of anatomic lag we would, therefore, expect them to have relatively wider heads, that is, to have a higher cephalic index. In so far as cephalic index is a function of head length, it follows that the fundamental sex difference is in absolute head length. Only when the cephalic index is significantly different between males and females having the same absolute head length (or head width) would cephalic index as such be a true sex trait as distinguished from a mere biometric trait.

A composite measure of "physical age" was reported by Dearborn (383) to be in process of construction. The procedure being employed is that of (a) transmuting raw values for stature, weight, bi-iliac diameter, carpal ossification, and dentition into age values; and (b) averaging the series of physical ages (stature age, weight age, hip age, carpal age, and dental age) for each individual.

Growth in Bodily Dimensions

General studies—Central tendency and variability values for thirty-three external dimensions taken on newborn white infants at two New York hospitals were reported by Bakwin and Bakwin (359). The infants born at one hospital represented homes of moderate income while those born at the other were from poor homes. For twenty-four dimensions, the basic data were obtained from measurement of 812 first-born infants (395 male, 417 female) and 841 later-born infants (423 male, 418 female). The remaining nine measurements were made on a shorter series of cases. Means, standard deviations, and coefficients of variations were given for each dimension by sex and order of birth. With few exceptions, the mean magnitudes were larger for males than for females and for later-born than for first-born infants. Coefficients of variation showed length of thigh, circumference of head, and body length as the least variable of the dimensions studied. The most variable measurements were body weight, bi-iliac diameter, and height of nose. The distributions of weight for first-born males and females were skewed positively. Later-born infants of each sex showed approximately normal distributions.

Tentative standards for five external dimensions were presented by Stuart (440): head circumference, thoracic circumference (in plane of ensiform at mid-respiration), interspinous diameter, vertex-sole length, and body weight. The subjects were approximately 110 white children of North European stock. They were measured at eight age periods between birth and twenty-four months of age. Tables, specific for dimension, sex, and age period, gave range, 5 percentile values, mean, standard deviation, and range of $\pm$ 1 standard deviation.

Bayley and Davis (362) analyzed data for nine anthropometric measurements secured by seriatim measurement of sixty-one well-nourished Berkeley infants (thirty female, thirty-one male). The measurements were taken at seventeen ages during the first thirty-six months following birth. Central tendency analysis showed that (a) boys were consistently a little larger than girls for all measurements throughout the three-year age span, and (b) of the transverse measures studied, bideltoid diameter was largest and grew the most, bitrochanteric diameter came next in size, thoracic width (at nipple level) was third, and thoracic depth smallest. By expressing the series of means for a given measurement as percents of the mean at one month of age, the following findings were obtained: (a) weight far outstrips all other measures; (b) during the first eighteen months the width measures increase greatly and it is not until the twenty-fourth month that the increment for height exceeds that for the three widths; (c) the first year shows practically equal proportionate growth for stem length and total length. "It is only after the 12th month that the legs begin to grow rapidly and cause relatively greater increase in the total height curve"; (d) "the dimension which shows the smallest percentage increment throughout the entire 36 months is chest depth. Head circumference shows the second smallest increment" (362:45).

A study of eighteen physical measurements obtained on 1,243 Iowa City white males ranging in age between birth and eighteen years was reported by Meredith (415). The sampling was homogeneous as to geographic location and sex, almost entirely of North European racial stock, and somewhat favored economically and culturally. A total of 93,232 measurement values constituted the data. Central tendency and variability constants were calculated for thirty-one successive age distributions of each measurement and central tendency curves drawn to the series of means for each measurement. Comparison of four curves for thickness of skin and subcutaneous tissue (at upper arm back, upper arm front, thorax back, and thorax front) revealed the original finding that all four trends were similar in form below eleven years, whereas beyond this age the two thorax curves climbed, each attaining an absolute magnitude in excess of that found at any previous age. At the same time the two upper arm curves descended, each falling to a mean magnitude at eighteen years lower than that found at any point between three months and this age. A second major finding of this study emerged when mean percent increment curves for each measurement were obtained and studied. Every measurement analyzed except the four for skin and subcutaneous tissue showed a decrease in relative growth rate during the eleventh year.

Palmer and Reed (420) studied the relationship between attained stature and annual increment in stature in elementary-school children aged six to fourteen years. The subjects were 2,414 white native-born children (1,254 boys and 1,160 girls) attending the elementary schools of Hagerstown, Maryland, during the years 1922-28. Each child had repeated annual stature measurements for four or more successive years. Analysis consisted of the calculation of means and standard deviations of distributions of annual absolute gains. In preparation for this analysis the subjects were grouped into age and sex specific classes and further separated into subgroups containing only individuals of the same stature to within one inch. Major findings were (420:327-34):

1. For girls, average annual rates of growth in height decrease regularly from the 6th through the 9th year, and are independent of attained height.
   For boys, mean annual rates of growth in height decrease regularly from the 6th through the 10th year of age.
   During these years "children, regardless of their actual height, grow like other children of the same age and sex."
2. During the 9th and 10th years, girls above 51 inches in height appear to grow more rapidly than those less than 51 inches.

> Between the tenth and eleventh years, boys above fifty-two or fifty-three inches in height grow more rapidly than the shorter ones. In general the adolescent acceleration of growth in height appears synchronized with actual height and tends to occur at certain points on the scale of height, i.e., fifty-one inches for girls and fifty-three inches for boys.

It was concluded that in the years immediately preceding the adolescent acceleration there was practically no association between average gain in height and attained height, while with the onset of the adolescent acceleration there was a definite and direct association between annual increments of height and height itself.

Boas (368) analyzed seriatim stature observations with reference to year of maximum adolescent growth. The subjects were 483 Horace Mann School girls, between the ages of nine and sixteen years, and 566 Newark Academy and City College boys, ranging in age from eleven to seventeen years. It was found:

> For girls, the mean age of maximum stature increase was 12.1 years, 34 percent had their maximum growth in the twelfth year, and 96 percent reached their maximum rate between the eleventh and the fourteenth years of age, inclusive.
>
> For boys, 14.5 years was the mean age of maximum rate, the fifteenth year was the year of maximum growth for 43 percent, and 88 percent attained their maximum rate in the fourteenth, fifteenth, or sixteenth years.

The investigator noted (368:309-10):

> Since the dates of measurement were irregularly distributed, ranging between about six months and a year and a half, it was necessary to interpolate for full year intervals. This was done so that the stature used corresponded to the full completed year. It will be understood that the measurements as taken are not sufficiently accurate for our purpose and that with greater accuracy and consideration of seasonal variations in growth the results would be slightly altered.

A preliminary study on the prediction of stature during the age interval from six years to maturity was reported by Meredith (415). Fifty individual stature curves for Iowa City white males were employed. The curves were drawn to semiannual measurement values covering the age period six to eighteen years. Bissett and Laslett (366) presented means and standard deviations for stature and weight at six-month intervals over the age period from thirteen to twenty-one years. Their basic data were 4,700 nude observations for each measurement made on 1,850 males in attendance at the Oakland Technical High School during the years 1925-30. Boas (368) published annual stature means for Hebrew boys and girls covering the age period four and one-half to fourteen and one-half years, inclusive. The data were collected between 1892 and 1924 from measurement of 2,453 girls and 2,547 boys at the time of their admittance to two institutions. Grandprey (399) compiled tables of variability for children between birth and six years of age which gave the 10th and 90th percentiles for each sex in weight for age, stature for age, and weight for stature. The data used were "those published in 'Statures and Weight of Children under Six Years of Age' by Robert M. Woodbury."

Diehl (384, 385) made an analysis of stature and body weight data taken on American college men and women during the years 1928-30. Height was determined without shoes and weight without clothing. The data were accumulated from a variety of institutions. Means at annual intervals from sixteen to twenty-one years, specific for measurement and sex, showed: (a) college men attain their maximum stature at nineteen years of age but continue to increase in weight until twenty-one years; (b) college women do not grow either in stature or weight between the ages of sixteen and twenty-one years; and (c) at twenty-one years of age, college men exceed college women by five inches in stature and twenty-four pounds in weight.

Studies on head and face—Head length and head breadth means for Old Virginians of each sex were reported by Bean (363). His subjects included twenty-two girls and twenty-four boys at age eight and one-half years, forty-three girls and thirty boys at age thirteen years, and sixty of each sex at age eighteen years. Major findings were: (a) the Old Virginian boys exceeded the girls in both dimensions at all ages studied; (b) in relation to status at eighteen years, girls were more precocious at thirteen years than were boys; (c) head length increased .4 cm. for boys and .5 cm. for girls from eight and one-half to thirteen, and 1.1 cm. for boys and .4 cm. for girls from thirteen to eighteen. With reference to this last finding Bean commented: "The extremely greater growth in the boys than in the girls from 13 to 18 may be partly because of the greater growth of the accessory sinuses of the nose in the boys at that time" (363:264).

Hellman (403) studied mean growth in total face height, bizygomatic width, and goniomenton depth between the fifth year of age and maturity. The data consisted of measurements made from two to seven times at yearly intervals on 670 females and 526 males. He found that (a) throughout the entire growth period studied the "transverse diameter of the face is greatest, the vertical is next in size, and the anteroposterior is smallest;" (b) the male face is larger than the female face in all three dimensions; and (c) the percent increment during the period covered was least for the largest dimension and greatest for the smallest dimension.

The mean length and breadth of the fleshy palate in the newborn were investigated by Ashley-Montagu (356). Length was measured from the incisivum to a chord between both postgingivae and maximum breadth was usually found to correspond to the greatest diameter between points slightly posterior of the molon point. The subjects were ninety white, living males born at Bellevue Hospital. Mean maximum length was 25.6 mm. Maximum breadth exceeded length by 5.0 mm. Goldstein and Stanton (398) studied seven dimensions of the alveolar arches over the age period from two to nine years. Their basic data were four width and three length measurements of each arch, derived from 522 sets of dentures for 300 children of North European stock. Means for each measurement, specific for sex, dental arch, and age, showed: (a) every width studied increased in magnitude between two and nine years; (b) the four maxillary widths were larger for males than females at every age (sex differences for the mandibular arch were in the same direction but less consistent); (c) female growth showed a greater average absolute gain per year than male growth for all widths and both arches; and (d) neither deciduous arch showed any increase in total length within the age limits considered.

One or more dimensions of the head or face were incorporated and analyzed in the general studies of Bakwin and Bakwin (359), Bayley and Davis (362), Stuart (440), Mohr and Bartelme (418), and Meredith (415).

Studies on trunk—Dunham and D'Amico (387) obtained and analyzed roentgenograms of the thoraxes of twenty-eight infants. The infants were born in New Haven Hospital and varied in birth weight between 2,705 and 4,106 grams. The roentgenograms included a series taken within twenty-four hours after birth and a series taken on the tenth day. All exposures were made in the prone position with arms and legs held in extension. Statistical reduction for diameter of the thorax at the first and eighth ribs yielded two findings: (a) a slight mean increase from the first hour to the tenth day, from 5.5 to 5.6 cm. at first rib and from 10.6 to 10.8 cm. at eighth rib; and (b) a lesser range in diameter at the first rib than at the eighth rib. The experimenters concluded: "The infant's chest does not appreciably change in size during the first ten days of life."

A study of growth of the cardiac silhouette and thoraco-abdominal cavity during the first year of post-natal life was reported by Bakwin and others (358). They took ten dimensions on 311 anteroposterior roentgenograms of the thorax and abdomen made with the infants supported in a sitting posture. A table gave smoothed means, sexes undifferentiated, for each dimension at monthly intervals. General findings were: "During the first year the heart grows rapidly, the frontal plane more than doubling in area. . . . The frontal plane of the thorax more than doubles in area during the first year of life, while the abdominal area increases only about 70 per cent" (358:866).

Davenport (379) presented individual and central tendency growth curves for biacromial width and bicristal diameter covering the age period from six to eighteen years. The central tendency curves for biacromial width (smoothed curves) showed the boys to have broader shoulders than the girls between six and nine years and after fifteen years. The interval between the two decussations (crossings of the curves) was six years. Analogous curves for bicristal diameter showed boys to exceed girls between six and nine years only. Individual curves were classified into two main types, the linear trend type and the concavo-convex type, with numerous intergrades. No indication was given as to the frequency with which each type of curve occurred for each sex. General findings on comparison of these curves with individual stature curves for the same children were: (a) stature spurts tend to precede spurts in pelvic width by about one year; and (b) shoulder width runs parallel to stature, i. e., "a spurt, or retardation, in one is apt to be reflected in the other, though not always simultaneously" (379:156).

Central tendency values and average percent increments for sitting height were reported by Bean (365). The subjects were third generation residents of Virginia and of North European stock. They ranged in age between six and one-half and sixty years. It was found that average sitting height

> ... is about the same in the Old Virginian boys and girls up to 11, at which time that of the girls becomes greater, to remain so until about the age of 15. ... From the age of fifteen onward throughout life the sitting height of the male is greater than that of the female. There is a sex difference in the adult of about 5 cm. (365: 450-51).

The percent rate findings are not reviewed since the number of cases in each age-sex group between six and one-half and sixteen and one-half years varied from thirty-five to as few as thirteen.

Studies on extremities—Bean (365) found that leg length was greater in girls than in boys between the ages of seven and twelve years but that thereafter the relationship was reversed to the extent that the average adult leg was 7 cm. longer in the male than in the female. He used a small sampling of Virginian children of North European stock. Davenport (379) analyzed individual curves for thigh length and lower leg length, extending over the age period from six years to maturity, and found that:

> The thigh, which is the longer, grows slowly in the juvenile period, increasing only 5 mm. in some cases, 20 mm. in others, in the course of single years. But at some time before puberty—it may be at 11 or 12 or 13 or 14 years—the thigh begins to grow more rapidly, 25 to 30 mm. per year. On the other hand, the lower leg grows in some cases fairly uniformly throughout the juvenile period at about 15 mm. per year, or it may grow 25 mm. or more during these juvenile years when the thigh is growing slowly. Its growth is thereafter damped off, at about 15 years, at the time when the thigh is growing fastest. The consequence is that the two curves of absolute growth of these respective segments of the leg tend to approach each other from childhood to the late juvenile period and thereafter to diverge (379:339-40).

Thigh length was measured as the distance from the articular surface of the inner condyle of the distal end of the femur to the mid-point between the symphysion and the iliospinale; lower leg length as the distance from tibiale to sphyrion.

Means, standard deviations, and coefficients of variation for twelve external dimensions of the upper and lower extremities of newborn white males and females were reported by Bakwin and Bakwin (359). The same investigators (358) obtained means and standard deviations for six roentgenographic measurements of the ulna and radius. In this study the sexes were pooled and the constants derived from eight age distributions of each measurement covering the period from birth to one year.

Davenport (380) studied the growth of the foot in length and breadth between five and sixteen years of age. The subjects were approximately 100 boys and 50 girls in the Brooklyn Orphan Asylum. Measurements were obtained at annual intervals or oftener and were taken in part on the contour form and in part directly on the foot. Foot length was taken as "the greatest distance from the back of the heel outline to the tip of the second toe" and foot breadth as "the distance of the processus styloideus metatarsi V from the tuberositas ossis navicularis." Means for each dimension, calculated at yearly age intervals, showed that in foot length boys increase from 16.5 cm. at five years to 25.7 cm. at sixteen years and in posterior foot breadth from 6.8 cm. at five years to 9.2 cm. at sixteen years. Corresponding means for girls were 16.1, 23.0, 6.0, and 8.9 cm., respectively. Analysis of individual curves for foot length and stature led to the conclusion: "The spurt in increasing foot growth may occur before or at the age of adolescent spurt in stature" (380:176).

Changes in Body Proportions

Head and face—Bean (363) found the mean cephalic index to decrease between eight and one-half and eighteen years and to increase slightly to adulthood. The decrease was greater between eight and one-half and thirteen years in the girls than in the boys, and more between thirteen and eighteen in the boys than in the girls. He considered the earlier reduction in the girls' index to show them more precocious than the boys. The adult indexes obtained were 78.1 for males and 79.3 for females, showing females to be shorter headed than males.

In a study covering the age period from five years to adulthood, Hellman (403:1143-44) found: (a) "during differentiation the face changes in proportion, becoming longer and deeper in comparison with its width; the female face becoming relatively longer and the male face relatively deeper;" and (b) "the relative dimensions of the upper and lower face heights decrease when compared to the total face height, the dental height making up the difference; but the ratio of upper to lower face remains the same throughout the course of development."

Ashley-Montagu (356) found the average palatal index for ninety newborn Caucasian males to be 119.9. The distribution of palatal types was 9 percent Dolichouranic, 44 percent Mesouranic, 45 percent Brachyuranic, and 2 percent Hyperbrachyuranic. Goldstein and Stanton (398) studied the relation of total length to total width of the deciduous dental arches and found a decrease between two and nine years, i.e., the arches, especially the mandibular, became relatively broader.

Trunk—Weisman (449) studied changes in thoracic index with increasing age, stature, and weight. His subjects were 18,000 Minneapolis school children (roughly 9,000 of each sex) ranging in age from five to eighteen years. The thoracic measurements were made at the nipple level with the children stripped to the waist. Data on each sex were treated separately throughout. For studying changes in mean thoracic index (ratio of thoracic depth to thoracic width) with age, one-year distributions were used. A gradual decrease in index was found, falling from 71 or 72 percent at five years to 68 percent at seventeen years. No consistent sex difference was indicated. The trends for mean index in relation to stature and weight paralleled those on age, showing a decreasing index with increasing stature and weight. Again sex differences were not marked though, in general, boys tended to have the flatter thorax after a weight of 125 pounds, and girls the flatter thorax (lower index) above a stature of 65 inches.

Age changes in mean thoracic index between six and eighteen years were also studied by Davenport (382). His method of study differed from that of Weisman in two respects: (a) the basic thoracic dimensions were taken with straight-armed calipers whereas Weisman used curved calipers; and (b) the thoracic index was computed as breadth divided by depth, i.e., as the converse of the ratio obtained by Weisman. The general finding was that the index rose until around the twelfth year and beyond this age first decreased slightly and then showed a slight increase. The index rose to eleven years for girls and twelve years for boys—reaching 135 in both sexes. Davenport (382:21) concluded that "in girls the maximum eccentricity of chest cross-section is achieved a year or two earlier than in boys; corresponding to the earlier adolescence of girls."

Freeman (397) and Davenport (379) investigated the relationship between upper trunk and hip widths. Freeman found that thoracic width was relatively broader than hip width at birth, became increasingly broader during the first eighteen months, and from eighteen months to the age of puberty became progressively narrower. The two measures became equal (gave an index of 100) between three and one-half and four and one-half years. The major finding of Davenport was that bicristal width increases in relation to biacromial width from about 70 percent at six years to 75 percent at fourteen years. Curves for boys participating in manual labor were considered to indicate that manual labor expands the shoulders and results in reduction of the trunk width index.

Extremities—Changes with age in intermembral index, crural index, brachial index, foot index, and leg-foot index were reported by Davenport (378, 380, 381). General findings were:

1. Arm length in relation to leg length, for males, undergoes rapid reduction from 125 percent at the third month of gestation to about 92 percent at birth. More gradual decrease in intermembral index continues to 84 percent at about fourteen years of age, and thereafter there is a slight increase in index to around 86 percent at twenty years.

2. The crural index, or ratio of lower leg length to thigh length, "tends to increase from 6 years to the late juvenile period (11 or 12 years) and then to diminish." Leg length grows relatively more rapidly during the childhood years and thigh length during adolescence.

3. Between the third month of gestation and birth the relative length of the lower arm to that of the upper arm rises from 74 percent to 90 percent. The postnatal trend consists of a decrease to approximately 78 percent at twelve or thirteen years, and a slight rise to about 80 percent at fifteen years. In interpretation of the "peculiar discontinuity" in the crural index trend Davenport wrote: ". . . The prenatal part follows the general Primate trend, preparing the child, as it were, for an arboreal, brachiating, life; but from birth on the brachial index deviates more and more from the brachiating plan and acquires that of adult man" (381:363).

4. "... The foot index of males tends to diminish slightly with age, (between 6 and 16 years) from 38.5 to 35 percent.... The female index shows no such trend, fluctuating between 37 and 39" (380:197-98).

5. Foot length divided by tibial length gives a progressively reduced ratio of from 80 to 67 percent during the years four to sixteen. This decline in leg-foot index with age is "due to exceptionally rapid growth of the lower leg during childhood" (380:183).

Miscellaneous—Bakwin and Bakwin (359) studied newborn infants of both sexes and found the proportion of a series of five dimensions to total body length identical for each sex. The dimensions were thoracic circumference, weight, bimalar diameter, biacromial diameter, and bi-iliac diameter. The relation of stem length to stature, thoracic circumference to stature, and thoracic circumference to stem length was studied by Bayley and Davis (362). Birth to three years was the age period covered. It was found: "The ratio of stem length to total length, after a slow decrease through the ninth month, falls off very rapidly. ... The same is true of the ratios of chest circumference to length, and of chest circumference to stem length" (362:54). The same investigators, after computing the ratios weight to stature, weight to square of stature, and weight to cube of stature, concluded: "All of the weight-length indices show that, for the most part, the boys are heavier relative to their length" (362:59). Bean (365) found girls and boys to have a mean sitting height index of approximately 55.2 at seven and one-half years and 52.5 at twelve years. At fifteen and one-half years the girls' index was 52.8 and the boys' index, 51.8. This decrease for the boys and increase for the girls, from twelve to fifteen and one-half, was considered to show that "the sitting height in the girls begins to grow more rapidly than the stature at an earlier age than in the boys." In the adult, the female index obtained was 53.5 and the male index, 52.5. Findings for leg length as a percent of sitting height were also reported by Bean.

Davenport (379, 380) drew the following generalizations from his study on Nordic children at the Brooklyn Orphan Asylum:

1. On the average, biacromial width is about 23 percent of stature at six years, and 21.7 percent at sixteen years. The ratio for girls exceeds that for boys between ten and one-half and sixteen years.

2. Bicristal width in relation to stature, on the average, is 16.1 percent at six years for both sexes. At sixteen years the boys' index is 15.7 percent and the girls' index, 16.5 percent.

3. "The bi-acromial width is roughly two-thirds of the sitting supersternale height; i.e., the height of the trunk is about 1½ times the breadth of the shoulders." The ratio for females is slightly less than this approximation since "the upper part of the female trunk is always relatively slenderer than that of the male" (379:160-62).

4. On the average, the inter-cristal diameter is roughly one-half the sitting-supersternal or torso height. The index for females is lower than that for males during the age period six to sixteen years.

5. For both boys and girls, foot length at six years of age is about 15.5 percent of stature. At sixteen years the ratio is 14.5 for girls and 15.3 for boys.

Factors Conditioning Growth

Race—Mean birth weights for 3,255 normal non-syphilitic negro infants and for 1,801 white infants were calculated by Bivings (367). Both groups of infants were born in Grady Hospital, Atlanta, Georgia, and were considered to represent the same economic level. The negro infants were found to have a mean birth weight of 6 pounds, 14 ounces, or ten ounces less than the white infants. Bakwin and Bakwin (359) studied twenty-four external dimensions of the newborn in relation to racial stock of parents. Mean and probable error of mean were obtained for each dimension by four racial groupings—North European, 234 cases; Central European, 103 cases; Mediterranean, 194 cases; and Jewish, 73 cases. No significant differences were found.

An investigation of differences in mean thoracic index according to nationality was made by Weisman (449). The subjects were Minneapolis school children ranging in age between five and fourteen years. Four nationality groups were employed. These were Scandinavian (over 1,300 of each sex), German (around 500 of each sex), Russian and Polish (approximately 500 of each sex), and Jewish (more than 300 of each sex). The mean thoracic indexes, specific for nationality, sex, and one-year age groups, showed no appreciable difference between the various nationalities.

Manuel (413) analyzed data for stature, weight, bideltoid and bitrochanteric diameter, anteroposterior diameter of thorax, and two measures of arm girth taken on approximately 1,800 Mexican children of each sex ranging between the ages of six and sixteen years. The data were obtained in the elementary schools of Laredo and El Paso, Texas, during the spring of 1930. Central tendency values for annual age-sex groups were calculated. The series for stature and for weight were compared with Baldwin-Wood averages and it was found that the Mexican children were both shorter and lighter. The average differences over the age period studied were approximately 7 pounds in weight for each sex and, in stature, 2.0 inches for boys and 1.8 inches for girls.

Family—A study of the resemblance of non-twin siblings in stature and weight during the age period from seven to twelve years was made by Palmer (419). Data for 193 pairs of brothers and 154 pairs of sisters were assembled with reference to a point where the two brothers (or two sisters) had reached a certain chronological age. Pearsonian product moment coefficients, specific for measurement, sex, and annual age groupings, gave the following findings:

1. The average coefficient of correlation, all ages seven to twelve, for both brothers and sisters together is .44 for height and .33 for weight.
2. The average of the coefficients, all ages, for both height and weight together is .47 for brothers and .30 for sisters.
3. The degree of correlation tends to decrease with age during the growth period studied. The decrease is considerably less for brothers than for sisters.

Boas (369) reported an investigation on the tempo of growth of fraternities. His data were stature observations on boys and girls from six to seventeen years of age made at the Hebrew Orphan Asylum, New York. The children of each sex were classified into a tall, a medium, and a short group, classification being made at seven, nine, eleven, and thirteen years. Mean absolute increments were computed for each group at each age. The general finding was (369:415):

... The brothers and sisters of the tall ones, who included many of those with rapid tempo of development, also have rapid tempo, an early time for the maximum rate of growth, a rapid rate and an early termination of growth, while the brother and sisters of the short ones, who include many of those with sluggish tempo of development, have a slow rate of growth of less intensity and longer duration.

No tables or specific figures were given, nor was the number of cases reported.

Physical measurement data for Harvard college men and the women of four eastern women's colleges were analyzed by Bowles (370). The major results were:

1. Means for each of thirty dimensions, based on measurement of 481 fathers and their sons, showed the sons to be larger than the fathers in all dimensions but breadth of head, breadth of hips, and shoulder-elbow length. For a larger series of 1,160 fathers and their sons, the fathers were 3.4 cm. shorter and 3.7 kilograms lighter than the sons.
2. Means for each of twelve dimensions, obtained from measurement observations for 413 mothers and their daughters, showed an increase of the daughters over the mothers in all dimensions except breadth of hips. The daughters exceeded the mothers by 2.9 cm. in stature and 1.8 kilograms in weight.
3. Data on thirty dimensions for seventy-nine couples of younger and older brothers showed the younger to excel the older, on the average, in every measurement except breadth of head and breadth of waist.
4. Mean stature and weight comparisons for 140 pairs of sisters by juniority and seniority of birth showed that the younger exceeded the older by .5 cm. in stature and 0.45 kilograms in weight.

The various samples were considered comparable for age, racial extraction, geographic location, and socio-cultural status.

Geographic area—Bivings (367) secured birth weight data on white infants from Iowa City, New Haven, Los Angeles, and Atlanta. Each locality was represented by 1,000 or more cases. He (367:726) found that "with the notable exception of Los Angeles, the weight rises considerably as we approach the southern portion of the United States." This trend was thought probably due to the quantity of ultraviolet reaching the earth. The significance of Bivings' finding is dubious, since (a) the sexes were neither differentiated nor shown to be represented in equal proportions in all samplings; (b) no evidence was given to show that the time and conditions of weighing were comparable for all localities; (c) the racial and socio-economic composition of the samples was not discussed; and (d) the mean difference in birth weight between the most northern and the most southern area was three ounces.

Palmer and Collins (429) analyzed data for seven physical measurements taken on approximately 30,000 children of native white parents and grandparents in four geographic sections of the United States. The children were between six and fifteen years of age and, except for a relatively small number in the western section, were all from large urban centers. Analysis was made in terms of annual means and annual mean increments for each geographic section, the data on each sex being treated separately. The authors (429:345) summarized their findings as follows:

1. On the whole, children from the northeastern section tend to be the largest, those from the north central area the next largest, children from the south central area are third largest, and those from the western section are the smallest.
2. Study of growth increments, calculated as the differences between averages of successive age classes, shows no consistent differences in mean increments for children in the various sections.

It should be noted particularly that the first finding is a gross generalization. Thus the difference between stature means for the different areas were found to fluctuate irregularly rather than to show any sectional consistency. Weight means, on the other hand, showed decided sectional differences and the weight-height index indicated that the stockiest children were in the northeast region and the least stocky in the western area.

Suski (442) compared obtained means for stature, thoracic circumference, and weight of American-born Japanese school children with analogous means for Japan-born Japanese children. The experimental group consisted of 573 girls and 498 boys ranging in age between six and one-half and seventeen and one-half years. They were measured at private schools in Los Angeles being conducted to supplement the public school education. The parents were stated to be full-blooded Japanese representing all walks of life. In round numbers, American-born Japanese were found to excel Japan-born Japanese by 7 percent in stature and thoracic circumference and by 20 percent in weight. Suski (442:349) concluded:

The children in this investigation are certainly growing faster, that is, taller and heavier, age for age, in comparison with children in Japan. It seems very likely that they will grow up to be taller and heavier adults than native born Japanese, inferring from the height and weight attained by these children at 16 or 17 years of age, which were already greater than those of adult Japanese.

The greater size of American-born Japanese was interpreted as being due to influence of geographic location.

A study of stature and weight of isolated mountain children (roughly 700 of each sex) of the Southern Appalachians was made by Wheeler (452). The subjects ranged in age from six through seventeen years, represented the agriculture and lumbering classes, and were largely of North European stock. Analysis consisted of (a) statistical description of the southern mountaineer children in terms of central tendency and variability of annual age-sex distributions; and (b) comparison of central tendency values with corresponding values for seven other samplings of American children. The general finding was that East Tennessee mountain children do not differ significantly in mean stature and weight from unselected children in various other parts of the country.

Season—The influence of season of birth on the external dimensions of the newborn was studied by Bivings (367) and by Bakwin and Bakwin (360). Neither study differentiated the data according to sex: both studies classified the data in terms of quarter year in which birth occurred. Bivings treated birth weight data accumulated from Iowa City, New Haven, Los Angeles, and Atlanta. He found a tendency for birth weight means to follow the curve of sunshine, i.e., to be low in winter, higher in spring and summer, and lower again in the fall. The obtained means were approximately 7 pounds, 4 ounces for winter, 7 pounds, 7 ounces for spring and summer, and 7 pounds, 6 ounces for fall. The data analyzed by Bakwin and Bakwin covered twenty-four dimensions taken on newborn infants at two New York hospitals. They reported their findings as below:

> The following dimensions showed seasonal changes, the diameters being smaller during the spring and summer and larger during the autumn and winter: bimalar diameter of the face, height of the upper part of the face, height of the lower jaw, nasal height and breadth, biacromial diameter, bi-iliac diameter, circumference of the thorax and dimensions of the hand (360:1236).

In contrast with Bivings' findings, birth weight means were higher in summer and winter than in fall and spring.

Palmer (426) made a study of fluctuations in the mean monthly weight increment occurring coincident with changes of season. His basic data consisted of approximately 80,000 weight values obtained on some 2,500 native born, white elementary-school children at Hagerstown, Maryland. Each child included had protocols which were 80 percent complete (weighings at monthly intervals between September and May of each school year) for a four-year period. The age range covered by the study was six to sixteen years. The major findings were:

1. At every age from six through fourteen years, the absolute monthly increment for weight is at a maximum during the month approximately delimited as September 15 to October 15, and at a minimum during the month April 15 to May 15.
2. The October rate is roughly one pound per child per month greater than is the May rate at all ages considered.
3. Both sexes show the same seasonal trend during the elementary-school years: maximum in October, marked decrease in November, horizontal or slightly downward trend during January to March, decided decrease again during April and May, and a definite rise during the summer.

Year or decade—An investigation on "the variation in successive calendar years of growth in body weight of children between six and fifteen years of age" was reported by Palmer (430). The data were serial weight observations for four years or more on approximately 2,500 children. They were obtained at Hagerstown between May, 1922, and May, 1928. The procedure in analysis was to calculate absolute annual increment means: (a) specific for age, sex, and year of measurement; and

(b) specific for age and sex but unspecified with regard to year of measurement. The mean gains in (a) were next expressed as percents of, and (b) the resulting series for percents for each sex and year of measurement averaged. It was found that 1924-25 was an inferior "growing" year and 1926-27 a good "growing" year. These two most divergent years of the six-year period studied showed that "in as short an interval as three successive calendar years, annual growth in weight may vary as much as 15 percent," from 91 percent of the average for the entire period to 106 percent in this average. Palmer (430-1004) considered this study to "break ground" for more refined studies relating secular trends to such factors as "total hours of sunshine, hours of cloudiness, amount of rainfall . . . amount of unemployment, per capita wages of the employed . . . incidence of epidemic diseases, fluctuations of endemic diseases . . . and similar variables."

Bowles (370) analyzed stature and weight data for approximately 3,000 Harvard men and 1,200 women of four eastern women's colleges according to decade of birth. His material covered the decades 1856-65 to 1906-15. He found:

1. For stature, a mean increase of .10 cm. per annum for college men and .08 cm. per annum for college women. Using 3 times the probable error as a criterion, a statistically significant difference occurred every 6.75 years for men and every 15.3 years for women.

2. For weight, an annual mean increase of .21 pounds for college men and .10 pounds for college women, with a statistically significant difference every 8.5 years for men and every 34.1 years for women.

The influence of date of birth on growth in stature was studied by Boas (368). The subjects were 5,000 Hebrew children (roughly 2,500 of each sex) measured at the time of their admittance to the Hebrew Orphan Asylum and the Hebrew Shelter and Guardian Society. For analysis, the stature observations were divided according to sex, grouped in one-year age intervals between four and fourteen years, and subdivided for quinquennial periods of birth from 1892-94 to 1920-24. Comparison of the obtained means for each quinquennial subgroup with means for each age regardless of quinquennial period of birth showed a "very considerable" mean increase in stature according to date of birth.

Socio-economic status—Bakwin and Bakwin (359) compared newborn males representing different socio-economic environments in regard to means for body length, weight, bimalar diameter, biacromial diameter, bi-iliac diameter, and thoracic circumference. The cases were 114 first- and ninety-one later-born males from Fifth Avenue Hospital (representing "homes of moderate income") and 205 first- and 265 later-born males from Bellevue Hospital (representing "very poor homes"). They (359: 617) found:

Infants born in the Fifth Avenue Hospital are regularly larger in all dimensions studied than are the Bellevue Hospital newborns. The differences are greater for first- than for later-born infants. In most instances the differences are statistically reliable.

A study of the median differences in thoracic index, stature, and weight between "children reared in poor and those reared in favorable social environments" was reported by Weisman (449). The subjects were approximately 4,000 Minneapolis school children ranging in age from five to fourteen years. There were 1,000 each of boys and girls from four representative schools in the best sections of the city and 1,000 each of boys and girls from four schools in the poorest sections. Boys and girls from the better districts were found, on the average, to be taller, much heavier, and to have a definitely flatter type of chest than boys and girls from the poorer districts.

Mitchell (417) studied the growth of white Puerto Rican school children with reference to socio-economic status. His subjects were 100 eight-year-old children of each sex and 900 ten-year-old children of each sex, all of Spanish origin and born in Puerto Rico. Socio-economic classification was made in terms of amount of house rent, number of rooms in the house, and average number of persons per room. The more privileged groups were found to be taller and to have greater hip width, larger arm girth, and greater amounts of subcutaneous tissue over the biceps than poorer groups.

Stature and weight data were collected from various types of college institutions by Diehl (384, 385). Means at successive annual intervals were calculated for men at each of ten institutions and for women at each of eight colleges. Findings were:

> In height, the [male] students of the private colleges, Princeton, Yale, and Stanford, exceed those of the state universities and the students of the state universities in turn are taller than the students of the municipal universities studied. In weight, a similar general grouping of institutions is found, although a certain amount of shifting of the positions of individual colleges and universities occurs (384:477).
>
> ... The heights and weights of the women from the various colleges show that the students of the two private colleges, Smith and Stanford, are both taller and heavier than the women of any of the other institutions from which data were obtained (385:628).

Diehl considered socio-economic selection to be the major factor accounting for these institutional differences.

Economic depression—Mean birth weights for approximately 1,000 negro infants born in Grady Hospital, Atlanta, during each of the years 1930, 1931, and 1932 were obtained by Bivings (367). The means showed a steady decline, from 7 pounds through 6 pounds and 14 ounces, to 6 pounds and 12 ounces. Bivings (367:728) concluded that "the falling birth weight undoubtedly is greatly influenced by nutritional deficiencies in the mother as a direct result of the depression."

Palmer (421, 422) contributed two papers treating the problem of whether or not the body weight of elementary-school children of Hagerstown, Maryland, differed in 1933 and 1934 in significant particulars from the body weight of children of the same sex and age and living in the same city during the economically more prosperous years of 1921-27.

Hagerstown was considered typical of the smaller urban communities of the United States in regard to the severity of its economic disturbance during the depression years. The data on each sex were analyzed separately. Means at annual age intervals were obtained for 1921-27, 1933, and 1934. Mean absolute annual gains were calculated for 1921-27, for 1933-34, and for each of the separate years from 1921 to 1927. Major findings were:

1. Corresponding weight means for children in 1933 and 1934 show no consistent or statistically significant differences from means of weight for the period 1921 through 1927.

2. At each age and for each sex the mean annual increment is lower for the year 1933-34 than is the mean for the period 1921-27 taken together. However, the mean gains for 1933-34 are not significantly lower than those for 1924-25.

With reference to the increment findings, Palmer (421:1462-63) wrote:

It becomes necessary to conclude, then, that the school year 1933-1934 was as good a "growing year," despite the depression, as at least one other year when the general economic status of the population was presumably much higher. On the other hand, since many of the factors which may be effective in making some years good and others poor "growing years" are not known, it is impossible to state conclusively that the depression has not affected adversely the growth in weight of children.

An investigation of stature and weight during the depression years 1929-33 in school children ages six to fourteen years was made by Palmer (423). The children were drawn from approximately 5,000 more or less typical working-class families of six large cities. They were grouped into three classes on the basis of family income throughout the four-year period: those whose families remained relatively comfortable, those whose families remained relatively poor, and those whose families changed from a relatively comfortable to a poor economic status. Forty-five percent of the subjects fell in this third class, which Palmer designated the "depression poor." For the age period from six through nine years it was found that the average weight of children from the continuously comfortable families was 4 to 5 percent greater than the average weight of all children taken together; that the relative weight of children from the poor families was 1 to 2 percent below the weight of all children; and that the relative weight of children from "depression poor" families descended from about 2 percent above the general average in 1928-29 to 1 percent below the general average in 1932-33. The conclusion was drawn that so far as the wage-earning class in large urban centers is concerned, "it is children from families whose income has fallen to a low level who have been affected by the depression" (423:1112). The specificity of this conclusion should not be overlooked: no downward trend for the "depression poor" was found for weight of children ten years and above or for stature of children at any of the ages studied.

Diet and disease—Two studies on the influence of undernutrition and mild infection upon growth during the first year of life were reported by Bakwin and others (358). Their experimental group consisted of

230 infants admitted to the wards of a New York hospital "as healthy boarders or because of mild infections of the upper respiratory tract. . . . They were retarded in growth in weight and total body length. . . ." (358:870). The control group was somewhat larger and was considered normally healthy and well nourished. Roentgenograms of the forearm and thoraco-abdominal cavity were obtained and central tendency values for sixteen roentgenologic dimensions calculated at eight age subdivisions of the first year. Findings were (358:872-83):

1. The cardiac silhouette of the undernourished infant grows more slowly in all its dimensions than that of the better nourished infant. . . .
2. The thoracic dimensions grow more slowly in the undernourished than in the healthy infant. . . .
3. For the same height, the malnourished infant has a smaller heart and thoracic cavity, a narrower mediastinum and a larger abdominal cavity than the well nourished infant. . . .
4. The ulna and radius of undernourished infants grow more slowly in all dimensions than those of normal infants. . . .
5. Ulna and radial length-width indices showed that the bones of the undernourished infants were narrowed in relation to the length of the bones. . . .

Bakwin and Bakwin presented some additional findings on ossification of the carpal centers. To quote (358:881-82):

During the first month of life about 20 per cent of infants showed ossification of one or more carpal centers. . . . after the thirty-first week of life only occasional infants fail to show ossified carpal centers. The rate is slightly accelerated in the girls. . . . No difference was found in the rate of ossification of the carpal centers in the normal and undernourished infants.

This latter finding appears contradictory to Todd's finding (444) that the carpal bones are "most susceptible to disturbance as a result of ill-health or nutritional deficiency."

Mitchell (417) studied the growth of ten-year-old white Puerto Rican school children with reference to urban and rural living conditions. He found the urban children "to be taller, have greater hip width, larger arm girths and greater amounts of subcutaneous tissue over the biceps than rural children." In view of the fact that hookworm and diet deficiencies were known to be more prevalent among the rural children, Mitchell interpreted his findings as primarily due to differences in dietary and disease conditions.

Hoefer and Hardy (405) took stature measurements on a representative sampling of Joliet public school children between the ages of eight and thirteen and found that in terms of the Baldwin-Wood norms shortness was more than five times as frequent as tallness. A concomitant finding was that the soil in which most of the vegetable supply for the town was grown showed deficiency in mineral content, particularly phosphorus. While definite statement as to the relationship between soil deficiency and growth retardation must await more intensive research, this study showed that the problem merits thorough investigation. It is clear that "the value to the growing child of an 'adequate diet' loses its significance if the recommended food items are lacking in nutritive content."

Health programs—A study of the influence of improved care on growth in external dimensions and proportions during the first year of life was made by Bakwin, Bakwin, and Milgram (358). Their experimental group was obtained at a health clinic where, at monthly intervals or more frequently

> advice was given regarding general care, with particular emphasis on diet. In some instances families were aided with milk . . . Cod liver oil was distributed freely . . . (358:1031).

The infants of both the experimental and the unsupervised group were born in Bellevue Hospital and represented the same poverty-stricken district. Means for the age period, birth to three weeks, gave weight advantages to the supervised group of 370 gm. for males and 340 gm. for females. At forty to forty-seven weeks the means for the experimental group exceeded those from the unsupervised group by 1,500 gm. and 950 gm., respectively. Ratios of each of five dimensions—thoracic circumference and bimalar, bigonial, biacromial, and bicristal diameters—to body length showed that during the first month of life the body proportions of the two groups were similar but after the eighth week the experimental group had relatively larger lateral dimensions than had the unsupervised group. There were subtle factors operating in the selection of the two samples which may have exaggerated the improvements found to accrue from more adequate care.

Hoefer and Hardy (406:368) summarized the major findings from "an experimental investigation in which a representative group of third-grade pupils who participated in a carefully planned three-year course of health instruction was compared with a similar group of pupils who had only the regular course in physiology and hygiene provided by the school curriculum." They (406:371-81) wrote:

> 1. In no instance were the variations large but, when two groups from the same socio-economic level who were alike as to age and size were compared at the close of the teaching projects, pupils who had participated in the health-instruction classes were consistently superior to the others. They were taller, weighed more, and were broader of shoulders than were the control pupils.
> 2. Test results on grip, muscle contraction of the upper arm, and vital capacity, all pointed to more marked improvement of the pupils in the health-education classes as compared with the control pupils of like ages and initial status.

Concomitant improvement for the experimental group as compared with the control group was found in dietary practices (consumption of leafy vegetables, milk, cereals, fruit), in number of children reporting sufficient sleep, in amount of dental attention, and in correction of posture defects.

Boas (368) investigated the influence of residence at the Hebrew Orphan Asylum, New York, upon growth in stature. The procedure was that of comparing children entering the institution with those of like age and sex who had been in residence for various periods of time. Comparisons were made for the period prior to 1918 and for the period 1918 to 1928. Children in residence during the later period showed positive differences as against negative differences for those in residence during the earlier period. In explanation of the improved stature growth during the later period, Boas noted that in 1918 the administrative policy of the institution was changed and thereafter there was less regimentation, more adequate diet, increased recreational facilities and rest hours, camping experience for one month each year, improved medical and dental care, and an increased effort to meet the needs of individual children.

Prematurity—Mohr and Bartelme (418) studied the physical growth of prematurely born white children during the age period from approximately one to seven years. The data were obtained from 477 examinations of 250 premature children and 173 examinations of 152 of their siblings. The range in birth weight for the prematures was from 900 to 2,500 grams. The entire premature group had received early post-natal care at the Premature Infant Station, Sarah Morris Hospital of Michael Reese Hospital, Chicago, and was measured through the social service department of the Station as part of a routine follow-up service. Major findings were:

1. The sibling boys excel prematurely born boys in stature until three years of age. Prematurely born girls attain sibling norms at two years. Beyond these ages no reliable differences are found.

2. The prematurely born boys consistently weigh less than the full-term sibling boys until the age of four years. After this the mean curves for the two groups closely approximate each other.

3. The prematurely born boys and girls do not differ reliably from the sibling boys and girls in head circumference.

4. Prematurely born boys and girls weighing 2,000 grams or more at birth grew more rapidly than those weighing 1,500 grams or less. Mean curves for the latter group were persistently below those for the former group, over the entire age period studied, in weight, stature, and head circumference.

These findings were obtained using chronological age for the sibling group and corrected chronological age (statutory age minus amount of prematurity) for the prematurely born children.

Ossification and Calcification

Ossification—Roentgenograms for the upper and lower extremities of 500 newborn infants were examined by Menees and Holly (414). They reported frequency of appearance of ossification centers in the shoulder, elbow, wrist and hand, hip, knee, ankle, and foot regions. Forty-seven percent of the females and 46 percent of the males showed a center for the head of the humerus, as against less than 1 percent for each sex showing a center for the head of the femur. The elbow showed no epiphyses: the lower epiphysis of the femur was present for 99 percent of the females and 98 percent of the males. Thirteen percent of the females and 4 percent of the males showed an ossification center for the capitate. Appearance of centers for the cuboid was found for 56 percent of the females and 35 percent of the males. The development of the two sides of the body was symmetrical for 96 percent of the cases and in only one individual did more than one asymmetrical center occur.

Flory (391) analyzed 6,600 roentgenograms of the right hand distributed over the age period from birth to maturity. He used both measurement and inspectional technics. Major consideration was given to the mean magnitude of sex differences in osseous processes from age to age. He (391:211) found that

> Girls are ahead of boys at birth; they are about one year ahead at school age; they are approximately one and a half years ahead at age nine; and about two years ahead of boys at the average age of the onset of puberty.

Tentative pictorial standards for ossification of the hand and foot were presented by Stuart (440). These standards showed carpal, tarsal, and epiphyseal development of the least mature, most mature, and those at percentiles 10, 25, 50, 75, and 90 for each quarterly interval of the first year and for semiannual ages covering the second year. Todd (455:264-79) tentatively described norms for appraising skeletal maturation during the age period from five to eighteen years. The descriptions were made for six-month age intervals and were considered to represent development of the mediocre or unselected average. They covered bony differentiation in the knee, elbow, hand, foot, and shoulder. J. W. Pryor (432) reviewed roentgenographic research on the time element in commencing ossification and epiphyseal union and gave case illustrations of how the marked acceleration of the female may be applied to the determination of sex.

Calcification—Logan and Kronfeld (412) studied the order of onset of calcification of the permanent teeth. Their material included twenty-two jaw specimens for subjects ranging in age between birth and four and one-half years. For both upper and lower jaw, they found onset to begin shortly after birth for the first permanent molars, between three and six months for the permanent central incisors and cuspids, and at about one and one-half years for first bicuspids, two years for second bicuspids, and two and one-half years for second permanent molars. Calcification of the lateral incisors was found to begin at three to six months for the lower jaw and at twelve to fifteen months for the upper jaw. The investigators recognized the paucity of observations upon which their findings were based and stressed time sequences rather than an exact age interpretation of their study.

The order of complete calcification of the permanent teeth was investigated by Kronfeld (408, 409). The first permanent molar was found to be characterized by fully calcified crown and completely matured enamel at two to three years. The incisors reached this stage at about the fifth year, the cuspids at about the sixth, the first bicuspids at six years, and the second bicuspids at about seven years. With reference to the incisors and cuspids, Kronfeld (409:1535) wrote:

... After the age of 4 or 5 years, it is unlikely that any form of disease, deficiency, or therapeutic measure can influence the enamel of the twelve anterior teeth, since by this time the crowns are fully formed and the enamel matured or nearly so.

Pubescence

Engle and Shelesnyak (389) analyzed first menstruation data for a group of 250 Jewish girls on whom the exact dates of birth and of menarche were known. The data were obtained from the files of the Hebrew Orphan Asylum, New York, and represented menarches occurring between 1926 and 1932. Cases with a history of endocrine dysfunction, thyroid trouble, obesity, and pneumonia were excluded. A twofold treatment of the data was made:

1. Central tendency and variability analysis showed the average age of first menstruation to be 13.5 years and the range in age to be from 11 years to 16.3 years.
2. Tabulation of the 250 menarches according to seasonal distribution of incidence showed that 18 per cent occurred in the summer months of June, July and August, 25 per cent in the autumn months, 30 per cent in the winter, and 27 per cent in the spring.

With reference to the low percent of menarches found to occur during the summer months, the authors (389:433) wrote:

We have satisfied ourselves that the condition is due not to faulty recording of data during the summer months, but is a true expression of a seasonal effect on menarche.

A study of the sexual development of 600 non-Hebrew white boys ranging in age from nine to eighteen years was reported by Kubitschek (410).

Dimock (386) investigated the relation of pubescence to stature and weight during the age period from twelve to sixteen years. The subjects were 200 boys examined annually for three successive years. Pubescent status was determined by the Crampton criteria. Means and mean annual increments, obtained for various subdivisions of the data, revealed the following findings:

1. The pubescent boy at twelve or thirteen is as tall and heavy as the boy two years older who is still prepubescent.
2. "At fourteen the post-pubescent boy exceeds the pre-pubescent of the same chronological age by over four and one half inches in height and almost 23 pounds in weight" (386:179).
3. There is a tendency for decreasing gain in height and weight as the boy becomes older if he remains preadolescent.
4. "The most rapid growth in height and weight comes in the year during which the boy passes from pubescence to post-pubescence. This is true whether actual growth or percent increase measures are used" (386:186).
5. The amount of growth that accompanies the change from pubescence to post-pubescence "is approximately the same for twelve-, thirteen-, and fourteen-year olds. ... These findings are at variance with the conclusions of other investigators to the effect that growth is more rapid and intense when pubescence is attained early" (386:184).

The relation between age of first menstruation and absolute increase in stature was studied by Boas (368). For 352 Horace Mann School girls, he found that the mean age of first menstruation was 13.1 years, that 80 percent of the dates fell between the age limits of 11.5 years and 14.5 years, and that the total age range was ten to seventeen years. The mean age of first menstruation for seventy-nine Horace Mann School girls observed continuously from ten to sixteen years was found to be 13.3 years. Classification of 483 Horace Mann School girls between nine and sixteen years of age according to year in which maximum absolute growth occurred gave a mean age of 12.1 years. Similar analysis for 222 Horace Mann School girls continuously observed from eight to seventeen years gave 12.0 years as the mean age of maximum absolute stature increment. Boas concluded that the mean age of maximum rate of stature growth preceded the mean date of first menstruation by one year.

Shuttleworth (438) reworked Van Dyke's material on the relation of first menstruation and stature for sixty girls. The material consisted of annual stature data over the period extending from two years prior to two years following first menstruation for twenty girls who matured at twelve or earlier and for nineteeen, sixteen, and five girls who matured at thirteen, fourteen, and fifteen years, respectively. Van Dyke had arranged the girls in rank order according to stature two years before puberty, selected the fifteen tallest and fifteen shortest, and calculated the mean age at which menstruation first appeared for these two groups. Shuttleworth arranged the girls in rank order according to stature at a given chronological age, selected the lowest and highest fourth of the age distribution, and calculated the mean age of first menstruation for each group. Van Dyke had obtained means of 12.5 years for the short group and 13.9 years for the tall group. The means obtained by Shuttleworth for girls aged thirteen years were 14.1 years for the short group and 12.2 years for the tall group. This twofold analysis of the same data pointedly illustrates the interrelatedness of methodology and findings. The two sets of findings are contradictory only when one fails to recognize that in one case tallness and shortness are a function of time of first menstruation and in the other case they are a function of chronological age.

A study purposing "to consider certain anthropometric measurements and osseous indices which will predict the age at which a given girl is likely to reach puberty" was reported by Flory (390). The data were obtained from records for eighty girls on file at the University of Chicago Laboratory Schools. These records gave date of first menstruation and, at yearly intervals for a ten-year period, roentgenograms of the right hand and a series of anthropometric measurements. Iliac diameter was found to be the best anthropometric predictor of puberty. This dimension correlated with first menstruation .41 at nine years and .57 at twelve years. Appearance of the sesamoid at the distal end of the first metacarpal correlated .76 with first menstruation. The mean age of appearance of this sesamoid was found to be eleven years, i.e., two years prior to the mean age of puberty. In no instance did first menstruation occur before the appearance of the sesamoid. Flory (390:5-6) concluded:

> Osseous development seems to be more closely related to puberty than is physical size. . . . The time of appearance of the sesamoid on the distal end of the first metacarpal is the simplest and best single indicator of puberty in girls.

Clinical Instruments

Tentative standards for use in clinical appraisement of infants were presented by Stuart (440). Ranges and five percentiles were given at seven age intervals during the first two years for ossification of hand and foot and for a series of anthropometric measurements. There were separate tables for each sex. Grandprey (399) constructed graphs of variability in weight for stature covering the age period from birth to six years. The graphs, one for each sex, were derived by calculating five percentiles at each of thirty-four stature intervals, plotting the obtained percentile values, and drawing a smooth curve through each of the five percentile series. H. B. Pryor and Stolz (431) published width-weight tables for each sex at yearly ages from six to sixteen years. These tables were an extension of the Baldwin-Wood height-weight tables. They gave seven normal weights for each stature and age depending on the width of the iliac diameter. Height-weight tables for Mexican school children of each sex, age range five and one-half to fifteen and one-half years, were presented by Manuel (413). Diehl (384, 385) constructed age-height-weight norms for college men and college women. Breathing capacity norms for boys and girls of given age, height, and weight were reported by Kelly (407). The age range covered was twelve to eighteen years.

The American Child Health Association (355) published a manual explaining the technic for determining three indexes of nutritional status and giving norms in each index for boys and girls seven to twelve years of age. These indexes assume that the relation of musculature, subcutaneous tissue, and weight to skeletal build offers the best objective approach to the appraisement of nutritional status. A less complex index for identifying children with small amounts of musculature and fatty tissue relative to body build was developed by Franzen and Palmer (394). This index incorporated measurements of arm girth, chest depth, and hip width and, in consequence, was designated the ACH index. Norms for each sex over the age period seven to twelve years were given.

Mitchell (416) discussed eight selected cases of elementary-school children on whom he had medical examination records and findings from application of the American Child Health Association indexes of nutritional status. The cases were selected to show the value of each of the three objective indexes and to illustrate the reciprocal relationship which should obtain between clinical standards and clinical observations. It was claimed that standards should help to release the clinician from the difficulties of individual judgment, while observations should serve to prevent the abuse of standards.

The relative adequacy of each of four methods of selecting malnourished children was studied by Franzen (395). The four methods were weight for height, weight for height and hip width, rating by a medical examiner, and the ACH screen or index. The criterion in terms of which each method was evaluated was complete application of the American Child Health Association indexes. It was found that if the objective was to select children who were underweight for their skeletal build the height-hip-weight method and the ACH method were about equally successful. If, however, the objective was to identify children with overlapping deficiency in weight, musculature, and subcutaneous tissue for body build, the ACH method was distinctly superior to the other methods. In evaluating this study it is pertinent to note that the ACH index was initially constructed to approximate, in abbreviated form, the results obtained with the criterion indexes.

Stix and Kiser (439) investigated the relation between physicians' estimates of nutrition and two widely used "expected weight" tables. They assumed that the children rated "poor" by the physicians were the truly undernourished children. Thus when it was found that only about 20 percent of the children appraised as "poor" were underweight according to the tables, they concluded that weight tables were not sufficiently accurate for satisfactory diagnosis of nutrition of school children.

Shuttleworth (437:91) proposed that research attention be given the hypothesis that "increments provide a better index of satisfactory development than the conventional height-weight-age-sex tables." Similar emphasis of individual progress was suggested elsewhere (402).

Needed Research

Rigorous research—Direct perusal of the research literature reviewed above leads to the summary evaluation: (a) an extensive list of physical growth problems has been investigated during the last three years; (b) comparatively few of the researches reported have made an explicit and unequivocal contribution to the problems studied; and consequently (c) a large body of inconclusive findings, suggestive leads, and inviting hypotheses await further research. Such research should be characterized by scientific rigor.

Investigations cannot be considered to afford more than tentative results or approximate generalizations where the investigators:

1. Fail to report the number of observations (369, 378, 382, 409)
2. Use a meager number of cases (398, 408, 412, 427)
3. Omit description of the measurement technic employed (365, 368, 381, 397)
4. Pool data obtained in part by one technic and in part by another (413)
5. Fail to differentiate the sexes (358, 367, 387)
6. Make comparisons of samples without showing that there are equal proportions of the two sexes in each sample (367)
7. Fail to mention the socio-economic status or racial stock of the subjects (367, 397)

8. Omit the method used to secure information on nationality (413, 449), first menstruation (368), or malnutrition (358)
9. Fail to indicate number of "accidental death" cases and number of cases of "death from disease" in sampling (403, 412, 427)
10. Fail to show that the experimental and control groups were equivalent with reference to the variables under study at the beginning of the experimental period (358)
11. Fail to make tabular analysis of findings (368, 369, 379, 382, 404, 410)
12. Do not indicate the measure of central tendency employed (365) and whether central tendencies were obtained from "full year" or "nearest birthday" distributions (452)
13. Apply standards based on one racial group to individuals of a different racial stock (417, 439)
14. Describe types of individual curves for various measurements without reporting whether all types are common to both sexes and with what frequency each type occurs (379, 382).

Longitudinal research—In 1895 Lincoln [1] attempted to show that further analysis in physical growth would fall short of their maximum significance unless the basic data were "continued observations on known individuals." During the forty-year period from Lincoln's paper to the present, frequent reiterations of this position have been made and a scattering of seriatim investigations has appeared. Today there is fairly wide recognition of the need for longitudinal research and numerous consecutive measurement studies are in progress. It is becoming increasingly evident, however, that to investigate the growth of the individual is a technically difficult task. Individual curves, drawn to observed values at reasonably frequent intervals, show spurious irregularities unless the values are highly reliable (415:102, 120). For the study of such problems as seasonal variation in growth or influence of disease on growth, the seriatim measurements must be made with great precision. Particularly in the case of transverse (width, depth, and girth) measurements of the body, changes in growth rate are a function of small differences in absolute magnitude.

Pattern research—Physical growth research to date has been largely patchwork research; that is, innumerable discrete investigations have been made but sequential investigations have been rare. Partial or superficial information is thus available on a great variety of problems, while few problems have been subjected to thorough study. The needed research is that which cumulatively emerges from a small number of clearly formulated and reasonably comprehensive problem clusters or research patterns. Such research, obviously, is adapted to the longitudinal method. In fact, it appears that longitudinal research is, at once, sterile unless it is rigorous, and unduly expensive unless it contributes to an organized pattern.

[1] Lincoln, D. F. "Anthropometry Individualized." *Report of the Tenth Annual Meeting of the American Association for the Advancement of Physical Education.* Concord, N. H.: Republican Press Assoc., 1896. p. 4-11.

CHAPTER V
Mental Development in Adolescence

THE DISCUSSION of mental development during adolescence is limited almost entirely to investigations reported in the United States, England, and other English speaking countries. No reference is made to the general bibliographies or abstracts covering mental and physical development because they are referred to in other chapters. For the same reason no reference is made to the literature on the problems of nature versus nurture in mental development during the teens.

As in other fields of research, the value of data on mental development during adolescence depends largely upon the methods employed. Since different rates of growth may be found among different individuals, on account of different environmental circumstances, or as the result of changes in environmental conditions, the selection of subjects for study is an important consideration in methodology. We scarcely need mention the necessity of using valid, reliable measuring instruments, since this is now regarded as an essential in all educational research. The instruments actually in use in measuring mental growth during adolescence are, however, far from satisfactory for that purpose. They do not meet the criticism leveled against them by Thurstone (494) who said of the Binet Scale: "It should be extended beyond the age of fourteen or sixteen by inserting tests on which older subjects succeed better than younger ones. It is difficult to find test questions of the ordinary type in which such differentiation is possible, but our inability to find them does not prove that the development of intelligence stops somewhere in the 'teens. Common sense judgment certainly favors the assumption that the average man of forty is more intelligent than the average boy of twenty, but so far we have not been able to measure that difference. Instead of acknowledging this limitation in our measurement methods, we have not infrequently attempted to juggle with the definition of intelligence to make it fit the measuring devices that are accessible." For the most part the tests now employed to determine mental development during adolescence are the same ones which were in use when Thurstone made this criticism. The writer (458) pointed out previously the relative value of retest and non-retest methods in determining development. By employing suitable measuring instruments and by using the retest method he secured data from which individual growth curves may be plotted. Such growth curves cannot be determined by testing large numbers of persons of each of the adolescent ages. Only a generalized curve can thus be found. Individual differences in mental development are concealed by non-retest data and significant laws of individual development cannot be drawn. However, the generalized growth curve from non-retest data does seem to have some theoretical value, even though it involves the assumption that those tested at any given age do represent what those a year younger will be in one year, for example, that the sixteen-year-olds truly represent what the fifteen-year-olds will be when they are one year older. Adequate statistical or other analysis is necessary. Inadequate analysis often involves unconscious assumptions which are contrary to fact and thus make the results worthless. If, however, basic data are worthless, elaborate statistical technics are likely to be of little value. In studying adolescent mental development, the way in which cases are selected should be known and other conditions affecting the results should be described. Cases selected at random are not necessarily a random sample nor does ignorance of the kind of sample drawn make it random. The inadequacies and limitations of many of the studies throwing light on the problems of mental development of adolescents arise from the fact that they were not planned primarily for that purpose.

Developmental studies should continue over a period of years so as to secure individual cumulative records. Often a research is begun, a tentative report is published, and then the research is abandoned. Perhaps there should be an unwritten law in educational research against such abandonment of "infant researches."

Research materials on mental development during adolescence are discussed under the following headings:

1. Age of cessation of mental development
2. Rate of mental growth; the mental growth curve during adolescence
3. Constancy of I.Q.
4. Range of individual differences in intelligence
5. Sex differences in mental development
6. Miscellaneous topics
7. Problems needing investigation.

Age of Cessation of Mental Development

Recent studies seem to support those reviewed in the April, 1933, issue of the *Review* indicating that mental growth continues beyond the age of thirteen or fourteen years, as was often inferred from mental testing in the army during the World War and from the widespread use of mental tests shortly thereafter.

Keen (478), Jones and Conrad (189), Miles and Miles (484), and Sorenson (489) used the non-retest method to determine the growth and decline of intelligence with age. Some of their results throw light on the age of cessation of mental growth. S. C. Garrison (472), McConnell (482), Freeman (468), Hollingworth and Kaunitz (173), Masters and Upshall (483), Baldwin (456), Moore (485), and Roberts (487) used the retest method. Keen (478) tested 200 children in thirty-five families, using the Stanford-Binet. Testing all of the children in large families would tend to give groups of different chronological ages and of homogeneity in intelligence; but they would not be equivalent to retests of the same individuals. One could hardly agree with the author (478:737) on the following: ". . . since tests of siblings have demonstrated that there is a correlation of .50 or more between the children of a family, testing all the members of a large family at one time is roughly equivalent to testing a single individual at intervals corresponding to the age of each child," because a correlation of .50 does not imply any such relative equivalence.

E. L. Thorndike's view (492) that maximum mental development is reached at age twenty-two was dismissed with the comment that "because the factor of experience is partly responsible for high scores at the upper age levels, it seems safer to assume the maximum at twenty or below." At the present time, the effect of experience upon the scores of younger children is seldom denied.

Jones and Conrad (189) used the Army Alpha intelligence examination (Forms 5 and 7) with 1,191 individuals in rural New England, ages ten to sixty. The individuals were cases selected as to homogeneity in "economic status and educational opportunity." They were entirely native-born of native-born stock and came from relatively stationary, limited districts comprising nine counties in central and north central New England (Massachusetts, New Hampshire, and Vermont). At each age from ten to eighteen, from thirty-four to seventy-five individuals were tested; at ages nineteen to twenty-one inclusive, a total of eighty-seven. Mental growth, as indicated by the mean or median scores of each of these age groups, seemed to reach its high point sometime between the ages of eighteen and twenty-one years, with a decline thereafter. An analysis of growth as measured by each of the eight subtests of Army Alpha was given. It showed that on some subtests the high point of development was reached around eighteen years, especially in test 3 (commonsense), test 6 (numerical completion), and test 7 (analogies); that on others a slight rise continued into the early twenties as in test 1 (oral directions) and test 5 (dissected sentences); and that on other tests there seemed to be a slight rise well into advanced maturity, as in test 4 (the opposites) and test 8 (general information). The authors note that "a distinction needs to be made between the peak of development and the mental age of adults." They point out that "the latter phrase is, as a matter of fact, no more justifiable than would be the expression 'the mental age of children.'" This point is well taken for all ages following that at which the maximum is reached. Obviously if the status of mental ability, as measured by the Army Alpha, at age fifty-five is about the fourteen-year level, a mental age of fifty-five would have no useful meaning. The mental age concept could not be used to characterize adults after decline begins. This seems to be inherent in the meaning of mental age. The authors make a distinction between basic intelligence and acquired abilities. At ages ten to eighteen the opposites and general information tests contributed from 25 to 30 percent of the total score; at ages fifty to sixty approximately 40 percent. From this they concluded that: "As reported in mental tests, then, the effective intellectual power of the adult, much more than that of the ten-year-old, is evidently derived from accumulative stocks of information." They seemed to find little evidence for a differential duration of growth between the bright and dull groups. They recognized a fundamental limitation of the non-retest method: "Any sweeping application of our average results to individual adults would be ill-advised." It seems clear that the best means of determining the age of cessation of mental growth is cumulative records from retests with proper allowance for practice effect and adequate care in respect to differences in motivation from one year to another. Even with the great care exercised by the authors in selecting the individuals for testing, conclusions must of necessity be highly tentative when based upon thirty-four to seventy-five different individuals of each of the ages up to eighteen and from thirty-three to 106 for each of the five-year age periods after twenty-one.

Miles and Miles (484) used the first sixty items in the Otis Self-Administering Test of Intelligence, Higher Examination, Form A with a fifteen-minute time limit. The examination was administered as an individual test to 823 persons ranging in age from seven to ninety-four years. From thirty-eight to fifty-one individuals were tested in each five-year age group from fifteen to forty-nine. Considerable care was used to secure good sampling of the literate citizens in each of two towns, particularly individuals who would "be homogeneous in general mental character from age to age." Although the numbers chosen may be large enough "for statistical reliability," the authors recognized that "conclusive evidence regarding the relation of age to intelligence test score will, of course, not be available until scores have been obtained year after year from childhood until old age from the same members of large representative populations." Conclusions about the age at which mental growth reaches its peak are hardly justifiable from the mean or median scores of fifty-one individuals ages fifteen to nineteen years, or forty individuals ages twenty to twenty-four years, or thirty-eight individuals twenty-five to twenty-nine years of age. If the data are taken at face value, mental growth seems to reach its peak sometime around the eighteenth or nineteenth year. We question seriously, however, the validity and reliability of conclusions based upon a fifteen-minute non-retest of approximately eight to ten individuals of each chronological age.

Sorenson (489) attacked the same problem, using a one-hour vocabulary test of 480 items and a reading test consisting of a six-minute vocabulary section of 100 items and a forty-minute paragraph reading section of thirty-five items. He selected 641 individuals from approximately 5,500 students attending late afternoon and evening classes of the General Extension Division of the University of Minnesota so as to have approximately seventy-five individuals for each five-year age group up to the age of fifty-five. The individuals of each age group were selected on the bases of their years of schooling and their occupational status. The author noted that "the younger adults had not reached as high an occupational level as had the older adults, nor had they completed quite as many years of schooling." Accordingly, those under twenty-five years of age were not as well selected as those older, but their full-time education was more recent. Taken at face value, the smoothed curves for vocabulary indicated the peak of development at the highest age tested. Paragraph reading scores, however, showed marked fluctuations; they were higher at twenty-two to twenty-four than at fifteen to nineteen. The smoothed curve from fifteen to sixty was a straight line with zero slope. The author pointed out that "vocabularies have been described as the best single tests of general intelligence," but that "possibly this does not apply to the intelligence of adults." His results roughly agreed with those of Jones and Conrad for the Army Alpha subtests for opposites and general information. Sorenson (489) argued as follows:

> One hardly dares to venture the statement, on the basis of these findings, that the intelligence of adolescents increases with age. Conceivably one can acquire a bigger vocabulary by living in an intellectually rich environment. Increased vocabulary then may not represent real mental growth. On the other hand, decreasing mental test ability of adults with age may not represent actual deterioration of real or intrinsic capacity. A decrease in test ability among adults probably is caused by the fact that adults, as they grow older, exercise their minds less and less with the materials found in psychological tests. It is the writer's opinion that most people's mental abilities begin to decline with their graduation from high school or college unless a vigorous post-school environment demands active mentation.[1]

Sorenson emphasized the effect of forgetting or lack of practice shown by adults as they get older. If it is true, as Kelley has pointed out, that presentday mental tests and batteries of educational tests have 90 percent community of function, then mental tests are made up largely of school materials and disuse would have something of the effect which Sorenson suggested. He also held that training, schooling, or practice determines very largely adult mental ability and that the mentality of pre-adults depends largely upon inherent mental growth or maturation and school training or practice. He expressed the view that "nature helps a pre-adult grow mentally to the age of twenty," although no evidence is available from his own investigation to support it.

S. C. Garrison (472) used the Yerkes-Bridges-Hardwick point scale in retesting thirty-two men and forty-one women after an interval of ten years. The average age of the men at the first testing was 30.4 years; that of the women 26.4 years. These were teachers attending the summer school of Peabody College. The men's scores were slightly higher when retested (that is, at age forty) than when first tested. The women's scores when retested (that is, at age thirty-six) were also slightly more than upon the first testing. The gains, however, were not significant, being but two-thirds to one and one-sixteenth times their standard errors. These data seem to indicate that these adults did about as well on the mental test at the age

---

[1] See Brooks (458:112) for a discussion of inadequacy of tests now used to measure growth of intelligence during and after adolescence.

of thirty-five or forty as at twenty-five or thirty. Whether they would have done better at an earlier age is unknown from the data available.

McConnell (482) retested seventy members of the senior class of 1932 at Cornell College, using the 1928 edition of the American Council Psychological Examination. These students had taken the 1927 edition as freshmen in September, 1928. Using Thurstone's equivalent scores on the early forms of the test, McConnell transmuted the 1927 scores into their 1928 equivalents. The ages were not given but they were probably around seventeen or eighteen at the time of the first test and approximately three and one-half years more at the retesting. The mean retest score was 185.2 and the original 144.8. The difference of slightly more than 40 points is more than eighteen times its probable error and is statistically significant. McConnell pointed out that the increase in scores may be due to some combination of the following factors: growth in an underlying capacity, growth in effective use of endowment, specific training and varying sets, emotional states, motivation as well as conditions under which the test was administered. Thus the increase in score on the analogies "might reflect refinement of habits of observation, analysis, and systematic effort to discover relationship." Increase of score on the artificial language test might be the result of the acquisition of better methods of attack on language learning situations. Then too, instruction in college may affect directly the students' performance on the examination. McConnell also pointed out that, although the emotional state of many freshmen while taking an intelligence examination was not conducive to the best performance, the average increase in score from freshman to senior year probably was not due to the better poise of the seniors because "these students as freshmen were more concerned with making good scores than they were as seniors." Of course college students represent a highly selected group, living under presumably intellectually stimulating conditions, and these results do not have significance for general population.

Freeman (468) reported results from the Chicago growth study. Repeated tests from several hundred children have been continued over a period of ten years. Many individuals were retested at the age of seventeen or eighteen years when graduating from the University of Chicago Laboratory Schools. A few were retested in college. A composite of four standardized tests (vocabulary, analogies, completion, and opposites) was used. The growth curves drawn from the raw scores showed mental development continuing well beyond the age of seventeen or eighteen years. Some evidence indicated that children of average ability might continue intellectual growth to a somewhat later age than the brighter children. Hollingworth and Kaunitz (173) retested 116 gifted children (Stanford-Binet I.Q. above 132) after an interval of ten years. Fifty-two of these were tested with Army Alpha at age of fifteen and again with a different form of Army Alpha four years later. The scores were noticeably higher at the later time. Hollingworth concluded that the group at the age of nineteen was close to maturity and "that subsequent increments for growth [as measured on Army Alpha?] will be slight if any." Some individuals' scores at fifteen were almost as large as at nineteen.

Masters and Upshall (483) reported retests using one or two forms of Part I of the Thorndike Intelligence Examination for High School Graduates. Three groups of students in the Bellingham, Washington, Normal School were used. The first consisted of 125 students first tested October, 1928, and retested in May, 1930; the second group of 113 was first tested in October, 1929, and retested in May, 1931; the third group of 125 was first tested in October, 1931, and retested in January, 1932, after an interval of three months. The average age of these three groups at the first testing was eighteen years. The average gain of the first group was 28 times its probable error, of the second group 26 times its probable error, and the third group 8 times its probable error. These results indicate a gain even for a three-month period which might be interpreted as practice effect; but the two groups tested at the beginning and the end of the two-year normal school course made gains which cannot be explained on the basis of practice effect. If the gain of the third group, tested after an interval of three months, be regarded as practice effect, the net gain of the other two groups would still be from 16 to 18 times their probable errors. The authors pointed out that the amount of time elapsing between high-school graduation and entrance into normal school bore no relation to the amount of gain from the beginning to the end of the two-year normal course, nor did age of entrance seem to have any part in determining the amount of gain. From a study of the gains of these groups on achievement tests (arithmetic reasoning and computation, English usage, history, and geography) they found that the gain on the Thorndike Intelligence Examination was considerably greater than on any of the five achievement tests used. They then faced the difficulty of (a) relatively large gains on the Thorndike Intelligence Examination from the eighteenth to the twentieth years; and (b) the frequently mentioned view that native intelligence ceases to grow after the age of sixteen years. They accepted the latter as basic and concluded that the Thorndike Intelligence Examination for High School Graduates, Part I, "is not a valid measure of general intelligence as that term is commonly defined and used." Brooks (459), Dearborn (463), E. L. Thorndike (493), Thurstone (494), and others have discussed this matter previously. We do not see the justification for calling increase in scores on an intelligence examination before age sixteen growth of native intelligence and then calling increase in scores on the same examination after age sixteen something else.

Baldwin (456) used a T-score scaling of the American Council Psychological Examination editions of 1924 to 1928 for testing and retesting students at the University of Kansas. The interval between tests and retests varied from one day to three years. Sixty-two students from freshman to senior year made a net gain (practice effect deducted) of 3.12 T-scale units (.312 standard deviation). This gain was 5 times its standard error.

Teagarden (491) found a gain of 8 T-scale units from thirteen to eighteen years. Other data indicated the curve was still rising in the senior year.

Moore (485) found that twenty-nine young students in college (graduating from high-school before age sixteen) when tested at sixteen, eighteen, and twenty years of age made Otis gross scores of 58, 63, and 67; the number was so small that the gains were not statistically significant. The scores, however, of approximately 1,200 high-school graduates (chronological age approximately eighteen, twenty, and twenty-two years at three testings) were 54, 59, and 63. These gains were statistically significant.

Roberts (487) studied 100 graduates in engineering and 100 graduates in liberal arts at the University of Kansas who had attended eight consecutive semesters. The average grade points increased slightly, from 1.61 to 1.71 for the engineers and from 1.51 to 1.81 for liberal arts. He says: "The average grade-point of the group studied increases in size during the eight semesters. This rise in grade points is due to the growth or maturation of the students. The students meet the situations in which they find themselves more and more intelligently which means that they are growing in intelligence." However, Roberts did not regard the marked drop in grade points in the sophomore year as evidence of a loss of intelligence. In view of the unreliability and subjectivity of marks and the varying bases of assigning them, one may fairly ask with what degree of precision increase in average grade points from year to year in college does measure intellectual growth. One may well question the equality of the units of measurement.

Stroud and Maul (314) found that ability to memorize poetry and nonsense syllables (measured by a fifteen-minute test and a ten-minute test, respectively) was greatest in a group of twenty-eight college freshmen, average chronological age 18 years; next greatest in twenty-six ninth-grade students, average chronological age 14.4 years; and that the score decreased at each age from eleven to seven years in the case of the 172 children tested at these five ages. Since (a) the number was small; (b) the individuals selected were not homogeneous in intelligence; (c) no retests were made; and (d) the equality of the units of measurement was unknown (the scores were the number of lines of poetry learned or the number of nonsense syllables learned and the relative difficulty of each might vary), no conclusions may be drawn about the age of cessation of growth or the rate of growth of this function.

Rate of Mental Growth

Jones and Conrad (189) presented growth curves for total Army Alpha and its eight subtests, basing them upon non-retest data of nearly 1,200 individuals, ages ten to sixty years, selected as indicated in an earlier section of this chapter (p. 87). Using 290 adults, ages twenty-five to thirty-nine years, they found T-score rescaling closely equivalent to Thorndike equal-unit rescaling. Growth curves were based upon T-scores and support the commonly accepted view of negative acceleration in the middle and late teens. A discussion of statistical technics included a treatment of methods of curve-fitting which is particularly in point: "As we have just implied, *there is no single, correct mathematical solution.* We hear about '*the* least squares solution,' when, as a matter of fact, any given set of data permits of numerous solutions, all depending on the type and degree of curve selected." Citations to Kelley (479), and Ezekiel (466) were given in support of their position.

Freeman (468) pointed out that retest raw scores showed differential rates of growth for bright and average adolescents which suggested that the average child may continue to grow intellectually somewhat longer than the bright ones. Data on equality of units of measurement are not given. Baldwin (456) reported negative acceleration in rate of growth for University of Kansas students from freshman to senior year, although the curve was plotted from one-year, two-year, and three-year gains made by different groups of students. The curve did not represent gains made by the same individuals during different intervals of time. Keen (478) attempted to plot a mental growth curve directly from the Stanford-Binet mental ages by choosing a vertical scale which assumed that the unit of measurement (one year of Stanford-Binet mental age) is equal throughout the entire age range, that is, that mental growth from eleven to twelve years equals growth from fifteen to sixteen or nineteen to twenty years.

A highly accurate measure of the rate of intellectual growth during adolescence has not yet been secured, even though several lines of evidence seem to point to a marked slowing down in the late teens.

Constancy of the I.Q.

Testing programs have been carried on long enough now for many cumulative records to be made. The methods used in studying constancy of the I.Q. have been (a) finding correlations between the I.Q.'s on two or more testings; and (b) finding the central tendency of differences in I.Q.'s or the Q. of differences in I.Q.'s on test and retest. If chronological age is partialled out or eliminated by grouping so as to avoid spurious index correlation, the correlation technic shows the relative ranks on test and retest, but it does not indicate the amount of variation in I.Q.'s from one testing to another. In order to know how constant a child's I.Q. is, the actual difference between test and retest I.Q. for each individual should be calculated and then these differences given suitable statistical treatment. Reports are now appearing on the constancy of the I.Q. in relation to the length of time elapsing between test and retest. Conclusions on constancy, based upon indiscriminate averaging after intervals of varying lengths of time, will have to be modified in the light of this more recent type of investigation. The effect of time upon constancy has been studied by Brown (106), R. L. Thorndike (318), Lorge (481), and Hollingworth and Kaunitz (173).

Brown (106) analyzed data on retests of 124 problem children tested in the Chicago Institute of Juvenile Research and retested after intervals of time varying from one month to 145 months. The Stanford-Binet test was used. The average change in I.Q. was least for those retested after an interval of one to twelve months. It was greater for those retested after twelve to twenty-four months, still greater for those retested after twenty-four to thirty-six months, etc., being greatest after six to seven years. The amount of change in I.Q. upon retest was somewhat smaller for those tested at intervals of more than seven years. Since not all of those retested at any one of these intervals were retested at all other intervals, these data are not entirely conclusive. However, fifty-eight individuals who were retested after one to twenty-four months were also retested after sixty to 145 months. The total average of individual changes in I.Q. was 5.8 points and 10.7 points, respectively. For 124 individuals retested after an interval of sixty to 145 months, the average of individual changes in I.Q. was 10.4 points. Age at time of retest was also considered in respect to the amount of change in I.Q. Thus the average change in I.Q. was 11.6 points for seventy-four individuals under sixteen years at final retest and 8.7 points for fifty individuals who were sixteen years or older at the last retest.

R. L. Thorndike (318) used the correlations between test and retest I.Q.'s reported by thirteen previous investigators to determine the effect of time interval (t) upon the constancy of I.Q. He fitted curves to the data (thirty-six correlations in which t ranged from zero to sixty months) and found that the theoretical coefficients ranged from r equals .89 when t equals 0, to r equals .70 when t equals 60 months. A second degree curve gave very little better fit than the linear, so the theoretical coefficients were determined by the latter. In this study the constancy of I.Q. at various ages was not studied, so no conclusions may be drawn from it on the correlations likely to be found between the I.Q.'s of adolescents of different ages when retested after varying intervals of time. Lorge (481) reported correlations upon scores of approximately 160 boys who were tested at the age of thirteen to fifteen years on the Thorndike-McCall reading scale, I.E.R. arithmetic test, Stenquist assembly test, and I.E.R. general clerical test, and retested on the same tests after an interval of ten years. The correlations ranged from .57 to .66, those on the Stenquist assembly test being highest. In the case of fifty-three girls the correlations between tests and retests on similar materials after an interval of five months were slightly higher. Possible causes of lowered coefficients after longer intervals of time were listed as initial reliability of tests, growth, environmental factors in time, and limitations of the tests themselves, the latter being regarded as the probable primary factor since tests usually are designed for a limited age or grade range. Hollingworth and Kaunitz (173) studied the results of retesting 116 gifted children who were in the top centile when first tested on the Stanford-Binet ten years earlier. The retest came when they were all near maturity and was designed to see if they maintained their high rank in intelligence. The Army Alpha scale was used for the retest. It showed that 82 percent of them made scores which would place them in the top centile of the military draft by Army Alpha. This was taken as evidence that gifted children tend to maintain their superiority (as measured by a verbal intelligence test) at maturity.

Rappaport (486) studied the effect upon constancy of I.Q. of using chronological ages fourteen, fifteen, and sixteen years as divisors in computing the I.Q. He used 150 clinical cases to whom the Stanford-Binet had been given before and after the age of fourteen in the Child Study Department of the Rochester Society for the Prevention of Cruelty to Children. The mean I.Q. was 80. The average time between initial and final tests was slightly more than four years. Cases were eliminated in which the element of emotional upset was present. The mean arithmetic deviation of those sixteen years of age and older at retest was 6.2 points. For those sixteen years of age or older at retest, sixteen years chronological age was the best divisor in finding I.Q., since it showed least change in I.Q. from test to retest; fifteen years as divisor showed slightly greater change, whereas fourteen years showed the greatest. Constancy, as measured by coefficients of correlation, was in the .80's. The effect of time between testings upon the constancy of I.Q. was not reported.

Lincoln (480) found changes in Stanford-Binet I.Q.'s of forty-five gifted boys and sixty-four gifted girls retested after an interval of five to eight years. The median changes were 8.1 points. Many of these were adolescents when retested. The mean I.Q.'s of the boys were slightly higher on the final than on the initial test; those of the girls were 4 or 5 points lower. A measure of the constancy of the I.Q.'s of gifted children is the extent to which later retests show them decreasing to the "average" group. This study showed the I.Q.'s of 13 percent of the boys and 22 percent of the girls dropping below 110 at the final test. The conclusion was reached that superior children tend to remain superior. We are inclined to believe that part of the drop in I.Q. was caused by the limitations of the Stanford-Binet at the higher ages.

Some of the cases tested by Lithauer and Klineberg (212) and by Gildea and Macoubrey (157) were adolescents. Lithauer and Klineberg found that the correlation between length of interval of time from test to retest (three to fifty-seven months) and amount of change in I.Q. was not significant. A preferable technic would be to find the actual amount of change in I.Q. for different intervals of time. Gildea and Macoubrey (157) sought to determine some of the factors affecting constancy of I.Q. of problem children. They matched for age, sex, and initial I.Q. seventy-three individuals whose I.Q.'s changed more than 10 points from test to retest with a group whose I.Q's changed 5 points or less. Degree of cooperation, attitude toward examiner, and speed on test were not related to variability in I.Q. Improvement in physical condition, parental attitudes, and symptomatic behavior were associated with variability in I.Q.

Range of Individual Differences

To determine the range of individual differences in mental traits, some measure of absolute variability should be used such as the standard deviation, Q., or range, rather than a measure of relative variability such as the Pearson coefficient of variation. The latter has much value in rendering variability comparable when different units of measurement have been used, such as measures of height, weight, and mental ability, and for other purposes, but if we are seeking to know the range of differences, a measure of absolute variability should be used.

The standard deviations of abbreviated Otis scores reported by Miles and Miles (484) for certain age groups were greatest at fifteen to sixteen years, next greatest at eleven to twelve, then at seventeen to eighteen, and least at thirteen to fourteen; but no reliance can be placed upon non-retest results of seventeen to thirty-five cases at each two-year-age group. According to data from Jones and Conrad (189), the standard deviations of Army Alpha scores increased from eleven to twenty-one with one exception; it was slightly less for the seventeen-year-olds tested than for the sixteen-year-olds. This may have been the result of selection. At any rate, we cannot know conclusively from non-retest data whether the range of individual differences in mental ability increases, decreases, or remains constant as children pass to early maturity and late adolescence.

According to McConnell (482), college students showed slightly greater variability on the American Council Psychological Examination as seniors than as freshmen, although the difference in variability was but 58 percent of its probable error. Baldwin (456) also found a slight increase in standard deviation from freshman to senior year in college on the American Council tests. On the other hand, Masters and Upshall (483) found normal school students slightly less variable on Part I of the Thorndike Intelligence Examination for High-School Graduates at the end of their two-year course than at the beginning, but a group retested after a three-month interval was slightly more variable than when first tested. The differences in variability, however, were not statistically significant. Moore (485) also found a very slight decrease in Q. of Otis scores of high-school graduates tested at ages sixteen, eighteen, and twenty years, and at ages eighteen, twenty, and twenty-two years. The retests reported by S. C. Garrison (472) covered individuals beyond adolescence at the first testing. On the retest ten years later they were slightly more variable but the differences in the standard deviations were only one to two times their standard errors. Brown (106) showed that the range of individual differences in Stanford-Binet mental age and I.Q. of 124 problem children tested at the Chicago Institute for Juvenile Research increased from the first test (average chronological age 8.2 years) to the retest (average chronological age 15.9 years), the mental age ranges being 9.8 years and 15.3 years respectively, and the I.Q. ranges, 85 and 117 respectively.

Sex Differences

Wellman (495) discussed sex differences in intelligence and gave a bibliography of 249 titles covering the more significant literature through 1932. On pages 629 to 630 she discussed sex differences in intelligence at adolescence.

Conrad, Jones, and Hsiao (120) reported sex differences of 271 boys and 238 girls, ages twelve to twenty-one on Army Alpha and each of its subtests. These individuals were selected, as indicated in an earlier section of this chapter, as to homogeneity in economic status and educational opportunity and were native-born of native-born stock from relatively stationary rural districts. Girls at all of these ages excelled the boys on the total Alpha score. They also excelled at all or nearly all of these ages on oral directions, commonsense, opposites, dissected sentences, and analogies. Boys at the later teen ages excelled girls in arithmetic problems and general information. The authors concluded that girls show a slight superiority over boys, the difference being greater during early adolescence; but at no age was it great enough to have any practical significance. The younger men and women tested and retested by S. C. Garrison (472) showed slight but unimportant differences on the Yerkes-Bridges-Hardwick scale in favor of the men. This was also true of the entire group of 541 adults. The thirty-two men tested and retested at an interval of ten years made slightly lower average scores than the forty-one women tested at the same times. The differences were too small to be statistically significant. Since selection was primarily enrolment in summer school classes in psychology, the group could not be regarded as representative of the two sexes.

Goodman (473) studied sex differences of nearly 1,400 New Haven high-school students who had failed one or more subjects. Nearly half of them had failed to graduate. Boys I.Q.'s (name of intelligence test used not given) average 5.1 points higher than those of girls, the critical ratio of this difference being 7.13. Dietze (464) compared immediate factual memory for printed material read by approximately 650 pairs of boys and girls (ages eleven to nineteen years) paired by age and grade. The tests were multiple choice of "a highly satisfactory degree of objectivity, reliability, and validity." On the whole, boys slightly excelled girls, the greatest difference being on a factual article on radium in which boys undoubtedly had greater interest than girls. The differences for three different sex paired groups on three different kinds of material were, respectively, 5, 1.5, and 3 times their probable errors. Wyatt (498) compared the sex differences of nearly 1,000 individuals (most of whom were from grades seven to twelve) on free word association. While the technic requires much time, some valuable data may be secured. Thus males showed a marked preference for feminine nouns, females a less marked preference for masculine nouns; this result "suggests that thinking of the opposite sex is stronger in males than in females, and that not only at the school age."

Hurd (476) reported sex differences in achievement on a unit of high-school physics. He selected 134 boys and 134 girls from more than 1,300 pupils in fifty-three classes in thirty-four schools. They were matched in age, grade, and instructor. Matching by age-grade status was used as a rough means of equating the groups in intelligence and since the members of each pair were under the same instructor for eighteen class periods of forty-five minutes each, the differences between preliminary and final tests were expected to depend "on inherent sex differences or different earlier training due to sex." The achievement test used had a reliability coefficient of .957. Boys' initial and final scores were higher than those of the girls. The difference between the sexes on the initial test was 9.8 times its standard error; on the final test it was 2.6 times its standard error. Girls gained more than boys, the difference in gain being 2.7 times its standard error.

Several studies on sex differences in mathematics have been made. Two of these were made by Foran and O'Hara (467) and by Eells and Fox (465). Foran and O'Hara (467) compared the scores of approximately 500 boys and 500 girls on the Webb geometry test in the Catholic high-schools of an eastern city. The boys made better scores than the girls, only 27 percent of the girls equaling or exceeding the boys' median. The difference was 9 times its standard error. The two sexes were almost the same in intelligence (measured by the Terman group test), the difference being but three-fifths of its standard error. The boys were clearly superior on four of the five parts of the test. The coefficient of variability of geometry scores was greater for girls than for boys, but the actual range of scores was probably greater for boys than for girls since the standard deviation of boys' scores was greater than the standard deviation of the girls' scores. Eells and Fox (465) compared the mathematics scores on the Iowa High School Content Examination of 6,000 men and women entering the freshman class in forty-seven junior colleges in California. They were all "low" freshmen. The men's mean score exceeded that of the women by an amount which was 40 times its probable error. The American Council Psychological Examination showed the men slightly superior to the women but the difference was not significant. The men, however, had taken approximately one-third more units of mathematics in high school than the girls. When compared according to units of mathematics in high school, the differences were still in favor of the men and were statistically significant for all who had three units or less of high-school mathematics. Approximately 100 of each sex had had no units of mathematics in high-school. Here again the men's scores were much greater than those of the women, the difference being 8 times its probable error.

Carroll (460) studied sex differences in the appreciation of literature, using the Carroll Prose Appreciation Test with 1,200 high-school students (100 boys and 100 girls of each grade from seven to twelve) and 100 college men and 100 college women. All subjects were reported as selected at random, although details of such selection were not given. The average scores of the girls in each grade were better than those of the boys, the critical ratios of the differences ranging from 3.7 to 8.6 (except in the eighth grade where it was 2.2). At the college level, 34 percent of the boys exceeded the girls' median; at the senior high-school level 30.9 percent; and at the junior high-school level 37.5 percent. Girls' standard deviations were greater in all groups (same in the tenth grade) but the variability coefficients were roughly the same. The range of scores varied, the girls' range being exceeded by the boys' only in grades eight and ten. Girls also made twice as many high scores as boys, whereas the latter made 58 percent of the lowest scores. To the extent that the test is a valid, reliable one and the sample really was random, clear and distinct sex differences were shown.

Miscellaneous Topics

Junge (477) studied the development of perception of complex relationships in the case of 522 individuals ages ten to fourteen years. The method used was to show two films under identical conditions, the subjects then writing descriptions of each film. Two reports, judged to be typical, were selected for each sex at each age and were analyzed. From these analyses, the author concluded that from the age of ten to fourteen "apperception" develops gradually. The method does not permit a quantitative expression of development.

Schmidt (488) conducted experiments with 200 boys ages nine to nineteen years, having them describe pictures. He concluded from a study of their descriptions that correct global perception begins at about the age of thirteen or fourteen years and that criticism and evaluation begin about the same time. Here again rate of development cannot be stated in quantitative terms. Cser (462), in the Municipal Pedagogical Psychological Laboratory in Budapest, studied the power of attention of 710 boys and 789 girls ages ten to fourteen years. They worked at a special kind of addition for a ten-minute period, the amount of work for each minute being calculated. There seemed to be a slowing down at fourteen years with greater individual differences. The boys seemed to be more rapid but less accurate than the girls. One cannot be sure, however, that the slowing down may not be a function of the difficulty of the test itself rather than a characteristic of development.

Willy and Lehman (497) used a questionnaire to study the reading preferences of a group of fifty intellectually gifted adolescents, I.Q.'s above 140. They were tested three times, the average ages being 10 years, 6 months; 15 years, 6 months; and 17 years, 6 months. Each individual listed the names of books which he preferred and checked his first, second, and third preferences on a printed list of fourteen types of reading material. From these answers the changes in reading preference with age were indicated. Bologa (457) studied the reading interests of 2,935 public school and high-school boys and girls ages eight to twenty years and drew conclusions on the ages at which various kinds of reading materials were of most interest. The author interpreted his findings as showing the following important incentives for reading: love of adventure until the age of fifteen; then eroticism; and still later, interest in knowledge and science. Wells (496) studied the tastes of 400 junior-senior high-school pupils for humorous literature, using forty samples of humorous literature from a wide variety of sources. In all grades the order of preference was absurdity, slap-stick, satire, or whimsy.

A fundamental difficulty in all questionnaire studies is to know how valid the results are. Some evidence exists showing that writing answers to questionnaires does not give the same results as putting check marks before items printed in a list; that is, if children are given a long list of books to check the ones they like best, the results are not likely to be the same as if they are merely asked to write a list of the books in the order of their preference. Attempts at the validation of interest questionnaires (the interview technic) involve the research worker in other difficulties. The intimate study of individuals by which the actual reading done from day to day for a short period of time is followed by a similar study of the same individuals for a short interval of time at a later age is difficult to carry on but probably will yield more valid results. Experimental and laboratory schools with their well-trained staffs and greater facilities for cumulative, individual records are in the best position to carry on such studies—subject, of course, to the possible limitation of selection of students above average in ability and socio-economic status.

Garrett, Bryan, and Perl (470) investigated the relationships of certain mental abilities at ages nine, twelve, and fifteen years, using a battery of six memory and four non-memory tests with 125 individuals of each sex and age. Analysis of correlations indicated that all tests measured much the same ability. They could not separate memory or retentivity from general intelligence at these three age levels. The part played by general ability seemed to decrease with age and that played by special abilities to increase with age. If this is true at later ages of adolescence and in adult years it may throw light on Sorenson's (489) and Jones and Conrad's (189) results from vocabulary, opposites, and general information.

Conklin (461) and K. C. Garrison (471) have brought out textbooks on adolescence which use the research literature on the topics discussed. Hollingworth (475) discussed some of the problems of adolescence and presented a bibliography of 100 titled to 1933.

Problems Needing Investigation

Probably the most pressing needs in research on mental development in adolescence include the following:

1. Measuring instruments suitable for measuring mental development in the late teens and early twenties which can be used to secure valid, reliable, developmental data on individuals. Thurstone's method of scaling data applied to the Stanford-Binet

or other tests gives a generalized curve, but yields no individual growth curves. Tests are needed which can be repeated at consecutive ages through adolescence and into adult life, if it is possible to construct them.

2. With such tests available, the retest method can be used to attack some of the major problems of adolescent mental development with a reasonable chance of finding satisfactory solutions. Such problems as those on which we have presented data from recent researches might well be attacked, as the following: (1) Determination of the actual individual mental growth curves of many persons living under a wide diversity of environmental conditions and with notable changes occurring in environment at different ages. Such studies would show: (a) the probable peak of mental development for individuals of varying degrees of intelligence under divergent environments; (b) divergence, convergence, or parallelism of curves of mental development under specified conditions and for individuals of various grades of ability; (c) sex differences as a function of age, ability, and differential environments; (d) individual variations in mental growth or the constancy of the I.Q. at adolescence. (2) A series of researches on problems of relationships involving mental ability and mental development, as discussed in Chapter VI.

CHAPTER VI
Relationships in Physical and Mental Development

THE PREVIOUS REVIEW on this topic (560), in the April, 1933, issue of the *Review of Educational Research,* reported results from over one hundred studies of physical-mental relationship. The variables considered were (a) anthropometric measurements, body build indexes, physical condition, anatomical or physiological age; and (b) intelligence measurements, scholarship, or other indexes of mental accomplishment or efficiency. The conclusion was reached that the correlation between any one measure of physical size (age constant) and any one measure of mental status was uniformly too low for predictive purposes, usually below .30 and quite commonly between .10 and .20. The use of compound physical traits, such as morphological indexes, or of developmental measures such as those based on dentition, pubescence, or physiological age in general failed to give indications of higher relationship. These results conform with theories which emphasize the relatively specific and independent character of human traits. Investigators have nevertheless been unwilling to abandon this field of research. Continued interest in the subject may be attributed to the following factors: (a) physical traits are objective, easily definable, easily measured (if they can be utilized in the prediction of other less easily measured aspects of growth, they will be of distinct value in research and in educational programs); (b) the concepts of "integration" and the "organism as a whole" have led to the conviction that in some manner structural and behavioral traits are significantly related, even though ordinary mass statistical methods fail to reveal this relationship; and (c) clinical indications of the intellectual effects of illness, physical handicap, endocrine dysfunction, etc., have led to attempts to place such evidence on a more quantitative basis.

A variety of suggestions has been offered as to the direction which further research should take. Paterson (592) indicated as important problems the relation between physical development and mental development at the preschool level, the investigation of nutritional relationships and of the physical basis of "stamina," and, in collaboration with physicians, the determination of the psychological effects of illness and of specific medical and surgical procedures. Minimizing results from comparisons of "ready-made" groups, Paterson advocates the use either of experimental technics or of correlational methods limited to single age levels. The present reviewer (560), after listing some of the difficulties involved in drawing conclusions from correlational material, suggested: "Our next stage of research must place its emphasis not in mass correlations but in individual growth studies, pursued intensively and with particular attention to concomitant changes in curves which express physiological functions, physical growth, and mental development."

Dearborn (383), accepting the above formulation, called attention to the fact that he has directed research of this character in connection with a twelve-year growth study in Massachusetts. He presented the following summary of findings, derived for the most part from doctoral dissertations in the Harvard School of Education:[1]

Correlation coefficients between carpal development and speed or quality of handwriting were found to be zero (Wittler).

Four hundred and thirty-eight coefficients of correlation between IQ and anthropometric measurements, mostly head measurements, have been presented by Estabrook. The average for girls was $+.06$; for boys $+.14$. The coefficients were higher for boys than for girls in every one of the eleven measurements.

Correlation coefficients between mental ages and Prescott's anatomic index within narrow age-range groups or when age was partialled out varied from $+.28$ to $+.03$. The anatomic rating of the children in a school for the feeble-minded was found to be about one year below the public school children (Prescott).

C. W. Smith found no relationship between Prescott's anatomic index and mental development. The coefficients between mental age and anatomic index obtained by Cattell for eight groups of from 50 to 100 cases averaged $+.04$. Wheeler found the dull children to be slightly but consistently below the average in anatomic development.

Correlation coefficients between dentition and mental age in one-year age groups varied from $+.04$ to $+.12$.

The anthropometric measurements of those pupils with IQ's below 90 have been compared with the total group. The measurements of the dull group are slightly, but consistently, below the average of the unselected group. In general about 65 percent of the subnormal were below the median of the unselected group (Wheeler). Similarly, those pupils with IQ's above 110 were found to be slightly but consistently above the average of the unselected group (Agee).

The difference between the height and weight of the children in the school for the feeble-minded was further below the unselected group than the dull children; namely, one year at the age of seven and three years at the age of seventeen. The adolescent spurt in growth took place about two years earlier than it did in the normal group (Smith).

The correlation coefficients between head measurements and intelligence are approximately the same as those between height and intelligence; i.e., about $r = +.15$ (Estabrook). When several physical measurements are combined the correlation coefficients are raised to around $+.20$ or $+.30$ (Latshaw, Cattell).

For the purpose of determining whether or not large or small annual increments of growth had any influence on school achievement, a group of over 1,000 children were studied during the two-year period in which on the average the greatest growth takes place. The methods of study were: correlation coefficients, comparisons of extreme groups and case studies of pupils who had made unusual gain or lack of gain in physical growth or school achievement. No relationship between spurts or lags in physical growth and achievement in school subjects was found (Hobson).

It does not appear to the reviewer that these investigations, as summarized, answer the questions previously raised as to the limitations of the customary type of correlational studies. Although dealing with cumulative data, the technics are primarily cross-sectional. It is only in the last study mentioned, by Hobson, that use is made of incremental data as such.

---

[1] Note also Lincoln's summary of the Harvard Growth Study (411).

In subsequent reports from this rich accumulation of records, the unique advantages of cumulative material will no doubt be more fully exploited. At the present time the Harvard contributions, both as to methods and results, appear to fall in line with the general body of mass statistical investigations which have indicated either little or no correspondence between physical and mental variables.

A number of other recent correlational studies may be mentioned. Lazarfeld (572) found no consistent positive correlation between size and intelligence. Bissett and Laslett (366), reporting on 350 high-school boys, found a negative correlation of —.185 between Miller Group Test I.Q. and height, and —.41 between I.Q. and weight. They seemed impressed by the unusual finding of negative r's, and stated that they have "no explanation to offer for this apparent anomaly." The anomaly is not in the correlations, but in the sampling represented. The school population ranged in age from thirteen to over twenty-one years. In such a group, selected on the basis of representation in a senior high school, the youngest, smallest individuals will of course be precocious children with high I.Q.'s, and the older, larger individuals will be grade repeaters with lower I.Q.'s.

In a group of New York college freshmen, Harris (554) found correlations of .10 $\pm$ .04 between weight and intelligence (Army Alpha) and .14 $\pm$ .04 between height and intelligence. Similar non-significant correlations were reported by Gittings (549) for Arizona freshman women: weight and intelligence (Army Alpha) .19 $\pm$ .11; height and intelligence .18 $\pm$ .11. Because of restricted range in the mental test scores, coefficients of correlation among college students may be expected to be lower than in an unselected school group. As representative of the latter, Stoke's results (621) may be quoted. For 499 children the correlation between I.Q. and a height index based on age and sex was .20 $\pm$ .029; between weight index and I.Q., 25 $\pm$ .028; and between anatomic index and I.Q., .09 $\pm$ .03 (computed from fivefold tables).

In a cumulative study Bayley (509) reported correlations between intelligence and a comprehensive series of physical variables (weight, height, head circumference, cephalic index, body build, ossification index, age of cutting first tooth, illness record, and physician's ratings of physical condition). All coefficients were close to zero. From forty-five to sixty-one cases were utilized, at various ages from infancy to five years.

Carter (524) advocated the use of factor analysis, as a means of isolating variables which may be of greater importance than those at present used in the study of physical-mental relationships:

Correlations in the neighborhood of .20 have been found repeatedly. These are not valuable for predictive work. However, it should be remembered that they are correlations between composites, naïvely put together, or naïvely accepted because found together in nature. On the side of the physical data, such measures as height and weight are very complex composites; even such measures as length of forearm are composites, since the length of one bone may be a resultant of the interplay of numerous forces. . . . Factor analysis may be expected to yield purified, uncorrelated factors, which will behave in a less routine, less monotonous, and more significant way than do overlapping variables. At present we have many measures, all so imbricated that they are all largely measures of the same thing (gross size). To the extent that the measures are correlated, defense of the present system amounts to insistence that only one thing in anthropometry is worth measuring, and that even this one thing is not worth measuring well. It is as if an engineer recording elevations always added the distance of a planet to each measurement, thereby minimizing all important differences on earth.

Only time will tell whether these statistically distilled and purified physical factors will yield a closer relationship to purified mental factors than is obtained in the variables at present investigated. Sanders (435) also reviewed the relationship of intelligence to height and weight.

Head Measurements

Earlier studies of head measurements failed to yield significant relationships with intelligence, whether a single dimension was used, or a "module" or average of several regarded as representative of head size. But the hypothesis might be advanced that intelligence is more likely to be a function of brain cubic capacity, than of linear measurements taken alone or crudely averaged. Broom (518) employed a formula devised to give brain capacity, when the length, breadth, and height of the cranium are entered in relation to certain constants (Lee formula No. 14). Among 100 college men a correlation of only .12 was found between this volume measure and Thorndike score (Intelligence Examination for High School Graduates). Among 100 college women the correlation was .24. It is apparent that this refinement of technic has no significant effect upon the correlations ordinarily obtained between anthropometric and intellectual measurements. Even this low correlation is subject to revision downward if the groups studied contain a heterogeneous racial mixture. It is not unlikely, for example, that in a mixed group containing persons of North and of South European origin, a small positive correlation would occur between head measurements and intelligence, although tending to disappear if computed for the two subgroups separately. In a homogeneous Japanese group, Okada (590) found a small difference in head circumference, when children of superior and inferior scholarships were compared, indicating a low positive relationship between these variables. Among the feebleminded, closer relationships may sometimes be found between head size and intelligence because of the presence of cases of cerebral hypoplasia (microcephaly).

Body Build

A careful study by Klineberg, Asch, and Bloch (565) involved a selection of 153 college men homogeneous as to age, education, and socioeconomic background. On the basis of a battery of anthropometric measurements, the sample was separated into a stocky or "pyknic" and a linear or "leptosome" group, intergrading cases being eliminated. A series of information, memory, perceptual, and personality tests was administered, but no reliable differences could be shown between the two groups. Similarly negative results were reported by the same investigators as to the relationship of body build to scholastic aptitude and other psychological traits among students in a women's college. In a recent study, Liefmann (208) found no relationship between body build, classified in terms of Kretschmer's types, and a series of motor abilities. Cameron and Pryor (522) used a case study method in dealing with the effects of extreme deviation in body build. Depending on circumstances, these deviations may operate either as social assets or as liabilities leading to social and emotional maladjustment. Indirect effects upon scholarship and intellectual "drive" can be inferred in individual cases. Theories concerning body build and psychological traits have been recapitulated by Landau (568).

Anatomical and Physiological Age: Pubescence

Little has been added to our former knowledge of relationships in this field. Stone and Barker (622), studying the relation of age at menarche to intelligence, in 594 college women, found a correlation of $-.175 \pm .036$ in one group and of $-.042 \pm .042$ in another. Menarcheal age also showed a low relationship to personality traits as measured by the Bernreuter test. A possible attenuating factor is unreliability in the measurement of age at menarche, depending upon memory of persons who at the time of the study had a mean age of eighteen years. Care was taken to keep the groups as homogeneous as possible, by eliminating students of Oriental, Semitic, or South European derivation. The results were similar to those of Brooks (517), who in an earlier study of freshman women reported correlations ranging from $-.04$ to $-.139$ between age at menarche and intelligence as measured by an eight-hour examination.

Body Chemistry: Endocrine Factors

The association of subthyroid conditions with mental defect (cretinism, myxedema) has led to an interest in studying relationships between thyroid function and mental performance within a normal range of subjects. The convenient index of thyroid function is basal metabolic rate (BMR). It must be pointed out that as ordinarily administered this is unsatisfactory as to reliability and that thyroid functioning is only one of the factors determining basal metabolism. In a group of fifty-two college women, Patrick and Rowles (593) found correlations of around zero between intelligence and BMR, blood pressure, and vital capacity. The authors seemed disappointed by these low relationships and suggested that a closer association could be demonstrated if the study were conducted over a wider age range. Such a study has been made by Rothbart (610) (not, however, with the use of repeated measures). Rothbart (610), after summarizing recent studies on psychological factors in relation to basal metabolism, reported results for a group of fifty-nine boys and thirty-nine girls in a state institution, ranging in age from nine to fifteen years, and in I.Q. from 60 to

120. No definite relation was found between I.Q. and BMR. It was also shown that between subjects of normal and of subnormal mentality there was no difference in blood cholesterol.

From a group of clinic children Levy (574) selected for basal metabolism determinations those who showed some indications of glandular imbalance. The correlation between I.Q. and BMR was, again, close to zero, and remained so when the relationship was studied for subgroups (non-problem cases, cases with I.Q. below 75, and cases with I.Q. above 110). Although in general no relation was found between BMR and behavior deviations, there was some slight indication that children with scholastic difficulties tended, in an unexpected proportion of cases, to have BMR's of −11 or lower. Levy concluded with an interrogation rather than with a declarative statement: "It has always been recognized that there is a group of cases in which scholarship difficulty is not due to lack of intelligence. Is it due to lack of interest? Does that lack of interest come from lack of drive as measured by basal metabolic rate?"

Studies of the psychological effects of glandular therapy have usually dealt with too few cases, and have presented the results in such form (599) that definite conclusions could not safely be drawn. An investigation by Marinus and Kimball (581) overcomes the former but retains the latter defect. Children in special classes in Detroit were examined for cases of suspected endocrine dysfunction; 233 of these were given glandular treatment and 151 reserved as controls; the procedure in matching controls was not stated. Results were given in terms of the percent showing increasing I.Q. percent with no change, and percent with decreasing I.Q. The data appear to indicate that the experimental group, as compared with the controls, showed a smaller percent making gains, but also a smaller percent suffering losses. Tests of achievement gave similarly uncertain results. Tests of motor function showed no significant trend. If any conclusion at all can be drawn from this material, it is that from the psychological standpoint treatment is advantageous for the congenitally hypothyroid, of no value for the pituitary deficient, and of uncertain value for other hypothyroid and for mixed cases. The writers stated: "Faulty thyroid function in pregnant women interferes with normal development of the central nervous system to a degree dependent on the severity of thyroid deficiency at different stages in the development of the fetus. Later thyroid feeding may enable the nervous system to function more efficiently, but without repairing damage already done." It seems desirable, however, to reserve judgment on this study until the data are reported in more adequate quantitative form.

Other clinical studies, not reported in the previous review, include the following: Konikow (567) reported scholastic improvement as the result of organo-therapy, in a case of gigantism. Geiger (548), in twenty cases, found indications of better school adjustment and of more consistent mental performance, as the result of pituitary extract administered hypodermically or thyroid extract administered orally, or a combination of the two.

Bronstein and Brown (516) treated twenty-one cases of hypothyroidism in children from one to sixteen years of age. They concluded that therapy tends to lessen the characteristic lethargy and unresponsiveness of the cretin, but that ability as indicated by tests remains substantially the same. Even when repeated tests were given over a period of two or more years, cases of I.Q. increase were no more common than cases of I.Q. decrease. Evidence is lacking as to the mental age level which the congenitally hypothyroid can attain under treatment. Gordan (552) believes that some cases can be brought to approximate normality. Kimball and Marinus (563) considered that the normal limit for untreated cretins is six years mental age and that under treatment instituted in infancy this may be increased to eight years. The importance of early treatment lies in the possibility of promoting, to some extent, differentiation during the period of the most rapid development of neural structures. Mental retardation is less marked and is perhaps more amenable to treatment, in cases of children of normal birth who develop hypothyroidism later in life.

The effects of pituitary disorders were investigated by Menninger (584). The majority of cases of pre-adolescent hypopituitarism were said to present evidence of mental retardation. Diabetic children, on the other hand, were described by Sherrill (615) as "mentally precocious." Insulin treatment permits normal growth in height and weight; the effects upon mental characteristics are not indicated.

A striking case of discrepancy in physical and mental growth was reported by McClure and Goldberg (578). At the age of five years and seven months a boy diagnosed as suffering from a pineal tumor showed: a mental age slightly below his chronological age; dentition normal for his chronological age; markedly advanced sexual development; and skeletal age, as determined from X-rays, equal to that of a boy of sixteen or eighteen years. This indicates a degree of specificity in development in conformity with what has previously been reported in the summaries on puberty precox (560:158).

In a large sample of Finnish children, Vuori (626) investigated the relationships of blood grouping to marks obtained in school. The distributions of grades were substantially the same for members of the different blood groups.

Studies of differential chemistry of emotional states and of neuroses and psychoses were fully reviewed by Dunbar (533). Relationships to mental ability are not at all clear and lack any systematic organization in relation to theory. Rich (605) reported a correlation of −.51 between intelligence and urinary excretion of phosphorus per unit of body weight. This was based on only twenty-eight subjects, and in a subsequent study with more cases Rich (606) found correlations of close to zero between intelligence and inorganic phosphorus in blood plasma, lipoid P, and total P. The correlation with blood calcium was also approximately zero. Powers (600), comparing twelve normal or superior persons with twenty idiots, reported that the latter were normal in calcium but high in inorganic phosphorus—supporting Rich's original finding. The present review will not attempt to consider studies of drug effects or applications of colloid chemistry in connection with problems of psychophysiology.

Relevant, however, to this field of inquiry is the study of variations in psychological functions in relation to the female sex rhythm. Herren (556), in a recent study, found premenstrual changes in cutaneous sensitivity to touch and pain and attempted to explain his results in terms of the influence of the female sex hormone upon the central nervous system. Other investigators have reported, in relation to the menses, changes in visual functions, neuromotor excitability, muscle strength, and motor coordination. A number of these effects appear to be well established on the basis of careful measurement, but the results are not at all clear as regards more complex mental functions and mental efficiency. This is a significant field for further work, not only because of its immediate practical importance, but also because of its bearing upon the theory of physical-mental relationships. A competent review of the literature up to 1934 was published by Seward (614).

Diurnal variations in performance have also been studied, in relation to changes in respiration, body temperature, metabolism, acid-base balance of the blood, etc. It would take us too far afield to deal with these in detail. The present state of the literature on diurnal variations is indicated in a review by G. L. Freeman and Hovland (543), who found twelve studies reporting a continuous rise in mental performance in the course of the day, twelve studies reporting a continuous fall, five reporting a morning rise and afternoon fall, and five reporting a morning fall and afternoon rise. Specific environmental factors are evidently of predominating importance, and evidence is lacking for a "natural rhythm" or a typical diurnal curve of performance.

Disease and Physical Handicap

Simpson (617) reported on behavior changes in tuberculous children, finding a high incidence of retardation and many indications of central nervous system involvement. Only forty cases were studied, and it is not clear that the possible influence of associated variables was excluded.

Richey (274) conducted a study on the effects of diseased tonsils and adenoids in which 104 school children received a tonsillectomy or adenectomy, 100 were classified as "needing attention," and 200 with normal tonsils or adenoids were paired, as controls, with members of the preceding groups. All received intelligence tests; in the case of the operated group six months were allowed, after the operation, before retesting. As in the studies by Rogers and Lowe, reported in the previous review, it could not be established that the removal of focal infections had on the average any beneficial effect upon intelligence, nor that the presence of infections produced a statistically significant impairment of mental ability. In an earlier study by Angell (505) the removal of tonsils or adenoids was indicated as having no effect upon intelligence (teachers' ratings were used rather than intelligence tests). In school work, however, improvement was registered in 48 percent of the cases. The sample studied is larger than in any other investigation in this field, but the methods of measurement and of statistical analysis are far from satisfactory.

Considerable attention has been given to the effects of intracranial birth lesions (596). Doll (529, 530, 531) pointed out that except for heredity, birth injury is the largest single etiological factor in mental deficiency. In a given case the growth of intelligence may or may not be disturbed; injuries to motor functions and interferences with normal development of the personality are common. Birth injury may affect intelligence primarily, without motor symptoms; where motor symptoms also occur, these may diminish in the course of growth, without necessary improvement in intellectual functions. Spastic cases tend to show more mental impairment than athetoids, probably because of the locus of the lesions involved (cortical pyramidal cells in the former case, basal nuclei in the latter). The picture derived from these observations is of a common factor which may influence one or several aspects of development, without implication of a direct interrelationship between the functions affected.

Draper and Johnson (532) discussed the role of enteric disease in producing emotional instability and mental retardation. Their point of view is indicated by the statement, "We have found that children or adolescents who begin to show abnormal alterations in personality are always physically sick." Improvement was reported in psychological traits following operation, but the data are not in statistical form.

A curious result has been reported by Balyeat (507, 508) in two studies of 120 allergic children. These were found to have higher I.Q.'s than a comparison group of non-allergic children, the difference being attributed to "greater activity of brain cells in children subject to allergy." The results are not in conformity with those more recently reported by Sullivan and Gahagan (623) who found among forty-five allergy cases in a children's hospital an I.Q. distribution similar to that of an unselected school population. The question should be raised as to whether the children referred to Balyeat may not have represented a superior school selection.

The relation of congenital syphilis to mental retardation is well known. Kiss and Rajka (564), using a Hungarian version of the Binet-Simon tests, reported an incidence of mental defect of 38 percent among syphilitic children. The incidence was reduced to 9 percent, however, among children who had received treatment beginning prior to the end of the second year. W. Lange (571) reported on the results of Binet-Simon-Bobertag tests administered to children who had been victims of epidemic encephalitis. The psychological effects of the disease were found to be most marked in children who contracted it under the age of five years. Subsequent testing indicated a tendency toward progressively diminishing I.Q.

Studies of epileptic children agree in finding subnormal average I.Q.'s. For different groups, average I.Q.'s ranging from 65 to 80 have been reported by Fetterman and Barnes (538); Fox, and Dawson and Conn (reviewed in 623). The proportion of feeble-minded among epileptics ranges from 6.5 percent (Paskind (591) reporting on cases in a private practice) to over 80 percent in some institutional samplings. In the most recent investigation in this field, a study of 103 clinic cases, Sullivan and Gahagan (623) reported a median I.Q. of 92; 18 percent received I.Q.'s at the moron level or below, but the marked variability of the group was shown by the substantial number of cases of superior intelligence. There appears to be a tendency for cases of primary or idiopathic epilepsy to rate higher in I.Q. than cases in which there is a definite organic diagnosis. I.Q.'s are also higher among those whose record shows the age of onset to have been subsequent to six years; this is in conformity with data concerning other disorders with central nervous system involvement. Deterioration with diminishing I.Q.'s has been reported by some writers, but this is by no means a universal finding (594). Retests frequently show wide fluctuations, both up and down. It may be suspected that this should be interpreted partly in terms of unreliability of measurement of epileptics who are tested too close to the time of a seizure.

A most exhaustive study on premature children was recently reported by Hess, Mohr, and Bartelme (38). In confirmation of previous results, it is apparent that the abnormal early environment and early physical condition of the premature have no necessary handicapping effect upon later mental development. Inman-Kane (40), however, found that premature birth and underweight at birth are more common among cases of mental deficiency than in the general population, and that in a group of school children born prematurely the incidence of mental defect is higher than expected. This association is considered to depend largely upon birth injury; if cerebral lesions have not occurred at birth the prognosis for later development may be satisfactory.

Troili (625) studied the effects upon the behavior of physically subnormal children of a régime in an open air school. Reviewing an earlier study by Fantini and Ciampi which had indicated gains in intelligence obtained through similar procedures, he recorded behavior changes in 118 third-grade children in the course of a school year. His conclusions are not well supported, since no control group was utilized.

Studies of special groups of handicapped children indicate, for the most part, a lower average intelligence than in the case of unselected children. Winkler (628) found crippled children retarded in intelligence as compared with the general school population. Witty and Smith (629) reported a mean I.Q. of 85 for 1,480 crippled children. Lee (573) obtained a mean I.Q. of 87, slightly higher for the poliomyelitis group, and markedly lower for the group with spastic birth paralysis. Nilson (255) compared 169 "disabled" children with 2,590 unselected children in the Minnesota public schools. The former had 15 percent below 80 I.Q., only 5 percent above 120 I.Q. The latter had 4 percent below 80 I.Q., 16 percent above 120. The Kuhlman-Anderson group intelligence test was used, but the comparison is somewhat vitiated by the fact that the disabled children cover a much wider age range, and the comparability of I.Q.'s is open to question in the upper ages.

Numerous studies have compared deaf and hearing children, with results which usually indicate some degree of mental retardation for the deaf. These investigations were summarized by Pintner (598) up to 1930. Madden (579), Waldman, Wade, and Aretz (627), Shirley and Goodenough (616), and MacKane (219) contributed further reports on this subject.

Other studies have indicated I.Q.'s lower than average for blind children (512), left-handed children (535, 539), and other special groups. These do not require detailed examination here; as in the case of the majority of studies in this section, they represent primarily not a functional interrelationship between mental abilities and physical traits, but the diverse operation of a common pathological factor. For related studies on the influence of disease upon motor development, see a recent review by Abramson (335).

Different in conception from any of the preceding studies is an investigation by Maller (224, 580) based on over 100,000 cases. These were fifth-grade children in 579 schools in New York City. The correlation between average I.Q. (N. I. T. and Pintner Survey Test) and the percent in each school having a given defect was as follows: visual defect, —.40; teeth defect, —.50; defective tonsils, —.26; malnutrition, —.28. These coefficients are considerably higher than correlations ordinarily reported because they represent averages from large samplings. Between average I.Q. and economic status of the neighborhood (based on value of home rentals) a positive correlation of .50 was found, and between average I.Q. and health, with economic status constant, a correlation of .28. This latter cannot be interpreted exclusively in terms of the influence of health on I.Q.; the inference should rather be made that in holding constant one measure of economic status, we have failed to account for all of the factors common to social, hygienic, and intellectual superiority.

The effect of physical factors upon intelligence quotients is suggested by Pintner and Forlano (271) in their study of 17,502 I.Q.'s classified by social level and by month of birth. In each social level the lowest average I.Q. occurs among children born in the winter months (January to March). The I.Q. difference between these months and the highest seasonal mean is small but statistically reliable. When the months are ranked as to average I.Q., sunshine, and temperature, correlations of .59 are found between I.Q. and amount of sunshine, and of .67 between I.Q. and temperature. These high values should not be misinterpreted; as in the case of Maller's study, they are, of course, correlations between means. Pintner and Forlano drew the inference that "children born in winter suffer more illness and are born of mothers weighted with more illness," with consequent effects upon mental development. It may be noted, however, that the social classification represents a coarse grouping into three categories, with considerable heterogeneity in each group; an alternative explanation might be offered in terms of differential birth control (children born in the summer are those who have survived a winter pregnancy). In a climate involving extreme seasonal variations in sunshine and temperature, Schiötz and Seland (612) found no relationship between month of birth and height or weight (1,952 Norwegian children). In a subsequent study of eminent men, Pintner and Forlano (271) found no relation of eminence to birth month. Reports on German children by K. Lange (570), and on American children by Palmer (426) agreed in indicating seasonal fluctuations, with maximum rate of growth in the fall. Palmer, however, disagreed with Emerson's inference (536) that seasonal fluctuations in growth are related to the incidence of illness.

Physical Abilities

The trend toward measurement has resulted in the development of standardized tests for "physical efficiency." These are concerned with such functions as strength, exercise tolerance, vital capacity, and the gross motor functions of jumping, running, dodging, throwing, etc. Correlational studies by Landis, Burtt, and Nichols (569), Cozens (527), and others indicated no relationship to intelligence among college students. Heaton (555), on the other hand, found that among school children "the average general level of physical development of the children who rate high on intelligence tests is distinctly superior to that of the children who rate low on intelligence tests." Tests included in these batteries are, more than most tests, subject to practice. If children of superior social status have more incentive or opportunity to practice certain athletic skills, this may result in a spurious correlation between tests of intelligence and tests of physical abilities. Subsequent work should attempt a control of the factor of social status. In a relatively homogeneous senior high-school group, McCloy (577) found slight negative correlations for both boys and girls between I.Q. and a series of tests of strength, posture, the Brace test, the Sargent jump test, etc. Such a relationship would perhaps be expected in a grade selection if, as is commonly the case, the brighter pupils are younger and smaller. Among 155 junior high-school boys, Ragsdale and Breckenfeld (601) reported a small negative relationship between I.Q. and speed in track events, a small positive relationship with accuracy and strength. Moore (586) found substandard athletic ability and inferior intelligence in a group of 150 problem boys. This may not indicate any general association between the variables considered, but merely the fact that in a sample selected as problem cases, inferiorities are likely to appear in a variety of traits. The relationship between athletic ability and scholarship was discussed by Davis and Cooper (528), who summarized results from over forty studies in colleges and secondary schools. Superior average scholarship is reported for non-athletes in eighteen studies, for athletes in fifteen studies. These varying results evidently depend upon local circumstances as to selection, admission standards, scholarship standards, and other factors irrelevant to our present interest. We are safe in concluding that on the basis of the total body of evidence available, the relationship between intelligence and gross motor functions is close to zero in any fairly homogeneous school population.

Physical Traits in Relation to Scholarship

Studies among college students by Chapin (525), Gittings (549), and Harris (554) indicated that physical traits are in general no more closely related to scholarship than to intelligence. One of the highest correlations reported is that by Chapin: .21 between academic grades and a measure of physical condition, for 250 women students. In a fairly homogeneous college group of foreign-born Jewish parentage, Harris selected subgroups consisting of those having numerous respiratory infections, those with a history of severe illness, those with poor physical development, and those below 63 inches in height. Each subgroup, containing from thirty-eight to eighty-one cases, showed scholarship grades and intelligence scores close to the average for the total class. F. S. Freeman (542) investigated forty-two cases in which there was a marked discrepancy between scholarship and intelligence. In only one of these was the scholarship deficiency attributed to illness.

Ohmann (589) conducted a study at the University of Iowa, making use not merely of quantitative measurements but also of a diagnostic interview. In 128 cases of scholastic defect, an attempt was made to determine causative factors. Physical factors were listed as of comparatively small importance, each of the following taking precedence: motivation, intelligence, emotional adjustment, educational preparation, study habits, environmental factors. A similar study by Remmers (604) at Purdue came to somewhat similar conclusions. In the smaller number of cases of scholastic deficiency attributed to lack of physical fitness, apparently visual defect was the major difficulty present. Nelson (588) reported a significant effect of visual correction upon scholarship in the case of ametropes. He pointed out, however, that for the total range of students there is no point in correlating visual efficiency with scholarship, since many students with good eyes are inferior students and many with poor eyes are particularly good students.

In the case of school children, positive results are somewhat more frequently reported. Beggs (510) found that children retarded in school three or more years have an excessive number of physical defects. His criterion for retardation was so severe as to result in the inclusion of many feebleminded in the retarded group. Liefmann (208), on the basis of a study of ten-year-old girls in Freiburg, concluded that "the healthier child is generally the abler one." Of thirty-three mentally superior children, eighteen were in the first and second groups in terms of physical condition; none was in the lowest group. Of thirty-three mentally inferior children, only three were in the first and second physical groups and five in the lowest group. The conclusion should have support from data presented in less cumbersome fashion. In a further study by Liefmann (575), children who were school repeaters were found to be inferior in physical measurements and physical condition and to show more cases with indications of rickets or of tubercular tendency. Liefmann (576) also noted that repeaters tended to be more inferior to the normal in chest measurements (including expansion and lung capacity) than in height and weight measurements.

These results are not supported by Blonsky (513), but Paull (595), in a study of over 10,000 normals and 1,446 repeaters in the schools of Karlsruhe, found that the latter were inferior in physical size at each age (six to fifteen) and in each sex. The interpretation emphasized genetic association rather than the influence of environmental factors. Rosell (608) made a study of skin capillaries, according to the methods of Jaensch, in relation to school status. Of sixty-one subnormal pupils (Hilfschülerinnen) 72 percent were classified as having "poor" capillaries, as compared with 33 percent in a normal sample. Müller (587) reported an unusually high correlation of .70 between school performance and social status, and .60 between school performance and family income, among preadolescent girls. Health was considered to be an important factor, but the data do not permit evaluating this factor independently. A number of German studies (520, 521, 557) investigated the effects of family unemployment upon the school performance of children. At all ages decrements found in achievement tests or in scholarship grades were attributed to the unemployment status of the father. Girls were said to show injurious effects to a more marked degree than boys, younger children more than older children. The latter effect was masked somewhat by the fact that disturbance to scholarship was cumulative, increasing with longer terms of unemployment. Busemann inferred that these effects are mediated primarily through poorer hygienic conditions and their influence upon child health and resistance to fatigue. Although large numbers of cases are dealt with, the differences considered are not in all cases statistically reliable. It is interesting to note that according to Fürst (547) children in Jena are considerably taller than corresponding age groups before the war, the difference averaging 8.9 cm. for the boys and 11.6 cm. for the girls. This is attributed to environmental effects. It is unfortunate that comparable data from psychological measurements are not available.

Keal (562) made a study of 109 boys entering Detroit High School, following them through four years and analyzing reasons for dropping school and for poor scholarship in cases with adequate intelligence. Results from physical examinations and from corrective work led to the conclusion that "health is the greatest single factor governing success in school." The study suffers from a lack of a sufficient number of cases to establish the thesis; there is no clear division of the sample into a group having corrective work and a control group, and the statistical treatment is of an elementary character. The study deserves attention, however, because it is one of the few in which children have been followed over a span of years and consecutive observations attempted.

Richard (607) studied the relation of scholastic overwork to physical disturbances. On the basis of clinical experience, he listed the symptomatology of overwork as: retardation in weight and height, shallow and insufficient respiration, rapid and unstable cardiac rhythm, constipation, nutritional and motor disturbances. This is apparently a one-sided view of the problem. From the reverse standpoint of Adler's individual psychology, it would be appropriate to consider overwork as a part of the symptomatology of physical inferiority. To support Richard's thesis more detailed quantitative data are necessary; how much "overwork," in what children, produces what specific symptoms, and through what time relations? Seham (613) studied chronic fatigue in the school child, finding evidence that "subefficient" children are inferior in anatomical measures, are less steady in motor tests, and have poorer health habits. Again, it is apparent that we are dealing with complex phenomena which cannot be explained in terms of a single causation.

Stedman (620) found a relationship between physical condition, I.Q., and scholarship among high-school pupils in Los Angeles. The results are sufficiently positive to justify presentation in some detail:

Physical condition	Number	Grade points	I.Q.
"Healthy"	39	11.4	104.0
Defective tonsils or adenoids	128	9.5	102.0
Eye defects	91	8.9	101.5
Defective teeth	136	8.3	100.0
Heart defects	70	8.9	99.5
Lung defects	13	7.3	98.0

The scholarship differences were said to remain when comparisons were made for children in different health groups but of the same I.Q. The subsamples, however, were too small to yield reliable differences. Stedman feels that she has presented evidence as to the effect of health upon intelligence and school grades, and comments on the futility of pouring money into education and at the same time "failing to furnish medical and dental care that would make education effective." It is not clear, however, whether her material shows an actual influence of health factors or whether the apparent relation is attributable to some common factor such as socioeconomic status.

A similar explanation may apply to Woehlert's findings (630) for a group of 500 children in a suburban school in Berlin. Woehlert compared the top 10 percent for scholarship with the lowest 10 percent, discovering an average difference in physical traits equivalent to about half a year of growth.

Evidence from Mental Defect

It is unnecessary to review here the very numerous studies which have convincingly indicated that feeble-minded children tend on the average to be shorter and lighter than normal (550), to show anomalies in dentition (502, 526), to have lower basal metabolism (515), and to be marked by stigmata in numerous structural characteristics (559:1062). In interpreting this enormous mass of material, we should bear in mind several points: (a) In a study of the lowest 2 percent of the population, relationships may emerge which are too slight to be detectable in the middle ranges of intelligence; (b) if we eliminate cases of secondary feeble-mindedness, constituting perhaps one-third of the total group, physical-mental relationships will be greatly reduced (these are cases in which a common pathological factor has affected both mental development, as dependent on the cerebral cortex, and some one or several aspects of physical growth or motor function); and (c) Duncan (534) reported physical measurements for a group of high-grade mental defectives, ages nine to sixteen years, under superior care. Of these, 95 percent were above weight for their height and the majority were above standard for both height and weight. The inference may be drawn that the commonly found physical inferiority of the feeble-minded is to some extent attributable to inferior nutrition and to substandard health habits.

Evidence from Sex Differences

The extensive literature on sex differences in mental characteristics may be utilized in connection with the problem of physical-mental relationships. Sex differences which are an outcome of differences in training and in the social environment of the two sexes would not be relevant for the present purpose; but differences which can be definitely attributed to a biological basis would be useful at least for pointing the way to further fundamental studies. A difficulty here is that the cause of sex differences is usually conjectured rather than known. Of more value than most is a report by Book (514) dealing with differences between a group of 475 college men and an equal number of college women, on a series of tests adapted from the Army Beta. In two tests the women excelled and in two the men were definitely superior. That these results are not due to differences in training during the period of school life is indicated by the fact that similar differences were found by Snoddy and Hyde (619) in their application of the same tests to elementary-school children. Book's interpretation assumes physiological sex differences due to unspecified metabolic or endocrine factors, resulting in a higher frequency in the transmission of neural impulses in women and shorter refractory periods; as a result women excel in activities where stimuli are constantly changing and where quick perceptual adaptation is required. Men have longer refractory periods and therefore fewer impulses per unit of time; their reactions are slower, more massive and deliberative, and they excel in tests requiring a more sustained analytic or integrative attitude. In general or composite functions, sex differences tend to be cancelled out. Interesting as these suggestions are, at the psychological level they appear to rest on results from too narrow a variety of tests, and at the physiological level they are far from empirical verification. Rosanoff and others (280) argued that a sex difference exists in intelligence, slightly favoring the female sex, and concluded that the major portion of this difference is due to the greater vulnerability of male fetuses to cerebral injury. Since in all mental characteristics the range within a sex is much greater than the difference between male-female averages, any study of causative factors in sex differences should aim towards an experimental phase in which the primary concern is with individual differences. For reviews of recent research on sex differences see Goodenough (551) and Allen (499, 500, 501).

Evidence from Growth Studies

In discussing the study of physical and mental relationships through the comparison of growth curves, F. N. Freeman (541) pointed out that the relative independence of physical and mental growth is shown by the following facts: mental growth curves for boys and girls are closely similar, but physical growth curves show conspicuous differences; negative acceleration is more marked in physical than in mental growth curves during adolescence, and intellectual growth continues after physical growth ceases; and finally, little relation has yet been found between periods of acceleration in mental and physical growth. These arguments are based upon the analysis of growth curves derived from population averages. Freeman recognized the possibility of more significant relationships emerging from the study of associated fluctuations in the growth curves of individuals. Moreover, both in individual and in average curves, fluctuations may be associated without being concomitant, since a common factor or group of factors may influence different functions with varying time lags. It is difficult, however, to point to actual results in this field. Bayley (509) analyzed mental and physical growth curves of children studied from birth to five years of age; individual cases show (a) concomitance of change, (b) correlated change after a time interval, and (c) complete lack of relationship. Honzik (558) studied data from mental tests and physical examinations given to 250 California children at twenty-one, thirty-six, forty-eight, and sixty months of age. Correlations close to zero were obtained between changes in mental test scores and changes in developmental status and physiological condition (as rated by the physician). There was, however, a tendency for children making an above-average gain in intelligence to make an associated above-average gain in height or weight (correlations for gains between twenty-one and sixty months were .17 for height and .13 for weight). These coefficients are more significant than cross-sectional correlations, since they are subject to greater correction for attenuation (436). An apparent rise in mental scores, relative to the group, was noted as occurring in the period of convalescence after a severe illness. A fuller discussion of this case study material will appear in subsequent reports.

Driscoll (24) conducted an interesting developmental study of fifty children in a nursery school follow-up. The prognostic value of various indexes was considered: mental test scores, special ability measures, physical measures in terms of deviation from Woodbury norms, and appraisals of personality adjustment. A "combined view" of these measures was attempted in the analysis of the case study material, preschool records being compared with records obtained during the school period. It is not clear that the combination of indexes, as proposed by Driscoll, was actually accomplished; i.e., while the various indexes for each child were made available for inspection, no method was suggested for integrating them in order to deal in a quantitative manner with problems of prognosis as involving interrelationships. Physical measures, as might be expected, were found to be of little or no value in predicting mental development; height in relation to age showed increasing age variability, but physical deviations were not associated with mental changes relative to the group.

Evidence from Studies of Later Maturity

A number of studies (566, 611) have made clear the essential facts concerning the decline, after maturity, of sensory acuity, reaction time, resistance to specific diseases, vital capacity, etc. Recent investigations by Jones, Miles, and their associates led to similar results concerning decline in complex mental functions. There is good evidence that the decrement in mental test abilities is not attributable to any large degree to losses of motivation, or to factors associated with the length of time individuals have been out of school. When samplings are kept uniform by comparing parents and children (in a rural group), Jones and Conrad (189) showed that at the age of fifty-five parents have dropped in intelligence test scores to about the test level of their fourteen-year-old children. If subtests particularly subject to the effect of length of experience are eliminated (general information, vocabulary) the recession is to about the thirteen-year-old level. Even apart from the more evident forms of senile pathology, it may be expected that in later life the correlations between physical and mental fitness will be higher than among children. Although it is probable that bodily changes play a highly important role in the age decrease in mental ability, at present we have little insight as to the physiological processes involved.

Relationships with Other Mental Traits

Continued work has been carried on at various centers on the relationship of physical factors to interests and attitudes. Earlier studies reporting conspicuous changes at puberty in play interests, vocational interests, social activities, etc., have commonly failed to take adequate account of the chronological age factor, and of the changing cultural patterns to which children become exposed at advancing ages. In subsequent reports by Furfey and his associates, an attempt was made to correlate various physical measures with an index of social and emotional maturity which Furfey termed "developmental age." This has been done (a) with chronological age partialled out, and (b) with chronological age restricted to a narrow range. Among pre-adolescents correlations tend to be zero or negative, but at the age of fourteen or fifteen increasing degrees of relationship are indicated. Thus, in the fourth grade Zalduondo (631) reported a correlation of $-.58$ between weight and developmental age; in the fifth grade the correlation became .00; in the seventh and eighth grades it was .36. Between physiological age (as determined from Crampton's norms) and developmental age, Rauth and Furfey (602) found bi-serial r's of $-.16$ at thirteen years, .42 at fourteen years, and .79 at fifteen years. As in the case of Zalduondo's study, the populations were small. For a series of five anthropometric measurements, Rauth and Furfey (603) compared correlations in pre-adolescent and in adolescent groups of boys of the same ages. Among the pre-adolescents, r's ranged from $-.13$ to .21; among adolescents from .22 to .60 (age constant). An exception to these findings is a correlation of .29, age constant, reported by Carey (523) for a group of 174 boys, ages eight to thirteen years.

Furfey (546), in reviewing these studies, concluded: "From these various lines of evidence it seems fair to conclude that puberty does cause an increase in DQ. Of course this is what one would expect. It is frequently asserted in the literature that the adolescent acquires, along with his physical maturity, a new maturity of behavior. The present data appear to give an interesting quantitative confirmation of this opinion."

It would be rash, however, to infer that this is wholly or even largely a direct physical effect. The effects are in an important way mediated through changes in the social environment; as he becomes larger, stronger, deeper voiced, the boy attains status in new social groups and is led to conform to stereotypes judged appropriate for his degree of maturity. Relevant to this point, is the finding of a correlation of .41 (corrected for attenuation) in the developmental ages of chums with each other, and Merwick's report (585) of a correlation of .186, for 800 boys, between developmental age and socio-economic status as measured by the Sims scale. The direct influence of social factors is also suggested by Merwick's finding that rural children have a lower average developmental age than urban children, and institutional children a lower developmental age than non-institutional children. Here we may assume that in restricted social groups physiological maturing is slower in its effect upon social relationships. The differences found by Merwick are consistent in three age groups, but data from more cases are desirable to establish statistical reliability.

Supplementary to the above, studies should be made, by various methods, of physical factors in relation to other, perhaps more specific, groups of interests and attitudes (intellectual, athletic, competitive, etc.). Such investigations are needed not merely because of their intrinsic significance but also because of their help in the interpretation of studies of relationships between mental and physical factors.

Nutrition

Experimentation with animals has provided the basis for extraordinary advances in the science of nutrition. Experiments have dealt typically with the relation of nutrition to physical condition and physical growth, but increasing interest is being shown in behavioral relationships. Research with animals has the advantage of superior control over the experimental conditions, the disadvantage (particularly in the case of behavior experiments) of uncertain applicability to problems in human biology. This disadvantage is all the more marked, in view of the fact that there has been a tendency to limit experimentation to one species of animal (the white rat) and to test only a single aspect of the effect upon behavior (performance in mazes).

Anderson and Smith (503, 504) conducted an experiment in which normal growth was handicapped in two ways: in one group of rats, through a diet unbalanced as to protein; in another group, through a diet which was balanced but restricted in amount. As compared with a control group of animals on a normal diet, the stunted animals showed no inferiority in maze performance; in some respects they appeared to be actually superior, due perhaps to stronger motivation. Somewhat similar results were obtained by Frank (540), in a comparison of normal rats with rats stunted from rickets. Mixed findings were reported by T'ang, Ch'in, and Tsang (624), as to the effects of a restricted vegetarian diet; in the case of female rats no effect was demonstrated, but in the case of male rats learning ability showed an apparent reduction. Fritz (545) studied the maze performance of rats restricted as to vitamin B and as to the intake of certain salts, finding no effect on maze performance. The foregoing negative findings from investigations of adult rats are in contrast to the work of Maurer and Tsai (582, 583) with suckling rats which, until they were weaned, were drastically depleted of vitamin B. After weaning they were brought to normal weight, and in the subsequent test of maze learning care was taken to maintain motivation factors comparable for the depleted and for the normal group. The conclusion was reached that "normal rats are about twice as efficient as depleted animals" in maze learning, with the implication that early vitamin B depletion produces permanently injurious effects upon the developing nervous system. Evidence supporting Maurer and Tsai has been given in a further study by Bernhardt (511).

This work led directly to a study of children by Balken and Maurer (506); the procedure in this case involved the study of possible favorable effects of vitamin B feeding among subjects who had presumably received inadequate diets in infancy. Children selected for the study (twenty-four boys and twenty-two girls) were from one of the poorest sections in Chicago and largely of foreign-born parents. A battery of intelligence and performance tests was given, before, during, and at the close of the experimental period. No average I.Q. gains were registered as the result of twenty weeks of vitamin B administration. Although improvement occurred in the performance tests, it is quite possible that this was due wholly to practice and to normal maturation during the period of the experiment; there was no control group.

Other studies of children have failed to show positive results from experimental changes in nutrition. Rosenberg (609) compared I.Q. gains in two groups of underweight children, one of which received a representative complete dietary, while the other received cereal, fruits, nuts, vegetables, and one quart of milk a day, but without eggs or meat. After six months the average I.Q. of each group remained substantially the same. To check the possibility that gains in nutrition may be followed by a delayed gain in I.Q., it would have been desirable to repeat the tests six months later.

Smith and Field (618) compared an experimental group of twenty-five underweight children with children who were approximately normal according to the Baldwin-Wood tables. Health lessons, school lunches, and various motivational devices were employed with the underweight group. The effectiveness of this procedure was shown by the fact that in a six-month period they gained in weight 26 percent more than the normal expectancy. Again, however, intelligence scores failed to show any accompanying increments.

A study by Graper and Park (553) involved a selection of children who were undernourished, revealed low I.Q.'s, and came from homes of poor socio-economic status. Improved feeding was said to be associated with I.Q. gains, but unfortunately the number of cases was too small (eight children) for definite conclusions.

Beebe (98) conducted an experiment with ten preschool children on learning to maintain equilibrium on a balancing board. Graphic records were made of the subjects' performance in a series of practice tests and in a subsequent retention series. The investigator felt that there was evidence of a slight positive relationship to body nutrition, but because of the small number of subjects this could not be established in a clear-cut fashion. The hypothesis was advanced that "optimal neuro-muscular learning is associated with optimal nutrition as affecting chemical balance of muscle cells and circulating fluids."

M. C. Jones and Davis (561) made a detailed case study of ten markedly overweight girls of adolescent age, compared with ten girls of approximately normal weight and of the same ages. There were no differences in intelligence or in achievement test scores, but differences emerged in a number of specific social and emotional traits.

Browne (519) studied the relationship between nutrition and scholarship among 1,600 pupils in a senior high school. Divided into four groups on the basis of deviation from the Wood-Baldwin-Woodbury tables, there was no evidence that the children of poorer nutritional status had a poorer average scholarship. The writer assumes that a relationship occurs at lower grade levels, but that this is lost, in the course of promotion, as a result of the elimination of the physically and mentally unfit.

Undismayed by negative findings, investigators in this field exhibit a tendency to assume that positive results are just around the corner, and will become visible if the experimental procedure is slightly changed. Common sense leads us to expect some direct or indirect influence of nutritional level upon mental performance; contrary evidence is accepted only very reluctantly. In view of this continuing faith, we may expect an increasing number of studies of the psychological effects of specifically restricted or extended diets. The future will undoubtedly bring closer cooperation between psychology, education, and the nutrition laboratory. Many nutrition investigations have been conducted which would be admirably adapted for the present purpose, if supplementary psychological measurements could have been made. The most promising field for present work appears to lie in studies beginning in infancy and employing homogeneous experimental and control groups, with experimental periods lasting for at least a year and with a program of physical and psychological measurements extending over several years. For a discussion of other related investigations, see a recent review by Fritz (544).

Emerson (537) offered the opinion that about 40 percent of children are malnourished and only about 20 percent in optimum condition. Although the experiments with animals involve an interference with normal nutrition of a more drastic character than is perhaps found within a normal range of developmental conditions in human infancy, such findings as those by Maurer and Tsai suggest the possible significance even of minor nutritional insufficiencies occurring at an early age. From a social standpoint, an agency which produces a small, perhaps unrecognized degree of retardation in a substantial number of individuals may be more important than one which produces an extreme degree of retardation limited to a fraction of 1 percent of the total population.

BIBLIOGRAPHY ON MENTAL AND PHYSICAL DEVELOPMENT

Chapter I. The Development of Intelligence and Motor Control in Infancy

1. BAYLEY, NANCY. *The California First-Year Mental Scale.* Syllabus Series, No. 243. Berkeley: University of California, 1933. 24 p.
2. BAYLEY, NANCY. "A Cumulative Study of Environmental Correlates of Intelligence." *Psychological Bulletin* 32: 702; November, 1935.
3. BAYLEY, NANCY. *Mental Growth During the First Three Years: A Developmental Study of Sixty-One Children by Repeated Tests.* Genetic Psychology Monographs, Vol. 14, No. 1. Worcester, Mass.: Clark University Press, 1933. 92 p.
4. BAYLEY, NANCY, and WOLFF, L. V. "Motor Development during the First Three Years." Abstract 801. *Child Development Abstracts and Bibliography* 7: 299-300; June, 1933.
5. BEASLEY, W. C. "An Investigation of Related Problems in the Vision of Newborn Infants." (Abstract.) *Psychological Bulletin* 30: 626; October, 1933.
6. BEASLEY, W. C. "Visual Pursuit in 109 White and 142 Negro Newborn Infants." *Child Development* 4: 106-20; June, 1933.
7. BREGMAN, ELSIE O. "An Attempt to Modify the Emotional Attitudes of Infants by the Conditioned Response Technique." *Pedagogical Seminary and Journal of Genetic Psychology* 45: 169-98; September, 1934.
8. BRIDGES, KATHERINE M. BANHAM. "Emotional Development in Early Infancy." *Child Development* 3: 324-41; December, 1932.
9. BRIDGES, KATHERINE M. BANHAM. "Measuring Emotionality in Infants: A Tentative Experiment." *Child Development* 5: 36-40; March, 1934.
10. BRIDGES, KATHERINE M. BANHAM. "A Study of Social Development in Early Infancy." *Child Development* 4: 36-49; March, 1933.
11. BÜHLER, CHARLOTTE. *The First Year of Life.* (Translated by Pearl Greenberg and Rowena Ripin.) New York: John Day Co., 1930. 281 p.
12. CASTNER, B. M. *The Development of Fine Prehension in Infancy.* Genetic Psychology Monographs, Vol. 12, No. 2. Worcester, Mass.: Clark University Press, 1932. p. 105-93.
13. CHANEY, BEVERLY, and MCGRAW, MYRTLE B. "Reflexes and Other Motor Activities in Newborn Infants. A Report of 125 Cases as a Preliminary Study of Infant Behavior." *Bulletin of the Neurological Institute of New York* 2: 1-56; January, 1932.
14. CUNNINGHAM, BESS V. "Infant I.Q. Ratings Evaluated after an Interval of Seven Years." *Journal of Experimental Education* 3: 84-87; December, 1934.
15. DENNIS, WAYNE. "The Age at Walking of Children Who Run on All Fours." *Child Development* 5: 92-93; March, 1934.
16. DENNIS, WAYNE. "A Description and Classification of the Responses of the Newborn Infant." *Psychological Bulletin* 31: 5-22; January, 1934.
17. DENNIS, WAYNE. "The Effect of Restricted Practice upon the Reaching, Sitting, and Standing of Two Infants." *Pedagogical Seminary and Journal of Genetic Psychology* 47: 17-32; September, 1935.
18. DENNIS, WAYNE. "An Experimental Test of Two Theories of Social Smiling in Infants." *Journal of Social Psychology* 5: 214-23; May, 1935.
19. DENNIS, WAYNE. "The Role of Mass Activity in the Development of Infant Behavior." *Psychological Review* 39: 593-95; November, 1932.
20. DENNIS, WAYNE. "Two New Responses of Infants." *Child Development* 3: 362-63; December, 1932.
21. DISHER, DOROTHY ROSE. "An Experimental Study of the Reactions of New-Born Infants to Olfactory Stimuli." (Abstract.) *Psychological Bulletin* 30: 582; October, 1933.
22. DISHER, DOROTHY ROSE, and OTHERS. *Studies in Infant Behavior.* Contributions in Psychology, No. 12. Columbus: Ohio State University, 1934. 93 p.

23. DOCKERAY, F. C. "Differential Feeding Reactions of Newborn Infants." (Abstract.) *Psychological Bulletin* 31: 747; November, 1934.
24. DRISCOLL, GERTRUDE PORTER. *The Developmental Status of the Preschool Child as a Prognosis of Future Development.* Child Development Monographs, No. 13. New York: Teachers College, Columbia University, 1933. 111 p.
25. DUDLEY, DONALDINE; DUNCAN, DOROTHY; and SEARS, ESTHER. "A Study of the Development of Motor Coördination in an Infant Between the Ages of Fifty-eight and Sixty-seven Weeks." *Child Development* 3: 82-86; March, 1932.
26. GESELL, ARNOLD, and OTHERS. *An Atlas of Infant Behavior: A Systematic Delineation of the Forms and Early Growth of Human Behavior Patterns.* New Haven, Conn.: Yale University Press, 1934. Vol. I, Normative Series; Vol. II, Naturalistic Series.
27. GESELL, ARNOLD. "Cinemanalysis: A Method of Behavior Study." *Pedagogical Seminary and Journal of Genetic Psychology* 47: 3-16; September, 1935.
28. GESELL, ARNOLD. *Films of Infant Development.* The Study of Infant Behavior; The Growth of Infant Behavior, Early Stages; Growth of Infant Behavior, Later Stages; Posture and Locomotion; From Creeping to Walking; A Baby's Day at Twelve Weeks; A Thirty-Six Week Behavior Day; A Behavior Day at Forty-Eight Weeks; Behavior at One Year; Learning and Growth; Early Social Behavior. New York: Erpi Picture Consultants, 1934.
29. GESELL, ARNOLD. *Infancy and Human Growth.* New York: Macmillan Co., 1928. 418 p.
30. GESELL, ARNOLD; THOMPSON, HELEN; and AMATRUDA, CATHERINE STRUNK. *Infant Behavior: Its Genesis and Growth.* New York: McGraw-Hill Book Co., 1934. 343 p.
31. GESELL, ARNOLD. "The Mental Growth of Prematurely Born Infants." *Journal of Pediatrics* 2: 676-80; June, 1933.
32. GILMER, BEVERLY VON HALLER. "An Analysis of the Spontaneous Responses of the Newborn Infant." *Pedagogical Seminary and Journal of Genetic Psychology* 42: 392-405; June, 1933.
33. GILMER, BEVERLY VON HALLER. "An Analysis of the Spontaneous Responses of the Newborn Infant." (Abstract.) *Psychological Bulletin* 30: 626-27; October, 1933.
34. HALLER, MARY WOODHULL. "The Reactions of Infants to Changes in the Intensity and Pitch of Pure Tone." *Pedagogical Seminary and Journal of Genetic Psychology* 40: 162-80; March, 1932.
35. HALVERSON, H. M. "The Acquisition of Skill in Infancy." Abstract 439. *Child Development Abstracts and Bibliography* 7: 164-65; April, 1933.
36. HALVERSON, H. M. *An Experimental Study of Prehension in Infants by Means of Systematic Cinema Records.* Genetic Psychology Monographs, Vol. 10, Nos. 2 and 3. Worcester, Mass.: Clark University Press, 1931. p. 107-286.
37. HALVERSON, H. M. "A Further Study of Grasping." *Journal of General Psychology* 7: 34-64; July, 1932.
38. HESS, JULIUS H.; MOHR, GEORGE J.; and BARTELME, PHYLLIS F. *The Physical and Mental Growth of Prematurely Born Children.* Chicago: University of Chicago Press, 1934. 449 p.
39. HURLOCK, ELIZABETH B. "Experimental Studies of the Newborn." *Child Development* 4: 148-63; June, 1933.
40. INMAN-KANE, CHRISTINE V. "The Relation of Premature Birth and Under-Weight Condition at Birth to Mental Deficiency." *Psychological Bulletin* 30: 596-97; October, 1933.
41. IRWIN, ORVIS C. "The Amount of Motility of Seventy-Three Newborn Infants." *Journal of Comparative Psychology* 14: 415-28; December, 1932.
42. IRWIN, ORVIS C. "The Distribution of the Amount of Motility in Young Infants Between Two Nursing Periods." *Journal of Comparative Psychology* 14: 429-45; December, 1932.
43. IRWIN, ORVIS C. "Infant Responses to Vertical Movements." *Child Development* 3: 167-69; June, 1932.
44. IRWIN, ORVIS C. "The Latent Time of the Body Startle in Infants." *Child Development* 3: 104-7; June, 1932.
45. IRWIN, ORVIS C. "Motility in Newborn Infants." (Abstract.) *Proceedings of the Iowa Academy of Science, 1932.* Vol. 39. Des Moines: State of Iowa, 1932. p. 243.

46. IRWIN, ORVIS C. "Motility in Young Infants." *American Journal for Diseases of Children* 45: 531-37; March, 1933.
47. IRWIN, ORVIS C. "The Organismic Hypothesis and Differentiation of Behavior. III. Differentiation of Human Behavior." *Psychological Review* 39: 387-93; July, 1932.
48. IRWIN, ORVIS C. "Proximodistal Differentiation of Limbs in Young Organisms." *Psychological Review* 40: 467-77; September, 1933.
49. IRWIN, ORVIS C. "The Relation of Body Motility in Young Infants to Some Physical Traits." *Journal of Experimental Education* 1: 140-43; December, 1932.
50. JENSEN, KAI. *Differential Reactions to Taste and Temperature Stimuli in Newborn Infants.* Genetic Psychology Monographs, Vol. 12, Nos. 5 and 6. Worcester, Mass.: Clark University Press, 1932. p. 361-479.
51. KASATKIN, N. I., and LEVIKOVA, A. M. "The Formation of Visual Conditioned Reflexes and Their Differentiation in Infants." *Journal of General Psychology* 12: 416-35; April, 1935.
52. KELLOGG, W. N., and KELLOGG, L. A. "Another Film of the Ape and the Child." (Abstract.) *Psychological Bulletin* 30: 581-82; October, 1933.
53. KELTING, LILLIAN SOPHIA. "An Investigation of the Feeding, Sleeping, Crying, and Social Behavior of Infants." *Journal of Experimental Education* 3: 97-106; December, 1934.
54. MCGRAW, MYRTLE B. "The Effect of Practice During Infancy upon the Development of Specific Behavior Traits." (Abstract.) *Psychological Bulletin* 30: 681-82; November, 1933.
55. MCGRAW, MYRTLE B. "The Effect of Specific Training upon Behavior Development During First Two Years." (Abstract.) *Psychological Bulletin* 31: 748-49; November, 1934.
56. MCGRAW, MYRTLE B. "Grasping in Infants and the Proximo-Distal Course of Growth." *Psychological Review* 40: 301-2; May, 1933.
57. MCGRAW, MYRTLE B. *Growth: A Study of Johnny and Jimmy.* New York: D. Appleton-Century Co., 1935. 319 p.
58. MARQUIS, DOROTHY POSTLE. "Can Conditioned Responses Be Established in the Newborn Infant?" *Pedagogical Seminary and Journal of Genetic Psychology* 39: 479-92; December, 1931.
59. MARQUIS, DOROTHY POSTLE. "A Study of Activity and Posture in Infants' Sleep." *Pedagogical Seminary and Journal of Genetic Psychology* 42: 51-69; March, 1933.
60. PRATT, KARL C. "The Effects of Repeated Auditory Stimulation upon the General Activity of Newborn Infants." *Pedagogical Seminary and Journal of Genetic Psychology* 44: 96-116; March, 1934.
61. PRATT, KARL C. "The Effects of Repeated Visual Stimulation upon the Activity of Newborn Infants." *Pedagogical Seminary and Journal of Genetic Psychology* 44: 117-26; March, 1934.
62. PRATT, KARL C. "Generalization and Specificity of the Plantar Response in Newborn Infants: The Reflexogenous Zone." *Pedagogical Seminary and Journal of Genetic Psychology* 44: 265-300; June, 1934. 45: 22-38, 371-89; September and December, 1934.
63. PRATT, KARL C. "A Note Upon the Relation of Activity to Sex and Race in Young Infants." *Journal of Social Psychology* 3: 118-20; February, 1932.
64. RAY, WILBERT S. "A Preliminary Report on a Study of Fetal Conditioning." *Child Development* 3: 175-77; June, 1932.
65. RICHARDS, T. W., and IRWIN, ORVIS C. "Experimental Methods Used in Studies on Infant Reactions Since 1900." *Psychological Bulletin* 31: 23-46; January, 1934.
66. RICHARDSON, HELEN M. "The Adaptive Behavior of Infants in the Utilization of the Lever as a Tool: A Developmental and Experimental Study." *Pedagogical Seminary and Journal of Genetic Psychology* 44: 352-77; June, 1934.
67. RICHARDSON, HELEN M. *The Growth of Adaptive Behavior in Infants: An Experimental Study at Seven Age Levels.* Genetic Psychology Monographs, Vol. 12, Nos. 3 and 4. Worcester, Mass.: Clark University Press, 1932. p. 195-359.
68. RIPIN, ROWENA. "A Comparative Study of the Development of Infants in an Institution with Those in Homes of Low Socio-Economic Status." (Abstract.) *Psychological Bulletin* 30: 680-81; November, 1933.

69. SHIRLEY, MARY M. *The First Two Years: A Study of Twenty-Five Babies.* Minneapolis: University of Minnesota Press, 1931-33. Vol. I, Postural and Locomotor Development, 227 p.; Vol. II, Intellectual Development, 513 p.; Vol. III, Personality Manifestations, 228 p.
70. SHIRLEY, MARY M. "Locomotor and Visual-Manual Functions in the First Two Years." *A Handbook of Child Psychology.* (Edited by Carl Murchison.) 2d ed. rev. Worcester, Mass.: Clark University Press, 1933. Chapter 5, p. 236-70.
71. SKEELS, HAROLD M. "The Use of the Conditioning Techniques in the Study of Form Discrimination of Young Children." *Journal of Experimental Education* 2: 127-37; December, 1933.
72. STAPLES, RUTH. "The Responses of Infants to Color." *Journal of Experimental Psychology* 15: 119-41; April, 1932.
73. STECKEL, MINNIE L. "Items of Gesell's Developmental Schedule Scaled." *Journal of Educational Psychology* 23: 99-103; February, 1932.
74. STUBBS, ESTHER, and IRWIN, ORVIS C. "A Note on Reaction Time in Infants." *Child Development* 5: 291; September, 1934.
75. SYMMES, EDITH F. "An Infant Testing Service as an Integral Part of a Child Guidance Clinic." *American Journal of Orthopsychiatry* 3: 409-30; October, 1933.
76. THOMPSON, HELEN. "The Development of Upright Posture." *Psychological Bulletin* 32: 693; November, 1935.
77. THOMPSON, HELEN. "The Growth and Significance of Daily Variations in Infant Behavior." *Pedagogical Seminary and Journal of Genetic Psychology* 40: 16-36; March, 1932.
78. THOMPSON, HELEN. "Measurement of Infant Behavior." *Journal of Experimental Education* 3: 230-32; March, 1935.
79. VALENTINE, W. L. *Films of Infant Development.* The Development of Manipulation in Infants. The Development of Creeping in a Human Infant. The Development of Prehension in a Single Child. The Development of Walking in the Human Infant. The Behavior of Newborn Infants. Columbus: Ohio State University.
80. VALENTINE, W. L., and WAGNER, ISABELLE F. "Relative Motility of the Arms of the Newborn Infant." (Abstract.) *Psychological Bulletin* 30: 582-83; October, 1933.
81. VANCE, THOMAS F., and OTHERS. "The Development of Children in the Home Management Houses of the Iowa State College." *Journal of Experimental Education* 2: 166-69; December, 1933.
82. WEISS, LABERTA A. "Differential Reactions of Newborn Infants to Different Degrees of Light and Sound Intensity." (Abstract.) *Psychological Bulletin* 30: 582; October, 1933.
83. WEISS, LABERTA A. "Differential Reactions of Newborn Infants to Different Degrees of Light Intensity." *Proceedings of the Iowa Academy of Science, 1933.* Vol. 40. Des Moines: State of Iowa, 1933. p. 198-99.
84. WEISS, LABERTA A. "Differential Responses of Newborn Infants to Sensory Stimuli." Abstract 1134. *Child Development Abstracts and Bibliography* 7: 434-35; August, 1933.
85. WEISS, LABERTA A. "Differential Variations in the Activity of Newborn Infants." (Abstract.) *Psychological Bulletin* 30: 680; November, 1933.
86. WENGER, M. A. "An Investigation of Conditioned Responses in Human Infants." (Abstract.) *Psychological Bulletin* 32: 691; November, 1935.

Chapter II. Mental Development from Two to Twelve Years

(See also Nos. 3, 14, 24)

87. ABEL, THEODORA M. "Tactual and Visual Perceptions of Extent Among Children and Adults." (Abstract.) *Psychological Bulletin* 31: 681; November, 1934.
88. ANDERSON, HAROLD H., and SMITH, RUTH SLOAN. "Motivation of Young Children: The Constancy of Certain Behavior Patterns." *Journal of Experimental Education* 2: 138-60; December, 1933.

89. ARMSTRONG, CLAIRETTE P. "Sex Differences in the Mental Functioning of School Children." *Journal of Applied Psychology* 16: 559-71; October, 1932.
90. ATTENBOROUGH, JOAN, and FARBER, MIRIAM. "The Relation Between Intelligence, Mechanical Ability, and Manual Dexterity in Special School Children." *British Journal of Educational Psychology* 4: 140-61; June, 1934.
91. BAILEY, MARJORY W. "A Scale of Block Constructions for Young Children." *Child Development* 4: 121-39; June, 1933.
92. BARKE, ETHEL M. "A Study of the Comparative Intelligence of Children in Certain Bilingual and Monoglot Schools in South Wales." *British Journal of Educational Psychology* 3: 237-50; November, 1933.
93. BATALLA, M. B. "An Experimental Study of Children's Behavior in a Spatial Complex." *Pedagogical Seminary and Journal of Genetic Psychology* 44: 127-38; March, 1934.
94. BAUMGARTEN, FRANZISKA. "Der Werdegang eines Wunderkindes (nebst einem Beitrag über die Beziehung des Gedächtnisses zur Begabung). (The Development of a Gifted Child: With a Contribution on the Relation of Memory to Talent.)" *Zeitschrift für angewandte Psychologie* 41: 473-98; February, 1932.
95. BECHER, ERIKA. "Untersuchungen zur kindlichen Theoriebildung. (Studies in Childish Theorizing.)" *Zeitschrift für Psychologie* 129: 43-120; May, 1933.
96. BECK, L. F. "The Rôle of Speed in Intelligence." *Psychological Bulletin* 30: 169-78; February, 1933.
97. BEEBE, ELINOR LEE. *Motor Learning of Children in Equilibrium in Relation to Nutrition.* Genetic Psychology Monographs, Vol. 15, No. 2. Worcester, Mass.: Clark University Press, 1934. p. 99-243.
98. BEEBE, ELINOR LEE. "Motor Learning of Children in Hand and Eye Coördination With Introduction of Prismatic Deflection." *Child Development* 4: 6-25; March, 1933.
99. BELLIS, CARROLL J. "Reaction Time and Chronological Age." *Proceedings of the Society of Experimental Biology and Medicine* 30: 801-3; March, 1933.
100. BENJAMIN, HAROLD. "Age and Sex Differences in the Toy-Preferences of Young Children." *Pedagogical Seminary and Journal of Genetic Psychology* 41: 417-29; December, 1932.
101. BESTOR, MARY FRANCES. "A Study of Attention in Young Children." *Child Development* 5: 368-80; December, 1934.
102. BIGELOW, ELIZABETH B. "School Progress of Under-Age Children." *Elementary School Journal* 35: 186-92; November, 1934.
103. BOGNÁR, C. "Térzemlelĕt. (Perception of Space.)" *Athenaeum* 18: 136-52; 1932.
104. BONTE, THEO. "Über die Suggestibilität von Eidetikern und Nichteidetikern. (The Suggestibility of Eidetic and Non-Eidetic Children.)" *Zeitschrift für angewandte Psychologie* 44: 161-92; January, 1933.
105. BOYNTON, PAUL L., and FORD, F. A. "The Relationship Between Play and Intelligence." *Journal of Applied Psychology* 17: 294-301; June, 1933.
106. BROWN, RALPH R. "The Time Interval Between Test and Re-test in Its Relation to the Constancy of the Intelligence Quotient." *Journal of Educational Psychology* 24: 81-96; February, 1933.
107. BRUNSWIK, EGON; GOLDSCHEIDER, L.; and PILEK, E. "Untersuchungen zur Entwicklung des Gedachtnisses. (Investigations of the Development of Memory.)" *Beihefte zur Zeitschrift für angewandte Psychologie* 19: 1-158; February, 1933.
108. BRYAN, ALICE I. *Organization of Memory in Young Children.* Archives of Psychology, No. 162. New York: Columbia University Press, 1934. 56 p.
109. BULLEY, MARGARET H. "An Enquiry as to Aesthetic Judgments of Children." *British Journal of Educational Psychology* 4: 162-82; June, 1934.
110. BURKS, BARBARA STODDARD. "The Relative Influence of Nature and Nurture upon Mental Development; a Comparative Study of Foster Parent-Foster Child Resemblance and True Parent-True Child Resemblance." *Nature and Nurture; Their Influence upon Intelligence.* Twenty-Seventh Yearbook, Part 1. National Society for the Study of Education. Bloomington, Ill.: Public School Publishing Co., 1928. p. 219-316.
111. CALHOON, STEPHEN WALLACE. "Influence of Length of Lists Upon Ability Immediately to Reproduce Disconnected Word-Series Auditorially Presented." *Journal of Experimental Psychology* 17: 723-38; October, 1934.

112. CALHOON, STEPHEN WALLACE. "Relative Seating Position and Ability to Reproduce Disconnected Word Lists After Short Intervals of Time." *Journal of Experimental Psychology* 17: 709-22; October, 1934.
113. CANIVET, NELLA, "Enquête sur l'Initiation Sexuelle. (A Study of Sexual Enlightenment.)" *Archives de Psychologie* 23: 239-78; Janvier, 1932.
114. CARTER, HAROLD D.; JONES, H. E.; and SHOCK, N. W. "An Experimental Study of Affective Factors in Learning." *Journal of Educational Psychology* 25: 203-15; March, 1934.
115. CARTER, HAROLD D. "Twin-Similarities in Personality Traits." *Pedagogical Seminary and Journal of Genetic Psychology* 43: 312-21; December, 1933.
116. CATTELL, PSYCHE. "Do the Stanford-Binet I.Q.'s of Superior Boys and Girls Tend to Decrease or Increase with Age?" *Journal of Educational Research* 26: 668-73; May, 1933.
117. CATTELL, PSYCHE. "Mental Development from Birth to Puberty." *Review of Educational Research* 3: 84-107, 163-68; April, 1933.
118. CHASE, LUCILE. *Motivation of Young Children; an Experimental Study of the Influence of Certain Types of External Incentives Upon the Performance of a Task.* University of Iowa Studies in Child Welfare, Vol. 5, No. 3. Iowa City: the University, 1932. 119 p.
119. CLAPARÈDE, ÉDUARD. "Das Bewusstsein der Ähnlichkeit und der Verschiedenheit beim Kinde. (The Consciousness of Similarity and Dissimilarity in the Child.)" *Psychologische Rundschau* 4: 60-65; 1932.
120. CONRAD, H. S.; JONES, HAROLD E.; and HSIAO, H. H. "Sex Differences in Mental Growth and Decline." *Journal of Educational Psychology* 24: 161-69; March, 1933.
121. COWAN, EDWINA A., and FOULKE, MARJORIE. "Variation in Susceptibility to the Conditioning of Inhibition as an Index of Constitutional Type." *Child Development* 5: 201-36; September, 1934.
122. COX, JOHN W. "Some Experiments on Formal Training in the Acquisition of Skill." *British Journal of Psychology* 24: 67-87; July, 1933.
123. CRUTCHER, ROBERTA. "An Experimental Study of Persistence." *Journal of Applied Psychology* 18: 409-17; June, 1934.
124. CUFF, NOEL B. "Social Status and Vocabulary." *Pedagogical Seminary and Journal of Genetic Psychology* 46: 226-29; March, 1935.
125. DANIELS, PARMELY CLARK. "Discrimination of Compositional Balance at the Pre-School Level." *University of Iowa Studies in Psychology No. 18.* Psychological Monographs, Vol. 45, No. 1. Princeton, N. J.: Psychological Review Co., 1933. p. 1-11.
126. DAVIDSON, HELEN P. "A Study of Reversals in Young Children." *Pedagogical Seminary and Journal of Genetic Psychology* 45: 452-65; December, 1934.
127. DAVIS, ALONZO J. "Personality, Parent Intelligence, and 'Scatter' on the Stanford-Binet." *Journal of Juvenile Research* 18: 175-78; July, 1934.
128. DAY, ELLA J. "The Development of Language in Twins. II. The Development of Twins: Their Resemblances and Differences." *Child Development* 3: 298-316; December, 1932.
129. DAYTON, NEIL A. "Influence of Size of Family Upon the Characteristics of the Mentally Deficient: Survey of 20,473 Retarded Children in the Public Schools of Massachusetts." *American Journal of Psychiatry* 91: 799-832; January, 1935.
130. DILLON, MIRIAM S. "Attitudes of Children Toward Their Own Bodies and Those of Other Children." *Child Development* 5: 165-76; June, 1934.
131. DUDYCHA, GEORGE J., and DUDYCHA, MARTHA MALEK. "Adolescents' Memories of Preschool Experiences." *Pedagogical Seminary and Journal of Genetic Psychology* 42: 468-80; June, 1933.
132. DUDYCHA, GEORGE J., and DUDYCHA, MARTHA MALEK. "Some Factors and Characteristics of Childhood Memories." *Child Development* 4: 265-78; September, 1933.
133. DÜKER, HEINRICH. "Willenspsychologische Untersuchungen an Schülern. (Studies of Volitional Ability of School Children.)" *Archiv für die gesamte Psychologie* 83: 429-56; February, 1932.
134. DUROST, WALTER NELSON. *Children's Collecting Activity Related to Social Factors.* Contributions to Education, No. 535. New York: Teachers College, Columbia University, 1932. 115 p.

135. DYSINGER, WENDELL S., and RUCKMICK, CHRISTIAN A. *The Emotional Responses of Children to the Motion Picture Situation.* New York: Macmillan Co., 1933. 122 p. (Published with: Peters, C. C. *Motion Pictures and Standards of Morality.*)
136. ELLESOR, MARTHA VANCE. "The Relation between Situation and Response in Vocalization of a Three Year Old Child." *Child Development* 5: 158-64; June, 1934.
137. ENGLE, T. L. "Home Environments and School Records." *School Review* 42: 590-98; October, 1934.
138. FAIRBANK, RUTH ELDRED. "The Subnormal Child—Seventeen Years After." *Mental Hygiene* 17: 177-208; April, 1933.
139. FAJANS, SARA. "Die Bedeutung der Entfernung für die Stärke eines Aufförderungscharakters beim Säuglings und Kleinkind. Untersuchungen zur Handlungs- und Affektpsychologie XII. (The Importance of Distance for the Strength of an Attraction Character in the Infant and Small Child. Studies of the Psychology of Action and Effect XII.)" *Psychologische Forschung* 17: 215-67; 1933.
140. FAJANS, SARA. "Erfolg, Ausdauer und Aktivität beim Säuglings und Kleinkind. Untersuchungen zur Handlungs- und Affektpsychologie XIII. (Success, Perseverance, and Activity in the Infant and Small Child. Studies of the Psychology of Action and Effect XIII.)" *Psychologische Forschung* 17: 268-305; 1933.
141. FARSON, MABEL R. "A Comparison of Orthogenic Backward Children and Regular Grade Children at the Six Year Performance Level." *Psychological Clinic* 22: 149-80; September-November, 1933.
142. FEDOROV, S. I. ["The Memory Peculiarities in Children With Defective Speech."] *Sovetskaja nevropatologia, psykhiatria i psychologia* 3: 95-99; 1934.
143. FINCH, F. H. "Sibling Resemblance and Its Relation to Age Interval." *Science* 77: 373-74; April 14, 1933.
144. FINCH, F. H. "A Study of the Relation of Age Interval to Degree of Resemblance of Siblings in Intelligence." *Pedagogical Seminary and Journal of Genetic Psychology* 43: 389-404; December, 1933.
145. FISHER, MARY SHATTUCK. *Language Patterns of Preschool Children.* Child Development Monographs, No. 15. New York: Teachers College, Columbia University, 1934. 88 p.
146. FRANK, A. ["Moral Evolution and Education in the 6-10-Year Period."] *Gyermek* 25: 57-71; 1933. (Budapest.)
147. FRANK, L. K. "The Problem of Child Development." *Child Development* 6: 7-18; March, 1935.
148. FREEMAN, FRANK N. "Individual Differences in Mental Growth." *Scientific Monthly* 37: 263-66; September, 1933.
149. FREEMAN, FRANK N., and OTHERS. "The Influence of Environment on the Intelligence, School Achievement, and Conduct of Foster Children." *Nature and Nurture; Their Influence upon Intelligence.* Twenty-Seventh Yearbook, Part 1. National Society for the Study of Education. Bloomington, Ill.: Public School Publishing Co., 1928. p. 103-217.
150. FREEMAN, FRANK S. *Individual Differences; the Nature and Causes of Variations in Intelligence and Special Abilities.* New York: Henry Holt and Co., 1934. 355 p.
151. FRIEDMANN, ALICE. "Über das Minderwertigkeitsgefühl phantasievoller Kinder. (On the Feeling of Inferiority in Imaginative Children.)" *Zeitschrift für pädagogische Psychologie* 33: 273-92; July-August, 1932.
152. FURFEY, PAUL HANLY. "A Note on the Relative Development-Age Scores of Urban and Rural Boys." *Child Development* 6: 88-90; March, 1935.
153. GANDY, ROXANA SMITH. *A Comparison of Certain Social Experiences of Third Grade Urban and Rural Children.* Philadelphia: Privately printed, 1933. 119 p. (Doctor's thesis, University of Pennsylvania, 1932.)
154. GANZ, ELISABETH, and LOOSLI-USTERI, MARGUERITE. "Le Test de Rorschach Applique a 43 Garçons Anormaux. (The Rorschach Test Applied to 43 Abnormal Boys.)" *Archives de Psychologie* 25: 245-55; Mars, 1934.
155. GARTH, THOMAS R., and PORTER, ELECTA PENINA. "The Color Preferences of 1032 Young Children." *American Journal of Psychology* 46: 448-51; July, 1934.

156. GELLERMAN, LOUIS W. "Form Discrimination in Chimpanzees and Two-Year-Old Children." *Pedagogical Seminary and Journal of Genetic Psychology* 42: 3-50; March, 1933.
157. GILDEA, HELEN, and MACOUBREY, CONSTANCE. "Factors Affecting the Constancy of the Intelligence Quotients of Problem Children." *Smith College Studies in Social Work* 3: 229-48; March, 1933.
158. GOODENOUGH, FLORENCE L. "The Development of the Reactive Process from Early Childhood to Maturity." (Abstract.) *Psychological Bulletin* 31: 701-2; November, 1934.
159. GOODENOUGH, FLORENCE L. "Expression of the Emotions in a Blind-Deaf Child." *Journal of Abnormal and Social Psychology* 27: 328-33; October-December, 1932.
160. GRAEWE, H. *Untersuchung der Entwicklung des Zeichnens.* (*A Study of the Development of Drawing.*) Halle: Schroedel, 1932. 180 p.
161. GRAY, J. L., and MOSHINSKY, P. "Studies in Genetic Psychology: The Intellectual Resemblance of Collateral Relatives." *Proceedings of the Royal Society of Edinburgh* 53 (Pt. 2): 188-207; 1933.
162. GRIGSBY, OLIVE JOHN. "An Experimental Study of the Development of Concepts of Relationship in Pre-School Children as Evidenced by Their Expressive Ability." *Journal of Experimental Education* 1: 144-61; December, 1932.
163. GRIPPEN, VELMA BOOKHART. "A Study of Creative Artistic Imagination in Children by the Contact Procedure." *University of Iowa Studies in Psychology, No. 18.* Psychological Monographs, Vol. 45, No. 1. Princeton, N. J.: Psychological Review Co., 1933. p. 63-81.
164. HANFMANN, E. "Some Experiments of Spatial Position as a Factor in Children's Perception and Reproduction of Simple Figures." *Psychologische Forschung* 17: 319-29; 1933.
165. HARROWER, M. R. "Social Status and the Moral Development of the Child." *British Journal of Educational Psychology* 4: 75-95; February, 1934.
166. HARTMANN, GEORGE W., and TRICHE, ANDREW. "Differential Susceptibility of Children and Adults to Standard Illusions." *Pedagogical Seminary and Journal of Genetic Psychology* 42: 493-98; June, 1933.
167. HATANO, I. "[The Picture Stories and Suggestions to the Education of Drawings.]" *Transactions of the Institute for Child Study (Hiroshima University)* 16: 811-30; 1934.
168. HEILMAN, J. D. "Sex Differences in Intellectual Abilities." *Journal of Educational Psychology* 24: 47-62; January, 1933.
169. HILDRETH, GERTRUDE. "Mental Ability Measured by Verbal and Non-Verbal Tests." *Teachers College Record* 34: 134-42; November, 1932.
170. HILDRETH, GERTRUDE. "Occupational Status and Intelligence." *Personnel Journal* 13: 153-57; October, 1934.
171. HILGARD, JOSEPHINE ROHRS. *The Effect of Early and Delayed Practice on Memory and Motor Performances Studied by the Method of Co-Twin Control.* Genetic Psychology Monographs, Vol. 14, No. 6. Worcester, Mass.: Clark University Press, 1933. p. 493-567.
172. HOLADAY, PERRY E., and STODDARD, GEORGE D. *Getting Ideas from the Movies.* New York: Macmillan Co., 1933. 102 p. (Published with: Charters, W. W. *Motion Pictures and Youth: A Summary.*)
173. HOLLINGWORTH, LETA S., and KAUNITZ, RUTH M. "The Centile Status of Gifted Children at Maturity." *Pedagogical Seminary and Journal of Genetic Psychology* 45: 106-20; September, 1934.
174. HOLMAN, PORTIA. "The Relationship Between General Mental Development and Manual Dexterity." *British Journal of Psychology* 23: 279-83; January, 1933.
175. HSIAO, H. H. "A Preliminary Study of the Formal Development of Memory." *Journal of Testing (Chinese)* 3: 55-75; 1933.
176. HSIAO, H. H. "Three Major Problems in Mental Growth." *Journal of Testing (Chinese)* 3: 51-54; 1933.
177. HULL, CLARK L., and FORSTER, MILTON C. "Habituation and Perseverational Characteristics of Two Forms of Indirect Suggestion." *Journal of Experimental Psychology* 15: 700-15; December, 1932.
178. HURLOCK, E. B., and THOMSON, J. L. "Children's Drawings: An Experimental Study of Perception." *Child Development* 5: 127-38; June, 1934.

179. HURLOCK, E. B., and BURSTEIN, M. "The Imaginary Playmate: A Questionnaire Study." *Pedagogical Seminary and Journal of Genetic Psychology* 41: 380-92; December, 1932.
180. HURST, C. C. "A Genetical Formula for the Inheritance of Intelligence in Man." *Proceedings of the Royal Society (London)* 112B: 80-97; December 1, 1932.
181. ILLGE, WILLI. "Das Religiöse im Seelenleben des Volksschülers. (Religion in the Mental Life of Primary School Pupils.)" *Zeitschrift für Pädagogische Psychologie* 33: 331-46, 366-75; September and October, 1932.
182. JACK, LOIS M. "An Experimental Study of Ascendant Behavior in Preschool Children." *Behavior of the Preschool Child.* (By L. M. Jack and others.) University of Iowa Studies in Child Welfare, Vol. 9, No. 3. Iowa City: the University, 1934. p. 7-65.
183. JASPER, CONSTANCE C. "The Sensitivity of Children of Pre-School Age to Rhythm in Graphic Form." *University of Iowa Studies in Psychology, No. 18.* Psychological Monographs, Vol. 45, No. 1. Princeton, N. J.: Psychological Review Co., 1933. p. 12-25.
184. JENKINS, R. L. "The Prediction of the Intelligence Quotients of Younger Siblings." *Pedagogical Seminary and Journal of Genetic Psychology* 42: 460-64; June, 1933.
185. JERSILD, ARTHUR T., and HOLMES, FRANCES B. *Children's Fears.* Child Development Monographs, No. 20. New York: Teachers College, Columbia University, 1935. 356 p.
186. JERSILD, ARTHUR T.; MARKEY, FRANCES V.; and JERSILD, CATHERINE L. *Children's Fears, Dreams, Wishes, Daydreams, Likes, Dislikes, Pleasant and Unpleasant Memories.* Child Development Monographs, No. 12. New York: Teachers College, Columbia University, 1933. 172 p.
187. JERSILD, ARTHUR T., and OTHERS. *Training and Growth in the Development of Children: A Study of the Relative Influence of Learning and Maturation.* Child Development Monographs, No. 10. New York: Teachers College, Columbia University, 1932. 73 p.
188. JONES, HAROLD E.; CONRAD, H. S.; and BLANCHARD, M. B. *Environmental Handicap in Mental Test Performance.* University of California Publications in Psychology, Vol. 5, No. 3. Berkeley: University of California Press, 1932. p. 63-99.
189. JONES, HAROLD E., and CONRAD, H. S. *The Growth and Decline of Intelligence: A Study of a Homogeneous Group between the Ages of Ten and Sixty.* Genetic Psychology Monographs, Vol. 13, No. 3. Worcester, Mass.: Clark University Press, 1933. p. 223-98.
190. JORDAN, A. M. "Parental Occupations and Children's Intelligence Scores." *Journal of Applied Psychology* 17: 103-19; April, 1933.
191. KAMARYT, S. "Die Frühesten Erinnerungen des Septimaner. (The Earliest Memories of Seventh-Grade Pupils.)" *Versammlung für Kinderforschung (Bratislava)* 4: 256-62; 1932.
192. KAWIN, ETHEL. *Children of Preschool Age.* Chicago: University of Chicago Press, 1934. Chapter 8, "Study III: Analysis of Stanford-Binet and Merrill-Palmer Test Results for Children of Preschool Age," p. 274-326.
193. KINTER, M. *Enquête sur un Groupe de Petits Parisiens: Leur Idees sur le Bien et le Mal: Leur Reactions de cooperation et l'Altruisme.* (Study of a Group of Parisian Children: Their Ideas of Right and Wrong: Their Reaction in Situations Involving Cooperation and Altruism.) Paris: L. Rodstein, 1933. 161 p.
194. KIRIHARA, H. *The Development of Intelligence in Relation to Socio-Economic Status.* Report of the Institute for Science of Labour No. 7, 1932. 22 p.
195. KOFFKA, KURT. *Principles of Gestalt Psychology.* New York: Harcourt, Brace and Co., 1935. 720 p.
196. LA BRANT, LOU LEV. *A Study of Certain Language Developments of Children in Grades Four to Twelve, Inclusive.* Genetic Psychology Monographs, Vol. 14, No. 5. Worcester, Mass.: Clark University Press, 1933. p. 387-491.
197. LACEY, JOY MUCHMORE. *Social Studies Concepts of Children in the First Three Grades.* Contributions to Education, No. 548. New York: Teachers College, Columbia University, 1932. 89 p.

198. LÄMMERMANN, HANS. "Die Konstanz und die Übbarkeit von Denkleistungen. (The Constancy and Improvability of Performances in Thinking.)" *Zeitschrift für angewandte Psychologie* 46-47: 3-87; February, 1934.
199. LANGHORNE, MAURICE CURTIS. "Age and Sex Differences in the Acquisition of One Type of Skilled Movement." *Journal of Experimental Education* 2: 101-8; December, 1933.
200. LAWRENCE, EVELYN M. *An Investigation into the Relation between Intelligence and Inheritance.* British Journal of Psychology, Monograph Supplements, No. 16. Cambridge, England: Cambridge University Press, 1931. 80 p.
201. LEAHY, ALICE M. *Nature-Nurture and Intelligence.* Genetic Psychology Monographs, Vol. 17, No. 4. Worcester, Mass.: Clark University Press, 1935. p. 235-308.
202. LEAHY, ALICE M. "A Study of Certain Selective Factors Influencing Prediction of the Mental Status of Adopted Children: Or Adopted Children in Nature-Nurture Research." *Pedagogical Seminary and Journal of Genetic Psychology* 41: 294-329; December, 1932.
203. LEBEDINSKI, M. S. ["The Problems of Heredity in Psychology and the Twin Method."] *Psikhologia* Nos. 1-2: 163-204; 1932.
204. LEHRER, L. "Dos yidishe in der psikhik fun amerikaner yidishn kind. (The Jewish Contents of the Mind of the American Jewish Child.)" *Jiwobleter* 4: 330-53; 4-5, 1932.
205. LEVY, DAVID M. "Relation of Maternal Overprotection to School Grades and Intelligence Tests." *American Journal of Orthopsychiatry* 3: 26-34; January, 1933.
206. LEVY, DAVID M. "Use of Play Technic as Experimental Procedure." *American Journal of Orthopsychiatry* 3: 266-77; July, 1933.
207. LICHTENBERGER, WALDEMAR. "V. Über das physikalischkausale Denken bei Hilfsschülern." *Archiv für die gesamte Psychologie* 87: 447-531; March, 1933.
208. LIEFMANN, ELSE. "Volksschülerinnen, ihre geisten und körperlichen Leistungen und die Beziehung zur Konstitution. (Girls in Public School, Their Mental and Physical Performances and the Relation to Their Constitution.)" *Zeitschrift für angewandte Psychologie* 42: 102-219; March, 1932.
209. LINCOLN, E. A. "Preliminary Report on the Stanford-Binet IQ Changes of Superior Children." *Journal of Experimental Education* 1: 287-92; March, 1933.
210. LINE, WILLIAM, and KAPLAN, E. "Variation in I. Q. at the Preschool Level." *Journal of Experimental Education* 2: 95-100; December, 1933.
211. LITHAUER, DONAH B. "A Follow-Up Report of the Later School Progress of Children of Primary School Age Trained in an Experimental Kindergarten." *Journal of Juvenile Research* 17: 175-78; July-October, 1933.
212. LITHAUER, DONAH B., and KLINEBERG, OTTO. "A Study of the Variation in IQ of a Group of Dependent Children in Institution and Foster Home." *Pedagogical Seminary and Journal of Genetic Psychology* 42: 236-42; March, 1933.
213. LORD, ARTHUR B. "A Survey of Special Class Pupils in Massachusetts." *Proceedings and Addresses, 1933.* Godfrey, Ill.: American Association for the Study of Mental Defectives (Groves B. Smith, sec., Beverly Farm), 1933. p. 249-54.
214. LUH, C. W., and OTHERS. *Word Association in Chinese Children.* Yenching Studies in Psychology, No. 1. China: Yenching University, 1932. 60 p. (Chinese); 7 p. (English).
215. MCGEOCH, GRACE O. "The Age Factor in Reminiscence: A Comparative Study of Preschool Children and College Students." *Pedagogical Seminary and Journal of Genetic Psychology* 47: 98-120; September, 1935.
216. MCGEOCH, GRACE O. "The Factor of Degree of Learning in Reminiscence." (Abstract.) *Psychological Bulletin* 31: 599; October, 1934.
217. MCGEOCH, GRACE O. "The Whole-Part Problem in Memorizing Poetry." *Pedagogical Seminary and Journal of Genetic Psychology* 43: 439-47; December, 1933.
218. MCGRATH, SISTER MARY. "Some Moral Concepts of Young Children." *Catholic Educational Review* 31: 477-87; October, 1933.
219. MACKANE, KEITH. *A Comparison of the Intelligence of Deaf and Hearing Children: A Study of the Reactions of Comparable Groups of Deaf and Hearing Children to Three Performance Scales and a Non-Language Test.* Contributions to Education, No. 585. New York: Teachers College, Columbia University, 1933. 47 p.

220. MACKINTOSH, HELEN K. *A Critical Study of Children's Choices in Poetry.* Studies in Education, Vol. 7, No. 4. Iowa City: University of Iowa, 1932. 128 p.
221. MCNEIL, CHARLES. "Heredity A Minor Factor in Mental Deficiency." *British Medical Journal* 1: 584-85; March 31, 1934.
222. MALLAY, HELENA. "The Latent Memory Span of the Preschool Child." *Child Development* 6: 110-19; June, 1935.
223. MALLER, J. B. "Mental Ability and Its Relation to Physical Health and Social Economic Status." *Psychological Clinic* 22: 101-7; June-August, 1933.
224. MALLER, J. B. "Psychological and Social Characteristics of Metropolitan Neighborhoods." (Abstract.) *Psychological Bulletin* 30: 554-55; October, 1933.
225. MANWELL, ELIZABETH MOORE, and MENGERT, IDA GAARDER. "A Study of the Development of Two- and Three-Year-Old Children With Respect to Play Activities." *Behavior of the Preschool Child.* (By L. M. Jack and others.) University of Iowa Studies in Child Welfare, Vol. 9, No. 3. Iowa City: the University, 1934. p. 67-111.
226. MARINESCO, G., and KREINDLER, A. "Des Reflexes Conditionnels: Premiere Partie. L'Organisation des Reflexes Conditionnels chez l'Enfant. (Conditioned Reflexes. I. The Organization of Conditioned Reflexes in the Child.)" *Journal de Psychologie* 30: 855-86; Novembre-Decembre, 1933.
227. MARKEY, FRANCES V. *Imaginative Behavior of Preschool Children.* Child Development Monographs, No. 18. New York: Teachers College, Columbia University, 1935. 139 p.
228. MARKEY, FRANCES V. "The Mental Hygiene Problems of School Attendants." *Psychological Clinic* 22: 277-80; December, 1933.
229. MARTZ, EUGENE W., and IRVINE, HELEN N. "The Results of Physical and Mental Training on Mentally Deficient, Birth Lesion Children." *Journal of Juvenile Research* 18: 42-51; January, 1934.
230. MARZI, A. "Sulle Attitudini Eidetiche visive nei Bambini Normali. (Concerning Visual Eidetic Aptitudes in Normal Children.)" *Scritti onore Kiesow*, 1933. p. 169-77.
231. MASON, SUE H. "A Comparative Study of Four Pairs of Twins Examined in Kindergarten and in Junior High School, with Special Reference to Personality." *Smith College Studies in Social Work* 4: 197-286; March, 1934.
232. MATTSON, MARION L. *The Relation Between the Complexity of the Habit to Be Acquired and the Form of the Learning Curve in Young Children.* Genetic Psychology Monographs, Vol. 13, No. 4. Worcester, Mass.: Clark University Press, 1933. p. 299-398.
233. MEAD, M. "An Investigation of the Thought of Primitive Children: With Special Reference to Animism: Preliminary Report." *Journal of the Royal Anthropological Institute of Great Britain and Ireland* 62: 173-90; January-June, 1932.
234. MEENES, MAX. "Eidetic Phenomena in Negro School Children." (Abstract.) *Psychological Bulletin* 30: 688-89; November, 1933.
235. MELCHER, RUTH TAYLOR. "Children's Motor Learning With and Without Vision." *Child Development* 5: 315-50; December, 1934.
236. MELLINGER, BONNIE E. *Children's Interests in Pictures.* Contributions to Education, No. 516. New York: Teachers College, Columbia University, 1932. 52 p.
237. MENDENHALL, JAMES E., and MENDENHALL, MARCIA A. *The Influence of Familiarity Upon Children's Preferences for Pictures and Poems.* New York: Teachers College, Columbia University, 1933. 74 p.
238. MESSERSCHMIDT, RAMONA. "Responses of Boys Between the Ages of Five and Sixteen Years to Hull's Postural Suggestion Test." *Pedagogical Seminary and Journal of Genetic Psychology* 43: 405-21; December, 1933.
239. MESSERSCHMIDT, RAMONA. "The Suggestibility of Boys and Girls Between the Ages of Six and Sixteen Years." *Pedagogical Seminary and Journal of Genetic Psychology* 43: 422-37; December, 1933.
240. MEYER, E. "Ordnen und Ordnung bei 3-6 jährigen Kindern. (Classification and Assortment in 3-6 Year Old Children.)" *Neue Psychologie Studien* 10: 100; 1934.
241. MILES, KATHARINE A. "Sustained Visual Fixation of Preschool Children to a Delayed Stimulus." *Child Development* 4: 1-5; March, 1933.
242. MILES, WALTER R. "Age and Human Ability." *Psychological Review* 40: 99-123; March, 1933.

243. MILLER, NEAL E. "The Perception of Children: A Genetic Study Employing the Critical Choice Delayed Reaction." *Pedagogical Seminary and Journal of Genetic Psychology* 44: 321-39; June, 1934.
244. MILLER, W. S. "Variation of IQ's Obtained from Group Tests." *Journal of Educational Psychology* 24: 468-74; September, 1933.
245. MINARD, RALPH D. *Race Attitudes of Iowa Children.* University of Iowa Studies in Character, Vol. 4, No. 2. Iowa City: the University, 1931. 101 p.
246. MIRENVA, A. N. "Psychomotor Education and the General Development of Preschool Children." *Pedagogical Seminary and Journal of Genetic Psychology* 46: 433-54; June, 1935.
247. MONNIN, J. "Correlations entre les Classements d'Ecoliers d'après untest d'intelligence et d'après le Travail scolaire. (Correlations Between Rankings of Pupils According to an Intelligence Test and According to Scholastic Work.)" *L'Année Psychologie* 33: 51-56; 1932.
248. MURPHY, MILES S. "The Relation Between Intelligence and Age of Walking in Normal and Feeble-Minded Children." *Psychological Clinic* 22: 187-97; September, 1933.
249. NEMZEK, CLAUDE L. "The Constancy of the I.Q." *Psychological Bulletin* 30: 143-68; February, 1933.
250. NEMZEK, CLAUDE L. "The Constancy of the IQ's of Gifted Children." *Journal of Educational Psychology* 23: 607-10; November, 1932.
251. NEWMAN, H. H. "The Effects of Hereditary and Environmental Differences upon Human Personality as Revealed by Studies of Twins." *American Naturalist* 67: 193-205; May-June, 1933.
252. NEWMAN, H. H. "Mental and Physical Traits of Identical Twins Reared Apart: Case VII. Twins Richard and Raymond." *Journal of Heredity* 24: 209-14; May, 1933.
253. NEWMAN, H. H. "Mental and Physical Traits of Identical Twins Reared Apart: Case VIII. Twins 'M' and 'R'." *Journal of Heredity* 25: 55-60; February, 1934.
254. NICE, MARGARET MORSE. "A Child's Attainment of the Sentence." *Pedagogical Seminary and Journal of Genetic Psychology* 42: 216-24; March, 1933.
255. NILSON, KENNETH. "Certain Intelligence Aspects of a Group of Physically Disabled Pupils in Minnesota Public Schools." *Journal of Educational Research* 26: 513-16; March, 1933.
256. OLNEY, ELIZABETH E., and CUSHING, HAZEL M. "*A Brief Report of the Responses of Preschool Children to Commercially Available Pictorial Materials.*" *Child Development* 6: 52-55; March, 1935.
257. ORGLER, A. "Über Zwillingsbeobachtungen. (Concerning Observations on Twins.)" *Internationale Zeitschrift für Individualle Psychologie* 10: 353-57; 1932.
258. OUTHIT, MARION CURRIE. *A Study of Resemblance of Parents and Children in General Intelligence.* Archives of Psychology, No. 149. New York: Columbia University, 1933. 60 p.
259. PARKER, H. T. *The Development of Intelligence in Subnormal Children.* Australian Council for Educational Research, Educational Research Series, No. 27. Melbourne, Australia: Melbourne University Press, 1934. 63 p.
260. PARKER, H. T. "Fluctuations in the Intelligence Quotients of Subnormal Children." *Journal of Juvenile Research* 18: 163-68; July, 1934.
261. PARKER, H. T. *Intelligence and Scholastic Attainment; a Study of the Educational Proficiency of Subnormal Children.* Australian Council for Educational Research, Educational Research Series, No. 17. Melbourne, Australia: Melbourne University Press, 1932. 64 p.
262. PARKER, P. A. "Variations in the Mental Development of Twins." *Proceedings, 1932.* Codfrey, Ill.: American Association for Study of the Feebleminded (Groves B. Smith, sec., Beverly Farm), 1932. p. 213-22.
263. PATERSON, DONALD G., and RUNDQUIST, EDWARD A. "The Occupational Background of Feeble-Mindedness." *American Journal of Psychology* 45: 118-24; January, 1933.
264. PECK, LEIGH, and WALLING, ROSEMARY. "A Preliminary Study of the Eidetic Imagery of Preschool Children." *Pedagogical Seminary and Journal of Genetic Psychology* 47: 168-92; September, 1935.
265. PECKHAM, ROBERT H. "Visual Discrimination in Preschool Children." *Child Development* 4: 292-97; December, 1933.

266. PENROSE, L. S. "A Study in the Inheritance of Intelligence. The Analysis of 100 Families Containing Subcultural Mental Defectives." *British Journal of Psychology* 24: 1-19; July, 1933.
267. PETERS, W. "Die Aufmerksamkeitskonzentration der Undeterminierten. (The Concentration of Attention of Indeterminates.)" *Zeitschrift für Psychologie* 127: 161-80; December, 1932.
268. PETERSON, RUTH C., and THURSTONE, L. L. *Motion Pictures and the Social Attitudes of Children.* New York: Macmillan Co., 1933. 75 p. (Published with: Shuttleworth, Frank N., and May, Mark A. *The Social Conduct and Attitudes of Movie Fans.*)
269. PHILIP, B. R. "Reaction-Times of Children." *American Journal of Psychology* 46: 379-96; July, 1934.
270. PIAGET, JEAN, and OTHERS. *The Moral Judgment of the Child.* New York: Harcourt, Brace and Co., 1932. 418 p.
271. PINTNER, RUDOLF, and FORLANO, GEORGE. "The Influence of Month of Birth on Intelligence Quotients." *Journal of Educational Psychology* 24: 561-84; November, 1933.
272. POYNTZ, LILLIAN. "The Efficacy of Visual and Auditory Distractions for Preschool Children." *Child Development* 4: 55-72; March, 1933.
273. RESTORFF, HEDWIG VON. "Beobachtungen über Nachahmungs- und Darstellungsfähigkeit jüngerer Kinder. (Observations Upon the Aptitude for Imitation and Expression in Young Children.)" *Zeitschrift für Kinderforschung* 38; 411-51; August, 1931.
274. RICHEY, AMYTIS. "The Effects of Diseased Tonsils and Adenoids on Intelligence Quotients of 204 Children." *Journal of Juvenile Research* 18: 1-4; January, 1934.
275. RIETI, E. "Le Attitudine Eidetiche Visive nei Bambini Ammalati di Mente. (Visual Eidetic Tendencies in Children Afflicted With Mental Diseases.)" *Scritti onore Kiesow,* 1933. p. 16-26.
276. ROBERTS, KATHERINE ELLIOTT. *Learning in Preschool and Orphanage Children; an Experimental Study of Ability To Solve Different Situations According to the Same Plan.* Studies in Child Welfare, Vol. 7, No. 3. Iowa City: University of Iowa, 1933. 94 p.
277. ROBERTS, MARY PRICE. "A Study of Children's Play in the Home Environment." *Researches in Parent Education II.* Studies in Child Welfare, Vol. 8, Iowa City: University of Iowa, 1934. p. 33-98.
278. RODGERS, FRANCES. "Variation in the Aesthetic Environment of Artistic and Non-Artistic Children." *University of Iowa Studies in Psychology, No. 18.* Psychological Monographs, Vol. 45, No. 1. Princeton, N. J.: Psychological Review Co., 1933. p. 95-107.
279. ROGERS, K. H. "'Intelligence' and 'Perserveration' Related to School Achievement." *Journal of Experimental Education* 2: 35-43; September, 1933.
280. ROSANOFF, AARON, J., and OTHERS. "Sex Factors in Intelligence." *Journal of Nervous and Mental Disease* 80: 125-37; August, 1934.
281. ROSENZWEIG, SAUL, and MASON, GWENDOLYN. "An Experimental Study of Memory in Relation to the Theory of Repression." *British Journal of Psychology* 24: 247-65; January, 1934.
282. ROSENZWEIG, SAUL. "Preferences in the Repetition of Successful and Unsuccessful Activities as a Function of Age and Personality." *Pedagogical Seminary and Journal of Genetic Psychology* 42: 423-41; June, 1933.
283. ROSTOHAR, M. "Die Entwicklung der Allgemeinbegriffe beim Kinde. (The Development of General Ideas in the Child.)" *Versammlung für Kinderforschung (Bratislava)* 4: 265-68; 1932.
284. ROSTOHAR, M. "Wie Entwickelt sich bei Kindern der konkrete Gegendstandsbegriff? (How Does the Idea of Concrete Objects Develop in Children?)" *Versammlung für Kinderforschung (Bratislava)* 4: 262-65; 1932.
285. RUSSELL, J. B. "The Relation of Intellectual, Temperamental and Other Qualities to Success at School—A Following Up Enquiry." *British Journal of Psychology* 24: 295-312; January, 1934.

286. SALLER, K. "Über die Stellung der Hilfsschulkinder von Regensburg und Göttingen in sozialen Aufbau der übrigen Bevölkerung. Beitrag IV zur Frage der Beziehungen zwischen Intelligenz, sozialer Schichtung und interschiedlicher Volksvermehrung. (Concerning the Position of the Opportunity School Children of Regensburg and Gottingen in the Social Structure of the Rest of Population. Contribution IV to the Question of the Relations Between Intelligence, Social Stratum, and Differential Rate of Reproduction.)" *Zeitschrift für Kinderforschung* 42: 447-62; 1934.
287. SALLER, K. "Über die Zusammenhänge von Schulleistungen, sozialer Schichtung und unterschiedlicher Volksvermehrung in einer vorwiegend katholischen und einer vorwiegend protestantischen Stadt (Regensburg und Göttingen). Beitrag III zur Frage der Beziehungen zwischen Intelligenz, sozialer Schichtung und interschiedlicher Volksvermehrung. (Relation Between School Work, Social Stratum, and Differential Rate of Reproduction in a Preponderantly Catholic City and in a Preponderantly Protestant City. (Regensburg and Gottingen). Contribution III to the Question of the Relations Between Intelligence, Social Stratum, and Differential Rate of Reproduction.)" *Zeitschrift für Kinderforschung* 42: 200-48; 1934.
288. SALLER, K. "Untersuchungen in Förderklassen (Sprachklassen) und Hilfsschulen der Stadt Hannover. Beitrag I zur Frage der Beziehungen zwischen Intelligenz, sozialer Schichtung und unterschiedlicher Volksvermehrung. (Investigations in the Advanced Classes (Language Classes) and in Opportunity Schools of the City of Hanover. Contribution I to the Relation Between Intelligence, Social Stratum, and Differential Rate of Reproduction.)" *Zeitschrift für Kinderforschung* 41: 181-211; 1933.
289. SALLER, K. "Untersuchungen in Landgebieten Ostfrieslands und des bayrischen Waldes. Beitrag II zur Frage der Beziehungen zwischen Intelligenz, sozialer Schichtung und unterschiedlicher Volksvermehrung. (Investigations in the Region of East Friesland and the Bavarian Forest. Contribution II to the Question of the Relation Between Intelligence, Social Stratum, and Differential Rate of Reproduction.)" *Zeitschrift für Kinderforschung* 41: 369-410; 1933.
290. SCHELL, MARGARET. "Infection by Intestinal Protozoa in Relation to the Intelligence of Siblings." *Child Development* 4: 253-58; September, 1933.
291. SCHIEL, WERNER. "Die Bedeutung des bewahrenden und verarbeitenden Gedächtnisverhaltens für die Strulstur des 11- bis 12-jährigen. (The Significance of Retentive and Elaborative Memorial Behavior for the Structure of the Child of 11-12 Years.)" *Zeitschrift für Psychologie* 132: 133-75; May, 1934.
292. SCHILDER, PAUL, and WECHSLER, DAVID. "The Attitudes of Children Toward Death." *Pedagogical Seminary and Journal of Genetic Psychology* 45: 406-51; December, 1934.
293. SCHLOTTER, B., and SVENDSEN, M. *An Experiment in Recreation With the Mentally Retarded.* Chicago: Behavior Research Fund, 1932. 75 p.
294. SCHNECKENBURGER, HANS. ["The Age Development and the Conditioning Influences of the Social-Ethical Understanding of the Proletarian Child. The Development to Maturity and the Conditioning Influence of the Social-Ethical Comprehension of the Child of the Proletariat."] *Zeitschrift für angewandte Psychologie* 42-43: 55-82, 42-47; 1932.
295. SCHWESINGER, GLADYS C. *Heredity and Environment: Studies in the Genesis of Psychological Characteristics.* New York: Macmillan Co., 1933. 484 p.
296. SHACTER, HELEN S. "Intelligence as a Causal Factor Determining Differences in Sustained Attention in Preschool Children." *Journal of Applied Psychology* 17; 487-88; August, 1933.
297. SHACTER, HELEN S. "A Method for Measuring the Sustained Attention of Preschool Children." *Pedagogical Seminary and Journal of Genetic Psychology* 42: 339-71; June, 1933.
298. SHACTER, HELEN S. "Personality Tendencies and Sustained Attention in Preschool Children." *Journal of Social Psychology* 5: 313-28; August, 1934.
299. SHALLIT, REBECCA. "The Dramatic Play of Ten Nursery School Children." *Child Development* 3: 359-62; December, 1932.
300. SHIMIDU, E. ["On the Development of Immediate Memory and Perception of Children."] *Transactions of the Institute for Child Study (Hiroshima University)* 16: 723-40; 1934.

301. SHIPLEY, WALTER C. "Stanford-Binet Test Scattering as Related to I. Q. in Clinical Cases." (Abstract.) *Psychological Bulletin* 31: 684-85; November, 1934.
302. SKEELS, HAROLD M. "The Use of Conditioning Techniques in the Study of Form Discrimination of Young Children." *Journal of Experimental Education* 2: 127-37; December, 1933.
303. SMITH, MADORAH E. "Grammatical Errors in the Speech of Preschool Children." *Child Development* 4: 183-90; June, 1933.
304. SMITH, MADORAH E. "The Influence of Age, Sex, and Situation on the Frequency, Form and Function of Questions Asked by Preschool Children." *Child Development* 4: 201-13; September, 1933.
305. SMITH, MADORAH E. "A Study of Some Factors Influencing the Development of the Sentence in Preschool Children." *Pedagogical Seminary and Journal of Genetic Psychology* 46: 182-212; March, 1935.
306. SMITH, MADORAH E. "A Study of the Speech of Eight Bilingual Children of the Same Family." *Child Development* 6: 19-25; March, 1935.
307. SMITH, WILEY F. "Direction Orientation in Children." *Pedagogical Seminary and Journal of Genetic Psychology* 42: 154-66; March, 1933.
308. SONTAG, L. W., and NELSON, V. L. "Monozygotic Dichorionic Triplets: Part II. Behavior of a Set of Identical Triplets." *Pedagogical Seminary and Journal of Genetic Psychology* 42: 406-22; June, 1933.
309. SONTAG, L. W., and NELSON, V. L. "A Study of Identical Triplets. Part I. Comparison of the Physical and Mental Traits of a Set of Monozygotic Dichorionic Triplets." *Journal of Heredity* 24: 473-80; December, 1933.
310. STALNAKER, ELIZABETH. "Language of the Preschool Child." *Child Development* 4: 229-36; September, 1933.
311. STAPLES, RUTH, and WALTON, WILLIAM E. "A Study of Pleasurable Experience as a Factor in Color Preference." *Pedagogical Seminary and Journal of Genetic Psychology* 43: 217-23; September, 1933.
312. STEINBERG, JANET. *The Relation Between Basal Metabolism and Mental Speed.* Archives of Psychology, No. 172. New York: Columbia University, 1934. 39 p.
313. STEVANOVIC, B. P. "The Development of the Child's Intelligence and the Beograd Revision of the Binet-Simon Scale: Summary of Data and Results." *Bullétin Academie Lettres serbe*, No. 1, 1935. p. 89-114.
314. STROUD, J. B., and MAUL, R. "The Influence of Age Upon Learning and Retention of Nonsense Syllables." *Pedagogical Seminary and Journal of Genetic Psychology* 42: 242-50; March, 1933.
315. SVENDSEN, MARGARET. "Children's Imaginary Companions." *Archives of Neurology and Psychiatry* 32: 985-99; November, 1934.
316. TEASDALE, H. "A Quantitative Study of Eidetic Imagery." *British Journal of Educational Psychology* 4:56-74; February, 1934.
317. THORNDIKE, EDWARD L., and FORLANO, GEORGE. "The Influence of Increase and Decrease of the Amount of Reward Upon the Rate of Learning." *Journal of Educational Psychology* 24: 401-11; September, 1933.
318. THORNDIKE, ROBERT L. "The Effect of the Interval Between Test and Retest on the Constancy of the IQ." *Journal of Educational Psychology* 24: 543-49; October, 1933.
319. THRUM, MARTHA E. "The Development of Concepts of Magnitude." *Child Development* 6: 120-40; June, 1935.
320. TIEBOUT, CAROLYN. "The Psychophysical Functions Differentiating Artistically Superior from Artistically Inferior Children." *University of Iowa Studies in Psychology, No. 18.* Psychological Monographs, Vol. 45, No. 1. Princeton, N. J.: Psychological Review Co., 1933. p. 108-33.
321. TUCKMAN, JACOB. *The Influence of Varying Amounts of Punishment on Mental Connections.* Contributions to Education, No. 590. New York: Teachers College, Columbia University, 1933. 45 p.
322. VAN ALSTYNE, DOROTHY. *Play Behavior and Choice of Play Materials of Pre-School Children.* Chicago: University of Chicago Press, 1932. 104 p.
323. VANCE, THOMAS F., and MCCALL, LOUISE T. "Children's Preferences Among Play Materials as Determined by the Method of Paired Comparisons of Pictures." *Child Development* 5: 267-77; September, 1934.

324. VANCE, THOMAS F., and TEMPLE, VERNA M. "The Food Preferences of Preschool Children: A Comparison of Rural Children with Children of the Iowa State College Nursery School." *Child Development* 4: 222-28; September, 1933.
325. VAN WAGENEN, M. J. "Effect of Test Content upon Intelligence Quotients." (Abstract.) *Psychological Bulletin* 31: 675; November, 1934.
326. VÉRTES, JOSEF O. "Das Gedächtnis taubstummer Kinder. (The Memory of Deaf-Mute Children.)" *Zeitschrift für pädagogische Psychologie* 32: 136-42; March, 1931.
327. WALTON, WILLIAM E. "The Sensitivity of Children and Adults to Color Harmony." *University of Iowa Studies in Psychology, No. 18.* Psychological Monographs, Vol. 45, No. 1. Princeton, N. J.: Psychological Review Co., 1933. p. 51-62.
328. WELLMAN, BETH L. "The Effect of Pre-School Attendance Upon the IQ." *Journal of Experimental Education* 1:48-69; December, 1932.
329. WHITE, KENNETH B. "A Clinical Study of Twenty-Six Pairs of Twins." *Psychological Clinic* 21: 243-52; December, 1932.
330. WHITESIDE, S. "Spontaneity of Normal and Mentally Deficient Subjects in Selective Learning." *Proceedings, 1934.* Godfrey, Ill.: American Association on Mental Deficiency (Groves B. Smith, sec., Beverly Farm), 1934. p. 344-84.
331. WHORLEY, KATHERINE SNOW. "An Experimental Investigation of the Sensitivity of Children to Compositional Unity." *University of Iowa Studies in Psychology, No. 18.* Psychological Monographs, Vol. 45, No. 1. Princeton, N. J.: Psychological Review Co., 1933. p. 26-45.
332. WILLIAMS, EILEEN JACKSON. "A Technique for Testing Color Harmony Sensitivity in Young Children." *University of Iowa Studies in Psychology, No. 18.* Psychological Monographs, Vol. 45, No. 1. Princeton, N. J.; Psychological Review Co., 1933. p. 46-50.
333. WITTY, PAUL A., and LEHMAN, HARVEY C. "The Collecting Interests of Town Children and Country Children." *Journal of Educational Psychology* 24: 170-84; March, 1933.
334. WOODALL, C. S. "The Children of Mentally Defective and Mentally Retarded Mothers." *Proceedings, 1932.* Godfrey, Ill.: American Association for the Study of the Feebleminded (Groves B. Smith, sec., Beverly Farm), 1932. p. 328-58.

Chapter III. Motor Development from Two Years to Maturity

(See also Nos. 90, 98, 118, 232, 235)

335. ABRAMSON, HAROLD. "The Influence of Disease upon Motor Development during Childhood." *Psychological Bulletin* 31: 800-14; December, 1934.
336. BAYLEY, NANCY. *The Development of Motor Abilities During the First Three Years.* Society for Research in Child Development Monograph No. 1, 1935. 26 p.
337. COWAN, EDWINA A., and PRATT, BERTHA M. "The Hurdle Jump As a Developmental and Diagnostic Test of Motor Coordination For Children From Three to Twelve Years of Age." *Child Development* 5: 107-21; June, 1934.
338. COX, JOHN WILLIAM. *Manual Skill; Its Organization and Development.* New York: Macmillan Co., 1934. 247 p.
339. CRIDER, BLAKE. "Unilateral Sighting Preference." *Child Development* 6: 163-64; June, 1935.
340. EELLS, WALTER CROSBY. "Mechanical, Physical, and Musical Ability of the Native Races of Alaska." *Journal of Applied Psychology* 17: 493-506; October, 1933.
341. EYRE, MARY B., and SCHMEECKLE, MARY M. "A Study of Handedness, Eyedness, and Footedness." *Child Development* 4: 73-78; March, 1933.
342. GOODENOUGH, FLORENCE L. "A Further Study of Speed of Tapping in Early Childhood." *Journal of Applied Psychology* 19: 309-19; June, 1935.
343. GOODENOUGH, FLORENCE L., and SMART, RUSSELL C. "Inter-Relationships of Motor Abilities In Young Children." *Child Development* 6: 141-53; June, 1935.
344. JOHNSON, BUFORD J. *Child Psychology.* Springfield, Ill.: Charles C. Thomas, 1932. 439 p.

345. LONG, JOHN A. *Motor Abilities of Deaf Children.* Contributions to Education, No. 514. New York: Teachers College, Columbia University, 1932. 67 p.
346. MCELWEE, EDNA WILLIS. "Standardization of the Stenquist Mechanical Assembling Test. Series III." *Journal of Educational Psychology* 23: 451-54; September, 1932.
347. MCNEMAR, QUINN. "Twin Resemblances in Motor Skills, and the Effect of Practice Thereon." *Pedagogical Seminary and Journal of Genetic Psychology* 42: 70-99; March, 1933.
348. NEMZEK, CLAUDE L.; CRONIN, MARION; and BRANNOM, EDNA. "Motor Ability of High-School Girls." *Journal of Educational Research* 26: 593-94; April, 1933.
349. STALNAKER, ELIZABETH M. "Responses of the Pre-School Child." *Child Development* 4: 195-99; June, 1933.
350. UPDEGRAFF, RUTH. "The Correspondence Between Handedness and Eyedness in Young Children." *Pedagogical Seminary and Journal of Genetic Psychology* 42: 490-92; June, 1933.
351. UPDEGRAFF, RUTH. "Preferential Handedness in Young Children." *Journal of Experimental Education* 1: 134-39; December, 1932.
352. VITELES, MORRIS S. "The Influence of Training on Motor Test Performance." *Journal of Experimental Psychology* 16: 556-64; August, 1933.
353. WESTPHAL, GRENAFORE. "An Experimental Study of Certain Motor Abilities of Stutterers." *Child Development* 4: 214-21; September, 1933.
354. YARMOLENKO, A. "The Motor Sphere of School-Age Children." *Pedagogical Seminary and Journal of Genetic Psychology* 42: 298-318; June, 1933.

Chapter IV. Physical Growth from Birth to Maturity

355. AMERICAN CHILD HEALTH ASSOCIATION. *Nutritional Status Indices.* New York: the Association, 1935. 66 p.
356. ASHLEY-MONTAGU, M. F. "The Form and Dimensions of the Palate in the New-born." *International Journal of Orthodontia and Dentistry for Children* 20: 694-704, 810-27; July and August, 1934.
357. ASHLEY-MONTAGU, M. F. "The Location of the Nasion in the Living." *American Journal of Physical Anthropology* 20: 81-93; April-June, 1935.
358. BAKWIN, HARRY; BAKWIN, RUTH MORRIS; and MILGRAM, LILLIAN. "Body Build in Infants." *American Journal for Diseases of Children* 48: 1030-40; November, 1934. 49: 861-83; April, 1935.
359. BAKWIN, HARRY, and BAKWIN, RUTH MORRIS. "Body Build in Infants: V. Anthropometry in the New-Born." *Human Biology* 6: 612-26; December, 1934.
360. BAKWIN, HARRY, and BAKWIN, RUTH MORRIS. "External Dimensions of the New-Born." *American Journal for Diseases of Children* 48: 1234-36; December, 1934.
361. BAYER, LEONA M., and GRAY, H. "The Hand: Method of Measurement." *American Journal of Physical Anthropology* 17: 379-415; January-March, 1933.
362. BAYLEY, NANCY, and DAVIS, FRANK C. "Growth Changes in Bodily Size and Proportions During the First Three Years: A Developmental Study of Sixty-One Children by Repeated Measurements." *Biometrika* 27 (Parts 1 and 2): 26-87; March, 1935.
363. BEAN, ROBERT BENNETT. "The Cephalic Index, Head Length and Breadth in Old Virginians." *American Journal of Physical Anthropology* 19: 247-88; July-September, 1934.
364. BEAN, ROBERT BENNETT. "Hair and Eye Color in Old Virginians." *American Journal of Physical Anthropology* 20: 171-204; July-September, 1935.
365. BEAN, ROBERT BENNETT. "Sitting Height and Leg Length in Old Virginians." *American Journal of Physical Anthropology* 17: 445-79; April-June, 1933.
366. BISSETT, LEE, and LASLETT, H. R. "A Study of Height, Weight, and Age Among High School Boys." *Journal of Juvenile Research* 16: 291-97; October, 1932.
367. BIVINGS, LEE. "Racial, Geographic, Annual, and Seasonal Variations in Birth Weights." *American Journal of Obstetrics and Gynecology* 27: 725-28; May, 1934.
368. BOAS, FRANZ. "Studies in Growth." *Human Biology* 4: 307-50; September, 1932. 5: 429-44; September, 1933. 7: 303-18; September, 1935.

369. BOAS, FRANZ. "The Tempo of Growth of Fraternities." *Proceedings of the National Academy of Sciences* 21: 415-18; July 15, 1935.
370. BOWLES, GORDON TOWNSEND. *New Types of Old Americans at Harvard and at Eastern Women's Colleges.* Cambridge, Mass.: Harvard University Press, 1932. 144 p.
371. BOYD, EDITH. "A Method of Establishing the Probable Limits of Normal Variation in the Weight of Organs." *Anatomical Record* 62: 1-6; April, 1935.
372. BOYD, EDITH. "Normal Variability in Weight of the Adult Human Liver and Spleen." *Archives of Pathology* 16: 350-72; September, 1933.
373. BOYD, EDITH. "The Specific Gravity of the Human Body." *Human Biology* 5: 646-72; December, 1933.
374. CATTELL, PSYCHE. "Preliminary Report on the Measurement of Ossification of the Hand and Wrist." *Human Biology* 6: 454-71; September, 1934.
375. COURTIS, S. A. "The Derivation of Norms." *Journal of Experimental Education* 2: 237-42; March, 1934.
376. COURTIS, S. A. "Maturation as a Factor in Diagnosis." *Educational Diagnosis.* Thirty-Fourth Yearbook, National Society for the Study of Education, Bloomington, Ill.: Public School Publishing Co., 1935. p. 169-87.
377. COURTIS, S. A. "The Prediction of Growth." *Journal of Educational Research* 26: 481-92; March, 1933.
378. DAVENPORT, CHARLES BENEDICT. "The Crural Index." *American Journal of Physical Anthropology* 17: 333-53; January-March, 1933.
379. DAVENPORT, CHARLES BENEDICT. "The Development of Trunk Width and the Trunk Width Index." *Human Biology* 7: 151-95; May, 1935.
380. DAVENPORT, CHARLES BENEDICT. "The Growth of the Human Foot." *American Journal of Physical Anthropology* 17: 167-211; October-December, 1932.
381. DAVENPORT, CHARLES BENEDICT. "Ontogeny and Phylogeny of Man's Appendages." *Proceedings of the National Academy of Sciences* 20: 359-64; June, 1934.
382. DAVENPORT, CHARLES BENEDICT. "The Thoracic Index." *Human Biology* 6: 1-23; February, 1934.
383. DEARBORN, WALTER F. "The Mental and Physical Development of Public School Children." *School and Society* 41: 585-93; May 4, 1935.
384. DIEHL, HAROLD S. "Height and Weights of American College Men." *Human Biology* 5: 445-79; September, 1933.
385. DIEHL, HAROLD S. "The Heights and Weights of American College Women." *Human Biology* 5: 600-28; December, 1933.
386. DIMOCK, HEDLEY S. "A Research in Adolescence: I. Pubescence and Physical Growth." *Child Development* 6: 177-95; September, 1935.
387. DUNHAM, ETHEL C., and D'AMICO, MICHAEL. "A Roentgenographic Study of the Thoraces of Newborn Infants." *Yale Journal of Biology and Medicine* 6: 385-401; March, 1934.
388. ELIOT, MARTHA M. *The Effect of Tropical Sunlight on the Development of Bones of Children in Puerto Rico.* U. S. Dept. of Labor, Children's Bureau Publication No. 217. Washington, D. C.: Government Printing Office, 1933. 122 p.
389. ENGLE, E. T., and SHELESNYAK, M. C. "First Menstruation and Subsequent Menstrual Cycles of Pubertal Girls." *Human Biology* 6: 431-53; September, 1934.
390. FLORY, CHARLES D. "Predicting Puberty." *Child Development* 6: 1-6; March, 1935.
391. FLORY, CHARLES D. "Sex Differences in Skeletal Development." *Child Development* 6: 205-12; September, 1935.
392. FRANK, L. K. "The Problem of Child Development." *Child Development* 6: 7-18; March, 1935.
393. FRANK, L. K. "Structure, Function and Growth." *Philosophy of Science* 2: 210-35; April, 1935.
394. FRANZEN, RAYMOND, and PALMER, GEORGE T. *The ACH Index of Nutritional Status.* New York: American Child Health Association, 1934. 12 p. (Also in *Child Health Bulletin* 10: 26-33; January, 1934.)
395. FRANZEN, RAYMOND. "Selection of Malnourished School Children." *American Journal for Diseases of Children* 47: 789-98; April, 1934.
396. FRANZEN, RAYMOND, and DERRYBERRY, MAYHEW. "Weight and Skeletal Build: A Reply." *American Journal of Orthopsychiatry* 3: 445-54; October, 1933.
397. FREEMAN, ROWLAND G., JR. "Chest Width-Hip Width Index." *Proceedings of the Society for Experimental Biology and Medicine* 30: 791-92; March, 1933.

398. GOLDSTEIN, MARCUS S., and STANTON, FREDERICK L. "Changes in Dimensions and Form of the Dental Arches with Age." *International Journal of Orthodontia and Dentistry for Children* 21: 357-80; April, 1935.
399. GRANDPREY, MEDORA B. "Range of Variability in Weight and Height of Children under Six Years of Age." *Child Development* 4: 26-35; March, 1933.
400. GRAY, HORACE. "Chest Depth." *American Journal of Physical Anthropology* 20: 1-4; April-June, 1935.
401. "Growth-Rates:—Physical and Mental." *Eugenical News* 18: 102-3; September-October, 1933.
402. "Height-Weight-Age Tables for Children." (Editorial.) *Journal of the American Medical Association* 101: 369-70; July 29, 1933. (Reprinted in *American Journal of Physical Anthropology* 18: 155-57; July-September, 1933.)
403. HELLMAN, MILO. "Growth of the Face and Occlusion of the Teeth in Relation to Orthodontic Treatment." *International Journal of Orthodontia and Dentistry for Children* 19: 1116-47; November, 1933.
404. HENSTELL, HENRY; KAUFMAN, ROBERT; and MIGNONE, JOSEPH. "The Physical Status of Underprivileged Boys of New Haven." *Yale Journal of Biology and Medicine* 6: 545-51; May, 1934.
405. HOEFER, CAROLYN, and HARDY, MARTHA CRUMPTON. "The Rôle of Health in the Child's Development." *Elementary School Journal* 35: 423-39; February, 1935.
406. HOEFER, CAROLYN, and HARDY, MARTHA CRUMPTON. "Some Influences of a Health-Education Program During the Elementary-School Years." *Elementary School Journal* 35: 368-82; January, 1935.
407. KELLY, HELEN GARSIDE. *A Study of Individual Differences in Breathing Capacity in Relation to Some Physical Characteristics.* University of Iowa Studies in Child Welfare, Vol. 7, No. 5. Iowa City: the University, 1933. 59 p.
408. KRONFELD, RUDOLF. "First Permanent Molar: Its Condition at Birth and Its Postnatal Development." *Journal of the American Dental Association* 22: 1131-55; July, 1935.
409. KRONFELD, RUDOLF. "Postnatal Development and Calcification of the Anterior Permanent Teeth." *Journal of the American Dental Association* 22: 1521-36; September, 1935.
410. KUBITSCHEK, PAUL E. "Sexual Development of Boys with Special Reference to the Appearance of the Secondary Sexual Characters and Their Relationship to Structural and Personality Types." *Journal of Nervous and Mental Disease* 76: 425-51; November, 1932.
411. LINCOLN, EDWARD A. "Methods and Results in the Harvard Growth Study." *Harvard Teachers Record* 5: 24-33; February, 1935.
412. LOGAN, WILLIAM H. G., and KRONFELD, RUDOLF. "Development of the Human Jaws and Surrounding Structures from Birth to the Age of Fifteen Years." *Journal of the American Dental Association* 20: 379-427; March, 1933.
413. MANUEL, H. T. "Physical Measurements of Mexican Children in American Schools." *Child Development* 5: 237-52; September, 1934.
414. MENEES, THOMAS O., and HOLLY, LELAND E. "The Ossification in the Extremities of the New-Born." *American Journal of Roentgenology and Radium Therapy* 28: 389-90; September, 1932.
415. MEREDITH, HOWARD V. *The Rhythm of Physical Growth: A Study of Eighteen Anthropometric Measurements on Iowa City White Males Ranging in Age Between Birth and Eighteen Years.* University of Iowa Studies in Child Welfare, Vol. 11, No. 3. Iowa City: the University, 1935. 128 p.
416. MITCHELL, HAROLD H. "Physical Measurement and Nutritional Status." *Journal of Pediatrics* 6: 316-21; March, 1935.
417. MITCHELL, HAROLD H. "A Study of Factors Associated with the Growth and Nutrition of Porto Rican Children." *Human Biology* 4: 469-508; December, 1932.
418. MOHR, GEORGE J., and BARTELME, PHYLLIS F. "Developmental Studies of Prematurely Born Children." *The Physical and Mental Growth of Prematurely Born Children.* (By J. H. Hess and others.) Chicago: University of Chicago Press, 1934. p. 55-120.
419. PALMER, CARROLL E. "Age Changes in the Physical Resemblance of Siblings." *Child Development* 5: 351-60; December, 1934.

420. PALMER, CARROLL E., and REED, LOWELL J. "Anthropometric Studies of Individual Growth. I. Age, Height, and Rate of Growth in Height, Elementary School Children." *Human Biology* 7: 319-34; September, 1935.
421. PALMER, CARROLL E. "Further Studies on Growth and the Economic Depression; a Comparison of Weight and Weight Increments of Elementary School Children in 1921-27 and in 1933-34." *U. S. Public Health Reports* 49: 1453-69; December 7, 1934.
422. PALMER, CARROLL E. "Growth and the Economic Depression: A Study of the Weight of Elementary School Children in 1921-27 and in 1933." *U. S. Public Health Reports* 48: 1277-92; October 20, 1933.
423. PALMER, CARROLL E. "Height and Weight of Children of the Depression Poor." *U. S. Public Health Reports* 50: 1106-13; August 16, 1935.
424. PALMER, CARROLL E. "Note on the Statistical Significance of the Difference of Two Series of Comparable Means." *Human Biology* 6: 402-5; May, 1934.
425. PALMER, CARROLL E. "The Relationship Between Attained Height and Growth in Height of Elementary School Children." *Anatomical Record*, Vol. 58, No. 4 (Supplement), March, 1934. 32 p.
426. PALMER, CARROLL E. "Seasonal Variation of Average Growth in Weight of Elementary School Children." *U. S. Public Health Reports* 48: 211-33; March 3, 1933.
427. PALMER, CARROLL E., and GAFAFER, WILLIAM M. "Selective Mortality in Childhood." *American Journal of Hygiene* 21: 608-12; May, 1935.
428. PALMER, CARROLL E. "Temporal Cycles of Growth." *School Physicians' Bulletin* 3: 12-14; September, 1933.
429. PALMER, CARROLL E., and COLLINS, SELWYN D. "Variation in Physique and Growth of Children in Different Geographic Regions of the United States." *U. S. Public Health Reports* 50: 335-47; March 8, 1935.
430. PALMER, CARROLL E. "Variations of Growth in Weight of Elementary School Children, 1921-28." *U. S. Public Health Reports* 48: 993-1005; August 18, 1933.
431. PRYOR, HELEN BRENTON, and STOLZ, HERBERT R. "Determining Appropriate Weight for Body Build." *Journal of Pediatrics* 3: 608-22; October, 1933.
432. PRYOR, J. W. "Roentgenographic Investigation of the Time Element in Ossification." *American Journal of Roentgenology and Radium Therapy* 29: 798-804; June, 1933.
433. ROSAHN, PAUL D. "A Graphic Method for Representing the Significance of the Difference Between Means." *Human Biology* 7: 267-71; June, 1935.
434. ROSENOW, CURTI. "Weight and Skeletal Build." *American Journal of Orthopsychiatry* 3: 55-64; January, 1933. 4: 258-61; April, 1934.
435. SANDERS, BARKEV S. *Environment and Growth.* Baltimore: Warwick and York, 1934. 375 p.
436. SHUTTLEWORTH, FRANK K. "The Reliability of Increments." *Journal of Educational Psychology* 26: 312-13; April, 1935.
437. SHUTTLEWORTH, FRANK K. "Standards of Development in Terms of Increments." *Child Development* 5: 89-91; March, 1934.
438. SHUTTLEWORTH, FRANK K. "Van Dyke's Data on the Relation of Menstruation to the Growth of Girls." *School Review* 42: 210-12; March, 1934.
439. STIX, REGINE K., and KISER, CLYDE V. "Relation of 'Correct' Weight and Blood Findings to Physicians' Estimates of Nutrition of School Children." *Journal of Pediatrics* 5: 763-70; December, 1934.
440. STUART, HAROLD C. "Standards of Physical Development for Reference in Clinical Appraisement: Suggestions for Their Presentation and Use." *Journal of Pediatrics* 5: 194-209; August, 1934.
441. STUNZ, DOROTHY I. "X-Ray Technic for Children." *Radiology* 22: 694-700; June, 1934.
442. SUSKI, P. M. "The Body Build of American-Born Japanese Children." *Biometrika* 25: 323-52; December, 1933.
443. THOMPSON, HELEN. "A Third Aspect of Growth." *Human Biology* 6: 405-7; May, 1934.
444. TODD, T. WINGATE. "The Developmental Health Examination." *Journal of Pediatrics* 3: 415-23; September, 1933.
445. TODD, T. WINGATE. "The Growing-Up Pattern." *Progressive Education* 11: 445-50; December, 1934.

446. Todd, T. Wingate. "Human Bodies and Human Beings." *Sigma Xi Quarterly* 21: 123-40; December, 1933.
447. Todd, T. Wingate. "The Progress of Physical Maturity and Mental Expansion in Childhood." *Proceedings of the Association for Research in Nervous and Mental Disease* 14: 56-65; December, 1933.
448. Wallis, Wilson D. "Anatomic Lag." *Human Biology* 6: 523-42; September, 1934.
449. Weisman, S. A. "Contour of the Chest in Children." *American Journal for Diseases of Children* 48: 502-6; September, 1934. 49: 47-59; 1180-84; January and May, 1935.
450. Wetzel, Norman C. "On the Motion of Growth." *Proceedings of the Society for Experimental Biology and Medicine* 30: 224-32, 1044-50; November, 1932 and May, 1933.
451. Wetzel, Norman C. "On the Motion of Growth." *Journal of Pediatrics* 3: 252-64; July, 1933. 4: 465-93; April, 1934.
452. Wheeler, Lester R. "A Comparative Study of the Physical Status of East Tennessee Mountain Children." *Human Biology* 5: 706-21; December, 1933.
453. Whitacre, Jesse. "Standing Heights of School Children as Determined by Two Techniques." *American Journal of Physical Anthropology* 18: 457-65; January-March, 1934.
454. White House Conference on Child Health and Protection. *Growth and Development of the Child: Part II. Anatomy and Physiology.* New York: Century Co., 1933. 629 p.
455. White House Conference on Child Health and Protection. *Growth and Development of the Child: Part IV. Appraisement of the Child.* New York: Century Co., 1932. "Physical Status," p. 231-336.

Chapter V. Mental Development in Adolescence

(See also Nos. 106, 120, 157, 173, 189, 212, 314, 318)

456. Baldwin, Onias Barber. "The Maturation of the College Student as Evidenced by Retests with the National Council Tests." *University of Kansas Studies in Psychology, No. 1.* Psychological Monographs, Vol. 44, No. 1. Princeton, N. J.: Psychological Review Co., 1933. p. 233-62.
457. Bologa, L. *Lectura Tineretului.* Cluj, Rumania: Inst. de Psihol., University Cluj, 1933. 116 p.
458. Brooks, Fowler D. "Mental and Physical Development in Adolescence." *Review of Educational Research* 3: 108-29, 168-74; April, 1933.
459. Brooks, Fowler D. *The Psychology of Adolescence.* Boston: Houghton Mifflin Co., 1929. 652 p.
460. Carroll, Herbert A. "Influence of the Sex Factor upon Appreciation of Literature." *School and Society* 37: 468-72; April 8, 1933.
461. Conklin, Edmund S. *Principles of Adolescent Psychology.* New York: Henry Holt and Co., 1935. 437 p.
462. Cser, J. "A Figyelem Kiserleti Vizsgalata a 10-14 Eves Korban" (Experimental Research on Attention in the Age Range 10-14 Years). *Gyermek* 25: 5-7, 99-115, 171-200; 1933. (Budapest.)
463. Dearborn, Walter Fenno. *Intelligence Tests; Their Significance for School and Society.* Boston: Houghton Mifflin Co., 1928. 336 p. (Especially Chapter 9.)
464. Dietze, Alfred G. "Some Sex Differences in Factual Memory." *American Journal of Psychology* 44: 319-21; April, 1932.
465. Eells, Walter Crosby, and Fox, Clement S. "Sex Differences in Mathematical Achievement of Junior College Students." *Journal of Educational Psychology* 23: 381-86; May, 1932.
466. Ezekiel, Mordecai. *Methods of Correlation Analysis.* New York: J. Wiley and Sons, 1930. 427 p.
467. Foran, T. G., and O'Hara, Colombiere. "Sex Differences in Achievement in High-School Geometry." *School Review* 43: 357-62; May, 1935.

468. FREEMAN, FRANK N. "Intellectual Growth of Children Based on Repeated Tests." *Abstracts of Papers at the Cleveland Meeting, 1934.* Yearbook No. 22. National Society of College Teachers of Education. Chicago: University of Chicago Press, 1934. p. 19-20.
469. FREEMAN, FRANK N. *Mental Tests; Their History, Principles and Applications.* Boston: Houghton Mifflin Co., 1926. 503 p. (Especially Chapter 13.)
470. GARRETT, HENRY E.; BRYAN, ALICE I.; and PERL, RUTH E. *The Age Factor in Mental Organization.* Archives of Psychology, No. 176. New York: Columbia University, 1935. 31 p.
471. GARRISON, KARL C. *The Psychology of Adolescence.* New York: Prentice-Hall, Inc., 1934. 377 p.
472. GARRISON, S. C. "Retests on Adults at an Interval of Ten Years." *School and Society* 32: 326-28; September 6, 1930.
473. GOODMAN, HELEN C. "IQ in Relation to Graduation after Failure." *Journal of Educational Psychology* 26: 195-205; March, 1935.
474. HAWTHORNE, J. W. "The Effect of Improvement in Reading Ability on Intelligence Test Scores." *Journal of Educational Psychology* 26: 41-51; January, 1935.
475. HOLLINGWORTH, LETA S. "The Adolescent Child." *A Handbook of Child Psychology.* (Edited by Carl Murchison.) 2d ed. rev. Worcester, Mass.: Clark University Press, 1933. Chapter 23, p. 882-908.
476. HURD, A. W. "Sex Differences in Achievement in Physical Science." *Journal of Educational Psychology* 25: 70; January, 1934.
477. JUNGE, K. R. *Beiträge zur Entwicklung der Auffassungsfähigkeit für komplexe Sachverhalte bei Kindern des 10.-14. Lebensjahres.* Tübingen: Tüb. Studentenwerk, 1934. 50 p.
478. KEEN, ANGELINE M. "Growth Curves and IQ's, as Determined by Testing Large Families." *School and Society* 32: 737-42; November 29, 1930.
479. KELLEY, TRUMAN L. *Statistical Method.* New York: Macmillan Co., 1923. 390 p.
480. LINCOLN, EDWARD A. "The Stanford-Binet I.Q. Changes of Superior Children." *School and Society* 41: 519-20; April 13, 1935.
481. LORGE, IRVING. "Retests after Ten Years." *Journal of Educational Psychology* 25: 136-41; February, 1934.
482. MCCONNELL, T. R. "Change in Scores on the Psychological Examination of the American Council on Education from Freshman to Senior Year." *Journal of Educational Psychology* 25: 66-69; January, 1934.
483. MASTERS, H. V., and UPSHALL, C. C. "Study of the Gains Made by Normal-School Students in Intelligence Test Scores." *Journal of Educational Research* 27: 446-52; February, 1934.
484. MILES, CATHARINE COX, and MILES, WALTER R. "The Correlation of Intelligence Scores and Chronological Age from Early to Late Maturity." *American Journal of Psychology* 44: 44-78; January, 1932.
485. MOORE, MARGARET WHITESIDE. *A Study of Young High School Graduates.* Contributions to Education, No. 583. New York: Teachers College, Columbia University, 1933. 78 p.
486. RAPPAPORT, MITCHELL E. "The Selection of the Intelligence Quotient Divisor for Clinical Cases Between Fourteen and Nineteen Years of Age." *Journal of Educational Psychology* 25: 101-14; February, 1934.
487. ROBERTS, ROY L. "The Maturation of College Students as Evidenced by the Eight Semester Average Grade Points." *University of Kansas Studies in Psychology,* No. 1. Psychological Monographs, Vol. 44, No. 1. Princeton, N. J.: Psychological Review Co., 1933. p. 263-81.
488. SCHMIDT, F. "Realgymnaziumi Tanulok Kopleirasai. (Descriptions of Pictures with Pupils of Real-Gymnasia.)" *Gyermek* 25: 158-71; 1933. (Budapest.)
489. SORENSON, HERBERT. "Mental Ability over a Wide Range of Adult Ages." *Journal of Applied Psychology* 17: 729-41; December, 1933.
490. SPALDING, A. W., and COMSTOCK, BELLE J. WOOD. *The Days of Youth; a Study of the Period of Adolescence.* Mountain View, Calif.: Pacific Press Publishing Association, 1932. 320 p.
491. TEAGARDEN, FLORENCE M. *A Study of the Upper Limits of the Development of Intelligence.* Contributions to Education, No. 156. New York: Teachers College, Columbia University, 1924. 112 p.

492. THORNDIKE, EDWARD L., and OTHERS. *Adult Learning.* New York: Macmillan Co., 1928. 335 p.
493. THORNDIKE, EDWARD L., and OTHERS. *The Measurement of Intelligence.* New York: Teachers College, Columbia University, 1926. 616 p.
494. THURSTONE, L. L. "A Method of Scaling Psychological and Educational Tests." *Journal of Educational Psychology* 16: 433-451; October, 1925.
495. WELLMAN, BETH. "Sex Differences." *A Handbook of Child Psychology.* (Edited by Carl Murchison.) 2d ed. rev. Worcester, Mass.: Clark University Press, 1933. Chapter 15, p. 626-49.
496. WELLS, RUTH E. "A Study of Tastes in Humorous Literature among Pupils of Junior and Senior High Schools." *Journal of Educational Research* 28: 81-91; October, 1934.
497. WITTY, PAUL A., and LEHMAN, HARVEY C. "The Reading and the Reading Interests of Gifted Children." *Pedagogical Seminary and Journal of Genetic Psychology* 45: 466-81; December, 1934.
498. WYATT, H. G. "Free Word Association and Sex Differences." *American Journal of Psychology* 44: 454-72; July, 1932.

Chapter VI. Relationships in Physical and Mental Development

(See also Nos. 24, 38, 40, 98, 143, 188, 208, 219, 225, 255, 271, 280, 335, 366, 383, 411, 426, 435, 436)

499. ALLEN, C. N. "Recent Research in Sex Differences." *Psychological Bulletin* 32: 343-54; May, 1935.
500. ALLEN, C. N. "Recent Studies in Sex Differences." *Psychological Bulletin* 27: 394-407; May, 1930.
501. ALLEN, C. N. "Studies in Sex Differences." *Psychological Bulletin* 24: 294-304; May, 1927.
502. ANDERSON, JOHN E., and COHEN, J. T. "Dentition and Mental Development." *Mouth Health Quarterly* 1: 13-17; January, 1932.
503. ANDERSON, JOHN E., and SMITH, ARTHUR H. "The Effect of Quantitative and Qualitative Stunting upon Maze Learning in the White Rat." *Journal of Comparative Psychology* 6: 337-59; October, 1926.
504. ANDERSON, JOHN E., and SMITH, ARTHUR H. "Relation of Performance to Age and Nutritive Condition in the White Rat." *Journal of Comparative Psychology* 13: 409-46; June, 1932.
505. ANGELL, EDWARD B. "Effect of Removal of Adenoids and Tonsils on Mental Development of the Child." *Archives of Neurology and Psychiatry* 13: 388-90; March, 1925.
506. BALKEN, EVA RUTH, and MAURER, SIEGFRIED. "Variations of Psychological Measurements Associated With Increased Vitamin B Complex Feeding in Young Children." *Journal of Experimental Psychology* 17: 85-92; February, 1934.
507. BALYEAT, RAY M. "The General Health and Mental Activity of Allergic Children." *American Journal of Diseases of Children* 37: 1193-1197; June, 1929.
508. BALYEAT, RAY M. "The Hereditary Factor in Allergic Diseases: With Special Reference to the General Health and Mental Activity of Allergic Patients." *American Journal of the Medical Sciences* 176: 332-45; September 1928.
509. BAYLEY, NANCY. "Some Aspects of Physical Growth in Young Children." *Psychological Bulletin* 32: 526-27; October, 1935.
510. BEGGS, S. T. "The Relationship of Physical Defects, the Intelligence Quotient, and the Quality of School Work." *Practitioner* 117: 392-95; December, 1926.
511. BERNHARDT, KARL S. "The Effect of Vitamin B Deficiency During Nursing on Subsequent Learning in the Rat." *Journal of Comparative Psychology* 17: 123-48; February, 1934.
512. BEST, HARRY. *Blindness and the Blind in the United States.* New York: Macmillan Co., 1934. 714 p.
513. BLONSKY, P. P. "Die faulen Schüler." *Zeitschrift für Kinderforschung* 36: 1-16; November, 1929.

514. BOOK, HANNAH M. "A Psychophysiological Analysis of Sex Differences." *Journal of Social Psychology* 3: 434-62; November, 1932.
515. BOWMAN, K. M., and GRABFELD, G. P. "Basal Metabolism in Mental Disease." *Archives of Neurology and Psychiatry* 34: 19; December, 1935.
516. BRONSTEIN, I. P., and BROWN, ANDREW W. "Hypothyroidism and Cretinism in Childhood." *American Journal of Orthopsychiatry* 4: 413-20; July, 1934.
517. BROOKS, FOWLER D. "The Organization of Mental and Physical Traits During Adolescence." *Journal of Applied Psychology* 12: 228-41; April, 1928.
518. BROOM, M. E. "Cranial Capacity and Intelligence." *School and Society* 36: 703-4; November 26, 1932.
519. BROWNE, THOS. J. "Nutrition and Scholarship." *American Physical Education Review* 33: 615-16; November, 1928.
520. BUSEMANN, ADOLF, and BAHR, GERDA. "Arbeitslösigkeit und Schulleistungen." *Zeitschrift für pädagogische Psychologie* 32: 417-21; September, 1931.
521. BUSEMANN, ADOLF, and HARDERS, G. "Die Wirkung väterlicher Erwerbslosigkeit auf die Schulleistungen der Kinder." *Zeitschrift für Kinderforschung* 40: 89-100; April, 1932.
522. CAMERON, W. JAFFREY, and PRYOR, HELEN B. *A Case Study of Children of Deviate Body Build.* Berkeley, Calif.: Institute of Child Welfare, University of California, October, 1935. (Unpublished manuscript.)
523. CAREY, THOMAS F. *A Study of the Relation Between Developmental Age and Dentition.* Master's thesis, Catholic University of America, 1932. 47 p.
524. CARTER, H. D. *Orthogonal Anthropometric Factors.* Berkeley, Calif.: Institute of Child Welfare, University of California, November, 1935. (Unpublished manuscript.)
525. CHAPIN, F. STUART. "Extra-Curricular Activities of College Students: A Study in College Leaderships." *School and Society* 23: 212-216; February 13, 1926.
526. COHEN, JOSEPH T., and ANDERSON, JOHN E. "Note on the Eruption of the Permanent Teeth in a Group of Subnormal Children, Including an Observation on the Frequency of Congenitally Missing Laterals." *Pedagogical Seminary and Journal of Genetic Psychology* 39: 279-84; June, 1931.
527. COZENS, FREDERICK W. "Status of the Problem of the Relation of Physical to Mental Ability." *American Physical Education Review* 32: 147-55; March, 1927.
528. DAVIS, ELWOOD C., and COOPER, JOHN A. "Athletic Ability and Scholarship." *Research Quarterly of the American Physical Education Association* 5: 68-78; December, 1934.
529. DOLL, EDGAR A. "Birth Lesion as a Category of Mental Deficiency." *American Journal of Orthopsychiatry* 3: 1-13; January, 1933.
530. DOLL, EDGAR A. "Mental Retardation as a Result of Birth Injury." *Pedagogical Seminary and Journal of Genetic Psychology* 42: 481-83; June, 1933.
531. DOLL, EDGAR A. "Psychological Significance of Cerebral Birth Lesions." *American Journal of Psychology* 45: 444-52; July, 1933.
532. DRAPER, JOHN WILLIAM, and JOHNSON, REDFORD K. "Personality Changes in Children and Adolescents: A Study of Their Relation to Enteric Disease." *American Journal of Surgery* 7: 568-72; October, 1929.
533. DUNBAR, HELEN F. *Emotions and Bodily Changes; a Survey of Literature on Psychosomatic Interrelationships, 1910-1933.* New York: Columbia University Press, 1935. 595 p.
534. DUNCAN, J. "Height, Weight, Growth and Diet of High-Grade Mental Defectives." *Medical Officer* 51: 65-68; February 17, 1934.
535. DUROST, WALTER N. *The Development of a Battery of Objective Group Tests of Manual Laterality, with the Results of Their Application to 1300 Children.* Genetic Psychology Monographs, Vol. 16, No. 4. Worcester, Mass.: Clark University Press, 1934. p. 223-335.
536. EMERSON, HAVEN. "Seasonal Variation in Growth of School Children: Based on Records of Eight Hundred and Thirty-Three Children in Honolulu, New York and Toronto." *Journal of the American Medical Association* 89: 1326-30; October 15, 1927.
537. EMERSON, WM. R. P. "Nutrition as a Factor in Child Development: Based on Studies of Children Covering the Entire Period of Growth." *Archives of Pediatrics* 51: 343-62; June, 1934.

538. FETTERMAN, JOSEPH, and BARNES, MARGARET R. "Serial Studies of the Intelligence of Patients with Epilepsy." *Archives of Neurology and Psychiatry* 32: 797-801; October, 1934.
539. FITT, ARTHUR B., and O'HALLORAN, K. H. "The Relation between Handedness and Some Physical and Mental Factors." *Journal of Educational Psychology* 25: 286-96; April, 1934.
540. FRANK, MARGARET. "The Effect of a Rickets-Producing Diet on the Learning Ability of White Rats." *Journal of Comparative Psychology* 13: 87-105; February, 1932.
541. FREEMAN, FRANK N. "The Concept of Intelligence as a Fixed or Unmodifiable Feature of the Personality." *Fourth Conference on Research in Child Development, 1933*. Washington, D. C.: National Research Council, 1933. Appendix H, 30 p. (Mimeographed.)
542. FREEMAN, FRANK S. "Elusive Factors Tending To Reduce Correlations between Intelligence Test Ranks and College Grades." *School and Society* 29: 784-86; June 15, 1929.
543. FREEMAN, G. L., and HOVLAND, C. IVER. "Diurnal Variations in Performance and Related Physiological Processes." *Psychological Bulletin* 31: 777-99; December, 1934.
544. FRITZ, MARTIN F. "The Effect of Diet on Intelligence and Learning." *Psychological Bulletin* 32: 355-63; May, 1935.
545. FRITZ, MARTIN F. "Maze Performance of the White Rat in Relation to Unfavorable Salt Mixture and Vitamin B Deficiency." *Journal of Comparative Psychology* 13: 365-90; June, 1932.
546. FURFEY, PAUL HANLY. "Social and Physical Factors in Developmental Age." *Fourth Conference on Research in Child Development, 1933*. Washington, D. C.: National Research Council, 1933. Appendix E, 16 p. (Mimeographed.)
547. FÜRST, THEOBALD. "Das vermehrte Längenwachstum der heutigen Jugend und seine pädagogische Bedeutung. (The Increased Growth in Height of Present-Day Youth and Its Pedagogical Significance.)" *Zeitschrift für pädagogische Psychologie* 36: 111-19; April, 1935.
548. GEIGER, SARA. "Some Results of Endocrine Therapy in Behavior Disorders of Children; a Preliminary Report." (Abstract.) *Archives of Neurology and Psychiatry* 18: 1050; December, 1927.
549. GITTINGS, INA E. "Correlation of Mental and Physical Traits in University of Arizona Freshman Women." *American Physical Education Review* 32: 569-83; October, 1927.
550. GODDARD, HENRY H. "The Height and Weight of Feeble-Minded Children in American Institutions." *Journal of Nervous and Mental Disease* 39: 217-35; April, 1912.
551. GOODENOUGH, FLORENCE L. "The Consistency of Sex Differences in Mental Traits at Various Ages." *Psychological Review* 34: 440-62; November, 1927.
552. GORDON, MURRAY B. "Childhood Myxedema or So-Called Sporadic Cretinism in North America." *Endocrinology* 6: 235-54; March, 1922.
553. GRAPER, FLORENCE M., and PARK, EDNA W. "The Effect of Improved Feeding on the Physical and Mental Development of Under-nourished and Backward Children." *Journal of Home Economics* 15: 627-32; November, 1923.
554. HARRIS, DANIEL. *The Relation to College Grades of Some Factors Other than Intelligence.* Archives of Psychology, No. 131. New York: Columbia University, 1931. 55 p.
555. HEATON, KENNETH L. "Physical Development of Children of High and Low Mental Ability Groups." *American Physical Education Review* 30: 127-30; March, 1925.
556. HERREN, R. YORKE. "The Effect of High and Low Female Sex Hormone Concentration on the Two-Point Threshold of Pain and Touch and Upon Tactile Sensitivity." *Journal of Experimental Psychology* 16: 324-37; April, 1933.
557. HOLZHAUER, H. "Die Umwelt der Kinder." *Hessiche Schulzeitung* 76: No. 51; 1932.
558. HONZIK, M. P. *Factors Related to Changes in Mental Test Performance During the Preschool Period.* Berkeley, Calif.: Institute of Child Welfare, University of California, October, 1935. (Unpublished manuscript.)
559. JELLIFFE, SMITH ELY, and WHITE, W. A. *Diseases of the Nervous System.* 5th ed. Philadelphia: Lea and Febiger, 1929. 1174 p.

560. JONES, HAROLD E. "Relationships in Physical and Mental Development." *Review of Educational Research* 3: 150-62; 177-81; April, 1933.
561. JONES, M. C., and DAVIS, H. *A Study of the Behavior Traits of Overweight and Average Girls.* Berkeley, Calif.: Institute of Child Welfare, University of California, September, 1935. (Unpublished manuscript.)
562. KEAL, HARRY M. "Mental Ratings, Scholarship and Health." *School and Society* 28: 277-80; September 1, 1928.
563. KIMBALL, O. P., and MARINUS, J. CARLTON. "The Relation of Endemic Goiter to Mental Deficiency." *Annuals of Internal Medicine* 4: 569-77; December, 1930.
564. KISS, PAUL V., and RAJKA, TIBOR. "Intelligenzprüfungen an Kindern mit angeborener Syphilis. (Intelligence Tests Upon Children With Inherited Syphilis.)" *Archiv für Kinderheilkunde* 102: 25-36; 1934.
565. KLINEBERG, OTTO; ASCH, S. E.; and BLOCK, HELEN. *An Experimental Study of Constitutional Types.* Genetic Psychology Monographs, Vol. 16, No. 3. Worcester, Mass.: Clark University Press, 1934. p. 140-221.
566. KOGA, Y., and MORANT, G. M. "On the Degree of Association between Reaction Times in the Case of Different Senses." *Biometrika* 15: 346-72; December, 1923.
567. KONIKOW, M. J. "A Case of Retarded Mentality in a Child, Treated by Organotherapy." *Endocrinology* 6: 218-20; March, 1922.
568. LANDAU, E. "Morphology and Character." *Character and Personality* 2: 238-41; March, 1933.
569. LANDIS, M. H.; BURTT, H. E.; and NICHOLS, J. H. "The Relation Between Physical Efficiency and Intelligence." *American Physical Education Review* 28: 220-21; May, 1923.
570. LANGE, KARLE. "Über Beziehungen zwischen Jahreszeiten und Wachstum des Kleinkindes. (The Relation Between Growth and Season in Children.)" *Archiv für Kinderheilkunde* 89: 259-72; February 28, 1930.
571. LANGE, WILHELM. "Erfahrungen und Ergebnisse auf Grund einer zehnjährigen Beobachtung in der Enzephalitiker-Abteilung Chemnitz-Altendorf." *Zeitschrift für Kinderforschung* 43: 263-99; November, 1934.
572. LAZARFELD, P. "Körperliche und geistige Entwicklung. (Physical and Mental Development.)" *Die Quelle* 79: 803-9; 1929.
573. LEE, MARY V. "The Children's Orthopedic Hospital: A Survey of the Intelligence of Crippled Children." *Journal of Educational Research* 23: 164-66; February, 1931.
574. LEVY, JOHN. "A Quantitative Study of the Relationship Between Basal Metabolic Rate and Children's Behavior Problems." *American Journal of Orthopsychiatry* 1: 298-310; April, 1931.
575. LIEFMANN, ELSE. "Körpermasse und Leistungsmessungen bei Kindern: Ein neues Verfahren der Berechnung." *Zeitschrift für Kinderheilkunde* 54: 230-35; 1933.
576. LIEFMANN, ELSE. "Über geistige und körperliche Leistungsfähigkeit von Repententen in der Volksschule." *Zeitschrift für pädagogische Psychologie* 34: 66-77; February, 1933.
577. MCCLOY, C. H. "The Measurement of General Motor Capacity and General Motor Ability." *Research Quarterly of the American Physical Education Association* 5 (Supplement.) : 46-61; March, 1934.
578. MCCLURE, W. E., and GOLDBERG, BRONETT. "A Clinical Study of 'Toledo's Strong Boy'." *Journal of Abnormal and Social Psychology* 27: 159-67; July-September, 1932.
579. MADDEN, RICHARD. *The School Status of the Hard of Hearing Child.* Contributions to Education, No. 499. New York: Teachers College, Columbia University, 1931. 64 p.
580. MALLER, J. B. "Vital Indices and Their Relation to Psychological and Social Factors; a Study of the 310 Health Areas of New York City with Reference to Birth Rate, Death Rate, Juvenile Delinquency, School Progress and Intelligence." *Human Biology* 5: 94-121; February, 1933.
581. MARINUS, CARLETON J., and KIMBALL, O. P. "Endocrine Dysfunctions in Retarded Children and Their Response to Treatment." *Endocrinology* 14: 309-18; September-October, 1930.
582. MAURER, SIEGFRIED, and TSAI, LOH SENG. "Vitamin B Deficiency and Learning Ability." *Journal of Comparative Psychology* 11: 51-62; October, 1930.

583. MAURER, SIEGFRIED, and TSAI, LOH SENG. "Vitamin B Deficiency in Nursing Young Rats and Learning Ability." *Science* 70: 456-58; November 8, 1929.
584. MENNINGER, WILLIAM C. "The Mental Disturbances Associated With Pituitary Disorders." *Journal of the American Medical Association* 91: 951-54; September 29, 1928.
585. MERWICK, JEROME. *A Study of Developmental Age and Social Factors.* Master's thesis, Catholic University of America, 1933. 45 p.
586. MOORE, H. K. "Is the Problem Boy a Weakling?" *Journal of Juvenile Research* 18: 79-89; April, 1934.
587. MÜLLER, ANDREAS. "Abhängigkeit der Schulleistungen von wirtschaftlichen und sozialen Einflüssen." *Archiv für die gesamte Psychologie* 83: 119-96; January, 1932.
588. NELSON, GEORGE E. "Correction of Visual Defects and Improvement in College Studies." *School and Society* 27: 107-8; January 28, 1928.
589. OHMANN, OLIVER ARTHUR. *A Study of the Causes of Scholastic Deficiencies in Engineering by the Individual Case Method.* University of Iowa Studies in Education, Vol. 3, No. 7. Iowa City: the University, 1927. 58 p.
590. OKADA, M. [A Study of Head Circumference.] *Nippon Gakko Eissei (Japanese School Hygiene)* 15, No. 3. 1927. (Seen in Abstract only.)
591. PASKIND, HARRY A. "Extramural Patients with Epilepsy; with Special Reference to the Frequent Absence of Deterioration." *Archives of Neurology and Psychiatry* 28: 370-85; August, 1932.
592. PATERSON, DONALD G. *Physique and Intellect.* New York: Century Co., 1930. 304 p.
593. PATRICK, JAMES R., and ROWLES, EMMETT. "Intercorrelations Among Metabolic Rate, Vital Capacity, Blood Pressure, Intelligence, Scholarship, Personality and Other Measures on University Women." *Journal of Applied Psychology* 17: 507-21; October, 1933.
594. PATTERSON, HAROLD A., and FONNER, DELMA. "Some Observations on the Intelligence Quotient in Epileptics." *Psychiatric Quarterly* 2: 542-48; October, 1928.
595. PAULL, HERMANN. "Körper-Konstitution und Begabung." *Archiv für Rassen- und Gesellschafts-Biologie, Einschliesslich Rassen- und Gesellschafts-Hygiene* 22: 21-36; July 15, 1929.
596. PHELPS, WINTHROP M. "Cerebral Birth Injuries: Their Orthopaedic Classification and Subsequent Treatment." *Journal of Bone and Joint Surgery* 14: 773-82; October, 1932.
597. PINTNER, RUDOLF, and FORLANO, GEORGE. "The Birth Month of Eminent Men." *Journal of Applied Psychology* 18: 178-88; April, 1934.
598. PINTNER, RUDOLF. *Intelligence Testing: Methods and Results.* New York: Henry Holt and Co., 1932. 555 p.
599. POTTER, HOWARD W. "Endocrine Therapy in Mental Deficiency." *Endocrinology* 7: 25-40; January, 1923.
600. POWERS, H. D. "Biochemistry in Relation to Intelligence." *Science* 73: 316; March 20, 1931.
601. RAGSDALE, C. E., and BRECKENFELD, IRVING J. "The Organization of Physical and Motor Traits in Junior High School Boys." *Research Quarterly of the American Physical Education Association* 5: 47-55; October, 1934.
602. RAUTH, J. EDWARD, and FURFEY, PAUL HANLY. "Developmental Age and Adolescence." *Journal of Social Psychology* 3: 469-72; November, 1932.
603. RAUTH, J. EDWARD, and FURFEY, PAUL HANLY. "The Maturational Factor in Adolescent Conduct." *Child Development* 4: 90-93; March, 1933.
604. REMMERS, H. H. *A Diagnostic and Remedial Study of Potentiality and Actually Failing Students at Purdue University.* Bulletin, Vol. 28, No. 12. Lafayette, Ind.: Purdue University, 1928. 164 p.
605. RICH, GILBERT J. "A Biochemical Approach to the Study of Personality." *Journal of Abnormal and Social Psychology* 23: 158-75; July-September, 1928.
606. RICH, GILBERT J. "Intelligence and Body Chemistry." *Science* 74: 21-22; July 3, 1931.
607. RICHARD, G. A. "Le Surmenage Scolaire et les Maladies de l'enfant et de l'adolescent. (Relation of Academic Overwork to Diseases of Childhood and Adolescence.)" *Le Bulletin Medical, Paris* 42: 1030-40; September 29, 1928.

608. ROSELL, C. "Über Kapillaruntersuchungen an Jugendlichen." *Zeitschrift für Kinderforschung* 39: 139-51; December, 1931.
609. ROSENBERG, L. CHARLES. "Malnutrition in Children: An Attempt at Standardization of a Dietary." *American Journal for Diseases of Children* 41: 303-36; February, 1931.
610. ROTHBART, H. B. "Basal Metabolism in Children of Normal and of Subnormal Intelligence: With Blood Cholesterol and Creatinine Values." *American Journal for Diseases of Children* 49: 672-88; March, 1935.
611. RUGER, HENRY A., and STOESSIGER, BRENDA. "On the Growth Curves of Certain Characters in Man (Males)." *Annals of Eugenics* 2: 76-110; April, 1927.
612. SCHIÖTZ, CARL, and SELAND, BORGNY. "Welche Bedeutung hat der Geburtsmonat für die Zukunft des Kindes. (What Significance Does the Birth Month Have for the Future of the Child?)" *Zeitschrift für Kinderheilkunde* 55: 348-56; 1933.
613. SEHAM, MAX. "Chronic Fatigue in the School Child: A Psychophysiologic Study. (Preliminary Report.)" *Boston Medical and Surgical Journal* 194: 770-77; April 29, 1926.
614. SEWARD, GEORGENE H. "The Female Sex Rhythm." *Psychological Bulletin* 31: 153-92; March, 1934.
615. SHERRILL, J. W. "Juvenile Diabetes; Growth and Stature Changes." *California and Western Medicine* 28: 788-94; June, 1928.
616. SHIRLEY, MARY, and GOODENOUGH, FLORENCE L. "A Survey of Intelligence of Deaf Children in Minnesota Schools." *American Annals of the Deaf* 77: 238-47; May, 1932.
617. SIMPSON, T. P. "Psychic Changes in Tuberculous Children." *Collected Papers, Psychiatric Clinic of the First Moscow State University* 2: 71; 1927.
618. SMITH, ANNIE J., and FIELD, ADA M. "A Study of the Effect of Nutrition on Mental Growth." *Journal of Home Economics* 18: 686-90; December, 1926.
619. SNODDY, GEORGE S., and HYDE, GEORGE E. *Mental Survey of Utah Schools and Adaptation of the Army Beta Tests.* Salt Lake City: University of Utah Press, 1921. 28 p.
620. STEDMAN, MELISSA BRANSON. "The Influence of Health upon Intelligence and School Grades of High School Pupils." *Journal of Applied Psychology* 18: 799-809; December, 1934.
621. STOKE, STUART M. *Occupational Groups and Child Development: A Study of the Mental and Physical Growth of Children in Relation to Occupational Grouping of Parents.* Harvard Monographs in Education, No. 8. Cambridge, Mass.: Harvard University Press, 1927. 92 p.
622. STONE, CALVIN P., and BARKER, ROGER G. "On the Relationships Between Menarcheal Age and Certain Aspects of Personality, Intelligence and Physique in College Women." *Pedagogical Seminary and Journal of Genetic Psychology* 45: 121-35; September, 1934.
623. SULLIVAN, ELLEN B., and GAHAGAN, LAWRENCE. *On Intelligence of Epileptic Children.* Genetic Psychology Monographs, Vol. 17, No. 5. Worcester, Mass.: Clark University Press, 1935. p. 309-76.
624. T'ANG, Y.; CH'IN, K.; and TSANG, Y. H. "The Effect of a Vegetarian Diet on the Learning Ability of Albino Rats." *Contribution of the National Research Institute of Psychology, Academy of Sinica* 1: 27-71; 1932.
625. TROILI, C. "Contributo Alla Psicopatologia Degli Alunni 'Gracili' Delle Scuole All' Aperto. (Contribution to the Psychopathology of Delicate Children in the Open-Air School.)" *Rivista di Psicologia* 29: 33-40; March, 1933.
626. VUORI, A. K. "Die Vererbung der Blutgruppen und deren Korrelation zu anderen konstitutionellen Eigenschaften. (Hereditary Transfer of Blood Group, and Its Relation to Other Constitutional Qualities.)" *Acta Societatis Medicorum Fennicae Duodecim* 12 (Fascicle 1): 1-137; 1929.
627. WALDMAN, J. L.; WADE, F. A.; and ARETZ, C. W. *Hearing and the School Children; Hearing, School Progress and Achievement of Public School Children.* Washington, D. C.: Volta Bureau, 1931. 222 p.
628. WINKLER, HERBERT. *Psychische Entwicklung und Krüppeltum.* Leipzig: L. Voss, 1931. 122 p.

629. WITTY, PAUL A., and SMITH, MURIEL B. "The Mental Status of 1480 Crippled Children." *Educational Trends* 1: 21-24; January, 1932.
630. WOEHLERT, HEINRICH. *Vergleichende Untersuchung schultüchtiger und schuluntüchtiger Volksschulkinder.* Berlin: Günther, 1934. 94 p.
631. ZALDUONDO, CELESTINA. *A Study of the Relation Between Developmental Age and Some Physical Measurements.* Master's thesis, Catholic University of America, 1930. 33 p.

REVIEW OF EDUCATIONAL RESEARCH

Official Publication of the American Educational Research Association, a department of the National Education Association.

The contents of the REVIEW are listed in the EDUCATION INDEX

| Volume VI | April, 1936 | Number 2 |

PUPIL PERSONNEL, GUIDANCE, AND COUNSELING
(Literature reviewed to October 1, 1935)

Prepared by the Committee on Pupil Personnel, Guidance, and Counseling: Fred C. Ayer, Harold H. Bixler, A. J. Brumbaugh, Ruth Strang, and Arch O. Heck, *Chairman;* with the cooperation of Leo J. Blaine, D. H. Eikenberry, Leston L. Love, Clifford Maddox, and Felix H. Ullrich.

TABLE OF CONTENTS

Chapter	Page
Introduction	155
I. School Attendance	157
ARCH O. HECK, *Ohio State University, Columbus, Ohio,* and LEO J. BLAINE.	
II. School Progress	164
FRED C. AYER, *University of Texas, Austin, Texas,* and FELIX H. ULLRICH.	
III. School Marks	169
HAROLD H. BIXLER, *Board of Education, Atlanta, Georgia.*	
IV. Recording and Reporting	174
HAROLD H. BIXLER, *Board of Education, Atlanta, Georgia.*	
V. Characteristics of Pupil Population	177
A. Elementary Education	177
RUTH STRANG, *Teachers College, Columbia University, New York, New York.*	
B. Secondary Education	185
D. H. EIKENBERRY, *Ohio State University, Columbus, Ohio.*	
C. Higher Education	188
A. J. BRUMBAUGH, *University of Chicago, Chicago, Illinois.*	
VI. Guidance and Counseling	194
A. Elementary Education	194
RUTH STRANG, *Teachers College, Columbia University, New York, New York.*	
B. Secondary Education	199
LESTON L. LOVE, *Ohio State University, Columbus, Ohio.*	
C. Higher Education	202
A. J. BRUMBAUGH, *University of Chicago, Chicago, Illinois.*	

Chapter	Page
VII. Extra-Curriculum Activities	207
A. Elementary Education	207

      RUTH STRANG, *Teachers College, Columbia University, New York, New York.*

   B. Secondary Education 208

      D. H. EIKENBERRY, *Ohio State University, Columbus, Ohio.*

   C. Higher Education 212

      A. J. BRUMBAUGH, *University of Chicago, Chicago, Illinois,* and CLIFFORD MADDOX.

VIII. Educational Adjustment 218

   A. Elementary Education 218

      RUTH STRANG, *Teachers College, Columbia University, New York, New York.*

   B. Secondary Education 219

      D. H. EIKENBERRY, *Ohio State University, Columbus, Ohio.*

   C. Higher Education 222

      A. J. BRUMBAUGH, *University of Chicago, Chicago, Illinois.*

IX. Special Schools and Classes 226

      ARCH O. HECK, *Ohio State University, Columbus, Ohio.*

X. Child Labor 235

      MIRIAM KEELER, *National Child Labor Committee, New York, New York.*

   Bibliography 243

Erratum

Owing to an unfortunate oversight, the name of Richard Wilkinson as co-author of the chapter entitled "Recent Developments in the Written Essay Examination" was omitted from the manuscript of the *Review of Educational Research,* Volume V, Number 5, December, 1935.—W. J. OSBURN.

Copyright, 1936
By National Education Association
Washington, D. C.

All Rights Reserved

INTRODUCTION

ATTENTION IS CALLED to one change in organization. The previous *Review of Educational Research*[1] on pupil personnel, guidance, and counseling used the topical method throughout; this issue uses essentially the same topics, but in four instances the reviewers dealt with them upon the basis of school organization. One reviewer was assigned all four topics as applied to elementary education; another was responsible for these topics at the secondary-school level; and a third dealt with the same areas for higher education. These topics were (a) characteristics of pupil population, (b) guidance and counseling, (c) extra-curriculum activities, and (d) educational adjustments. The remaining topics were treated as units covering the entire school life of the pupil.

The review covers essentially the period from October 1, 1932, to October 1, 1935. Chapter X dealing with child labor is the only chapter which departs radically from this rule. The previous issue of the *Review* omitted this topic. In order to bring the research in this area up to date many references previous to October 1, 1932, have been included. The remaining chapters depart from this general regulation only when important researches have been discovered which were omitted in the previous number.

As one reads the researches in the field of pupil personnel, one is impressed with the increased attention which is being given to the pupil. The traditional topics are treated, but they are being treated in the light of their effect upon children; they are means whereby the child is aided in self-development. Attendance service is being liberated from the hand of the police and the truant officer. Researches show that we are still faced with a big problem of enrolling and of securing regularity of attendance of all children who should attend school. It is not perfect attendance, however, that we now strive for; we strive to discover why youths do not attend; we try to understand the child. Forced attendance without such understanding and consequent adjustment may be even worse than useless.

Such a program assumes a progressive school staff (superintendents, principals, and teachers) who can forget the curriculum and think in terms of the needs of the youths they are guiding. It assumes a group of pupil personnel workers who can help the regular staff to understand better the needs of the pupils whom they would serve; these workers include field workers (attendance workers and visiting teachers), counselors, psychologists, psychiatrists, school nurses, and school physicians.

During the past few years the importance of these specialized pupil personnel services has been increasingly recognized. Cincinnati has placed these services in one bureau under the supervision of a trained worker. Minneapolis has appointed an assistant superintendent of schools in charge of pupil personnel services. Salt Lake City has a newly established depart-

---

[1] Heck, Arch O., chairman. "Pupil Personnel, Guidance, and Counseling." *Review of Educational Research* 3: 183-278; June, 1933.

ment of pupil personnel which includes all the specialized services enumerated above. Clearly the child-centered school is on the way. These new departments of pupil personnel may be the means of leavening the whole school organization.

Such trends point clearly to needed research. What records should be kept? How should they be kept? What types of data are worthwhile? How effectively can the teacher utilize these records? How effective is the field worker in helping problem children make satisfactory adjustments? What effect does the counselor have upon those youths being counseled? What evidences are there that the unification of pupil personnel services promotes child study? Numerous other problems have been suggested by the reviewers in their respective chapters.

ARCH O. HECK, *Chairman,*
Committee on Pupil Personnel, Guidance, and Counseling.

CHAPTER I
School Attendance

SIGNIFICANT RESEARCH dealing with school attendance is scarce. This may be due to the idea that problems within this field are unimportant; it may be due to an uncritical acceptance of the notion that problems of school attendance are already largely solved. Certainly the action of the various states with respect to increasing compulsory school attendance legislation during the past two decades, as well as the startling increases in enrolment in secondary schools, would indicate that society considers the problem an important one; possibly these very facts have tended to develop within us a complacency toward problems within the field which has been detrimental to research. At the close of this chapter a brief analysis will be made of certain problems which face school attendance workers.

History

The previous *Review of Educational Research* dealing with pupil personnel problems (14) called attention to the need for careful research in each of the forty-eight states relative to the development of school attendance legislation. We need to know more about the agencies responsible for the development of such legislation. Stamy (32) interestingly contrasted the development of school attendance legislation for North Carolina and Pennsylvania; he began with the first efforts to provide schooling of any type and traced these efforts down to the present. He recognized the belated beginnings in North Carolina and related these to the delayed arrival in the state of a type of settler similar to Pennsylvania's early settlers. Meadows (24) drew a picture of these beginnings in Alabama; he showed that there developed at an early date a system of education which conformed to the educational ideals of Alabama's early settlers; compulsory school attendance legislation did not arrive until 1915, although it was recommended by the state superintendent of schools in 1900. A realistic picture of the conditions of education in the state prior to 1878 is given. His sources are, however, largely secondary. Tarpley (36) dealt very briefly with the development of school attendance legislation in England, France, Germany, Italy, Ireland, Japan, the Netherlands, Russia, Scotland, South America, Switzerland, and the United States. It is hoped that the next three years will see more work accomplished in this field.

Legislation

Probably the best analysis of the school attendance legislation for the forty-eight states was that made by Deffenbaugh and Keesecker (8). The laws of all states were examined and data concerning their compulsory school attendance ages presented. During the past three years no additional states have adopted the eighteen-year limit for compulsory school attendance; several, however, with low limits previously have increased these limits by one or more years. Five states require attendance until eighteen years of age. Other data reported by Deffenbaugh and Keesecker related to the number of years youths must attend school, the length of the compulsory school year, the possible exemptions from school attendance, and various provisions for the enforcement of such legislation.

Allen (1) not only brought up to date certain school attendance legislation but related it to the percent of the population affected by such regulations. The five states, for example, which require attendance until eighteen years of age represent 8.1 percent of the whole population of the United States. Thirty-two states require attendance until sixteen years; they have 73.4 percent of the entire population. The six states requiring a seventeen-year limit have only 3.8 percent of the whole population. On the other hand, sixteen states or 29.8 percent of the population do not require children to enter school until eight years of age; only two states or 5.6 percent expect children to enter at six years of age. Reed (29) studied the legislation of the states as of 1910 and 1924 for the purpose of showing the shifts in legal requirements. She concluded that legislation is a factor in the control of elimination. The increases in legislative requirements during this fourteen-year period are quite marked.

Esser (11) made an analysis of present compulsory attendance laws for the forty-eight states and the District of Columbia. He found twenty different provisions such as ages, length of year, exemptions, and the like; he then compared the percent of attendance of each state with the number of these provisions found on its statutes. States with the most complete legislation had the best attendance.

Enrolment

Research dealing with enrolment in the public schools points to two most interesting developments. First, we find that high-school enrolments are continuing to increase very rapidly. This tendency was noted in the previous *Review* (14); it has not only continued but seems to be even more pronounced than three years ago. The United States Office of Education (33) presented data for the two-year period beginning in 1931-32 and ending in 1933-34; the change in total enrolment in the full-time day schools of forty-one states was an increase of 0.3 of a percent. The percent of increase jumped rapidly for each successive high-school grade; the increase was 1.5 percent for the ninth, 8.7 percent for the tenth, 11.3 percent for the eleventh, 12.5 percent for the twelfth, and 70.4 percent for postgraduates. Deffenbaugh and Keesecker (8) showed that 88.8 percent of those fourteen and fifteen years old are enrolled as well as 57.3 percent of these who are sixteen and seventeen years old. They also pointed out that, despite great increases in high-school enrolment, most of the non-enrolment was at the secondary-school level; of the 29,066,072 youths six to seventeen years of age in the United States, according to the 1930 census, 14.3 percent or 4,173,951 were not enrolled; 60.3 percent of these were of high-school age, fourteen to seventeen years inclusive; the remaining 39.7 percent belong to the eight age groups six to thirteen inclusive.

An editorial in the *School Review* (25) gave data on enrolments; it showed that in 1929-30, 51.5 percent of the total population fifteen to eighteen years of age were enrolled in high schools; by 1934-35 it was estimated that this percent had increased to 70.49; when youths of high-school age who are enrolled in special classes and in elementary schools are counted, it was estimated that 75 to 80 percent of those of high-school age attend school. With such complete popularization of the high school, it concluded that the old issue "shall high-school instruction be provided at public expense" has finally been laid to rest.

Kefauver and Rusk (21) studied high-school popularization. Data from the United States Bureau of the Census were used. They determined the percent of the sixteen- and seventeen-year-olds enrolled in school in 1910, 1920, and 1930. Great increases are shown. The states vary greatly; the South and East have the smallest percent figures; the greatest is in the West; the North Central states are between these extremes. Rhode Island is lowest with 40.4 percent, Ohio has 67.7 percent, and California has 82.1 percent enrolled. Trenham (37), in his study of California, emphasized the popularization of high-school work in still another way. Over a thirty-two-year period the state's population increased 297 percent; elementary-school enrolment increased 226 percent; kindergarten enrolment 1,563 percent; and high-school enrolment 3,183 percent. He also expressed high-school enrolment figures in terms of the whole population.

The second big development in public school enrolments is their tendency to decrease or remain stationary at the elementary-school level. Phillips (28) showed that the birth rate for the nation is decreasing. In 1915 it stood at 25.1 per thousand; in 1929 it stood at 19.0 per thousand. Upon this basis he estimated that the first-grade enrolment for 1935-36 would be 3,242,247 or a 25 percent drop from the number enrolled eighteen years ago. During the two years 1931-32 to 1933-34 kindergarten enrolment decreased 10.8 percent, first-grade enrolment 4.8 percent, second-grade 5.6 percent, and the entire elementary-school enrolment through the eighth grade had decreased 1.6 percent upon the basis of data from forty-one states (33). Trenham (37) found that elementary enrolments in California, expressed in terms of the ratio between enrolment and the whole population, decreased from 17.33 percent in 1900 to 13.63 percent in 1931. We are interested to know whether this trend is temporary—depending upon various social conditions—or whether it has become a fixed characteristic of American development.

School Attendance

Enrolment is important but the extent to which those enrolled actually attend is just as important a measure of the extent to which schools today meet the needs of children. Deffenbaugh and Keesecker (8) assembled data on attendance; of 25,678,015 enrolled daily, 4,413,129 are absent daily, or there is an average absentee list of 17.2 percent. Stamy (32) showed, for North Carolina, that the percent of attendance increased from 52.7 in 1900 to 80.1 in 1930 in white schools; in negro schools the percent changed from 49.6 to 71.8. During this period the average number of days on which schools were in session changed from 71 to 154. Meadows (24), reporting for Alabama, indicated that the percent of attendance has increased greatly; it was 44.1 percent for white children in 1900 and 77.3 percent in 1930; these percents for negro children were 52.0 and 75.5, respectively. Negro children who enrolled attended about as well as the white, but not nearly so many were enrolled. Trenham (37) showed for California that the percent of attendance for the kindergarten, from 1905 to 1931, only changed from 49.0 to 53.1 percent; the elementary grades during this period changed from 73.2 percent to 86.1. These studies indicated that the schools are still unable to hold from a fifth to a sixth of their pupils; it constitutes a real challenge to school people to discover the causes of this condition.

Causes of Non-Attendance

Many studies of the causes of non-attendance were based, in the past, upon the explanations made by pupils or parents as to why the child was not in school. Freeman (13) placed the responsibility of discovering the cause upon the teachers; the study was planned in advance; the teachers kept records. Six counties in North Carolina took part in the study; 11,647 pupils were enrolled and 7,257 had absences; there were 14,916 days of absence. Reed (29) reported that parents, teachers, and others as well as pupils were canvassed in order to ascertain the causes of absence. Sullenger (35) made an analysis of each non-attendance problem by interviewing persons likely to know the cause.

Other investigators such as Jones (19), Clements (6), Lippe (23), and Wilson (39) related various factors to the amount of non-attendance in order to discover what, if any, relation existed between the two. College marks (19), overageness and type of school (6), activity in athletics (23), and failure in junior high school (39) were some of the factors thus related.

In contrast to the studies reported in the previous *Review* (14), these studies tend to emphasize the significance of big social problems as causes of non-attendance rather than such specifics as illness, work, and the like. Parental neglect or home conditions constantly recur as causes. One report (8) suggested that 84.8 percent of the absences were due to parental neglect; another (32) stated that an outstanding factor was "the types of people that make up the population"; another (4) concluded "that there is a definite relation between the average number of days attended by the pupils in each grade and the type of schools"; and still another (35) stated that non-cooperation of parents or lack of a superior home was the chief cause.

We find, in addition to the above, the kind of legislation, the enforcement of attendance legislation, and the efficiency of attendance service as factors which are thought to be important in determining the amount of non-attendance. In all of the conclusions it is not ignored that illness does keep children out of school, that pupils do stay out to work, that weather is a hindrance, and that poverty is a real cause, but it is implied that these latter factors are subservient to the larger social problems and conditions enumerated above. A socially-minded community is more likely to take preventive measures with respect to contagious disease, more likely to have families which take all possible precautions to prevent illness, more likely to prefer to have its children in school instead of at work, more likely to provide a kind of school which will challenge the interest of children, and more likely to take an attitude toward school work which will cause the child to want to attend. This shift in emphasis is significant.

How To Improve School Attendance

These causes of non-attendance suggest steps which might be taken to improve attendance. Many of the investigators accordingly made such proposals, but failed to test experimentally their worth. In general they emphasized the necessity of child study through well-trained field workers capable of sympathetically and efficiently dealing with parents as well as with children. One study was discovered which attacked the problem of improving school attendance. Erestein and Perez (10) introduced interesting exercises, visited parents, communicated with parents through cordial notes, and planned Friday afternoon programs for parents. Over a period of time the percent of attendance increased from 86.5 to 93.9. We need experimentation to check the effectiveness of all procedures for improving attendance.

Lippe (23) approached the problem differently. He studied the attendance of varsity men in high school during (a) periods of athletic activity, and (b) periods of inactivity. He did the same for those active in intramurals. He then compared with these groups the attendance of those who never participated in athletics. He concluded that "intramural athletics do have a tendency to improve habits of regularity in school attendance." Similar conclusions were not justified for the varsity group. Brace (3) pointed out that "adequate school programs of health and physical education" would save the taxpayer many dollars "by preventing absences" and the resulting retardation.

Results of Non-Attendance

Chappell (4), Clements (6), Finch and Nemzek (12), Murray (27), and Van Kersen (38) presented data to discover whether there is a relation between attendance and scholarship. Chappell (4) distributed the school marks of those regular and those irregular in attendance; 45.4 percent of the irregular group are rated as just passing or lower; this percent is only 10.7 for those with regular attendance. Van Kersen (38) concluded that there is little or no such relation. Studies which show a relationship between poor attendance and certain other conditions frequently do little more than this; cause and effect relationships are difficult to discover. Perhaps only first-hand contact and personal study of given cases can uncover the real results of non-attendance.

Attendance Officers

In order better to enforce compulsory attendance legislation, officials known as "truant officers" or "compulsory school attendance officers" were and still are required by state law to be appointed. It was not uncommon to find that sheriffs, their deputies, or the police are asked to enforce the law (24).

According to Clapp and Strong (5) these attendance officers are frequently part time and then serve for as little as $25 per year to as high as $750. The average annual pay for full-time officers was $2,100. The number of children per full-time worker ranged from 2,150 to 18,575 with 7,000 as an average. London had one for every 2,500 to 3,000 children.

More lately emphasis upon enforcement has been shifting. Heck (15) found that during the depression child study has begun to displace the older idea of just forcing children to attend school regardless of the reason for not attending. The "truant officer" of an earlier day is being displaced by skilled, socially-minded field workers, by psychologists, by psychiatrists, by school nurses, and by school counselors. We need facts concerning the effectiveness or lack of effectiveness of these newer ideals respecting the enforcement of present school attendance legislation.

Plans for Improving School Attendance

Strayer and others (34) studied practices in Chicago's junior and senior high schools. In the junior high schools, teachers kept a seating plot of their groups and a permanent record of attendance in a class book; the office required excuses from parents and filed these excuses; most schools checked the signatures on the excuses; parents were required to come to school with pupils who had played truant; and cases of chronic truancy were turned over to a visiting teacher or an attendance worker. Senior high schools followed similar procedures. Reese (31) and Keller (22) studied the plans of administering attendance in various high schools; the questionnaire technic was used in both studies. Keller concluded the local districts needed the help of a centralized state department of school attendance; he would have this department responsible for the prosecution of parties guilty of violation of the law.

Heck (15) collected from 92 of the 93 cities of one hundred thousand or more population data concerning the number of persons dealing directly and indirectly with attendance problems. He found an increased emphasis being placed upon social service work, child study, and health work as a means of improving attendance. The administrative organization for performing all such services is being called a department or a bureau of pupil personnel; attendance service in such cases is just one of some four or five services which are a part of the bureau and which are designed to provide better child adjustment; thus attendance problems are handled by the bureau along with all other pupil problems.

Truancy

Baker (2) studied girls who were truant for the first time; each truant was matched with a non-truant of the same sex, school grade, home language, intellectual status, and social status. Baker concluded that the cause is more likely to be found in out-of-school experiences than in school situations.

Costs of Attendance Service

Herlihy (17) reported a study of 215 cities in the United States. The cost of attendance service in the five cities above 1,000,000 was 85¢ per pupil; in the 8 cities between a half million and a million the cost was 67¢; in the remaining 61 cities above 100,000 the cost was 43¢ per child. We need to analyze more carefully the effectiveness of various means of improving attendance against costs; this important problem is rarely studied.

Certain Conclusions

Clearly the problem of attendance (8) is not a minor one. The dependence upon "truant officers" and "police officers" as a means of securing effective school attendance is being questioned more and more widely. The necessity of discovering why a given child does not attend and then devising ways of removing those causes is gaining general acceptance among school people. The trained home visitor or field worker, the psychologist, the psychiatrist, the nurse, and the counselor are pupil personnel workers who are rapidly making the typical "truant officer" unnecessary to a modern school system; attendance problems are still with us but our method of solving them is gradually shifting from an emphasis upon force to an emphasis upon scientific study.

This very conflict in method demands research during the coming few years. We need (a) a better analysis of the extent of non-attendance, (b) more reliable data about general causes, (c) more detailed case studies showing why children do not attend school, (d) controlled experiments showing the effect or lack of effect of various amounts of non-attendance, and (e) controlled experiments giving some idea of the effectiveness of different measures for dealing with non-attendance.

CHAPTER II
School Progress

IN A VERY BROAD SENSE, every aspect of education might be related to *school progress*. A number of important aspects of school progress have been treated in this or other numbers of the *Review of Educational Research*. A more limited use of the term confines its meaning to those factors which appear to play a definite part in the acceleration or retardation of pupils. This chapter will be confined to six topics which relate to this more limited view of school progress.

In spite of the many investigations previously reported (46), which have revealed numerous unsatisfactory school progress practices, current methods of classification, promotion, and school failure still need much improvement. For example, "in one of our . . . cities a pupil who fails in one subject in the eighth grade must repeat that grade for a year, in another city the same pupil would repeat only a half year, and in another city close by he would not repeat at all" (41). The number of different promotion plans actually in operation was approximately two hundred (102). One city in Alabama failed only 17.1 percent of all elementary pupils, whereas another city failed 69.6 percent, and both cities had the same length of school term (93). Schools in the same system differed in the rate of non-promotion as much as 30 percent (58).

Age-Grade and Age-Grade-Progress Status

Inasmuch as age-grade and age-grade-progress studies continue to show a lack of uniformity in the method of computing ages, it is difficult to make comparisons. Furthermore, space limitation permits the presentation of only a few significant findings which have been revealed by important investigations in this field.

Statewide studies in Alabama, Arizona, and Texas were reported by Meadows (93), Larson (82), and Ayer (44, 45), respectively. Meadows (93) reported that the percents of rural high-school pupils making rapid, normal, and slow progress were 5.4, 34.4, and 62.2, respectively, while for city high-school pupils the percents were 16.1, 53.6, and 30.3. In the city elementary schools 2.4 percent made rapid progress, 60.3 percent made normal progress, and 37.3 percent made slow progress. Larson (82) indicated the status of age-grade conditions at four intervals between 1922 and 1934, inclusive. In the elementary schools there has been a steady decline in overageness, from 42.7 percent to 31.0 percent. The percent underage increased from 5.9 to 9.5 during the same period. In the high schools the trend was not as great. Ayer (44) found that the percents of pupils overage in the first, second, third, and fourth grades were 23, 30, 30, and 33, respectively, resulting in a total loss of 19,855 years by non-promotion. Also, as many as fifty different combinations of age and progress were found in the same grade. The following year he (45) found that out of 15,846 pupils, who entered school five years previously, 54 pupils were still in the first grade and only 8,910 pupils, or 56 percent, had made normal progress and entered the sixth grade. Age-grade conditions among Mexican pupils were found to be decidedly less favorable than among non-Mexican white pupils. In the same cities 72 percent of the former made slow progress, while only 46 percent of the latter made slow progress. The percent of Mexican pupils making rapid progress was 3 as compared to 7 for the non-Mexican white pupils. Pupils entering school at six years made better progress than those entering at five or seven (44, 45). Bigelow (50) indicated that if a child's chronological age was between six years and six years four months and his I.Q. was 110, he was practically certain to succeed, but if the child was below six years of age and his I.Q. was 110 his chance of success was small. In contrast Hayes (76) reported that chronological age at school entrance seemed to have no relation to school success.

Annual and Semiannual Promotions

A considerable number of studies have been made in an attempt to determine the advantages and disadvantages of annual promotions as compared to semiannual promotions. Chism (60) found that among 490 cities, 55.7 percent promoted pupils in the elementary schools only once a year. Lindsay (83), who used the residuum difference technic, found that neither the annual nor semiannual plan of promotion was strong enough to cause distinct superiorities in those school systems in which it was practiced. Steiner (113), who compared the percent of pupils promoted yearly under the annual promotion plan to the percent promoted semiannually in the same school system, reported that his data indicated a decrease of 5.9 percent in overage pupils and a slight increase in the percent of underage pupils during the period of semiannual promotion. In Texas (45), in a study including 388 cities paired according to population, the average group loss per pupil was less under the annual than under the semiannual plan of promotion. The average loss under the annual plan was .43 years as compared to .51 years under semiannual conditions. In a study made by Feingold (70) which was confined to data on honor students, midyear promotions were responsible for reducing school efficiency 30 percent. In another study (69) he reported that in a high school enrolling 2,000 students, ten classes could have been eliminated under the annual promotion plan with an approximate saving of $25,800. The number of repeaters under the semiannual promotion plan was 62 percent greater than the number under the annual plan. The detailed study by French (71), who attempted to contrast the effects of the two plans in 424 secondary schools, revealed that (a) subject offering to the midyear group is reduced about 40 percent of that offered to the class entering in the fall; (b) a larger percent of midyear entries than fall entries withdraw during the first semester; (c) there is more early graduation under the semiannual plan; (d) there is more continuity of teacher-pupil relationship under the annual plan.

Promotion, Non-Promotion, and Promotional Progress

Numerous attempts have been made to determine the significance of various factors, in school and outside of school, which accelerate or retard the school progress of pupils. Likewise, various technics have been utilized in interpreting the data. Sandon (109) devised and applied statistical methods in his analysis of school marks. A prediction index by means of which the rate of progress in a given school may be predicted from social, economic, biological, and ethnic data, was utilized by Maller (89). Caswell (58), in a comprehensive treatment of non-promotion in elementary schools, reported that the rate of non-promotion in cities and states ranged from approximately 2 percent to 20 percent and was significantly higher in grade one and varied as much as 30 percent between schools in the same system. The rate of non-promotion for boys and for B sections was higher. In the large majority of school systems, grade standards were used as a basis for regulating pupil progress. The status of school progress among first-grade pupils in South Carolina was reported (108) according to the size of the school. In the following groups of figures the figure to the left of the dash represents the number of teachers in the school and the figure to the right of the dash represents the percent of non-progress as revealed by the statewide study: 1—44.9; 2—44.1; 3—44.7; 4—41.8; 5—28.7; 16 to 26—28.8; 26 to 51—22.5; 51 to 100—22.9; 101 to 176—10.7. The size of the school was definitely related to the amount of retardation. In recent years there has been a tendency to favor 100 percent promotion through the elementary grades (99, 102). Kline (81) pointed out in his study that between 1900 and 1929 elimination had been postponed, on the average, two and one-half to three years. Various studies have been made to show the relationship between intelligence and progress in school (68, 89, 91). Many plans of promotion and remedies for retardation have been recommended (51, 58, 60, 83, 85, 86, 91, 92, 96, 99, 102, 107, 111, 115).

Status of Pupil Failure

This section is confined to the extent of pupil failures as reported by various investigators. Brueckner (56) reported that twenty years ago variations in failure ranged from 2 percent in one school to 80 percent in another. Pugsley (104) reduced the studies on school failures to general trends and conclusions, and reported the following: (a) from one-third to one-sixth of first-grade children failed; (b) 90 percent of first-grade failures were in reading; (c) a child who had attended kindergarten had 33 percent more of a chance to complete his first grade in one year than had the child who has not attended kindergarten; and (d) children who were overage for their grade showed the largest amount of failure. Data collected on 116,651 white pupils in elementary schools revealed that the chances of failing pupils to continue in school were small (52). Clem and Coon (61) reported interesting data on pupil failures in a "typical junior high school." Thirty-six percent of the pupils entering the school failed in one or more subjects and the largest percent of failures occurred in Latin and mathematics. In spite of the fact that the fall term was considerably shorter than the spring term, 56 percent of the subject failures occurred in the spring term, while 44 percent occurred in the fall. Forty-eight percent of the failing pupils had an I.Q. above 100. A study (67) of college failures indicated that the chances were less than 4 out of 100 that a failing student would reach the upper classes. Students in the college of arts and sciences found physics III and beginners' French most difficult. Education students seemed to find psychology and educational psychology most difficult. Failure among boys was more frequent than among girls (49, 62, 73, 93, 104).

Causes of Pupil Failure

It appears that during recent years more study has been devoted to causes of failure than to the extent of failure. A variety of approaches have been utilized in an attempt to discover why pupils fail. Some of these were: mental ability (40, 42, 61, 62, 63, 95, 114, 117); why teachers say they fail pupils (40, 61, 73, 88, 117); health (42, 62, 76, 95); family life and background (47, 62, 94, 114); sex differences (61, 62, 73, 93, 109); why pupils say they fail (61, 73, 75, 117); juvenile delinquency (64, 78); emotional life (47, 80, 114); interest (40, 61, 95); elementary- and secondary-school experience (47, 95, 117); attitudes (47, 102, 106); social distractions (42, 62); difficulty of subjectmatter (40, 61, 73); and racial differences (73). Among the chief causes of failure as given by the students were: dislike of teacher and too much work (61, 75); lack of effort (73, 75); illness and lack of funds (117); and work too difficult (75). Causes of failure as given by the teachers included the following: lack of effort (72); lack of ability (40, 61, 88, 117); lack of interest or appreciation (40, 61, 88, 117); and work too difficult (40, 88). Among the many reasons which teachers have given as a cause of failure none has ever listed poor teaching (88). Studies pertaining to failure among elementary pupils revealed that failure to do normal work may be due to a great variety of causes. Children in grades two and five who were periodically reminded that all of them would be promoted at the end of the semester did as well on a comprehensive achievement test as the control group who were told that anyone who did not work hard would have to repeat the grade (100). Unsatisfactory home conditions appeared to be a factor in causing failure (62, 94). Juvenile delinquents were mentally retarded as a group (64, 78). The percent of failure due to health or physical defects did not appear significant (62, 76). Fear reactions (114) and lack of mental ability (59, 62, 76, 84, 114) were direct causes of failure.

Mitchell (95) studied data on high-school failures as revealed in investigations extending over several years, and reported low intelligence as one of the chief causes of failure. He found a correlation of .65 between grade failures and high-school failures. According to his study, 62 percent of the pupils who had been informed of their low intelligence test score passed all subjects at the end of the year, while only 15 percent of the group which had not been notified passed all of their subjects. Thirty-three percent of the failing high-school pupils had not failed any subject in the grades. Karlan (80) made a careful study of the emotional life of thirty-one failing high-school students and found that emotional problems were the cause or contributed to the cause of two-thirds of the failures.

College students have most frequently failed because of illness, lack of funds, lack of ability, death of parent, frequent promotion in the elementary grades, emotional disturbances, social distractions, and lack of definite purpose (42, 47, 112, 117).

Reducing Pupil Failures

Many plans of reducing failures which have been put into practice as a result of related research have not been reported. However, a considerable number of suggested plans have been published in recent years. There has been a distinct tendency to recognize the value of a more complete diagnosis of failing students and the evils of repeating grades or subjects. Lithauer (84), in reporting the progress of pupils in a special kindergarten whose I.Q.'s at entrance ranged from 65 to 97, indicated how valuable this special kindergarten was in preventing failures. Seventy-three percent of failures could have been eliminated if the mentally immature group had been excluded from the first grade until maturity was reached according to Hayes (76). Karlan (80) recommended that all failing students of high intelligence should be investigated from a psychiatric point of view and proper treatment instituted. Numerous writers (59, 91, 97, 99, 102, 104) have recommended the abandonment of the traditional grade organization; others (48, 51, 92, 102) have favored the use of trial promotions. Curriculum adjustments (91, 104), special classes (63, 104, 108), a special high school for failing students (116), and a case study of each child (63, 104) are some of the devices which have been suggested for reducing pupil failure. To meet the situation in colleges, Alter (42) suggested that no student should be permitted to take more hours of work than he can carry with an average grade of "C."

From the foregoing review of school progress it appears that this problem is being more widely recognized as one of the major problems of public school administration. The introduction of many administrative devices such as semiannual promotion, special classes, and trial promotions has failed to solve the problem in its entirety. In recent years the importance of the problem of pupil progress has been emphasized through studies which have included a large number of pupils. Also, the technic employed and the methods of presenting the data have helped to make the results of the investigation more meaningful. The marked tendency of children, from every social level and with greatly varying abilities, to enter and continue in school, has complicated the problem to the extent that further study and experimental work are exceedingly essential.

CHAPTER III
School Marks

THE TERM *school marks* applies both to marks given on tests or examinations and marks given on report cards. There have been a number of studies of present practice during the three-year period covered by this report, but few experimental studies of the new widely advocated marking systems.

Distribution and Reliability of Teachers' Marks

Despite all of the research studies during the past twenty years and all of the efforts to improve marks, the latest studies present the same familiar picture. Bixler (123) showed that the variation among high schools of the scholastic aptitude of their graduates and the variations in the standards of marking are so great that any index based on school marks is subject to gross misinterpretation. After giving the American Council Psychological Examination in 1931 to fifty high-school graduation classes, he found that the University of Chicago could have admitted every member of the graduating classes of three of the schools without lowering the scholastic aptitude of the freshman class as measured by this test. But the scholastic aptitude of this class would have been lowered by the admission of the upper quarter only of the classes in ten other high schools. Bixler (124) further found that if the minimum high-school work mark acceptable for college entrance were 85, this grade might mean anything from 75 to 180, in terms of the scholastic aptitude test.

Various investigators have attempted to provide a basis for a more valid distribution of school marks. Moffitt (138) reported an index rating based upon a battery of tests and a personality test. This rating sets a standard which the pupil must attain before credit for work is given. Snedecor (145) proposed a complicated statistical procedure to determine the limits within which marks for a given group may be assigned.

Edmiston (132) concluded, after a careful piece of research, that the standard deviation method provides for an accurate distribution of teachers' marks. He recommended that the median of each converted set of marks should be 50 with a standard deviation of 10. He then proposed a scale whereby scores of 51 to 62 may represent "B," 45 to 50 "C," and so on. Obviously, however, this is not practical in the average class. It is questionable whether it is worth the time necessary.

Factors Affecting Teachers' Marks

A number of writers have reported the effects of various factors on teachers' marks. Dexter (130) found that in grading papers there is usually a consistent tendency for increasing severity or increasing leniency caused by fatigue or boredom. Richardson (143) reported that pupils of high intelligence can be scheduled for few or no study periods in high school without affecting their marks. The number of study periods has little effect on the marks of a group between 90 to 109 I.Q., but he found a correlation of $.34 \pm .04$ (boys) and $.11 \pm .04$ (girls) between the number of study periods and the marks in the group below 90 I.Q. Chapman (128) found that part-time employment tends to lower the marks of some types of pupils, such as those who dislike their work, those who frequently change jobs, and those who are fourteen years of age or under, but that the evidence is not conclusive, and that the influence of employment on the marks of a pupil is small. Logsdon (135), studying the marks of pupils in homes receiving relief, found a slight superiority in the pupils from homes economically independent. Sex bias was studied by Maney (136). Over a period of ten years he found that the grading by women instructors was not as objective as the grading by men in Transylvania College. Yates (151), however, found that the sex of the teacher had little or no effect. Farnsworth (133) reported that seating in the classroom had some effect on marks, since the best scores came from the front central section of the room, presumably because the instructor directs his attention more to this area. Charles (129) showed that when freshmen were scheduled for courses in competition with juniors and seniors they received all of the inferior marks. Similar studies with other groups led him to conclude that the practice of closing some courses to freshmen is justified.

Summary of Present Practice

Billett (122) reported that in the 258 school systems selected for study there are 100 different marking systems, counting the minor varieties. In 20 percent of the school systems uniform practice in marking does not exist even in the secondary schools of the system.

As to the type of marks employed, Billett showed that 80 percent of the schools issue marks in the form of letters or equivalent symbols. In 25 percent of the schools percents alone or in combination with letters or other symbols are used. The five-point marking scale predominates. A few schools are trying out new marking systems, such as percentile rank, class rank, accomplishment quotients, sigma scores, and written records or logs showing pupils' progress.

Hill (134) also made a survey of present practice; he analyzed 443 report cards now in use. The interesting finding of his study was that 52 percent of all systems issue report cards six times a year; 20 percent monthly. He found that 80 percent of the cards carry some message to the parent; 96 percent report attendance, and 45 percent health. Seventy-six percent of the kindergarten-primary, 84 percent of the elementary, 93 percent of the junior high-school, and 94 percent of the high-school cards have a failing mark. Practically all of the cards have at least one character trait or conduct habit mentioned, the distribution being as follows: 95 percent of the kindergarten-primary, 98 percent of the elementary, 86 percent of the junior high, and 69 percent of the high-school cards.

Elementary-school report cards in cities over 100,000 population were studied by Weber (148). He obtained the opinions of judges selected at random throughout the United States. These judges included superintendents, principals, teachers, directors of research, professors of school administration, and outstanding parents. His recommendations, as might be expected, did not depart very widely from present practice. In view of the method of procedure used it is hardly accurate to claim that the result represents an ideal report card.

Smith (144), in an interesting article on marking in the negro colleges, showed that there is no established plan for marking in many of the colleges. In the high schools the five-way plan of letters is most generally used. This research, based on questionnaires, was marred by the fact that almost half of the institutions failed to respond.

Other investigators have made surveys of present practice in particular areas. Thus Boardman (125) sent questionnaires to 128 high-school principals in Minnesota. The majority of this group used the five-point letter system. However, there were numerous variations, and as a result of this study a committee (140) recommended the adoption of a uniform system which was later adopted. The percent system was abandoned and the symbols "A," "B," "C," "D," "E," and "F" will be used in Minnesota high schools hereafter. For purposes of obtaining honor point averages or other averages the various letters are assigned values as follows: "A," 4; "B," 3; "C," 2; "D," 1. They also agree that these marks should represent scholastic attainment, not behavior. A similar summary of practice in New York state was made by Reed (142). Likewise Diettert (131) summarized present practice in Indiana. One significant indication in his report is that 25 out of 149 high-school principals were satisfied not to mark. The Indiana group also agreed that the deportment mark has questionable value. A similar survey in the state of Kansas was made by Williams (149). These county and city superintendents believed that a uniform system should be adopted for the state of Kansas. In general they favored the usual type of card, although they agreed that the letter is a valuable supplement to the original report card. Thus we find general dissatisfaction with the present marking system, but, as yet, little agreement as to the direction in which to go.

The Educational Research Service of the National Education Association (139) prepared a practical contribution on new developments in pupil report cards. The report contained summaries of studies of ratings on behavior or character, messages to parents, and health items; the names of cities that were experimenting with new methods; local procedures in revising report cards, a particularly significant section on guiding principles in developing reports to parents; and a tabulated analysis of certain elements in 108 pupil report cards adopted during the four years 1931 to 1934. Particularly valuable for planning the revision of report cards will be the reproduction of report forms from 28 different cities. The cards reproduced include elementary, junior, and senior high-school reports.

New Developments in Marking

Many writers report experiments with new types of marking systems. Beatty (121) described a new type of report card or goal card used in elementary and secondary schools in Bronxville, New York. In the elementary grades the report lists detailed objectives or goals for two years of work in each of the school subjects. Students advance as their individual abilities permit. When the topics on the goal card are completed achievement is further checked by objective tests. It will be recognized that this plan is similar to the Winnetka, Illinois, plan. In the Bronxville High School the work of each subject is divided into six-week units, with the goals set up in similar fashion. Students who demonstrate knowledge of facts receive a P (Pass). Students who also use these facts in the solution of problems receive an R (Recommend for College).

Ball (120) reported an experiment carried out voluntarily by six teachers in Pasadena in which they attempted to develop a report that would put child growth ahead of acquisition of subjectmatter. Their plan requires an evaluation of each pupil's work by pupil and teacher. This report card includes a heading such as "What kind of a boy or girl am I?" "What kind of work do I do?" Pupils comment and sign. Teachers comment and sign. We note that this author indicates that the competitive attitude among the children has disappeared and that there develops a personal friendship shared by pupil, parent, and teacher.

Worlton (150) described a two-year experiment in Salt Lake City, during which the report contained no mark indicating scholarship rank, but only attendance and citizenship record. In determining the pupil's ability a clean card indicates satisfactory progress. Lack of satisfactory progress in any subject is indicated by a check; improvement by a plus sign. Inquiries to 28 principals and 513 teachers indicate that 78.4 percent of the principals and 48.5 percent of the teachers mention advantages in the new plan. The parents have also expressed satisfaction.

Warren (147) reported on the Newton, Massachusetts, plan, in which the report to parents is couched in descriptive sentences. Letters are written by teachers twice a year to parents of children from kindergarten through grade nine. After a year's trial, a questionnaire, filled out by the teachers, indicates that on the whole they were in agreement with the principles involved. But in operation the plan was not wholly satisfactory. The plan was, therefore, revised as follows:

1. In the primary grades no reports are issued, except that every child's home must be informed concerning his progress once during the year.
2. In grades four, five, and six a report blank consisting of statements to be completed by the teacher with space for comments is issued four times a year. In the junior high school there is sent home four times a year a collection of individual comments by subject teachers. One sheet may be used for each subject.

A school administrator seeking help to improve his marking system will do well to read the Pennsylvania bulletin (141). The Office of Education in Washington also has sample books of report cards contributed by fifty school systems. Upjohn (146) and Brooks (126) have attempted to enunciate the fundamental prnciples of report card construction. However, more experimental work needs to be done here. Upjohn asserted, for example, "It is not enough to report upon subjects in general, as upon arithmetic . . . there must be a breakdown of the elements of these fields of information or acquisition of skills." On the other hand, many writers have pointed out that marks are necessary since proper grade placement of curriculum materials will make 100 percent promotion practicable, at least in the elementary schools. No one has studied the fundamental problem of whether or not marks are necessary in any comprehensive way.

As indicated above, many writers are urging a mark or report of some type on moral or character qualities. However, Chambers (127), discussing new departures in England, pointed out the risks we run in labeling the child's moral qualities. Miller (137) studied the conduct mark and found a great lack of uniformity in the attitude of teachers toward conduct. One hundred teachers were given a questionnaire dealing with forms of misconduct, and were asked to list them in order of seriousness. Truancy was given every place on the list from second to twentieth; lying, every place from first to twentieth. Carelessness and whispering ranged from third place to twentieth. This study raises serious questions as to the validity of conduct marks in view of this tremendous difference in teachers' attitudes.

Summary

Much of the material which has appeared during the three-year period has been descriptive in nature, or summaries of current practices. Many fundamental issues have not been adequately attacked. The new marking systems which have received experimental try-outs in a few systems need to be subjected to critical analysis and further experimental study under carefully controlled conditions.

CHAPTER IV
Recording and Reporting

Records

THERE HAS BEEN MUCH DISCUSSION about the chaotic condition of school records and reports. Little research, however, has been done in this field. Johnson (153) made a study of 349 permanent record cards used in secondary schools. He had 47 high-school principals and 13 specialists rank the uses of permanent record cards. Their ranking of uses is as follows:

1. To assist in guidance of pupils (including classification and placement)
2. To improve teaching by giving teachers access to information regarding individual differences of pupils
3. To assist in research
4. To meet requirements of and provide basis for reports to state, county, and local authorities
5. To motivate pupils' work by their knowledge that a permanent record of their activities is kept.

After thus determining the uses, Johnson had the 237 items found on permanent record cards rated according to their contribution to these criteria. He concluded by listing the following items which were ranked high and which, therefore, deserve consideration in the construction of permanent record forms:

1. Objective information about pupils
2. Achievement and intelligence test results
3. Character traits
4. Extra-curriculum activities
5. Vocational plans
6. Marks and credit information
7. Data regarding school entrance
8. Attendance data.

Robertson (160) described the cumulative personnel record forms fostered by the American Council on Education. For several years the College Presidents' Association, the Department of Public Instruction, and the Carnegie Foundation for the Advancement of Teaching, cooperating with a number of schools in Pennsylvania, have experimented with the American Council Cumulative Personnel Record in connection with a study of the relations of secondary and higher education. The Pennsylvania Department of Public Instruction (157) published the report of a committee on records and reports, which showed that the American Council Record is the most satisfactory instrument yet devised for recording cumulative information concerning individual pupils. This bulletin also described a modified form of the American Council folder which has been developed by the Pennsylvania Committee. As an outgrowth of their experiment, the Committee has prepared directions for making entries, particularly on such disputed matters as personality qualities. On the whole this bulletin may be of practical help to any administrator seeking to improve his record system. Campbell (162) gave samples of various records.

Reports

The term *report* is used here to mean the report of the superintendent of schools, principal, or any other school official. As many writers have pointed out, present accounting, both fiscal and pupil, is inadequate. Reavis (159) found that approximately half of the reports of city superintendents are statistical in character and that, in about a third of the reports, the data are not adequately interpreted or explained. Reports seldom describe the services rendered, the administrative organization for control, the personnel, and the plant necessary for the program. Reavis (159) further showed that reports should indicate the services needed in the community served. He asserted that reports should and can be measured by their effects upon the board, the staff, the community, and the immediate administrative policy. Unfortunately, however, we do not find that any writers have attempted to measure the effects of such reports.

In the field of higher education the National Committee on Standard Reports (156) attempted to achieve general uniformity, not only in the financial reports of educational institutions, but also in reports required by governmental, accrediting, statistical, and controlling bodies. The recommendations have been adopted by some 2,000 colleges and many other groups, including the United States Office of Education.

It has been advocated by Brown (152) that the superintendent's monthly report be improved. He outlined criteria by which to determine the effectiveness of a report, as well as a checklist of topics. Although mainly descriptive, this study has value in pointing the need for experimental studies in this field.

Smith (161) discussed reports of high-school principals and reported a questionnaire study in Montana. The especial interest in this article was the criteria for judging the vitality of the secondary school as set up by Judd. Judd's list is in itself a fine checklist for any principal who is preparing such a report. Murphy (155) analyzed the high-school principal's annual report, giving ratings by 153 superintendents and 104 principals on 35 items found most frequently in such reports. Of the group investigated 93 principals made reports, but 142 did not.

Jorden (154), after analyzing 45 superintendents' annual reports, found that reports served several uses, namely:

1. A means of publicity
2. A record of important data
3. A professional stimulant.

He listed the following desirable features to be included in an annual report:

1. Table of contents
2. School calendar

3. Introductory statement
4. Official directory, including the board of education, staff, etc.
5. Trends, over a period of five or more years, in enrolment, attendance, etc.
6. Changes in policies, curriculum, rules, etc.
7. Special problems and what is being done to solve them
8. Class schedule of junior and senior high schools
9. Program of studies, time allotments, etc.
10. Mental and achievement test results
11. Age-grade and progress facts
12. Scholarship, acceleration, and causes of non-promotion
13. Health program
14. Physical education program, aside from competitive athletics
15. Salary schedule; other data concerning teaching staff
16. Budget; interpretation of significant features; auditor's statement; balance sheet
17. Extra-curriculum activities
18. Brief review of the school plant and equipment
19. Pictures of buildings, classes, equipment, etc.
20. Recommendations
21. Bibliography of important articles in the newspapers, or separate publications of the schools
22. Attractive educational quotations
23. A space "In Memoriam."

Summary

There is need for more research regarding permanent record cards, particularly for extensive controlled experiments with some of the better forms that have been devised, such as the American Council folder and the form issued by the Department of Secondary-School Principals of the National Education Association. The Committee on Records and Reports of the Progressive Education Association (158) has been systematically studying this problem. Their present and forthcoming publications will undoubtedly provide material which other investigators should carefully study. There have been several critical investigations of superintendents' and principals' annual reports. It will be of interest to study the effects of an improved report on the various groups for which it is intended.

CHAPTER V
Characteristics of Pupil Population
A. ELEMENTARY EDUCATION

RESEARCH on characteristics of children makes three main contributions to the development and guidance of pupils in the elementary school: (a) it supplies distributions of abilities on which to locate the position of a particular child; (b) it suggests relationships among factors in the child's development; and (c) it describes methods of studying individuals. The first two of these contributions will be summarized in this section. The third is included in Chapter VI.

Abilities and Problems of Elementary-School Children

Surveys have been made of pupils' intelligence, achievement, recreation, physical proficiency, mechanical ability, personality, character, and problems of adjustment. Of these characteristics, intelligence has been most extensively studied.

Intelligence—Several outstanding summaries of research on intelligence have been recently published. One of these is Pintner's annual summary (230) of research on intelligence tests. Others are in the *Review of Educational Research* (166, 249) covering such topics as the mental development of the school child, mental growth of intellectually inferior and of gifted children, growth from birth to maturity, relationships in physical and mental development, and applications of intelligence testing.

Because these topics are primarily the province of other issues of the *Review of Educational Research* only certain findings of special significance to guidance will be reviewed in this section. The research on intelligence of special interest to personnel workers is that which deals with the growth of intelligence, the constancy of the intelligence quotient, and the intelligence of various elementary-school populations.

Smoothed curves showing a linear growth were found to be characteristic of the elementary-school period (199, 218). By eleven years of age, the developmental curve had attained 80 percent of maturity (235). Development in different intellectual abilities, however, is not uniform (235, 199)—decline in intelligence during adult years was pronounced in numerical completions, common sense, and analogies but was negligible in the opposites and general information tests of the Army Alpha (199). Any evaluation of research on growth of intelligence must consider three points: (a) whether the test measures mental ability as it functions to best advantage at different ages; (b) whether the units of the tests used are of equal value; and (c) whether the average level of different ages truly represents the developmental curve of individuals.

Sex differences and race differences in intelligence are of minor concern to the personnel worker because the individual differences within groups are so infinitely larger than the differences between groups. Heilman (189), Conrad and others (177), and Armstrong (164) found differences in general intelligence to be negligible, but reported a true sex difference in spelling and other verbal abilities in favor of girls and a tendency for boys to excel in arithmetical reasoning, nature study, science, and psychomotor abilities.

Although it is not yet known how the peoples of the earth compare in mental ability, there is evidence that American elementary-school children of various national and racial origins differ in mean scores on intelligence tests. Overlapping among all groups is characteristic of the distributions reported (166:212-14, 234).

Whether an intelligence quotient means the same thing at different ages and whether it remains fairly constant for a particular individual is of concern to counselors who use tests in the appraisal of pupils' ability. Nemzek (222), in 1933, summarized 249 investigations on the constancy of the intelligence quotient. The median of a distribution of 97 retest correlations for the Stanford-Binet was .83; of 27 retest correlations for group tests, .85. Almost identical results were obtained with 50 nine-year-old German children (203). A glance at a scatter diagram, however, will show that a reasonably high coefficient of correlation does not necessarily imply a constancy of the intelligence quotient. The fact that fluctuations ranging from $+32$ to -18 points were obtained under standard conditions of testing (226) is a warning to counselors not to base any important decision regarding an individual on the results of a single test. In general, constancy of the intelligence quotient decreased with time interval (171, 253) and varied with the intelligence level of the subjects (174, 192, 226). The Terman Group Test of Mental Ability, given to children in the eighth grade and repeated in another form thirty months later, yielded fairly constant intelligence quotients for the middle range of ability, a mean decrease of twelve points for children of 120 I.Q. or above, and an increase of five or six points, on the average, for dull pupils.

Surveys of children's mental ability ranged in scope from a single class in a small school to a sampling of the child population of an entire country. There have been recently extensive surveys of the intelligence of elementary-school children in England, Scotland, and Australia. Collmann and his colleagues (176) reported almost identical mean intelligence test scores for the various age groups of American and Victorian children. A survey of all children born in Scotland during 1921—a total of 87,498 children of chronological ages from 10.5 to 11.5—revealed, both in the group tests and in a sampling of 1,000 of the same children tested with the Stanford-Binet Test, a mean intelligence quotient slightly below 100. Of this population, 1.5 and 3 percent were below 70 I.Q. (243). Extensive yearly surveys of private schools by the Educational Records Bureau (262, 263, 265) consistently showed higher scores for pupils in the private or independent schools than for the public school population. For example, the median intelligence quotient of one group of 3,674 children in grades four to eight was 115. The results of testing programs in public school systems approximate the norms of the tests used (266).

Of special value in the educational guidance of elementary-school pupils is information concerning the intelligence necessary for certain courses of study and occupations. Reifenrath (233) found pupils in the German gymnasium ranking highest on a general intelligence test and those in the commercial and trade school ranking lowest. In the United States, a similar relationship between the college preparatory and other courses exists. The United States Children's Bureau (175), from a follow-up study of 949 boys and girls having intelligence quotients ranging from below 40 to 88, obtained detailed data regarding the kind of occupations in which they were employed, their earnings, the duration of their various employments, the extent to which they had been employed since they started work, and the number of positions they had held. The jobs held by these boys and girls fell chiefly in the semi-skilled operatives classification, but included also some work in the fields of transportation, trade, personal and domestic service, and clerical occupations. Fryer and Sparling (186) found a significant relationship between the scores on intelligence tests and the capacity to learn tasks of various levels of difficulty. They published tentative minimum critical scores on the Army Alpha for occupational success of clerical workers.

Achievement—Comparative studies of achievement as well as of intelligence have been made. MacGregor (213) found the eleven-year-old pupils in the county of Fife, Scotland, to be considerably ahead of American children on an American achievement test. The fact, however, that these children had a mental age four months ahead of the norm for all Scottish children should be taken into consideration in drawing conclusions regarding the greater teaching efficiency of the Scottish schools.

A wealth of detailed data on the achievement of pupils in independent schools is available in the Educational Records Bureau bulletins (261, 264). In spite of the fact that the educational objectives of private schools frequently differ from those of the traditional schools, the median achievement of private school pupils on standardized tests generally reached the grade norms of the test, though achievement was not always commensurate with the children's intelligence. In the primary grades, however, Hopkins and Mendenhall (194) found that the pupils' achievement on standardized tests was below the average.

Three conclusions of practical importance concerning the education of mentally retarded children were suggested by Parker's investigation (227): (a) the correlation between test scores and actual school achievement may be expected to vary in different subjects and to be higher for the dull group than for the normal but retarded children; (b) it is uneconomical to begin instruction in the tool subjects at the zero learning age; (c) the typical feeble-minded child does not reach his scholastic limit during ordinary school ages.

Rose (239) found that pupils tended to hold their initial rank on successive forms of the Stanford Achievement Test except where the initial score was so high that no appreciable gain could be made. The pupils whose gain was above the average on the standardized test did not make a grade gain equal to their test gain, while those below average in test gain made a correspondingly larger grade gain. The promotion policy of the school system was plainly reflected in the relationship between achievement on standardized tests and annual grade gain.

The effect of administrative organization was studied by Beatley (167), who found no significant differences in pupils' achievement in the ninth grade on standardized tests in the 8-4 organization and in the 6-3-3 organization.

Recreation—McPherson (214) uncovered a need for guidance of ten-year-old children during vacation in the wise use of leisure. Davis (181) found that listening to the radio, attending clubs, reading, housework, school activities, church activities, and listening to music were the activities most frequently participated in by the younger girls who were members of the Y.W.C.A. Hardy (188) compared the out-of-school activities of well-adjusted and poorly adjusted elementary-school pupils. The maladjusted attended movies more frequently, had a smaller number of playmates, and preferred more vigorous play than did the well-adjusted children. The most outstanding difference was the higher general intelligence of the well-adjusted group.

Physical proficiency—Extensive scales and standards for achievement in athletic events were published by Neilson and Cozens (221). These tests and norms make possible a more objective measurement of achievement in physical education activities on the elementary-school level than has previously been possible; whether they measure the most important objectives of physical education might be questioned. If their effect is to focus attention on these specific athletic skills, there is a danger that social and recreational values may be neglected.

Mechanical ability—Contrary to general opinion, experimental evidence does not always show a superiority in certain kinds of mechanical ability on the part of subnormal children (224), or inferiority on the part of young gifted children (190).

Personality and character—Studies in character and personality in German psychological literature were reviewed by Maller (215, 216), who also summarized research on measurement in this field in 1934 and 1935. Similar summaries were made by Watson (255, 256) in 1932 and 1933. The study of this aspect of child development has been limited by inadequate measuring instruments.

One of the most significant contributions in this field has been made by means of interviews and observations (228). Piaget's method was to question and to converse with a large number of school children, taking care to maintain a naive attitude, to formulate questions in the child's language, and to endeavor to grasp the child's mental orientation. The results provide a background against which the spontaneous remarks of children become more meaningful. The following are a few of Piaget's significant generalizations regarding the moral judgments of children in the lower grades of the elementary school: the child of about seven grows from a regard of rules as sacred and untouchable to a concept of rules as laws due to mutual consent; he tends to emphasize motives more than the external effects of an action as he becomes more mature; his sense of justice is largely independent of adult influences and "requires nothing more for its development than the mutual respect and solidarity which holds among children themselves." Development is not in distinct stages; the processes partially synchronize, but central tendencies are evident at different ages. Schulz (241) studied the motives of lying in an experimental situation. Kinter-Remmlein (201) reported a specificity of response on certain of the C. E. I. tests in a small group of French children similar to that which Hartshorne and May found in American children. This apparent lack of organization of character, however, may be merely a function of the test situation. If the children were studied individually and the reasons for their behavior ascertained, far less specificity might have been evident. Sears (244) concluded from his study of the philosophy of punishment and from an analysis of discipline cases that effective punishment was as rare as ineffectual punishment was common. These investigations throw light on the problem of discipline in the elementary school and seem to be of more value than the results obtained by means of the character and personality tests now available. Few attempts have been made to understand the unique course of an emotion or the real structure of a particular individual's personality (258).

Rogers (238) obtained evidence in a small group of children ten to sixteen years old of a general factor of perseveration quite different from Spearman's "G" factor. Reusser (234) found a more critical attitude toward "average" boys, more peculiar attitudes, interests, and ideas, and less ability to estimate the feelings of others characteristic of a group of delinquent boys.

Maladjustment.—Surveys of behavior and personality defects in school children have been made in England and in the United States. McFie (212) discovered personality difficulties and behavior disorders in 46 percent of 697 Canadian children between the ages of twelve and fourteen. Among the signs of maladjustment most frequently noted were personality deviations such as timidity, sensitiveness, and lack of sociability; behavior disorders such as bullying, quarreling, and truancy; habit disorders such as nail-biting; and scholastic difficulties other than those due to mental defect. Yourman (267) reported practically the same percent, 44 percent, of pupils in twelve schools of a large city in the United States as having more or less serious difficulties in adjustment. He found the ratio of mean score of the problem group to the unselected group to be 5 to 1 on the following items: disinterest in school work, cheating, lying, defiance to discipline, marked overactivity, temper outbursts, bullying, imaginative lying, and truancy. The borderline (I.Q. 70-80) and the dull-normal (I.Q. 80-90) made up most of the problem group. Children with a median intelligence quotient of 79 were rated much lower by parents and teachers on a scale of personality and behavior maladjustments than were children with a median I.Q. of 121 (206). Maller (217) reported a startling increase in the proportion of girls arraigned in the Children's Court, New York City, during the years 1902-32. The ratio of boys to girls in the first decade studied was sixty to one; in the latest decade, it was eight to one.

Laycock (207) in Canada, McFie (212) in England, Yourman (267), and Snyder (248) in the United States all obtained results similar to those of Wickman in his well-known study of children's behavior and teachers' attitudes. Stogdill (250) found that parents and advanced college students resembled teachers in their estimates of the seriousness of certain forms of child behavior: they considered fears, suspiciousness, excessive modesty, shyness, and day dreaming as far less serious than did the mental hygienists.

It is true that serious maladjustment should be recognized early; then research on signs of maladjustment that become evident in school years has special significance for guidance (240). Equally important are methods of preventing these early symptoms from developing. Moreno (220) applied the principle that satisfactory adjustment is possible for certain individuals in some groups but not in others and devised technics for measuring and recording the attractions and repulsions that exist in social groups.

The effect of skill or lack of skill upon the adjustment of children is an excellent problem for research. Jack's significant experimental study (195), in which shy and submissive behavior of five preschool children changed to ascendant behavior as the result of their acquiring certain skills, might well be repeated with elementary-school children. Kirk (202) and Damerau (178) both studied the effect of improved reading ability on behavior disorders but with different results. Kirk obtained decided improvement in personality adjustment following improvement in reading, while Damerau found little relation between improvement in reading and improved behavior.

Comment—Surveys of pupils' needs and abilities enable the counselor to characterize the position of a given individual in a group, but they do not warrant sweeping applications of average results to individual cases. Within a given sample, individual differences are far greater than differences between the central tendencies of groups. What is true "on the average" is not necessarily true in individual cases. There are merely different degrees of probability that an individual will follow the average path of development in any respect. Accordingly, from the standpoint of guidance, interpretive and descriptive work such as that of Piaget and others (228) is of more value than mass statistics.

Relationships among Characteristics

Although the information obtained from surveys is of limited value in the guidance of individuals, it becomes more meaningful when significant relationships of the survey items are known. Researches of such relationships have been summarized in a previous issue of the *Review of Educational Research* (166). Accordingly, only a limited number of investigations will be mentioned in this section.

Relationships between intelligence and reading ability—One page of a previous *Review of Educational Research* (166:63) was devoted to this problem. The results of most significance to guidance workers were: (a) the correlation between mental age as determined by group verbal tests of intelligence and reading age is usually above .60, but is decidedly lower when a non-language test is used; (b) the group test of intelligence is an unfair measure of the mental ability of poor readers; (c) achievement test scores could be used instead of mental ages for purposes of school classification; and (d) reading ability of less than a grade score of 4.3 is detrimental to the progress of children in grades four and above, regardless of their intelligence quotients.

Relationships between intelligence and environmental factors—This topic, too, has already been summarized (166:209-12). It is well for counselors to know the following results of research in this area: (a) the correlation of intelligence between a single child and a single parent was found to be slightly higher than .50 and between a single child and the mid-parent from .54 to .73 (223); (b) the results of Hollingworth's and Gray's investigation (193) gave no support to the theory of intellectual achievement as a compensation for smallness of physique; (c) the mean intelligence of children of professional parents was reported as highest; that of children of traveling salesmen, insurance agents, merchants, bankers, and lumbermen next highest; and that of children of mill workers, other types of laborers, and farmers the lowest (200); and (d) there is some evidence that children develop intelligence in accordance with the demands of their environment (198, 246). Schwesinger (242) made a detailed summary of recent investigations on the relation of genetic and environmental factors to intelligence.

Relationships between intelligence and social and emotional adjustment—Research on gifted children has shown good social adjustment to be associated with high intelligence. Correlations between intelligence test scores and scores of personality measurements, on the other hand, have been low. Dellaert (183) is one of the few investigators who reported a correlation as high as $+.56$ between ratings of social adjustment and scores on individual intelligence tests. Jastak (196) found vocabulary unaffected by mental instability. He accordingly suggested discrepancy between performance and vocabulary tests as a measure of personality difficulties. Mean intelligence quotients of various groups of delinquent children hovered around 80 (163, 172, 180, 210, 219, 237, 238).

Lord (209) presented an encouraging report of the social and vocational adjustment of 230 mentally retarded boys who had been in the special classes of the public school. Glueck and Glueck (187), on the other hand, found the results of juvenile court and psychological clinic treatment very disappointing. During a five-year period after court treatment, 88 percent of the children continued their delinquencies. The results of these investigations suggest the effectiveness of school pre-delinquency education over clinical post-delinquency treatment.

Relationships of environment to personality—The influence of the environment upon the personality of children from five to twenty years of age in two different environments—a crowded, dirty district and a good residential section—was intensively studied by Francis and Fillmore (185). The environmental influences found to be most significantly related to personality development were good health of parents, parents' care of the home and interest in the child and his playmates, the giving of freedom and responsibility in certain areas, and parents' participation in recreation. The main conclusion was that "parental attitudes do shape the personality of a child while his material surroundings are not of vital importance." One section of the White House Conference on Child Health and Protection (257), after a still more extensive investigation, came to a similar conclusion. Smith (247) made a study of the factors most significant in a school situation affecting groups of children who were difficult to deal with constructively. After summarizing the investigations of the personality adjustments of "only" children, Campbell (173) concluded that the mere presence or absence of siblings apparently does not play a crucial role. Over-protection, however, seems to be related to superiority in verbalization and to inferiority in arithmetic (208), and to maladjustment (258).

Relationships between speech and development—Decroly (182) concluded from a study of the development in speech in children that bilingualism usually impedes mental development and that the maternal language should be well established first of all and the second language begun about the age of ten. Johnson (197) used a variety of technics to gain information about the influence of stuttering on the personality of eighty stutterers from seven to forty-two years of age. The effect of stuttering seemed to vary with the individual's perception of the defect: "Whenever the stutterer's situation-as-perceived changes, his adaptations and attitudes change accordingly" (197:22).

Relationships between health and other factors—Hoefer and Hardy (191) obtained evidence that good health seemed to be related to physical growth, intelligence and school achievement, social traits, good health in parents, superior home environment, and good early developmental history. The summary of relationships between health, motor ability, and other factors is the province of another issue of the *Review* (251).

Comment—Since the personnel worker focuses attention on what the individual may become, research on existing relationships is less valuable than the study of development that might take place as a result of effective education. Accordingly, there seems to be a need for the following types of investigation:

1. The effect of the best kind of instruction on the reading ability of children of different levels of non-verbal intelligence
2. The effect of the acquisition of certain skills on the personality of elementary-school children
3. The methods of education that are most effective in preventing delinquency among children of low mentality
4. The environmental influences which are most significantly related to good adjustment.

B. SECONDARY EDUCATION

Edgerton's summary of research studies relating to characteristics of the pupil population, in the *Review of Educational Research* (184) classified the studies under the following headings: high-school seniors, superior children, character studies, sex and race differences, mechanical ability, and physical growth. During the three-year period covered by this review studies of the secondary-school population have been numerous and have covered a number of aspects. The partial nature of the researches is indicated by the following brief summary.

Changes in the secondary-school population during the period 1880-1930 were studied by Kefauver, Noll, and Drake (276); intelligence by Kefauver, Noll, and Drake (276), Dowd (271), Lamson (277), Moore (279), and Portenier (281); honor society pupils by Engle (272); behavior problem children by Kaplan (273); persistence by Caliver (269) and Clem and Hovey (270); high-school graduates by Caliver (269), Dowd (271), and Moore (279); leadership by Brown (268) and Partridge (280); physical defects by Smith (282); emotional maladjustment by Maller and Lundeen (278); educational and vocational plans by Kefauver, Noll, and Drake (274); continuation and evening school pupils by Kefauver, Noll, and Drake (275); and negro pupils by Caliver (269). The present review will be limited to the following phases: changes in the secondary-school population, intelligence, behavior problem children, high-school graduates, and leadership.

Changes in the Secondary-School Population

Every student of secondary education is keenly aware of the fact that the secondary-school population of the present is different in quantity and quality from that of a generation ago. These differences were the subject of special study by the National Survey of Secondary Education. Kefauver, Noll, and Drake (276) reported the following major changes:

1. In the fifty-year period 1880-1930 the public secondary-school population increased from 110,277, or 2.8 percent of persons aged fourteen to seventeen inclusive, to 4,354,815 or 46.6 percent of persons aged fourteen to seventeen.
2. A repetition in Seattle and Bridgeport of Counts' study of 1920 of the selective character of American secondary education showed large increases in 1930 in all oc-

cupational groups. The average increase reported was 193 per 1,000 for the managerial, proprietary, and professional groups; 118 per 1,000 for the commercial and clerical groups; 153 for the transportation and public service groups; 112 for the trade groups; and 86 for the personal service and common labor groups.

3. Intelligence test data secured from eleven schools showed a median I.Q. of 102 for all schools combined and 91 for the four trade schools included. The median I.Q. of all schools combined is three points lower than the median found by Terman in 1919 and four points lower than that found by Proctor in 1925. "A highly important conclusion from the evidence presented is that intellectual democratization is being achieved by extension of the offering to include vocationalized and other non-college preparatory curriculums in the secondary schools."

Intelligence of Secondary-School Pupils

The intelligence of secondary-school pupils is also reported in the National Survey of Secondary Education (274). Tabulation of I.Q.'s of pupils in two comprehensive, four general, four trade or vocational, and one commercial school showed such significant facts as the following: Among boys the highest median I.Q., 114.0, was in the preparatory curriculum of the technical school; followed in order by the scientific curriculum of the general school, 108.0; the general curriculum of the general school, 107.6; the academic curriculum of the general school, 106.2; the academic curriculum of the comprehensive school, 105.9; and on down to the commercial curriculum of the comprehensive school, 100.0; the industrial arts curriculum of the general school, 94.6; and the trade school, 92.4. Among girls a similar situation was found. The highest median I.Q. was found in the academic curriculum of the general school, 109.7; the lowest in the trade school, 89.1. The selection taking place between the ninth and twelfth grades was indicated by the medians which were 98.6, 101, 103.7, and 104.5, respectively, for all schools combined. The authors said, "There is evidence that in many communities the secondary-school population as a whole is not far from a representative cross-section of at least the total literate population."

In a study of high-school pupils of low mentality Portenier (281) secured data from representative high schools throughout the country in an attempt to answer two questions: (a) Has the marked increase in high-school enrolment during the decade 1921-31 been accompanied by a greater range in intelligence and a lowering of the mean level of intelligence? and (b) Has the percent of pupils who remain to graduate increased with the increased enrolment? The author concluded that the mean intelligence quotient decreased a few points during the decade and that there was a small increase in the percent of pupils of low mentality who remained in high school to graduate. Part II of the study was concerned with differences other than intelligence between an experimental group ranging in I.Q. from 70 to 85 and a control group ranging from 99 to 129. The data showed that the most marked differences between the two groups were revealed by the tests for paragraph meaning, geography and arithmetic, in teachers' marks in academic subjects, teachers' ratings for intelligence, and in leadership, originality, books read per year, and home study. Least differences were found in such things as dictation tests, teachers' marks in music, physical education, industrial arts and citizenship, self-control, industry, and dependability. The author concluded that "much time and effort on the part of the school as well as of the pupils is being misdirected, which, if guided into proper channels, should result in a more wholesome and more adequate adjustment to the problems that these young people will be called upon to meet."

Behavior Problem Pupils

Kaplan's study (273) of behavior problem children in the Central High School of Philadelphia compared delinquents with non-delinquents with respect to intelligence and progress in school work, with respect to the incidence of certain hereditary and environmental characteristics, and emphasized teachers' attitudes as a possible factor in contributing to delinquency. Kaplan concluded that pupils of superior intelligence are in general less likely to become behavior problems than those of inferior or average intelligence, that delinquents as a group are seriously retarded, that retardation, although associated with delinquency, is in most cases the resultant of more subtle conditioning factors, that the home seems to be a primary factor in developing and nurturing delinquent tendencies, and that delinquency is not the result of one factor but of a combination of influences varying with the individual case.

High-School Graduates

Dowd (271) studied the intelligence of 913 pupils who graduated from Cincinnati high schools in 1929, 1930, and 1931, and who were included in the 4,184 sixth-grade pupils tested with the Otis Group Intelligence Test in 1923-24. The median P.R. of these 913 graduates was 73.8 as compared with 45.87 for the entire 4,184. Graduates of the classical curriculum had a median P.R. of 93.75, graduates of the general curriculum 77.33, music 69.7, industrial arts 68.75, household arts 62.50, commercial arts 61.67, and art 44.17. Dowd concluded that pupils with percentile ranks under 25 might succeed in graduating from high school but that the chances are slight since only 1.9 percent of the graduates had ratings that low.

Moore (279) studied 308 Pennsylvania students who graduated from high school before they were sixteen years of age. The study consisted of two main parts: (a) a comparison of the 308 young graduates with 27,000 graduates in the statewide group, and (b) a comparison of the gifted students in the group of 308 with equally gifted students who were older. The author found that the 308 young students had proportionately more foreign-born parents, more fathers from the higher occupational levels, and better educated parents than the statewide group. Fifty-four percent of the young group attended college as compared with 34 percent for the statewide group. The results of the comprehensive examinations given at the end of the sophomore and of the senior year in college showed that students graduating from high school at the age of fifteen maintained their superiority as they progressed through college. The author concluded "that so far as college achievement as measured by objective tests and college grades is concerned, it is desirable to encourage gifted students to enter college at an age as young as fifteen or sixteen years. There is no evidence of any loss since the young gifted hold their own with the older gifted, and there is obvious reason for believing that these young people have saved something like two years, and have probably avoided habits of indolence which they might have acquired if they had refrained from occupying themselves with studies which constituted a real challenge to their intelligence and industry."

Leadership

Two studies of leadership deserve special mention. Brown (268) showed that among high-school pupils leaders were selected pupils in intelligence, scholarship, and socio-economic status, but were a non-homogeneous group with respect to personal qualities, interests, degrees of leadership, range of intelligence, age, and scholarship. Partridge's study (280) of leadership among adolescent boys showed that leadership is associated with age, intelligence, athletic ability, scout rank and tenure, and physical size.

In the judgment of the reviewer, research concerning the pupil population should in the future be concerned less with intelligence, persistence, socio-economic status, etc., concerning which we have had hundreds of studies in the last decade and a half. It should deal much more with attitudes and beliefs. What is modern American youth thinking about the crucial problems of presentday life? What is the school, along with other social agencies, doing to provide opportunities for pupils to think through these crucial problems and to arrive at intelligent conclusions?

C. HIGHER EDUCATION

Numerous studies of the characteristics of college students have been published during the period covered by this review. These studies have dealt with the age of students entering college; the attitudes of college students; intelligence and achievement; reading and study habits; personality and behavior traits; racial and nationality traits; study loads; vocational interests and choices; and enrolments.

Age

A study of the age of freshmen entering the University of Wisconsin (284) showed a much larger percent who entered at eighteen or under in 1932-33 than in 1908-09. Other studies showed that the younger students entering college held their own in scholarship with older students of equal ability (327, 329, 339), that average college marks tended to decrease as age at entrance increased (329), and that the younger students tended to remain in college as long as, or longer than, those of equal ability who entered at the normal age (329, 339). There is general agreement that the acceleration of the superior student is desirable.

Attitudes and Beliefs

Angell (285) showed the depression to have had a maturing and sobering influence upon university students. Other studies reported that students tended to become more liberal as they progressed from the freshman to the senior year, or as they advanced in age (290, 310), social-science courses particularly exerting a definite liberalizing influence (290, 311, 338). The same studies showed a positive correlation when intelligence and scholarship were compared with increases in liberality as measured by tests of attitudes. A definite change in attitude toward crime as a result of studying certain courses dealing with psychology and sociology was reported by Telford (345). Summaries of an investigation of the attitudes of a group of seniors in one university (287, 295) indicated on the whole an unfavorable attitude toward prohibition, a favorable attitude toward pacifism and birth control, a neutral or indifferent attitude toward communism, and a bimodal distribution, some antagonistic, others favorable to the reality of God. Women, on the average, were more favorable to prohibition than were men; women, likewise, expressed a stronger belief in the reality of God than did the men. Physical science majors were not as favorable toward communism and pacifism as were majors in the social sciences. Gelwick (310) found that women were more conservative than men, that religious students were most conservative, and that there is less tendency toward double standards by college students than in 1925.

A study of the religious beliefs of college freshmen and seniors in six liberal arts colleges (303) indicated that freshmen and seniors believed essentially the same religious propositions, but the freshmen showed a greater inclination to believe the propositions than did the seniors. In both groups, a proposition suggesting pleasantness, e.g., the existence of heaven, was believed by a larger number than a proposition suggesting unpleasantness, e.g., the existence of hell. Telford (345) also investigated the attitudes of a group of university students toward the church by the use of the Thurstone and Chave Scale. The data showed that students in the University of North Dakota had on the whole a more favorable attitude toward the church than did students in the University of Chicago, about whom comparable data were available. The study showed the comparative attitudes of the larger groups—Catholic, Protestant, Jewish, and those having no affiliation—also the order of attitudes from most favorable to the least favorable among certain Protestant denominations.

Other investigators reported on attitudes and reactions to the future (319), and on traits attributed to different national and racial groups (320).

Achievement and Intelligence

Most of the studies dealing with either achievement or intelligence, or the interrelation of the two, were limited in scope and in some instances contained certain generalizations not wholly justified by the data. While intelligence test scores identified fairly accurately those who were unlikely to succeed (325), it was demonstrated that high scholastic aptitude ratings did not assure success in college (286). The multiplicity of factors that affect achievement was clearly brought out in a report by Upshall and Masters (348). This study, as well as the one by Bayliss (286), laid emphasis on the fact that many items of information must be taken into account in advising students who rate high as well as those of less promise. A warning against attaching too much weight to a college aptitude rating as a basis for predicting ultimate success both in college and in vocational pursuits appeared in a study made at the University of Minnesota (289). Another investigation at the same institution indicated that students who failed a particular course two or more times, or failed three or more courses, had less than four chances out of a hundred of reaching the upper classes. Failure as defined in the study was advocated as a sound basis for guidance (307). The conclusions reached by Byrns and Henmon (293), after analyzing the records of 687 seniors at the University of Wisconsin, supported the results of other investigations to the effect that the work done in mathematics and foreign language in high school does not develop a student's capacity for successful college work.

An analysis of superior college students at the University of Buffalo showed, on the other hand, that this group took more than two years of Latin in high school and predominated in advanced mathematics. The study showed further that superior students spent less time in high school, excelled in high school, came from the city rather than small towns or rural high schools, were graduated at a younger age, studied more, had keener memories, read more rapidly, took less interest in fraternities or athletic activities, participated in the more intellectual type of activities, and tended toward liberalism but were less suggestible than the average or poor students (304).

A comparison between the records, at the University of Kentucky, made by graduates from private schools and the records made by graduates from public schools showed that the latter have a slightly higher achievement (296). McCullough (324) concluded that, upon the basis of ability and preparation, selective women's colleges might well admit a larger percent of graduates from public schools.

Other studies presented data regarding the general cultural information of undergraduates (316); the intelligence and knowledge of Czechoslovak students (336); the bearing of various factors upon achievement in a school of social work (326); and the comparative achievements of students transferring to Stanford University from junior colleges and four-year colleges and of students doing their work continuously in the University (340).

A few research articles dealt primarily with the scholastic ability of students in college. The results of intelligence tests used widely among colleges showed an increase in the last four years among entering students in the average or median scores in most institutions (346). It appeared also that students made a significant gain in intelligence test scores from the freshman to the senior year and that those who ranked lowest made the largest gains (323, 352). In a comparison of students in collegiate centers of Buffalo with students at the University of Buffalo, it was found that the two groups differed very little in age and in marks obtained on the New York State Regents examination but that the university group was slightly superior in the Ohio State University Psychological Test, Form 17, and in rank in the graduating class (343). A report based upon the average grade points of 3,000 undergraduates at the University of Colorado stated that men were not superior intellectually to women. In fact, "without a single exception the women are ahead of the men by a few points." Several factors bearing upon the relative achievements of the men and women were summarized (298). A somewhat unusual study of the relation of color-blindness to intelligence was made by Lorenz and McClure (322). Students classified as color-blind made intelligence test scores averaging 11.39 points higher than those not color-blind. The academic records of the color-blind group, on the other hand, were slightly lower than for the other group. The total number in the color-blind group was too small to warrant any conclusive generalizations.

Reading Ability and Study Habits

A continued interest in the reading technics and skills of college students is reflected in the investigations reported in this field. A photographic study of eye-movements in reading, of students matched upon the basis of a number of important factors, revealed no significant differences between probation students and successful students as to the average number of fixational pauses or as to the duration of pauses and the number of regressive movements. The successful students tended to make higher scores in reading comprehension but no significant differences in rate of reading were found (308). Broom (292) likewise found that "reading comprehension is important for successful academic study, since the average student who demonstrates reading comprehension on a standardized test on his entrance into the college earns on the average a better academic record than does the student who is weak in reading comprehension." While the author showed that both mental ability and reading comprehension contributed to academic achievement, he did not show the intercorrelation between these two factors.

There was found no high correlation for adult subjects between visual apprehension of meaningless material and achievement in reading or in intelligence tests (321).

Some investigations have dealt with the nature and amount of reading done by college students (306). Reports along this line indicated that there was a significant relationship between the total amount of time spent in reading and study and the number of pages read; that although there were no significant differences among classes as to the amount of time spent in reading and study, seniors read a significantly greater number of pages than sophomores. The average number of pages read was twenty-two to thirty-nine per hour. There were no significant differences between the sexes in either the amount of time spent in reading or the number of pages read, and the amount of reading had no significant relation to scholarship or intelligence.

The amount of time students spent in reading and study ranged from twelve hours per week in one institution to forty-four hours per week in another (301, 306, 312, 350). About 50 percent of the students in one institution spent as much time in study as professors expected (301), in another the average time per week devoted to academic ends exceeded the amount that faculty members believed could be profitably used (340). According to Hotz and Trice (317), students who varied in their total academic load from semester to semester by either carrying an abnormally heavy schedule or less than a normal program, on the whole, showed more improvement than those who carried the same load from semester to semester. No data were given in this study regarding the study habits of the different groups. Reeder (334) reported little relationship to exist between study habits measured by Wrenn's Study Habits Inventory and intelligence. A knowledge of the results of the study habits test combined with suggestions for improving study technics resulted in improvement.

Personality and Behavior Traits

College cribbers have a more or less distinctive combination of personality traits according to Coiner (299). According to their score on the Bernreuter Inventory, the cribbers were more neurotic, less self-sufficient, more introverted, and more prone to overstate the extent of their knowledge. Approximately 50 percent of the subjects included in this study cheated to some degree. Those who cheated but did not admit it varied more from the normal combination of personality traits than did those who were honest or those who admitted cheating.

There was found no significant relationship between menarcheal age and Bernreuter ratings for neurotic tendency, self-sufficiency, introversion, or dominance; nor was there any significant relationship between Bernreuter's ratings and height or weight, or the height-weight ratio. Likewise, intelligence test scores and menarcheal age showed no significant relation.

There was a small but significant positive correlation between menarcheal age and height (341). An extensive study of the physique of women students in a college in the South was published by Gould (314).

A comparison of personality traits between negro and white students, North and South, indicated certain racial as well as sectional differences, but the inferences were admittedly tentative and need to be verified further (331).

Vocations

Little appears to have been done recently in studying college students from the standpoint of vocational interests, aptitudes, or achievement. One investigation presented an analysis of vocations entered by women from land-grant colleges, giving the median salaries earned, the marital status of the members of different vocational groups, and their relation to vocations subsequent to marriage (353).

Another investigator (294) reported a survey of the vocations entered and the avocational activities participated in by graduates from forty-five southern colleges and universities. He found that 81.3 percent of the graduates from private and denominational colleges engaged in gainful employment as compared with 92 percent of the graduates from the state colleges for women and 93.8 percent of the graduates from coeducational institutions. The avocational interests including politics, church, books, and a wide range of amusements cannot be presented in detail in this connection. The specialized vocational interests of students who entered a technical school were investigated by Remmers (335). An analysis of the relation of curriculums of different schools in the University of Pennsylvania to both vocational and subjectmatter interests of students and the relation of subject preferences to performance in those subjects was presented by Chauncey (297).

Enrolments

Several studies dealt with enrolment trends (349), conditions affecting enrolment trends (300), and the geographical distribution of enrolments in selected institutions (330, 342).

CHAPTER VI
Guidance and Counseling
A. ELEMENTARY EDUCATION

RESEARCH ON GUIDANCE in the elementary school is conspicuous by its absence. This dearth of research may be due to three causes: (a) the difficulty in evaluating guidance programs and procedures; (b) the essential nature of guidance which demands a utilization and synthesis of research in other more specialized fields; and (c) the integration of guidance and education in the elementary years. The principles underlying progressive education coincide with the principles of guidance, but neither the methods of progressive education nor the more specialized guidance functions in the elementary school have been subjected to scientific evaluation. This section will, therefore, necessarily be limited to a brief summary of surveys and descriptive accounts of guidance programs in the elementary school and to the more technical aspect of the use of tests in counseling.

Programs of Guidance

Surveys misleading—Guidance is functioning anonymously in the majority of elementary schools. The process of helping children to attain their potentialities is carried on to some extent in every school, though it is seldom labeled *guidance* or *personnel work*. Only in work with deviates does this process become differentiated from education and acquire a specific name, usually that of *child guidance*. Thus we find *child guidance clinics* established in certain elementary-school systems, and less frequently *pupil personnel bureaus*. Allen (355) summarized the situation as follows:

> Results of a recent questionnaire on guidance in the elementary schools of the United States indicated that apparently few cities had undertaken the task and little had been accomplished. Such a report may be very misleading. Every progressive elementary-school system has always performed many guidance functions rather effectively. The difficulty has been that such functions have not been regarded as guidance and consequently have not been recognized for their real nature and purpose. Often, moreover, they have not been effectively coordinated (355:81).

Child guidance clinics—The child guidance clinics are an important teaching agency and supplement to the guidance program in the elementary school. The development and present status of child guidance clinics is described in one of the excellent publications of the Commonwealth Fund (389). The service functions of these clinics are threefold: to study and treat patients, to cooperate with other agencies in the prevention and treatment of maladjustment, and to reveal to the community the unmet needs of children.

View of the program as a whole—The guidance program as a whole described by Weglein (397) begins in the elementary school and includes the following features: cumulative records kept from the time the child enters school, guidance service in making educational and vocational plans, group work largely through classes in educational information, and cooperation with high-school personnel workers in bridging the gap between elementary school and high school.

McCarthy (374) discussed the history of the guidance movement, the need of guidance below the junior high school, and the activities of progressive systems. His survey made in 1932 was based on replies of twenty-eight cities to this main question: "Do you make definite provision for guidance in grades one through six?" Eighteen of these cities answered "yes"; ten answered "no"; and only six reported provision for vocational guidance. Although in most cases the regular teachers were responsible for the guidance of pupils, there were six cities that reported having special teachers known as teachers of vocational and educational guidance, visiting teachers, or counselors. Several cities mentioned the service rendered by child study laboratories or clinics and one, a bureau of child guidance. In these cities, with one exception, only isolated features rather than comprehensive programs of guidance were reported. The exception was Milwaukee which did not attempt to separate guidance into its educational, vocational, social, moral, and physical aspects but rather emphasized the unified best development of every child. In the kindergarten, this objective involved the collection of information about every child from his parents, observation and records of his social and emotional status, and a physical inventory. This early study of the child was continued throughout the grades by means of questionnaires, rating scales, objective tests, and records of significant incidents in the child's experience which contributed to the ever-growing cumulative record. The principal coordinated the problem and utilized the services of such specialists as were available. Child study and adjustment were continuous. Pittsburgh reported the most carefully planned study of occupations correlated with the regular courses of study from the first through the sixth grade and having a twofold purpose to acquaint pupils with the various kinds of work done in the city and to give them a respect for the dignity of all useful labor. The proposed ideal program included as its main features education of teachers in the personnel point of view and procedures, child study, adjustment to individual needs and abilities, cumulative records of each pupil available for use by teachers, and the service of experts for specialized diagnosis and counseling.

The success of the guidance program in the majority of elementary schools rests chiefly upon the teacher who at present is poorly prepared for this task. "Teachers have been trained to educate. Have they been educated to guide?" (390:101, 399).

Vocational guidance—Vocational guidance is a specialized phase of guidance. Kitson (372) summarized the functions of the vocational counselor as follows: to help the individual to become interested in worthy vocations and to find information about them; to make an inventory of his present assets—physical, psychological, social, and economic; to direct him in securing the best educational preparation for occupational endeavor; and to assist him in finding a job and progressing in it. All of these functions have a place in the eight-year elementary school. Wales (396) compared vocational guidance methods in Berlin with those in London. She found in London a definite attempt to prepare the child for the transition from school to industry, and a more adequate program of individual counseling which takes the form of case conferences with every child due to leave school. This preliminary guidance is followed by a system of industrial supervision. The Berlin program, on the other hand, does not attempt to advise each child individually, nor is there as comprehensive and active an industrial supervision and after-care service as in London. Since choice of occupation is relatively limited, the London emphasis on adjustment on the job seems more promising than the American emphasis on elementary-school or junior high-school classes in occupations (360).

A specialized phase of this total program was studied by Thorndike and others (392), namely, the relation between certain test scores and certain criteria of subsequent educational and vocational success. Approximately two thousand children tested at the age of fourteen with the best tests of intelligence, clerical capacity, and mechanical adroitness then available were followed up for eight years and retested at the age of twenty-two. It was found that the grade which an individual will reach can be predicted with substantial accuracy, but that none of the measures used predicted vocational success as measured by the criteria set up. In spite of the limitations of the investigation as research in vocational guidance, Thorndike's results (380) contribute to the professional body of subjectmatter in this field accurate facts concerning certain definite relationships.

Macrae's results (376) bear on the same problem. He concluded that by the age of ten, if not before, a reliable measure of the child's general educable capacity can be obtained, but vocational predictions must be reserved for the age period of thirteen to fifteen or thirteen to seventeen. In a follow-up of nearly two hundred vocationally advised cases, Macrae (375) found 97 percent of the successful cases had followed the institute's advice. As Macrae pointed out, however, "the estimate of actual success is almost as difficult as the estimation of potential success." Menger's study (378) of the vocational choices of children of different ages likewise showed the need for guidance in the elementary school.

The efficacy of a vocational guidance program, however, can be ascertained only by control group experiments in which a large number of persons who have had vocational guidance of the most approved kind are compared with a similar group who have not had it (372, 376).

Counseling

The counseling process in its broad sense comprises both the appraisal and the adjustment of the individual. Appraisal by means of tests has been recognized as a research problem; the experimental study of other phases of counseling has been neglected.

Much of the research on tests significant for guidance has already been summarized. Baker and others (356) in the *Review of Educational Research* reported not only a critical evaluation of tests of intelligence, aptitude, character, personality, emotional adjustment, and social attitudes, but also measures of character and personality through conduct and information. Nor was this issue of the *Review* confined to the tests themselves; the applications of results to specific situations, groups, and populations were also considered. In this section, therefore, only a selected number of investigations of especial interest to pupil personnel workers will be included.

Tests used in clinics—The intelligence test most frequently reported as used by twenty-eight child guidance clinics in the United States was the Stanford-Binet which was used by all the clinics reporting (362). The personality test most frequently reported, the Bernreuter, was used by only six clinics. The most popular vocational guidance test, the O'Connor Wiggly Block, was used by four clinics. A wide variety of tests of special abilities were used, of which the Stenquist Test of Mechanical Ability and the Stanford Achievement Test were reported most frequently.

Intelligence tests—Reference has already been made to summaries of the extensive investigations of intelligence tests (356, 382).

Measurement of achievement—A similar service has been rendered by Jones and others (367, 368, 369) in the field of achievement testing. In France, a critical study of the traditional examination given to pupils at approximately twelve years of age (373) showed a marked discrepancy between the results of the certificate examinations and the experimental tests. The correlation between the two was only .20. Certain pupils clearly showed superiority in the experimental tests and yet were lowest in the list in the academic examinations. The good pupil of the examination was not the one possessing the important mental abilities measured by the experimental tests. Laugier and others (373) reported a lack of agreement in the marks given by two experienced examiners which was similar to that reported earlier by American investigators of the subjectivity of teachers' marks. The French authors concluded that, except for French composition, subjective valuations should be replaced so far as possible by objective measures. They recognized the need for measures of two goals—the acquisition of knowledge and the determination of special abilities of children or of young people who could profit by a specialized educational development. It is interesting to note that France, Scotland, and England seem to have the implicit faith in standardized tests that characterized educators in America some years ago.

The major issue in the measurement of achievement in this country seems to be that between objective reliable measures of specific abilities manifested in controlled situations and a less reliable but more relational study of achievement under natural conditions. Considerable dissatisfaction has been expressed with available tests (370) which reenforced the tendency to include in an adequate repertory of educational measurements, not only paper and pencil tests but also recorded observation of the pupils' work and records of their reading and participation in other cultural activities (394).

Tests of personality and character—Tests of personality appropriate for the elementary school are less numerous than similar instruments devised for high-school and college students. Experimental work with the Rorschach ink-blot test was reported by Kerr (371) in England, Giehm (363) in Germany, and Beck (358) and Meltzer (377) in the United States, all of whom have reported favorably on the validity of this instrument in measuring emotional stability of elementary-school children. This is one of the few personality tests which is suitable for elementary-school children and for children of different nationalities. It represents one of the rare attempts to devise a usable objective instrument which is diagnostic of the personality as a whole.

Other personality measures that have been used experimentally with elementary-school children are Maller's Character Sketches, Symonds' and Block's student questionnaire, Woodworth-Matthews Questionnaire, Sweet's Personal Attitudes Test, and Pintner and others' Pupil Portraits. The conflicting results obtained with these tests (356) suggest that the total score on this type of questionnaire used with children of elementary-school age is of less value in guidance than a study of the specific responses made by individuals.

The summary (361) of research on methods of measuring attitudes included a relatively small number of references in the elementary-school field.

Vernon (395), in an able discussion of the problem of the attitude of the subject in personality testing, called attention to the fundamental difficulty, that the subject who knows that his personality is under investigation cannot react normally. Because of this difficulty, the observational technics of studying personality under natural conditions seem to be far the most promising and the desirability of taking into consideration the meaning of the test to the subject, extremely important.

Observation—Consecutive short sample observations of the overt behavior of selected individuals distributed over a period of months were described by Thomas and others (391), and this technic was applied to groups of kindergarten children and to older boys in a trade school. Such an analytical study of disparate phases of behavior with little or no coordination and articulation of the whole was criticized by Bott (359). Her method was to begin with an all-inclusive diary record which made possible an interpretation of each event in terms of its context. Rating, which is essentially directed observation, was studied by Williams (398). He analyzed more than a thousand personality reports of the essay type written by teachers at the Chicago University Elementary School and, on the basis of the list of traits thus obtained, constructed a personality rating scale.

Choice of tests for different purposes—Although this is a problem constantly confronting the counselor, little research has been done on it. Hildreth (364) found that verbal and non-verbal tests show equally well the superiority of young bright children over average children. Senour (388) and Sanchez (384) both emphasized the necessity of using a non-language mental test with bilingual groups. Schiller's analysis (386) of the verbal, numerical, and spatial abilities of 395 children in grades three and four indicated the presence of a central factor and of differentiable abilities measured by the sub-tests within a general intelligence battery. The role of speed in intelligence is another topic that confronts counselors in their choice of tests. Research on this subject has been summarized by Beck (357). Segel (387) described a method of differential diagnosis as a means of making more effective use of test results in the individual guidance of children and in the enrichment of their experience in accordance with their strengths and weaknesses.

Comment—Most of these researches throw little light on the dynamics of behavior; they are concerned primarily with the end results, not with the process by which certain characteristics are acquired. They are useful to the counselor in diagnosis; they aid him only indirectly in the equally important function of adjustment.

From the standpoint of the personnel worker, further research is needed along at least six lines:

1. Improvement of the best tests now available
2. Construction of tests and other measurements in new areas of educational objectives
3. Development of cumulative record systems by means of which the results of measurement will be used to best advantage
4. Formulation of a philosophy of educational measurement
5. Study of the background needed by the investigator in the interpretation and use of the results of tests, observations, and interviews
6. Study of the relativity of an individual's responses to one another and to the total situation that evokes them.

B. SECONDARY EDUCATION

Significant research in guidance at the secondary level has been startlingly lacking in the last three years. In comparison with the nationwide publication and discussion of guidance, its needs and effective practice, little scientific study in the field has been conducted recently. Apparently there has been a great deal of "wishful thinking" with respect to programs and practices as now carried out. Perhaps the greatest needs at present are evaluation of present practices, and further occupational studies. The latter are needed particularly in occupations which do not call for college training. Although much less than half of the high-school graduates attend college, although large numbers of boys and girls do not finish high school, although many in college perhaps should not attend as colleges are now constituted, still it is almost impossible to find reliable information on occupations which require training of non-collegiate grade. Many doctoral dissertations could be written on the evaluation of guidance practices.

More could be written on occupational studies. At least one could be written in every state on the opportunities for occupational training of non-collegiate grade.

Guidance Programs

Reavis (412) studied the kind and extent of guidance in a large number of schools through personal visitation. He found four major types of organization: (a) centralized bureaus of guidance for secondary schools in city system; (b) city school systems with a central guidance organization but with the individual secondary school considered the unit in the program; (c) centralized bureaus or departments in individual secondary schools; and (d) central guidance organizations in individual secondary schools which utilize regular officers and teachers as guidance functionaries. Virtually the same guidance activities are undertaken in all schools though procedures and organization employed vary. Using regular officers and teachers as guidance functionaries reduces cost.

Cunliffe and others (402) made a detailed "status" study of guidance in 188 New Jersey high schools. Strength seemed to lie in educational, curriculum, and homeroom guidance, while activities of a definitely vocational guidance nature, such as a course in occupations and placement, tended to be weak. Junior high schools presented better balanced programs than did senior high schools. Schools of 300 to 1,000 pupils had better balanced programs than the very large or very small schools.

Kefauver, Noll, and Drake (405) found that guidance practices in specialized high schools differ little from those in comprehensive high schools. They concluded that both types of school have a long way to go in the development of their guidance programs.

Vocational Choice

Menger (410) investigated the occupational choices of 3,083 pupils in grades nine to twelve. The number of occupations chosen at each grade level was: ninth—boys, 95, girls, 51; tenth—boys, 74, girls, 48; eleventh—boys, 72, girls, 43; twelfth—boys, 62, girls, 42. Barr scale values for the occupations chosen tended to increase from grade to grade. This study confirmed the findings of other investigations: narrow range of choice centered in "white-collar" jobs, and wide dissimilarity between choices and distribution of workers in occupations. Accelerated boys tend to choose professions; retarded boys choose commercial and mechanical pursuits.

Johnson (404) found that joy and pleasure in the work plus interest predominated as reasons given for occupational choice by high-school boys in a statewide survey. More than two-thirds of the boys were interested in engineering. No significant differences were discerned between city and country boys.

Occupational Information

Proffitt (411) found in an investigation of 1,100 high schools that 68.5 percent provide occupational information for students. Of these, 43.8

percent report the instruction given as a separate course, while 51.3 percent provide it as a part of other courses.

A most significant evaluation study was made by Hand (403). He compared 391 senior high-school students who had had the "Life-Career" course with 250 who had not. He used tests on occupational information, information on false guidance, educational information, an adjustment test, and a questionnaire. The study showed that on all measurements there were practically no statistically significant differences in the two groups. Not all aspects of all objectives of the course were measured. This would seem to indicate that serious attention should be given to the "Life-Career" class everywhere to determine whether or not the values claimed for such a course are really being achieved.

Thorndike and others (414) made a very detailed study following up a large group of children who were studied in 1922. At that time information was collected concerning school record, general intelligence, clerical ability, and mechanical adroitness. Many items were found valuable for prediction of vocational and educational advancement, while others were of little or no significance.

Guidance Problems

Love (409) studied the vocational, educational, and personal problems of high-school seniors as determined by analysis of interview records, personnel data, and questions asked in personal conferences by 3,000 high-school seniors over a two-year period. The study included a list of 1,500 separate and distinct questions asked of the counselor by the seniors. The problems were analyzed and classified from many standpoints: e.g., for both sexes, highly intelligent seniors presented comparatively more educational and personal problems and fewer vocational problems than the less intelligent. By showing what the guidance problems of seniors actually were this study gave a valuable factual basis for training guidance workers.

Richardson (413) pointed out some of the fallacies of placing too much dependence on intelligence quotients in guidance.

Miscellaneous

Brammell (401) studied certain aspects of articulation between high school and college. There is confusion to the extent that there are no generally recognized standards in the pattern of admission requirements. The value of current requirements has not been clearly demonstrated. The four outstanding hindrances to improved articulation listed by colleges are quoted:

1. Lack of specific subject guidance in the secondary schools for pupils planning to enter college
2. Lack of secondary-school guidance of pupils into appropriate activities after graduation
3. Lack of well-organized guidance work in colleges and universities
4. Lack of effectiveness in colleges and universities in properly orientating and instructing the freshmen.

The problem of articulation is not to be solved at the point of transition from the secondary school to college. The abilities, habits, characteristics, interests, and health of pupils ought to be studied during their secondary-school careers.

The studies reported by Koos and Kefauver (407) and the article by Kitson and Stover (408) offer much material on the status of guidance and attempts at evaluation.

Kefauver and Davis (406) found that only 140 out of 461 articles dealing with guidance in five leading educational journals involved some systematic investigation. Ten directors of guidance felt that the greatest need was for measuring the results of existing forms of guidance, while 51 professors of guidance attached largest importance to the proposition: "Set up well-planned programs of guidance, make complete records at each step or grade level, and make a careful measure of the results obtained by this well-planned guidance service."

C. HIGHER EDUCATION

The Need of Guidance

The need of guidance is reflected in studies of the problems of students. In the Pasadena Junior College by far the largest percent of problems pertained to educational adjustments. Other problems in the order of their frequency of occurrence were classified as vocational, attendance, social, economic, health, avocational, and moral (475). Problems reported in a study at the University of Minnesota in the order of their frequency were educational, social, personal, emotional, vocational, health and physical disabilities, and financial (482). One writer (483) found that transfer students had several problems that were different from those of students who enter the same university as freshmen. Other studies have likewise reported educational and vocational problems to be of major significance (425, 435, 477). The studies by Hartmann (435) and Emme (425) included detailed analyses of problems too extensive in scope to be enumerated in this issue of the *Review*. A few studies were devoted to special disabilities and difficulties, e.g., arithmetical and algebraic (446), social (453), educational (457).

Educational Counseling

The most important studies bearing upon educational counseling dealt with the prediction of success in college. While there was general agreement among the investigators that college grades could be predicted with sufficient reliability to make the predictions of practical value, there was marked disagreement as to the single measures that give the best prediction. Kriner (442) found that the judgments of administrative officers correlated more highly with achievement than did high-school rank or the results of objective tests and, further, that a psychological test and rank in high-school graduating class had practically the same correlation with first semester grades in college. Wagner (478) found that the average of all regents examinations correlated better with college marks than did any one of a number of other measures that were employed. Reitz (458) reported that the score on scholastic aptitude, as measured by the American Council Psychological Examination, gave the highest correlation with comprehensive examinations at the University of Chicago. Among the investigators who combined two or more measures, there was general agreement that the predictions were better than when only one measure was employed (440, 458). Flemming (428) reported a correlation of .67 between a number of measures and achievement in college, but he did not discuss the relative predictive value of the different measures. A study of the value of various measures for prediction in the University of Chicago was reported in a survey of the institution (454). Some of the investigations were given to the prediction of achievement in specific subjects or fields of study in college. Particularly striking was the agreement of two investigators to the effect that achievement in college could be predicted approximately as well from data secured in the freshman year in high school, or even earlier, as from data secured at the time of graduation (419, 427). Wagner (478) found it easiest to predict language achievement and most difficult to predict achievement in mathematics; English, social science, and physical science fell between these extremes. An exceptionally high correlation, .61, between two English placement tests combined with a college aptitude test and final grades in first quarter of college English, was reported by Starbuck (469). Other studies dealt with the prediction of success in mathematics (451), and in nurses' training (460). Remmers (459) found that an institution that emphasizes technical training tended to select students who were less successful in the formal aspects of English but who rated relatively high on tests of mathematical, chemical, and technical knowledge. The size of the high school from which a student graduated was found to have no significant bearing in the prediction of first quarter average college grades (450). Personality scores were reported to bear little direct relation to academic achievement, but because of the indirect effect of personality factors upon achievement were, nevertheless, considered important in counseling students (468, 476).

With the exception of two studies of limited importance, dealing with methods of preparing for objective tests (422, 424), no significant reports bearing upon other aspects of educational counseling were found.

Vocational Guidance

A study of the vocational satisfactions of 2,424 graduates of Stanford University showed that 19 percent of the group would not reselect their present vocation. Fifty-two percent of those dissatisfied were in professions or vocations demanding college training (484). A comprehensive study of the vocations entered by graduates of the College of the City of New York, covering the period from 1849 to 1934 illustrated trends toward and away from certain vocations (441). A third investigation of the vocational adjustments of college graduates presented data showing that graduates with high scholarship records more often followed vocations in line with their undergraduate fields of specialization than did those having low records (466). In apparent disagreement with this conclusion was the report by Hillman (436) that the higher the intelligence of an individual the less likely is he to follow a vocation for which he has been trained. Houston (437) concluded from an extensive study at the University of Colorado that students who made a definite vocational choice upon entering the university had higher intelligence scores than did those who were undecided and that a larger percent majored in fields related to their vocational choice. He concluded further that "favorite studies" were more closely related to vocational choices than were "highest mark" studies. Achilles (415) found likewise that a larger percent of those having made a definite vocational choice were above the average in ability. The greatest need and desire for further vocational guidance existed among undecided students. This group had a much smaller percent of students with grades above average than did the decided group.

Lehman and Witty (444) stressed the need for vocational guidance by showing that the vocational choices of boys are inconsistent with the opportunities in many occupations. One of the most comprehensive and valuable studies analyzed the factors affecting the educational and vocational plans of a large group of seniors in colleges of Pennsylvania (471). The scope of the study was such that a detailed statement of all the results cannot be included here. Of special importance in this connection is the conclusion that many colleges failed to provide vocational guidance adequate to the needs and desires of the students (471). The inadequacy of provisions for vocational guidance in colleges and universities was further confirmed by Huston (438) in a survey of the practices followed in forty-three institutions.

Most of the investigations pertaining to the prediction of occupational success and the definition of measures for guidance purposes were outside of the college field. Mention should be made of them, nevertheless, because of their bearing upon the subject of guidance. Dodge (423) and Trabue (474) have each reported on occupational ability patterns. There is evidence in the latter study that occupations may be differentiated to some degree by distinctive patterns of ability that characterize those who are successfully and happily employed in them. The former study confirmed Trabue's conclusions, although exception was taken to certain phases of the procedure. Thorndike and others' study (470), quite widely known, dealt primarily with the possibility of vocational guidance at the precollege level, but it is noted here because it was carried over into the college period with a small group. He reported that educational careers could be predicted with greater accuracy at the ages of fourteen, fifteen, or sixteen than could the vocational future. The study as a whole is significant. Sparling (467) reported upon the basis of information secured from 888 students of Long Island University that the majority of students expected to enter vocations in which they would have a handicap in intelligence.

Points of special significance that appeared in a study at Ohio State University by Zorbaugh (485) were the nature of the part-time employment problem as a phase of vocational counseling, the inadequacy of vocational counseling, and the relation of preparation for a career to marriage on the part of college women.

Housing Students

The housing and boarding of students present definite problems that bear upon student welfare. Some of these problems belong to administrative officers other than student counselors; others bear directly upon counseling. A bulletin of the United States Office of Education (429) summarized the provisions for housing students found in various types of institutions. This report showed that, generally, better provisions were made for housing women than for men; that college-owned residence halls were preferable to other types of housing; and that it was advantageous to students who lived in private rooms to rent only rooms approved by the institution. One investigator (461) reported a study of the management problems of fraternities and sororities with a view to finding how, and to what extent, colleges and universities were assisting the fraternities and sororities in their management problems. The investigation showed clearly the wide divergence of practice with reference to such problems as supervision, ownership of property, regulation of building costs, locations, business management, and auditing.

Two well-organized studies dealt with the relation of student housing to success in a university. There was close agreement in the two studies to the effect that residents in dormitories excelled students who lived in private rooms, at home, or in fraternity and sorority houses (456, 479).

Health and Hygiene

Many articles and books have been written that stress the importance of physical and mental health to college students, but comparatively few are of a research nature. Reeves and others (455) summarized the provisions made for student health service in a group of liberal arts colleges. Griswold and Spicer (433) investigated the organization, services rendered, and costs of the health service in six large colleges and universities. While some variations appeared in the type of services rendered and the general plan of rendering the services, these institutions provided services far superior to those of typical liberal arts colleges as reported by Reeves and others (455). Patrick and Rowles (449) reported a number of intercorrelations between certain indexes of health and of scholastic promise of success, e.g., metabolic rate, vital capacity, blood pressure, intelligence, scholarship, and personality. In only a few items—age and health index, systolic and diastolic blood pressure, and percentile rank and point-hour-ratio—were there low reliable positive correlations found.

Guidance Programs and Procedures

Several surveys showed the extent to which guidance programs were in operation in colleges and universities and the types of guidance provided. Townsend (473) made a comprehensive study of practices in guidance among teachers colleges together with an evaluation of specific items that should be included in a guidance program. This study is valuable for use in organizing and administering guidance.

Other investigations pertained to specific methods of guidance, particularly orientation (416, 429, 452, 472). Bennett (416) reported that most public junior colleges gave group guidance through an orientation course. Only in twelve out of thirty-three of these institutions was individual guidance tied up with the orientation courses. The data indicated favorable results from orientation courses and an increase in the number of such courses. In content the courses were pointed more toward aiding students in solving individual problems of life adjustment and less toward the larger problems of group adjustment. Frazier and others (429) found that 80.1 percent of 417 colleges and universities studied had some form of orientation and about the same percent had a definite program of guidance in operation. Data were also secured regarding financial aid to students—aid in providing employment for self-help students and the placement of graduates. Two studies indicated that, on the whole, student opinions favored the orientation courses in which they participated (452, 472).

While skepticism was expressed by one writer regarding the value of personnel data, the results of objective tests in particular (434), the weight of opinion supported by research data was favorable to the effectiveness of counseling and to the use of objective data in counseling (421, 431, 447, 465, 477, 480). One investigation (475) indicated that generally men should counsel men students and women should counsel women students, except in social problems. The number of cases upon which the conclusions were based was too limited to justify any far-reaching generalization.

The value and effectiveness of an administrative plan coordinating the counseling procedures in the University of Minnesota were presented in two reports (481, 482). The number of counseling contacts made with students, the nature of the problems, and the relationship between certain objective data and the recurrence of certain types of problems were summarized.

The publications of a non-research type that were examined in selecting materials for this review dealt with other aspects of guidance not included among the topics of this section. The absence of research data on some of these aspects, as well as the limited data available on some of the topics included here point the way for much more extensive research in the field of guidance.

CHAPTER VII
Extra-Curriculum Activities
A. ELEMENTARY EDUCATION

THE TERM, *extra-curriculum activities*, is unfamiliar in the elementary school. Few references of any kind dealing with this subject were located. This does not mean, however, that activities of an extra-curriculum nature are absent from the elementary school. On the contrary, the curriculum of many progressive schools is extra-curriculum in spirit and is characterized by spontaneity, interest, initiative, freedom, and participation in planning of the extra-curriculum activities.

Since research on extra-curriculum activities in the elementary school is practically nil, this section is brief and will include only (a) several descriptive accounts of activities carried out voluntarily by pupils in addition to the regular classroom requirement either after school hours or in a period designated for such purpose, or as an integrated part of the school day; and (b) contribution of outside organizations to the extra-curriculum program.

Types of Activities and Extent of Participation

Porter (487) defined extra-curriculum activities as events in which *all* pupils participate voluntarily. The chief activities carried on in one school system over a period of ten years were (a) drives such as a magazine drive in which children raised money for a piano by selling old magazines; (b) performances and exhibits such as operettas, pageants, and art exhibits; (c) handwork projects such as weaving; (d) excursions; (e) service activities such as the management of the cafeteria and the provision of free milk, food, and clothing for needy children; (f) organized groups such as the Scouts, Junior Red Cross, and Young Citizens' League; and (g) competitive sports and games. The description of this extra-curriculum program led the reader to wonder whether its aim was primarily financial or educational.

Washburne's program (488) of group and creative activities is extra-curriculum in nature, though it is part of the official school day, and constitutes an essential part of the education of the "whole child." The participation varies with the group and may include organized play, clubs, committees, self-governing assemblies, a school newspaper, and a school bazaar. These activities always include creative expression through handwork, informal composition, art, and dramatization. They include a wide variety of projects which, although they often grow out of the individualized academic work, are essentially an end in themselves. In many other progressive elementary schools, these same kinds of activities are integrated with the regular work of the school; in fact, they form the core from which academic endeavor emanates.

Outside Organizations Associated with the School

The Scouts are the strongest outside organization affiliated with the elementary school. Wyland (489) obtained information on scouting in the schools from 536 elementary-school principals as well as from superintendents and high-school principals. He found this organization prevalent and approved. Scouts constituted slightly over 50 percent of all the boys in the school studied. Schoolmen expressed general goodwill toward scouting and recognized it as an educational agency. The most significant differences in the records of Scouts and non-Scouts were in respect to the number of Scouts holding positions of leadership and participating in student activities.

About half of the Girl Reserves in the cities studied by Davis (486) were below the ninth grade and about one-third were fourteen years of age or younger. This investigation showed a large but transient participation of girls of elementary-school age in the Y. W. C. A. activities.

Comments

The lack of emphasis on the constructive side of guidance is indicated by the few references in this section. Personnel work broadly defined is not primarily remedial. It is not chiefly concerned with problem behavior, delinquency, and other forms of deviation from the desirable. It is concerned with a constructive program for the development of every child. What kind of research can contribute to the realization of such a program? It seems to the writer that one type of research is essential—a study of the changes produced in individuals by certain kinds of activities or programs. Successful research of this kind presupposes reliable and valid technics for studying individuals. Such technics are not available. The need, therefore, is first of all the development of measuring instruments. This is research basic to research.

B. SECONDARY EDUCATION

The literature on extra-curriculum activities has developed with amazing rapidity during the period since about 1920. During the three-year period under review several books and monographs and hundreds of magazine articles appeared as well as many unpublished theses. Nineteen selected research studies falling within the period may be classified as follows: general surveys, Brammell (490), Reavis and Van Dyke (504), Ferriss, Gaumnitz, and Brammell (495); administration, Draper and Corbally (493), Holroyd (498), and Noble (501); athletics, Brammell (490), Cormany (492), Eaton and Shannon (494), and Perry (502); homeroom, McKown (500); pupil participation, Spence (505) and Wyman (508); clubs, Proffitt (503); relation to curriculum, Jones (499); teacher preparation, Briggs (491); evaluation, Henninger (496) and Holland (497); and bibliographies, Terry (506, 507). Due to space limitations the present review will be limited to surveys of extra-curriculum activities, administration, homerooms, relation to the curriculum, teacher preparation, and evaluation.

Surveys of Extra-Curriculum Activities

Two of the monographs of the National Survey of Secondary Education are devoted entirely and one in part to the status of extra-curriculum activities in the secondary schools of the United States. Reavis and Van Dyke (504) traced the development of extra-curriculum activities in four secondary schools for the three decades 1900-30, and presented the status of activities in 224 representative high schools. Data were presented on such problems as limitation of participation, the organization of new activities, credit toward graduation, extra-curriculum guidance, finances, administration, training of pupil officers, and interscholastic non-athletic contests. Twenty-four of the 224 schools were studied intensively by visitation with particular reference to purposes, membership, meetings and programs, finances, and sponsorship. An attempt at appraisal of non-athletic activities was made by securing data from 529 graduates of private and 293 graduates of public high schools. In the words of the authors: "The responses revealed a strong consensus of opinion in support of extra-curriculum activities as a necessary part of secondary education."

Brammell (490) presented data for 327 secondary schools cited as doing outstanding work in athletics, both intramural and interscholastic. The status of intramural athletics in the 327 schools was presented with respect to scope, administration, finances, relation to other activities, experiments, and trends. Likewise data were presented showing the status of interscholastic athletics with respect to scope, administration including tournaments and meets, athletic associations, girls athletics, finances, and interschool relationships. The author concluded that "interscholastic competitions are confined mainly to a few sports, most of which have no carry-over value" and "the schools in general are recognizing the close relationship between intramural sports, physical education, health work, and interscholastic athletics."

Ferriss, Gaumnitz, and Brammell (495) described both athletic and non-athletic activities in the smaller schools of the country. In summary the authors said: "The data on extracurriculum and related activities show clearly that the smaller schools are giving considerable attention to this phase of secondary education. They show also that, in general, the smaller the schools the more limited the range of activities offered and the smaller the proportion of schools fostering each activity."

Administration

The administration of extra-curriculum activities was described in considerable detail by the National Survey of Secondary Education (490, 504). Draper and Corbally (493) studied the practices of eighteen carefully selected junior, senior, and junior-senior high schools "which were experimenting in administratively organizing their schools so that the educational values of the extra-class activities could be evaluated adequately and credit for participation in these activities could be allowed the students toward graduation from their respective organizations." Data were presented on the stimulation and limitation of activities, the director of activities, academic and non-academic credit for activities, records and forms used, and articulation of the extra-curriculum activities. Some of their conclusions were: all point systems include scholarship as a prerequisite for participation or for the earning of awards, all point systems differentiate between activities by assigning a different number of points for different kinds of participation, a new officer—the director of activities—and a new program are being developed in progressive schools, the practice of granting awards other than credit is quite general, and junior and senior high schools are recognizing the need of some method of checking and evaluating pupil participation in activities. Noble (501) analyzed the problems involved in the accounting of extra-curriculum funds, and organized his materials into the form of a manual or textbook for use of student finance officers and faculty supervisors.

Homerooms

The outstanding contribution to the literature of the homeroom was by McKown (500). In his preface the author stated:

Because of the magnitude of the home room opportunity, the presentations of the book are not designed to be complete but rather to suggest extents and possibilities in each of the various fields. Nor are the programs offered as examples of perfect home room material. But they do represent what is now being done in the home rooms of many schools and what, after an exhaustive study of thousands of such programs, appears to the author to be good present practice.

With materials gathered from many sources McKown discussed the homeroom from many points of view including purposes, administration, membership, internal organization, selection and placement of homeroom program materials, principles of homeroom program making, homeroom sponsorship, orientation of pupils, and guidance including educational, vocational, moral, citizenship, health, manners, thrift, and recreational. The book abounds in illustrations of practices in junior and senior high schools.

Relation of Extra-Curriculum Activities to the Curriculum

For a decade or more the literature of extra-curriculum activities has been concerned with the "curricularization of extra-curriculum activities." Jones' study (499) was the first serious attempt to show present theory and practice with respect to the relationship between what we have traditionally called "curriculum" and "extra-curriculum" activities. Data were secured from 269 schools representing all sections of the country and ranging in enrolment from approximately 400 to more than 2,250 concerning the status of twenty-eight activities. The study dealt with the time of inception of the activities, status at introduction, change in status and present status, trend of activities in their relation to the curriculum, extent of participation in activities, opinion and theory as to the proper status of activities, and evaluation of activities with reference to their relation to the curriculum. The author's summarizing conclusions were: (a) the newspaper, music organizations, dramatics, and debating are definitely tending toward a curriculum status; (b) the student council, assembly, clubs, and homeroom are either wholly or almost wholly extra-curriculum; and (c) athletic activities are largely extra-curriculum, although there is a slight tendency to make them an integral part of the health and physical education program.

Teacher Preparation for Extra-Curriculum Activities

The professional preparation of secondary-school teachers for guiding and directing extra-curriculum activities has been recognized more in theory by teacher-training institutions than in practice. Typically, teachers in training receive little more than a mere introduction to the responsibilities which will be theirs when they secure their first teaching position. Briggs (491) undertook "to discover the extent of the demand for teachers trained to guide and direct extra-class activities, to find out the provisions now being made in state teachers colleges to give such training, to analyze these provisions, and to suggest a program for state teachers colleges which will make adequate provision for training teachers in guiding and directing extra-class activities." Data were secured from 161 high-school principals and 115 state teachers colleges. Some important findings were:

1. Seventy-six percent of all high-school teachers participate in guiding and directing extra-curriculum activities.
2. A large majority of high-school principals desire teachers who have been trained to guide and direct these activities.
3. Ninety-seven percent of the high-school principals advocate participation of secondary-school teachers in extra-curriculum activities while in college.
4. Eighty-eight percent of teachers college students are actually participating in one or more activities.

The program of training proposed by Briggs included a regular activity period each day to be used for counseling, clubs, assembly, class meetings, student council, forensics, student publications, music organizations, dramatics, social organizations, religious organizations, intramural sports, intercollegiate athletics, all-school affairs, and the study of extra-curriculum activities in a carefully planned course.

Evaluation

An important attempt to evaluate a program of activities was that made by Henninger (496) in the Pittsburgh high schools. Data were secured from students, teachers, and alumni. Conclusions drawn were as follows:

1. From the students' point of view extra-curriculum activities furnish so much of value that they form an essential part of the educational program.
2. From the teachers' standpoint extra-curriculum activities are not a fad; teachers should have or develop expert skill in one or more phases of activities.
3. From the standpoint of the alumni extra-curriculum activities are heartily approved, yet the majority consider them of less importance than regular classroom instruction.

The trend of much presentday thinking with respect to secondary education is distinctly in the direction of breaking down the traditional dualism between "curriculum" and "extra-curriculum" activities. Subscribing to a definition of the term "curriculum" which includes all activities of educative value, the reviewer believes that major emphasis in future research should be given the problems involved in fusing into one integrated whole our present "curriculum" and "extra-curriculum" activities. Jones' study (499) marks the beginning of what the reviewer hopes will be a series of studies addressed to this important problem.

C. HIGHER EDUCATION

Extent and Classification of Extra-Curriculum Activities

No complete and satisfactory classification of all extra-curriculum activities was attained in the reports of research published from 1932 to 1935. Maney (531) classified the extra-curriculum activities of Transylvania College into cultural, ethical, athletic, political, and social groups. Frazier and others (523) classified the student activities of 209 universities, colleges, and junior colleges into twenty-three groups. Christensen (517) reported that forty-two non-athletic student activities were found in the eighty public junior colleges studied by him. Intercollegiate basketball appeared in 98 percent of these institutions. Football and track tied for second place with 76 percent of the colleges participating in each.

Participation and Leadership in Extra-Curriculum Activities

Of eighty public junior colleges investigated by Christensen (517), 36 percent reported that some organized effort was made to stimulate the indifferent student to greater participation and a total of fourteen different devices for acquainting new students with the opportunity in student activities was used. Assembly programs headed the list with 94 percent of the junior colleges using them. The organized freshman week and the junior college yearbook each was utilized for the enlistment of students in extra-curriculum activities in only one college. In the same study Christensen found that 64 percent of the junior colleges attempted to limit the number of activities in which any student was allowed to participate. At Hunter College (512), participation was limited to members of the Student Self-Government Association. At one liberal arts college the fraternity members had a monopoly on every type of activity. This predominance was most marked in social and political activities and least apparent in cultural and ethical activities (531). For 507 students at Hunter College (512), the activities engaged in by scholarship students ranged from 1 to 7 with a mean of 1.43; for the non-scholarship students, the range was from 1 to 6 with a mean of 0.98. In the same institution the scholarship holders surpassed the non-scholarship group in the leadership of student activities. Archer (511) found that the scholarship holders of the University of the State of New York proved themselves not to be unsocial ascetics; 60 percent participated in at least one student activity.

Relation of Intelligence and Scholarship to Extra-Curriculum Activities

It has been recognized that accurate comparisons of the relative scholastic attainments of various groups of students demand a knowledge of the abilities of the groups compared.

Intelligence—In a study of the intelligence of sixty-five students at Northern State Teachers College at Aberdeen, South Dakota, McMurtrey (529) found that members of athletic teams were intellectually and scholastically inferior to non-members, and that students who attended movies most frequently were lower in intelligence yet higher in scholarship than those who attended less frequently.

Similarly, students having no "dates" while in college were decidedly brighter than students having "dates." On the other hand, students earning all or part of their expenses had a higher average intelligence than those students who earned nothing, and brightness increased with increase in percent earned.

For 114 fraternity and 65 non-fraternity men at Albion College, Carter (513) found no significant difference in the "average indexes of promise" for the two groups. Chase (514), however, reported that the average "index of scholastic expectancy" at the University of Illinois was somewhat higher for men pledged to fraternities than for men who did not join fraternities, but at the end of the first semester the fraternity men who lived in fraternity houses showed a lower performance than the non-fraternity men.

Scholarship—In a study by Mehus (535) of two institutions, the data indicated that students who were most active in campus activities tended to receive the highest grades in academic subjects. The author suggested that possibly extra-curriculum activities were a means whereby those of higher mentality expended some of their surplus mental energy.

The fact that the athletes were about equally inferior both in scholarship and in intelligence led McMurtrey (529) to the conclusion that intelligence rather than participation in athletics was the determining factor in securing high academic rating and that with more time to spend on academic work non-athletes should achieve much more satisfactory results than athletes of equal ability. The same writer reported that the more active participants in movies and dances, even though slightly inferior in ability, made higher scholastic records than those who participated less. The small number of students investigated and the selected nature of students attending a teachers college made it unsafe to generalize concerning either the intelligence or the scholastic standing of students who danced, and of students who attended movies. In a study of the grades earned by football men, by non-football men, and by women of Transylvania College for a period of ten years, Maney (532) concluded that the superiority of the women and non-football men over the football men was to be attributed to motivation rather than to any advantage due to native ability. The value of Maney's explanation is lessened by the absence of objective measurements of the intelligence of the various groups studied. In a carefully controlled experiment in which 159 athletes from seven institutions were paired with non-athletes, with extra-curriculum men, and with non-extra-curriculum men on the basis of scores on freshman intelligence tests and were then compared as to achievement by means of objective achievement tests, Cooper (518) found that the non-athletic groups showed a slight superiority in achievement and that the non-athlete worked in slightly closer parallelism with his ability than did the athlete. In a summary study of both college and high-school athletics, Davis and Cooper (520) stated the conclusion that "in most cases the non-athlete performs slightly better school work than the athlete although the differences are of no statistical significance."

When the median scholarship of all fraternity men was compared with that of all non-fraternity men at Wittenberg College (534), no significant difference was found between the two groups. For the freshman sorority women, the rank in scholarship was higher than that of non-sorority women. In a carefully controlled comparison of 100 equated pairs of fraternity and non-fraternity students made at Brown University by MacPhail (530), a superiority in favor of the non-fraternity group was found but the difference was not significant statistically. It was evident, however, that for the freshman year the lowest fourth of the two groups did about equally well but that a decrease for the fraternity group and a marked increase for the non-fraternity group took place during the remaining years. For both groups, the upper fourth did well in the freshman year, but the non-fraternity group started at a higher level and maintained it throughout the entire four years although the fraternity group improved. Carter (513) discovered that the average achievement of 114 fraternity men at Albion College was almost exactly the same as that for 65 non-fraternity men. For students having indexes of promise above the average, however, Carter showed that the indexes of achievement were likely to be higher than the indexes of promise if they did not join fraternities. Students having indexes of promise lower than the average were more likely to attain indexes of achievement higher than their indexes of promise by joining fraternities. In spite of the fact that there was a general tendency at the University of Ohio for the spring-semester marks to improve over those of the preceding semester (525), there was a uniform decrease in marks for both the fraternity men and the sorority women. Maney (531) found that for ten consecutive semesters at Transylvania College the majority of the students of superior scholarship were not members of social fraternities or sororities.

Evaluation of Extra-Curriculum Activities

Little research has been done to determine the direct values obtained from participation in extra-curriculum activities. MacKenzie (527) made a study to determine the relative values to be derived from the different physical activities. At three different times he measured the physical condition of a number of freshman students, participating in the selected physical activities, by means of the Physical Fitness Index. The more important conclusions were (a) that "general corrective programs, exercise to improve abdominal conditions, cross country, and hockey yielded the greatest dividends in physical development," and (b) that "football was least productive" and that wrestling was not much better. According to Frazier and others (523), "the values of athletics in the preparation of teachers are confined largely to the vocational training given public-school athletic coaches and to the improvement of the health of the limited number of students who participate."

Attitudes toward Intercollegiate Athletics

By means of an attitude scale developed according to the Thurstone technic (547), it was found that all of the eleven representative groups who were questioned were favorable to intercollegiate athletics. When ranked from those most favorable to those least favorable, the athletes and their parents took first and second places while the faculty and college presidents took the tenth and eleventh places.

Organization and Administration of Extra-Curriculum Activities

Rutledge and Briscoe (542) sent forty-eight selected principles for the administration of extra-curriculum activities in teachers colleges to sixty college presidents throughout the country. To these they received forty replies from college presidents and five from authorities in the field of the administration of teachers colleges. When the percent of those assenting to each of the principles was obtained, it was found "that thirty of the principles were approved by 90 percent or more of the jurors; that thirty-three of the principles were approved by more than 85 percent of the jurors; that only nine of the principles were approved by less than 80 percent of the jurors and that only one principle was approved by less than 75 percent of the jurors." Some essential points of these principles were that the stimulation and guidance of extra-curriculum activities should be placed in the hands of a general faculty committee appointed by the president and coordinated under the sponsorship of a general student organization, that advisers for each of the activities should be appointed by the president for each of the separate activities, and that the veto power concerning all extra-curriculum activities should be vested in the president.

In his study of junior colleges, Christensen (516) found that 40 percent of these colleges had no committee on student activities. In 79 percent of the colleges which have such committees the final responsibility was vested in the dean. At the University of Chicago (539), the control of all extra-curriculum activities was placed under the dean of students in order that the weaknesses inherent in a highly decentralized system of control might be corrected. In that institution, the participation of alumni in the management of athletics was eliminated by placing the management under the control of the University Board of Athletics and Physical Culture of which the Dean of Students was chairman.

As a fundamental postulate of financial administration, Savage (543) asserted that "any budget not related to function has little administrative value" and suggested several pertinent questions which should be considered by administrators who desire to secure greater values from funds spent on athletics.

Self-Support of Students

A survey of conditions at the University of Minnesota (550) revealed the fact that 55.5 percent of the students at that institution earned at least a part of their expenses. A similar survey of conditions at the University of Colorado (509) brought out the fact that, in 1933, 42.3 percent of all men and only 18.5 percent of all women earned all or a part of their expenses. As early as 1930-31, Reeves and Russell (538) reported that 72 percent of the men and 51 percent of the women holding scholarships at the University of Chicago were engaged in part-time employment.

The importance of well-organized employment service is shown by the fact that "Yale students who found it necessary to support themselves suffered relatively less than have those of many institutions where campus employment has been less stabilized" (521). Gentzler (510) and Zorbaugh (552) presented valuable suggestions concerning part-time placement. Sharpe (544) gave the following pertinent advice: "In cases where academic failure seems certain because of need of employment, it may be wiser and more charitable to refuse admission."

In an attempt to determine the effects of self-help and other factors on freshmen during their first term at North Carolina State College (536), the tentative conclusions were reached that (a) the grades of freshman students were not affected to any appreciable extent by their efforts to earn a part of their expenses, and (b) there were no data to support the general conclusion that self-help students are superior in scholarship to nonworking students.

Student Self-Government and the Honor System

From the responses of eighty-one institutions to a questionnaire, Wahlquist (551) found that honor societies were more common in private colleges than in public universities, that more institutions have adopted and abandoned the honor system than are now using it, and that the lack of student cooperation is the most common cause of failure. At Ohio Wesleyan University, Mathews (533) secured the cooperation of faculty and students in checking a list of thirty-six questionable actions. The data secured indicated that in the opinion of students and faculty members, some of the thirty-six actions were much more worthy of condemnation than others and that the students were much more willing to condone questionable practices than were the members of the faculty.

CHAPTER VIII

Educational Adjustment

A. ELEMENTARY EDUCATION

EDUCATIONAL ADJUSTMENT is inextricably associated with adjustment as a whole. To attempt to separate educational guidance from guidance in general is to destroy the psychological unity of the process. In fact, the development and guidance of individual children in the elementary school involves far more than knowing the characteristics of pupils, counseling them, providing extra-curriculum activities for them, or giving them a narrow type of educational guidance. This phase of education permeates home, school, and community; it has the unity of personality itself. In reality, it cannot be separated from the curriculum (560), instruction (557), school buildings (559), home and community contacts. All these factors in the matrix of the life of a child provide the necessary conditions for his development and guidance. As education provides a more and more adequate basis on which pupils may make life choices, the areas in which actual guidance at the time of choice needs to be given will be reduced.

The chief purpose of this short section is to call attention to the psychological unity of guidance and to refer the reader to sources of summaries of specific aspects of educational adjustment.

Gifted Children

After reviewing four provisions for the needs of gifted children, namely, enrichment of the curriculum, acceleration, ability grouping, and special classes in selected subjects, Grover (558) advocated a flexible program based on a counseling system and adequate cumulative records which would early locate gifted children. He suggested the need for their continuous adjustment as they progress through school, acceleration for pupils who expect to continue their education beyond high school, and special classes in certain subjects.

Individual Instruction and Special Remedial Instruction

These topics are reviewed very completely for each subject of the elementary school in a previous issue of the *Review of Educational Research* (559).

Ability Grouping

This subject, too, has been presented in previous issues of the *Review of Educational Research* (562, 563) and in another section of this issue. Wyndham's more detailed summary (568) is of special interest to personnel workers because of its emphasis on provision for the capacities, needs, and abilities of every individual within any existing administrative organization. He pointed out the danger of thinking that the educational adjustment of pupils has been secured merely by the grouping of pupils alike in one or even in several respects. Barthelmess and Boyer (553), in their comparison of five schools having homogeneous grouping with control groups in the same city, found that "in improvement of arithmetic, reading, and technical English skills, there is a statistically significant difference in favor of homogeneously grouped pupils as compared with heterogeneously grouped pupils." Douglass (555) critically reviewed some of the research on so-called homogeneous grouping and made a plea for an open-minded attitude toward the problem. Investigations of this problem to date neither unreservedly sanction nor do they condemn ability grouping as one step toward the individualization of education. West (567) presented evidence of the possibility of reducing through grouping the variability in achievement in certain schools. Whether a reduction in variability is to be desired is another question.

Certain Factors Contributing to Educational Adjustment

Retan (564) found that the socio-economic status, emotional stability, and health habits were the factors that exerted the greatest influence on the progress of children through the grades of the elementary schools.

Cummings (554) presented evidence from 100 cases of maladjusted school children to show that most school failure can be prevented. Smith (565) surveyed presentday practices and opinions regarding various phases of home study held by teachers, principals, pupils, and parents.

Otto and Melby (561) obtained evidence from a semicontrolled experiment that the practice of failing some pupils as an insurance against low standards of achievement is not necessary. In other words, threat of failure was not essential as a motivating device in the eighteen second- and fifth-grade classes studied. There was practically no difference in scores on the new Stanford Achievement Test between the group which was told that all would be promoted the following term and the group which was told that anyone who did not work hard would have to repeat the grade.

Comment

The effectiveness of what at present appears to be the best methods of educational adjustment needs to be studied. Such an investigation would involve the measurement of the complex outcomes of a complex situation, for the best adjustment is not a function of a single procedure. It always involves appraisal of the individual pupil, counseling, and the making of environmental changes. It frequently involves home and community contacts. Research in this field should take the form of the study of individuals rather than the form of mass investigations.

B. SECONDARY EDUCATION

A review of educational research in the field of educational adjustment reveals five studies of primary significance. These include two surveys

(569, 573), one study dealing with home environment and adjustment (575), one with high-school promotion plans (571), and one with the adjustment of behavior problems (572).

Surveys of Adjustment Programs

Billett (569) reported data from 8,594 high schools representing all types of schools and ranging in enrolment from 50 or less to more than 1,000. In addition to his preliminary inquiry sheet Billett used 13 follow-up inquiry forms totaling 201 pages of information. These secured detailed information from selected schools concerning homogeneous or ability grouping, scientific study of problem cases, Dalton, Winnetka, and Morrison plans, problem and project methods, marking systems, and promotional plans. Among the many important findings of this monograph were the following:

1. Homogeneous grouping may refer either to grouping into class sections or within class sections. Sixteen different bases of grouping were found in use in a wide variety of combinations. The I.Q. from a group mental test is the most common basis. A larger percent of schools having enrolments of 500 or more reported unusual success with the plan used than of the schools under 500 enrolment. Differentiation of teaching procedure has made more progress than differentiation of subjectmatter.

2. Special classes are formed for those pupils who deviate from the norm in needs, in capacity, or in both. Special classes for the very slow pupils are created for the purpose of enabling them to succeed with regular school work after all other provisions for individual differences have failed. Classes for the very capable are created to bring capable but retarded pupils up to normal, to accelerate, or to enrich the programs of capable pupils.

3. Of the 8,594 responding schools, 737 reported use of the Morrison plan, 162 the Dalton plan, and 119 the Winnetka plan. From a critical study of the plans in actual operation and of the project method, problem method, differentiated assignments, long-unit assignments, contract plan, laboratory plan, and individualized instruction, Billett concluded that the technics or procedures were essentially one and the same thing.

4. Among 258 schools investigated with respect to marking systems, 100 different systems, counting minor variations, were found. In a fifth of the schools uniform practice does not exist within the secondary schools of the local system. The five-point scale is the dominant marking system.

5. In the large majority of schools studied the passing mark entitles the pupil to promotion. Factors taken into account are attendance, age, ability, handicaps, and the probable effect of promotion or non-promotion upon the pupil's future success. More than half of the schools studied use trial promotion.

As a part of the survey of the Chicago public schools, Mort, Wright, and Featherstone (574) studied articulation, progress, and adjustment in the junior and senior high schools. With respect to provisions for adjustment their data showed the following:

1. A report on 12 percent of junior high-school pupils showed for a period of eighteen weeks only 1.64 adjustments per pupil. These adjustments in order of frequency were: adjustments to unusual proficiency in ordinary school work, to low ability, to special disabilities in ordinary school work, correction of deficiencies in school subjects, social adjustments, adjustments to health and physical defects, correction of other educational deficiencies, adjustments to special abilities, and adjustments to limited stay in school.

2. Elementary schools in Chicago enrolling eighth-grade pupils made only .619 adjustments per pupil during an eighteen weeks' period. Social adjustments stood first followed by adjustments to special disabilities in ordinary school work, to low ability, to health and physical defects, to unusual proficiency in ordinary school work, correction of deficiencies in school subjects, adjustments to special abilities, and corrections of other educational deficiencies.

3. In the high schools a report on 8,100 pupils for eighteen weeks showed 1.21 adjustments per pupil. Correction of deficiencies in school subjects stood first, followed by adjustments to unusual proficiency in ordinary school work, to low ability, to special disabilities in ordinary school work, to health and physical defects, correction of other educational deficiencies, social adjustments, adjustments to special abilities, and adjustments to limited stay in school.

Home Environment and Adjustment

Myers (575) studied 700 junior-senior high-school pupils for the purpose of developing a measure of various factors in the home environment commonly assumed to be important in determining pupil adjustment and behavior, and of discovering relationships between the factors in the home environment of pupils and their adjustment and behavior in school. Responses of pupils to an extensive questionnaire were compared with the responses of twenty parents, twenty-six teachers, and fourteen members of a parent education group. Among the important findings were these:

1. The education of parents is a factor highly associated with the adjustment of pupils.
2. For younger pupils there is an association between poor adjustment and unsupervised out-of-school activities.
3. There is disagreement among the responding groups with respect to the relationship of church attendance to adjustment and with respect to the relationship between parental approval of a pupil's friends and adjustment.
4. There is a relationship between good adjustment and discipline by means of partially withdrawing privileges.
5. For older pupils there is a relationship between poor adjustment and punishment for serious misconduct.
6. Unquestioning obedience demanded by parents is associated with good adjustment for younger pupils and poor adjustment for older pupils.

High-School Promotional Plans

French (571) studied high-school promotional plans from data secured from 424 high schools, 170 of which employed semiannual plans and 254 annual plans of promotion. In summary the author said:

Annual and semi-annual promotions are simply two variations in an administrative procedure, the principal result of either form of which is the regular, uniform movement of groups of students through the high school from entrance to graduation. The annual promotional plan as administered has the advantage of simplicity. The semiannual promotional plan as administered usually involves the expenditure of more time, effort, energy, and, probably in small schools, more money. In addition, some concomitant disadvantages commonly, but not always necessarily, follow. To balance these disadvantages there is some evidence of greater school progress by withdrawals and some early graduation, principally by mid-year entries. The principal result of its operation, however, is practically the same regular, uniform group progress through school as under annual promotion. Any high school willing to be satisfied with this degree of adjustment of its program to the individual needs of its students may obtain it, as far as this study shows, with annual promotion approximately as well as with semi-annual promotion.

Adjustment of Behavior Problems

Martens and Russ (572) reported an experiment in treating behavior problems in a group of 109 pupils in the Berkeley, California, schools. These pupils were considered the most serious cases and were referred to the behavior clinic for treatment. For comparative purposes two other groups of children were studied according to the same technic. One was a group of 109 non-problem children and the other a group of 50 problem children who were not given clinical attention. The 109 pupils who constituted the experimental group were predominantly boys, came from all age groups and levels of intelligence, were slightly below normal in average intelligence, and showed educational achievement not significantly different from other children of the same age and intelligence. Both problem groups included a significantly larger percent of children coming from broken homes than did the non-problem group. The authors concluded that it is time for the school to give up its attitude of aloofness and to take its place among the numerous social agencies that are concerned with the development of childhood in a well-organized effort to modify the undesirable behavior of children before it assumes serious proportions.

C. HIGHER EDUCATION

Numerous plans for adapting college instruction to the needs of students who differ in ability and background are being tried. One may conclude from the reports that were made during the past few years that the idea of providing for individual differences at the college level is gaining ground, but the number of studies that gave objective data or experimental evaluations of the different plans was very limited.

Honors Courses

Honors courses appear to be growing in favor as a means of providing for students of superior ability and as a means of developing individual initiative and responsibility. Some institutions have extended the privilege of honors work to a larger percent of the students (616). The Massachusetts Institute of Technology, after an eight-year experiment with honors courses in the field of electrical engineering, reported favorable results (592). Umstattd (626) summarized the opinions of students who participated in an honors course in education at the University of Minnesota. The most significant advantages listed were that honors work (a) developed an appreciation of the relationship between basic courses in education; (b) gave a broader perspective of the field covered; (c) made greater competition within the group, because the homogeneous grouping was more stimulating; (d) recognized individual differences; (e) gave opportunity for individual expression of opinion; (f) developed individual responsibility; and (g) developed initiative. The disadvantages most commonly mentioned were that it (a) caused waste of time at the outset, due to lack of understanding of aims and requirements; (b) encouraged a tendency to procrastinate; (c) did not provide sufficient and proper motivation for some students; (d) provided no periodic check of progress; (e) permitted some students not to participate in discussion; and (f) did not insure the student against omitting important aspects of the course.

Individual Instruction

Reports made by institutions experimenting with individual instruction were favorable to various plans being tried (606, 624, 595). The advantages of the tutorial plan at Colgate as reported by fifty students were presented by Thurber (624). The judgments of these students were strongly in favor of the method. Gerberich and Roberds (595) reported the results of an experiment that compared individual and group instruction in physics. The number participating was too small to permit any significant generalizations, but the method employed could well be applied to a larger group. MacLean (605) of the University of Minnesota's General College, where the tutorial plan has been extended downward for the use of the lower grade students, reported a favorable change in student attitudes toward the plan but gave no data to support his conclusions. Greene (597), in experiments conducted at Columbia University, the City College of New York, and the University of Michigan, found guided reading vastly superior to either the lecture or unguided reading. He stated that the test "results indicate that for this situation there is not as much as one chance in five thousand statistically calculated that any student from these groups would do as well after either lecture or unguided reading as after the guided reading periods."

Special Remedial Instruction

Reports of remedial instruction through either credit or non-credit courses, in fundamental tool subjects, and in how-to-study courses were made by various writers (582, 590, 591, 593, 594, 609, 612, 613, 622, 629). Behrens (580) announced the successful extension of the work in remedial classes to cover a physical remedial program and the social and emotional problems of students. Moore (609) evaluated a how-to-study course at Mount Holyoke College as follows: (a) lectures on how to study were of little value unless accompanied by exercises on the specific points discussed; (b) conferences between the freshmen and seniors were of as much value as were class discussions; over 70 percent of the freshman group reported the freshman-senior conferences as the most valuable part of the experiment; (c) vocabulary weakness was primarily due to unfamiliarity with word roots and affixes; improvement was best made by word analysis after the common prefixes and suffixes were known; and

(d) the most common weakness was in the field of meanings and central issues in paragraphs.

Courses in remedial reading have generally resulted in significant gains in reading efficiency. One of the most important experiments by Deal (590), produced a gain in reading comprehension of "as much as one hundred per cent in short training periods over a few weeks." There was continued improvement in comprehension for two semesters (590). The author of the reports stressed the need for an investigation of the permanence of gains in reading ability and of the extent to which an increase in reading ability carries over into all subjects taken by the students. Other investigators reported favorable results from remedial work in reading, but the data were generally limited in scope (594, 629). Strang (622) evaluated the investigations of remedial work in reading as follows: "There is abundant experimental evidence that college students improve in certain reading abilities as the result of individualized instruction in some aspects of reading. . . . Enforced rapid reading either results in an undesirable tenseness, or in the eventual mastery of more economical ways of grasping larger reading units."

Sectioning Classes on the Basis of Ability

Jones (600), in an investigation of the extent to which college classes were divided into sections according to the ability of students, found among ninety colleges that 37.8 percent had no sectioning and 62.2 percent had some sectioning. The criteria generally employed in grouping students were: intelligence test scores, high-school grades, scores in standardized and unstandardized placement tests, and previous records in college (625, 620, 627). Very valuable data showing the advantages of sectioning were reported by Monroe and Gausewitz, in the fields of romance and modern languages, respectively (625). Meyer presented a method of remedial service (625).

Articulation of High School and College

Closely related to the sectioning of classes upon the basis of ability are various plans used to permit capable students at the high-school level either to do advanced work or to do extra work for which they receive advanced standing. Jones (600) found that 76.7 percent of ninety colleges gave no credit for work done at the high-school level. Twenty percent gave credit only if the work was in excess of fifteen or sixteen units, 3.3 percent gave credit for not more than nine hours, and 4.4 percent gave credit only after successful completion of advanced work in college. Among the institutions reporting such plans were the University of Chicago (583), Yale University (615), University of Buffalo (601), and Stephens College (619). An experiment at Stephens College in which students who had not finished high school were enrolled in junior college classes resulted in no significant difference between the scholastic success of the high-school and the regular college students when the two groups were matched in terms of mental ability (581). Under a plan in effect at the University of Buffalo (607), whereby students in high school may take examinations along with college students for advanced credit, 190 examinations were taken by high-school students and 114 were passed. At least one student passed in every subject in which an examination was taken except chemistry.

Other Types of Adjustment

Among the special adjustments not already mentioned are endocrinological diagnosis and treatment of students whose work is of a low grade (581), special emphasis upon motivation (588, 599), and special counseling of low-grade students (593).

CHAPTER IX
Special Schools and Classes

RECENT RESEARCH concerning special education has dealt with a diversity of problems. Billett (637) studied some 8,594 high schools in an endeavor to discover what was being done for handicapped and gifted children. State surveys were made in North Carolina (645) and Washington (678) to discover how extensively special schools and classes had been established. Feldman (654) did the same thing for 78 cities scattered throughout the United States. Kunzig (662) and Otto (688) assembled a great amount of pertinent data relating to the public school program for educating atypical children. Other topics such as state aid (663), preparation of teachers (673, 693), state administrative organization governing special education (674), the special class curriculum (652), overageness of the physically handicapped (685), and ways and means of better coordinating the work of various social agencies interested in the education of exceptional children (672) have been considered.

In addition to the more general studies which cover the entire field of special education, there is a great amount of research dealing with particular groups of handicapped or gifted children. This research deals not only with the educational programs which are being and which have been developed; it is tending also to give considerable emphasis to causation, particularly with respect to the socially handicapped. This emphasis is important. We are ceasing to be interested in special education just as a means of remedying a condition which handicaps these children socially and vocationally; workers in special education are eager to prevent those conditions which so seriously handicap young people. This emphasis upon causation is a necessary first step in any program which aims at prevention. We are interested, of course, in any research which gives us data concerning the need, the size, and the success of special education's remedial program; the handicapped must be cared for and educated. To stop at this point, however, would be ignoring special education's more important function—that of *prevention*.

General Studies

Billett (637) studied the extent to which high schools throughout the country provide special classes or special help for handicapped or gifted children. He used the questionnaire plus considerable visitation. Replies were received from 8,594 high schools having enrolments which ranged from less than 50 to more than 1,000. Approximately 75 percent of these high schools provided special help or coaching; this was provided with about the same frequency in small schools and in large schools; special classes appeared much less frequently. Special classes for pupils who have failed were provided in 30 percent of the high schools; only 11 percent provided opportunity rooms for slow pupils; 8 percent had special coaching to help capable pupils to skip; 6 percent reported adjustment classes;

4 percent opportunity rooms for gifted children; and 2 percent had restoration classes. These classes were usually found in the large schools; the smaller high schools rarely provided them.

Cuthbertson (645), in her study of special education in North Carolina, concluded that "the gifted child is perhaps the most neglected of any of our children." Masters and Upshall (678) reported that of 15 first-class cities in the state of Washington, 11 had special work for subnormals, 9 for dull normals, 7 for impaired hearing, 5 for defective speech, 4 for cripples, 4 for gifted, 4 for impaired vision, and 4 for the tubercular. Two cities reported no special provisions for exceptional children. The investigators concluded that "the data indicate that the provisions are very inadequate in most of our first-class cities and, it is safe to say, that in the smaller towns and rural areas, any special organization or equipment to more adequately provide for exceptional children is practically unknown."

Feldman (654), using the questionnaire, had reports for 78 of 130 cities. He confirmed other studies in showing that subnormal children are much more generally provided for than any other types; special classes for this group were provided by 73 percent of the cities reporting; the gifted were cared for in only 3 percent. From 20 to 30 percent of these cities had special classes for the partially sighted, the deaf, the cripples, and those needing special help to restore them to their regular grade; 10 to 14 percent provided disciplinary, nutrition, and open air classes; and only 3 to 7 percent had special classes for the non-English speaking, the blind, the hard of hearing, the speech defective, the tubercular, and the cardiac. He said in concluding that "the states in the North East and the North Central sections of the country have moved far ahead of the other sections."

Thus far only 17 states (663) grant state aid by statute for special classes for physically and mentally handicapped children. Thirteen states have a state division or bureau in charge of the state's program of special education (674). Martens (672) pointed out the necessity of coordinating the efforts of all agencies interested in special education if the problem is to be adequately solved. The training of teachers for special classes has been given attention by state boards in eleven states according to Schleier (693); these requirements range from 15 semester hours to one year of specialized training. Five states demand from one year to three years' teaching experience in the regular grades. He concluded that "the few standards formulated at present for teachers of the various types of physically handicapped children are too general and inadequate." He reported that 37 teachers colleges and 8 normal schools in 22 states and 54 colleges and universities in 32 states had from 1 to 12 courses for preparing teachers of special education. Martens (673) gathered data concerning courses for the preparation of teachers. Questionnaires were sent to 600 institutions. Catalogs were also studied. She listed offerings of the various institutions and gave a brief description of each course.

The Blind

Best (636) assembled an amazing amount of data regarding the blind. He considered society's treatment of the blind historically, the various public institutions which care for them, legal and constitutional provisions for the blind, and their general physical, mental, social, and economic status. Part III of his report dealt with their education. He concluded that "some three-fourths (77 percent) of the blind children in the country are in the special schools." In order to reach all blind children he urged compulsory attendance laws for the blind which will require "attendance for a sufficient number of years and for a sufficient length of time, each year. . . ." The Joint Committee on Health Problems (684) has made a multitude of specific suggestions for public school officials with regard to conserving the sight of school children. Andrews (630) studied the mentally retarded blind in the United States. He found that neither the state institutions for the feeble-minded nor the state school for the blind did much for this doubly handicapped group. Doraiswamy (649) studied the reading difficulties of blind children in the elementary grades; child study aimed at child growth is the core of the remedial measures proposed. Merry (679) traced the development of programs for caring for and educating those with defective vision.

Cutsforth (646) presented a picture of the blind which no sighted worker in this field can afford to ignore. His contribution is not the typical research; it is, however, based upon some of the most significant research done within this field and is made by a man who has been blind since his eleventh year. The phantasy life, the emotional life, and the esthetic life of the blind are considered in the light of available facts. French (655) brought together much valuable data by tracing the historical development of society's care for and education of the blind. The progress made is marked and yet much remains to be done; he stated:

> The housing of children in barnlike barracks is surely out-of-date. Housing must begin with a strict segregation of the sexes and a division, according to age, into relatively small groups. The groups may be assigned to cottages with preferably a private room for each boy or girl. . . . A group of from twelve to twenty boys or girls may live in a cottage under the care of one matron and assistant. . . . The greatest need in the education of the blind is the close correlation of subject with subject and of the whole with life. . . .

The Cripple

Wallace (696) gave an excellent historical account of the education of crippled children in England, France, Germany, and the United States; she described the educational programs provided, the organizations interested, and the legislation passed.

The state of Michigan has given considerable attention to crippled children; three studies (694, 681, 682) dealt with the work in that state. Upson and Matson (694) made a statewide survey of the problem; they concluded that all the cripples were not being discovered by the usual methods and that the total number was probably "twice the generally accepted estimate." The study dealt with all facilities now provided to care for and educate the cripple. The Michigan Crippled Children Commission (681) studied some 10,274 crippled children. One thousand, five hundred twenty-seven were crippled at birth; 1,908 after birth but before six years of age; 1,053 between six and sixteen; 48 between sixteen and twenty-one; no data as to age of the onset of the crippling condition available for the remainder. The report emphasized the need for discovering crippled children immediately. Musser (682) studied the vocational program which is provided for crippled children; he studied in some detail the work done at the Hospital School of the University of Michigan; a questionnaire was sent to 227 hospitals and to 131 public schools for cripples throughout the United States and Canada. In addition to discovering what is being done vocationally for these children, the vocational opportunities now open to youths disabled in (a) one hand, (b) both hands, (c) one arm, (d) both arms, (e) one leg, (f) both legs, (g) one hand plus one arm, (h) one hand and one leg, and (i) one arm and one leg, were studied.

Feick (653) studied, by the case study method, a group of twenty-two cripples enrolled in an Ohio public school for cripples. Their social and economic status was low; 22 percent were congenitally crippled. He presented, however, a "hopeful picture with regard to educational and vocational potentialities." B. McLeod (668) assembled most helpful data regarding the problems of the regular teacher in dealing with those who are crippled. McBride (665) brought together a great amount of data concerning numerous technical problems involved in dealing with cripples; he considered physical therapy, the physical care of the child, and the causes of crippling conditions.

The Deaf and Hard of Hearing

Waldman and others (695) studied the effect of varying degrees of hearing upon school progress and the extent to which school children have losses in hearing. They concluded that 5.5 percent of school children have a hearing loss of nine units in one or both ears. An audiometer was used. Of 63 cases detected by the audiometer only 14 had been discovered by the teachers and only 5 by the regular physical examination given at the school. "There can be no question that there is a marked relationship between hearing and school achievement," said these investigators.

MacKane (666) compared the intelligence of deaf and hearing children when sex, age, socio-economic status, and nationality of the parents are kept constant. By pairing, 130 deaf and 130 hearing children were used in the experiment. These youths were ten, eleven, and twelve years of age. American investigators had found that deaf children were retarded two to three years, whereas, Drever and Collins found less than a year of retardation at all age levels. MacKane concluded that "the study plainly shows that the same deaf children may be less than a year retarded in their responses to performance scales and yet be two years retarded in their responses to the non-language test." Meyer (680) urged that the deaf be taught shorthand. He advocated its use from the third year on, and presented case studies to show results. B. McLeod (667) assembled and discussed the problems of a regular grade teacher in dealing with hard-of-hearing children in her class group. Groff (656) made a study of the first-year vocabulary of children in public residential schools for the deaf.

Delicate Children

Delicate children, referred to by B. McLeod (669) as of "lowered vitality," are numerous among public school pupils and cause the regular teaching staff much trouble. Wallin (697) sent questionnaires to 29 city superintendents to discover how well fresh air classes were being maintained during the current depression. He reported upon number of classes, enrolment, cost, lunches, transportation, and service of cooperating agencies.

Speech Defect

There are a vast number of researches that deal with such topics as influence of stuttering upon personality (660), motor capacities of stutterers (644), but not much research that relates directly to a program of education for children with speech defects.

Gifted Children

During the past two decades considerable attention has been given to plans which segregate superior children for purposes of academic instruction. Wilkins (700), on the other hand, studied children in regular junior and senior high-school classes who were accelerated at graduation; they were examined with regard to mental, educational, physical, and social characteristics. He concluded that pedagogical acceleration "merits more widespread adoption," since it "is associated with desirable adjustment in all types of development for which data were assembled." Bell (634), after studying provisions for superior children in New York state, concluded that "progressive education is the answer to the problem of the gifted child for the vast majority of schools."

Dransfield (650) studied the possibilities of bringing enrichment to superior children while allowing them to remain in regular classes. His idea was to prepare complete instructions for the regular teachers showing specific ways of enriching the regular curriculum. Units of study were prepared, including references, activities, objectives, guiding questions, and tests, which were self-administering. Two groups of gifted children were paired. One group followed the experimental work and the other the regular school work. Regular teachers during three months used 12.6

hours to make the experimental method operate. The plan was administratively feasible; it eliminated the need of withdrawing gifted children from regular classes in order to form special groups, and the experimental group made greater advances in educational age than did the control group. Henderson (657), after a study of superior children in a large high school, concluded that a variety of practices should be utilized in order to help such youths adjust; she recommended (a) case study records, (b) a testing program, (c) better library facilities, (d) acceleration, (e) ability grouping, (f) an adaptation of the House plan, and (g) intelligent cooperation between home and school.

The inadequacy of the school working alone in making satisfactory adjustments for its superior children is noted by Regensburg (691). She studied fifty gifted children who had been referred to the New York City clinic for study. She says "that school success or failure . . . is part and parcel of the child's personality adjustment to life, with roots deep in the home situation." Certainly merely the act of organizing classes for gifted children will not help these children adjust; the special class ought to make possible that more careful study which is needed as a preliminary to satisfactory adjustment. Martens (675) pointed out the problems which regular teachers face in helping their superior pupils. R. B. MacLeod (670) and Lincoln (664) studied the constancy of the I.Q. The latter concluded that though the I.Q. of superior children decreased more frequently than it increased, despite the decreases, they still must be classified as superior children.

Mental Defectives

If special schools and classes for mental defectives are to continue to receive needed financial support, we will need to define more clearly our objectives in educating such defectives; we then need to determine by means of careful measurement the effectiveness of the special class and school in attaining these objectives as compared to the extent to which those same objectives are achieved when these children are retained in regular classes. Bennett (635) used two groups paired on mental age, chronological age, and I.Q. One group was in special classes while the other was in a regular grade group. He found them similar in most respects.

Wassman (699) interested herself in the same problem. She matched the children with respect to (a) age, (b) sex, (c) I.Q., (d) M. A., and (e) nationality. She also tried to keep the socio-economic condition of the children's families the same. She measured both groups with respect to scholastic achievement, behavior, and extroversion-introversion traits. The measures were taken at the opening and at the close of the year in order to determine progress. In general, children in regular classes seemed to make greater gains in achievement; the special class groups gained slightly more in behavior but the difference was not statistically significant. The special class group was more extrovertive. She concluded that until further data are gathered "the advantage of one kind of class over the other on the items measured is questionable."

Several investigations were reported which deal with the work being done by special classes. Beckett (633) studied a group of 160 negro children in a special class center in Philadelphia. She pointed out the need for a careful diagnosis of each case. Petit (689) studied the educational opportunities of the Prevocational School at Dayton, Ohio. Croke (643) studied the adjustment classes in a New York City junior high school. There were 200 pupils, about 5 percent of the school's population, in these classes. These pupils were the 5 percent of poorest ability and therefore "very dull." According to the teachers they were inclined to be rebellious, liked to inflict pain, tended to be impudent, had no regard for authority, and could scarcely read. They came from homes where poverty, filth, inability to speak English, and lack of spirit seem to be common conditions. Farson (651) compared orthogenic backward and regular grade children at the six-year level and concluded that "it is possible to select upon their admission to school a certain number of children who can never function adequately in the regular grades." Descoeudres (648) and Ingram (659) assembled a great amount of illustrative curriculum materials for the use of special class teachers. Martens (676) called attention to the numerous problems which regular teachers face when teaching these mental defectives.

Truants and Delinquents

The size of the truant and delinquent problem needs to be given wide publicity. Data published by the Research Division of the National Education Association (683) indicated that 200,000 delinquents were dealt with in the United States in 1928; the cost of all crime was estimated at $2,000,000,000. Oas (686) discovered in Van Buren County, Michigan, 130 cases on file in the juvenile court during a ten-year period or an average of thirteen per year; most of these were male offenders.

We are recognizing that the problem of delinquency will not be solved by remedial measures alone; we must prevent. This implies ability to prevent, provided we can discover the reasons for the delinquency. Likewise we must remember that even remedial work must rest upon the sure foundation of discovered causes. Numerous studies (631, 632, 641, 642, 647, 661, 683, 686, 692) have called attention to causes; Babcock (631), Courthial (642), Daniel (647), and Kaplan (661) have all compared groups of delinquents with non-delinquents.

Babcock (631), using five measures of personality adjustment, concluded that delinquent boys cannot be clearly differentiated from non-delinquents; "there is," however, "a tendency for delinquents to be slower in response in a new activity after change from an established habit; and they become more disturbed making more errors than non-delinquents, by this change." Emotional differences between delinquent and non-delinquent girls were found to exist according to Courthial (642), despite keeping chronological age, intelligence, and environment the same for both groups. Daniel (647), after a study of 100 delinquent negro boys, 80 problem negro boys in school, and 120 non-problem negro boys, concluded that a check on character and personality traits "may be of value in picking out those boys from public schools that are likely to become maladjusted, or they may serve as points of departure for the further study of the individual case."

Kaplan (661) studied boys entering Central High School, Philadelphia, in 1925, 1926, and 1927; data for 1,747 white and 232 negro boys were secured. Those who were non-delinquent were compared with the delinquent upon the basis of (a) intelligence, (b) progress in school, (c) environment, and (d) teacher attitudes. He concluded that "delinquency is generally a resultant of no one factor but of a combination of influences varying with the individual case." Carl (641) likewise concluded that there are many causative factors; he did not show any causal relation between increased enrolment in secondary schools and increase in juvenile delinquency, though the title might point to that as an aim. Hill (658), in a study of 1,500 young men at the Illinois State Reformatory, concluded that "being in school is somewhat of a safeguard against delinquency."

Ruggles (692), in a study of 103 white delinquents, found that broken and unhappy homes were closely associated with juvenile delinquency. Martens and Russ (671) called attention to the numerous factors causing delinquency; they insist "that prolonged intensive study and clinical attention by a group of psychiatric, psychological, medical, and social specialists has a direct positive relationship to a progressive change for the better in the overt problem behavior of children." Olson (687) urged that we check by means of research the effectiveness of various procedures now used in dealing with delinquents.

Burkey (640) studied the initial and successive offenses of 100 boys of normal intelligence and 98 who were subnormal. She concluded that the normals were more likely to begin their delinquent careers by stealing; the subnormals more generally began with sex offenses. The successive offenses of those whose first offense was stealing were 67.9 percent stealing; those who began with truancy had 58.3 percent of all later offenses classified as stealing.

Beard (632) studied the records of 500 children of the Judge Baker Guidance Clinic who had been placed on probation. She concluded from a study of these youths, whose probation took place from five to seven years earlier, that "of paramount importance" is the training of probation workers. Parental education, adequate family income, periodic medical examinations, adequate recreation, school work adjusted to needs, vocational guidance for all children, and better court facilities are also suggested as essential, if delinquency is to be prevented. Bowler and Bloodgood (639) studied five state schools for delinquent boys; they pointed out the necessity of judging such a school in terms of how well it succeeds in helping the boy make satisfactory adjustment to life upon his release. The educational program of the school must help him satisfactorily solve his daily problems while at the school just as he will have to do when released. The community must be helped to receive him properly upon his release. He, too, must come to appreciate the reasons for his placement in the school and to lose whatever resentment he may have had due to such placement.

The effect of the movie upon delinquency and crime has been studied by Blumer and Hauser (638). In general they concluded that "the child in the high-rate delinquency area tends to be sensitized and the child in the low-rate delinquency area immunized to delinquent and criminal attitudes and forms of behavior depicted on the screen."

Future Research

In addition to the research reported in this chapter, we need better evaluations of the work being done by special schools and classes; we need much more experimentation in methods, and a better testing of the different ways of organizing to educate the atypical child. Research on causation must continue if we are to develop the preventive side of the work of special education but we need to check more carefully than has been done in the past the accomplishment of special schools and classes.

CHAPTER X
Child Labor

CHILD LABOR may be defined as the harmful or unsuitable employment of children under commercialized conditions. Whether or not the child is paid directly, it is the exploitation of his labor that counts. In vocational training and genuine apprenticeship, on the other hand, the educational or vocational value of the work done to the child himself is the first consideration. The continued existence of child labor, therefore, is inimical to the development of vocational training and apprentice training.

A comprehensive investigation of child labor in the United States was carried on under Neill (748) pursuant to a Senate Resolution in 1907 and led to the establishment of the Federal Children's Bureau in 1912. From that time on, the Children's Bureau, the National Child Labor Committee, and other organizations engaged in many studies of child labor conditions which led to the building up and gradual improvement of a body of state laws, varying widely, however, from state to state.

For nationwide statistics on the extent of child labor, United States Census volumes beginning with 1880 have been the chief reliance. Edwards (765, 766) brought together the statistics from the 1930 Census relating to children in gainful occupations by age groups and by occupations. More recent figures, based on employment certificates issued in 1933 by individual states, were published by the United States Children's Bureau (741).

The White House Conference on Child Health and Protection (780) summarized research in the field of child labor up to 1930, under nonagricultural and agricultural occupations, industrial accidents and workmen's compensation, and administration of laws affecting the employment of minors, with extensive bibliography. This review, therefore, will confine itself for the most part to researches undertaken since the White House Conference and not covered in that report.

Research has always played a threefold role in the progress of child labor regulation. Pioneer investigations into conditions of exploitation such as lighted the way for early legislation, have continued to be a vital need, especially in such fields as industrial home work, industrialized agriculture, and street trades, where legislation has lagged. With the establishment of legislative control, statistical studies and comparative surveys of legislation and administration have assumed importance. Lastly, investigations of conditions as affected by the laws are indispensable, with special attention to problems such as illegal employment, industrial injuries, or lack of suitable employment.

Legislation and Administration

The report by Otey (753), published in 1910, gave the most extensive account of early child labor legislation in the United States. It was followed by those of Loughran (734) and Ogburn (752). Current laws of each state were analyzed by the National Child Labor Committee (745) and by the United States Children's Bureau (773), both of which revised them to include 1935 legislation and also issued comparative summaries (744, 770) revised to 1933.

Cheyney (711) compared the labor standards of each state, including its child labor standards, with those prescribed for member countries under the draft conventions of the International Labor Organization. The latter (731) published a compilation of the laws of all countries pertaining to child labor as of early 1935, with a 50-page bibliography.

Chamberlain (707) made a study of the putative validity of the proposed Child Labor Amendment to the United States Constitution, based on court decisions and constitutional law.

The administration of the child labor and school attendance laws of Ohio was studied by Gibbons and Stansbury (720), Heck (726), and Widener (782). The operation of the compulsory school attendance law and of the employment certificate system in Illinois was investigated by Simons (760).

Two studies scheduled for early publication deserve mention. The study by Lumpkin and Douglas (735) of some 600 non-retarded child workers in Massachusetts and in Alabama will be included in a book on the general child labor problem. The Texas Child Welfare Survey carried on between 1933 and 1935 under Benjamin (704) and covering data on more than 800 child laborers, will contain chapters on employment permits, school attendance, and illiteracy.

Accidents, Workmen's Compensation, and Hazardous Occupations

As the number of children under fourteen in industry was gradually reduced, research concerned itself increasingly with the economic and human wastage involved in industrial injuries to minors up to the age of eighteen years. The frequency and seriousness of accidents to minors in the coal mining industry in Pennsylvania were investigated by the Pennsylvania Department of Labor and Industry (757). This study demonstrated that the rate of accidents to minors was definitely higher than that of coal mine workers of all ages. One out of every seven employees under eighteen years in Pennsylvania coal mines incurred an injury in 1930. The Pennsylvania Industrial Board promptly prohibited minors under eighteen from a number of hazardous occupations in and about coal mines.

Matthews (739) made a study of accidents to minors working as telegraph messengers, a field where there was previously almost no information available to the public. Studies of industrial injuries to minors in individual states were made, subsequent to the White House Conference report (780), by Marsh (738) for Georgia, and by Stone (761) for California.

The United States Children's Bureau (772), in cooperation with an advisory committee of experts, appointed pursuant to the recommendations of the Committee on Vocational Guidance and Child Labor of the White House Conference, prepared a list of occupations involving mechanical or health hazards which the experience of specialists in labor law administration, safety engineers, and industrial hygienists demonstrated should be barred to minors under eighteen; additional occupations which should be closed to children under sixteen; and general recommendations as to the employment of minors in hazardous occupations. Provision was made for revising the lists as required by changes in industrial processes. These lists were relied upon by many Code Authorities under the National Recovery Administration in determining what hazardous occupations and processes should be closed to minors under eighteen.

Interest centered especially on the effectiveness of legislation under the workmen's compensation laws providing additional compensation for minors injured while illegally employed, both as a measure of justice to the unfortunate children and as a deterrent to illegal employment. Studies were published by the Illinois Department of Labor (728), which, however, discontinued its annual reports after 1932, and by the New York Department of Labor (752). In both these states the double compensation provision was shown to benefit the injured children substantially. The Pennsylvania Department of Labor and Industry (736) attributed a marked decrease in accidents to employed minors during 1932 in part to depression conditions and in part to the double compensation provision in operation that year for the first time. Matthews (740) analyzed the status of illegally employed minors under the workmen's compensation laws of the various states and made a detailed comparison of their status under the laws of one state, Wisconsin, which provided for additional compensation, and one, Indiana, which at that time excluded minors illegally employed from all benefits under the compensation law.

Gibbons and others (723) investigated the after-effects of industrial accidents involving permanent injury to 167 minors in the states of Tennessee, Illinois, and Wisconsin, analyzing not only the operation of the different laws but the legal advise and medical service received by the children, the use they made of the compensation payments, the effect of the injury on earning capacity, reeducation, and rehabilitation.

Sweatshop Employment

The reversion to the sweatshop type of factory during the depression was studied in relation to its effect on child employment in the cotton garment industry for 1932 and 1933, with comparison of conditions under the code in 1934, by the Pennsylvania Department of Labor and Industry (756); and in the shirt industry and the women's dress industry by the Connecticut Department of Labor (714, 715). The United States Women's Bureau in its report on the employment of women in the sewing trades in Connecticut in 1932 (776) stated that in some factories as many as

20 percent of the employees were children under sixteen. The United States Department of Labor (768) made a quick survey of the labor of women and children in the shirt industry of nine states through a study of payroll data, in the late spring of 1933.

Industrial Home Work

Investigations in the field of industrial home work disclosed significant data on the labor of children. The National Child Labor Committee (747) found children five to fifteen years of age earning as little as four cents an hour in the artificial flower industry in the New York City district in March, 1934, just before the date when the code for that industry required the abolition of home work. The Connecticut Department of Labor (712, 713) found in 1933 and 1934 extremely bad conditions involving extensive labor of young children, long working hours, and earnings ranging from $3 to $4 per week per family, in the lace and the fabricated metals industries, where home work was not forbidden by the codes. The Pennsylvania Department of Labor (754, 755) in 1934 found children illegally employed in 7 percent of the homes where industrial home work was done, in spite of a reduction of about one-third in the number of home work certificates issued, due to the prohibition of home work under the codes of the men's clothing and certain other industries.

The United States Department of Labor (769), in a survey of industrial home work in twenty-four industries scattered over seven states during 1934, reported that one-third of the home workers making dolls' dresses and 8 percent of the home workers in all the industries covered were children under sixteen years.

Industrialized Agriculture

Although 85 percent of all children between seven and fifteen years of age among Colorado families working sugar beets on contract, who were visited by Gibbons (721) in 1933, worked in the fields, the average income of the families was only $53 per person per year, as compared with $129 per year in 1924 as computed by Brown and others (705). Consequently, most of the families, it was found, had been on public relief during the winter and spring. Abbott (701) used studies of the cost of living and family budgets to determine the wage necessary to maintain beet workers at a self-supporting level, making allowance for the elimination of child labor and a reduction in working hours. These reports were used by the Agricultural Adjustment Administration in determining child labor and minimum wage provisions for sugar beet benefit agreements operative for 1935 and 1936.

Aside from the sugar beet experiment, no attempt was made to extend federal control to child labor in industrialized agriculture, and studies of various crops and localities indicated no reduction comparable to that in factory employment in the extent of agricultural child labor subsequent to the 1930 Census. The New Jersey Department of Labor (749) submitted to the State Legislature a detailed report on the work done and school time lost by 1,342 migratory children six to fifteen years of age on New Jersey farms in 1930, although in the same year the United States Census (766:1057) reported only 706 children ten to fifteen years, inclusive, doing agricultural work in the entire state of New Jersey. Hathway (725) investigated the work of migratory farm families in the state of Washington, throwing considerable light on the educational difficulties of migrant children arriving in each region just as the harvest opened and the school closed.

Taylor, whose earlier studies of Mexican labor in the United States had included valuable material on the labor and education of Mexican children in Colorado beet fields (764) and in the Winter Garden section of Texas (763), published a report on Nueces County, Texas (762) giving similar data for a cotton-growing section.

Street Trades

Gibbons and Stansbury (722) found in 23 elementary schools in Detroit, 1,216 or 7.6 percent of the pupils in the second to the sixth grades engaged in street trading; 2,385 or 12.6 percent of the pupils in the seventh and eighth grades; and 829 or 12.4 percent of those in five intermediate schools (seventh, eighth, and ninth grades). He estimated on this basis that some 17,000 elementary- and intermediate-school children in Detroit were working in street trades in 1930-31, over 45 percent of them selling or delivering newspapers. The United States Census (766:851) for the same year gave only 450 children ten to seventeen years of age, inclusive, working as newsboys in Detroit.[1]

Shulman (759), from welfare agency and official law-enforcing agency records supplemented by field observation, estimated that 5,000 children were engaged in selling or delivering daily newspapers in New York City during 1931, about 20 percent of whom worked illegally at night.

The United States Children's Bureau (771) made a rapid survey of 4,000 street traders under sixteen, in 17 representative cities in March, 1934, in cooperation with the Research and Planning Division of the National Recovery Administration, to meet the request of President Roosevelt for a factual basis on which to determine standards for the employment of minors under the newspaper publishing code, the child labor provisions of which were unsatisfactory. The median age for newspaper sellers was 13.7 years; for newspaper carriers, 14.3 years; and for magazine distributors, 12.7 years. In Atlanta, Omaha, and Paterson, which had been studied previously by McGill (737), conditions were much improved in 1934, and the percent of newsboys under twelve years of age had decreased, although in Atlanta the number of young children dis-

---
[1] Compare advertisement of *Detroit News* in *Editor and Publisher*, October 5, 1935, p. 23, claiming 3,000 carrier boys for that paper alone.

tributing magazines had greatly increased. In Wilkes-Barre, due to the severe depression in coal mining, older boys and adults had replaced young boys in newspaper work almost entirely.

Unemployed Youth

During the recent depression period, when employment was difficult to find, an increasing number of children, instead of being prematurely inducted from school into industry, were left dangling between the two for months or even years. It became more and more evident that it was not enough to keep children in school until their training was completed or to advise them what type of occupation to prepare for. The work of guidance in other words is not carried to a satisfactory conclusion until the pupils have completed the transition from school to industry and have found work in line with their training and abilities. Up to the end of 1934, when, according to the Children's Bureau there were 3,000,000 young people sixteen to twenty-one years of age who were neither in school nor employed, a beginning had scarcely been made in studying the tremendous and urgent problems presented by this unprecedented situation.

Of 60 youth surveys undertaken in urban communities as the result of a conference on youth problems called by the United States Commissioner of Education in June, 1934, only one comprehensive report—that of the Indianapolis survey (729)—was available by the fall of 1935. This showed 62 percent of the sixteen-year-old children in school full time, as compared with 11 percent reporting part-time employment and 3 percent full-time employment. Of the seventeen-year-olds, 47 percent were attending school full time, 14 percent had part-time employment, and 6 percent were employed full time. Although rich in materials, the Indianapolis survey lacked the interpretative handling which would make it readily assimilable.

Local studies of the employment experience of minors leaving school in a period of unemployment were made showing the comparative extent of employment, under-employment, and unemployment by Layton and Hennigar (733) for Detroit; by Whitney and Walker (781) for Cincinnati; by the Milwaukee Vocational School (742) and the University of Denver (779); and by Alper and Lodgen (703) for unemployed youth in Boston.

The Connecticut State Employment Service (716) analyzed applications for employment by persons sixteen to twenty-five years of age in 1933-34, totaling 43,106. The fact that of 5,273 applicants under eighteen only 966 or 18.5 percent were placed, as compared with 31.3 percent of those twenty-one to twenty-four years of age, was attributed to an acute shortage of trade schools or other opportunities for training young people for skilled industrial jobs in which openings were found to exist. This report could well be used as a model for similar studies in other states, both because it handled the problem of suitable employment for youth on a statewide basis, and because the statistical procedures were simplified so that the bulk of the work could be and was done by untrained workers as a Federal Emergency Relief Administration project.

In September, 1935, the newly organized American Youth Commission announced plans to obtain further and more comprehensive information as to the problems and employment status of youth.

The primary investigation of the alarming increase in transiency among unemployed youth was made by the United States Children's Bureau (774) and served as the text for dozens of magazine articles. The hearings before a United States Senate Subcommittee (777), although not strictly research, provided additional data on transient youth and adults, leading to the establishment of federal transient camps in 1933; and the federal transient program and its effect on the problem of transiency was in turn analyzed by Reed (758). Minehan (743) contributed a popular study of transient boys and girls covering two years during which he collected over 500 case histories, "associated on terms of intimacy and equality with several thousand, traveled in six states as a transient, experienced in all seasons and under all conditions the daily life of a boy or girl living in box cars." Innocent of statistics except for a few simple tables in the appendix, his informal treatment was nevertheless able to throw new light on the education, background, habits, and manner of life of a group too mobile, furtive, and shifting to be reached by the usual research methods. According to the Works Progress Administration (778) there were 54,430 transient youths sixteen to twenty-four years of age inclusive, being cared for under the federal transient program in May, 1935.

Fields for Further Research

Among fruitful topics for future research, the following might be suggested as especially needed:

1. Investigations of the pioneering type:
    a. Local studies of the whole problem of the vocational and occupational adjustment of youth who have left school and of solutions applicable in different types of communities.
    b. Child employment in the various ramifications of the amusement industry, including booths at beaches and amusement parks, radio broadcasting and nightclubs, as well as the legitimate theater. Woodbury (782, 783) made a promising start with studies of stage children in Buffalo and golf caddies in Erie County, New York.
    c. Children working as domestic servants. A field untouched by the industrial codes and almost untouched by state laws. In many states children of compulsory school age may be exempted from school for domestic service and random reports during the depression indicated serious exploitation of young girls in domestic service—long working hours, little or no pay, and unsatisfactory living conditions.
    d. A study of errand and delivery boys, with especial attention to traffic and motor vehicle hazards.
2. Studies of the administration and enforcement of the various types of sixteen-year minimum age laws enacted by five states since 1932 (Connecticut, Pennsylvania,

Utah, Wisconsin; and after a new law becomes operative in September, 1936, New York). Especial attention to any variation in numbers of industrial injuries to minors.
3. Statistical studies:
   a. Accident rates among employed minors by age groups and by type of work, similar to Illinois and New York reports (730, 751). Comparative rates for minors under and over sixteen years, in states which prohibit hazardous employment only up to sixteen years and in states which continue this protection to eighteen years, would be particularly useful.
   b. Comparative health rating of children who had left school and been working at least one year, with control group of children originally in same classes who had continued in school during the same period.
4. Recheck of child labor conditions under state laws:
   a. In selected industries after the industrial codes ceased to operate in May, 1935; the cotton garment and textile industries should be especially interesting.
   b. Follow-up studies of children receiving work permits in selected cities, to determine any conditions below the standard set by the industrial codes; permanency of employment; and whether the employment is in line with the child's previous vocational training and aptitudes or merely a "stop-gap."
   c. In the sugar-beet fields under the regulations of the AAA benefit agreements (due to expire in 1936).
   d. In industrial home work after the industrial codes ceased to operate; with especial attention to work done by school children and its effect on health and school standing and amount of retardation.
5. Studies of delinquent, truant, or retarded children, including in the social data secured a history of their employment outside of school hours, in order to throw light on any factors in their employment which seem to be contributory to maladjustment at school.

BIBLIOGRAPHY ON PUPIL PERSONNEL, GUIDANCE, AND COUNSELING

Chapter I. School Attendance

1. ALLEN, HOLLIS P. *Universal Free Education.* School Economy Series. Stanford University, Calif. Stanford University Press, 1934. 100 p.
2. BAKER, EDITH MAYWOOD. *A Study of Certain Factors Involved in Truancy Among Girls (First Offenders).* Master's thesis, Brown University, 1933. 55 p.
3. BRACE, DAVID KINGSLEY. "Some Objective Evidence of the Value of Physical Education." *Journal of Health and Physical Education* 4: 38-41, 62; April, 1933.
4. CHAPPELL, ALETHEA. "How Does Overcutting Affect the Grades?" *School and Society* 32: 677-78; November 15, 1930.
5. CLAPP, MARY A., and STRONG, MABEL A. *The School and the Working Child.* Boston: Massachusetts Child Labor Committee, 1928. p. 153-71.
6. CLEMENTS, JOHNNIE R. *A Study of Age-Grade-Progress and Attendance in the White Schools of Lamar County, Alabama.* Master's thesis, University of Alabama, 1932. 63 p.
7. COON, WILBUR DEWEY. *The Determination of Causes of Elimination in Maple Heights, Ohio, High School Through a Comparative Study of Graduates and Withdrawals.* Master's thesis, Ohio State University, 1933. 70 p.
8. DEFFENBAUGH, WALTER S., and KEESECKER, WARD W. *Compulsory School Attendance Laws and Their Administration.* U. S. Dept. of the Interior, Office of Education, Bulletin, 1935, No. 4. Washington, D. C.: Government Printing Office, 1935. 96 p.
9. DYER, RAY E. *A Study of the Working of the Bing Law in the Rural Schools of Morgan County.* Master's thesis, Ohio State University, 1931. 65 p.
10. ERESTEIN, IRENES, and PEREZ, GRACIANO M. "Studies on the Problem of Tardiness and Attendance and Suggestions for Its Solution." *Philippine Journal of Education* 14: 399-400; March 1932.
11. ESSER, E. SIGURD. *Recent Tendencies in Compulsory Attendance in the United States.* Master's thesis, University of North Dakota, 1933. 189 p.
12. FINCH, F. H., and NEMZEK, C. L. "Attendance and Achievement in the High School." *School and Society* 41: 207-8; February 9, 1935.
13. FREEMAN, J. N. *School Attendance in North Carolina; a Survey of Six Counties.* Special Bulletin No. 11. Raleigh: North Carolina State Board of Charities and Public Welfare, 1931. 67 p.
14. HECK, ARCH O., chairman. "Pupil Personnel, Guidance, and Counseling." *Review of Educational Research* 3: 183-278; June, 1933.
15. HECK, ARCH O. "Pupil Personnel Services in the Public Schools." *Educational Research Bulletin (Ohio State University)* 14: 57-61, 98-102, 155-61, 182-91, 214-16; March, April, September through November, 1935.
16. HENDERSON, LOUISE. "A Study of Absences on Account of Sickness Among High-School Girls." *School and Society* 36: 797-800; December 17, 1932.
17. HERLIHY, LESTER B. "What It Costs to Enforce Attendance Laws." *Nation's Schools* 15: 28; April, 1935.
18. HEWES, AMY. "Why Pupils Leave High School." *School Review* 43: 287-94; April, 1935.
19. JONES, LONZO. "Class Attendance and College Marks." *School and Society* 33: 444-46; March 28, 1931.
20. KAPLAN, ALBERT J. "The N. R. A. Codes and Secondary School Efficiency." *School and Society* 41: 471-74; April 6, 1935.
21. KEFAUVER, GRAYSON N., and RUSK, JAMES. "Variation in Popularization of Secondary Education." *School Review* 43: 112-18; February, 1935.
22. KELLER, GEORGE MEAD. *Study of Administrative Solutions of Attendance Problems.* Master's thesis, University of Michigan, 1933. 166 p.
23. LIPPE, NATHAN MAX. *The Relationship Between Athletic Activity and the Attendance of Boys in School.* Master's thesis, University of Pittsburgh, 1933. 67 p.

24. MEADOWS, AUSTIN RUEL. *The Progress of School Attendance in the Public Schools of Alabama Since 1900.* Master's thesis, University of Alabama, 1932. 144 p.
25. "A Mighty 'Issue' Laid to Rest." *School Review* 43: 241-43; April, 1935.
26. MORGAN, WALTER E. "Estimates of Population, 1934." *California Schools* 6: 200-5; June, 1935.
27. MURRAY, MATTHEW J. *School Attendance and Its Relation to Senior High School Achievement.* Doctor's thesis, Fordham University, 1934. 96 p.
28. PHILLIPS, FRANK M. "Where Are the Children?" *School and Society* 32: 324-25; September 6, 1930.
29. REED, ANNA YEOMANS. *Human Waste in Education.* New York: Century Co., 1927. p. 72-363.
30. REED, CARROLL R. "Postschool Adjustment of Pupils Who Withdraw from the Upper Grades." *Elementary School Journal* 31: 653-54; May, 1931.
31. REESE, CARL RICHARD. *A Survey of Attendance Procedures in City Junior High Schools.* Master's thesis, Ohio State University, 1933. 79 p.
32. STAMY, A. REESE. *Some Factors Influencing School Attendance in Pennsylvania and North Carolina.* Master's thesis, Drake University, 1933. 106 p.
33. "Statistics of State School Systems." *School and Society* 42: 238-39; August 17, 1935.
34. STRAYER, GEORGE D., director. *Report of the Survey of the Schools of Chicago, Illinois.* New York: Teachers College, Columbia University, 1932. Vol. II. p. 209-11.
35. SULLENGER, T. EARL. "Some Social Factors in School Non-Attendance." *School and Society* 41: 238-40; February 16, 1935.
36. TARPLEY, MARVIN FRANK. *The Major Judicial Decisions Relating to Compulsory School Attendance in the United States.* Master's thesis, Ohio State University, 1933. 161 p.
37. TRENHAM, N. BRADFORD. "Educational Growth in California." *Tax Digest (California Taxpayers' Association)* 10: 232-36, 277-85; July and August, 1932.
38. VAN KERSEN, E. PHILIP. *A Study of the Causes of Irregular Attendance and Its Effect on Pupil Achievement.* Master's thesis, University of Michigan, 1932. 41 p.
39. WILSON, IRENE BLAKELY. *A Comparison of Attendance and Failure in a Junior High School.* Master's thesis, University of Pittsburgh, 1933. 82 p.

Chapter II. School Progress

40. ADAMS, W. L. "Why Teachers Say They Fail Pupils." *Educational Administration and Supervision* 18: 594-600; November, 1932.
41. ALLEN, CHARLES F. "The Bunk in Grade Classification of Pupils." *Junior-Senior High School Clearing House* 7: 301-2; January, 1933.
42. ALTER, DINSMORE. "Students Whose Academic Work Is Inferior." *Bulletin of the American Association of University Professors* 20: 333-36; May, 1934.
43. AYER, FRED C. *The Progress of Pupils in the State of Texas, 1931-1932.* Research Bulletin of the Section of Superintendence, Texas State Teachers Association. Austin, Texas: the Association, November, 1932. 35 p.
44. AYER, FRED C. *The Progress of Pupils in the State of Texas, 1932-1933.* Research Bulletin of the Section of Superintendence, Texas State Teachers Association. Austin, Texas: the Association, November, 1933. 36 p.
45. AYER, FRED C. *The Progress of Pupils in the State of Texas, 1933-1934.* Research Bulletin of the Section of Superintendence, Texas State Teachers Association. Austin, Texas: the Association, November, 1934. 35 p.
46. AYER, FRED C. "School Progress." *Review of Educational Research* 3: 194-200, 249-53; June, 1933.
47. BAYLISS, ZOE BURRELL. "A Study of the Factors Contributing to the Unsatisfactory Scholastic Attainment of First Year Women Students." *Journal of Educational Research* 27: 687-97; May, 1934.
48. BEHRENS, H. D. "Effects of a 'How to Study' Course." *Journal of Higher Education* 6: 195-202; April, 1935.
49. BENNETT, ANNETTE. "A Comparative Study of Subnormal Children in the Elementary Grades." *Teachers College Record* 34: 63-65; October, 1932.
50. BIGELOW, ELIZABETH B. "School Progress of Under-Age Children." *Elementary School Journal* 35: 186-92; November, 1934.

51. BILLETT, ROY O. *Provisions for Individual Differences, Marking, and Promotion.* U. S. Dept. of the Interior, Office of Education, Bulletin, 1932, No. 17. National Survey of Secondary Education, Monograph No. 13. Washington, D. C.: Government Printing Office, 1933. p. 462-72.
52. BLOSE, DAVID T., and SEGEL, DAVID. "The School-Life Expectancy of Failures in the Elementary Grades." *American School Board Journal* 86: 29-30; March, 1933.
53. BREED, FREDERICK S. *Classroom Organization and Management.* Yonkers-on-Hudson, N. Y.: World Book Co., 1933. p. 197-218.
54. BROWN, EDWIN J. *Everyday Problems in Classroom Management.* Boston: Houghton Mifflin Co., 1933. p. 125-41.
55. BROWNELL, CLIFFORD L. "Educational Progress and Hard Times." *Journal of Health and Physical Education* 4: 10-11, 61; April, 1933.
56. BRUECKNER, L. J. "The Cumulative Effects of the Policy of Non-Failing." *Journal of Educational Research* 28: 289-90; December, 1934.
57. CALDWELL, FLOYD F. "Speed as a Factor with Children of Superior and Inferior Intelligence." *Journal of Educational Research* 26: 522-24; March, 1933.
58. CASWELL, H. L. *Non-Promotion in Elementary Schools.* Field Studies No. 4. Nashville, Tenn.: George Peabody College for Teachers, 1933. 100 p.
59. CHEYNEY, WALKER W., and BOYER, PHILIP A. "Is Non-Promotion a Defensible Policy?" *Elementary School Journal* 33: 647-51; May, 1933.
60. CHISM, LESLIE L. "Classification and Promotion Practices in the Elementary School." *Elementary School Journal* 33: 89-91; October, 1932.
61. CLEM, ORLIE M., and COON, LEON. "Factors in Pupil Failure in a Typical Junior High School." *High School Teacher* 10: 114-16, 123; April, 1934.
62. CUTRIGHT, PRUDENCE, and ANDERSON, WALTER A. "An Experimental Study of Pupil Failures in the First Grade." *Elementary School Journal* 34: 570-74; April, 1934.
63. DRESDEN, B. M. "Use of Tests as a Means of Discovering Causes of Failures in High School." *Educational Method* 13: 267-71; February, 1934.
64. DURLING, DOROTHY, and POWELL, WEBSTER. "Improper School Placement as a Factor in Juvenile Delinquency." *Journal of Applied Psychology* 16: 519-24; October, 1932.
65. ECKERT, RUTH E. "Intellectual Maturity." *Journal of Higher Education* 5: 478-84; December, 1934.
66. EGINTON, DANIEL P. "Classifying and Promoting Pupils." *Nation's Schools* 14: 22-25; August, 1934.
67. EURICH, ALVIN C. "College Failures." *School and Society* 37: 692-96; May 27, 1933.
68. FARLEY, E. S.; FREY, A. J.; and GARLAND, GERTRUDE. "Factors Related to the Grade Progress of Pupils." *Elementary School Journal* 34: 186-93; November, 1933.
69. FEINGOLD, GUSTAVE A. "Annual and Semiannual Promotions." *School Review* 41: 747-58; December, 1933.
70. FEINGOLD, GUSTAVE A. "Midyear Promotions and School Efficiency." *School and Society* 37: 662-64; May 20, 1933.
71. FRENCH, WILL. *Promotional Plans in the High School.* Contributions to Education, No. 587. New York: Teachers College, Columbia University, 1933. 90 p.
72. GERLING, HENRY J. "Educational Problems." *School and Society* 42: 101-4; July 20, 1935.
73. GLESSNER, HARRY H., and GRAHAM, LEO J. "A Study of Retardation and Failure in a Junior High School." *Educational Administration and Supervision* 19: 81-90; February, 1933.
74. GRAVES, S. MONROE. "Are School Failures Necessary?" *Journal of Education* 116: 322, 326; June 19, 1933.
75. GUILFORD, CHARLES C. "Why Pupils Fail." *Educational Method* 12: 219-22; January, 1933.
76. HAYES, ELEANOR H. "Why Pupils Fail." *Educational Method* 13: 25-28; October, 1933.
77. HEWES, AMY. "Why Pupils Leave High School." *School Review* 43: 287-94; April, 1935.

78. HILL, GEORGE E. "Educational Attainments of Young Male Offenders." *Elementary School Journal* 36: 53-58; September, 1935.
79. HOOKER, GROVER C. "Did the Pupils Fail?" *Educational Method* 12: 367-68; March, 1933.
80. KARLAN, SAMUEL C. "Failure in Secondary School as a Mental-Hygiene Problem." *Mental Hygiene* 18: 611-20; October, 1934.
81. KLINE, E. J. "Significant Changes in the Curve of Elimination Since 1900." *Journal of Educational Research* 26: 608-16; April, 1933.
82. LARSON, EMIL L. "Arizona's Educational Progress." *Arizona Teacher* 24: 8-12; September, 1935.
83. LINDSAY, J. ARMOUR. *Annual and Semi-Annual Promotion.* Contributions to Education, No. 570. New York: Teachers College, Columbia University, 1933. 170 p.
84. LITHAUER, DONAH B. "A Follow-up Report of the Later School Progress of Children of Primary School Age Trained in an Experimental Kindergarten." *Journal of Juvenile Research* 17: 175-78; July, 1933.
85. LORD, ARTHUR B. "A Survey of Four Hundred Forty-Nine Special Class Pupils." *Journal of Educational Research* 27: 108-14; October, 1933.
86. MCELWEE, EDNA WILLIS. "Homogenous Grouping of Retarded Pupils." *Elementary School Journal* 34: 118-21; October, 1933.
87. MCELWEE, EDNA WILLIS. "School Progress and Grade Placement." *School Executives Magazine* 53: 114; December, 1933.
88. MCGINNIS, WILLIAM C. "Dodging the Blame for Failures." *Journal of Education* 117: 209-11; April 16, 1934.
89. MALLER, J. B. "Economic and Social Correlatives of School Progress in New York City." *Teachers College Record* 34: 655-70; May, 1933.
90. MANUEL, HERSCHEL T. "A Comparison of Spanish-Speaking and English-Speaking Children in Reading and Arithmetic." *Journal of Applied Psychology* 19: 189-202; April, 1935.
91. MANUEL, HERSCHEL T., and VOYER, MARY T. "What Shall We Expect of the Child Who Enters School at Six Years of Age." *Educational Administration and Supervision* 19: 521-28; October, 1933.
92. MARSHALL, HENRY C. "Trial Promotion—An Administrative Device for the Improvement of Learning." *Educational Administration and Supervision* 20: 373-81; May, 1934.
93. MEADOWS, A. R. "Grade Progress During 1935." *Alabama School Journal* 53: 24-25; September, 1935.
94. MILLER, JOSEPH. "Causes of Failure and Success in School." *Educational Method* 12: 364-66; March, 1933.
95. MITCHELL, CLAUDE. "Why Do Pupils Fail?" *Junior-Senior High School Clearing House* 9: 172-76; November, 1934.
96. "A New Plan of Promotion in the Schools of Rochester, New York." *School and Society* 38: 698-99; November 25, 1933.
97. "New York Commission Recommends Abandonment of Traditional Grade Organization." *Elementary School Journal* 35: 728-30; June, 1935.
98. "Non-Promotion in the First Grade and Future Progress of Pupils." *Elementary School Journal* 34: 731-32; June, 1934.
99. OTTO, HENRY J. "Administrative Control of Pupil Promotion in Elementary Schools." *Educational Trends* 2: 28-33; January, 1933.
100. OTTO, HENRY J., and MELBY, ERNEST O. "An Attempt to Evaluate the Threat of Failure as a Factor in Achievement." *Elementary School Journal* 35: 588-96; April, 1935.
101. OTTO, HENRY J. *Elementary School Organization and Administration.* New York: D. Appleton-Century Co., 1934. p. 198-271.
102. OTTO, HENRY J. "Promotion of Pupils in Elementary Schools." *American School Board Journal* 87: 19-21, July; 21-22, August; 21-22, September, 1933.
103. OTTO, HENRY J. "Pupil Failure as an Administrative Device in Elementary Education." *Elementary School Journal* 34: 576-89; April, 1934.
104. PUGSLEY, C. A. "Reducing and Handling Student Failures." *American School Board Journal* 86: 18-20; March, 1933.
105. "Retardation in the First Grade." *Elementary School Journal* 34: 88-91; October, 1933.

106. "Retardation in the Schools of New York City." *School and Society* 41: 861; June 29, 1935.
107. ROBIE, EVERETT E. "A Study of Over-Age Distribution in the Grades." *American School Board Journal* 87: 22; October, 1933.
108. SAMLER, JOSEPH. "Report of an Experiment with Failing Students." *Junior-Senior High School Clearing House* 9: 235-40; December, 1934.
109. SANDON, FRANK. "Progress Through a Secondary School as Measured by School Marks." *British Journal of Educational Psychology* 3: 269-90; November, 1933.
110. SARBAUGH, MARY E. "The Young College Student." *School and Society* 40: 823-24; December 15, 1934.
111. "A Saturday School for Talented Children." *School and Society* 38: 699; November 25, 1933.
112. SMITH, MARK. "Causes for Failures in College Freshmen." *High School Quarterly* 21: 145-49; April, 1933.
113. STEINER, M. A. "Should Pupils be Promoted Annually or Semi-Annually?" *Nation's Schools* 12: 49-50; December, 1933.
114. STREET, ROY F. "Factors Related to Maladjustment in School." *Elementary School Journal* 34: 676-80; May, 1934.
115. THOMSON, JENNIE LLOYD. "Chronological Age Does Count." *Journal of Education* 115: 661-64; December 5, 1932.
116. THORNE, NORMAN. "A High School Which Turns Failure into Success." *American School Board Journal* 88: 23, 71; April, 1934.
117. ULLRICH, O. A. "Why College Students Fail." *Texas Outlook* 17: 11-12; August, 1933.
118. VINSON, MARIETTA R. "Retardation Problems." *Volta Review* 36: 206; April, 1934.
119. WITTY, PAUL A., and WILKINS, LAROY W. "The Status of Acceleration or Grade Skipping as an Administrative Practice." *Educational Administration and Supervision* 19: 321-46; May, 1933.

Chapter III. School Marks

120. BALL, IDA GRACE. "An Evolutionary Report Card." *Progressive Education* 12: 89-94; February, 1935.
121. BEATTY, W. W. "Objectifying School Marks." *American School Board Journal* 87: 27-28; July, 1933.
122. BILLETT, ROY O. *Provisions for Individual Differences, Marking and Promotions.* U. S. Dept. of the Interior, Office of Education, Bulletin, 1932, No. 17. National Survey of Secondary Education, Monograph No. 13. Washington, D. C.: Government Printing Office, 1933. p. 424-61.
123. BIXLER, ROY W. "Rating the College Entrant." *Journal of Higher Education* 3: 361-65; October, 1932.
124. BIXLER, ROY W. "Variable Standards of Marking in High Schools." *School and Society* 38: 159-60; July 29, 1933.
125. BOARDMAN, C. W. "Uniform Marking Advocated by Secondary School Principals." *Minnesota Journal of Education* 15: 139-40; December, 1934.
126. BROOKS, H. B. "What Can Be Done About Comparative Marks and Formal Report Cards?" *California Journal of Secondary Education* 10: 101-6; January, 1935.
127. CHAMBERS, B. "Reports—The Break With Tradition." *New Era* 14: 117-21; May, 1933.
128. CHAPMAN, H. F. *Influence of Part Time Employment on the Marks of High School Students.* Detroit, Mich.: Detroit Public Schools. 15 p. (Typewritten manuscript.)
129. CHARLES, JOHN W. "Competition for Marks." *Journal of Applied Psychology* 16: 315-21; June, 1932.
130. DEXTER, EMILY S. "The Effect of Fatigue or Boredom on Teachers' Marks." *Journal of Educational Research* 28: 664-67; May, 1935.
131. DIETTERT, CHESTER C. "Deportment Grading in Indiana." *High School Teacher* 10: 310-12; December, 1934. (Similar article in September, 1934. p. 216-18.)
132. EDMISTON, R. W. "A Method of Providing a More Valid Distribution of School Marks." *Journal of Experimental Education* 3: 194-97; March, 1935.

133. FARNSWORTH, P. R. "Seat Preference in the Class Room." *Journal of Social Psychology* 4: 373-76; August, 1933.
134. HILL, GEORGE E. "The Report Card In Present Practice." *Educational Trends* 3: 6-14; February, 1934.
135. LOGSDON, J. DESMOND. *A Comparative Study of Pupils from Homes Not Receiving Relief with Pupils from Homes Which Are Receiving Relief.* Chicago: University of Chicago. 9 p. (Typewritten manuscript.)
136. MANEY, C. A. "Sex-Bias in College Marking." *Journal of Higher Education* 4: 29-31; January, 1933.
137. MILLER, JOSEPH. "Conduct Mark." *Educational Method* 13: 193-98; January, 1934.
138. MOFFITT, J. C. "Substitute for Report Cards." *Education* 55: 147-50; November, 1934.
139. National Education Association, Department of Superintendence and Research Division. *New Developments in Pupil Report Cards.* Educational Research Service, Circular No. 4, 1934. Washington, D. C.: the Association, May, 1934. 36 p.
140. PALM, R. R., chairman "A Proposed Secondary School Uniform State Marking System." *Minnesota Journal of Education* 15: 213-15; February, 1935.
141. Pennsylvania Department of Public Instruction. *Reporting Pupil Progress.* Curriculum Studies Bulletin No. 88. Harrisburg: the Department, 1935. 31 p.
142. REED, HAROLD F. "Report Cards." *New York State Education* 21: 145-47, 175-76; November, 1933.
143. RICHARDSON, ALLEN B. "A Study of the Relation Between Number of Study Periods and Pupils' Marks." *School Review* 42: 104-10; February, 1934.
144. SMITH, LUCIUS. *Status of Marking in Negro Colleges.* Bluefield, W. Va.: Bluefield State Teachers College, 1935. 40 p.
145. SNEDECOR, G. W. "Analysis of Co-variance of Statistically Controlled Grades." *Journal of the American Statistical Association* 30: 263-68; March (Supplement), 1935.
146. UPJOHN, H. S. "New Type of Report Card for the Elementary Grades." *Elementary School Journal* 35: 730-31; June, 1935.
147. WARREN, J. E. "School Reports to Parents on Pupil Progress." *American School Board Journal* 90: 16-17, 81, 83; May, 1935.
148. WEBER, ORVILLE E. "A Study of Pupil Reports Issued by the Public Elementary Schools in Cities Having a Population of More than 100,000." *Pittsburgh Schools* 9: 95-98; January-February, 1935.
149. WILLIAMS, MARY R. *Critical Study of the Individual Reports Made by Kansas Administrators to Parents.* Studies in Education No. 8. Emporia, Kan.: Kansas State Teachers College, 1934. 32 p.
150. WORLTON, J. T. "Shall We Eliminate the Comparative Marking System from the Report Card?" *Elementary School Journal* 33: 176-84; November, 1932.
151. YATES, L. "Grading Students in Sections of Freshmen English." *Kentucky Personnel Bulletin* May, 1934.

Chapter IV. Recording and Reporting

152. BROWN, JOSEPH C. "Superintendents' Monthly Reports to Board of Education." *Educational Research Record* 5: 18-25; April, 1933.
153. JOHNSON, B. L. "Permanent Record Form in the Secondary School." *School Review* 41: 114-22; February, 1933.
154. JORDEN, EDWARD L. "Improving the Superintendent's Annual Report." *School Executives Magazine* 52: 151-52; December, 1932.
155. MURPHY, J. FRED. "The High-School Principal's Annual Report." *American School Board Journal* 85: 41-42; November, 1932.
156. National Committee on Standard Reports for Institutions of Higher Education. *Financial Reports for Colleges and Universities.* Chicago: University of Chicago Press, 1935. 285 p.
157. Pennsylvania Department of Public Instruction. *Cumulative Pupil Personnel Records, Elementary and Secondary Schools.* Bulletin 81. Harrisburg: the Department, 1933. 23 p.

158. Progressive Education Association, Committee on Reports and Records. *Manual of Directions for Trait Study.* Chestnut Hill, Mass.: E. R. Smith, chairman (Beaver Country Day School), 1935.
159. REAVIS, W. C., chairman. "Topic Group H: A National Coordination of School Statistics, Records and Reports." *Official Report.* Washington, D. C.: Department of Superintendence, National Education Association, 1934. p. 228-29.
160. ROBERTSON, DAVID ALLAN. "The American Council Cumulative Record Forms for Colleges and Secondary Schools." *Educational Record* 14: 81-93; January, 1933.
161. SMITH, LEO. "Our High School Records." *Montana Education* 10: 22-23, March; 22-24, April; 13-15; May, 1934.
162. White House Conference on Child Health and Protection. *Vocational Guidance.* Report of the Subcommittee on Vocational Guidance. (M. Edith Campbell, chairman.) New York: Century Co., 1932. 369 p.

Chapter V. Characteristics of Pupil Population

A. ELEMENTARY EDUCATION

163. ARMSTRONG, CLAIRETTE P. "Juvenile Delinquency as Related to Immigration." *School and Society* 38: 61-64; July 8, 1933.
164. ARMSTRONG, CLAIRETTE P. "Sex Differences in the Mental Functioning of School Children." *Journal of Applied Psychology* 16: 559-71; October, 1932.
165. BABCOCK, MARJORIE E. *A Comparison of Delinquent and Non-Delinquent Boys by Objective Measures of Personality.* Honolulu: the Author, 1932. 74 p. (Doctor's thesis, Columbia University.)
166. BAKER, HARRY J., chairman. "Psychological Tests." *Review of Educational Research* 5: 185-331; June, 1935.
167. BEATLEY, BANCROFT. *Achievement in the Junior High School.* Harvard Studies in Education, Vol. 18. Cambridge, Mass.: Harvard University Press, 1932. 92 p.
168. BOYNTON, PAUL L., and MCGRAW, BONNIE H. "The Characteristics of Problem Children." *Journal of Juvenile Research* 18: 215-22; October, 1934.
169. BROOM, M. E., and DE SILVA, F. W. "Achievement Test Scores as Measures of the Mental Ability of Junior High School Pupils." *School and Society* 38: 715-16; November 25, 1933.
170. BROWN, FRED. *An Experimental Study of the Psychoneurotic Syndrome in Childhood.* Doctor's thesis, University of Ohio, 1933. 175 p.
171. BROWN, RALPH R. "The Time Interval Between Test and Retest in Its Relation to the Constancy of the Intelligence Quotient." *Journal of Educational Psychology* 24: 81-96; February, 1933.
172. CALDWELL, M. G. "Is the Reformatory Reforming the Prisoner?" *Journal of Juvenile Research* 18: 90-102; April, 1934.
173. CAMPBELL, ALBERT A. "The Personality Adjustments of Only Children." *Psychological Bulletin* 31: 193-203; March, 1934.
174. CATTELL, PSYCHE. "Do the Stanford-Binet I. Q.'s of Superior Boys and Girls Tend to Decrease or Increase with Age?" *Journal of Educational Research* 26: 668-73; May, 1933.
175. CHANNING, ALICE. *Employment of Mentally Deficient Boys and Girls.* U. S. Dept. of Labor, Children's Bureau Publication, No. 210. Washington, D. C.: Government Printing Office, 1932. 107 p.
176. COLLMANN, R. D.; MARSHALL, A. J.; and THOMAS, RUTH. *Three Studies in the Comparative Intelligence of English, American and Australian Children.* Educational Research Series, No. 22. Melbourne, Australia: Melbourne University Press, 1934. 70 p.
177. CONRAD, H. S.; JONES, H. E.; and HSIAO, H. H. "Sex Differences in Mental Growth and Decline." *Journal of Educational Psychology* 24: 161-69; March 1933.
178. DAMERAU, RUTH. "Influence of Treatment on the Reading Ability and Behavior Disorders of Reading Disability Cases." *Smith College Studies in Social Work* 5: 160-83; December, 1934.
179. DANIEL, ROBERT P. "Negro-White Differences in Non-Intellectual Traits, and in Special Abilities." *Journal of Negro Education* 3: 411-23; July, 1934.

180. DANIEL, ROBERT P. *A Psychological Study of Delinquent and Non-Delinquent Negro Boys.* Contributions to Education, No. 546. New York: Teachers College, Columbia University, 1932. 59 p.
181. DAVIS, HELEN E. *The Report of the Study of Work with Younger Girls in the Y. W. C. A.* New York: Woman's Press, 1935. 24 p.
182. DECROLY, O. *Comment l'enfant arrive à parler.* Brussels: Centrale du P. E. S. de Belgique, 1934. 2 vol.
183. DELLAERT, R. "L'intelligence des anormaux du caractere." *L'Année Psychologique* 34: 200-16; 1933.
184. EDGERTON, H. A. "Recording and Reporting." *Review of Educational Research* 3: 205-8, 256-59; June, 1933.
185. FRANCIS, KENNETH V., and FILLMORE, EVA. *The Influence of Environment Upon the Personality of Children.* Studies in Child Welfare, Vol. 9, No. 2. Iowa City: University of Iowa, 1934. 71 p.
186. FRYER, DOUGLAS, and SPARLING, E. J. "Intelligence and Occupational Adjustment." *Occupations* 12: 55-63; June, 1934.
187. GLUECK, S., and GLUECK, E. T. *One Thousand Juvenile Delinquents, Their Treatment by Court and Clinic.* Cambridge, Mass.: Harvard University Press, 1934. 341 p.
188. HARDY, MARTHA CRUMPTON. "The Out-of-School Activities of Well-Adjusted and Poorly Adjusted Elementary School Pupils." *Journal of Educational Psychology* 26: 455-67; September, 1935.
189. HEILMAN, J. D. "Sex Differences in Intellectual Abilities." *Journal of Educational Psychology* 24: 47-62; January, 1933.
190. HILDRETH, GERTRUDE H. "Mental Ability Measured by Verbal and Non-Verbal Tests." *Teachers College Record* 34: 134-42; November, 1932.
191. HOEFER, CAROLYN, and HARDY, MARTHA CRUMPTON. "The Role of Health in the Child's Development." *Elementary School Journal* 35: 423-39; February, 1935.
192. HOLLINGWORTH, LETA S., and KAUNITZ, RUTH M. "The Centile Status of Gifted Children at Maturity." *Pedagogical Seminary and Journal of Genetic Psychology* 45: 106-20; September, 1934.
193. HOLLINGWORTH, LETA S., and GRAY, HOWARD A. "Juvenile Achievement as Related to Size." *Teachers College Record* 32: 236-44; December, 1930.
194. HOPKINS, L. THOMAS, and MENDENHALL, JAMES E. *Achievement at Lincoln School: A Study of Academic Test Results in an Experimental School.* Lincoln School Research Studies. New York: Teachers College, Columbia University, 1934. 65 p.
195. JACK, LOIS M. "An Experimental Study of Ascendant Behavior in Preschool Children." *Behavior of the Preschool Child.* (By L. M. Jack and others.) University of Iowa Studies in Child Welfare, Vol. 9, No. 3. Iowa City: the University, 1934. p. 7-65.
196. JASTAK, JOSEPH. *Variability of Psychometric Performances in Mental Diagnosis.* New York: Spinner Press, 1934. 100 p.
197. JOHNSON, WENDELL. *The Influence of Stuttering on the Personality.* University of Iowa Studies in Child Welfare, Vol. 5, No. 5. Iowa City: the University, 1932. 140 p.
198. JONES, HAROLD ELLIS; CONRAD, H. S.; and BLANCHARD, M. B. *Environmental Handicap in Mental Test Performance.* Publications in Psychology, Vol. 5, No. 3. Berkeley, Calif.: University of California Press, 1932. p. 63-99.
199. JONES, HAROLD ELLIS, and CONRAD, II. S. *The Growth and Decline of Intelligence; a Study of a Homogeneous Group Between the Ages of Ten and Sixty.* Genetic Psychology Monographs, Vol. 13, No. 3. Worcester, Mass.: Clark University Press, 1933. p. 223-98.
200. JORDAN, A. M. "Parental Occupations and Children's Intelligence Scores." *Journal of Applied Psychology* 17: 103-19; April, 1933.
201. KINTER-REMMLEIN, MADALINE. "Study of a Group of Paris Children: Their Ideas of Right and Wrong; Their Reactions in Situations Involving Cooperation and Self-Sacrifice." *Journal of Social Psychology* 6: 91-104; February, 1935.
202. KIRK, S. A. "The Effects of Remedial Reading on the Educational Progress and Personality Adjustment of High-Grade Mentally Deficient Problem Children: Ten Case Studies." *Journal of Juvenile Research* 18: 140-62; July, 1934.

203. LAMMERMANN, H. "Die Konstanza und die Ubbarkeit von Denkleistungen. (Ubungsversuche mit Intelligenztests)." *Zeitschrift für angewandte Psychologie* 46: 3-87; February, 1934.
204. LANE, H. A., and WITTY, P. A. "The Educational Attainment of Delinquent Boys." *Journal of Educational Psychology* 25: 695-702; December, 1934.
205. LANE, H. A. *The Social and Educational Backgrounds of Young Delinquent Boys.* Doctor's thesis, Northwestern University, 1934. 164 p.
206. LAYCOCK, SAMUEL RALPH. "Adjustments of Superior and Inferior School Children." *Journal of Social Psychology* 4: 353-66; August, 1933.
207. LAYCOCK, SAMUEL RALPH. "Teachers' Reactions to Maladjustments of School Children." *British Journal of Educational Psychology* 4: 11-29; February, 1934.
208. LEVY, DAVID M. "Relation of Maternal Overprotection to School Grades and Intelligence Tests." *American Journal of Orthopsychiatry* 3: 26-34; January, 1933.
209. LORD, ARTHUR B. "A Survey of Four Hundred Forty-Nine Special Class Pupils." *Journal of Educational Research* 27: 108-14: October, 1933.
210. McCLURE, W. E. "Intelligence of 600 Juvenile Delinquents." *Journal of Juvenile Research* 17: 35-43; January, 1933.
211. McELWEE, EDNA WILLIS. "Profile Drawings of Normal and Sub-normal Children." *Journal of Applied Psychology* 18: 599-603; August, 1934.
212. McFIE, BERNICE STEWART. "Behavior and Personality Difficulties in School Children." *British Journal of Educational Psychology* 4: 30-46; February, 1934.
213. MACGREGOR, GREGOR. *Achievement Tests in the Primary School; a Comparative Study with American Tests in Fife.* Scottish Council for Research in Education Publications, Vol. 6. London: University of London Press, 1935. 136 p.
214. McPHERSON, ORPHA R. *Summer Vacation Activities of 100 Ten Year Old Farm Children in a Selected Area.* Doctor's thesis, Teachers College, Columbia University, 1933. 123 p.
215. MALLER, J. B. "Character and Personality Tests." *Psychological Bulletin* 31: 501-24; July, 1934. 32: 500-23; July, 1935.
216. MALLER, J. B. "Studies in Character and Personality in German Psychological Literature." *Psychological Bulletin* 30: 209-32; March, 1933.
217. MALLER, J. B., "The Trend of Juvenile Delinquency in New York City." *Journal of Juvenile Research* 17: 10-18; January, 1933.
218. MILES, CATHARINE COX, and MILES, WALTER R. "The Correlation of Intelligence Scores and Chronological Age from Early to Late Maturity." *American Journal of Psychology* 44: 44-78; January, 1932.
219. MOORE, H. K. "Is the Problem Boy a Weakling?" *Journal of Juvenile Research* 18: 79-89; April, 1934.
220. MORENO, J. L. *Who Shall Survive? A New Approach to the Problem of Human Interrelations.* Nervous and Mental Diseases Monologue, Series No. 58. Washington, D. C.: Nervous and Mental Disease Publishing Co., 1934. 440 p.
221. NEILSON, N. P., and COZENS, FREDERICK W. *Achievement Scales in Physical Education Activities for Boys and Girls in Elementary and Junior High Schools.* New York: A. S. Barnes and Co., 1934. 171 p.
222. NEMZEK, CLAUDE L. "The Constancy of the I. Q." *Psychological Bulletin* 30: 143-68; February, 1933.
223. OUTHIT, MARION C. *A Study of Resemblance of Parents and Children in General Intelligence.* Archives of Psychology, No. 149. New York: Columbia University, 1933. 60 p.
224. PAGE, MARJORIE L. "The Mechanical Ability of Subnormal Boys." *Journal of Applied Psychology* 17: 164-81; April, 1933.
225. PARKER, HENRY T. *The Development of Intelligence in Subnormal Children.* Educational Research Series, No. 27. Melbourne, Australia: Melbourne University Press, 1934. 63 p.
226. PARKER, HENRY T. "Fluctuations in the Intelligence Quotients of Subnormal Children." *Journal of Juvenile Research* 18: 163-68; July, 1934.
227. PARKER, HENRY T. *Intelligence and Scholastic Attainment.* Educational Research Series, No. 17. Melbourne, Australia: Melbourne University Press, 1932. 62 p.
228. PIAGET, JEAN, and OTHERS. *The Moral Judgment of the Child.* New York: Harcourt, Brace and Co., 1932. 418 p.

229. PINTNER, RUDOLF. "Intelligence and Month of Birth." *Journal of Applied Psychology* 15: 149-54; April, 1931.
230. PINTNER, RUDOLF. "Intelligence Tests." *Psychological Bulletin* 29: 93-119; February, 1932. 30: 488-504; July, 1933. 31: 453-75; July, 1934. 32: 453-72; July, 1935.
231. PINTNER, RUDOLF, and FORLANO, GEORGE. "Sibling Resemblance on Two Personality Tests." *School and Society* 42: 70-72; July 13, 1935.
232. PRICE, J. ST. C. "Negro-White Differences in General Intelligence." *Journal of Negro Education* 3: 424-52; July, 1934.
233. REIFENRATH, H. "Vergliechende Intelligenzprufungen in Handels-und Gewerbschulen." *Industrielle Psychotechnick* 10: 48-52; February, 1933.
234. REUSSER, JOHN LEWIS. "Personal Attitudes of Delinquent Boys." *Journal of Juvenile Research* 17: 19-34; January, 1933.
235. RICHARDSON, CYRIL A., and STOKES, C. W. *The Growth and Variability of Intelligence.* British Journal of Psychology Monograph Supplements, No. 18. Cambridge, England: Cambridge University Press, 1933. 84 p.
236. RICHARDSON, H. D. "The Intelligence Quotient and Secondary-School Guidance." *School Review* 43: 49-59; January, 1935.
237. ROGERS, K. H., and AUSTIN, O. L. "Intelligence Quotients of Juvenile Delinquents." *Journal of Juvenile Research* 18: 103-6; April, 1934.
238. ROGERS, K. H. "'Perseveration' in a Group of Subnormal Children." *Journal of Experimental Education* 2: 301-9; March, 1934.
239. ROSE, ANNA LORETTE. *Ability in Relation to School Progress.* Mansfield, Penn.: Mansfield Advertiser, 1933. 131 p.
240. SCHOTT, E. L. "School Maladjustments of Some Mentally Superior Patients in a Psychiatric Clinic." *Psychological Clinic* 21: 202-7; September-November, 1932.
241. SCHULZ, O. "Experimentelle Untersuchungen uber Luge und Charakter." *Untersuchungen zur psychologie; philosophie und Padagogik* Vol. 8, No. 2, 1934. 60 p.
242. SCHWESINGER, GLADYS C. *Heredity and Environment.* New York: Macmillan Co., 1933. 484 p.
243. Scottish Council for Research in Education. *The Intelligence of Scottish Children; a National Survey of an Age-Group.* Publications, 5. London: University of London Press, 1933. 160 p.
244. SEARS, LAURENCE. *Responsibility; its Development Through Punishment and Reward.* New York: Columbia University Press, 1932. 198 p.
245. SHELDON, DONALD R. "Children's Interests." *Elementary School Journal* 33: 205-14; November, 1932.
246. SHERMAN, MANDEL, and KEY, CORA B. "The Intelligence of Isolated Mountain Children." *Child Development* 3: 279-90; December, 1932.
247. SMITH, HELEN RAYMOND. *The Difficult Child and the Teacher. A Study of Factors in the Situations of Children Whom Teachers Found It Difficult to Handle Constructively.* Doctor's thesis, Teachers College, Columbia University, 1933. 193 p.
248. SNYDER, LOUISE MAY. *The Problem Child in School: A Study of the Differences Between Problem and Non-Problem Children in the Elementary Schools of Jersey City.* Doctor's thesis, New York University, 1933. 178 p.
249. STODDARD, GEORGE D., chairman. "Mental and Physical Development." *Review of Educational Research* 3: 81-181; April, 1933.
250. STOGDILL, RALPH M. "Attitudes of Parents, Students, and Mental Hygienists Toward Children's Behavior." *Journal of Social Psychology* 4: 486-89; November, 1933.
251. STRANG, RUTH. "Health and Physical Education." *Review of Educational Research* 5: 48-53, 106-10; February, 1935.
252. STREET, ROY F. "Factors Related to Maladjustment in School." *Elementary School Journal* 34: 676-80; May, 1934.
253. THORNDIKE, ROBERT L. "The Effect of the Interval Between Test and Retest on the Constancy of the I. Q." *Journal of Educational Psychology* 24: 543-49; October, 1933.
254. WARNER, FLORENCE MARY. *Juvenile Detention in the United States.* Doctor's thesis, University of Chicago, 1933. 166 p.

255. WATSON, GOODWIN. "Character and Personality Tests." *Psychological Bulletin* 30: 467-87; July, 1933.
256. WATSON, GOODWIN. "Measures of Character and Personality." *Psychological Bulletin* 29: 147-76; February, 1932.
257. White House Conference on Child Health and Protection. *The Adolescent in the Family; a Study of Personality Development in the Home Environment.* New York: D. Appleton-Century Co., 1934. 473 p.
258. WILE, I. S., and OTHERS. "The Continuity of the Neurotic Processes." *American Journal of Orthopsychiatry* 4: 49-72; January, 1934.
259. WILLIAMS, H. D. "A Survey of Predelinquent School Children of Ten Midwestern Cities." *Journal of Educational Sociology* 7: 365-70; February, 1934.
260. WITTY, P. A., and JENKINS, M. D. "The Educational Achievement of a Group of Gifted Negro Children." *Journal of Educational Psychology* 25: 585-97; November, 1934.
261. WOOD, BEN D., director. *1934 Fall Testing Program in Independent Schools.* Bulletin No. 14. New York: Educational Records Bureau (437 W. 59th St.), 1934. 42 p.
262. WOOD, BEN D., director. *1935 Achievement Test Program in Independent Schools.* Bulletin No. 15. New York: Educational Records Bureau (437 W. 59th St.), 1935. 94 p.
263. WOOD, ELEANOR PERRY. *Achievement Testing in Independent Schools.* Bulletin No. 10. New York: Educational Records Bureau (437 W. 59th St.), 1933, 46 p.
264. WOOD, ELEANOR PERRY. *1933 Fall Testing Program in Independent Schools.* Bulletin No. 12. New York: Educational Records Bureau (437 W. 59th St.), 1933. 66 p.
265. WOOD, ELEANOR PERRY. *1934 Achievement Test Program in Independent Schools.* Bulletin No. 13. New York: Educational Records Bureau (437 W. 59th St.), 1934. 64 p.
266. WOODY, CLIFFORD. *Results of the Testing Program in the Ironwood Public Schools.* Bureau of Educational Reference and Research Bulletin, No. 146. Ann Arbor, Mich.: University of Michigan, 1933. 114 p.
267. YOURMAN, JULIUS. *Children With Problems. A Mental Hygiene Study of Maladjustment in the Elementary Schools of New York City.* Doctor's thesis, New York University, 1932. 2 vol.

B. SECONDARY EDUCATION

268. BROWN, MARION. *Leadership Among High School Pupils.* Contributions to Education, No. 559. New York: Teachers College, Columbia University, 1933. 166 p.
269. CALIVER, AMBROSE. *Secondary Education for Negroes.* U. S. Dept. of the Interior, Office of Education, Bulletin, 1932, No. 17. National Survey of Secondary Education, Monograph No. 7. Washington, D. C.: Government Printing Office, 1933. 121 p.
270. CLEM, ORLIE M., and HOVEY, CHESTER W. "Comparative High-School Persistence of Pupils from Village and Rural Elementary Schools." *Journal of Educational Sociology* 8: 98-107; October, 1934.
271. DOWD, CONSTANCE E. "A Study of High School Graduates with Reference to Level of Intelligence." *Journal of Educational Psychology* 23: 687-702; December, 1932.
272. ENGLE, T. L. "A Personality Study of a Group of High School Honor Society Pupils." *Journal of Applied Psychology* 18: 293-96; April, 1934.
273. KAPLAN, ALBERT JACOB. *A Study of the Behavior Problem Pupil in a Secondary School.* Philadelphia: Temple University, 1933. 187 p. (Doctor's thesis, Temple University, 1933.)
274. KEFAUVER, GRAYSON N.; NOLL, VICTOR H.; and DRAKE, C. ELWOOD. *The Horizontal Organization of Secondary Education.* U. S. Dept. of the Interior, Office of Education, Bulletin, 1932, No. 17. National Survey of Secondary Education, Monograph No. 2. Washington, D. C.: Government Printing Office, 1934. 273 p.
275. KEFAUVER, GRAYSON N.; NOLL, VICTOR H.; and DRAKE, C. ELWOOD. *Part-Time Secondary Schools.* U. S. Dept. of the Interior, Office of Education, Bulletin, 1932, No. 17. National Survey of Secondary Education, Monograph No. 3. Washington, D. C.: Government Printing Office, 1933. 98 p.

276. KEFAUVER, GRAYSON N.; NOLL, VICTOR H.; and DRAKE, C. ELWOOD. *The Secondary-School Population.* U. S. Dept. of the Interior, Office of Education, Bulletin, 1932, No. 17. National Survey of Secondary Education, Monograph No. 4. Washington, D. C.: Government Printing Office, 1933. 58 p.
277. LAMSON, EDNA E. "High School Achievement of Fifty-Six Gifted Children." *Pedagogical Seminary and Journal of Genetic Psychology* 47: 233-38; September, 1935.
278. MALLER, J. B., and LUNDEEN, G. E. "Superstition and Emotional Maladjustment." *Journal of Educational Research* 27: 592-617; April, 1934.
279. MOORE, MARGARET WHITESIDE. *A Study of Young High School Graduates.* Contributions to Education, No. 583. New York: Teachers College, Columbia University, 1933. 78 p.
280. PARTRIDGE, ERNEST DEALTON. *Leadership Among Adolescent Boys.* Contributions to Education, No. 608. New York: Teachers College, Columbia University, 1934. 109 p.
281. PORTENIER, LILLIAN GERTRUDE. *Pupils of Low Mentality in High School.* Contributions to Education, No. 568. New York: Teachers College, Columbia University, 1933. 109 p.
282. SMITH, SARAH JANE. "A Study of Physical Defects and Their Significance in Vocational Guidance and Counseling." *Michigan Vocational News* 11: 5; May, 1934.
283. SPILMAN, CARL J. *A Comparative Critical Analysis and Evaluation of Youth and Its Problems.* Doctor's thesis, New York University, 1933. 308 p.

C. HIGHER EDUCATION

284. "The Ages of Freshmen at a State University." *School Review* 41: 333-35; May, 1933.
285. ANGELL, ROBERT C. "The Trend Toward Greater Maturity Among Undergraduates Due to the Depression." *School and Society* 38: 391-96; September 23, 1933.
286. BAYLISS, ZOE BURRELL. "A Study of the Factors Contributing to the Unsatisfactory Scholastic Attainment of First Year Women Students." *Journal of Educational Research* 27: 687-97; May, 1934.
287. BELLOWS, ROGER M. "Attitudes of Undergraduate Students." *Journal of Higher Education* 5: 498-99; December, 1934.
288. BIRD, CHARLES, and BEERS, F. S. "Maximum and Minimum Inner Speech in Reading." *Journal of Applied Psychology* 17: 182-87; April, 1933.
289. BOARDMAN, CHARLES W., and FINCH, FRANK H. "The Educational and Vocational Status of University of Minnesota Students Having Low College Aptitude Rating." *Journal of Educational Psychology* 25: 447-58; September, 1934.
290. BOLDT, W. J., and STROUD, J. B. "Changes in the Attitudes of College Students." *Journal of Educational Psychology* 25: 611-19; November, 1934.
291. BOND, GUY L. *Auditory and Speech Characteristics of Poor Readers.* Contributions to Education, No. 657. New York: Teachers College, Columbia University, 1935. 48 p.
292. BROOM, M. EUSTACE. "A Note on Silent Reading Comprehension and Success in Academic Achievement in a State Teachers College." *Journal of Applied Psychology* 18: 561-65; August, 1934.
293. BYRNS, RUTH K., and HENMON, V. A. C. "Entrance Requirements and College Success." *School and Society* 41: 101-4; January 19, 1935.
294. CAMPBELL, DOAK S. *Problems in the Education of College Women.* Field Studies No. 6. Nashville, Tenn.: George Peabody College for Teachers, 1933. 80 p.
295. CARLSON, H. B. "Attitudes of Undergraduate Students." *Journal of Social Psychology* 5: 202-13; May, 1934.
296. CHAMBERLAIN, LEO M. "Comparisons of Achievement." *Journal of Higher Education* 4: 15-18; January, 1933.
297. CHAUNCEY, MARLIN RAY. *The Educational and Occupational Preferences of College Seniors.* Contributions to Education, No. 533. New York: Teachers College, Columbia University, 1932. 72 p.
298. COCKERELL, T. D. A. "The Relative Ability of Men and Women." *Journal of Heredity* 25: 163-64; April, 1934.

299. COINER, GLADYS EDNA. *The Personality of the College Cribber.* Master's thesis, University of Southern California, 1933.
300. CONSTANCE, C. L. "University and College Enrolments, 1931 and 1933." *School and Society* 39: 485-88; April 14, 1934.
301. DONOVAN, H. L., and JONES, W. C. "Study Habits of College Students." *High School Quarterly* 21: 61-62; January, 1933.
302. DUDYCHA, GEORGE J. "Moral Beliefs of College Students." *International Journal of Ethics* 43: 194-204; January, 1933.
303. DUDYCHA, GEORGE J. "The Religious Beliefs of College Students." *Journal of Applied Psychology* 17: 585-603; October, 1933.
304. ECKERT, RUTH E. "Analyzing the Superior College Student." *School and Society* 41: 69-72; January 12, 1935.
305. ECKERT, RUTH E. "Intellectual Maturity." *Journal of Higher Education* 5: 478-84; December, 1934.
306. EURICH, ALVIN C. "The Amount of Reading and Study Among College Students." *School and Society* 37: 102-4; January 21, 1933.
307. EURICH, ALVIN C. "College Failures." *School and Society* 37: 692-96; May 27, 1933.
308. EURICH, ALVIN C. "The Photographic Eye-Movement Records of Successful and Unsuccessful College Students." *Journal of Applied Psychology* 17: 604-13; October, 1933.
309. FENDRICK, PAUL. *Visual Characteristics of Poor Readers.* Contributions to Education, No. 656. New York: Teachers College, Columbia University, 1935. 54 p.
310. GELWICK, MYRTLE. "Responses of College Students to the Pressey X-O Test, Form B, Part 1." *Educational Research Record* 6: 16-19; October, 1933.
311. GERBERICH, J. R., and JAMISON, A. W. "Measurement of Attitude Changes During an Introductory Course in College Sociology." *Journal of Educational Sociology* 8: 116-24; October, 1934.
312. GERBERICH, J. R., and JONES, CHARLES. "The Optional and Required Reading of College Students." *School and Society* 38: 93-96; July 15, 1933.
313. GILBERT, L. C. "Professional Reading of Young Students of Education." *School Review* 40: 606-12; October, 1932.
314. GOULD, HARLEY N. "Physique of Women Students at Newcomb College of Tulane University." *Research Quarterly of the American Physical Education Association* 3: 111-16; October, 1932.
315. HARRIMAN, PHILIP L. "Auditory Acuity and Success in College Courses." *Peabody Journal of Education* 11: 25-31; July, 1933.
316. HARTMANN, GEORGE WILFRIED, and BARRICK, FLOYD M. "Fluctuations in General Cultural Information Among Undergraduates." *Journal of Educational Research* 28: 255-64; December, 1934.
317. HOTZ, H. G., and TRICE, J. A. "The Relation of an Abnormal Weekly Schedule to Grade Point Average." *School and Society* 39: 422-24; March 31, 1934.
318. HUNTER, ELDEN. "A Study of the Periodical Reading Done by College Students." *School and Society* 40: 70-72; July 14, 1934.
319. ISRAELI, NATHAN. "Measurement of Attitudes and Reactions to the Future." *Journal of Abnormal and Social Psychology* 28: 181-93; July-September, 1933.
320. KATZ, DANIEL, and BRALY, KENNETH. "Racial Stereotypes of One Hundred College Students." *Journal of Abnormal and Social Psychology* 28: 280-90; October, 1933.
321. LITTERER, OSCAR F. "An Experimental Study of Visual Apprehension in Reading." *Journal of Applied Psychology* 17: 266-76; June, 1933.
322. LORENZ, ALICE B., and MCCLURE, WILLIAM E. "The Influence of Color Blindness on Intelligence and Achievement of College Men." *Journal of Applied Psychology* 19: 320-30; June, 1935.
323. MCCONNELL, T. R. "Change in Scores on the Psychological Examination of the American Council on Education from Freshman to Senior Year." *Journal of Educational Psychology* 25: 66-69; January, 1934.
324. MCCULLOUGH, CONSTANCE M. "Preparation for College Success in Public Versus Private High Schools." *Education* 54: 629-31; June, 1934.
325. MALOTT, JAMES L. "Relation of Intelligence to Success in College Studies." *Wisconsin Journal of Education* 67: 271-72; February, 1935.

326. MERRIAM, THORNTON WARD. *Relations Between Scholastic Achievement in a School of Social Work and Six Factors in Students' Background.* Contributions to Education, No. 616. New York: Teachers College, Columbia University, 1934. 136 p.
327. MOORE, MARGARET WHITESIDE. *A Study of Young High School Graduates.* Contributions to Education, No. 583. New York: Teachers College, Columbia University, 1933. 78 p.
328. NEMZEK, CLAUDE L. "Intelligence Testing at the College Level." *Journal of Educational Research* 26: 617-18; April, 1933.
329. ODELL, CHARLES W. "The Effect of Early Entrance Upon College Success." *Journal of Educational Research* 26: 510-12; March, 1933.
330. "Origin of the Students of Columbia University." *School and Society* 40: 57; July 14, 1934.
331. PATRICK, JAMES R., and SIMS, VERNER M. "Personality Differences Between Negro and White College Students, North and South." *Journal of Abnormal and Social Psychology* 29: 181-201; July, 1934.
332. PAYNE, ARTHUR F., and PERRY, JAMES D. "The Intelligence Ranking of 250 City College Honor Students." *School and Society* 42: 383-84; September 14, 1935.
333. PINTNER, RUDOLF. "Neurotic Tendency and Its Relation to Some Other Mental Traits." *School and Society* 36: 765-67; December 10, 1932.
334. REEDER, C. W. "Study Habits." *School and Society* 42: 413-15; September 21, 1935.
335. REMMERS, H. H. "Vocational Selectivity of an Institution of Higher Learning." *School and Society* 38: 178-80; August 5, 1933.
336. ROUCĚK, JOSEPH S. "Experiments in the Measuring of Intelligence and Knowledge of Czechoslovak University Students." *School and Society* 38: 709-10; November 25, 1933.
337. RUGG, HAROLD. "Who Are the Superior Peoples? New Evidence on Racial Differences and the Nordic Myth." *Scholastic* 25: 15-16, 20; December 15, 1934.
338. SALNER, E., and REMMERS, H. H. "Affective Selectivity and Liberalizing Influence of College Courses." *Journal of Applied Psychology* 17: 349-54; August, 1933.
339. SARBAUGH, MARY E. "The Young College Student." *School and Society* 40: 823-24; December 15, 1934.
340. STAGER, HENRY W. "Comparative Study of the Achievement of Junior College Transfers in Certain Subjects." *California Quarterly of Secondary Education* 9: 341-49; June, 1934.
341. STONE, CALVIN PERRY, and BARKER, ROGER G. "On the Relationships Between Menarcheal Age and Certain Aspects of Personality, Intelligence and Physique in College Women." *Pedagogical Seminary and Journal of Genetic Psychology* 45: 121-35; September, 1934.
342. STOWE, ANSEL ROY MONROE. "Residential Distribution of Students of Selected American Women's Colleges in 1931-32." *Social Forces* 12: 84-87; October, 1933.
343. STRABEL, EUNICE. "How Academically Apt Are Collegiate College Students?" *School and Society* 41: 814-16; June 15, 1935.
344. TAYLOR, S. W. "Catholic Student in the Non-Catholic College." *Catholic World* 137: 202-5; May, 1933.
345. TELFORD, C. W. "Experimental Study of Some Factors Influencing the Social Attitudes of College Students." *Journal of Social Psychology* 5: 421-28; August, 1934.
346. THOMPSON, W. H. "Intelligence Tests in American Colleges." *School and Society* 39: 790-92; June 16, 1934.
347. TRAXLER, ARTHUR E. "The Relation Between Rate of Reading and Speed of Association." *Journal of Educational Psychology* 25: 357-65; May, 1934.
348. UPSHALL, C. C., and MASTERS, HARRY V. "Differences Between Good and Poor Students Chosen on the Basis of College Entrance Test Scores." *Educational Administration and Supervision* 19: 507-10; October, 1933.
349. WALTERS, RAYMOND. "Statistics of Registration in American Universities and Colleges." *School and Society* 38: 781-95; December 16, 1933. 40: 785-801; December 15, 1934.
350. WHITNEY, FREDERICK LAMSON, and ARMENTROUT, WINIFIELD DOCKERY. "The Total Load of Students." *Journal of Higher Education* 3: 427-30; November, 1932.

351. WILLIAMS, J. HAROLD. "Attitudes of College Students Toward Motion Pictures." *School and Society* 38: 222-24; August 12, 1933.
352. WOLCOTT, WILLA. "Changes in Thorndike Intelligence Test Scores at the End of the College Course." *School and Society* 37: 630-32; May 13, 1933.
353. WOODHOUSE, MRS. CHASE GOING. *After College—What?* Institute of Women's Professional Relations Bulletin, No. 4. Greensboro, N. C.: North Carolina College for Women, 1932. 200 p.
354. WOOLSTON, HOWARD. "Discrimination: A Study of Social Determinants." *Journal of Social Psychology* 5: 248-54; May, 1934.

Chapter VI. Guidance and Counseling

A. ELEMENTARY EDUCATION

355. ALLEN, RICHARD DAY. *Organization and Supervision of Guidance in Public Education.* New York: Inor Publishing Co., 1934. 420 p.
356. BAKER, HARRY J., chairman. "Psychological Tests." *Review of Educational Research* 5: 185-331; June, 1935.
357. BECK, L. F. "The Role of Speed in Intelligence." *Psychological Bulletin* 30: 169-78; February, 1933.
358. BECK, SAMUEL J. *The Rorschach Test as Applied to a Feebleminded Group.* Archives of Psychology, No. 136. New York: Columbia University, 1932. 84 p.
359. BOTT, HELEN MCMURCHIE. *Personality Development in Young Children.* Child Development Series, No. 2. Toronto: University of Toronto Press, 1934. 139 p.
360. CUNLIFFE, REX BARNARD. *Trends in Vocational Guidance.* Studies in Education No. 4. New Brunswick, N. J.: Rutgers University, 1932. 42 p.
361. DROBA, D. D. "Methods for Measuring Attitudes." *Psychological Bulletin* 29: 309-23; May, 1932.
362. FENTON, NORMAN, and WALLACE, RAMONA. "Use of Tests in Twenty-Eight Child Guidance Clinic Centers in the United States." *Journal of Juvenile Research* 18: 115-18; April, 1934.
363. GIEHM, G. "Experimentelle-psychologische Ermittlung des aktuellen Kernproblems einer Personlichkeit." *Zeitschrift für die gesamte Neurologie und Psychiatrie* 150: 100-9; 1934.
364. HILDRETH, GERTRUDE. "Mental Ability Measured by Verbal and Non-Verbal Tests." *Teachers College Record* 34: 134-42; November, 1932.
365. HUGHES, A. G. "Discrepancies Between the Results of Intelligence Tests and Entrance Examinations to Secondary Schools." *British Journal of Educational Psychology* 4: 221-36; November, 1934.
366. JENNESS, ARTHUR. "The Recognition of Facial Expressions of Emotion." *Psychological Bulletin* 29: 324-50; May, 1932.
367. JONES, VERNON, and CROOK, MASON. "Educational Tests." *Psychological Bulletin* 29: 120-46; February, 1932.
368. JONES, VERNON, and NEET, CLAUDE. "Educational Tests." *Psychological Bulletin* 30: 518-31; July, 1933.
369. JONES, VERNON, and BROWN, ROBERT H. "Educational Tests." *Psychological Bulletin* 31: 476-500; July, 1934. 32: 473-99; July, 1935.
370. KELLEY, TRUMAN L., and KREY, A. C. *Tests and Measurements in the Social Sciences.* Report of the Commission on the Social Studies of the American Historical Association, Part IV. New York: Charles Scribner's Sons, 1934. 635 p.
371. KERR, MADELINE. "The Rorschach Test Applied to Children." *British Journal of Psychology (General Section)* 25: 170-85; October, 1934.
372. KITSON, HARRY DEXTER. "Vocational Guidance Is Not Fortune Telling" *Teachers College Record* 35: 372-76; February, 1934.
373. LAUGIER, H., and OTHERS. *Études Docimologiques sur le Perfectionnement des Examens et Concours.* Publications du Travail Humain, Série A, No. 3. Paris: Conservatoire National des Arts et Métiers (292 Rue Saint-Martin), 1934.
374. MCCARTHY, EDWARD JAMES. *Guidance Procedures Below the Junior High School.* Master's thesis, Boston University, 1933. 114 p.
375. MACRAE, ANGUS. "A Second Follow-up of Vocationally Advised Cases." *Human Factor* 6: 42-52; February, 1932.

376. MACRAE, ANGUS. "Vocational Guidance in Fife." *Human Factor* 9: 85-93; March, 1935. (Summary of *A Vocational Guidance Research in Fife*. 101 p.)
377. MELTZER, H. "Personality Differences Among Stutterers as Indicated by the Rorschach Test." *American Journal of Orthopsychiatry* 4: 262-80; April, 1934.
378. MENGER, CLARA. *The Significance of Vocational Choices of School Children and College Students.* St. Louis, Mo.: the Author (5176 Raymond Ave.), 1932. 177 p.
379. MUNKRES, ALBERTA. *Personality Studies of Six-Year-Old Children in Classroom Situation.* Doctor's thesis, Teachers College, Columbia University, 1934. 221 p.
380. PATERSON, DONALD G., and MACRAE, ANGUS. "A Target for Critics: Professor Thorndike's Findings Draw Fire Both Here and Abroad." *Occupations* 13: 18-29; October, 1934.
381. PEATMAN, JOHN GRAY, and GREENSPAN, ISRAEL. "The Reliability of a Questionnaire on Superstitious Beliefs of Elementary School Children." *Journal of Abnormal and Social Psychology* 30: 208-21; July-September, 1935.
382. PINTNER, RUDOLF. "Intelligence Tests." *Psychological Bulletin* 29: 93-119; February, 1932. 30: 488-504; July, 1933. 31: 453-75; July, 1934. 32: 453-72; July, 1935.
383. RETAN, GEORGE AUSTIN. *A Study of Environmental Factors Influencing the Progress of Children Through the Grades of the Elementary School.* Doctor's thesis, New York University, 1932. 92 p.
384. SANCHEZ, G. I. "Bilingualism and Mental Measures." *Journal of Applied Psychology* 18: 765-72; December, 1934.
385. SAYLES, MARY B. *Child Guidance Cases.* New York: Commonwealth Fund, 1932. 584 p.
386. SCHILLER, BELLE. *Verbal, Numerical, and Spatial Abilities of Young Children.* Archives of Psychology, No. 161. New York: Columbia University, 1934. 69 p.
387. SEGEL, DAVID. *Differential Diagnosis of Ability in School Children.* Baltimore: Warwick and York, 1934. 86 p.
388. SENOUR, A. C. "Necessity for Use of a Non-Language Mental Test in Group Intelligence Testing." *Journal of Educational Research* 27: 435-41; February, 1934.
389. STEVENSON, GEORGE S., and SMITH, GEDDES. *Child Guidance Clinics: A Quarter Century of Development.* New York: Commonwealth Fund, 1934. 186 p.
390. STRANG, RUTH. *The Rôle of the Teacher in Personnel Work.* Rev. and enl. New York: Teachers College, Columbia University, 1935. 417 p.
391. THOMAS, DOROTHY SWAINE, and OTHERS. *Observational Studies of Social Behavior.* Social Behavior Patterns, Vol. 1. New Haven: Institute of Human Relations, Yale University, 1933. 271 p.
392. THORNDIKE, EDWARD L., and OTHERS. *Prediction of Vocational Success.* New York: Commonwealth Fund, 1934. 284 p.
393. THORNDIKE, EDWARD L. "Rebounds from the Target." *Occupations* 13: 329-33; January, 1935.
394. TYLER, RALPH WINFRED. "Evaluation: A Challenge and an Opportunity to Progressive Education." *Educational Record* 16: 121-31; January, 1935.
395. VERNON, PHILIP E. "The Attitude of the Subject in Personality Testing." *Journal of Applied Psychology* 18: 165-77; April, 1934.
396. WALES, JEAN A. "Vocational Guidance Methods in Berlin." *Human Factor* 9: 13-21; January, 1935.
397. WEGLEIN, DAVID E. "Guidance in a Large City." *Occupations* 14: 10-20; October, 1935.
398. WILLIAMS, EULA S. "A Personality Rating Form for Elementary-School Pupils." *Elementary School Journal* 34: 16-29; September, 1933.
399. WOOD, BEN D., and BEERS, F. S. "The Major Strategy of Guidance." *Occupations* 12: 8-12; April, 1934.
400. WRIGHTSTONE, J. WAYNE. "Measuring Personal and Social Adjustments." *Teachers College Record* 36: 224-28; December, 1934.

B. SECONDARY EDUCATION

401. BRAMMELL, P. ROY. *Articulation of High School and College.* U. S. Dept. of the Interior, Office of Education, Bulletin, 1932, No. 17. National Survey of Secondary Education, Monograph No. 10. Washington, D. C.: Government Printing Office, 1933. 96 p.

402. CUNLIFFE, REX B., and OTHERS. *Guidance Practice in New Jersey.* Studies in Education No. 2. New Brunswick, N. J.: Rutgers University, 1932. 31 p.
403. HAND, HAROLD C. *An Appraisal of the Occupations or Life-Career Course.* Palo Alto, Calif.: the Author, 1934. 67 p.
404. JOHNSON, EDWARD C. "The Vocational Preferences of High School Students in Washington." *Washington Education Journal* 13: 154-56; April, 1934.
405. KEFAUVER, GRAYSON N.; NOLL, VICTOR H.; and DRAKE, C. ELWOOD. *The Horizontal Organization of Secondary Education.* U. S. Dept. of the Interior, Office of Education, Bulletin, 1932, No. 17. National Survey of Secondary Education, Monograph No. 2. Washington, D. C.: Government Printing Office, 1934. Chapter 4, p. 108-18.
406. KEFAUVER, GRAYSON N., and DAVIS, ALBERT M. "Investigations in Guidance." *Occupations* 12: 17-25; November, 1933.
407. KOOS, LEONARD V., and KEFAUVER, GRAYSON N. *Guidance in Secondary Schools.* New York: Macmillan Co., 1932. 640 p.
408. KITSON, HARRY DEXTER, and STOVER, E. M. "Measuring Vocational Guidance; a Summary of Attempts." *Personnel Journal* 11: 150-59; October, 1932.
409. LOVE, LESTON LEWIS. *Guidance Problems of High-School Seniors.* Doctor's thesis, Ohio State University, 1932. 232 p.
410. MENGER, CLARA. *The Significance of Vocational Choices of School Children and College Students.* St. Louis, Mo.: the Author (5176 Raymond Ave.), 1932. 177 p.
411. PROFFITT, MARIS M. *Courses in Occupational Information.* U. S. Dept. of the Interior, Office of Education, Bulletin, 1934, No. 11. Washington, D. C.: Government Printing Office, 1934. 47 p.
412. REAVIS, WILLIAM C. *Programs of Guidance.* U. S. Dept. of the Interior, Office of Education, Bulletin, 1932, No. 17. National Survey of Secondary Education, Monograph No. 14. Washington, D. C.: Government Printing Office, 1933. 144 p.
413. RICHARDSON, H. D. "Intelligence Quotient and Secondary School Guidance." *School Review* 43: 49-59; January, 1935.
414. THORNDIKE, EDWARD L., and OTHERS. *Prediction of Vocational Success.* New York: Commonwealth Fund, 1934. 284 p.

C. HIGHER EDUCATION

415. ACHILLES, PAUL S. "Vocational Motives in College; Extent and Significance of Career Decisions." *Occupations* 13: 624-28; April, 1935.
416. BENNETT, MARGARET E. "Trends in Junior College Orientation Courses." *Junior College Journal* 4: 353-57; April, 1934.
417. BOYD, PAUL P. "Freshmen and Seniors." *School and Society* 38: 842-44; December 23, 1933.
418. BRUMBAUGH, A. J. "Adjustments and Classifications in Colleges and Universities." *Review of Educational Research* 3: 234-37, 272-74; June, 1933.
419. BYRNS, RUTH, and HENMON, V. A. C. "Long-range Prediction of College Achievement." *School and Society* 41: 877-80; June 29, 1935.
420. CATTELL, RAYMOND B. "Occupational Norms of Intelligence, and the Standardization of an Adult Intelligence Test." *British Journal of Psychology (General Section)* 25: 1-28; July, 1934.
421. COWLEY, W. H. "An Experiment in Freshmen Counseling." *Journal of Higher Education* 4: 245-48; May, 1933.
422. CRAWFORD, C. C. "How to Study for Objective Tests." *Education* 53: 413-16; March, 1933.
423. DODGE, ARTHUR F. *Occupational Ability Patterns.* Contributions to Education, No. 658. New York: Teachers College, Columbia University, 1935. 97 p.
424. DOUGLASS, HARL R., and TALLMADGE, MARGARET. "How University Students Prepare for New Types of Examinations." *School and Society* 39: 318-20; March 10, 1934.
425. EMME, EARLE EDWARD. *The Adjustment Problems of College Freshmen.* Nashville, Tenn.: Cokesbury Press, 1933. 126 p.
426. FERGUSON, GEORGE O., JR. "Some Factors in Predicting College Success." *School and Society* 37: 566-68; April 29, 1933.

427. FINCH, F. H., and NEMZEK, C. L. "Prediction of College Achievement from Data Collected During the Secondary School Period." *Journal of Applied Psychology* 18: 454-60; June, 1934.
428. FLEMMING, EDWIN G. "College Achievement, Intelligence, Personality and Emotion." *Journal of Applied Psychology* 16: 668-74; December, 1932.
429. FRAZIER, BENJAMIN W., and OTHERS. *Special Survey Studies*. U. S. Dept. of the Interior, Office of Education, Bulletin, 1933, No. 10. National Survey of the Education of Teachers, Vol. V. Washington, D. C.: Government Printing Office, 1935. Chapter 6, "Orientation, Guidance and Adjustment Services." p. 215-32.
430. FREEMAN, FRANK N.; BUSWELL, G. T.; and FLORY, CHARLES D., compilers. "Selected References on Educational Psychology." *School Review* 41: 379-86; May, 1933.
431. GIBB, LOUISE. "Evaluating a Conference." *Occupations* 13: 546; March, 1935.
432. GRAY, RUTH A., compiler. "Higher Education." *Bibliography of Research Studies in Education, 1932-1933*. U. S. Dept. of the Interior, Office of Education, Bulletin, 1934, No. 7. Washington, D. C.: Government Printing Office, 1934. p. 181-94.
433. GRISWOLD, DON MORSE, and SPICER, HAZEL I. *University Student Health Service*. Committee on the Cost of Medical Care Publications, No. 19. Chicago: University of Chicago Press, 1932. 114 p.
434. HARRIS, DANIEL. "Are Personnel Data Really Useful?" *Personnel Journal* 12: 341-44; April, 1934.
435. HARTMANN, G. W. "Classification of Adjustment Problems Among College Students." *Journal of Abnormal and Social Psychology* 28: 64-69; April, 1933.
436. HILLMAN, LOUIS F. "Training for Vocations in Those of High and Low Intelligence." *Journal of Applied Psychology* 18: 401-8; June, 1934.
437. HOUSTON, CLIFFORD G. *Vocational Choices of University Freshmen*. Doctor's thesis, University of Colorado, 1933.
438. HUSTON, C. G. "Significance of College Guidance: A Survey of Contemporary Vocational Guidance and Its Significance in Forty-three Universities in the United States." *Vocational Guidance Magazine* 11: 31-34; October, 1932.
439. HUTSON, PERCIVAL W., compiler. "Selected References on Guidance." *School Review* 41: 539-46; September, 1933. 42: 540-46; September, 1934. 43: 540-46; September, 1935.
440. JOHNSTON, JOHN BLACK, and WILLIAMSON, E. G. "A Follow-up Study of Early Scholastic Predictions in the University of Minnesota." *School and Society* 40: 730-38; December 1, 1934.
441. KARPP, MORTIMER. "Vocations of College Men, 1849-1934; a Study of the Alumni of the College of the City of New York." *Personnel Journal* 13: 158-68; October, 1934.
442. KRINER, HARRY L. "Preliminary Report on a Five-Year Study of Teachers College Admissions." *Educational Administration and Supervision* 19: 691-95; December, 1933.
443. KURANI, HABIB AMIN. *Selecting the College Student in America*. Contributions to Education, No. 503. New York: Teachers College, Columbia University, 1932. 124 p.
444. LEHMAN, HARVEY C., and WITTY, PAUL A. "Vocational Guidance; Some Basic Considerations." *Journal of Educational Sociology* 8: 174-84; November, 1934.
445. LINGENFELTER, MARY REBECCA, and STEELE, REA J., compilers. "Educational Books of 1933: Guidance and Personnel Service; Higher Education." *School and Society* 39: 387-88, 389-91; March 24, 1934.
446. LUECK, WILLIAM R. *The Arithmetical and Algebraic Disabilities of Students Pursuing First Year College Physics*. Studies in Education, Vol. 8, No. 1, Iowa City: University of Iowa, 1932. 48 p.
447. MORRIS, ELIZABETH H. "Some Results Secured in Personnel Work in a Teachers College." *School and Society* 39: 574-76; May 5, 1934.
448. NEEL, MARY OAKS, and MATHEWS, C. O. *The Guidance Needs of Superior College Students*. Delaware, Ohio: Ohio Wesleyan University, 1933.
449. PATRICK, JAMES RUEY, and ROWLES, EMMETT. "Intercorrelations Among Metabolic Rate, Vital Capacity, Blood Pressure, Intelligence, Scholarship, Personality and Other Measures on University Women." *Journal of Applied Psychology* 17: 507-21; October, 1933.

450. PETTENGILL, TRUE E. "Size of High School and Predictive Value of Class Rank and Aptitude Test Rank." *Bulletin of the American Association of Collegiate Registrars* 9: 190-93; 1934.
451. PERRY, ROBERT D. *Prediction Equations for Success in College Mathematics.* Contributions to Education, No. 122. Nashville, Tenn.: George Peabody College for Teachers, 1934. 58 p.
452. PIPER, R. F. "Freshmen Preferences: Studies in College Orientation." *School and Society* 41: 374-76; March 16, 1935.
453. PRICE, LOUISE. "Social Adjustments in the Junior College." *Junior College Journal* 3: 456-61; May, 1933.
454. REEVES, FLOYD W., and RUSSELL, JOHN DALE. "Comparison of One Hundred Best and One Hundred Poorest Graduate Students in Education; A Proposed Plan for the Selection of Graduate Students in Education; Summary of Findings Regarding the Admission and Retention of Graduate Students in Education." *Admission and Retention of University Students.* University of Chicago Survey, Vol. V. Chicago: University of Chicago Press, 1933. Chapters 25 through 27, p. 230-44.
455. REEVES, FLOYD W., and OTHERS. "Health Service." *The Liberal Arts College.* Chicago: University of Chicago Press, 1932. p. 375-77.
456. REEVES, FLOYD W., and RUSSELL, JOHN DALE. *Some University Student Problems.* University of Chicago Survey, Vol. X. Chicago: University of Chicago Press, 1933. Chapter 7, "The Relationship Between Grades and Living Environment," p. 121-37.
457. REINHARDT, EMMA. "Freshman Difficulties." *Journal of Higher Education* 4: 307-9; June, 1933.
458. REITZ, WILHELM. "Forecasting Marks of New Plan Students at the University of Chicago." *School Review* 43: 34-48; January, 1935.
459. REMMERS, H. H. "Vocational Selectivity of an Institution of Higher Learning." *School and Society* 38: 178-80; August 5, 1933.
460. RHINEHART, JESSE BATLEY. "An Attempt to Predict the Success of Student Nurses by the Use of a Battery of Tests." *Journal of Applied Psychology* 17: 277-93; June, 1933.
461. ROBSON, BARBARA REID. *House Management Problems of Fraternities and Sororities.* New York: Teachers College, Columbia University, 1933. 93 p.
462. RUSSELL, JOHN DALE; REEVES, FLOYD W.; and CLAPP, GORDON R., compilers. "Selected References on Higher Education." *School Review* 41: 780-86; December, 1933.
463. RUSSELL, JOHN DALE, compiler. "Selected References on Higher Education." *School Review* 42: 780-86; December, 1934.
464. SEGEL, DAVID. "Differential Prediction of Scholastic Success." *School and Society* 39: 91-96; January 20, 1934.
465. SEGEL, DAVID. *Prediction of Success in College.* U. S. Dept. of the Interior, Office of Education, Bulletin, 1934, No. 15. Washington, D. C.: Government Printing Office, 1934. 98 p.
466. SMITH, V. T. "Occupational Adjustment of College Graduates as Affected by Scholarship in Their Undergraduate Majors." *School and Society* 41: 237-38; February 16, 1935.
467. SPARLING, EDWARD JAMES. *Do College Students Choose Vocations Wisely?* Contributions to Education, No. 561. New York: Teachers College, Columbia University, 1933. 110 p.
468. STAGNER, ROSS. "The Relation of Personality to Academic Aptitude and Achievement." *Journal of Educational Research* 26: 648-60; May, 1933.
469. STARBUCK, A. "The Freshman's First Hurdle." *English Journal (Coll. Ed.)* 22: 643-49; October, 1933.
470. THORNDIKE, EDWARD LEE, and OTHERS. *Prediction of Vocational Success.* New York: Commonwealth Fund, 1934. 284 p.
471. THRELKELD, HILDA. *The Educational and Vocational Plans of College Seniors.* Contributions to Education, No. 639. New York: Teachers College, Columbia University, 1935. 194 p.
472. TIBBITTS, F. L. "An Experiment in Junior College Orientation." *Junior College Journal* 3: 84-86; November, 1932.

473. TOWNSEND, MARION ERNEST. *Administration of Student Personnel Services in Teacher-Training Institutions of the United States.* Contributions to Education, No. 536. New York: Teachers College, Columbia University, 1932. 115 p.
474. TRABUE, M. R. "Occupational Ability Patterns." *Personnel Journal* 11: 344-51; February, 1933.
475. TURRELL, A. M. "The Guidance Interview in the Junior College." *Junior College Journal* 3: 240-45; February, 1933.
476. TURRELL, A. M. "Relation of Personality to Scholarship." *Junior College Journal* 5: 355-57; April, 1935.
477. TYLER, HARRY EDWARD. "Student Personnel Work at Sacramento." *Junior College Journal* 5: 346-51; April, 1935.
478. WAGNER, MAZIE EARLE. "Prediction of College Performance." *Studies in Articulation of High School and College.* University of Buffalo Studies, Vol 9. Buffalo, N. Y.: the University, 1934. p. 125-44.
479. WALKER, ERNEST TIMOTHY. *The Relation of the Housing of Students to Success in a University.* Doctor's thesis, University of Chicago, 1935. 76 p.
480. WALTERS, J. E. "Measuring Effectiveness of Personnel Counseling." *Personnel Journal* 11: 227-36; December, 1932.
481. WILLIAMSON, E. G., and PATERSON, D. G. "Co-ordinating Counseling Procedures." *Journal of Higher Education* 5: 75-78; February, 1934.
482. WILLIAMSON, E. G.; LONGSTAFF, H. P.; and EDMUNDS, J. M. "Counseling Arts College Students." *Journal of Applied Psychology* 19: 111-24; April, 1935.
483. WRENN, C. GILBERT, and GARRETT, MILDRED. "Adjusting Youth to College Life." *Occupations* 12: 38-41; March, 1934. (Section One.)
484. WRENN, C. GILBERT. "Vocational Satisfaction of Stanford Graduates." *Personnel Journal* 13: 21-24; June, 1934.
485. ZORBAUGH, GRACE S. M. "Part-Time Placing and Vocational Counseling of Women." *Educational Research Bulletin (Ohio State University)* 11: 426-32; December 7, 1932.

Chapter VII. Extra-Curriculum Activities

A. ELEMENTARY EDUCATION

486. DAVIS, HELEN E. *The Report of the Study of Work with Younger Girls in the Y. W. C. A.* New York: Woman's Press, 1935. 24 p.
487. PORTER, CAROLINE W. *A Description of the Extra-Curricular Activities of an Elementary School from 1922 to 1932.* Master's thesis, Teachers College, Columbia University, 1933. 42 p.
488. WASHBURNE, CARLETON. *Adjusting the School to the Child.* Yonkers-on-Hudson, N. Y.: World Book Co., 1932. 189 p.
489. WYLAND, RAY O. *Scouting in the Schools.* Contributions to Education, No. 631. New York: Teachers College, Columbia University, 1934. 200 p.

B. SECONDARY EDUCATION

490. BRAMMELL, P. ROY. *Intramural and Interscholastic Athletics.* U. S. Dept. of the Interior, Office of Education, Bulletin, 1932, No. 17. National Survey of Secondary Education, Monograph No. 27. Washington, D. C.: Government Printing Office, 1933. 143 p.
491. BRIGGS, EUGENE S. *The Preparation of Secondary Teachers in Teachers Colleges for Guiding and Directing Extra-Class Activities.* Jefferson City, Mo.: Midland Printing Co., 1935. 115 p.
492. CORMANY, W. J. B. "High-School Athletics and Scholarship Measured by Achievement Tests." *School Review* 43: 456-61; June, 1935.
493. DRAPER, EDGAR MARIAN, and CORBALLY, J. E. *Extracurricular Credits.* New York: A. S. Barnes and Co., 1932. 142 p.
494. EATON, DOROTHY, and SHANNON, J. R. "College Careers of High-School Athletes and Non-Athletes." *School Review* 42: 356-61; May, 1934.
495. FERRISS, EMERY N.; GAUMNITZ, W. H.; and BRAMMELL, P. ROY. *The Smaller Secondary Schools.* U. S. Dept. of the Interior, Office of Education, Bulletin, 1932, No. 17. National Survey of Secondary Education, Monograph No. 6. Washington, D. C.: Government Printing Office, 1933. 236 p.

496. HENNINGER, MARIE J. "Evaluation of Extra-Curricular Activities in the Pittsburgh High Schools." *Pittsburgh Schools* 8: 4-41; September, 1933.
497. HOLLAND, MARY N. "Extra-Curriculum Activities in High Schools and Intermediate Schools in Detroit." *School Review* 41: 759-67; December, 1933.
498. HOLROYD, GEORGE HENRY. *Organization of School Societies and Other School Activities.* New York: Pitman Publishing Corporation, 1933. 261 p.
499. JONES, GALEN. *Extra-Curricular Activities in Relation to the Curriculum.* Contributions to Education, No. 667. New York: Teachers College, Columbia University, 1935. 99 p.
500. McKOWN, HARRY C. *Home Room Guidance.* New York: McGraw-Hill Book Co., 1934. 447 p.
501. NOBLE, L. SCOTT. *Student Body Finances and Accounting.* Cincinnati: South-Western Publishing Co., 1931. 256 p.
502. PERRY, JOHN M. "Differences between High School Major Sports Participants and Non-Athletes in Certain Characteristics." *High School Teacher* 9: 339-40; November, 1933.
503. PROFFITT, MARIS M. *High School Clubs.* U. S. Dept. of the Interior, Office of Education, Bulletin, 1934, No. 18. Washington, D. C.: Government Printing Office, 1934. 64 p.
504. REAVIS, WILLIAM C., and VAN DYKE, GEORGE E. *Nonathletic Extracurriculum Activities.* U. S. Dept. of the Interior, Office of Education, Bulletin, 1932, No. 17. National Survey of Secondary Education, Monograph No. 26. Washington, D. C.: Government Printing Office, 1933. 174 p.
505. SPENCE, RALPH W. *Pupil Participation in the Control of Activities in the Senior High Schools of Hamilton County and Cincinnati.* Master's thesis, Ohio State University, 1935. 366 p.
506. TERRY, PAUL W., compiler. "Selected References on the Extra-Curriculum." *School Review* 41: 299-306; April, 1933. 42: 300-6; April, 1934.
507. TERRY, PAUL W. "Summary of Investigations of Extra-Curricular Activities in 1931." *School Review* 40: 505-14, 613-19; September and October, 1932.
508. WYMAN, LILLIAN KENNEDY. *Character and Citizenship Through Student Government.* Philadelphia: John C. Winston Co., 1935. 173 p.

C. HIGHER EDUCATION

509. ADEN, FRED E. "Some Facts Related to Student Life as Found in a Survey at the University of Colorado, March, 1933." *School and Society* 39: 182-83; February 10, 1934.
510. "The Appointments Bureau of Columbia University." *School and Society* 39: 109-10; January 27, 1934.
511. ARCHER, JOHN K. "Achievements of Scholars." *New York State Education* 22: 375, 414-16; February, 1935.
512. BILDERSEE, ADELE. "Participation in Extra-Curricular Activities; Participation in Social Service." *State Scholarship Students at Hunter College of the City of New York.* Contributions to Education, No. 540. New York: Teachers College, Columbia University, 1932. p. 46-66.
513. CARTER, T. M. "The Effect of College Fraternities on Scholarship." *Journal of Applied Psychology* 18: 393-400; June, 1934.
514. CHASE, H. W. "Fraternities Under Present-Day Conditions." *Transactions and Proceedings of the National Association of State Universities, 1932.* Vol. 30. Oxford, Ohio: the Association (A. H. Upham, sec., Miami University), 1932. p. 60-84.
515. CHILDS, HARWOOD L. "Ranking Motives in Voting; Questionnaire Study of Students at Bucknell, Princeton, and Syracuse Universities." *American Journal of Sociology* 41: 59-66; July, 1935.
516. CHRISTENSEN, ALFRED. "The Administration of Student Activities." *Junior College Journal* 3: 138-40; December, 1932.
517. CHRISTENSEN, ALFRED. "Student Activities in Public Junior Colleges." *Junior College Journal* 3: 251-54; February, 1933.
518. COOPER, JOHN ANDREW. *The Effect of Participation in Athletics Upon Scholarship Measured by Achievement Tests.* Doctor's thesis, Pennsylvania State College, 1932. 22 p.

519. COWLEY, W. H. "Evaluating the Fraternity." *Journal of Higher Education* 5: 281-84; May, 1934.
520. DAVIS, ELWOOD C., and COOPER, JOHN A. "Athletic Ability and Scholarship." *Research Quarterly of the American Physical Education Association* 5: 68-78; December, 1934.
521. "Difficulties of Self-Supporting Students at Yale University." *School and Society* 36: 748; December 10, 1932.
522. EATON, DOROTHY, and SHANNON, J. R. "College Careers of High-School Athletes and Non-Athletes." *School Review* 42: 356-61; May, 1934.
523. FRAZIER, BENJAMIN W., and OTHERS. "Health and Physical Education, and Athletics; Extracurriculum Activities." *Special Survey Studies*. U. S. Dept. of the Interior, Office of Education, Bulletin, 1933, No. 10. National Survey of the Education of Teachers, Vol. 5. Washington, D. C.: Government Printing Office, 1933. p. 188-214.
524. FREEARK, C. H. *College Career, and the American College Fraternity System*. Lincoln, Nebr.: Fraternity Management, Inc., 1935. 32 p.
525. LEHMAN, HARVEY C. "Motivation; College Marks and the Fraternity Pledge." *Journal of Applied Psychology* 19: 9-28; February, 1935.
526. LINGENFELTER, MARY REBECCA, and STEELE, REA J. compilers. "Educational Books of 1933; Extracurricular Activities." *School and Society* 39: 388-89; March 24, 1934.
527. MACKENZIE, DONALD H. "Effects of Various Physical Activities on the Physical Fitness of University Men." *Research Quarterly of the American Physical Education Association* 6: 125-43; March (Supplement), 1935.
528. MCMAHON, ERNEST E., and FOSTER, C. R., JR. "The Undergraduate Point of View on Student Participation." *School and Society* 35: 768-70; June 4, 1932.
529. MCMURTREY, G. W. "A Study of the Relationship Between Some Factors Which Affect School Work." *Journal of Educational Psychology* 23: 553-58; October, 1932.
530. MACPHAIL, ANDREW H. "A Comparative Study of the Quality of Academic Work Done by Fraternity and Non-fraternity Students at Brown University." *School and Society* 38: 873-76; December 30, 1933.
531. MANEY, CHARLES A. "The Distribution of Memberships in the Extra-Curricular Activities of the Liberal Arts College." *School and Society* 39: 63-64; January 13, 1934.
532. MANEY, CHARLES A. "The Grades of College Football Students." *School and Society* 38: 307-8; September 2, 1933.
533. MATHEWS, C. O. "The Honor System." *Journal of Higher Education* 3: 411-15; November, 1932.
534. MEHUS, O. MYKING. "Academic Achievement of College Students in Different Kinds of Extra-Curricular Activities." *Journal of Educational Sociology* 8: 50-56; September, 1934.
535. MEHUS, O. MYKING. "Extracurricular Activities and Academic Achievement." *Journal of Educational Sociology* 6: 143-49; November, 1932.
536. MOORE, JOE E. "A Study of Certain Variables Among Self-Help Freshmen." *Vocational Guidance Magazine* 11: 120-22; December, 1932.
537. MOSSMAN, LOIS COFFEY. "Discovering Interests Through Extra-Curricular Activities." *The New Deal in Education*. Twenty-first Annual Schoolmen's Week Proceedings. Philadelphia: University of Pennsylvania, 1934. p. 325-28.
538. REEVES, FLOYD W., and RUSSELL, JOHN DALE. *Some University Student Problems*. University of Chicago Survey, Vol. X. Chicago: University of Chicago Press, 1933. Chapter 3, "Adequacy of Student Aid Grants," p. 55-68.
539. REEVES, FLOYD W., and OTHERS. *The Organization and Administration of the University*. University of Chicago Survey, Vol. II. Chicago: University of Chicago Press, 1933. Chapter 6, "Non-Curriculum Interests of Students," p. 83-95.
540. RICHARDSON, LUCY, and OTHERS. "Student Participation in Government." *Problems in Teacher-Training, Vol. VIII*. (Alonzo F. Myers, Ed.) Proceedings of the 1933 Spring Conference of the Eastern States Association of Professional Schools for Teachers. New York: Prentice-Hall, Inc., 1934. p. 305-10.
541. ROBINSON, RUTH G. "Students Mean Business in This College." *Texas Outlook* 17: 12, 40; September, 1933.

542. RUTLEDGE, SAMUEL A., and BRISCOE, ALONZO O. "Guiding Principles for the Administration of Extra-Curricular Activities in the Teachers College." *Educational Administration and Supervision* 19: 129-40; February, 1933.
543. SAVAGE, HOWARD J. "The Carnegie Foundation's Study of American College Athletics—Three Years Later." *Research Quarterly of the American Physical Education Association* 4: 15-25; March, 1933.
544. SHARPE, R. T. "The Present Problem of Student Employment." *Bulletin of the American Association of University Professors* 18: 502-4; November, 1932.
545. SHEEDER, FRANKLIN I. "The Honor Spirit on the College Campus." *Religious Education* 27: 735-41; October, 1932.
546. STACKMAN, HARVEY A., JR. "Handwriting and Extra-Curricular Activity." *Journal of Applied Psychology* 18: 819-25; December, 1934.
547. STALNAKER, JOHN M. "Attitudes Toward Intercollegiate Athletics." *School and Society* 37: 499-504; April 15, 1933.
548. TERRY, PAUL W., compiler. "Selected References on the Extra-Curriculum." *School Review* 41: 299-306; April, 1933. 42: 299-306; April, 1934. 43: 300-6; April, 1935.
549. THISTED, MOSES N. "Participation in College Athletics and Vocational Success." *Doctoral Theses in Education I.* Studies in Education Vol. 9, No. 1. Iowa City; University of Iowa, 1934. p. 131-49.
550. UMSTATTD, JAMES G. *Student Self-Support at the University of Minnesota.* Minneapolis: University of Minnesota Press, 1932. 205 p.
551. WAHLQUIST, JOHN T. "The Honor System in American Colleges and Universities." *School and Society* 37: 757-60; June 10, 1933.
552. ZORBAUGH, GRACE S. M. "Part-Time Placing and Vocational Counseling of Women." *Educational Research Bulletin (Ohio State University)* 11: 426-32; December 7, 1932.

Chapter VIII. Educational Adjustment

A. ELEMENTARY EDUCATION

553. BARTHELMESS, HARRIET M., and BOYER, PHILIP A. "An Evaluation of Ability Grouping." *Journal of Educational Research* 26: 284-94; December, 1932.
554. CUMMINGS, HELEN F. *A Study of One Hundred Cases of Maladjusted School Children with a View to Showing that Most School Failure Can Be Prevented.* Doctor's thesis, Boston College, 1934. 122 p.
555. DOUGLASS, HARL R. "Certain Aspects of the Problem of Where We Stand with Reference to the Practicability of Grouping." *Journal of Educational Research* 26: 344-53; January, 1933.
556. FARLEY, E. S., and OTHERS. "Factors Related to the Grade Progress of Pupils." *Elementary School Journal* 34: 186-93; November, 1933.
557. GATES, ARTHUR I., chairman. "Special Methods and Psychology of the Elementary-School Subjects." *Review of Educational Research* 5: 1-120; February, 1935.
558. GROVER, CHARLES C. "Gifted Children in Elementary School." *Nation's Schools* 16: 12-16; July, 1935.
559. HOLY, T. C., chairman. "The School Plant." *Review of Educational Research* 5: 333-439; October, 1935.
560. NORTON, MARGARET ALLTUCKER, chairman. "The Curriculum." *Review of Educational Research* 4: 121-252; April, 1934.
561. OTTO, HENRY J., and MELBY, ERNEST O. "An Attempt to Evaluate the Threat of Failure as a Factor in Achievement." *Elementary School Journal* 35: 588-96; April, 1935.
562. PIERCE, PAUL R. "Internal Organization of School Divisions: The Elementary School." *Review of Educational Research* 4: 382-96; 437-40; October, 1934.
563. RANKIN, PAUL T. "Pupil Classification and Grouping." *Review of Educational Research* 1: 200-30, 233-44; June, 1931.
564. RETAN, GEORGE AUSTIN. *A Study of Environmental Factors Influencing the Progress of Children Through the Grades of the Elementary School.* Doctor's thesis, New York University, 1932. 92 p.

565. SMITH, W. RAY. *Home Study Practices in the Elementary Schools of Certain School Districts in Western Pennsylvania.* Doctor's thesis, University of Pittsburgh, 1933. 172 p.
566. TILTON, J. W. "The Feasibility of Ability Grouping." *Journal of Educational Research* 28: 30-35; September, 1934.
567. WEST, PARL. *A Study of Ability Grouping in the Elementary School.* Contributions to Education No. 588. New York: Teachers College, Columbia University, 1933. 70 p.
568. WYNDHAM, HAROLD S. *Ability Grouping; Recent Developments in Methods of Class-Grouping in the Elementary Schools of the United States.* Educational Research Series, No. 31. Melbourne, Australia: Melbourne University Press, 1934. 234 p.

B. SECONDARY EDUCATION

569. BILLETT, ROY O. *Provisions for Individual Differences, Marking, and Promotion.* U. S. Dept. of the Interior, Office of Education, Bulletin, 1932, No. 17. National Survey of Secondary Education, Monograph No. 13. Washington, D. C.: Government Printing Office, 1933. 472 p.
570. DURLING, DOROTHY, and POWELL, WEBSTER. "Improper School Placement as a Factor in Juvenile Delinquency." *Journal of Applied Psychology* 16: 519-24; October, 1932.
571. FRENCH, WILL. *Promotional Plans in the High School.* Contributions to Education, No. 587. New York: Teachers College, Columbia University, 1933. 90 p.
572. MARTENS, ELISE H., and RUSS, HELEN. *Adjustment of Behavior Problems of School Children.* U. S. Dept. of the Interior, Office of Education, Bulletin, 1932, No. 18. Washington, D. C.: Government Printing Office, 1932. 78 p.
573. MILLER, JOSEPH. "Causes of Failure and Success in School." *Educational Method* 12: 364-66; March, 1933.
574. MORT, PAUL R.; WRIGHT, W. W.; and FEATHERSTONE, W. B. "Fitting the School to the Pupil." *Report of the Survey of the Schools of Chicago, Illinois.* Vol. II. New York: Teachers College, Columbia University, 1932. p. 1-141.
575. MYERS, THEODORE R. *Intra-Family Relationships and Pupil Adjustment.* Contributions to Education, No. 651. New York: Teachers College, Columbia University, 1935. 115 p.
576. PECK, LEIGH. "Teachers' Reports of the Problems of Unadjusted School Children." *Journal of Educational Psychology* 26: 123-38; February, 1935.
577. RIDENOUR, NINA A. "A Study of the Backgrounds of Withdrawing Children." *Journal of Educational Research* 28: 132-43; October, 1934.

C. HIGHER EDUCATION

578. AIKEN, WILFORD M. "Report of Commission on the Relation of Secondary School and College." *Bulletin of the Department of Secondary-School Principals of the National Education Association* 50: 174-85; March, 1934.
579. ALTER, DINSMORE. "Students Whose Academic Work is Inferior." *Bulletin of the American Association of University Professors* 20: 333-36; May, 1934.
580. BEHRENS, H. D. "Effects of a 'How to Study' Course." *Journal of Higher Education* 6: 195-202; April, 1935.
581. BENJAMIN, HARRY J. "Endocrinology and the Problem College Student." *Progressive Education* 12: 348-51; May, 1935.
582. BLAKE, MABELLE B., and DEARBORN, WALTER F. "The Improvement of Reading Habits." *Journal of Higher Education* 6: 83-88; February, 1935.
583. BOUCHER, C. S. "New Articulation Plan at Chicago." *Progressive Education* 10: 381-85; November, 1933.
584. BRAMMELL, P. ROY. *Articulation of High School and College.* U. S. Dept. of the Interior, Office of Education, Bulletin, 1932, No. 17. National Survey of Secondary Education, Monograph No. 10. Washington, D. C.: Government Printing Office, 1933. 96 p.
585. BROOM, M. E. "Importance of Reading for College Study." *Educational Administration and Supervision* 20: 189-92; March, 1934.
586. BROWN, FRANK EMERSON, and COONS, R. R. "Treatment of Students Earning Low Grades." *Journal of Chemical Education* 11: 579-81; October, 1934.

587. CLEETON, GLEN U. "Clinical Treatment of Maladjusted College Students." *Journal of Engineering Education* 25: 405-10; February, 1935.
588. COREY, STEPHEN M. "The Effect of Motivation upon the Relationship Between Achievement and Intelligence." *School and Society* 41: 256-57; February 23, 1935.
589. CRAWFORD, STANTON C. "The University of Pittsburgh's Program of Cooperation with High Schools." *School and Society* 38: 772-73; December 9, 1933.
590. DEAL, ROY W. "The Development of Reading and Study Habits in College Students." *Journal of Educational Psychology* 25: 258-73; April, 1934.
591. ECKERT, RUTH E., and JONES, E. S. *Value of a How to Study Course for College Students.* University of Buffalo Studies, Vol. 10, No. 2. Buffalo, N. Y.: the University, 1935. 46 p.
592. FRAZIER, RICHARD H. "An Experiment in the Honors Treatment of Students in Electrical Engineering." *School and Society* 39: 271-72; March 3, 1934.
593. FREEMAN, HOMER J., and JONES, LONZO. "Final Report of the Long-Time Effect of Counseling Low-Percentile Freshmen." *School and Society* 38: 382-84; September 16, 1933.
594. GERBERICH, J. R. "Five Years of Experience with a Remedial Reading Course for College Students." *Journal of Experimental Education* 3: 36-41; September, 1934.
595. GERBERICH, J. R., and ROBERDS, W. M. "Individualized Instruction for Superior Students in Introductory College Physics." *Science Education* 18: 28-33; February, 1934.
596. GRAY, WILLIAM S. "Provisions for Individual Differences in Reading Efficiency." *Provisions for the Individual in College Education.* Proceedings of the Institute for Administrative Officers of Higher Institutions, 1932. Chicago: University of Chicago Press, 1932. p. 144-58.
597. GREENE, EDWARD B. "Certain Aspects of Lecture, Reading and Guided Reading." *School and Society* 39: 619-24; May 12, 1934.
598. "High School and College Relationships." *Bulletin of the Association of American Colleges* 20: 227-39; May, 1934.
599. JONES, EDWARD S. "The Grade-Test Correlation as an Index of Motivation." *School and Society* 36: 478-80; October 8, 1932.
600. JONES, EDWARD S. "Integrating High School and College." *Journal of Higher Education* 4: 131-32; March, 1933.
601. JONES, EDWARD S., editor. *Studies in Articulation of High School and College.* University of Buffalo Studies, Vol. 9. Buffalo, N. Y.: the University, 1934. 319 p.
602. LEARNED, WILLIAM S. "Study of the Relations of Secondary and Higher Education in Pennsylvania; Knowledge as a Factor in Education—The Tests and Their Implications." *Twenty-eighth Annual Report of the President and of the Treasurer.* New York: Carnegie Foundation for the Advancement of Teaching, 1933. p. 39-63.
603. LEIGHTON, R. W. *Studies to Determine the Relative Achievement of Students at Different Potentiality Levels.* Studies in College Teaching Vol. 1, Bulletin 1. Eugene: University of Oregon, 1933. 39 p.
604. McCLUSKY, HOWARD YALE. "An Experiment on the Influence of Preliminary Skimming on Reading." *Journal of Educational Psychology* 25: 521-29; October, 1934.
605. MACLEAN, MALCOLM S. "The Minnesota Junior College." *Educational Record* 14: 301-9; July, 1933.
606. MCNEELY, JOHN H. "Changes in Traditional Methods of Collegiate Instruction." *School and Society* 41: 213-17; February 16, 1935.
607. MILLS, HENRY C. "Anticipating College Credits." *School and Society* 38: 577-80; October 28, 1933.
608. MILLS, HENRY C. "Duplication of Effort Between High School and College." *School Review* 43: 363-70; May, 1935.
609. MOORE, HERBERT. "Training College Freshmen to Read." *Journal of Applied Psychology* 18: 631-34; October, 1934.
610. NANNINGA, S. P., and KNODE, JAY C., editors. *Articulation of High School and College in New Mexico.* Report of Conference held July 21-22, 1933. Bulletin Vol. 7, No. 2. Albuquerque: University of New Mexico, 1933. 96 p.

611. PADELFORD, NORMAN J. "Sophomore Tutorial Work." *Journal of Higher Education* 6: 59-62; February, 1935.
612. PARR, F. W. "Teaching Ways of Study." *Journal of Higher Education* 5: 377-81; October, 1934.
613. PEARSON, PETER HENRY. "Reducing Waste in the Work of Students." *Education* 54: 495-97; April, 1934.
614. "Placement Examinations at LaFayette College." *School and Society* 38: 762; December 9, 1933.
615. "The Program of High-School Articulation at Yale University." *School and Society* 39: 470; April 14, 1934.
616. "Provision at Yale University for Students of Special Ability." *School and Society* 40: 439-40; October 6, 1934.
617. REMMERS, H. H., and OTHERS. *Exemption from College Semester Examination as a Condition of Learning.* Studies in Higher Education No. 23. Bulletin Vol. 34, No. 3. Lafayette, Ind.: Purdue University, 1933. 52 p.
618. RYDER, STEPHEN PAUL. *An Experimental Study of Potential Failures in College.* Doctor's thesis, University of Chicago, 1934. 114 p.
619. SHOFSTALL, W. P. "The Achievement of High-School and College Students in the Same Classes." *School Review* 43: 184-88; March, 1935.
620. STEVENSON, MARY LOU. "The Use of Modern Language Placement Tests at the University of Pittsburgh." *Modern Language Journal* 18: 433-50; April, 1934.
621. STOCKRAHM, ROY L. *Tentative Analysis of Learning to Read, With a Study of the Reading Ability of College Freshmen.* Bloomington: Indiana University Graduate Council, 1932. 64 p.
622. STRANG, RUTH. "Improving Students' Reading." *Journal of Higher Education* 5: 426-32; November, 1934.
623. STRATTON, DOROTHY C. *Problems of Students in a Graduate School of Education.* Contributions to Education No. 550. New York: Teachers College, Columbia University, 1933. 168 p.
624. THURBER, CLARENCE HOWE. "The Colgate Plan." *Journal of Higher Education* 4: 59-66; February, 1933.
625. TYLER, RALPH W., and OTHERS. *Service Studies in Higher Education.* Bureau of Educational Research Monographs, No. 15. Columbus: Ohio State University, 1932. 283 p.
626. UMSTATTD, J. G. "Students' Appraisal of Independent Study." *Journal of Higher Education* 6: 240-43; May, 1935.
627. WAGNER, MAZIE E., and STRABEL, EUNICE. "Predicting Success and Failure in College Ancient and Modern Foreign Languages." *Modern Language Journal* 19: 285-93; January, 1935.
628. WARD, PAUL W. "Attitudes of Average and Superior Students Towards Survey Courses." *School and Society* 40: 398-99; September 22, 1934.
629. ZELENY, FLORENCE KELLY. "Remedial Instruction in Reading at the Freshman Level in a Teachers College." *Educational Administration and Supervision* 18: 607-20; November, 1932.

Chapter IX. Special Schools and Classes

630. ANDREWS, FRANCES MARSHALL. *The Educational Status of the Blind Mentally Retarded in the United States.* Master's thesis, Boston University, 1933. 60 p.
631. BABCOCK, MARJORIE E. *A Comparison of Delinquent and Non-delinquent Boys by Objective Measures of Personality.* Doctor's thesis, Columbia University, 1932. 74 p.
632. BEARD, BELLE B. *Juvenile Probation: An Analysis of the Case Records of 500 Children Studied at the Judge Baker Guidance Clinic and Placed on Probation in the Juvenile Court of Boston.* New York: American Book Co., 1934. 219 p. (Doctor's thesis, Bryn Mawr College, 1933.)
633. BECKETT, VERONA E. *A Study of Types of Handicapped Children in the Eugene Field School, Philadelphia.* Master's thesis, Temple University, 1932. 120 p.
634. BELL, ROBERT E. *The Provision for the Education of Gifted Children in the Elementary Schools of New York State.* Doctor's thesis, New York University, 1933. 175 p.

635. BENNETT, ANNETTE. *A Comparative Study of Subnormal Children in the Elementary Grades.* Contributions to Education, No. 510. New York: Teachers College, Columbia University, 1932. 81 p.
636. BEST, HARRY. *Blindness and the Blind in the United States.* New York: Macmillan Co., 1934. 714 p.
637. BILLETT, ROY O. *Provisions for Individual Differences, Marking, and Promotion.* U. S. Department of the Interior, Office of Education, Bulletin, 1932, No. 17. National Survey of Secondary Education, Monograph No. 13. Washington, D. C.: Government Printing Office, 1933. p. 195-226.
638. BLUMER, HERBERT, and HAUSER, PHILIP M. *Movies, Delinquency, and Crime.* New York: Macmillan Co., 1933. 233 p.
639. BOWLER, ALIDA C., and BLOODGOOD, RUTH S. *Institutional Treatment of Delinquent Boys: Part I.* U. S. Dept. of Labor, Children's Bureau, Publication No. 228. Washington, D. C.: Government Printing Office, 1935. 324 p.
640. BURKEY, RUTH E. "A Statistical Study of the Sequence of Successive Delinquencies." *Journal of Juvenile Research* 16: 133-44; April, 1932.
641. CARL, PAUL REVERE. *A Study of Enrolment in Secondary Schools and the Increase in Juvenile Delinquency.* Master's thesis, Temple University, 1932. 52 p.
642. COURTHIAL, ANDRÉE. *Emotional Differences of Delinquent and Non-delinquent Girls of Normal Intelligence: A Study of Two Groups Paired by Chronological Age, Intelligence, and Environment.* Doctor's thesis, Columbia University, 1932. 102 p.
643. CROKE, M. FRANCIS. *The Adjustment Child in Junior High School.* Master's thesis, Fordham University, 1933. 72 p.
644. CROSS, HILDRETH MARIE. *The Motor Capacities of Stutterers.* Doctor's thesis, State University of Iowa, 1933. 63 p.
645. CUTHBERTSON, DAISY JANE. *The Exceptional Child in the Elementary Schools of North Carolina.* Master's thesis, North Carolina College for Women, 1929. 36 p.
646. CUTSFORTH, THOMAS D. *The Blind in School and Society.* New York: D. Appleton-Century Co., 1933. 263 p.
647. DANIEL, ROBERT PRENTISS. *A Psychological Study of Delinquent and Non-delinquent Negro Boys.* Contributions to Education, No. 546. New York: Teachers College, Columbia University, 1932. 59 p.
648. DESCOEUDRES, ALICE. *The Education of Mentally Defective Children* (Translated by Ernest F. Row). Boston: D. C. Heath and Co., 1928. 312 p.
649. DORAISWAMY, CHINNISH. *An Analysis of Reading Difficulties Among the Blind Children in Primary Grades.* Master's thesis, Boston University, 1934. 63 p.
650. DRANSFIELD, JOHN EDGAR. *Administration of Enrichment to Superior Children in the Typical Classroom.* Contributions to Education, No. 558. New York: Teachers College, Columbia University, 1933. 107 p.
651. FARSON, MABEL R. "A Comparison of Orthogenic Backward Children and Regular Grade Children at the Six Year Performance Level." *Psychological Clinic* 22: 149-80; September-November, 1933.
652. FEATHERSTONE, WILLIAM BLAND. *The Curriculum of the Special Class; Its Underlying Principles.* Contributions to Education, No. 544. New York: Teachers College, Columbia University, 1932. 157 p.
653. FEICK, EVANGELINE HOUGHTALING. *A Study of the Psychological and Social Status of Crippled Children in a City of 25,000 Population.* Master's thesis, Ohio State University, 1934. 75 p.
654. FELDMAN, BENJAMIN. *Trends in the Education of Exceptional Children.* Master's thesis, Temple University, 1933. 96 p.
655. FRENCH, RICHARD SLAYTON. *From Homer to Helen Keller.* New York: American Foundation for the Blind, 1932. 298 p.
656. GROFF, MARNE LAURITSEN. *An Analysis of First Year Vocabulary of the Public Residential Schools for the Deaf in the United States.* Doctor's thesis, University of Pennsylvania, 1932.
657. HENDERSON, MARY. *Proposed Adjustment Procedures for the Superior Pupils of Bellinger Hill School, Montgomery, Alabama.* Master's thesis, University of Alabama, 1933. 97 p.
658. HILL, GEORGE E. "Educational Attainments of Young Male Offenders." *Elementary School Journal* 36: 53-58; September, 1935.

659. INGRAM, CHRISTINE P. *Education of the Slow-Learning Child.* Yonkers-on-Hudson, N. Y.: World Book Co., 1935. 419 p.
660. JOHNSON, WENDELL. *The Influence of Stuttering on the Personality.* Studies in Child Welfare, Vol. V, No. 5. Iowa City: University of Iowa, 1932. 140 p.
661. KAPLAN, ALBERT JACOB. *A Study of the Behavior Problem Pupil in a Secondary School.* Doctor's thesis, Temple University, 1933. 187 p.
662. KUNZIG, ROBERT W. *Public School Education of Atypical Children.* U. S. Dept. of the Interior, Office of Education, Bulletin, 1931, No. 10. Washington, D. C.: Government Printing Office, 1931. 160 p.
663. LEHMAN, CLARENCE OLIVER. *The Legal Status of State Aid for Special School Projects in the United States.* Doctor's thesis, Ohio State University, 1929. 167 p.
664. LINCOLN, E. A. "Stanford-Binet I. Q. Changes of Superior Children." *School and Society* 41: 519-20; April 13, 1935.
665. MCBRIDE, EARL D. *Crippled Children, Their Treatment and Orthopedic Nursing.* St. Louis, Mo.: C. V. Mosby Co., 1931. 12 p.
666. MACKANE, KEITH. *A Comparison of the Intelligence of Deaf and Hearing Children; A Study of the Reactions of Comparable Groups of Deaf and Hearing Children to Three Performance Scales and a Non-Language Test.* Contributions to Education, No. 585. New York: Teachers College, Columbia University, 1933. 47 p.
667. MCLEOD, BEATRICE. *Teachers' Problems with Exceptional Children: IV. Deaf and Hard-of-Hearing Children.* U. S. Dept. of the Interior, Office of Education, Pamphlet No. 54. Washington, D. C.: Government Printing Office, 1934. 29 p.
668. MCLEOD, BEATRICE. *Teachers' Problems with Exceptional Children: V. Crippled Children.* U. S. Dept. of the Interior, Office of Education, Pamphlet No. 55. Washington, D. C.: Government Printing Office, 1934. 18 p.
669. MCLEOD, BEATRICE. *Teachers' Problems with Exceptional Children: VI. Children of Lowered Vitality.* U. S. Dept. of the Interior, Office of Education, Pamphlet No. 56. Washington, D. C.: Government Printing Office, 1934. 16 p.
670. MACLEOD, ROBERT BRODIE. *An Experimental Investigation of Brightness Constancy.* Archives of Psychology, No. 135. New York: Columbia University, 1932. 102 p. (Doctor's thesis, Columbia University, 1931.)
671. MARTENS, ELISE H., and RUSS, HELEN. *Adjustment of Behavior Problems of School Children.* U. S. Dept. of the Interior, Office of Education, Bulletin, 1932, No. 18. Washington, D. C.: Government Printing Office, 1932. 78 p.
672. MARTENS, ELISE H., compiler. *Coordination of Effort for the Education of Exceptional Children.* U. S. Dept. of the Interior, Office of Education, Bulletin, 1935, No. 7. Washington, D. C.: Government Printing Office, 1935. 82 p.
673. MARTENS, ELISE H. *Opportunities for the Preparation of Teachers of Exceptional Children.* U. S. Dept. of the Interior, Office of Education, Bulletin, 1931, No. 21. Washington, D. C.: Government Printing Office, 1932. 42 p.
674. MARTENS, ELISE H. *Organization for Exceptional Children Within State Departments of Education.* U. S. Dept. of the Interior, Office of Education, Pamphlet No. 42. Washington, D. C.: Government Printing Office, 1933. 35 p.
675. MARTENS, ELISE H. *Teachers' Problems with Exceptional Children: II. Gifted Children.* U. S. Dept of the Interior, Office of Education, Pamphlet No. 41. Washington, D. C.: Government Printing Office, 1933. 45 p.
676. MARTENS, ELISE H. *Teachers' Problems with Exceptional Children: III. Mentally Retarded Children.* U. S. Dept. of the Interior, Office of Education, Pamphlet No. 49. Washington, D. C.: Government Printing Office, 1934. 42 p.
677. MARTIN, WILLIAM H. *The Legal Status of Vaccination in 48 States and the District of Columbia.* Master's thesis, Ohio State University, 1933. 89 p.
678. MASTERS, HARRY V., and UPSHALL, C. C. *Provisions for Exceptional Children in the Public Schools of Washington, 1932-33.* Bureau of Research Studies No. 34. Bellingham: Washington State Normal School, 1933. 12 p.
679. MERRY, RALPH VICKERS. *Problems in the Education of Visually Handicapped Children.* Studies in Education, Vol. 19. Cambridge, Mass.: Harvard University Press, 1933. 243 p.
680. MEYER, MAX F. *Fitting into a Silent World, the First Six Years of Life.* Studies, Vol. 9, No. 2. Columbia: University of Missouri, 1934. 106 p.

681. MICHIGAN CRIPPLED CHILDREN COMMISSION. *Report, 1927-1932.* Lansing: the Commission, 1932. 36 p.
682. MUSSER, LAWRENCE L. *A Study of Vocational Guidance and Vocational Education for Crippled Children.* Master's thesis, University of Michigan, 1933. 203 p.
683. NATIONAL EDUCATION ASSOCIATION, RESEARCH DIVISION. "Crime Prevention Through Education." *Research Bulletin* 10: 133-202; September, 1932. Washington, D. C.: the Association.
684. NATIONAL EDUCATION ASSOCIATION and the AMERICAN MEDICAL ASSOCIATION, JOINT COMMITTEE ON HEALTH PROBLEMS IN EDUCATION. *Conserving the Sight of School Children.* Publication 6. New York: National Society for the Prevention of Blindness, 1935. 54 p.
685. NILSON, KENNETH. *Physically Disabled Persons in Minnesota, and an Analysis of Certain Factors in Their Education and Vocational Rehabilitation.* Doctor's thesis, University of Minnesota, 1931.
686. OAS, REYNOLD G. "A Study of Juvenile Delinquency in Van Buren County, Michigan." *Education News Bulletin* 5: 2-7; June, 1935. Kalamazoo, Mich.: Western State Teachers College.
687. OLSON, WILLARD C. "Needed Research in the Prevention of Delinquency." *University of Michigan School of Education Bulletin* 6: 102-3; April, 1935.
688. OTTO, HENRY J. *Elementary School Organization and Administration.* New York: D. Appleton-Century Co., 1934. p. 479-517.
689. PETIT, EDITH. *Opportunities for Unadjusted Boys.* Master's thesis, University of Cincinnati, 1933. 47 p.
690. PORTENIER, LILLIAN GERTRUDE. *Pupils of Low Mentality in High School.* Contributions to Education, No. 568. New York: Teachers College, Columbia University, 1933. 109 p.
691. REGENSBURG, JEANETTE. *Studies of Educational Success and Failure in Supernormal Children.* Archives of Psychology, No. 129. New York: Columbia University, 1931. 150 p.
692. RUGGLES, EDWARD W. "An Analytical Study of Various Factors Relating to Juvenile Crime." *Journal of Juvenile Research* 16: 125-32; April, 1932.
693. SCHLEIER, LOUIS MARTIN. *Problems in the Training of Certain Special-Class Teachers.* Contributions to Education, No. 475. New York: Teachers College, Columbia University, 1931. 138 p.
694. UPSON, LENT D., and MATSON, OPAL V. *Crippled Children in Michigan.* Detroit: George H. Cummings Fund (3400 Union Guardian Bldg.), 1931. 188 p.
695. WALDMAN, JOHN L.; WADE, FRANCIS A.; and ARETZ, CARL W. *Hearing and the School Child; Hearing, School Progress and Achievement of Public School Children.* Washington, D. C.: Volta Bureau, (Doctor's thesis, Temple University), 1930. 222 p.
696. WALLACE, CORA JEANETTE. *Educational Opportunities for Crippled Children in England, France, Germany, and the United States.* Master's thesis, University of Cincinnati, 1933. 155 p.
697. WALLIN, J. E. WALLACE. "The Support of Fresh-Air Classes During the Economic Depression." *Elementary School Journal* 35: 597-605; April, 1935.
698. WARNER, FLORENCE MARY. *Juvenile Detention in the United States.* Doctor's thesis, University of Chicago, 1933. 166 p.
699. WASSMAN, KATHERINE. *A Comparative Study of Mentally Deficient Children in Regular and in Special Classes.* Master's thesis, George Washington University, 1935. 41 p.
700. WILKINS, LAROY WALTER. *Certain Characteristics of Pedagogically Accelerated Children in the High School.* Doctor's thesis, Northwestern University, 1933. 196 p.

Chapter X. Child Labor

701. ABBOTT, W. LEWIS. *Report for the Committee on Labor Conditions in the Growing of Sugar Beets.* Washington, D. C.: U. S. Dept. of Labor, 1934. 55 p. (Mimeographed.)
702. ALABAMA CHILD WELFARE DEPARTMENT. *Summary of a Survey of 100 Minors under 17 Working After School in Huntsville, Alabama, May, 1932.* Montgomery: the Department, 1932. 3 p. (Mimeographed.)

703. ALPER, BENEDICT S., and LODGEN, GEORGE E. "Youth Without Work." *Survey* 70: 285-86; September, 1934.
704. BENJAMIN, GRACE E., director. *Texas Child Welfare Survey, 1933-1935.* Austin: Bureau of Research in the Social Sciences, University of Texas, 1935.
705. BROWN, SARA A.; SARGENT, ROBIE O.; and ARMENTROUT, CLARA B. *Children Working in the Sugar Beet Fields of Certain Districts of the South Platte Valley, Colorado.* Publication No. 333. New York: National Child Labor Committee, 1925. 167 p.
706. CALLCOTT, MARY STEVENSON. *Child Labor Legislation in New York; the Historical Development and the Administrative Practices of Child Labor Laws in the State of New York, 1905-1930.* New York: Macmillan Co., 1931. 267 p.
707. CHAMBERLAIN, JOSEPH P. *Child Labor Amendment: Argument for Ratification.* New York: Non-Partisan Committee for Ratification of the Federal Child Labor Amendment (419 Fourth Ave.), 1934. 33 p.
708. CHANNING, ALICE. *Employed Boys and Girls in Milwaukee.* U. S. Dept. of Labor, Children's Bureau, Publication No 213. Washington, D. C.: Government Printing Office, 1932. 71 p.
709. CHANNING, ALICE. *Employed Boys and Girls in Rochester and Utica, New York.* U. S. Dept. of Labor, Children's Bureau, Publication No. 218. Washington, D. C.: Government Printing Office, 1933. 74 p.
710. CHANNING, ALICE. *Employment of Mentally Deficient Boys and Girls.* U. S. Dept. of Labor, Children's Bureau, Publication No. 210. Washington, D. C.: Government Printing Office, 1932. 107 p.
711. CHEYNEY, ALICE. *International Labor Standards and American Legislation (A Comparison).* Geneva Special Studies, Vol. 2, No. 8. Washington, D. C.: International Labor Organization, 1931. 62 p.
712. CONNECTICUT DEPARTMENT OF LABOR, MINIMUM WAGE DIVISION. *Homework in the Connecticut Lace Industry.* Hartford: the Department, 1933. 20 p. (Mimeographed.)
713. CONNECTICUT DEPARTMENT OF LABOR, MINIMUM WAGE DIVISION. *Homework in the Fabricated Metal Industry in Connecticut.* Hartford: the Department, 1934. 20 p. (Mimeographed.)
714. CONNECTICUT DEPARTMENT OF LABOR, MINIMUM WAGE DIVISION. *Hours and Earnings in Connecticut Shirt Factories, 1933 and 1934.* Hartford: the Department, 1935. 27 p. (Mimeographed.)
715. CONNNECTICUT DEPARTMENT OF LABOR, MINIMUM WAGE DIVISION. *Hours and Earnings in the Women's Dress Industry, 1933 and 1934.* Hartford: the Department, 1935. 22 p. (Mimeographed.)
716. CONNECTICUT STATE EMPLOYMENT SERVICE. *Youth in Search of Jobs! FERA Project C. P. S.-F2-87.* Hartford: the Service, 1935. 36 p. (Mimeographed.)
717. CRESSMAN, L. S., and SPENKER, EDNA C. "Federal Regulation of Child Labor in Oregon." *Commonwealth Review* 14: 154-57; July, 1932.
718. DINWIDDIE, COURTENAY. "Controlling Child Labor Through Code Procedure." *American Federationist* 41: 34-41; January, 1934.
719. FULLER, RAYMOND G. "Child Labor." *Encyclopaedia of the Social Sciences.* Vol. 3. New York: Macmillan Company, 1930. p. 412-24.
720. GIBBONS, CHARLES E., and STANSBURY, CHESTER T. *Administration of the Child Labor Law in Ohio.* Publication No. 363. New York: National Child Labor Committee, 1931. 66 p.
721. GIBBONS, CHARLES E. *Statement on Conditions Relating to Sugar Beet Workers in Colorado, at the Hearing on the Sugar Stabilization Agreement, August 11, 1933.* New York: National Child Labor Committee, 1933. 14 p. (Mimeographed.)
722. GIBBONS, CHARLES E., and STANSBURY, CHESTER T. *Street-Trading in Detroit.* New York: National Child Labor Committee, 1931. 34 p. (Mimeographed.)
723. GIBBONS, CHARLES E.; STANSBURY, CHESTER T.; and ZIMAND, GERTRUDE FOLKS. *When Children Are Injured in Industry: Report of a Follow-up Study of 167 Children Injured in Industrial Accidents in Tennessee, Illinois, and Wisconsin.* Publication No. 367. New York: National Child Labor Committee, 1933. 43 p.

724. GOLDBERGER, ANTHONY M. *Variability in Continuation School Populations.* Contributions to Education, No. 454. New York: Teachers College, Columbia University, 1931. 52 p.
725. HATHWAY, MARION. *The Migratory Worker and Family Life: the Mode of Living and Public Provision for the Needs of the Family of the Migratory Worker in Selected Industries of the State of Washington.* Social Service Monographs, No. 21. Chicago: University of Chicago Press, 1934. 240 p.
726. HECK, ARCH O. *A Study of the Ohio Compulsory Education and Child Labor Law.* Educational Research Monographs, No. 9. Columbus: Ohio State University, 1931. 210 p.
727. HICKMAN, MILDRED M. *Junior Wage Earners in Cleveland: A Statistical Study.* Occupational Information Series, No. 5. Cleveland: Board of Education, Bureau of Educational Research, 1930. 71 p.
728. ILLINOIS DEPARTMENT OF LABOR. "Additional Compensation for Illegal Employment of Minors in Illinois: Fifth Annual Report, July 1, 1931-June 30, 1932." *Labor Bulletin* 12: 109-11; December, 1932.
729. INDIANA GOVERNOR'S COMMISSION ON UNEMPLOYMENT RELIEF. *Indianapolis Youth Survey: A Report of the Situations and Needs of Representative Indianapolis Youths Between the Ages of 16 and 25.* Indianapolis: the Commission, 1935. 96 p. (Mimeographed.)
730. INTERNATIONAL LABOR CONFERENCE. *Unemployment Among Young Persons.* Report III, Nineteenth Session, 1935. Geneva: International Labor Office, 1935. 189 p.
731. INTERNATIONAL LABOR OFFICE. *Children and Young Persons Under Labor Law.* Studies and Reports, Series 1, No. 3. New York: World Peace Foundation, 1935. 342 p.
732. KEELER, MIRIAM. *Child Labor Legislation: Annual Summary.* New York: National Child Labor Committee, 1935. 14 p. (Mimeographed.)
733. LAYTON, WARREN K., and HENNICAR, A. N. "A Follow-up of Drop-out Boys Who Left School before Graduation to Enter Employment." *Vocational Guidance Magazine* 10: 202-7; February, 1932.
734. LOUGHRAN, MIRIAM E. *The Historical Development of Child Labor Legislation in the United States.* Washington, D. C.: Catholic University of America, 1921. 111 p.
735. LUMPKIN, KATHERINE D., and DOUGLAS, DOROTHY W. "The Effect of Unemployment and Short-time During 1931 in the Families of 200 Alabama Child Workers." *Social Forces* 11: 548-58; May, 1933.
736. MCCONNELL, BEATRICE. "A Decrease in Accidents to Children." *Labor and Industry (Pennsylvania Department of Labor and Industry)* 21: 4, 11; March, 1934.
737. MCGILL, NETTIE P. *Children in Street Work.* U. S. Dept. of Labor, Children's Bureau, Publication No. 183. Washington, D. C.: Government Printing Office, 1928. 353 p.
738. MARSH, MARGUERITE. *Youth in Danger: A Study of Young Workers Injured in Georgia Industries.* New York: National Consumers' League, 1930. 12 p.
739. MATTHEWS, ELLEN NATHALIE. "Accidents to Telegraph Messengers." *Monthly Labor Review* 38: 14-31; January, 1934.
740. MATTHEWS, ELLEN NATHALIE. *The Illegally Employed Minor and the Workmen's Compensation Law.* U. S. Dept. of Labor, Children's Bureau, Publication No. 214. Washington, D. C.: Government Printing Office, 1932. 226 p.
741. MERRITT, ELLA ARVILLA. "Child Labor Under the N. R. A. as Shown by Employment Certificates Issued in 1934." *Monthly Labor Review* 41. 1477-91; December, 1935.
742. MILWAUKEE VOCATIONAL SCHOOL, DIVISION OF INSTRUCTION AND RESEARCH. *Survey of Employment and School Status of Milwaukee High School Graduates—Class of June, 1933.* Milwaukee: the School, 1934. 28 p. (Mimeographed.)
743. MINEHAN, THOMAS. *Boy and Girl Tramps of America.* New York: Farrar and Rinehart, 1934. 267 p.
744. NATIONAL CHILD LABOR COMMITTEE. *Child Labor Facts.* Publication No. 366. New York: the Committee, 1932. 31 p.
745. NATIONAL CHILD LABOR COMMITTEE. *Child Labor Laws and Child Labor Facts: An Analysis by States.* Revised to 1935. New York: the Committee, 1935.

746. NATIONAL CHILD LABOR COMMITTEE. *Handbook on the Federal Child Labor Amendment.* New York: the Committee, 1935. 64 p.
747. NATIONAL CHILD LABOR COMMITTEE. *Investigation of Homework in the Artificial Flower and Feather Industry.* New York: the Committee, 1934. 20 p. (Mimeographed.)
748. NEILL, CHARLES P., director. *Report on Condition of Woman and Child Wage-Earners in the United States.* 61st Congress, 2nd Session, Senate Document No. 645. Washington, D. C.: Government Printing Office, 1910-13. 19 vols.
749. NEW JERSEY DEPARTMENT OF LABOR. *Report of the Commission to Investigate the Employment of Migratory Children in the State of New Jersey.* Trenton: the Department, 1931. 131 p. Supplement, 1932. 64 p.
750. NEW YORK DEPARTMENT OF LABOR, DIVISION OF STATISTICS AND INFORMATION. "Compensated Accidents to Minors in 1934." *Industrial Bulletin* 14: 262-63; October, 1935. (See also previous issues.)
751. NEW YORK DEPARTMENT OF LABOR, DIVISION OF WOMEN IN INDUSTRY. *The Social Aspects of the Administration of the Double Compensation Law in New York State.* Special Bulletin No. 168. New York: the Department, 1931. 114 p.
752. OGBURN, WILLIAM F. *Progress and Uniformity in Child-Labor Legislation.* New York: Columbia University Press, 1912. 219 p.
753. OTEY, ELIZABETH LEWIS. *The Beginnings of Child Labor Legislation in Certain States; a Comparative Study.* Report on Condition of Woman and Child Wage-Earners in the United States. Vol. VI. 61st Congress, 2nd Session, Senate Document, No. 645. Washington, D. C.: Government Printing Office, 1910. 225 p.
754. PENNSYLVANIA DEPARTMENT OF LABOR AND INDUSTRY, BUREAU OF WOMEN AND CHILDREN. *Industrial Home Work in Pennsylvania Under the NRA.* Harrisburg: the Department, 1935. 27 p. (Mimeographed.)
755. PENNSYLVANIA DEPARTMENT OF LABOR AND INDUSTRY, BUREAU OF WOMEN AND CHILDREN. *Pennsylvania's Experience with Certificated Home Workers.* Harrisburg: the Department, 1935. 8 p. (Mimeographed.)
756. PENNSYLVANIA DEPARTMENT OF LABOR AND INDUSTRY, BUREAU OF WOMEN AND CHILDREN. *The Quest for a Living Wage.* Pennsylvania Labor and Industry in the Depression, Part V. Special Bulletin, No. 39. Harrisburg: the Department, 1934. p. 54-70.
757. PENNSYLVANIA DEPARTMENT OF LABOR AND INDUSTRY, BUREAU OF WOMEN AND CHILDREN. "Reducing the Hazards of Employment for Boys in the Coal-mining Industry." *Labor and Industry* 19: 8-15; August, 1932.
758. REED, ELLERY F. *An Evaluative Survey of the Federal Transient Program, May to July, 1934.* New York: Committee on Care of Transient and Homeless (1270 Sixth Ave.), 1934. 143 p.
759. SHULMAN, HARRY M. *Newsboys of New York: A Study of Their Legal and Illegal Work Activities During 1931.* New York: New York Child Labor Committee (105 East 22nd St.), 1932. 48 p.
760. SIMONS, SAVILLA MILLIS. *A Study of the Issuance of Employment Certificates, the Provisions of Junior Placement, and the Procedure for Enforcing the Compulsory School Attendance Law in Illinois.* Report of Illinois Committee on Child Welfare Legislation. Springfield: Journal Printing Co., 1931. p. 149-97.
761. STONE, MARIAN FAAS. "Industrial Accidents to Employed Minors in California in 1932." *Monthly Labor Review* 39: 1078-94; November, 1934.
762. TAYLOR, PAUL S. *An American-Mexican Frontier, Nueces County, Texas.* Chapel Hill: University of North Carolina Press, 1934. "The Educational Problem." p. 199-214.
763. TAYLOR, PAUL S. *Mexican Labor in the United States: Dimmit County, Winter Garden District, South Texas.* Berkeley: University of California Press, 1930. "Education," p. 372-87.
764. TAYLOR, PAUL S. *Mexican Labor in the United States: Valley of South Platte, Colorado.* Berkeley: University of California Press, 1929. "Education," p. 192-207.
765. U. S. DEPARTMENT OF COMMERCE, BUREAU OF THE CENSUS. *General Report on Occupations.* Fifteenth Census: Population, Vol. 5. Washington, D. C.: Government Printing Office, 1933. Chapter 6, "Children in Gainful Occupation," p. 341-401.

766. U. S. DEPARTMENT OF COMMERCE, BUREAU OF THE CENSUS. *Occupations, By States.* Fifteenth Census: Population, Vol. 4. Washington, D. C.: Government Printing Office, 1933. 1796 p.
767. U. S. DEPARTMENT OF LABOR. "Labor Conditions in the Onion Fields of Ohio." *Monthly Labor Review* 40: 324-35; February, 1935.
768. U. S. DEPARTMENT OF LABOR. "Labor in the Shirt Industry, 1933." *Monthly Labor Review* 37: 499-510; September, 1933.
769. U. S. DEPARTMENT OF LABOR. *A Study of Industrial Home Work in the Summer and Fall of 1934: A Preliminary Report to the National Recovery Administration.* Washington, D. C.: the Department. 62 p. (Mimeographed.)
770. U. S. DEPARTMENT OF LABOR, CHILDREN'S BUREAU. *Child Labor Facts and Figures.* Publication No. 197, revised October, 1933. Washington, D. C.: Government Printing Office, 1933. 85 p.
771. U. S. DEPARTMENT OF LABOR, CHILDREN'S BUREAU. *Children Engaged in Newspaper and Magazine Selling and Delivering.* Publication No. 227. Washington, D. C.: Government Printing Office, 1935. 60 p.
772. U. S. DEPARTMENT OF LABOR, CHILDREN'S BUREAU. "Report of Advisory Committee on Employment of Minors in Hazardous Occupations." *Monthly Labor Review* 35: 1315-22; December, 1932.
773. U. S. DEPARTMENT OF LABOR, CHILDREN'S BUREAU. *State Compulsory School Attendance Standards Affecting the Employment of Minors; State Child-Labor Standards.* Washington, D. C.: Vocational Education Division, Office of Education, January, 1935. 54 p. (Mimeographed.)
774. U. S. DEPARTMENT OF LABOR, CHILDREN'S BUREAU. "Transient Boy." *Twentieth Annual Report of the Chief of the Children's Bureau, 1932.* Washington, D. C.: Government Printing Office, 1932. p. 5-9.
775. U. S. DEPARTMENT OF LABOR, CHILDREN'S BUREAU. "Trend of Child Labor in the United States, 1920 to 1931." *Monthly Labor Review* 35: 1322-36; December, 1932.
776. U. S. DEPARTMENT OF LABOR, WOMEN'S BUREAU. *The Employment of Women in the Sewing Trades of Connecticut.* Bulletin No. 97. Washington, D. C.: Government Printing Office, 1932. 13 p.
777. U. S. SENATE, 72ND CONGRESS, 2ND SESSION. *Relief for Unemployed Transients.* Hearings before a Subcommittee of the Committee on Manufactures on S. 5121, January 13-25, 1933. Washington, D. C.: Government Printing Office, 1933. 203 p.
778. U. S. WORKS PROGRESS ADMINISTRATION. *Statistics of Youth on Relief.* Research Bulletin, Series I, No. 16. Washington, D. C.: the Administration, January, 1936. 31 p.
779. UNIVERSITY OF DENVER, BUREAU OF BUSINESS AND SOCIAL RESEARCH. *Occupations of Denver High-School Graduates.* Report, Vol. 10, No. 3. Denver: the University, 1934. 8 p.
780. WHITE HOUSE CONFERENCE ON CHILD HEALTH AND PROTECTION. *Child Labor.* Report of the Subcommittee on Child Labor. New York: Century Co., 1932. 592 p.
781. WHITNEY, FRANCES R., and WALKER, MIRIAM. *Out of School—Out of Work? What Happened to 100 Cincinnati Children Withdrawing from School for Work in a Period of Unemployment.* Cincinnati: Consumers' League of Cincinnati, 1932. 34 p.
782. WIDENER, HARRY W. *Attitude of Employers Towards the Ohio Compulsory Education and Child Labor Law.* Bureau of Business Research Special Bulletin No. 32. Columbus: Ohio State University, 1931. 74 p.
783. WOODBURY, ROY F., and CLAFLIN, CHARLOTTE I. *Caddying, Erie County, N. Y.* Buffalo: Juvenile Protective Department, Children's Aid and Society for the Prevention of Cruelty to Children of Erie County, N. Y., 1935. 44 p.
784. WOODBURY, ROY F., and CLAFLIN, CHARLOTTE I. *Children on the Stage in Buffalo, New York, and Elsewhere: A Report of the Juvenile Protection Department.* Buffalo: Children's Aid and Society for the Prevention of Cruelty to Children of Erie County, N. Y., 1932. 30 p.

REVIEW OF EDUCATIONAL RESEARCH

Official Publication of the American Educational Research Association, a department of the National Education Association.

The contents of the REVIEW are listed in the EDUCATION INDEX

| Volume VI | June, 1936 | Number 3 |

PSYCHOLOGY OF LEARNING, GENERAL METHODS OF TEACHING, AND SUPERVISION

(Literature reviewed from January 1, 1933 to January 1, 1936)

Prepared by the Committee on Psychology of Learning, General Methods of Teaching, and Supervision: W. A. Brownell, Prudence Cutright, M. E. Irwin, E. O. Melby, and G. T. Buswell, *Chairman.*

TABLE OF CONTENTS

Chapter	Page
Introduction	279
I. Theoretical Aspects of Learning and Transfer of Training	281
W. A. BROWNELL, *Duke University, Durham, North Carolina.*	
II. Types of Learning and General Conditions Affecting Learning	291
G. T. BUSWELL, *University of Chicago, Chicago, Illinois.*	
III. Motivation, Emotional Responses, Maturation, Intelligence, and Individual Differences	300
M. E. IRWIN, *Public Schools, Detroit, Michigan.*	
IV. Methods of Teaching	310
PRUDENCE CUTRIGHT, *Public Schools, Minneapolis, Minnesota.*	
V. Supervision	324
E. O. MELBY, *Northwestern University, Evanston, Illinois.*	
Bibliography	337

Copyright, 1936
By National Education Association
Washington, D. C.

All Rights Reserved

Erratum

Through an unfortunate circumstance, the following names were omitted from the manuscript of the chapters entitled "School Marks" and "Recording and Reporting" in the *Review of Educational Research*, Volume VI, No. 2, April, 1936:

WILLIAM A. MCCALL, *Teachers College, Columbia University, New York, New York*

FLORENCE MAPES, *Paterson, New Jersey*

B. DUKE SMALL, *Board of Education, Atlanta, Georgia*

ADELAIDE P. BOSTICK, *New York, New York*

DOROTHEA WALSH, *New York, New York*

FREDA SMULKER, *Long Island City, New York.*

—ARCH O. HECK, *Chairman,*
Committee on Pupil Personnel,
Guidance, and Counseling.

INTRODUCTION

WITH ONE OR TWO EXCEPTIONS the literature reviewed in this issue is limited to the period from January 1, 1933, to January 1, 1936. The general organization followed is the same that was used in the previous *Review of Educational Research* issued in October, 1933. In the introduction to that bulletin the committee expressed its position in regard to the topic of supervision and explained in some detail the difficulties encountered in finding research studies which could be clearly allocated to this topic. The position of the committee was criticized by some of the members of the Association who thought that the bulletin did not give adequate treatment to supervision. For the present bulletin the committee encountered the same type of difficulties which were described in the introduction to the 1933 report. In order to get an entirely independent treatment of the topic in the present issue, the assignment was given to Dean E. O. Melby, who was not a member of the earlier committee.

In many cases studies could be classified with equal propriety under the general heading of learning or methods of teaching. In the present issue the principle followed was to include under methods those studies which were more or less directly related to classroom situations, and to include under learning, studies which were carried on under conditions resembling the laboratory more than the classroom. Readers who are interested in either learning or methods of teaching are advised to read the chapters dealing with both topics.

As in the previous report, it should be understood that the committee does not in any sense guarantee the validity of conclusions except in the case of such studies as are the object of explicit criticism.

G. T. BUSWELL, *Chairman,*
Committee on Psychology of Learning, General
Methods of Teaching, and Supervision.

CHAPTER I

Theoretical Aspects of Learning and Transfer of Training

THEORETICAL ASPECTS OF LEARNING [1]

THE SELECTION OF STUDIES on the theoretical aspects of learning for this summary presents peculiar difficulties. One wishes to note all "significant" researches—that is, significant for education as a practical enterprise. But it is precisely at this point that selection becomes unsatisfactory. What studies *are* significant? How direct and how immediate must this significance be? Studies now passed over as not being "significant" may well, in the course of a few years, be better recognized for their true worth.

The reviewer can only set limits which to him seem to be judicious. The studies selected according to these limits are grouped and discussed below under five heads. For the benefit of readers who want to set wider or different limits the bibliography includes references (7, 8, 26, 29, 36, 37, 44, 52, 53, 70), which contain classified lists of studies on learning published in the years 1933-35, and in earlier years as well. Or they may consult the index numbers of *Psychological Abstracts* for these three years, referring to the topic "learning."

Theories of Learning

Gengerelli (26:1) recognized that it "requires presumption, if not considerable foolhardiness, to advance at the present time any neurological considerations in an effort to unify some of the many and varied phenomena which constitute the field of learning. In this respect we are suffering from a reaction to the unbridled physiological speculations in which psychologists even slightly interested in this highly important field of study have indulged." Nevertheless he ventured "the skeleton framework of a possible neurological theory." Listing five necessary postulates, he developed a theory which repudiates completely the "telephone" conception of the nervous system and which lends support, he believes, to the Gestalt position.

Washburne (69) outlined his "Closure Theory" in some detail. Finding the synaptic theory "reasonable but inadequate" with respect both to physiology and to psychology, he proposed an "electro-chemical theory." "The closure theory proposes that in the interrelation between these two polarizations (transverse and longitudinal in the resting nerve) lies the

---
[1] Chapters II and III, also on learning, necessarily raise questions concerning the theoretical aspects of learning—a fact which will lead the reader himself to supplement the references and discussions in this chapter.

explanation of all learning phenomena. It proposes that the fundamental change which occurs in human learning is a change in patterns of the polarization of resting neurones" (69:101). The theory, Washburne claimed, rests upon admitted facts of physiology and physics.

In addition to these attempted descriptions of the neurological bases of learning, mention should be made of several efforts to formulate coherent accounts of the learning process itself. Guthrie (28, 29) sought to explain all learning in terms of a single principle, namely, the law of association by temporal contiguity. McDougall (50), for the first time giving space to a chapter on learning in one of his texts, presented an outline of a theory which agreed with the principles of his particular dynamic psychology. The literature on the conditioned reflex was organized by Hull (36), and new data were offered by Liddell (47). Probably the most authoritative statement of the Gestalt theory of learning is to be found in Koffka's new text (42). McGeoch's views on learning have been summarized (52).

The Functions of Various Muscular and Neural Mechanisms

Under this head it will be possible only to sample the many available studies. The function of the cerebrum in learning has been the object of continued investigation and discussion. Lashley's summary (44) covered the work done prior to 1934 on the cerebrum as well as on other neural mechanisms. Franz and his associates (24) reported studies on cerebral dominance in visual learning.

Krechevsky (43) departed from traditional experimental practice by attempting to secure measures other than those of rate and errors in maze learning. Using 100 rats whose cortical areas had been destroyed in varying degrees he secured data which could not be explained purely in terms of the gross amounts of cortical tissue which had been destroyed. Instead, learning seemed to be a complex function of at least two anatomically delimited cortical areas. This hypothesis, Krechevsky insisted, does not contradict Lashley's views of cerebral functioning, but rather "attempts to reconcile the facts of functional specialization in the brain with the facts and principles of the 'field' theories, by postulating the presence of anatomically localized 'structuring' areas in the brain."

The extreme difficulty of experimental work on the function of subcortical mechanisms in learning was explained and illustrated by Brown (8), who also reviewed and criticized earlier studies in this field.

Harlow and Stagner (31) reported what they claim to be the first experimental attempt to test directly the importance of the end-movement in learning. None of their animals, whose skeletal muscles had been completely paralyzed by means of curare, was able even with thirty repetitions to learn a simple reaction which was mastered by control animals with less than three repetitions. The authors (31:293) saw certain implications for educational psychology: "The importance of pupil activity in the learning process is emphasized since it appears that the presentation of stimuli alone will not cause learning if no reaction is made." Such implications are, however, extremely debatable.

The last of the studies in this group presents few quantitative data. Hunter (38) criticized adversely two popular notions regarding the effects of learning. He contended that proprioception does not take over the control of behavior as learning progresses, and further that "consciousness" does not eventually lapse in favor of complete automaticity.

Controversial Articles

One does not wonder that the practical educationist loses patience when he reads the confusing and confused arguments between the various psychological schools. Reading, for example, that Gestalt represents a direct attack upon behaviorism, one is hardly prepared for the claim of a prominent exponent of its doctrines that he is a "radical behaviorist" (57). Again, understanding from the words of its advocates that Gestalt is an effective answer to mechanistic psychology, one is surprised to learn that the mechanistic conceptions of Gestalt are among its chief merits (9).

The situation is bewildering. It is more than that. To an impartial psychologist it is even "a depressing thing to note the acrimony that is allowed to creep into what purports to be scientific discussion of natural science events, the acrimony varying pretty directly with the youthfulness of the schools represented, and taking its saddest form in a vituperative reading out of the field of learning any phenomena of change or improvement that fails to qualify by coinciding with a given school's favorite formulation" (19).

On the one hand, Brown and Feder (9) attempted the difficult feat of spanking Thorndike for his "ignorance" of experimental work done by the Gestalt school, ending with a plea that Thorndike repent of his error and lead his flock back to the fold of the true faith of Gestalt. On the other hand, Curti (18), reviewing a text written by two Gestalt psychologists, finds in these authors similar evidence of "ignorance"—this time of the work of non-Gestalt psychologists on learning.

As might have been expected, the announcement of a reformulation of his views of learning by Thorndike, always a preferred target for Gestalt supporters, has been met by attack. Thus, Brown and Feder (9) attempted to show that Thorndike's five new concepts are really postulates of the Gestalt system. They are especially certain that the concept of "belongingness" is a good Gestalt term, and should be so recognized by Thorndike. The same concept of "belongingness" has been subjected to criticism and to experimentation by Hsiao (33), who secured data inconsistent with Thorndike's statements concerning the nature of "belongingness." Not the least of Hsiao's objections to the concept is that its logical implications are "undesirable for theory and experimental research."

Ogden (57) attempted to explain in simple language just what Gestalt is. "A Gestalt theory of learning posits a completely integrated behavior which can be improved by the elaboration of partial patterns within the whole." Failure to accept Gestalt is due, he thinks, to the following facts: (a) the theory was "made in Germany"; (b) it is not correctly understood; and (c) it is opposed by a "naive adherence . . . to a mechanistic interpretation of behavior and its phenomena."

Bellows (4) presented an interpretation of memory in terms of Gestalt that is full of interesting possibilities; and, as already mentioned, Koffka (42) elaborated the Gestalt view of learning into a coherent theory.

Gestalt psychology, or at least the Wheeler-Perkins formulation of Gestalt, was examined carefully by Curti (18) and by McGeoch (51) in references which can be recommended.

Applications of Gestalt to Educational Practice and Theory

Taylor (65) wrote on the significance of Gestalt psychology for engineering education, and Wheeler (71) applied his system of thinking to the teaching of arithmetic. Carr (13) saw in Gestalt psychology much which parallels the philosophy behind progressive educational theory and practice.

One study, that by McConnell (49), purported to submit the Gestalt theory of learning to a practical test in teaching the number combinations in the primary grades. A system of instruction approved as adequately meeting the criteria of the Gestalt approach was tried against a system based upon drill technics. Accuracy and time measures favored the traditional methods by statistically reliable differences. When the measures taken were those of transfer and of methods of thinking, a slight, but statistically unreliable, advantage lay with the Gestalt methods.

Common Ground among the Conflicting Schools

Three articles (18, 19, 51) already referred to have suggested the desirability of holding to the gains already made at the same time that room is made for the newer findings of Gestalt on learning.

The article by Dashiell (19) presented this position with special clarity and force. He asserted that there are many points of agreement between the different schools. These schools he subsumed "without violence" under three categories—(a) the conditioned-response school, (b) the trial-and-error school, and (c) the Gestalt school. Citing experimentation by members of the three schools, Dashiell showed that all agree with respect to eleven main features of learning:

1. The subject must be motivated.
2. A field or complication of motives exists.
3. Obstruction is offered to the principal motive.
4. Hyperactivity is aroused.
5. The response is multiple and varied.
6. The response is to relations of stimuli.
7. The most important relationship is between means and objective.
8. Selection or least action occurs.

9. The selected responses originally occur fortuitously.
10. The effects of the responses are crucial.
11. The rate of learning varies in degree from gradual to abrupt.

Divergence of opinion, Dashiell asserted, is due to (a) an apparent attempt to identify types of learning with the phylogenetic or genetic series and to (b) rationalization from the technics themselves. (Thus, the conditioned-response psychologist deals with elements in isolation and wants to interpret all behavior accordingly.) The data found and the interpretation placed thereon depend in turn upon how far the investigator goes (a) in his experimental analysis and (b) in testing the capacity to respond to relationships. In conclusion, there is "no such thing as an *isolated* conditioned response . . . or *pure* trial-and-error . . . or wholly spontaneous insight" (19:275).

Concluding Statement

Whether or not psychologists of the different schools accept the position outlined by Dashiell, that position has much to commend it both for the practical business of educating children and for the direction of educational research on learning. Quite apart from the unpleasant emotions engendered by disputation, other unfortunate outcomes are apt to result from premature and too exclusive formulations of learning theories.

In the first place, the theories, rather than learning itself, tend to become the objects of research interest. This is precisely what happened upon the announcement of Thorndike's original conception of the learning process. If part of the energy expended upon testing the validity of the law of effect, for example, had gone into the investigation of learning itself, psychology and education alike would have profited. It is to be hoped that Gestalt psychologists will not precipitate another period of misdirected effort.

In the second place, inference from any learning theory is an uncertain means of deriving educational practice (10). Witness the common citation of the principle of "learning by doing," to justify the most unlike procedures. As a consequence the principle, however valid when carefully interpreted, has led perhaps as frequently to error as to sound gain. Now the Gestalt folk, with their statements about the relations between "wholes" and "parts," about learning as "differentiation" and "emergence," are on the point of furnishing educationists with a new vocabulary which may be as empty and misleading as was the vocabulary furnished by the connectionists.

In the third place, the educationist has his own learning problems to study. These problems he must study directly, and he can do so without leaning upon any particular theory of learning. What teachers need to know is how to teach spelling, for instance. That method is best which brings the best results, regardless of whether it gains support from or lends support to, Gestalt, conditioning, or trial-and-error theories. (As a matter of fact, its effectiveness will be explained equally well by the exponent of any of the three theories, in terms of his particular theory.)

TRANSFER OF TRAINING

With the exception of neurological investigations, the studies on transfer, unlike those on the theoretical aspects of learning, can be rather completely listed, classified, and summarized.

Critical Reviews and Practical Discussions

Bond (5) outlined the present status of the doctrine of transfer as it affects the teaching of arithmetic, and Fawcett (23) showed how mathematics may actually be taught to insure transfer. The latter article is listed, not because of any quantitative data it reports, but because of the suggestiveness of its concrete detail—badly needed in a school subject for which unbridled claims of transfer values are made without any apparent responsibility for specifying means and methods.

An attempt was made by Bruce (11) to formulate five laws to cover the main objective conditions under which positive and negative transfer may be expected and can be predicted.

Orata's article (58) listed most of the educational experiments on transfer made since 1927, when his first summary appeared. "In round figures," he (58:267) stated, "70% of the studies (since 1927) support the proposition that the effect of practice is general, and that therefore transfer takes place most effectively through *conscious generalization,* whereas about 30% may be classified as supporting the theory that practice is specific and that transfer therefore takes place through *identical elements.*" Orata argued that transfer is now essentially a problem of educational engineering. The same position was taken by Uhl (68) who concluded that " 'common sense' and science agree" on the fact of transfer, and that the educational problem is to discover how best to secure transfer in abundance. Nevertheless, "for some inexplicable reason, professors of education are opposed to 'transfer.' "

To Poffenberger (59) the reason is not, however, so "inexplicable." Tracing the history of experiment and discussion on transfer, this author advanced two reasons why twentieth century faith in transfer all but disappeared during the first quarter of this century. These reasons are (a) the unfortunate emphasis of the original studies "upon *limitation* of spread of influence as against unlimited spread" and (b) the "use of the term 'identical' " to account for the results obtained.

Laboratory Studies of Transfer[2]

Nine of the fifteen subjects in Shipley's experiment (63) showed what appeared to be transfer, when they withdrew their hand upon the flash of a light which had been previously presented simultaneously with a blow on

---

[2] The term "transfer" appears in certain theories designed to explain the phenomena of retroactive inhibition (7). The reader is advised that in such discussions "transfer" applies to neural elements supposed to be active in the behavior in question, a usage which in many respects agrees with Thorndike's neural conception of identical elements.

the right cheek (the conditioned S) and an electric shock on the right index finger (unconditioned S).

Using series of paired words and numbers, accompanied by letters which were irrelevant to the learning situation, Thorndike and others (67:435) found that "a reward influences not only the rewarded connection itself but also a contemporaneous neural connection attached to the rewarded connection."

Cook (14) reported that in his experiment in cross education transfer from foot to hand and from hand to foot did not differ materially.

Hulin and Katz's study (34) showed transfer in reading Braille. The subjects taught to read by tactual methods revealed more transfer to visual reading than did those trained and tested in the reverse order.

In the case of learning stylus mazes Britt (6:116) obtained evidence "that if the associations for a learning problem are of the same strength but are of unequal age, the older association is more subject to positive transfer to a second problem than is the younger association." The author was careful to point out, however, that this difference is probably not due to the age of the association alone, but to factors that must necessarily vary with its age.

The experimental study of maze learning supplied Hull (35) with data which he employed to develop a theory of transfer much like the Thorndike theory of identical elements.

McKinney (54) trained his subjects to identify four simple geometric figures, then altered one of the figures in amounts varying from 10 percent to 30 percent and from perfect symmetry to apparent asymmetry. Transfer was measured in terms of percent of responses to the altered patterns as though they were in their original form. A definite relationship was found between degree of transfer and amount of alteration. Furthermore, symmetrical changes yielded more transfer than did those which led to asymmetry. The results are interpreted as favoring the generalization theory of transfer.

Two laboratory studies approach more nearly the types of school learning. Arons (2), using measures of serial learning (playing cards) and of problem solving (Yerkes multiple choice apparatus), obtained coefficients of correlation of only $.08 \pm .087$ and $.10 \pm .086$. Cox (16) found that a group of students set to assemble and to take to pieces the parts of an electric lamp holder learned to perform this task quickly, but showed relatively little skill in manipulating other similar materials. Another group, whose practice was accompanied by systematic instruction on points to be observed, learned the task in hand and also demonstrated relatively greater skill with other materials.

Transfer in the School Subjects

Two investigations deal with mathematics. McConnell (49) produced evidence that instruction which puts the emphasis on meaning in primary numbers may result in improved types of quantitative thinking which are susceptible to transfer. Lehman (46) found that only 4 percent of his college students solved arithmetic problems by algebraic methods which they showed they knew. His data point "forcibly to the fact that application of knowledge is one type of transfer" and that "the existence of identical elements is of itself no guarantee that transfer will take place."

In an unusually careful statistical analysis in which every precaution was taken to control selective factors, Whelden (72) investigated the effect of Latin upon the quality of other academic work at Yale. Students who had had more than thirty hours of Latin (and Greek) were compared with those who had had less than this amount. In terms of average marks the extra study of Latin seemed to function only in the fields most closely related (French composition, for example), in which the subjectmatter was similar to some extent. No evidence at all was secured for the extended study of Latin as "an intellectual discipline, serving to extend the scope of intellectual capacity in whatever field it might be applied" (72:497).

In another study (40), involving foreign language, 202 pupils in grades 7-12, 148 with varying experience with one to three languages, were tested on their ability (a) to translate and (b) to detect the meaning of certain words in a Spanish article on football. Transfer values were demonstrated from both sets of measures. The first year of foreign language study seemed to make the largest contribution. In subsequent study it mattered little whether the work was concentrated in a single language or was spread over as many as three.

Cooper (15) tested "the hypothesis that functional grammar taught at the college level (freshman year) and deliberately taught for transfer will carry over into composition ability." Her results, impaired somewhat by experimental difficulties, showed that the hypothesis is at least tenable.

Two studies have been made of transfer in spelling. Gilbert's investigation (27), made in grade 9, showed that pupils profited considerably in their ability to spell new words merely from meeting these words in reading. The best spellers profited most from such reading. Improvement was not dependent upon a slow rate of reading. Gates (25) reported a large-scale study (3,800 pupils, grades 2-8, 106 classes), in which two types of spelling instruction were compared. Half of the children learned each word as a specific unit. The other half studied the words in special groupings and had various generalizations and rules called to their attention. The end-tests showed (a) equal ability to spell the words set for each grade and to spell familiar words which permitted use of generalizations and rules, but (b) superiority for the generalization groups in spelling new words to which their rules would apply and in converting unstudied base forms by adding suffixes, etc.

Bedell (3) and Downing (21) discussed generalization, inference, and "scientific thinking" as these abilities are set as outcomes of instruction in science.

Jacobson (39) and Salisbury (61, 62) investigated the carry-over of improved study and reading habits to the content subjects. Salisbury's subjects (grades 7, 9, and 12), who were shown the possible applications of their newly acquired technics, clearly revealed transfer. In Jacobson's first experiment, in which the training in work-type reading was given in the English classes (grade 9), no transfer to other subjects was noted. In the second experiment, in which the training was given in the content of the subjects themselves, application of the new study technics was clearly observable.

Character Training

In a statistical investigation admittedly "preliminary," Sinclair and Tolman (64) failed to obtain any evidence that the study of science increases "open-mindedness." Their method, that of comparing measures from different collegiate institutions and from different classes within the same institution, suffered from the usual influence of selective factors.

A series of investigations have been reported on the value of *incidental* moral and character instruction in connection with plane geometry (1), the social studies (12, 41), athletics (30), and Latin (55). In the main, the conclusions agreed in being negative.

On the other hand, the effect of *direct* instruction on such traits as honesty, leadership, and attitudes toward war, patriotism, etc. (17, 22, 32, 48, 56, 60), seems to be positive. Thus, Longstreet (48) in perhaps the most carefully controlled of these studies found that changed attitudes were to be expected in the high-school social studies only when a deliberate attempt was made to instil new attitudes. The report by Hobson (32) is especially interesting as showing a method for deriving a program of direct instruction in a moral trait—honesty in this case.

Concluding Statement

It would seem to be high time to abandon the controversy between the relative merits of the "generalization" and the "identical elements" (and now the Gestalt "functional similarity") theories of transfer. The dispute served a useful purpose by keeping the issue alive during a critical period, but there seems to be no purpose in prolonging it.

The Judd theory (generalization) has consistently emphasized the importance of *subjective* factors in transfer. It is possible to interpret Thorndike's definition of identical elements [3] so as to include this same recognition of subjective factors. On the other hand, unfortunately, whether Thorndike meant it so or not, identical elements have commonly been regarded as wholly *objective* in nature. As a consequence, attempts have been made time and time again to explain the presence or absence of expected transfer

---

[3] "By identical elements are meant mental processes which have the same cell action in the brain as their physical correlate. It is of course often not possible to tell just what features of two mental abilities are thus identical" (66:269).

in terms of the external conditions of learning. As a matter of fact, neither of the two theories provides a basis for prediction. Both are *ex post facto* explanations: they account for the event after it has happened. There is transfer if the learner has generalized, which is to say, if he has observed identity—or vice versa. The question promptly resolves itself if one asks the question, Identical *to whom?* To experimenter or to subject, to teacher or to pupil? If this position is sound, as Orata (58:270) seems to think, then it becomes almost an absurdity to say that there is no transfer in spite of the presence of identical elements.

The position taken by Orata (58) and by Uhl (68) seems to be the sensible one so far as education is concerned. The possibility and the desirability of transfer cannot be questioned. The problem then becomes one of so organizing the materials and methods of instruction to guarantee the largest possible amount of positive transfer.

CHAPTER II
Types of Learning and General Conditions Affecting Learning

FOLLOWING THE TREATMENT of the theoretical aspect of learning and transfer of training in the preceding chapter, this chapter will review studies of certain types of learning, such as motor learning and skill, memory and association, the formation of concepts, and problem solving, and will also deal with some of the conditions affecting learning. All studies dealing with the motivation of learning, individual differences, and the relation of general intelligence to learning are reserved for treatment in Chapter III.

A number of excellent studies relating to learning in the various school subjects have been omitted from those treated in this chapter due to the fact that special numbers of the *Review of Educational Research* (92, 125) are devoted to the psychology of school subjects. However, many of the studies of the psychology of school subjects consist in applications of basic studies of learning, such as are reported in this chapter. Some other investigations which deal with the same types of learning reported here are reserved for treatment in Chapter IV, where they are reviewed as illustrations of the way methods of teaching affect learning.

Motor Learning and Skill

Ten of the studies reviewed in this chapter have to do with the formation of skills of one type or another. Since most of these experiments are basic in character, the findings are applicable to a great many of the kinds of motor learning which are carried on in the schools. Mattson (119) studied the relationship between the complexity of the skill to be acquired and the shape of the learning curve with young children. She found that the patterns of learning in the case of simple and complex skills are quite different and that while in the case of simple skills practice tended to make the different subjects more alike, the reverse was true in the case of complex skills where the greater the practice the larger were the differences in performance of the different individuals. From the data of the experiment she concluded that no amount of practice may be able to make children of low-level ability equal the performance of children of very high-level ability. Smith and Fitch (137) reported a target experiment in which seventy-five men were used as subjects. They studied the rate of learning when postural cues were artificially distorted while aiming at the target, and then followed this by studying the duration of the habits formed when the subjects returned to their natural posture, thereby getting a measure of both the establishment of a new habit and the interference of an old one.

They found that return to the old, that is, the regular posture, was impeded about two-thirds as much as the original habit impeded the performance when the posture was artificially distorted. The findings have a significant application to the many school tasks where habit interference constitutes one of the important factors in new learning. Hyde (101) used archery as the medium for studying certain characteristics of motor skill. She found a definite practice effect at each distance and that achievement in archery follows the usual form of the learning curve. She found no marked positive correlations between ability in archery and mental ability, as measured by the Otis Test. Scott and Henninger (133) reported an interesting body of data showing the relationship between length and difficulty of materials in motor learning, and also compared the results in motor learning with those in verbal learning. They found that a considerable similarity exists between motor learning and verbal learning in respect to the relationships between length of materials and relative difficulty of mastering them, but found that longer materials are somewhat more difficult in motor learning than in verbal learning.

Several studies have to do with the basic problem of method in motor learning. Crafts and Allen (84) studied two groups of subjects in learning to trace mirror images with both hands, in which they found the successive method produced better results than the simultaneous method. The implications of this study touch upon so many fields, for example, learning to play a piano or to write on a typewriter, that the reviewer should point out a considerable lack of agreement which still exists among the conclusions of various studies which are in the literature. Young (151) studied the comparative efficiency of varied and constant methods of sensori-motor learning. He found a superiority of 30 percent for the constant method as compared with the varied method in the groups of 162 subjects which he studied. He also found that a directed constant method was superior to an undirected constant method. The experiment had to do with such simple types of learning as ball tossing, quoits, and "gowf." Although the relative efficiency of varied and constant methods is a perennial one in educational discussions, the contributions of experimental studies to the solution of the problem would seem to be more promising if they dealt with the higher learning processes, which are more characteristic of typical situations to which such studies are applied.

Two reports deal with the part-whole method as applied to motor learning. Shay (134) made a brief report of the results of two groups of subjects in learning the "upstart on a horizontal bar," in which he found that the groups using the whole-learning method achieved superior results to the group using the part-learning method. Hanawalt (96), in using a maze experiment, also found the whole method superior to the part method or a modified part method. He observed that the patterns were easier to learn when they were kept unbroken, and then pointed out some of the causes why part methods are wasteful.

Two reports by Beebe (75, 76) dealt with the motor learning of young children. One of the studies was a very elaborate report of the effect of nutrition on motor ability, in which she found individual differences to be marked and highly variable. Other findings of the study were reported in detail. The report deserves careful reading by any who are interested in this problem. Her second study made an analysis of data from a controlled aiming test in which hand-eye coordinations were measured. Again she noted marked individual differences, and in general found that boys were superior to girls.

Memorization

In spite of the enormous number of studies of memory which have appeared in the literature, experimenters still find specific problems to investigate. Gordon (94) restudied the effect of practice in memorizing poetry, using ten sonnets in paired groups of five each. Her results were quite consistent in showing that the fifth trial was the best in the series, but from the evidence at hand she was not able to say whether this was due to possible differences in the difficulty of the material or whether it was due to position in the practice series. The fact that the improvement from Trial 1 to Trial 5 was fairly steady tended to show that position in the series is the primary factor. J. A. McGeoch (112) also observed that practice changes the percent learned in successive units of learning time. With unpracticed subjects and difficult materials he found that the curve of memorization tends to be S shaped. Mitchell (122) studied the presumed warming up effect in memorization. Experimenting with two lists of ten three-place numbers he found no reliable quantitative differences between number of trials or number of errors in learning the two lists consecutively, and concluded that there is no conspicuous warming up effect. In a second report the same writer (123) concluded that the effect of primacy is much more widespread and definite than the effect of finality. In still a third study, Mitchell (124) found that in memorizing three-place numbers the most frequent error was to give no response, the next frequent to give a three-digit response, with errors of one and two digits respectively appearing least commonly.

Ross (132) reported a study dealing with the technic of experimentation in which he showed the optimum order for the presentation of pairs in the method of paired comparisons. Persons who are setting up experiments of this type will find Ross' study worth careful reading.

Studies Using Mazes of Various Types

Ten studies relating to the various aspects of memory were carried on through the use of some type of maze situation. While many of the maze situations are subject to the same types of criticism which have been brought against the use of nonsense syllables, nevertheless, the susceptibility of maze situations to specific control makes them very useful for studying certain types of learning problems. The kinesthetic cues in learning a maze have frequently been described as the outstanding factor in the process. Chase (82) took exception to this view and proposed that maze learning is chiefly ideational rather than kinesthetic motor learning. Insight comes gradually as the maze pattern is grasped and is coordinated in some symbolic manner by the mind. Students of psychology who are interested in the concepts of insight will doubtless find that the maze furnishes a flexible technic for their purpose.

Kellogg and White (102) employed a stylus maze to test Dunlap's theory of learning. They used seventy-five adult subjects divided into three groups. One group used the ordinary method of trial and error in learning the maze; a second group followed the method of repeating blind alleys as a test of Dunlap's Beta hypothesis; while a third group was used as a control. They found some support of Dunlap's theory as far as it relates to frequency and exercise. McKinney (117) reported a study of the retention of interrupted learning activities, using data from learning stylus mazes. He tested the hypothesis that interruption of a task before its mastery leads to better retention than non-interruption. Experimenting with both maze and verbal learning McKinney found some beneficial effects of interruption, particularly where the interruption comes near to the end of the task which is being learned. His findings have a relation to the distribution of practice which should be studied by persons preparing drill and practice materials in any field.

An extensive study of the relationship between anticipation and erroneous responses was reported by Lumley (107). He used evidence from finger mazes and also tested pupils in anticipation of numbers in a radio speech. He found that pupils' memory for numbers given in a radio talk was in accordance with the anticipation generalization. The study contained some significant implications for methods of teaching. Smith (136) presented a brief report of a maze experiment, using forty subjects, in which he showed the values of specific cues in maze learning.

An elaborate study of the behavior of young children in body mazes was reported by Wenger (148) in which different maze patterns were used. Above a necessary age minimum he found neither mental nor chronological age to be a factor in determining rapidity of learning in the types of maze situations employed. Individual differences in motivating conditions were considered of great importance. The study is a good example both of a careful experimental technic and of good scientific analysis and evaluation of a large body of data. Duncan (85) reported a comparative study of learning a finger maze by blind and sighted subjects. She found that the blind group made more errors and that the sighted group had a wider range of performance. The blind group experienced greater difficulties in the early part of the learning but found them easier during the later trials. Thurstone (143) developed a quantitative method to use in analyzing maze performances so as to reveal functional continuities that are not ordinarily revealed by the customary methods of analyzing maze data. The statistical technic proposed was described in some detail. Wagner (146) reported a study to demonstrate the number maze as a useful technic for the study of the nature of learning.

While few of the maze experiments deal with situations which are typical of those found in school, they possess a value for the educational psychologist in that they aid in analyzing and abstracting certain elements of learning which should be restudied in typical school situations.

Forming Concepts, Problem Solving, and Insight

An interesting study of the value of positive and negative instances in learning new concepts was reported by Smoke (138). In describing the characteristics of a sedan automobile a positive method would be to point out that this car is a sedan and has these and these characteristics, whereas a negative method would be to point to cars which are not sedans and describe their characteristics. The study reported dealt with both the time of learning the new concept and the accuracy of the concept once learned. The investigator found no statistically significant difference in the time of learning by either method, but found that negative instances do improve the accuracy of the concepts which are formed. He also reported that most subjects preferred to learn by both positive and negative instances. The report dealt with a problem which has been studied so much less than the topic of memory, reviewed in the last two sections, that it would seem to furnish a profitable field for more frequent investigation. Furthermore, the problem occurs as such in most typical school situations, and is significant at all levels of education.

A study of the application of two divergent theories of learning was reported by McConnell (108) using arithmetic as the medium for study. A comparison was made of the learning of two groups of pupils, one of which follows the theories of the connectionist, whereas the other follows the theories of the Gestaltist. The data show that the connectionist group is superior in immediate and automatic responses, whereas the Gestaltist group is superior in the transfer of training and in manipulating the number facts learned in mature ways. The problem involved in the study is significant and the hypothesis presented should be tested in other school situations in subsequent studies.

Morgan (126) reported the characteristics of problem-solving behavior of adults. His data were drawn from three sources: a puzzle experiment and two experiments making use of mental mazes. Another study of problem solving was reported by Hartmann (97) who analyzed the factors involved in "insightful learning" and compared them with factors found in the trial-and-error learning in the solution of problems. Data were drawn from a series of tests of various forms. Different varieties of insight were identified, such as immediate, gradual, partial, complete, and sudden. The results indicated that insight learning is present as an end product of trial-and-error activity, and that an act is learned only when insight has been achieved. The study was limited by the difficulty involved in giving any adequate and satisfying definition of the concept "insight" and in relating it to the terminology which was common before this word was introduced in its technical sense. Another study involving the role of insight in analytical thinking was reported by Henry (99). Thirty-two high-school students solved 9 originals and 14 theorems in geometry, and their reactions were studied to test the operation of insight. Insight as defined by the author was found in certain instances of solving geometric originals, although he reported that this does not characterize the typical behavior of successful students. A bibliography of twenty-eight articles is appended to the study.

Alteneder (73) proposed the use of jig-saw puzzles as useful material for classroom demonstration to show the various characteristics of the learning curve and also to show fluctuations in efficiency, the effect of physiological limits, plateaus, etc. The learning curves reported in his study were negatively accelerated.

Two studies were reported which have to do with learning in college classes. Welborn (147) reported a series of measurements made of the retention of meaningful material by recognition-type tests, showing results which emphasized the use of meaningful material. Cooke (83) reported two experiments in learning educational statistics from which he concluded that an equal distribution of the students' time should be given to working problems and to reading statistical literature.

Retention, Recall, and Forgetting

A considerable group of studies was found dealing with the conditions concerning the permanence of learning. Kolberg (103) reported a test given to 236 pupils in May and again in September to measure the amount of forgetting which occurred during the summer vacation. For easy material he found that improvement rather than forgetting takes place during the summer. For the difficult materials the amount of forgetting was roughly proportional to the degree of difficulty. He found no relationship between intelligence and retention, except that difficult materials were retained better by pupils having I.Q.'s above 120 than by pupils having I.Q.'s at the low 90's. In another study the investigators (89) reported a series of eight experiments with something over 1500 college students, using meaningful prose. They found the paradoxical situation of a progressive increase in recognition scores over a two-month interval, without practice. Furthermore, they found little relationship between this type of negative forgetting and the degree of mastery of the subjectmatter learned. Easley (87) reported an analysis of the curves of learning and forgetting code material, and showed that learning and forgetting curves of the traditional type may not accurately represent the true process of learning and forgetting.

A study reported briefly by Tyler (145) showed that the learning of scientific principles and their applications is more permanent than the learning of information and technical terms. The data for this study were drawn from 82 college students in classes in zoology. Although the study was brief it dealt with an extremely important problem, and its implications have a marked significance for the curriculum maker. Eurich (90) reported a study of the retention of knowledge acquired in a course in general psychology, using a new type test of 150 items. He found that after a nine-month interval the median score on a general psychology test was at the third percentile, as compared with a test of the same group at the end of the course. It is to be regretted that the study did not make possible the type of comparison reported by Tyler (145). Bedell (74) reported a study of the relationship between the ability to recall and the ability to infer in specific learning situations. He concluded that the ability to recall specific facts and the ability to infer a generalized idea from these facts were different abilities. The low I.Q. subjects, that is, those in the lower fourth of the group, had greater difficulty in inferring than had the brighter members of the group.

Four studies by J. A. McGeoch, and J. A. McGeoch and McKinney (114, 115, 116) deal with the general problem of retroactive inhibition in learning. They considered that forgetting is, to a large extent, the function of the events interpolated between learning and the measurements of retention. In view of the fact that the permanence of learning is so often considered purely in terms of the materials learned rather than in the subsequent learning experiences, this group of studies is of a good deal of importance to the school. Another study dealing with the same problem was reported by Gibson and Gibson (93) in which they showed that the interpolation of a task similar to the primary learning either in operation or in material results in poorer retention than does the interpolation of a task similar in neither operation nor material. Considerations of this sort have received entirely too little attention in relation to the organization of curriculum material and the programming of pupil activities. Two studies of reminiscence by G. O. McGeoch (109, 110) showed that reminiscence, which is the improvement in memory after an interval of time without intervenient formal review or relearning, occurs independently of casual revival or intentional review. This phenomenon of reminiscence is another factor conditioning permanence which has received little consideration in methods of teaching at the present time.

General Factors Which Condition Learning

A miscellaneous group of studies is reviewed in this section of the chapter. In the main there is little excuse for grouping them together except to say that they do not fit in conveniently in the previous sections.

Educators who trust greatly to the efficacy of drill have fared badly at the hands of investigators during the last three years. Numerous studies have shown the inadequacy of sheer repetition. Thorndike (139) reported a study of the changes in the relative frequency with which letters are given in response to words, where the letters are neither right nor wrong. From the data in the study he (139:428) generalized as follows: "When any one connection is as satisfactory as any other the brain's choice amongst them depends upon causes about which little is known, because such studies have been so little studied. . . . Two things we know about them. They are sensitive and shift notably; their shifts are not in the direction of strengthening the more frequent or strong at the expense of the less frequent or weak." In another study Thorndike (142) found the law of effect much more important than sheer repetition, while in a third study (140) he pointed out as a basal fact in mental dynamics that the last of two different connections made with a situation is stronger regardless of what happens before or after to that situation.

Siipola and Israel (135) reported a significant study related to habit interference in which they showed that when two incompatible habits are learned successively, so that interference appears in the learning of the second habit, there is in the initial stages of training an inverse relationship between the amount of interference and the stage of previous training, whereas in the advanced stages of training the relationship is positive. Maslow (118) reported a body of data on the effect of varying time intervals between acts of learning where the learning consisted of mastering one hundred lists of nine meaningful terms. He found mutual interference as well as retroactive inhibition. Short rest periods between practices were beneficial. Lepley (106) studied a factor in incidental learning by measuring in two large classes the amount of retention of names in the roll call. He found that retention was decidedly greater for names preceding and following the student's own name with somewhat higher scores for those preceding than for those following. Although the study is simple there are some rather interesting implications involved in the findings.

Carter (80), in studying errors in learning in the sixth and seventh grades, found a tendency for children to replace correct unpleasant words with incorrect pleasant ones. Factors of this type have received relatively little emphasis up to the present time in studies of learning, but they are doubtless important elements in many school situations. Emmons (88) studied the relationship between self-assurance and skill in a group of sixteen young children. She found a positive relationship between self-assurance and skill, and that both increase with chronological age. She found also that self-assurance varied directly with intelligence, although the measure of self-assurance consisted of a subjective rating and is open to some question. Betts (77) has made a rather extensive study of time limits versus work limits in learning. He found that the time-limit method produced more errors than the work-limit method. However, other factors of learning seemed to be more significant than either of these two. He found that the work-limit method was of greater value in raising the rank of an individual and in decreasing individual differences.

Reviews of Learning with Bibliographies

Three reports consisted primarily in critical reviews of studies of learning and contained sufficient bibliographies to be of considerable interest to the general student of learning. J. A. McGeoch (113) wrote an extensive critical article dealing with the learning and retention of verbal materials, to which he appended a bibliography of 244 titles. The reference affords an excellent guide for a general survey of this field. Peterson (129) presented a critical article on certain aspects of learning to which a bibliography of one hundred titles is appended. A third general review (128), somewhat more limited in scope, dealt with a critical evaluation of forty-eight experiments on transfer of training. In this article the authors found that they can consider only six of the forty-eight studies as valid, with four more as of possible validity. The reference will supply a useful background for students in educational psychology who wish to become acquainted with the significant experiments in the literature of transfer.

CHAPTER III

Motivation, Emotional Responses, Maturation, Intelligence, and Individual Differences

Effect of Motivation on Learning

MOTIVATION, as used in many of the studies reported here, is rather an inclusive term. It includes those factors which in an individual and in the situation determine the nature of his acts. For this reason, reward and punishment, annoyance, knowledge of results, and purposing are classified as belonging to the general term "motivation."

There seems to be no doubt, at least judging by the number of studies reported, that the law of effect as stated by Thorndike has caused more controversy and more experimentation during the last three years than any other question of motivation. At least thirty-nine different articles dealing with rewards and punishment, all reporting one or more experiments have been published. The results of the experiments are conflicting, although there is a great deal of evidence showing that rewards have a beneficial effect on learning. The degree of benefit received from reward varies with the type and amount of rewards given. The effect of punishment is more doubtful.

Brenner (156) described an experiment in which he used 403 pupils of twelve third-grade classes. The classes were divided into the following six groups: immediate praise, immediate control, immediate blame, delayed praise, delayed control, and delayed blame. The groups were matched by average chronological age, I.Q., and initial spelling tests. The learning task consisted of learning eighty words from the Ayres Measuring Ability in Spelling. The examiner praised the work or blamed the pupils or said nothing as the case might be after the pupils had taken spelling tests. The author concluded that immediate praise tends to be more effective than delayed praise and immediate blame and delayed blame tend to be equally effective. No difference statistically significant was found between the recall performance of the different groups.

Crafts and Gilbert (160), in an experiment with one hundred college students divided into two groups with twenty-five men and twenty-five women each, found that punishment for error was advantageous, not only for the learning of a maze but also for retention of learning. Gilbert and Crafts (168) reported another study, the aim of which was to determine the effect upon the learning and retention of a stylus maze of giving an auditory signal for error during the learning. The experimental group, after a week, were markedly superior in recall, in relearning, and in percent saved on the number of per trial errors.

Guthrie (172) concluded from a study on reward and punishment that stimuli acting at the time of satisfaction or annoyance tend to reexcite whatever behavior was in evidence at the time. Muenzinger (194) reported on the effect of motivation in learning with three groups of white rats. In the first experiment the rats formed a black and white discrimination habit. The first group of rats was shocked in the correct alley, the second group was shocked in the wrong alley, and the third group was not shocked at all. The "no shock" group was definitely inferior to either of the other two. The "shock wrong" group was slightly better than the "shock right" group. His results contradict rather flatly that part of the law of effect which deals with the after-effects of annoyers. In another experiment, Muenzinger (195) tried to discover the function of punishment in learning upon college students. No significant differences were found between the groups that received an electric shock and those that did not. The same conclusions were reached whether the shocks were for right or for wrong responses.

After an experiment with white rats, Ni (196) presented data to show that the punishment for errors in learning to run a maze increased the efficiency in both learning and relearning. Ni (197) repeated his experiment using two groups of white rats, one of which was punished and the other was not. The punishment for errors during the learning of the first maze had not only a beneficial effect on the learning but also had a beneficial effect upon the mastery of a second maze.

Stephens (217) stated that the results of his study indicate that reward strengthens and punishment weakens connections even with initially weak connections. In another study with college students as the subjects, Stephens (218) found that punishment has no uniform stamping-in influence but that its effects vary with the conditions. "When conveyed by flashing lights, punishment stamps-in. When conveyed by a spoken word, punishment stamps-out. When a signal carrying no information of success is given, it has a decided stamping-in effect. When the same signal tells when the subject is right, strengthening is enhanced. When the same signal tells the subject that he is wrong, the strengthening is diminished." The author concluded that punishment and reward seem to have distinctly opposite effects, "if not equal."

Garrison (167) reported that there is a close relation between motivation and learning. He stated that interest, knowledge of progress, praise and reproof, and competition are important factors in motivation.

Crafts and Gilbert (159) presented data to show that knowledge of results on maze learning and retention has no significant effect. Thorndike (225), in an experiment with nineteen college students as subjects, came to the conclusion that the effect of relevant reward in general is not great. However, he found that money reward is effective. His evidence favored the decision that a satisfying after-effect strengthens somewhat the connection to which it is attached, even though it is irrelevant to the purpose in the interest of which the connection was made and highly incongruous with the cravings and expectations of the person at the time. Thorndike (220) reported another study on the direct action of rewards upon mental connections and their indirect action versus the stimulation of inner equivalents of the connections. Human adults were used as subjects. Results indicated a small and unreliable advantage from inner repetition for multiple response situation.

The amount of strengthening that can be attributed to inner repetition is perhaps ten percent. The strengthening by the attachment of the satisfying after-effect in multiple choice experiments in which a new situation follows very soon after the after-effect of the previous connection is almost exclusively due to direct action on the connection, not to the incitement of an inner repetition to it.

Regarding the influence of punishment, Thorndike with Lorge, Tuckman, Stephens, and Rock, after several experiments, concluded that in multiple choice learning by human subjects where the situation vanishes immediately after the choice, is replaced by another, and recurs only after intervals of fifty to two hundred seconds filled by other situations and responses, a connection punished by the announcement of "wrong," or "wrong" plus one or more electric shocks, or "wrong" plus a money fine is strengthened by the occurrence in spite of the annoying after-effect (228:72).

Similar results were found by Rock (208) in a word learning experiment in which fifty educated adults and seventy-five children twelve and thirteen years of age in grades six, seven, and eight participated. In an experiment in which ball-tossing was the task, 125 educated adults were the subjects. For the children at least, the mere satisfaction at success in these tasks was small in comparison with the satisfaction at even the smallest money reward and the increments of satisfaction with increases in the money reward were presumably large. Rock stated that neither the addition of a money reward nor the increase in its amount causes a demonstrably greater strengthening over that found by the mere announcement of "right."

Thorndike and Forlano (223) reported on five experiments. In each experiment there were ten subjects, all boys, ten to eleven years of age. Although money was used as the reward for improvement and the reward was increased with the number of trials, the authors concluded that the increase of money seems not beneficial. In a second experiment with new subjects where smaller amounts of money were given as rewards, the gains were smaller. In their conclusion they stated, "We can then be fairly certain that the increases of the money part of the reward acts to increase the rate of learning up to 0.4¢ but the increase to 0.8¢ seems to do as much or more harm as it does good by arousing and maintaining attention to the work, satisfaction at success, and the like." They added, however, that the evidence is not conclusive.

Eisenson (165), in an experiment with 120 college students, found evidence to support the work of Thorndike and Lorge, namely, that multiple choice learning is a function of rewards and not of punishment. Irwin and others (177) repeated Thorndike and Rock's experiment trying to control additional factors which in their opinion afford no evidence of learning without knowledge.

Jensen (178) studied the effect of punishment by electric shock on performance. Fifty-five college students were selected as subjects. Eleven pairs of students learned a maze. With each error an electric shock was given. Eleven other pairs learned without the electric shock. They discovered that the control groups did better than the experimental groups. In fact, the control group learned the maze in 14.64 trials, while the experimental group required 19.59 trials.

Many current articles are critical statements and reviews of other published articles. Waters (230) reviewed seventy-three articles which criticize Thorndike's original statement of the law of effect. Stephens (216) presented a theoretical discussion of the need for change in the interpretation of the law of effect, and H. E. Jones (179) studied the laws of emphasis and effect in children's learning. He described three experimental situations which were used to test trial-and-error conditions. The subjects were 150 junior high-school pupils. He concluded that laws of emphasis and effect are inadequate in explaining trial-and-error learning in the experimental conditions used.

Gilliland (169) reported that in an experiment with rats in which such factors as primacy, recency, and intensity were held constant, the law of effect *is* a factor in learning. The rats learned to go where they were fed, but they learned more slowly than in regular maze running. Gulliksen (171) developed an equation of the learning curve based on Thorndike's law of effect which gives the relation between cumulative errors and cumulative correct responses. He presented only theoretical data to show how the equation is used. Gray (170) gave a preliminary report of the effect of fatigue on learning and the selection and consumption of food materials. The report appears to offer many interesting suggestions for an experimental set-up, but no results were given.

Effect of Knowledge of Results on Learning

Several studies have been made to determine the effect of knowledge of achievement upon learning, only three of which are given here. Ross (209), in an experiment with 467 college students in which he gave full knowledge, partial knowledge, vague knowledge, and no knowledge of their results on a series of tests, concluded that a knowledge of progress such as is afforded by students seeing their test papers or hearing their test scores need not be a factor of practical significance in the ordinary classroom situation in college. Smith (213) described an experiment in which students estimate the length of a line without knowledge of the results. He gave no data. Waters (231), after having students judge the length of strips of cardboard, concluded that there is no relation between improvement and degree of information given. In another experiment he found that the improvement is roughly proportional to the degree of information given. He concluded that knowledge of results helps in complex learning tasks but is of little help in the simple learning tasks.

Other Types of Motivation

Drever (162) described an experiment with a series of geometrical diagrams some of which had a certain feature in common. He found that insight into the nature of the common feature developed gradually rather than suddenly. Keys (181, 182), Meyer (193), and Remmers (206) studied the effect of tests on learning. Keys (182), in an experiment to study the influence on learning and retention of weekly as opposed to monthly tests, found that retention is 7 percent superior when tests are administered without warning from five to thirteen weeks after the corresponding periodic tests. Keys (181) also presented data to show the influence of true-false items on specific learning. The tests were given to 286 students in educational psychology five weeks after the completion of the subject.

Rankin (204) called attention to four community factors that affect learning. These factors were (a) the public agencies, (b) the private commercial agencies, (c) the organizations in the community that affect learning more or less directly, and (d) the characteristics of the neighborhood.

Hansen (174), in attempting to find the effect of motion pictures upon the retention of informational learning, selected pupils in grades seven, eight, and nine as subjects. Eighty-two pairs matched by intelligence and previous knowledge of the subject were used. The results showed that the pupils using motion pictures surpassed the control group by 12.1 percent and by 17.5 percent on the permanency of learning. He concluded that motion pictures are an aid to learning and that knowledge gained by pictures is fully as permanent in its nature as that gained through reading and oral presentation.

Effect of Emotional Responses on Learning

No less than eleven studies and several more individual experiments have been made to determine the effect of emotional responses on learning. In general, it would seem that pleasant experiences, and the arousal of pleasurable emotions are more conducive to learning than unpleasant experiences or the arousal of unpleasant emotions. Olson (198) called attention to the need for considering the emotional behavior of children in the school program. Moreover, there is some evidence to show that the act of learning is, itself, accompanied by an emotional reaction. Baker (152) found evidence that pulse and breathing rates increased over the normal, while the subject was attempting to learn. There was generally an increase in the amount learned when an artificial change in pulse occurred as a result of stimulation.

Carter and H. E. Jones (158) studied the response to pleasant, unpleasant, and indifferent words. They found that the words were learned most efficiently in the order just given. The differences in the results were statistically reliable. Although the retention of the learning is the same, the difference between the retention of unpleasant and indifferent words is not reliable. Carter, H. E. Jones, and Shock (157) reported another study of 102 children in grades six and seven. The task was the learning of a list of words classified as pleasant, unpleasant, and indifferent. The ease of learning correlated .40 with estimated pleasantness, .49 with galvanometric deflections, and .65 with an emotional indifference. The learning scores of individuals were highest for pleasant words, next for unpleasant words, and lowest for indifferent words. In this experiment the group differences between any two of the three categories were statistically reliable.

White and Ratcliff (233) reported three experiments to determine the memory value of pleasant and unpleasant words. The results of these three experiments, in which the subjects were 150 students in psychology, support a theory of active forgetting. In the first experiment practically no difference was found between pleasant and unpleasant words in the ease of learning. In the other two experiments a difference was found. More pleasant than unpleasant words were remembered in delayed recall in every experiment. The longer the time interval the greater the superiority of the pleasant words over the unpleasant words. Eisenson (165) also found that a pleasant word generally caused a higher percent of repetition than an unpleasant word but slightly less than an indifferent word. The differences, however, were not statistically reliable.

Whitely and Blankfort (234) studied the influence of certain prior conditions on learning. In one experiment three kinds of learning material were employed, letter-digit substitution, poetry, and monosyllabic words. In another experiment three types of words were utilized which differed in each instance with regard to affective tone, namely, suffering and dejection, joy or hilarity, and neutral. They came to the conclusion that when using a story as a means of arousing a set of joy or sorrow, the best learning is obtained under the normal condition for the three kinds of learning material. With reference to the utilization of pictures as a means to arousing an emotional set, the total scores revealed no significant differences for the three conditions of learning.

Patrick (200) attempted to find the influence that certain emotional stimuli have on the types of reaction made by normal human adults—college students. The emotional stimuli consisted of pain by means of electric shock, cold shower, and blast of a horn. The results revealed a marked reduction in efficiency in the quality of types of reaction tendencies made by these adults while operating under the influence of emotional stimuli. McKinney (192) reported a study of 135 college students divided into three groups who learned a maze and a list of twelve nonsense syllables, performed a motor task, and solved a group of multiplication problems. While one group went through these tasks, an automatic clock buzzed each minute. In another group, in addition to the above set-up, the subjects were told that the average person could do the task in six minutes and at the end of that time an automatic interval timer rang. The third group worked under normal laboratory conditions. Errors in the task increased greatly with the introduction of the clock ringing each minute and increased more with the suggestion of intellectual inferiority. Time and trials were affected in both directions and both tended to increase. There was a noticeable change in the expressed attitude of the subjects as well as a change in social behavior and steadiness of movement due to the experimental conditions. The results evince that emotion affects learning and that a strong emotion cannot act as a motive in an intellectual task or a skill.

Whitely (235) reported four different experiments concerning the influence of music upon learning. In one experiment the subjects learned joy and sorrow words with music as a prior condition. In the second experiment monosyllabic words were learned with music as context during the learning period. In the third experiment, monosyllabic words were learned and after an interval of fifteen minutes recalled and relearned by the anticipation method. Four different types of music were employed in this experiment. The results showed that both fast and slow music exert a slight detrimental influence upon learning. When memorization is accomplished by the anticipation method, the fewest number of trials are needed with slow music and the greatest number of trials under the song condition. Recall scores fifteen minutes after the learning do not reveal any significant differences although the song condition appears to be best for retention. In the memorization of poetry the results indicated clearly the superiority of the normal condition over the two musical conditions "Largo" and "The Storm." Least returns were obtained when music of a tempestuous character served as context.

Zyve and Smith (238) studied the effect of radio music accompaniment on accomplishment in school work. They concluded that there was no significant difference in the results of tests taken normally and those accompanied by jazz instrumental music. In fact, they found no evidence to show that the playing of music in the home while pupils were studying either helped or hindered their learning.

Hartmann and Hamm (176) reported an interesting device to find the proportions of a course which students in educational psychology were interested in and which parts affected them pleasurably.

Effect of Maturation on Learning

The relation of maturity, in terms of chronological age, to learning is reported in fourteen studies. These studies deal with all age levels of humans. More studies of infants are reported than of any other group. Wenger and Williams (232) reviewed ninety-nine studies of learning in infants and preschool children. The authors summarized the studies as follows:

> The work on learning is similar in many respects to experimentation in child psychology as a whole. . . . There has been an increasing use of controls important in studies of learning in rapidly growing organisms. Interest has shifted from the try-out of techniques and the achievement type of research to more analytical studies of the learning process. The more refined researches thus far, however, may be characterized as being samples of many types of problems rather than as units in an integrated program.

Halverson (173) studied eight infants at lunar month intervals. Motion picture records of the movements of the children were kept. He found three stages in the development of these infants. The first stage consisted of simple sensory motor responses, the second stage consisted of voluntary movements reaching from crude groping to direct reaching, and the third stage was largely automatic. Reaching began at twelve to twenty weeks, was discontinuous and jerky. From twenty to sixty weeks the movements became more continuous.

Bayley (154) studied sixty-one infants at regular intervals from birth to thirty-six months. He found that gross motor coordinations mature more rapidly than mental functions during the first two years, while after two years motor progress is comparatively slower. There was less consistency in motor development made by the same child over different age levels than was found on mental series. The coefficient of correlation between mental and motor scores after two years was .50, while no relation was found between the motor test scores and parents' education.

Roberts (207) studied twenty-one four-year-old children enrolled in the preschool laboratories of the Iowa Child Welfare Research Station and nineteen children from four to seven years of age in the Iowa Soldiers' Orphans' Home. Learning ability was more closely related to mental age than to chronological age. According to this study, children's responses to direct questioning may or may not yield reliable information concerning their ability to solve problems. Failure to respond verbally should not be taken as inability to respond, nor should failure to verbalize in a learning or problem-solving situation be considered as indicative of inferior ability in learning or problem solving of the type represented by this experiment. A child may give no evidence of ability to generalize verbally, whereas his performance in problem situations may show that he can generalize correctly.

Bathhurst (153) found a constant increase in reaction time and muscular coordination with advancing chronological age from six to eighteen years inclusive. Langhorne (184) studied seventy-six children whose ages varied from seven to seventeen. These children were trained to operate the Wrenshaw Pursuitmeter. Each child ran thirty-six cycles of four minutes each during eighteen consecutive days. He found that the limit and rate of improvement from practice increased directly with age. Maximum acceleration in improvement appeared about the beginning in the age of adolescence (thirteen to fourteen years). Sorenson and Price (214) arrived at the conclusion that adults have by no means lost their ability to learn.

At least one study has been made to show the relation of chronological age to achievement in subjectmatter. Finch and Floyd (166) reported a study of 147 pupils ranging in chronological age from eleven to nineteen years who were studying French. The pupils were equated on intelligence quotient obtained from an average of five group intelligence tests. The achievement was measured by American Council Alpha Foreign Test. The results showed a correlation of .10 between age and achievement for the vocabulary part of the test and .12 for the grammar part. When intelligence was partialed out, the relationship was raised to .27 for vocabulary and reduced to .09 for grammar. There seems to be no evidence in this study to indicate that French should be reserved to senior high schools or that pupils in grades seven and eight are too young to begin the study.

In another study on the effect of age differences Langhorne (185) drew the following conclusions: (a) rates and limits of improvement from practice increase with an increase in chronological age; (b) the period of greatest improvement appears during or near the beginning of the adolescent period; (c) the subjects seemed to fall into age groups separated from each other by different intervals; and (d) an increase in age does not bring a conflict between the various manipulatory responses involved in the acquisition of this skill.

Ruch (210) studied the effect of learning motor tasks and verbal tasks at three different age levels. Forty persons divided into three groups were studied. The subjects in the first group were twelve to seventeen years of age, in the second group thirty-four to fifty-nine years of age, and in the third group sixty to eighty-two years of age. The motor tasks showed the greater deficit of the aged as compared with the younger learners. The verbal learning tasks showed the amount of deficit increased in the following order of learning skills, paired associates, nonsense materials, and false products. The differences between the aged and the other two groups were statistically significant. The results between the young and the middle age groups fluctuated so that no specific conclusions regarding the superiority of one group over the other could be drawn.

Stroud and Maul (219) studied 226 subjects from grades two through six and grade nine and from college, who were tested on the memorizing of three poems and six lists of nonsense syllables. The learning scores increased with age, but chronological age was found to be less important than mental age. No consistent relation appeared between age and retention. Cruze (161), in an extensive laboratory experiment with chicks, studied the effect of practice at different levels of maturity in picking and swallowing reactions.

Effect of Intelligence on Learning

Relatively few studies have been made in the last three years to determine the effect of intelligence on learning. Eckert (164) reported in a study of superior and inferior college students that reliable differences were found in their success in college English and social studies, New York State Regents Examinations, total freshman-sophomore college average, and high-school English, social studies, and Latin. Thorndike and Woodyard (226) reported a series of experiments related to intelligence and learning. They concluded that there is little or no fundamental depression of the intellectual apparatus by work with infrequent success for which a suitable voluntary control cannot compensate. Frequent frustration caused irritation and loss of interest but not any large loss in power to attend to frustrating tasks. Bathhurst (153) reported a low positive correlation between abstract intelligence and scores to measure muscular reaction.

Effect of Sex and Individual Differences on Learning

Langhorne (185) found that boys learned to manipulate a machine more readily than did girls. Scott and Underwood (212) studied the effect of sex in learning a maze. Perl (201) studied the changes in individual differences in ninety-nine pupils, forty-six boys, and fifty-three girls in grade 4B. The pupils were matched by chronological age and intelligence. Four tasks were used in the study; namely, (a) making gates test, (b) Whipple's symbol-digit test, (c) Turkish-English vocabulary test, and (d) arithmetic test of a "peculiar type." She found that individual differences increase with practice in all the tests for both boys and girls when an increased sigma was used as the criterion of an increase in individual differences. The results tended to confirm the hypothesis that in simple tasks individual differences decrease with practice, while in the case of more complex tasks, they increase. Harter (175) found support for Snoddy's theory of learning as the capacity of neuromuscular patterns to endure stimulation.

Effect of Drugs on Learning

Two studies have been made to show the effect of drugs on learning. Omwake (199) reported a study of the effect of barbital, an effective sleep producing drug, on white rats. The barbital group was consistently less active than the control group. For five-minute periods the barbital group showed lower learning rate but for thirty-minute periods there was no significant difference in the two groups. J. R. Jones (180) studied the effects of aspirin and quinine upon the rate of learning twelve nonsense syllables of college students. The average number of trials for learning these syllables were for the aspirin group 10.48, for the quinine group 10.28, and for the control group 10.00. The differences were not statistically significant. The authors concluded that quinine and aspirin may be said to have a neutral effect on learning. The variations appeared to be due to chance. However, an early rise in the quinine curve may be due to action of quinine; but this, too, is probably a chance factor.

CHAPTER IV
Methods of Teaching

MUCH HAS BEEN WRITTEN about the difficulties of conducting research on methods of teaching. No one can review studies in this field without being impressed with the illusive nature of many of the factors which may influence the results of experimentation in this area. In any controlled experiment in methods of teaching, there are chance fluctuations in pupil-interest, pupil-industry, pupil-experimental background, pupil-teacher relationships which may affect growth in achievement in such a manner as to obscure differences in the relative effectiveness of different methods. The teacher's zeal in employing one of the two or more methods under investigation may be only partially controlled even when methods and teachers are rotated. For this reason the problem of measuring growth during the experimental period presents many difficulties. In practically all reported experiments, the conclusions are based on measurements of growth in terms of subjectmatter tests. As to the relative effect of different experimental methods upon pupils' concepts, attitudes, relationships with life situations, one may only speculate.

Since methods of teaching must be investigated in teaching situations closely resembling actual teaching, it has been quite impossible in this summary to avoid overlapping with those summaries of research which treat the teaching of special subjects, and to some extent with those which deal with the psychology of school subjects. Although the reviewer has made an attempt to focus attention in this section on "general method" rather than upon the different subject areas, it has been impossible to make a clean-cut separation. The studies in this section have been confined to the general areas of: remedial teaching, training in study, procedures using audio-visual aids, newer-type procedures, and special methods.

Remedial Teaching

Studies in this division are for the most part related to remedial teaching in reading, English composition and grammar (including correct usage), handwriting, and spelling.

The summaries of reading investigations by Gray (264, 265) and the contributions of research in the teaching of curriculum making in English by D. V. Smith (292) include additional materials on the problem of remedial teaching in the field of English.

Traxler (294, 296) reported a study made in the University of Chicago High School to determine the value of teaching corrective reading, to discover technics to be used in correcting reading defects, and to ascertain the permanence of gains made during the period of corrective teaching with seventh- and ninth-grade pupils. The study was of three-year duration. During the first-year experimental period, both the seventh- and the ninth-grade remedial groups showed much greater growth in rate and comprehension than did the control groups. During the second year and during the third year of experimental teaching, the remedial groups made significant and substantial gains over the gains made by the control groups, and decidedly larger gains than the norms given by the publishers of the tests which were used. While some pupils showed losses when retested several months later, most of the backward readers derived considerable permanent benefit.

Gatto (259) reported the results of a remedial reading program in thirteen high schools in Pittsburgh in which use was made of factual material to insure transfer to the work of the regular classes. Persons (284) reported the procedure used in the Theodore Roosevelt High School, New York City. A three-week period was reserved in all freshman English classes for intensive work in reading. The results indicated that such a plan secures desirable returns.

Shuchowsky and Flemming (290) and Farbish (252) conducted studies with ninth-grade pupils and reported significant gains on the part of the remedial groups. Shuchowsky and Flemming used a composite of activities designed for improving ability in reading, while Farbish used only a series of lessons, each lesson consisting of a single paragraph with a number of questions on each paragraph.

Miller (279) tested the possibility of increasing comprehension of literature on the part of ninth- and twelfth-grade pupils by using short comprehension drills on literary materials. The technic proved effective. The ninth-grade pupils improved more than the twelfth-grade pupils and the plan was most effective for the poor and average readers.

Gibbs (260) used free reading as means of improving the reading ability of sophomores. Pupils selected their own books from a library of 45 books ranging in difficulty from the fifth-grade to the ninth-grade level, and the report indicated that a number of comprehension checks in the form of dramatizations, answering questions, making out test questions, and giving out sub-headings to selections were used. The Thorndike-McCall and the Monroe Reading Tests indicated a median improvement of 2.5 grades. Only two pupils failed to show real progress.

Hinchman (270) used remedial procedures in instructing a group of dull pupils in the ninth-grade level, in English. The twenty-five pupils in the group had a median I.Q. of eighty and came largely from foreign-born parents. Tests administered before and after the remedial program indicated an advance in median scores from sixth-grade to ninth-grade level of attainment. Parkhill (283) also reported improvement in reading with low-mentality groups on the seventh-grade level secured by using a variety of easy reading materials. Unfortunately neither Hinchman nor Parkhill used a control group.

Attempts to meet the needs of poor readers on the elementary-school level by carefully planned programs of remedial reading are well illustrated by Gates (257) in a report of a series of diagnostic and remedial studies carried on in New York City. The report described the effective work done with "non-readers" from grades two to four inclusive, in forty coaching days. Lamoreaux and others (273) reported successful work with sixth-grade groups.

Orr (282) reported a study conducted in two elementary schools of Atlanta, Georgia. Orr was interested in setting up a program of remedial teaching which might be carried along with regular class duties. The technics used for selecting and diagnosing pupil difficulties and for conducting remedial teaching were based largely on the procedures outlined by Monroe (281). Improvement was shown by practically all the children for whom records were kept. Because the results reported were based on a small number of cases, the outcomes of this study are not at all conclusive; but the problem is one of considerable interest to public school workers. MacLatchy and Beavers (277) reported a study which gave evidences of the effectiveness of reading for enjoyment as a means of improving the reading ability of sixth-grade children.

Studies of attempts to correct the difficulties of pupils in reading and to secure improvement in rate and comprehensions are encouraging in that they seem to indicate that whenever intelligent effort is directed toward securing improvement, such improvement is forthcoming.

Bonar (241) summarized nineteen studies relative to the comparative values of systematic and incidental training in reading and concluded that the evidence was decidedly on the side of systematic training. Bonar's conclusion seems to be sustained by the results obtained in the field of remedial instruction in reading. More studies on the permanence of the improvement secured in remedial classes as well as on the transfer of the improvement secured under various conditions to reading activities in other classes seem desirable.

The correction of errors in composition has received considerable attention. Guiler (267) reported a remedial project conducted with college students. The Guiler-Henry Diagnostic Test in Grammatical Usage was given to 346 students. The scores of these students ranged from zero to seventy-five. Those having scores below forty-three, 163 students, were selected for remedial work. The remedial work was organized on an individual and self-administering basis. The results showed a marked improvement in ability to apply principles of grammatical usage. The average student's score increased from 26.8 in the initial test to 8.4 in the final, or from less than eleventh-grade ability to a standard far above that attained by a typical college sophomore. Guiler suggested that because students manifested marked individuality in the types of errors made, individualized remedial instruction is advisable.

Another study by Guiler (266) conducted on the elementary-school level, showed clearly the possibility of improving pupil mastery of mechanical and usage skills in language through remedial instruction.

Warner and Guiler (298) studied the relative effectiveness of individualized remedial drill versus group instruction as a means of improving grammatical usage with ninth- and tenth-grade students. Again the results indicated that individual instruction based on individual needs is much more effective than mass instruction.

Two methods of correcting eight errors in English, oral drill and grammar study, were investigated by Crawford and Roger (247) using two groups of seventh-grade children. The major feature in the oral approach was having the class read in concert a series of sentences containing the correct form of the error on which attention was being focused. The major feature of the grammatical approach was the explanation of the grammatical principle involved and the memorization of rules. Methods were rotated so that each group of pupils used both methods. The final test showed the two methods to be equally effective. No tests for permanency were given.

Ransom (287) investigated the value of having pupils carry on a semi-individualized type of practice to correct language errors. All drill in the experimental group was directed toward the elimination of sixteen types of errors made by the pupils. The experimental group made significantly greater progress in eliminating errors than did the control group.

Six methods of eliminating twenty selected errors in grammatical usage over a six-week period in thirteen classes in grades 5, 6, and 7, were investigated by Cutright (248). The rank order of the successful methods was: (a) choice of two forms followed by oral repetition of corrected sentences to accustom pupils to the *sound* of the correct forms; (b) combination of all methods, a different one each week; (c) the Beta-hypothesis procedure of practicing error rather than the correct form [better with older pupils than with younger]; (d) choice of two forms [same as (a) but without oral repetition]; (e) proofreading; and (f) language games.

One study of remedial teaching in fields closely related to English composition is that of Traxler and Anderson (295) in group corrective handwriting and group corrective spelling. Traxler and Anderson gave corrective instruction in handwriting to two groups of seventh- and eighth-grade students, sixty-nine pupils in all, whose handwriting scored below fifty in the Ayres Scales for Measuring Handwriting, Gettysburg Edition, for one period a week for eight weeks. At the end of the period of corrective teaching, the students in the corrective classes had lost slightly in average rate of writing while those in a control group had gained. These students in the corrective group made marked improvement in quality while those in the control made only a small gain. All groups were retested after the summer vacation and it was found that all groups had increased in mean rate and that there was only a small loss in quality by the corrective groups. The net gain of the corrective groups from February to October was approximately nine-tenths of a step on the Ayres Scale.

As a result of group corrective instruction in spelling Anderson and Traxler (239) reported that two groups of students, seventh- and eighth-grade level, made one year's growth in a period of thirteen weeks, with one class period a week devoted to class work. The gain in spelling ability was permanent. The corrective groups retained about 80 percent of the gain when they were retested after the summer vacation.

Studies of remedial and corrective teaching in general seem to indicate that whenever attention is focused on the learning difficulties of the individual child and some intelligent and systematic type of help is given, improvement is secured.

Study Habits

Studies of the value of special training in specific study habits are closely related to those reported in the section on corrective and remedial teaching. Three such studies were located in the literature. Jacobson (272) reported a series of studies on the effect of work-type reading exercises on the reading comprehension of pupils, on their achievement in general science, and on their general achievement in all academic subjects. The exercises proved to be more effective with poor initial readers than with good initial readers. The studies gave some evidence that reading instruction in the field in which content is to be mastered is superior to giving it in one subjectmatter field and expecting the ability to be transferred to another field.

Mills, Eckert, and Williams (280) evaluated a "How To Study" unit of instruction. Instruction in how to study took the form of lectures and discussions on the mechanics of reading, analysis of methods of deriving more meaning from the printed pages, extra vocabulary work, and the use of large number of exercises designed to increase speed and comprehension. After six weeks' training the experimental group was compared with a control group. The experimental group was superior in speed only and in a retest several months later even this advantage had disappeared. In comprehension the results favored the control group, but the difference was not significant.

A more encouraging report is that of Salisbury (289) who gave thirty special training lessons on outlining to secondary-school pupils who were matched with pupils in a control group on the basis of mental age and reading ability. The pupils in the control group studied English in the usual way. The results implied that definite training in outlining will secure decided improvement in reading and that such instruction measurably increases a child's chances for general school success. Likewise Leggitt (276) secured encouraging results by providing guidance in (a) becoming informed about a new book, (b) using a general reference book, (c) the reading of a newspaper, (d) interpreting a diagram or chart, a picture graph, or a statistical table, (e) summarizing, and (f) outlining.

Audio-Visual Aids

The effectiveness of audio-visual equipment as instructional aids is a comparatively new subject for experimental investigation. Clark (243) compared sound films with silent films as aids in teaching a survey course in science. Sound films were found to be as effective as the lecture demonstration and more effective than the silent films in arousing interest. Sound films were less effective than silent films in securing high scores on a comprehension test. Einbecker (251) conducted a somewhat unique study which compared the effects of various forms of verbal accompaniments to films. He compared the effect of silent films without captions or oral comments of any kind, silent films with oral comments by the teacher, and sound films. So far as science films are concerned, the results indicated that verbal accompaniments increased the comprehension over that secured from the film without captions or comments, but that it is immaterial whether it is the teacher or the speaker in a sound film who comments. Einbecker suggested that the function of verbal accompaniments to films is to furnish word symbols which may be used to represent the more concrete experiences which the films portray, and to direct attention to the important terms or features of the pictures. Rulon (288) compared three groups in general science; one group used the usual textbook method, another group used the textbook and a sound film, and a third group acted as a control. The groups were carefully equated. On an information test the film group exceeded the control group by 20.5 percent more than the textbook group exceeded the control group. Sound films according to this study furnish much supplemental information.

Arnspiger (240) measured the effectiveness of carefully prepared sound film units as compared with traditional methods in teaching natural science and music. This controlled experiment was carried on in five cities in the same geographic area using fifth- and seventh-grade pupils. The investigator concluded: (a) the superiority of the sound picture method (as used in the study) was 26 percent in the science group and 27 percent in the music group; (b) the average gain was 22 to 30 percent in the science group and 18 to 34 percent in the music group, using the sound pictures; (c) on the film unit items, all cities combined showed 50 percent superiority in science, and 31 percent in music for the sound pictures; (d) pupils, both below and above the average 1A, showed distinct learning gains from the use of the films; and (e) the average recall test gains over the initial test were greater for the experimental group. In natural science the percents of superiority ranged from 9 to 18; in music, from 14 to 32.

Only one study was located concerning the effectiveness of the radio as an instructional aid. This study was reported by Carpenter (242). He measured the factual knowledge in general science gained by radio instruction given to seventh-grade pupils. Twenty-five groups, each in a different school and without science equipment or trained science teachers, were compared with fourteen groups in schools with well equipped science rooms and well-trained science teachers. The radio group was given thirty lessons by radio, two lessons a week. Each lesson consisted of a thirty-minute radio presentation and a twenty-minute follow-up period. Teachers of the radio groups were supplied with a brief outline of the work for each week along with directions for the follow-up period. Pupils took notes during the broadcast and at the end of the presentation were asked to select the most important thing and the most interesting fact given. Tests which were given at the end of the experimental period and which were based on the syllabus used in the school system, showed the radio classes to have a higher percent of correctness in fifty-two of seventy questions than did the regular science groups. While the investigator did not feel that the study necessarily indicated that instruction by radio was superior to regular class instruction by trained teachers, still it does indicate a satisfactory means of giving science instruction to small, scattered classes where teachers trained in science are not available.

Newer-Type Procedures in Teaching

The educational outcomes in schools using the activity type of curriculum were reported by two investigators, Collings and Wrightstone. Collings (245) reported a study which compared the achievement of pupils in grades seven, eight, and nine in an "activity" school with pupils of the same grades in a "subject" school. Sixty-four pupils in an "activity" school were paired with 64 pupils in a "subject" school. The seventh-grade pupils in each school were then given a series of subjectmatter tests, 13 tests in all. These tests covered the fundamentals taught in the various subjects in the "subject" school. The eighth- and ninth-grade pupils were given the same battery of tests with a test in science added. In the seventh-grade groups, the average mean score was 4.7 higher for the "activity" group. The "activity" group excelled in 9 of the 13 tests. In the eighth grade, the average median score was 4.0 higher for the "activity" school and they excelled in 9 of the 14 tests. The average mean score for the ninth grade was 5.9 higher for the "activity" group. Collings concluded that the study indicated that pupils taught in a school where an activity curriculum prevailed did as well or better than did pupils in a school with the conventional subject curriculum.

Wrightstone (300) compared four communities with reference to the educational outcomes in schools using the newer type of curriculum and in standard type schools using the standard subject-centered type of curriculum. He used a matched-pair technic. The study was concerned with "areas of intellectual factors, with dynamic factors, and with social performance factors." The results were uniformly in favor of new-type procedures.

Many studies have as their subject the investigation of the relative effectiveness of a type of teaching which allows more pupil initiative and activity as contrasted with a type of teaching such as the textbook method which is usually very limiting to pupils' activity. Wrightstone (301) also reported a study which evaluated the more informal pupil-activity type of teaching with the conventional textbook and topical method of teaching American history. Groups of 30 pupils each were used. The groups were carefully equated in the basis of intelligence, socio-economic status, and phases of school experience. The experimental group approached their study of American history through problems chosen from current events which the teachers and pupils found in periodicals and newspapers. Each pupil chose topics for investigation according to his interest. The teacher was guide and counselor to individuals and groups. There were discussions, and both oral and written reports. The conventional group used a textbook in the conventional manner.

At the end of the experimental period, both groups were given the Cooperative American History Test, Form 1933. The mean score of the experimental group was 96.9 and that of the textbook group was 88.6. This difference led Wrightstone to conclude that, in the teaching of the social studies, the "new" approach is just as effective as the conventional approach, if not more so. When the pupils were tested for liberal versus conservative civic attitudes and beliefs, it was found that the activities used in the experimental teaching were more effective than the conventional method in leading pupils to liberal points of view on civic problems.

Wrightstone (303) also investigated the new-type method of teaching mathematics as compared with the traditional method. The new-type method consisted of a fused course in which the various branches of mathematics were correlated with other courses such as the natural sciences and the social studies. The work was organized in units about such themes as "The Financial Relationships of Children to Parents." The subjects so taught were arithmetic, elementary algebra, intermediate algebra, and geometry in the seventh-, eighth-, ninth-, tenth-, and eleventh-grade levels. He reported that in arithmetic, elementary algebra, and plane geometry the classes taught by the newer-type method achieved better scores than did the classes taught according to the traditional method, but that the differences were statistically significant only in plane geometry. The conventional or traditional method was significantly superior in intermediate algebra.

Wrightstone (302) investigated the comparative value of the traditional separate subject plan of teaching of grammar, spelling, reading, composition, and literature versus the newer type of functional-individualized teaching, correlating all phases of English instruction with other departments to produce such projects as plays, newspapers, etc. He concluded that the newer or functional approach to the teaching of language arts produced equal or superior knowledge and skills according to the tests used in the experiment. In literary acquaintance, the activity method gave significantly superior results. The investigator suggested a more extensive study of the value of this new-type program in English.

Lee and Root (274) reported an experiment with a program which integrated the social studies, English, and art. The three subjects were taught separately to the control group and were integrated for the experimental group. In grade 7B, the results favored the integrated program, but in grades 7A and 8B the separate subjects seemed more effective. The authors concluded that the results varied directly with the personality, training, and adaptability of the teacher.

Hazelrigg (269) found that a group of pupils taught by the informal method in English composition showed a markedly greater reduction in the number of errors for each 100 words written than did another group of pupils of like ability, taught by a formal method. Also the informal method seemed to stimulate pupils to write more than did the more formal method. Taggart and Haefner (293) reported on two methods used in teaching Macbeth. An experimental method in which the students led all the discussions and carried on other activities largely of their own selection, individually or in groups, was compared with a more traditional method of the teacher-question type. The pupils in the experimental group were slightly superior to those in the traditional method group in intelligence. At the end of the experimental period, the experimental group had less factual knowledge concerning the play, Macbeth, than did the traditional group. The results, however, were such that no significance could be attached to them.

Lee (275) evaluated an activity program in relation to learning to read by measuring the reading ability of first-grade children grouped according to the teacher's estimate of the amount of time given to "activity work" into groups doing "a great deal," doing "some activity," doing "very little," and doing "none." The tests indicated that pupils in schools doing a "great deal" of activity work had somewhat less ability in silent reading than had those children in schools doing somewhat less activity work. No particular significance can be attached to the results since teachers' estimates of how much activity work they were doing were no doubt somewhat unreliable.

Howell, Dunn, and Stoker (271) tested the efficiency of a plan of giving one hour a day to drill on skills not growing directly out of an integrated program. They used the Stanford Achievement Test in grades three to six inclusive to test the efficiency of the plan, and concluded that skills can be maintained in an integrated program when one hour a day is allotted to drill on skills not growing out of regular units of work. Spelling may be the one exception but the investigators questioned the extent to which the Stanford Achievement Test really measured the pupils' ability to spell the words which they were using.

Dransfield (250) made an investigation of the value of a method of meeting the needs of superior children within the limits of an ordinary classroom situation. His method was one of supplying superior children with self-administering instructional units. The pupils selected for this experiment had I.Q.'s of 110 or better, and E.Q.'s of 100 or better. They were located in nine schools, ranging from the rural to the junior high school, and in grades three, five, and seven. The experimental group was equated with a control group. The experimental group spent approximately 38 percent of their time working on their self-administering and self-checking units, while the control group continued their regular class work. The subjectmatter test used to measure pupil-growth during the experimental period favored the experimental group as did the subjective judgment of teachers.

Special Methods

Classroom teachers continue to be interested in special methods described by such terms as the contract method, the project method, the

Dalton laboratory method, etc. While none of these terms have definite connotations, still they indicate, in general, attempts to modify teaching methods in such a way as to furnish a greater challenge to pupil interest, to utilize more lifelike materials, and to permit more pupil activity.

C. G. Smith (291) investigated the relative merits of the project method and the traditional method of teaching senior high-school biology. He used four classes of equal ability for experimental teaching. A fifth group of pupils used the traditional method throughout the experiment. The work was divided into two units of eighteen days each. The first unit was presented in the traditional manner, two days of laboratory work and three days of recitation, to two classes while the other two classes had the same unit presented by a project method wherein the pupils worked individually or in groups on projects selected from a posted list or substituted with the teacher's permission. During the second unit the methods were reversed. Mimeographed objective tests were used to gauge improvement. Scores on the objective tests were 34.94 for the traditional method and 17.85 for the project method. Difference in skill in using the two methods may have influenced the results of Smith's experiment. Powers and Black (286) attempted to ascertain the measurable results of a panel discussion method of teaching the social studies as compared with the Morrison unit method. They used the three-group method for experimentation. Group A used the modified Morrison plan and acted as the control group, Group D used the panel plan, and Group C used the Morrison plan. The experiment ran for eight weeks. At the end of the first four weeks, the panel group and the Morrison group exchanged methods. Tests were given at the end of the first four weeks and at the end of eight weeks. On these tests, both at the end of the first four weeks and at the end of the second four-week period, the methods ranked in this order: (a) the group using the panel method, (b) the control group, and (c) the Morrison group. The authors concluded that the panel method of teaching social studies produced better results as measured by teacher-made objective tests than did the Morrison method; that the pupils in the panel group assimilated more facts and more understandings; that pupils of the lowest intelligence did as well by the panel method as by the Morrison method; that pupils of average or high intelligence did consistently better in the panel method than in the Morrison method. Studies by Fowler (253) and Gadske (254) gave results more favorable to attempts in vitalizing methods of teaching.

Macomber (278) compared the contract method and the discussion method for teaching the social studies in the seventh grade using the matched-pairs technic. The results in general favored the contract method, but the number of cases used were too few to permit the drawing of conclusions. Fowler (253) made an investigation comparing a laboratory or modified Dalton plan with the traditional plan of teaching history on the secondary-school level to discover which of the two methods caused the larger number of students to study history for "interest" rather than for "credit." The results indicated that the laboratory or modified Dalton plan aroused the greater degree of desirable interest in history. Gadske (254) compared a "unit method" in which instruction was quite individualized, with the traditional recitation plan in the teaching of ninth-grade algebra using equated groups. The results were significantly in favor of the individualized unit method.

Peters (285) made a study which may well be included in this section on special methods. Teachers of foreign languages have long discussed the comparative value of the grammar translation method and the direct method of teaching a language. Peters compared the relative values of the two methods in the teaching of French, using a group of college freshmen. A group of students was divided into two sections, equated as to mental ability. One group was taught by the grammar translation method and the other by the direct method. The grammar translation method had the advantage of more concrete progress in the early stages of teaching, whereas the direct method students seemed to achieve more at the end of their first year. The advantages of the grammar translation method seemed to be: (a) it secures better results during the first semester; and (b) it secures better results in translation both in vocabulary and comprehension, as of written questions. The advantages of the direct method seemed to be: (a) it secures better results during the second semester; and (b) it secures better results in dictation, in reading, in pronunciation, aural comprehension, appreciation, and grammar. The number of cases used in Peters' study was far too small to permit the drawing of any hard and fast conclusions.

Drake (249) investigated the relative merits of an individual method and an individualized group method in the teaching of algebra. The pupils comprising the two were ninth-grade algebra classes, matched according to intelligence quotient, achievement during the first few weeks of school under the same method of instruction, results of a survey list, arithmetic achievement, and chronological age. Under the specific conditions of the experiment, these conclusions were reached:

> Students with superior ability attain a higher standard of achievement under the group method than under the individual method; the group method is also to be preferred for students with low ability. Both methods require about the same amount of outside preparation on the part of the students. Pupils taught under the individual method make slower progress than those taught under the group method. Pupils under the group method achieve consistently higher on tests throughout the year as well as on tests given at the end of the year.

The results of Drake's investigations are somewhat at a variance with other studies in the field of remedial teaching which indicate that attention to individual needs is effective. This investigation should possibly be extended both in the number of pupils involved and in the use of typical school situations.

Hartmann (268) investigated the effectiveness of student-instructor conferences in relation to student achievement. He used 56 equated pairs of students in elementary psychology as the subjects of a parallel group experiment in which one-half served as control by attending recitations and lectures regularly three times a week. The other half constituted the experimental group which was allowed private conferences with the instructor in the place of the third weekly class period. In five out of the six measures of pupil attainment, four measures being objective tests, the interview group did more poorly. The investigator suggested that the alleged benefits of greater student-teacher contact are either fictitious or are effective in some other way than in the overt manifestation of scholarship.

Gates and Bennett (255) compared the daily plan of teaching spelling with the weekly plan in grades two to six inclusive. The inconsistency of the results led the investigators to conclude that the features of the general method of teaching spelling matter little in comparison "with the ability of enabling pupils to learn and use the technic of learning to spell by themselves." Gates and Graham (258) compared a program based almost exclusively upon direct study of work lists by the study-test and test-study plan with a program wherein part of the time was devoted to spelling games, puzzles, problems, etc., on the basis of the interest aroused and the spelling ability developed. Two tests were used to measure the improvement; one test on words, selected from the list which had been studied, and the other a survey test. The results seemed to indicate:

1. The two methods increase spelling ability in roughly equal degree, but that the book-directed programs combining word study with word games and other activities are more interesting under the conditions of the experiment.

2. The two programs of word study and game type used in the experiment were relatively slightly more successful with the third of the pupils highest in spelling and intelligence test scores than with the third lowest in these respects.

Still another study by Gates (256) on spelling was an investigation of the comparative superiority of teaching spelling by a method designed to foster generalization and a method of specific study of words as isolated items. More than three thousand pupils in 106 classes in a public school in Brooklyn, New York, were used in this investigation. Pupils were divided into generalization and non-generalization groups. The same basal list of words was used for both groups. The weekly list contained the same number of words and the amount of time spent in study and review was identical. For the generalization group, the list each week consisted of words grouped according to some common element as those falling under the ei, ie rule, or having some common phonetic element as in or eep. A variety of devices were used in which learning rules was but one, and a minor feature. For the non-generalization group, the words in the word list were arranged without grouping according to word-form characteristics, but were arranged in lists on the basis of a combined difficulty and frequency of use criteria. Each word was treated as a specific spelling problem. No rules were introduced, and attention was not called to common word characteristics. It was found that a broad and varied program of generalization, while it did not increase ability to spell the words studied during the term more than the specific learning method, did tend to increase to some extent the power to spell new words and especially to handle the specific derivatives and other elements to which the generalization program was especially directed. This study also gave some information concerning the value of certain rules and generalization devices which should be of special interest.

Watson (299) summarized the findings of several experiments comparing methods of teaching and found a preference (a) for the use of individual practice with access to formulated rules over individual drill with reference to rules, (b) for class study of rules over class drill without rules, and (c) for individual drill over class drill.

Miscellaneous Studies

Unzicker (297) reported a study of the effects of typewriting on learning to read in the first grade, supplementing modern methods of teaching reading with from seventy-five to ninety minutes per week of typewriter practice. This controlled experiment included some 226 pupils in ten first-grade classes, in five schools, in Elizabeth, New Jersey, and in the demonstration school at Teachers College. The results indicated a slight but constant superiority on the part of the pupils who used the typewriter.

Crawford and Malin (246) reported an investigation of the effectiveness of three approaches to water color work: (a) a preliminary detailed pencil drawing, (b) a preliminary chalk sketching, and (c) free painting. They used three equivalent groups of 30 pupils each. The groups were equated in age, intelligence, and previous art experience. The three methods were rotated. Group 1 used pencil drawing with one group of subjects, chalk drawing with another group, and free painting with the third. The drawings were evaluated by 20 competent judges. When the evaluations were summarized, it was found that the pencil drawing method received the highest mean rating, with chalk sketching and free painting of about equal value. The number of cases used in the experiment was small, and it is possible that pencil drawing may not lead to the best ultimate development in advanced water color work.

Goetsch (263) investigated the effect of early handwriting. The subjects were children in grades three, four, and five, in two cities in which manuscript writing was taught in grades one and two, and in two cities in which only cursive writing was taught in grades one and two. Samples of handwriting were collected and scored. The results indicated that (a) pupils taught manuscript writing in grades one and two have but little difficulty in shifting to the cursive form of writing, and that (b) speed of writing in the intermediate grades is not affected by the type of handwriting instruction given in the lower grades. Pupils who have had manuscript writing write more slowly right after the shift, but they are equal or superior to the cursive group in later grades.

Clemensen (244) evaluated the worth of study outlines based on the application of the laws of learning to the general aims and specific subject-matter objectives of a course in physics. Classes of three types were organized: (a) an outline group, one using the prepared study outlines; (b) the non-outline group, with the same teachers as the outline group, paired with the pupils of the outline group, and taught in exactly the same way as the outline group except that the study outlines were not used; and (c) an outside control group, composed of classes whose teachers were not familiar with the outlines, and who simply gave the tests for comparative purposes. The results gave strong evidence on the value of study outlines as a teaching device.

Gilbert (262) reported a study on the effect of reading on spelling on the junior, senior, and graduate university level. Gilbert (261) previously reported a study of the same problem on the ninth-grade level. This study used as subjects 389 men and women of junior, senior, and graduate levels. The conclusions were quite similar to those outlined for the ninth grade: that college students improve their spelling through reading when attention is not directed toward it (the pick-up through reading for words recently brought to one's attention is probably greater than the pick-up from words encountered more remotely); that the amount of learning of spelling through reading is highly significant; that good spellers are able to pick up more spelling through their reading than poor spellers; that superior achievement for good spellers is not effected by virtue of a slow reading rate; that there are large deviations from average rate for both good and poor spellers; and that there is no significant difference in the reading rates of those who acquired little spelling and those who acquired much.

CHAPTER V
Supervision

As a subdivision in a review of educational research, the term "supervision" presents a number of very serious difficulties. According to usual definition, supervision is concerned with those aspects of educational administration which are directly related to instruction. Thus such activities as classroom visitation and teacher meetings come to be looked upon as supervisory while oversight of buildings and grounds and purchase of supplies are viewed as administrative in character. This is, of course, a purely artificial assumption since all administrative activities carried on in a school system do have a relationship to instruction if they have any significance at all. Thus, our first difficulty grows out of the problem of determining just how widely the term "supervision" should be interpreted.

Even if we restrict the meaning of supervision to its traditional sense, we are confronted with another equally serious problem. How shall we distinguish between studies in methods of teaching, curriculum, and supervision? If, for example, a supervisor makes a study of eye movements of children, shall we classify this study under the head of "learning" or "supervision"? In all probability the supervisor would use the same technic in a study of eye movements as would be used by a teacher were he to make a similar study. It is obvious that if we follow the practice of classifying research activities according to the titles of the persons who engage in them, we shall be led into all manner of confusion in regard to both our activities and the meanings of our terms.

The result of past practices in defining what constitutes research in supervision, can be plainly seen in the organization of courses in professional education. Many schools present courses in the teaching of reading, for example. They also present courses in the supervision of reading. In addition, courses are presented in the broader aspects of supervision. Simultaneously in these schools courses are offered in the psychology of reading. It is thus entirely possible that a student may take several successive courses that have somewhat different titles but which have a more or less common scientific basis. The net effect is that the student must cover the material in a certain field three or four times in as many different courses in order to complete a given program toward a degree.

It will, of course, be argued by some that the supervisor, while using the same technics that are employed by the teacher, possesses a broader background of understanding and employs these technics on a higher level or with a higher degree of skill. Such persons would, no doubt, insist that the difference in the manner in which the various technics are employed justifies the creation of a separate category for their classification. The presentation of such a point of view forces us to a consideration of the basic assumptions underlying the existing organization of the school with their implications regarding the roles of both teachers and supervisors as well as their bearing upon our present problem of classification of research.

Our present supervisory practices have their origin in an effort to protect the public against the most harmful forms of teaching in the school. Early supervision was essentially inspectorial in character. It sought to isolate and eliminate the highly incompetent teachers from the school system. Gradually this form of supervision undertook also to improve the practices of the teachers who were retained. We began to talk about supervision as the improvement of instruction. In this work of improving instruction there was an underlying assumption to the effect that the teacher was relatively ignorant and incompetent and at the same time the supervisor was highly competent and knew what should be done. We thus adopted the industrial principle of separation of planning and performance. The supervisor became a planner and the teacher became a performer. Through this pattern, authority became the method for the discovery of truth in a school. If the teacher wanted to know what should be done in any educational situation, his obvious approach was to ask the supervisor. In a sense this system of separation of planning and performance came to be a method of compensating for the ineffectiveness of poorly prepared teachers. It was assumed that we might get along with incompetence on the part of teachers if we only had a competent supervisor.

It is this underlying assumption of separation between planning and performance which has led some authorities to classify research largely on the basis of the titles of the persons who carry on the activity rather than in terms of the activities themselves. The science of education has come to be viewed as the property and principal domain of the supervisor. The teacher has been looked upon as an individual who does *not* in the main understand the science of education but who merely does the bidding of the supervisor who *does* understand this science. Under this scheme of organization, the teacher is somewhat analogous to a nurse in a hospital. In medical practice nursing is, of course, viewed as a somewhat different field of activity than the practice of medicine, although there are no doubt many common elements. While it is extremely dangerous to draw analogies between different professions and types of activity, there is enough of a rough comparison so that it is worthwhile for us to examine it here. If the teacher is analogous to a nurse, and if the supervisor is comparable to a physician, then our past practice in classifying research in this field is no doubt justified.

Far-reaching changes are, however, taking place in the organization of American schools. Teachers are gradually acquiring far better preparation for their work. Many school systems have a considerable number of teachers whose qualifications for their work are as good as or better than those possessed by their supervisors. There is no longer any justifiable assumption to the effect that the supervisory officer is competent and the teacher is incompetent. Moreover, we are gradually discovering that our science of education cannot be utilized unless it becomes the property of the teachers in our classrooms. Separation of planning and performance, however successful it may have been in industry, is not appropriate in education. We are slowly discovering that the effort to compensate for incompetence on the part of teachers through such separation of planning and performance is futile.

The growth of the scientific method has also brought into question the appropriateness of authority as a pattern for the discovery of truth in the modern school. The mere fact that a supervisory officer holds to a certain point of view gives us no guarantee that that point of view is correct. Authority is concerned only with *who* is right; science is concerned with *what* is right. The two do not mix.

One must not overlook the considerations growing out of our basic social philosophy of democracy. There are many who believe that it is too much to expect children to acquire the meaning of democracy if they live in a school which is itself a dictatorship. Such persons will hold that teachers are likely to treat children in the same way in which they are treated by their supervisory officers. Thus, our more recent psychology, our educational science, and our basic social philosophy all point in the direction of a school organization which depends less upon authority and separation of planning and performance and more upon a mastery of educational science by the classroom teacher.

Rather obviously, if we demand that the teacher possess an adequate mastery of educational science, the teacher will be assigned a new role in American education. There must, of course, be corresponding modifications in the role of the supervisor. It is out of the question to delineate such roles in a situation of this kind. We must limit ourselves to the mere statement that the teacher in the future will be one who practices our educational science. The supervisor will be a leader who creates the setting in which teachers can make the greatest professional growth. This supervisor's knowledge of learning, for example, will perhaps be no different from the knowledge of learning possessed by the teacher. Neither will his knowledge of curriculum or methods of teaching be any different in kind.

If the above concepts of educational organization become basic to our classification of research, it is clear that the literature in supervision must take on different limits than it has been given in the past. Thus, psychological studies, or method studies, or curriculum studies will naturally be classified under the head of learning, methods, or curriculum. They will be viewed as elements in educational science irrespective of the role of the person who utilizes this educational science.

What then constitutes research in the field of supervision? Generally speaking, it is research which has to do with the relationships between supervisors and teachers and the activities which are carried on in this relationship. A few examples may be helpful. Studies of the classroom activities of teachers through the utilization of various technics for objective analysis of classroom procedure can be viewed as being studies in supervision. Likewise, studies of the effectiveness of teachers meetings, demonstration teaching, individual conferences, may be looked upon as supervisory. It will, of course, be objected that the supervisor will cooperate in making curriculum studies, method studies, and the carrying of experiments in learning. This will be admitted. But in such cooperation, the supervisor is merely engaged in the practice of educational science. This science is as much the property of the teacher as the supervisor.

As indicated earlier in this discussion, it is extremely difficult and perhaps unwise to attempt to draw a line between supervision and administration. The term "educational leadership" might be used to describe both of these activities. If this plan were followed, the term "leadership" would include not only the activities now carried on directly in relationship to the problems of improving instruction but also the activities less closely related to instructional improvement such as finance, buildings, salary schedules, and the like. It is obviously outside the province of the present review to undertake so comprehensive an enterprise. In attempting to limit the present review to the areas closely related to instruction, many very arbitrary divisions have been made. Studies of the status of elementary-school principals have not, for example, been included, although it is clear that they may include material which has a direct bearing on supervision. Studies of practice teaching have likewise been left out on the assumption that they belong more properly in the field of teacher education.

Many persons actively engaged in the field of supervision either from a practical or theoretical point of view may feel that through the above assumptions we are restricting the field of supervision in an unfortunate manner. Without any question the amount of research which can be listed under this concept is considerably less than that which could be listed under certain concepts held in the past. It may, however, be argued with equal force that it is highly important for those interested in supervision to make a realistic appraisal of the situation in which they find themselves in the face of current educational developments. No good can come to the field of supervision through the careless appropriation of technics and researches from a number of related fields without any very clear notion as to their origin or appropriateness in the field of supervision. If supervision as a field of endeavor lacks a scientific basis in research today, it would be much better for us to face this fact squarely, take inventory of our position, and address ourselves to the task of studying our field of activity and through the years providing ourselves with as sound a scientific basis as possible. If a different and somewhat more rigid classification of research in the field covered by the present monograph helps to clarify our thinking on the status of supervision and its scientific basis, it is the judgment of the authors that such a classification will have served a useful purpose.

From one point of view existing research in supervision is of doubtful value. So often the studies have been made under the conditions of questionable organization for supervision, under outmoded concepts of what constitutes effective supervision, and using technics of questionable soundness that it is very difficult to appraise the net value of the whole body of research in this field. One of the first steps in furthering research in supervision is a careful rethinking of the field.

We should not fail to point out in this connection that the term "supervision" has many unfortunate connotations in view of the developments which have taken place in this field in recent years. It implies oversight with the power to control—authoritarian in origin. It has years of traditional association with the concept of separation of planning and performance. It is out of harmony with the scientific method, with our knowledge of child growth, and with our basic social philosophy of democracy. Through the continued use of the term we tend to confuse the thinking of educators and to perpetuate anachronistic concepts of educational leadership. We are therefore stressing the term "educational leadership" in the subsequent discussion.

A few observations are in order concerning the plan of classification of studies in educational leadership. The subdivisions chosen are:

1. Philosophy of Educational Leadership
2. Organization for Educational Leadership
3. Leadership Activities
4. Evaluation of Educational Leadership.

The first of these—Philosophy of Educational Leadership—is as yet without much significant research. It is included in a separate category largely in an effort to call attention to the need for studies in this field.

The Philosophy of Educational Leadership

The entire field of educational administration at present lacks an expressed philosophy. The Sixth Yearbook of the Department of Supervisors and Directors of Instruction of the National Education Association (321) included certain studies of the judgments of teachers and supervisors concerning certain elements in a philosophy of leadership. There is need for a rethinking of the basic assumptions in leadership. Especially do we need to make a careful study of democracy as our basic social philosophy in order to secure its implications for leadership; of science as our basic pattern for the discovery of truth in order to learn its suggestions for leadership activities; of our knowledge of the child and his growth and development in order to learn what kind of school environment is most conducive to growth. Finally we need experimentation with types of organization and activities in order to determine their appropriateness to education and its peculiar demands.

Organization for Educational Leadership

The authoritarian character of past leadership has been clearly shown in such studies as those reported in the Sixth Yearbook of the Department of Supervisors and Directors of Instruction (321). Teachers in this study definitely assumed that it was the supervisor's function to determine methods to be used, content to be taught, and in general to dominate the school. In fact this study gave little evidence that teacher initiative was an important factor in present leadership. For some time, however, theorists have been advocating more dependence upon teacher initiative. One instance is the advocacy of so-called visitation "on call." Thomson (328) and Ringo (323) reported experiments in an effort to apply the principles of teacher initiative in an actual school situation. Thomson kept a card on record of all the calls which teachers sent her for help. Thus she was able not only to keep a record of the number of calls but the nature of the requests and the characteristics of the teachers who made them. Many critics of the teacher initiative plan insist that when it is used only the really competent teachers will call for help. Thomson proved that in her experiment at least this was not true for she provided for the rating of the teachers and the teachers with the lower ratings asked for more help than those with the higher ratings. Thomson followed the development of a supervisory plan from the traditional to the teacher-initiative form over a period of four years and stated that the data "clearly indicated the feasibility" of the program. It was, in her opinion "constructive, stimulating, enlightening." She made this further comment:

> Teachers with university training react more favorably to call supervision than teachers with teachers college training. Teachers who had taught less than six years accepted the new program more readily than those with more experience.

Ringo's study (323), which covered a period of three years, set forth the benefits of supervision based on teacher initiative both to the teacher and the supervisor, and its disadvantages, among which was cited the fact that some teachers call for too much help. However, Ringo declared that under the new plan "there was general growth in independence."

Without doubt the success of the teacher-initiative plan is largely dependent upon the degree of professional interest which prevails in a school system, or which the leader is able to arouse. These studies should be repeated in a variety of ways to give more dependable conclusions.

The tenacity of the authoritative concept of leadership was, however, well shown by a study by Herron (312). It was clear that teachers, leaders, and even specialists in the field hold that most of the really important activities and decisions in the school belong in the province of the supervisor. Ninety percent of the supervisors, superintendents, and recognized leaders in education who expressed themselves made the supervisor responsible for 92 out of 123 specific activities. With the exception of one item, the construction of standardized tests, 60 percent of these judges checked the entire list to the province of the supervisor. More than

90 percent made her responsible for all the activities connected with the planning of the supervisory program and the constructing and revising of the course of study, and almost 80 percent considered that one of her activities should be the performance of clerical duties. It is interesting to note that the judges agreed unanimously on three specific activities: keeping in touch with the latest developments in the field of education; making self-preparation for group conferences; and making self-preparation for supervisory visits. Also, out of the entire list of 123 activities, there were only 15 upon which the judges were not in accord as to their being of major or minor importance.

It is impossible to expect that any widespread progress toward a higher type of teacher leadership could be accomplished without adequate training facilities; and from studies made, one in the field of general supervision by Herron (311) and one in music by Thomas (326), we can do no better than to quote from their conclusions. Herron (311:128) stated:

> Obviously, further evidence of the inadequacy of the present opportunities for the training of general elementary supervisors is unnecessary. If thirty-eight per cent of the teacher training institutions which have set up a specific curriculum for general elementary supervisors do not list a single course in supervision in the curriculum, and fifty-four per cent require but one course, what has otherwise seemed a worthy effort to improve supervision is but an empty farce. The mere labeling of curricula and adding of courses will not suffice. An adequate curriculum for the professional training of general elementary supervisors and directors will obtain only when teacher-training institutions, or those who are responsible for curriculum planning, become thoroughly familiar with the needs of general supervisors, and the instructional materials of the required courses are selected on the basis of their fitness in training for the specific duties and activities of such officers.

Thomas (326) found that according to the standards set for music supervisors by the Music Education Research Council, "Teachers colleges fail to reach the mark in numbers of hours of music theory and applied music required by approximately twenty-one semester hours."

Leadership Activities

In considering studies in the field of leadership activities, little space has been given to the traditional activities such as visitation, teachers meetings, demonstration teaching, and intervisitation. Older studies of these activities made through inventory of teachers' judgments concerning the value of these activities present a discouraging picture. An example is to be found in a study by Hughes and Melby (314) which showed that over 60 percent of the teachers interviewed held that the visits which had been made to their classrooms and the conferences which followed had not changed their teaching in any way. In McGinnis' study (317), 208 elementary-, 101 junior high-, and 99 senior high-school teachers were asked this question:

> Do supervisory visits help you solve problems of (a) classroom management, (b) methods of teaching, (c) diagnosis of pupils' difficulties, (d) the selection of subjectmatter, and (e) the selection of materials of instruction?

From the data collected, three things were evident:

1. Supervisory visits are effective to a high degree in helping the teachers to solve problems of classroom management in the elementary, junior high, and high school.
2. Supervisory visits are considerably less effective in the matter of problems of methods of teaching than in problems of management.
3. In helping teachers to solve problems of diagnosis, selection of subjectmatter, and selection of materials supervisory visits are effective to a high degree in the elementary and junior high school and to a low degree in the high school.

Many reasons have been assigned for the lack of faith in these activities on the part of teachers. Important among these may be the general spirit in which they are carried on and the nature of the technics employed.

Technics for analyzing classroom procedure—One of the most important issues with reference to the various technics has to do with their objectivity, reliability, and validity. Barr (304:565) for instance, after investigating results of the use of nineteen more or less typical instruments for the measuring of teacher ability, said:

> . . . In general, the values calculated were exceedingly low, the most of them, when expressed in terms of coefficients of correlation, falling between 0 and .35. It is unnecessary to say that such results for so large a number of more or less typical instruments for the measurement of teaching ability, are, of course, disappointing . . . . There is undisputable evidence that there is much more work to be done before we can be said to measure teaching ability accurately . . . . Other data showed just how inaccurate our ordinary judgments about teaching ability really are.

McGinnis (317) asked nearly 3,000 teachers this question: "In your opinion as a teacher, to what degree does the use of checklists and teacher rating devices represent good supervisory practice?" Less than 14 percent thought they were valuable to a high or even fairly high degree, while 86 percent expressed the opinion that they were valuable to a low or very low degree. On the other hand, of the 200 or more supervisors who were asked the same question, 50 percent held them to be valuable to a high or fairly high degree; and only 19 percent rated them as being valuable to a very low degree in comparison with 51 percent of the teachers who gave them that rating. McGinnis (317:46-47) made this comment:

> The number of cases . . . is small in comparison with the total number of teachers and supervisors in the American schools . . . no claim is made that these data are reliable for the country as a whole. But they are reliable as representing the opinion of nearly 3,000 teachers of an unselected group in three states. The fact that 86.2 percent of these teachers think the use of check lists and teacher rating devices represents good supervisory practice to only a low or very low degree is strong evidence that there is something decidedly wrong with such devices as now used.

Present devices for analyzing classroom precedure thus seem to have little statistical merit and in addition appear to be given little weight in the opinions of teachers. The concern for the statistical merits of the various technics seems to suggest that leaders in the field have been primarily concerned with the rating function rather than with the problem of helping teachers to improve. Thus one may find that a particular device may possess only a rough accuracy, yet it may be helpful in making a teacher aware of her problems. If it serves this purpose well, we need not be greatly concerned about statistical merit. Of course, if we want technics for rating teachers for salary purposes or status, that is a different matter.

It is possible that teachers have yet to be convinced that the various checklists and devices for analyzing and describing classroom procedure are really used in an effort to help them become better teachers. Perhaps they still believe that supervisors use them primarily for rating purposes. It is likely that this feeling is responsible for the low regard in which the various technics are held rather than their lack of statistical merit.

Relatively little has been done with self-checking, and self-evaluation. This fact probably throws light on the amount of teacher initiative prevailing in our current educational leadership. The teacher is not assumed capable of evaluating herself. This may be true of teachers at present since they have had little practice. One study by Rankin (322) indicated that teachers rate themselves too high. In this case, several hundred teachers were asked to check the items in which they needed supervisory assistance in music. It is a well-known fact that grade teachers have scant preparation for the teaching of music; yet substantial numbers of these teachers indicated that they felt fully competent to handle music work.

In past leadership the rating function has loomed so large that most teachers are probably fearful of any checking or rating scheme lest its use reflect on their standing as teachers. Until supervisors can establish a different relationship with teachers, self-rating or self-analysis will not make much progress.

Cooperative efforts such as those described by McClure (315) are promising. Many of the devices for analyzing or describing classroom procedure could be adapted to self-analysis. Illustrations may be mentioned in the studies by Brand (306), Fields (309), and McCracken (316).

One interesting outcome of the application of the various technics for analyzing and describing classroom procedure seems to be the general disappointment with the conditions they reveal. For years various theorists have attacked the barren question and answer recitation; yet a study by Hughes and Melby (314), in the large, well-supported high schools, showed this method to be used in over 70 percent of the classes observed in social studies. In general, one feels that attempts to describe classroom procedure tend to show an enormous lag between our theory and practice in education. This situation would seem to suggest that the use of such devices by supervisory officers might become a stimulating procedure.

The development of some of the more recent methods of classroom procedure such as the Morrison mastery technic and the activity school have created new problems in the analysis of classroom procedure. When existing technics are applied to some of these newer procedures, they do not appear to be appropriate. New technics must be developed. Since these newer methods depend very largely on a rich classroom experience for their effectiveness and since their outcomes are difficult to measure by means of traditional tests, there is greater need than ever for technics of describing the learning activities of children. Another way to state it is that the educators are more interested in the nature of the learning activities than they are in the exact facts or skills learned. If we can devise methods for describing the learning activities of children we can at least know how children live while they are learning even though we cannot measure all that is learned.

The nature of some of the newer methods also attaches a greater importance to self-analysis and description. Occasional classroom visits are of little value in describing a classroom activity which is continuous over a period of several weeks. In fact, in such cases the teacher herself is probably the best judge of the effectiveness of her own work. We, therefore, need technics for describing and recording classroom activities so that teachers can appraise their own work.

Teacher difficulties—Studies of teacher difficulties are in many ways closely related to technics for analyzing classroom procedure. The chief difference lies in the fact that the difficulties are usually secured as reported by teachers themselves. A study by Brayton (307) indicated that sophomores in a training institution were less aware of their difficulties than juniors and seniors and that experienced teachers report a still larger number of difficulties. Apparently the teacher must acquire considerable theoretical knowledge and practical experience before she can locate her own problems. This same study lists 49 items, 32 of which are generally agreed to be of "very serious difficulty." Out of 20 of these listed in their rank order, only 5 are personality traits while the other 15 have more to do with education, or professional attitude.

Serious difficulties are presented to the traditional supervisor who asks teachers to report their difficulties to her. One teacher said, "How can you expect me to reveal my difficulties today to a person who comes tomorrow to rate me with regard to my status in the school system?" If supervisors are to make serious use of inventories of teacher difficulties, they will need to establish a different relationship to teachers.

Evaluation of Leadership

The effectiveness of a program of leadership should not be assumed without subjecting it to critical analysis. Greenfield (310:123), in his study of elementary supervision, gave three reasons for evaluation:

1. Because, while supervisors have been content to take for granted the effectiveness of their supervision, teachers have long since questioned its worthwhileness
2. Because, if the supervisor's position is to withstand the barrage of economic scrutiny, it will have to be justified by productiveness . . . and

3. Because a critical evaluation of the products of supervision should stimulate supervisors to improve supervision.

These were his conclusions at the close of the two-year period over which the study was made:

1. The time spent in bringing teachers into coöperative working relationship, stimulating them to consciousness of a professional attack upon teaching problems, and enthusing them with a modern philosophical viewpoint of education which shifts the emphasis from factual subject matter to child interest and activity, may not result in a statistically significant difference in the amount of factual material learned. The fruits of such a program should be cumulative and any indication of improvement is indicative of the functioning of such a program.

2. While an average critical ratio of positive .524 is not statistically significant, it can be assumed from these data that teaching can be modernized without jeopardizing factual learning.

3. The fact that the results of a supervisory program such as this do not reveal themselves materially in achievement tests impresses the writer with the necessity for the use of data gathering devices which will measure the more elusive developments in child personality.

4. The teachers coöperating in this program made some definite improvement in their teaching practices. It is interesting to note that the teachers making the greatest improvement were also the persons whose groups made the most significant gains in pupil achievement.

Ullemeyer (329), in an endeavor to learn "to what extent music supervision has kept pace with developments in education and in supervision generally," drew these conclusions:

1. Modern educational movements as a whole are not expressed in the practice of public school music teaching.

2. Supervisory activities employed in schools observed are designed for didactic supervision.

3. Absence of initiative and originality and lack of understanding of the purposes of supervision on the part of teachers who teach music are characteristics of teachers who retard progress of classroom music.

4. The lack of preparation in music on the part of classroom teachers constitutes a major problem in music supervision.

5. Music supervisors as a whole are well-trained and progressive in their own specific field but they are not trained in the field of general educational philosophy and supervision.

6. There is a need for problem solving and research by supervisors and teachers of music.

The findings by Brady (305) in his study of the objectives and functions of supervision follow:

1. The supervisor must have a plan and a philosophy of general education and of education in his own special field.

2. His activities must be an attempt to evaluate and improve the procedures within his department in the light of this philosophy.

3. He must keep abreast of the findings in his field and modify his plan when it has been demonstrated it is advisable for him to do so.

4. He must be understanding, sympathetic, constructive, and impersonal in his supervisory functions.

5. So far as is possible, he should effect modification of teaching methods and departmental procedures through the efforts of his stronger teachers. Discussion by a small group of teachers facing the same problem, with the intelligent, sympathetic leadership of the supervisor, will undoubtedly result in plans much more effective than by declaration of the supervisor alone.

6. Supervision should be upon an objective basis whenever possible. Visitation and the conference are supplemented by check-lists, unit tests, and departmental tests as the means employed to accomplish this aim (305: 141).

The existing literature on evaluation, a few samples of which have been submitted above, is exceedingly disappointing. The whole project of evaluating leadership is beset with difficulties. In the first place we are not clear on the place or role of the leader in educational progress. Suppose that in a certain school there is no supervisor. This fact does not prevent educational progress in that school. There might be curriculum projects, experimentation, and many other evidences of growth on the part of teachers and improvement in educational procedure. Let us now assume that a supervisor is employed. How shall we evaluate her presence and leadership? Suppose she changes the curriculum and methods used. Will there be greater learning on the part of children? We cannot tell. Suppose children learn less under the new curriculum? Has the supervisor failed? Not necessarily. She may have been in error in her choice of procedures. It should be noticed that in this instance we are confusing leadership and problems of curriculum or method. It would seem that curriculums and other elements in education must be evaluated as such, apart from supervision. Nearly all of our experiments in evaluation so far confuse the various factors involved.

Teacher growth is probably the best measure of the supervisor's effectiveness. That is not to say that teacher growth is impossible without a supervisor. Does the presence of the supervisor or of a certain supervisory set-up, accelerate or enrich teacher growth? Here we have practically no studies.

In evaluating leadership complete dependence cannot be placed upon controlled experimentation. Probably the most helpful work will come from case studies. In these we shall keep careful record of the nature of the organization for leadership and its activities. We shall also describe what happens in the school in teacher activities along lines of professional growth. In these cases we shall not be able to say what growth would have occurred if different procedures had been followed. We can only say that in a given situation certain things were done and here is a picture of what happened. If we have a large number of such cases, certain generalizations will be possible. In such procedures we would be following technics somewhat similar to those utilized in medical case studies.

Research in leadership is essentially a problem of evaluation. We shall probably make progress here largely as our leaders learn to describe and record their activities and their attendant development. We need to accumulate such data in regard to a wide variety of leadership activities and types of organization. It is especially important that the various types of research undertaken should take proper cognizance of the educational program in the schools. In existing practice there is too often a conflict between the objectives of the school and those of the leadership; between the principles basic to learning on the part of children and those which are basic to the activities of the supervisor. Sound evaluation will be possible only as leaders have clear objectives and as they are consistent in their application.

BIBLIOGRAPHY ON PSYCHOLOGY OF LEARNING, GENERAL METHODS OF TEACHING, AND SUPERVISION

Chapter I. Theoretical Aspects of Learning and Transfer of Training

1. ALLEN, GRACE E. "Individualized Method and Character Education." *Journal of Educational Sociology* 7: 254-58; December, 1933.
2. ARONS, LEON. "Serial Learning and Generalizing Abstraction." *American Journal of Psychology* 45: 417-32; July, 1933.
3. BEDDELL, R. C. "Relationship between the Ability to Recall and the Ability to Infer in Specific Learning Situations—Abstract." *Science Education* 18: 158-62; October, 1934.
4. BELLOWS, R. M. "Configurational Interpretation of Memory as Related to the Learning Process." *Journal of Experimental Education* 3: 1-10; September, 1934.
5. BOND, ELIAS A. *The Professional Treatment of the Subject Matter of Arithmetic for Teacher-Training Institutions, Grades I to VI.* Contributions to Education, No. 525. New York: Teachers College, Columbia University, 1934. p. 15-25.
6. BRITT, S. H. "The Relationship between Transfer of Learning and Age of Previous Associations." *American Journal of Psychology* 46: 113-16; January, 1934.
7. BRITT, S. H. "Retroactive Inhibition: A Review of the Literature." *Psychological Bulletin* 32: 381-440; 1935.
8. BROWN, C. W. "Subcortical Mechanisms in Learning." *Psychological Review* 42: 307-34; July, 1935.
9. BROWN, J. F., and FEDER, D. D. "Thorndike's Theory of Learning as Gestalt Psychology." *Psychological Bulletin* 31: 426-37; June, 1934.
10. BROWNELL, WILLIAM A. "Educational Research on Learning." *Educational Outlook* 8: 210-19; May, 1934.
11. BRUCE, ROBERT W. "Conditions of Transfer of Training." *Journal of Experimental Psychology* 16: 343-61; June, 1933.
12. CAMPBELL, DON W., and STOVER, G. F. "Teaching International-Mindedness in the Social Studies." *Journal of Educational Sociology* 7: 244-48; December, 1933.
13. CARR, J. W., JR. "The Relationship between the Theories of Gestalt Psychology and Those of a Progressive Science of Education." *Journal of Educational Psychology* 25: 192-202; March, 1934.
14. COOK, THOMAS W. "Studies in Cross Education: III. Kinæsthetic Learning of an Irregular Pattern." *Journal of Experimental Psychology* 17: 749-62; October, 1934.
15. COOPER, BERENICE. "Can We Teach Grammar for Composition?" *English Journal* (*Coll. Ed.*) 22: 826-33; December, 1933.
16. COX, J. W. "Some Experiments of Formal Training in the Acquisition of Skill." *British Journal of Psychology* 26: 67-87; 1933.
17. CRESSMAN, ELMER W. "Workbook versus Oral Instruction." *Journal of Educational Sociology* 7: 250-53; December, 1933.
18. CURTI, MARGARET W. Book Review of *Principles of Mental Development* by Raymond H. Wheeler and Francis T. Perkins. *Psychological Bulletin* 31: 438-49; June, 1934.
19. DASHIELL, J. F. "A Survey and Synthesis of Learning Theories." *Psychological Bulletin* 32: 261-75; 1935.
20. DAVIS, ROBERT A. *Psychology of Learning.* New York: McGraw-Hill Book Co., 1935. 490 p.

21. DOWNING, ELLIOT R. "Does Science Teach Scientific Thinking?" *Science Education* 17: 87-89; April, 1933.
22. EICHLER, GEORGE A., and MERRILL, ROBERT R. "Can Social Leadership Be Improved by Instruction in its Techniques?" *Journal of Educational Sociology* 7: 233-36; December, 1933.
23. FAWCETT, HAROLD P. "Teaching for Transfer." *Mathematics Teacher* 28: 465-72; December, 1935.
24. FRANZ, S. I., and OTHERS. *Studies in Cerebral Function: Parts I-III.* Publication in Education, Philosophy, Psychology, Vol. I, No. 3-5. Berkeley: University of California, Southern Branch, 1933. p. 65-98.
25. GATES, ARTHUR I. *Generalization and Transfer in Spelling.* New York: Teachers College, Columbia University, 1935. 80 p.
26. GENGERELLI, J. A. *Brain Fields and the Learning Process.* Psychological Monographs, Vol. 45, No. 4. Princeton, N. J.: Psychological Review Co., 1934. 115 p.
27. GILBERT, LUTHER C. "Effect of Reading on Spelling in the Ninth Grade." *School Review* 42: 197-204; March, 1934.
28. GUTHERIE, EDWIN R. "Discussion: Pavlov's Theory of Conditioning." *Psychological Review* 41: 199-206; March, 1934.
29. GUTHERIE, EDWIN R. *Psychology of Learning.* New York: Harper and Brothers, 1935. 258 p.
30. HACKENBURG, J. L.; YEICH, E. B.; and WEISENFLUH, L. A. "The Effect of Athletics on Certain Character Studies." *Journal of Educational Sociology* 7: 264-68; December, 1933.
31. HARLOW, HARRY F., and STAGNER, ROSS. "Effect of Complete Striate Muscle Paralysis Upon the Learning Process." *Journal of Experimental Psychology* 16: 283-94; April, 1933.
32. HOBSON, CLOY S. "Is Instruction in the Principles of Honesty Effective?" *Educational Research Bulletin (Ohio State University)* 13: 78-87; April, 1934.
33. HSIAO, H. H. "The Belongingness of Non-belonging Impressions." *Journal of Experimental Psychology* 18: 227-45; April, 1935.
34. HULIN, WILBUR S., and KATZ, DANIEL. "Transfer of Training in Reading Braille." *American Journal of Psychology* 46: 627-31; October, 1934.
35. HULL, CLARK L. "The Concept of the Habit-Family Hierarchy and Maze Learning." *Psychological Review* 41: 33-54, 134-52; January-March, 1934.
36. HULL, CLARK L. "Learning: II. The Factor of the Conditioned Reflex." *A Handbook of General Experimental Psychology.* (Edited by Carl Murchison.) Worcester, Mass.: Clark University Press, 1934. Chapter 9, p. 382-455.
37. HUNTER, WALTER S. "Learning: IV. Experimental Studies of Learning." *A Handbook of General Experimental Psychology.* (Edited by Carl Murchison.) Worcester, Mass.: Clark University Press, 1934. Chapter 11, p. 497-570.
38. HUNTER, WALTER S. "The Stimulus-Neural Control of Behavior during and after Learning." *Science* 79: 145-51; February 16, 1934.
39. JACOBSON, PAUL B. *Two Experiments with Work-Type Reading Exercises in Ninth Grade.* Studies in Education, Vol. 8, No. 5. Iowa City: University of Iowa, 1933. 85 p.
40. JOHNSON, LAURA; HINDERMAN, ROY A.; and RYAN, H. H. "Language Transfer." *Journal of Educational Research* 26: 579-84; April, 1933.
41. KNISS, F. R.; ROBB, E. K.; and GLATFELTER, E. A. "The Results of the Incidental Method of Instruction in Character Education." *Journal of Educational Sociology* 7: 259-63; December, 1933.
42. KOFFKA, KURT. *Principles of Gestalt Psychology.* New York: Harcourt, Brace and Co., 1935. 720 p. (Chapters X-XIII.)
43. KRECHEVSKY, ISADORE. "Brain Mechanisms and 'Hypotheses'." *Journal of Comparative Psychology* 19: 425-68; June, 1935.
44. LASHLEY, K. S. "Learning: III. Nervous Mechanisms in Learning." *A Handbook of General Experimental Psychology.* (Edited by Carl Murchison.) Worcester, Mass.: Clark University Press, 1934. Chapter 10, p. 456-96.
45. LASHLEY, K. S.; McDONALD, W. T.; and PETERS, H. N. "Studies of Cerebral Function in Learning. X. The Effect of Dilatation of the Ventricles upon Maze Learning." *American Journal of Psychology* 104: 51-61; April 1, 1933.
46. LEHMAN, HARVEY C. "A Class Experiment in the Transfer of Training." *Journal of Applied Psychology* 17: 77-82; February, 1933.

47. LIDDELL, H. S.; JAMES, W. T.; and ANDERSON, O. D. *The Comparative Physiology of the Conditioned Motor Reflex; Based on Experiments with the Pig, Dog, Sheep, Goat, and Rabbit.* Comparative Psychology Monographs, Vol. 11, No. 1. Baltimore: Johns Hopkins University Press, 1934. 89 p.
48. LONGSTREET, RUPERT J. "Experiments with the Thurstone Attitude Scales." *School Review* 43: 202-8; March, 1935.
49. MCCONNELL, T. RAYMOND. "Discovery vs. Authoritative Identification in the Learning of Children." *Studies in the Psychology of Learning, II. Studies in Education,* Vol. 9, No. 5. Iowa City: University of Iowa, 1934. p. 13-62.
50. MCDOUGALL, WILLIAM. *The Energies of Men.* New York: Charles Scribner's Sons, 1933. Chapter 23, "Learning and the Steering Processes," p. 335-67.
51. MCGEOCH, JOHN A. "The Configurational Psychology of Learning." *Journal of Applied Psychology* 17: 83-96; February, 1933.
52. MCGEOCH, JOHN A. "Learning." *Psychology.* (Edited by E. G. Boring and others.) New York: John Wiley and Sons, 1935. Chapter 13.
53. MCGEOCH, JOHN A. "Learning and Retention of Verbal Materials." *Psychological Bulletin* 31: 381-407; June, 1934.
54. MCKINNEY, FRED. "Quantitative and Qualitative Essential Elements of Transfer." *Journal of Experimental Psychology* 16: 854-64; December, 1933.
55. MEEK, ELIZABETH B. "The Effect of the Study of Latin upon Character Traits." *Journal of Educational Sociology* 7: 241-43; December, 1933.
56. MILSOM, ALICE K. "The Teaching of Courtesy in the Junior High School." *Journal of Educational Sociology* 7: 249; December, 1933.
57. OGDEN, R. M. "The Gestalt Theory of Learning." *School and Society* 41: 527-33; April 20, 1935.
58. ORATA, PEDRO T. "Transfer of Training and Educational Pseudo-Science." *Mathematics Teacher* 28: 265-89; May, 1935.
59. POFFENBERGER, ALBERT T. "Psychology and Life." *Psychological Review* 43: 9-31; January, 1936.
60. ROBB, E. K., and FAUST, J. F. "The Effect of Direct Instruction." *Journal of Educational Sociology* 7: 237-40; December, 1933.
61. SALISBURY, RACHEL. "Integration and Transfer in the Junior High School." *Junior-Senior High School Clearing House* 9: 423-27; March, 1935.
62. SALISBURY, RACHEL. "A Study of the Transfer Effects of Training in Logical Organization." *Journal of Educational Research* 28: 241-54; December, 1934.
63. SHIPLEY, WALTER C. "An Apparent Transfer of Conditioning." *Journal of General Psychology* 8: 382-91; April, 1933.
64. SINCLAIR, J. H., and TOLMAN, RUTH SHERMAN. "An Attempt to Study the Effect of Scientific Training upon Prejudice and Illogicality of Thought." *Journal of Educational Psychology* 24: 362-70; May, 1933.
65. TAYLOR, EARL B. "What does the Configurationist Say?" *Journal of Engineering Education* 23: 365-76; January, 1933.
66. THORNDIKE, EDWARD L. *Educational Psychology: Briefer Course.* New York: Teachers College, Columbia University, 1914. 442 p.
67. THORNDIKE, EDWARD L., and OTHERS. "The Spread of the Influence of Reward of Connections Irrelevant to the Learner's Purpose." *Pedagogical Seminary and Journal of Genetic Psychology* 44: 428-36; June, 1934.
68. UHL, WILLIS L. "Timidity about the Transfer of Training." *Junior-Senior High School Clearing House* 7: 493-94; April, 1933.
69. WASHBURNE, J. N. "An Electro-Chemical Theory of Learning." *Journal of Educational Psychology* 26: 99-122; February, 1935.
70. WATERS, R. H. "The Law of Effect as a Principle of Learning." *Psychological Bulletin* 31: 408-25; June, 1934.
71. WHEELER, RAYMOND HOLDER. "The New Psychology of Learning." *The Teaching of Arithmetic.* Tenth Yearbook, National Council of Teachers of Mathematics. New York: Teachers College, Columbia University, 1935. p. 233-50.
72. WHELDEN, CHESTER HOWARD, JR. "Training in Latin and the Quality of other Academic Work." *Journal of Educational Psychology* 24: 481-97; October, 1933.

Chapter II. Types of Learning and General Conditions Affecting Learning

73. ALTENEDER, LOUISE E. "The Learning Curve in Solving a Jig-Saw Puzzle." *Journal of Educational Psychology* 26: 231-32; March, 1935.
74. BEDELL, RALPH CLAIRON. *The Relationship between the Ability to Recall and the Ability to Infer in Specific Learning Situations.* Doctor's thesis, University of Missouri, 1934.
75. BEEBE, ELINOR LEE. *Motor Learning of Children in Equilibrium in Relation to Nutrition.* Genetic Psychology Monographs, Vol. 15, No. 2. Worcester, Mass.: Clark University Press, 1934. p. 99-243.
76. BEEBE, ELINOR LEE. "Motor Learning of Children in Hand and Eye Coördination with Introduction of Prismatic Deflection." *Child Development* 4: 6-25; March, 1933.
77. BETTS, EVELYN W. *Time-Limit vs. Work-Limit in Learning.* Baltimore: Williams and Wilkins Co., 1934. 58 p.
78. BRUECKNER, LEO J. "Pedagogical Factors Associated with Learning Difficulty." *Educational Diagnosis.* Thirty-fourth Yearbook, National Society for the Study of Education. Bloomington, Ill.: Public School Publishing Co., 1935. p. 49-62.
79. CALHOON, STEPHEN WALLACE. "Influence of Length of Lists upon Ability Immediately to Reproduce Disconnected Word-Series Auditorially Presented." *Journal of Experimental Psychology* 17: 723-38; October, 1934.
80. CARTER, HAROLD D. "A Study of Errors in Learning." *Psychological Bulletin* 31: 589; October, 1934.
81. CASON, HULSEY. "The Role of Verbal Activities in the Conditioning of Human Subjects." *Psychological Review* 41: 563-71; November, 1934.
82. CHASE, WILTON P. "The Role of Kinesthesis in Ideational Maze Learning." *Journal of Experimental Psychology* 17: 424-38; June, 1934.
83. COOKE, DENNIS H. "Two Experiments in Learning Educational Statistics." *Journal of Educational Research* 26: 674-78; May, 1933.
84. CRAFTS, LELAND W., and ALLEN, R. MORRIS. "A Comparison of Simultaneous and Successive Methods of Motor Learning." *American Journal of Psychology* 46: 459-61; July, 1934.
85. DUNCAN, BERTHA K. "A Comparative Study of Finger-Maze Learning by Blind and Sighted Subjects." *Pedagogical Seminary and Journal of Genetic Psychology* 44: 69-95; March, 1934.
86. DUNLAP, JACK W. *The Organization of Learning and Other Traits in Chickens.* Comparative Psychology Monographs, Vol. 9, No. 4. Baltimore: Johns Hopkins University Press, 1933. 55 p.
87. EASLEY, HOWARD. "An Analysis of the Curves of Learning and Forgetting Code Material." *Journal of Educational Psychology* 24: 634-40; November, 1933.
88. EMMONS, ARDITH L. "A Study of the Relation between Self-Assurance and Skill in Young Children." *Child Development* 4: 323-28; December, 1933.
89. ENGLISH, HORACE B.; WELBORN, E. L.; and KILLIAN, C. D. "Paradoxical Forgetting or Learning Without Overt Practice." *Psychological Bulletin* 30: 697-98; November, 1933.
90. EURICH, ALVIN C. "Retention of Knowledge Acquired in a Course in General Psychology." *Journal of Applied Psychology* 18: 209-19; April, 1934.
91. FEHRER, ELIZABETH V. "An Investigation of the Learning of Visually Perceived Forms." *American Journal of Psychology* 47: 187-221; April, 1935.
92. GATES, ARTHUR I., chairman. "Special Methods and Psychology of the Elementary-School Subjects." *Review of Educational Research* 5: 1-120; February, 1935.
93. GIBSON, ELEANOR J., and GIBSON, JAMES J. "Retention and the Interpolated Task." *American Journal of Psychology* 46: 603-10; October, 1934.
94. GORDON, KATE. "Some Records of the Memorizing of Sonnets." *Journal of Experimental Psychology* 16: 701-8; October, 1933.

95. HAMILTON, HUGHBERT C. "The Relation between Length of Task and Amount of Work Required to Learn with Finger Maze and Nonsense Syllable Material." *Psychological Bulletin* 30: 674-75; November, 1933.
96. HANAWALT, ELLA M. "Whole and Part Methods in Trial and Error Learning." *Journal of Experimental Psychology* 17: 691-708; October, 1934.
97. HARTMANN, GEORGE W. "Insight vs. Trial-and-Error in the Solution of Problems." *American Journal of Psychology* 45: 663-77; October, 1933.
98. HELSON, HARRY. "The Relation between Instructions and Past Experience in a Simple Observational Task." *Journal of Educational Psychology* 25: 29-38; January, 1934.
99. HENRY, LYLE K. "The Role of Insight in the Analytic Thinking of Adolescents." *Studies in the Psychology of Learning, II.* Studies in Education, Vol. 9, No. 5. Iowa City: University of Iowa, 1934. p. 65-102.
100. HILL, L. B. "A Quarter Century of Delayed Recall." *Pedagogical Seminary and Journal of Genetic Psychology* 44: 231-38; March, 1934.
101. HYDE, EDITH I. "The Measurement of Achievement in Archery." *Journal of Educational Research* 27: 673-86; May, 1934.
102. KELLOGG, W. N., and WHITE, ROSE E. "A Maze Test of Dunlap's Theory of Learning." *Journal of Comparative Psychology* 19: 119-48; February, 1935.
103. KOLBERG, O. W. "A Study of Summer-Time Forgetting." *Elementary School Journal* 35: 281-87; December, 1934.
104. LANGER, WALTER C. "An Apparatus for Studying Sensorimotor Learning, Retention and Reaction Time." *Journal of General Psychology* 12: 228-38; January, 1935.
105. LANGLIE, T. A. "A New Device for Studying Learning." *Journal of General Psychology* 11: 218-23; July, 1934.
106. LEPLEY, WILLIAM M. "A Gradient in Incidental Learning." *Journal of Experimental Psychology* 18: 195-201; April, 1935.
107. LUMLEY, FREDERICK H. "Anticipation and Erroneous Responses." *Journal of Experimental Psychology* 17: 48-64; February, 1934.
108. MCCONNELL, T. RAYMOND. "Discovery vs. Authoritative Identification in the Learning of Children." *Studies in the Psychology of Learning, II.* Studies in Education, Vol. 9, No. 5. Iowa City: University of Iowa, 1934. p. 13-62.
109. MCGEOCH, GRACE O. "The Conditions of Reminiscence." *American Journal of Psychology* 47: 65-89; January, 1935.
110. MCGEOCH, GRACE O. "The Factor of Degree of Learning in Reminiscence: A Second Comparative Study of Preschool Children and College Students." *Pedagogical Seminary and Journal of Genetic Psychology* 46: 455-62; June, 1935.
111. MCGEOCH, JOHN A. "Changes Accompanying Practice upon Successive Samples of Verbal Material." *Journal of General Psychology* 9: 117-29; July, 1933.
112. MCGEOCH, JOHN A. "Curves of Memorization after Different Amounts of Practice." *American Journal of Psychology* 45: 678-90; October, 1933.
113. MCGEOCH, JOHN A. "Learning and Retention of Verbal Materials." *Psychological Bulletin* 31: 381-407; June, 1934.
114. MCGEOCH, JOHN A., and MCKINNEY, FRED. "Retroactive Inhibition in the Learning of Poetry." *American Journal of Psychology* 46: 19-33; January, 1934.
115. MCGEOCH, JOHN A. "Studies in Retroactive Inhibition." *Journal of General Psychology* 9: 24-57; July, 1933.
116. MCGEOCH, JOHN A., and MCKINNEY, FRED. "The Susceptibility of Prose to Retroactive Inhibition." *American Journal of Psychology* 46: 429-36; July, 1934.
117. MCKINNEY, FRED. "Studies in the Retention of Interrupted Learning Activities." *Journal of Comparative Psychology* 19: 265-96; April, 1935.
118. MASLOW, A. H. "The Effect of Varying Time Intervals between Acts of Learning with a Note on Proactive Inhibition." *Journal of Experimental Psychology* 17: 141-44; February, 1934.
119. MATTSON, MARION L. *The Relation between the Complexity of the Habit to Be Acquired and the Form of the Learning Curve in Young Children.* Genetic Psychology Monographs, Vol. 13, No. 4. Worcester, Mass.: Clark University Press, 1933. p. 299-398.

120. MELTON, A. W. "The Final Spurt in Memorization Curves as an Artifact of the Method Used for Averaging Individual Curves." *Psychological Bulletin* 31: 719; November, 1934.
121. MELTON, A. W. "The Relation between Repetitions and Length of List in the Learning of Meaningless and Meaningful Materials." *Psychological Bulletin* 30: 542; October, 1933.
122. MITCHELL, MILDRED B. "The Alleged Warming-up Effect in Memorization." *Journal of Experimental Psychology* 16: 138-43; February, 1933.
123. MITCHELL, MILDRED B. "The Effect of Serial Position in the Continuous Memorization of Numbers." *American Journal of Psychology* 45: 493-94; July, 1933.
124. MITCHELL, MILDRED B. "Errors in the Memorization of Numbers." *American Journal of Psychology* 45: 1-16; January, 1933.
125. MONROE, WALTER S., chairman. "Psychology and Methods in the High School and College." *Review of Educational Research* 4: 445-563; December, 1934.
126. MORGAN, CLELLEN L. "Characteristics of Problem-solving Behavior of Adults." *Studies in the Psychology of Learning, II.* Studies in Education, Vol. 9, No. 5. Iowa City: University of Iowa, 1934. p. 105-43.
127. MORGAN, CLELLEN L. "Meaning versus Repetition, Recency, and Effect in the Determination of Choices of Alternative Letters of a Mental Maze." *Journal of Experimental Psychology* 17: 839-46; December, 1934.
128. NOREM, G. M., and WIEDERAENDERS, M. F. *Studies in the Psychology of Learning.* Studies in Education, Vol. 8, No. 6. Iowa City: University of Iowa, 1933. 75 p.
129. PETERSON, JOSEPH. "Aspects of Learning." *Psychological Review* 42: 1-27; January, 1935.
130. RAFFEL, GERTRUDE. "The Effect of Recall on Forgetting." *Journal of Experimental Psychology* 17: 828-38; December, 1934.
131. ROCKWELL, JOHN GUNDERSEN. "Physical Conditioning Factors in Learning." *Educational Diagnosis.* Thirty-fourth Yearbook, National Society for the Study of Education. Bloomington, Ill.: Public School Publishing Co., 1935. p. 17-36.
132. ROSS, ROBERT T. "Optimum Orders for the Presentation of Pairs in the Method of Paired Comparisons." *Journal of Educational Psychology* 25: 375-82; May, 1934.
133. SCOTT, T. C., and HENNINGER, L. L. "The Relation between Length and Difficulty in Motor Learning; a Comparison with Verbal Learning." *Journal of Experimental Psychology* 16: 657-78; October, 1933.
134. SHAY, CLAYTON T. "The Progressive-Part vs. the Whole Method of Learning Motor Skills." *Research Quarterly of the American Physical Education Association* 5: 62-67; December, 1934.
135. SIIPOLA, ELSA M., and ISRAEL, HAROLD E. "Habit-Interference as Dependent upon Stage Training." *American Journal of Psychology* 45: 205-27; April, 1933.
136. SMITH, STEVENSON. "The Principle of Specific Conditioners." *Pedagogical Seminary and Journal of Genetic Psychology* 46: 296-302; June, 1935.
137. SMITH, STEVENSON, and FITCH, ESTHER E. "Skill and Proprioceptor Pattern." *Pedagogical Seminary and Journal of Genetic Psychology* 46: 303-10; June, 1935.
138. SMOKE, KENNETH L. "Negative Instances in Concept Learning." *Journal of Experimental Psychology* 16: 583-88; August, 1933.
139. THORNDIKE, EDWARD L. "The Influence of the Repetition of a Situation." *American Journal of Psychology* 46: 420-28; July, 1934.
140. THORNDIKE, EDWARD L. "Measurements of the Influence of Recency." *American Journal of Psychology* 47: 294-300; April, 1935.
141. THORNDIKE, EDWARD L. "Primitive Forms of Belief and Knowledge." *Psychological Review* 41: 403-11; September, 1934.
142. THORNDIKE, EDWARD L. "A Proof of the Law of Effect." *Science* 77: 173-75; February 10, 1933.
143. THURSTONE, L. L. "The Error Function in Maze Learning." *Journal of General Psychology* 9: 288-301; October, 1933.
144. TRAVIS, LEE EDWARD. "Intellectual Factors." *Educational Diagnosis.* Thirty-fourth Yearbook, National Society for the Study of Education. Bloomington, Ill.: Public School Publishing Co., 1935. p. 37-47.

145. TYLER, R. W. "Permanence of Learning." *Journal of Higher Education* 4: 203-4; April, 1933.
146. WAGNER, ROBERT P. "An Experiment with the Number Maze as a Measure of Learning." *Journal of Applied Psychology* 17: 614-20; October, 1933.
147. WELBORN, ERNEST L. "A Study of Logical Learning in College Classes." *Twentieth Annual Conference on Educational Measurements.* Bulletin of the School of Education, Vol. 10, No. 1. Bloomington: Indiana University, 1933. p. 12-20.
148. WENGER, M. A. "Path-Selection Behavior of Young Children in Body-Mazes." *Journal of Experimental Education* 2: 197-236; December, 1933.
149. WHITE, M. M. "The Relation of Instructions to Electrical Resistance and Performance." *Journal of General Psychology* 12: 383-96; April, 1935.
150. WOLFLE, DAEL L. "The Relative Efficiency of Constant and Varied Stimulation during Learning." *Journal of Comparative Psychology* 19: 5-27; February, 1935.
151. YOUNG, A. L. "The Comparative Efficiency of Varied and Constant Methods in Sensorimotor Learning." *Journal of Experimental Psychology* 18: 133-40; February, 1935.

Chapter III. Motivation, Emotional Responses, Maturation, Intelligence, and Individual Differences

152. BAKER, LAWRENCE M. "A Study of the Relationship between Changes in Breathing and Pulse Rate, and the Amount Learned Following Supposed Emotional and Supposed Non-Emotional Stimuli." *Journal of General Psychology* 11: 348-68; October, 1934.
153. BATHHURST, JAMES E. "The Maturation and Learning of Serial Reaction-Time and Muscular Coördination Involving Visual Stimuli." *Psychological Bulletin* 31: 701; November, 1934.
154. BAYLEY, NANCY. "Some Comparisons between Growth in Motor and in Mental Abilities in Young Children." *Psychological Bulletin* 31: 608; October, 1934.
155. BRANDT, HYMAN. *The Spread of the Influence of Reward to Bonds Remote in Sequence and Time.* Archives of Psychology, No. 180. New York: Columbia University, 1935. 45 p.
156. BRENNER, BENJAMIN. *Effect of Immediate and Delayed Praise and Blame upon Learning and Recall.* Contributions to Education, No. 620. New York: Teachers College, Columbia University, 1934. 52 p.
157. CARTER, H. D.; JONES, H. E.; and SHOCK, N. W. "An Experimental Study of Affective Factors in Learning." *Journal of Educational Psychology* 25: 203-15; March, 1934.
158. CARTER, H. D., and JONES, H. E. "A Study of Emotional Factors in Learning and Retention." *Psychological Bulletin* 30: 586; October, 1933.
159. CRAFTS, L. W., and GILBERT, R. S. "Effect of Knowledge of Results on Maze Learning and Retention." *Journal of Educational Psychology* 26: 177-87; March, 1935.
160. CRAFTS, L. W., and GILBERT, R. W. "The Effect of Punishment during Learning upon Retention." *Journal of Experimental Psychology* 17: 73-84; February, 1934.
161. CRUZE, WENDELL W. "Maturation and Learning in Chicks." *Journal of Comparative Psychology* 19: 371-409; June, 1935.
162. DREVER, J. I. "The Pre-Insight Period in Learning." *British Journal of Psychology (General Section)* 25: 197-203; October, 1934.
163. ECKERT, RUTH E. "The Problem of Intellectual Maturity." *Studies in Articulation of High School and College.* University of Buffalo Studies, Vol. 9. Buffalo: the University, 1934. p. 103-22.
164. ECKERT, RUTH E. "Who Is the Superior Student?" *Studies in Articulation of High School and College.* University of Buffalo Studies, Vol. 9. Buffalo: the University, 1934. p. 11-50.
165. EISENSON, JON. *Confirmation and Information in Rewards of Punishment.* Archives of Psychology, No. 181. New York: Columbia University, 1935. 37 p.

166. FINCH, FRANK H., and FLOYD, O. R. "The Relation of Chronological Age to Achievement in the Study of French." *Journal of Educational Psychology* 26: 52-58; January, 1935.
167. GARRISON, KARL C. Motivation and Learning." *Peabody Reflector* 7: 171-72; 1934.
168. GILBERT, R. W., and CRAFTS, L. W. "The Effect of Signal for Error upon Maze Learning and Retention." *Journal of Experimental Psychology* 18: 121-32; February, 1935.
169. GILLILAND, A. R. "The Law of Effect in Learning." *Psychological Bulletin* 30: 721-22; November, 1933.
170. GRAY, WENDELL L. "The Effect of Forced Activity on Maze Learning and Selection of Food in White Rats." *Psychological Bulletin* 30: 615-16; October, 1933.
171. GULLIKSEN, HAROLD. "A Rational Equation of the Learning Curve based on Thorndike's Law of Effect." *Journal of General Psychology* 11: 395-434; October, 1934.
172. GUTHRIE, E. R. "Reward and Punishment." *Psychological Review* 41: 450-60; September, 1934.
173. HALVERSON, H. M. "The Acquisition of Skill in Infancy." *Pedagogical Seminary and Journal of Genetic Psychology* 43: 3-48; September, 1933.
174. HANSEN, JOHN ELMER. "The Effect of Educational Motion Pictures upon the Retention of Informational Learning." *Journal of Experimental Education* 2: 1-4; September, 1933.
175. HARTER, RICHARD S. "A Study of Individual Differences in Associative Capacity." *Pedagogical Seminary and Journal of Genetic Psychology* 44: 139-53; March, 1934.
176. HARTMANN, GEORGE W., and HAMM, ANSON MARK. "Variations in Affective Tone of Different Areas of Educational Psychology." *Journal of Educational Psychology* 25: 115-35; February, 1934.
177. IRWIN, F. W., and OTHERS. "On Learning without Awareness of What Is Being Learned." *Journal of Experimental Psychology* 17: 823-27; December, 1934.
178. JENSEN, MILTON B. "Punishment by Electric Shock as Affecting Performance on a Raised Finger Maze." *Journal of Experimental Psychology* 17: 65-72; February, 1934.
179. JONES, HAROLD E. "The Laws of Emphasis and Effect in Children's Learning." *Psychological Bulletin* 31: 597-98; October, 1934.
180. JONES, JAMES RICHARD. "The Influence of Some Antipyretic Drugs on Learning." *Journal of General Psychology* 9: 472-75; October, 1933.
181. KEYS, NOEL. "The Influence of True-False Items on Specific Learning." *Journal of Educational Psychology* 25: 511-20; October, 1934.
182. KEYS, NOEL. "The Influence on Learning and Retention of Weekly as Opposed to Monthly Tests." *Journal of Educational Psychology* 25: 427-36; September, 1934.
183. KORINS, MEYER. "A Study in Eye-Hand Coördination." *Journal of Experimental Psychology* 17: 878-84; December, 1934.
184. LANGHORNE, MAURICE CURTIS. "Age and Sex Differences in Pursuitmeter Learning." *Psychological Bulletin* 30: 623-24; October, 1933.
185. LANGHORNE, MAURICE CURTIS. "Age and Sex Differences in the Acquisition of One Type of Skilled Movement." *Journal of Experimental Education* 2: 101-8; December, 1933.
186. LEEPER, ROBERT. "The Role of Motivation in Learning: A Study of the Phenomenon of Differential Motivational Control of the Utilization of Habits." *Pedagogical Seminary and Journal of Genetic Psychology* 46: 3-40; March, 1935.
187. LORGE, IRVING, and THORNDIKE, EDWARD L. "The Comparative Strengthening of a Connection by One or More Occurrences of It in Cases Where the Connection Was Punished and Was Neither Punished nor Rewarded." *Journal of Experimental Psychology* 16: 374-82; June, 1933.
188. LORGE, IRVING. "The Effect of the Initial Chances for Right Responses upon the Efficacy of Intensified Reward and of Intensified Punishment." *Journal of Experimental Psychology* 16: 362-73; June, 1933.

189. LORGE, IRVING. "The Efficacy of Intensified Reward and of Intensified Punishment." *Journal of Experimental Psychology* 16: 177-207; April, 1933.
190. LORGE, IRVING; EISENSON, JACK; and EPSTEIN, BERTRAM. "Further Experiments in the Strength of Connections Where the Connection is Punished or Rewarded or Neither Punished nor Rewarded." *Journal of Experimental Psychology* 17: 412-23; June, 1934.
191. LORGE, IRVING, and THORNDIKE, EDWARD L. "The Influence of Delay in the After-Effect of a Connection." *Journal of Experimental Psychology* 18: 186-94; April, 1935.
192. MCKINNEY, FRED. "Certain Emotional Factors in Learning and Efficiency." *Journal of General Psychology* 9: 101-16; July, 1933.
193. MEYER, GEORGE. "An Experimental Study of the Old and New Types of Examinations: I. The Effect of the Examination Set on Memory." *Journal of Educational Psychology* 25: 641-61; December, 1934.
194. MUENZINGER, KARL F. "Motivation in Learning. I. Electric Shock for Correct Response in the Visual Discrimination Habit." *Journal of Comparative Psychology* 17: 267-77; April, 1934.
195. MUENZINGER, KARL F. "Motivation in Learning. II. The Function of Electric Shock for Right and Wrong Responses in Human Subjects." *Journal of Experimental Psychology* 17: 439-48; June, 1934.
196. NI, CHUNG-FANG. "An Experimental Study of the Influence of Punishment for Errors during Learning upon Retention." *Journal of Comparative Psychology* 17: 279-301; April, 1934.
197. NI, CHUNG-FANG. "The Influence of Punishment for Errors during the Learning of the First Maze upon the Mastery of the Second Maze." *Journal of Comparative Psychology* 18: 23-28; August, 1934.
198. OLSON, WILLARD C. "Emotional and Social Factors in Learning." *Educational Diagnosis.* Thirty-fourth Yearbook, National Society for the Study of Education. Bloomington, Ill.: Public School Publishing Co., 1935. p. 63-77.
199. OMWAKE, LOUISE. "The Influence of Barbital on the Activity and Learning of White Rats." *Journal of Comparative Psychology* 16: 317-25; December, 1933.
200. PATRICK, J. R. "Studies in Rational Behavior and Emotional Excitement." *Journal of Comparative Psychology* 18: 153-95; October, 1934.
201. PERL, RUTH E. *The Effect of Practice upon Individual Differences.* Archives of Psychology, No. 159. New York: Columbia University, 1934. 54 p.
202. PESSIN, JOSEPH. "The Comparative Effects of Social and Mechanical Stimulation on Memorizing." *American Journal of Psychology* 45: 263-70; April, 1933.
203. PESSIN, JOSEPH, and HUSBAND, R. W. "Effects of Social Stimulation on Human Maze Learning." *Journal of Abnormal and Social Psychology* 28: 148-54; July, 1933.
204. RANKIN, PAUL T. "Environmental Factors Contributing to Learning." *Educational Diagnosis.* Thirty-fourth Yearbook, National Society for the Study of Education. Bloomington, Ill.: Public School Publishing Co., 1935. p. 79-92.
205. REMMERS, H. H., and OTHERS. *Exemption from College Semester Examinations as a Condition of Learning.* Studies in Higher Education, No. 23. Lafayette, Ind.: Purdue University, 1933. 52 p.
206. REMMERS, H. H. *Learning, Effort, and Attitudes as Affected by Three Methods of Instruction in Elementary Psychology.* Studies in Higher Education, No. 21. Lafayette, Ind.: Purdue University, 1933. 48 p.
207. ROBERTS, KATHERINE ELLIOTT. *Learning in Preschool and Orphanage Children; an Experimental Study of Ability to Solve Different Situations According to the Same Plan.* Studies in Child Welfare, Vol. 7, No. 3. Iowa City: University of Iowa, 1933. 94 p.
208. ROCK, R. T. *Influence upon Learning of the Quantitative Variation of After-Effects.* Contributions to Education, No. 650. New York: Teachers College, Columbia University, 1935. 78 p.
209. ROSS, C. C. "The Influence upon Achievement of a Knowledge of Progress." *Journal of Educational Psychology* 24: 609-19; November, 1933.
210. RUCH, F. L. "The Differential Decline of Learning Ability in the Aged as a Possible Explanation of Their Conservatism." *Journal of Social Psychology* 5: 329-37; August, 1934.

211. RUCH, F. L. "The Differentiative Effects of Age upon Human Learning." *Journal of General Psychology* 11: 261-86; October, 1934.
212. SCOTT, T. C., and UNDERWOOD, E. "Sex of Experimenter and Intelligence as Factors in Maze Learning: A Further Comparison of Maze and Sex Difference." *Pedagogical Seminary and Journal of Genetic Psychology* 44: 239-46; March, 1934.
213. SMITH, FRANKLIN O. "Repetition Without Knowledge of Results as a Factor in Learning." *Psychological Bulletin* 30: 673-74; November, 1933.
214. SORENSON, HERBERT, and PRICE, RICHARD R. "Horizontal Development." *Journal of Adult Education* 6: 436-39; October, 1934.
215. SPRAGG, S. D. S. "Anticipation as a Factor in Maze Errors." *Journal of Comparative Psychology* 15: 313-29; April, 1933.
216. STEPHENS, J. M. "A Change in the Interpretation of the Law of Effect." *British Journal of Psychology* 24: 266-75; 1934.
217. STEPHENS, J. M. "Further Notes on Punishment and Reward." *Pedagogical Seminary and Journal of Genetic Psychology* 44: 464-72; June, 1934.
218. STEPHENS, J. M. "The Influence of Punishment on Learning." *Journal of Experimental Psychology* 17: 536-55; August, 1934.
219. STROUD, J. B., and MAUL, RUTH. "The Influence of Age upon Learning and Retention of Poetry and Nonsense Syllables." *Pedagogical Seminary and Journal of Genetic Psychology* 42: 242-50; March, 1933.
220. THORNDIKE, EDWARD L. "The Direct Action of Rewards upon Mental Connections and Their Indirect Action via the Stimulation of Inner Equivalents of the Connections." *Journal of Experimental Psychology* 18: 91-96; February, 1935.
221. THORNDIKE, EDWARD L., and OTHERS. "An Experimental Study of Rewards." Contributions to Education, No. 580. New York: Teachers College, Columbia University, 1933. 72 p.
222. THORNDIKE, EDWARD L., and ROCK, ROBERT T., JR. "A Further Note on Learning without Awareness of What Is Being Learned." *Journal of Experimental Psychology* 18: 388-89; June, 1935.
223. THORNDIKE, EDWARD L., and FORLANO, GEORGE. "The Influence of Increase and Decrease of the Amount of Reward upon the Rate of Learning." *Journal of Educational Psychology* 24: 401-11; September, 1933.
224. THORNDIKE, EDWARD L., and OTHERS. "Influence of Irrelevant Continuing Discomfort upon Learning." *Pedagogical Seminary and Journal of Genetic Psychology* 44: 444-48; June, 1934.
225. THORNDIKE, EDWARD L. "The Influence of Irrelevant Rewards." *Journal of Educational Psychology* 24: 1-15; January, 1933.
226. THORNDIKE, EDWARD L., and WOODYARD, ELLA. "The Influence of the Relative Frequency of Successes and Frustrations upon Intellectual Achievement." *Journal of Educational Psychology* 25: 241-50; April, 1934.
227. THORNDIKE, EDWARD L., and ROCK, R. T. "Learning without Awareness of What is Being Learned or Intent to Learn It." *Journal of Experimental Psychology* 17: 1-19; February, 1934.
228. THORNDIKE, EDWARD L., and OTHERS. *The Psychology of Wants, Interests, and Attitudes.* New York: D. Appleton-Century Co., 1935. 301 p.
229. TUCKMAN, JACOB. *The Influence of Varying Amounts of Punishment on Mental Connections.* Contributions to Education, No. 590. New York: Teachers College, Columbia University, 1933. 45 p.
230. WATERS, R. H. "The Law of Effect as a Principle of Learning." *Psychological Bulletin* 31: 408-25; June, 1934.
231. WATERS, R. H. "The Specificity of Knowledge of Results and Improvement." *Psychological Bulletin* 30: 673; November, 1933.
232. WENGER, M. A., and WILLIAMS, H. M. "Experimental Studies of Learning in Infants and Pre-School Children." *Psychological Bulletin* 32: 276-305; 1935.
233. WHITE, M. M., and RATCLIFF, MARGARET McLEOD. "The Relation of Affective Tone to the Learning and Recall of Words." *American Journal of Psychology* 46: 92-98; January, 1934.
234. WHITELY, PAUL L., and BLANKFORT, GERALD. "The Influence of Certain Prior Conditions upon Learning." *Journal of Experimental Psychology* 16: 843-53; December, 1933.

235. WHITELY, PAUL L. "The Influence of Music on Memory." *Journal of General Psychology* 10: 137-51; January, 1934.
236. WOOD, THEODORE W. "The Effect of Approbation and Reproof on the Mastery of Nonsense Syllables." *Journal of Applied Psychology* 18: 657-64; October, 1934.
237. WYMAN, H. B. "Satisfaction: Its Source and Function in Learning." *Progressive Education* 12: 224-29; April, 1935.
238. ZYVE, CLAIRE, and SMITH, EVELYN. "Effect of Radio Musical Accompaniment on Accomplishment in School Work." *Educational Method* 13: 366-68; April, 1934.

Chapter IV. Methods of Teaching

239. ANDERSON, HAROLD A., and TRAXLER, ARTHUR E. "Group Corrective Spelling in the Junior High School—An Experiment." *School Review* 41: 595-603; October, 1933.
240. ARNSPIGER, V. C. "The Relative Effectiveness of the Sound Motion Picture in Teaching Elementary Science and Music." *Education* 53: 333-35; February, 1933.
241. BONAR, HUGH S. "Systematic versus Incidental Training in Reading." *Elementary English Review* 10: 90-94, 112; April, 1933.
242. CARPENTER, HARRY A. "Teaching Science by Radio." *Junior-Senior High School Clearing House* 8: 421-27; March, 1934.
243. CLARK, CLARENCE C. "The Effectiveness of Sound Films as Aids in Classroom Teaching." *Education* 53: 337-42; February, 1933.
244. CLEMENSEN, JESSIE WILLIAMS. *Study Outlines in Physics.* New York: Teachers College, Columbia University, 1933. 154 p.
245. COLLINGS, ELLSWORTH. "Learning the Fundamentals in the Activity Curriculum." *Journal of Experimental Education* 1: 309-15; June, 1933.
246. CRAWFORD, C. C., and MALIN, MARY ALICE. "An Experiment with Three Ways of Teaching Water-Color Painting." *Elementary School Journal* 36: 40-43; September, 1935.
247. CRAWFORD, C. C., and ROGER, MADIE M. "Oral Drill versus Grammar Study." *Elementary School Journal* 36: 116-19; October, 1935.
248. CUTRIGHT, PRUDENCE. "A Comparison of Methods of Securing Correct Language Usage." *Elementary School Journal* 34: 681-90; May, 1934.
249. DRAKE, RICHARD. "A Comparison of Two Methods of Teaching High School Algebra." *Journal of Educational Research* 29: 12-16; September, 1935.
250. DRANSFIELD, J. EDGAR. *Administration of Enrichment to Superior Children in the Typical Classroom.* Contributions to Education, No. 558. New York: Teachers College, Columbia University, 1933. 107 p.
251. EINBECKER, WILLIAM FRANCIS. "Comparison of Verbal Accompaniments to Films." *School Review* 41: 185-92; March, 1933.
252. FARBISH, SYDNEY A. "An Experiment in Remedial Reading." *English Journal* 22: 585-87; September, 1933.
253. FOWLER, DONALD W. "An Experiment in the History Laboratory." *Historical Outlook* 24: 252-54; May, 1933.
254. GADSKE, RICHARD E. "A Comparison of Two Methods of Teaching First Year High School Algebra." *School Science and Mathematics* 33: 635-40; June, 1933.
255. GATES, ARTHUR I., and BENNETT, CHESTER C. "The Daily versus the Weekly Lesson Plan in Spelling." *Journal of Educational Research* 28: 203-6; November, 1934.
256. GATES, ARTHUR I. *Generalization and Transfer in Spelling.* New York: Teachers College, Columbia University, 1935. 80 p.
257. GATES, ARTHUR I. "Recent Developments in Diagnostic and Remedial Teaching in Reading." *The Application of Research Findings to Current Educational Practises.* Official Report of the American Educational Research Association, 1935. Washington, D. C.: National Education Association, 1935. p. 83-91.
258. GATES, ARTHUR I., and GRAHAM, FREDERICK B. "The Value of Various Games and Activities in Teaching Spelling." *Journal of Educational Research* 28: 1-9; September, 1934.

259. GATTO, FRANK M. "Remedial Reading in Pittsburgh High Schools." *Pittsburgh Schools* 9: 3-12; September-October, 1934.
260. GIBBS, ELSIE FRANCES. "Remedial Work through Free Reading." *English Journal* 23: 827-31; December, 1934.
261. GILBERT, LUTHER C. "Effect of Reading on Spelling in the Ninth Grade." *School Review* 42: 197-204; March, 1934.
262. GILBERT, LUTHER C. "A Study of the Effect of Reading on Spelling." *Journal of Educational Research* 28: 570-76; April, 1935.
263. GOETSCH, WALTER R. "The Effect of Early Handwriting Instruction." *Elementary School Journal* 36: 290-98; December, 1935.
264. GRAY, WILLIAM S. "Summary of Reading Investigations (July 1, 1933 to June 30, 1934)." *Journal of Educational Research* 28: 401-24; February, 1935.
265. GRAY, WILLIAM S. "Summary of Reading Investigations (July 1, 1934 to June 30, 1935)." *Journal of Educational Research* 29: 407-32; February, 1936.
266. GUILER, WALTER SCRIBNER. "Improving Instruction in English Mechanics in the Elementary School." *Elementary School Journal* 34: 427-37; February, 1934.
267. GUILER, WALTER SCRIBNER. "Remediation of College Freshmen in Grammatical Usage." *School Review* 42: 283-93; April, 1934.
268. HARTMANN, GEORGE W. "Comparative Pupil Gains under Individual Conference and Classroom Instruction." *Journal of Educational Psychology* 26: 367-72; May, 1935.
269. HAZELRIGG, BLANCHE. "An Experiment in Teaching Composition." *English Journal* 22: 486-90; June, 1933.
270. HINCHMAN, FLORENCE M. "Teaching the Dull Freshman." *English Journal* 22: 830-34; December, 1933.
271. HOWELL, ETTA; DUNN, MAUDE WILSON; and STOKER, DORA. "Measuring the Skills in an Integrated Program." *Journal of Experimental Education* 1: 316-19; June, 1933.
272. JACOBSON, PAUL B. *Two Experiments with Work-Type Reading Exercises in Ninth Grade.* Studies in Education, Vol. 8, No. 5. Iowa City: University of Iowa, 1933. 85 p.
273. LAMOREAUX, LILLIAN A., and OTHERS. "Remedial Reading Instruction in Sixth Grade Groups." *California Journal of Elementary Education* 3: 116-22; November, 1934.
274. LEE, J. MURRAY, and ROOT, E. RAYMOND. "An Experiment in Integration." *California Quarterly of Secondary Education* 9: 247-55; April, 1934.
275. LEE, J. MURRAY. "Reading Achievement in First-Grade Activity Programs." *Elementary School Journal* 23: 447-51; February, 1933.
276. LEGGITT, DOROTHY. "Measuring Progress in Working Skills in Ninth-Grade Civics." *School Review* 42: 676-87; November, 1934.
277. MACLATCHY, JOSEPHINE H., and BEAVERS, ETHEL B. "Reading for Enjoyment in the Sixth Grade." *Educational Research Bulletin (Ohio State University)* 14: 38-44; February 13, 1935.
278. MACOMBER, F. G. "A Study in Social Science Teaching Method." *Journal of Educational Research* 27: 115-22; October, 1933.
279. MILLER, GEORGIA E. "A Technique for Developing Comprehension of Literature." *English Journal* 23: 810-18; December, 1934.
280. MILLS, HENRY C.; ECKERT, RUTH E.; and WILLIAMS, MURIEL W. "Study Habits of High-School Pupils." *School Review* 42: 755-61; December, 1934.
281. MONROE, MARION. *Children Who Cannot Read.* Chicago: University of Chicago Press, 1932. 205 p.
282. ORR, DOROTHY. "An Experiment in Remedial Reading." *Peabody Journal of Education* 13: 141-51; November, 1935.
283. PARKHILL, JEAN. "Methods Used in Teaching L10 Reading to a 'Z' Section." *California Quarterly of Secondary Education* 8: 363-66; June, 1933.
284. PERSONS, GLADYS. "Silent Reading with First-Term Pupils in the Theodore Roosevelt High School." *High Points* 16: 5-15; November, 1934.
285. PETERS, MARY OLGA. "An Experimental Comparison of Grammar-Translation Method and Direct Method in the Teaching of French." *Modern Language Journal* 18: 528-42; May, 1934.

286. POWERS, J. ORIN, and BLACK, FLORENCE MASSEY. "Exploring the Panel Method Scientifically." *Progressive Education* 12: 85-88; February, 1935.
287. RANSOM, GRACE. "Remedial Methods in English Composition." *English Journal* 22: 749-54; November, 1933.
288. RULON, PHILLIP J. "The Teaching Effectiveness of the Sound Motion Picture in General Science." *Education* 53: 335-37; February, 1933.
289. SALISBURY, RACHEL. "Some Effects of Training in Outlining." *English Journal* 24: 111-16; February, 1935.
290. SHUCHOWSKY, RUTH E., and FLEMMING, CECILE WHITE. "The English Teacher Makes Room for Remedial Reading." *English Journal* 24: 122-28; February, 1935.
291. SMITH, CHARLES G. "The Project Method in Biology." *School Science and Mathematics* 35: 83-88; January, 1935.
292. SMITH, DORA V. "The Contributions of Research to Teaching and Curriculum-Making in English. January, 1933 through June, 1934." *English Journal* 23: 718-31; November, 1934. 24: 363-74, 451-61; May and June, 1935.
293. TAGGART, LOUISE, and HAEFNER, GEORGE E. "Two Methods of Teaching Macbeth." *English Journal* 23: 543-53; September, 1934.
294. TRAXLER, ARTHUR E. "Corrective Reading." *English Instruction in the University High School.* Publications of the Laboratory Schools of the University of Chicago, No. 4. Chicago: University of Chicago, 1933. p. 121-36.
295. TRAXLER, ARTHUR E., and ANDERSON, HAROLD A. "Group Corrective Handwriting in the Junior High School—An Experiment." *School Review* 41: 675-84; November, 1933.
296. TRAXLER, ARTHUR E. "Group Corrective Reading in the Seventh Grade—An Experiment." *School Review* 41: 519-30; September, 1933.
297. UNZICKER, CECILIA E. *An Experimental Study of the Effect of the Use of the Typewriter on Beginning Reading.* Contributions to Education, No. 610. New York: Teachers College, Columbia University, 1934. 95 p.
298. WARNER, PAUL C., and GUILER, WALTER SCRIBNER. "Individual versus Group Instruction in Grammatical Usage." *Journal of Educational Psychology* 24: 140-51; February, 1933.
299. WATSON, ALICE E. *Experimental Studies in the Psychology and Pedagogy of Spelling.* Contributions to Education, No. 638. New York: Teachers College, Columbia University, 1935. 144 p.
300. WRIGHTSTONE, J. WAYNE. *Appraisal of Newer Practices in Selected Public Schools.* New York: Teachers College, Columbia University, 1935. 117 p.
301. WRIGHTSTONE, J. WAYNE. "Appraising Newer Practices in Teaching Social Studies." *School Review* 42: 688-93; November, 1934.
302. WRIGHTSTONE, J. WAYNE. "Comparison of Newer with Conventional Practices in English." *English Journal* 24: 399-403; May, 1935.
303. WRIGHTSTONE, J. WAYNE. "Comparison of Varied Curricular Practices in Mathematics." *School Science and Mathematics* 35: 377-81; April, 1935.

Chapter V. Supervision

304. BARR, A. S. "The Measurement of Teaching Ability." *Journal of Educational Research* 28: 561-69; April, 1935.
305. BRADY, DAVID B. "An Analysis of the Objectives and Functions of Supervision as Viewed by the Department Heads of the Rochester Secondary Schools." *Educational Method* 13: 137-41; December, 1933.
306. BRAND, ANNA R. *Activities in the Teaching of Pitch and True Intonation; an Inventory of Practices in Selected Elementary School Classes.* Master's thesis, Northwestern University, 1933.
307. BRAYTON, MARGARET. *Classroom Difficulties of the Student Teachers in the Kindergarten.* Master's thesis, Northwestern University, 1933.
308. DUFF, JOHN CARR. *Creative Supervision.* Doctor's thesis, New York University, 1933.
309. FIELDS, FRANCES FLORENCE. *An Analysis of Teaching Practices in Selected Seventh and Eighth Grade Music Classes.* Master's thesis, Northwestern University, 1933.

310. GREENFIELD, B. L. "A Study of the Effectiveness of a Program of Elementary School Supervision." *Journal of Educational Research* 27: 123-26; October, 1933.
311. HERRON, ALLEN M. "An Evaluation of the Available Training Programs for General Elementary Supervisors." *Educational Administration and Supervision* 19: 124-28; February, 1933.
312. HERRON, ALLEN M. "The Relative Importance of the Duties and Activities of the General Elementary Supervisor in City Schools." *Educational Method* 12: 325-32; March, 1933.
313. HIGGINS, SISTER M. XAVIER. *Reducing the Variability of Supervisors' Judgments; an Experimental Study.* Studies in Education, No. 23. Baltimore: Johns Hopkins Press, 1936. 69 p. (Doctor's thesis, Johns Hopkins University, 1933.)
314. HUGHES, J. M., and MELBY, E. O. *Supervision of Instruction in High School.* Bloomington, Ill.: Public School Publishing Co., 1930. 191 p.
315. McCLURE, WORTH. "Supervision; a Study in Cooperative Effort." *School Executives Magazine* 52: 131-33; December, 1932.
316. McCRACKEN, SUZANNAH. *A Comparison of Teaching Activities in Music Classes Using Different Types of Methods.* Master's thesis, Northwestern University, 1933.
317. McGINNIS, W. C. "Supervisory Visits and Teacher Rating Devices." *Journal of Educational Research* 28: 44-47; September, 1934.
318. McKEE, MARGARET C. *An Analysis of Supervisory Activities of Supervising Principals In Allegheny County.* Master's thesis, University of Pittsburgh, 1933. (Abstract in University of Pittsburgh's *Abstracts of Theses, Researches in Progress, and Bibliography of Publications*, Vol. 9, p. 413-14.)
319. MOORE, EOLINE WALLACE. *Difficulties Recognized by Elementary Teachers and Their Implications for Supervision.* Contribution to Education No. 137. Nashville, Tenn.: George Peabody College for Teachers, 1934. 70 p. (Abstract in *Educational Administration and Supervision* 21: 51-55; January, 1935.)
320. MORITZ, RUTH KEPPLE ARNOLD. *A Survey of the Certification of and Need for Supervisors in Secondary Education.* Master's thesis, University of Southern California, 1933.
321. NATIONAL EDUCATION ASSOCIATION, DEPARTMENT OF SUPERVISORS AND DIRECTORS OF INSTRUCTION. *Effective Instructional Leadership.* Sixth Yearbook. New York: Teachers College, Columbia University, 1933. 183 p.
322. RANKIN, LOIS CORNELIA. *The Development of a Check List for the Self-Improvement of Music Teachers in the Elementary Grades.* Master's thesis, Northwestern University, 1933.
323. RINGO, LUCILLE. *The Development of a Supervision Program in Music for the Elementary Grades of a City School System.* Master's thesis, Northwestern University, 1933.
324. RUSSELL, MARGARET S. *Visitation and Conference as a Technique of Supervision.* Master's thesis, University of Pittsburgh, 1933. (Abstract in University of Pittsburgh's *Abstracts of Theses, Researches in Progress, and Bibliography of Publications*, Vol. 9, p. 447.)
325. SMITH, C. CURRIEN. *An Evaluation of a Supervisory Program in a City School System.* Doctor's thesis, George Peabody College for Teachers, 1933.
326. THOMAS, MILDRED LUCILE. *Programs for the Training of Music Supervisors.* Master's thesis, Northwestern University, 1932.
327. THOMPSON, GLENN STEWART. *An Evaluation of the Scientific Movement in Secondary School Supervision.* Doctor's thesis, Ohio State University, 1933. (Abstract in Ohio State University's *Abstracts of Doctors' Dissertations*, Vol. 13, p. 234-42.)
328. THOMSON, BLANCHE C. *The Development of a Supervisory Program in Music Based upon Teacher Initiative.* Master's thesis, Northwestern University, 1933.
329. ULLEMEYER, GRACE ELIZABETH. *Practices in Music Supervision in Selected School Systems.* Master's thesis, Northwestern University, 1933.
330. WATTLES, GEORGE S. *A Study To Determine the Efficiency of Supervision of Instruction.* Master's thesis, University of Colorado, 1934. (Abstract in University of Colorado's *Abstracts of Theses for Higher Degrees*, 1934, p. 71.)
331. WILEY, EDWARD O. *An Evaluated Check-List of Supervisory Activities Performed by Supervisors in Laboratory Schools of Teacher-Training Institutions.* Doctor's thesis, University of Texas, 1934.

Available Issues of the REVIEW OF EDUCATIONAL RESEARCH

The Curriculum
Vol. I, No. 1, January, 1931. 64 pp........................$1.00
Teacher Personnel
Vol. I, No. 2, April, 1931. 96 pp.......................... 1.00
School Organization
Vol. I, No. 3, June, 1931. 84 pp........................... 1.00
Special Methods in the Elementary School
Vol I, No. 4, October, 1931. 82 pp........................ 1.00
Psychology of the School Subjects
Vol I, No. 5, December, 1931. 127 pp..................... 1.00
Special Methods on High-School Level
Vol. II, No. 1, February, 1932. 96 pp..................... 1.00
Finance and Business Administration
Vol. II, No. 2, April, 1932. 89 pp........................ 1.00
Tests of Personality and Character
Vol. II, No. 3, June, 1932. 88 pp......................... 1.00
Tests of Intelligence and Aptitude
Vol. II, No. 4, October, 1932. 72 pp...................... 1.00
School Buildings, Grounds, Equipment, Apparatus, and Supplies
Vol. II, No. 5, December, 1932. 89 pp..................... 1.00
Educational Tests and Their Uses
Vol. III, No. 1, February, 1933. 80 pp.................... 1.00
Mental and Physical Development
Vol. III, No. 2, April, 1933. 100 pp...................... 1.00
Pupil Personnel, Guidance, and Counseling
Vol. III, No. 3, June, 1933. 95 pp........................ 1.00
Psychology of Learning, General Methods of Teaching, and Supervision
Vol. III, No. 4, October, 1933. 88 pp..................... 1.00
Legal Basis of Education
Vol. III, No. 5, December, 1933. 114 pp.................. 1.00
Methods and Techniques of Educational Research
Vol. IV, No. 1, February, 1934. 96 pp.................... 1.00
The Curriculum
Vol. IV, No. 2, April, 1934. 132 pp...................... 1.00
Teacher Personnel
Vol. IV, No. 3, June, 1934. 100 pp....................... 1.00
School Organization
Vol. IV, No. 4, October, 1934. 92 pp..................... 1.00

Psychology and Methods in the High School and College
  Vol. IV, No. 5, December, 1934. 119 pp $1.00

Special Methods and Psychology in the Elementary School
  Vol. V, No. 1, February, 1935. 120 pp 1.00

Finance and Business Administration
  Vol. V, No. 2, April, 1935. 64 pp 1.00

Psychological Tests
  Vol. V, No. 3, June, 1935. 150 pp 1.00

The School Plant
  Vol. V, No. 4, October, 1935. 111 pp 1.00

Educational Tests and Their Uses
  Vol. V, No. 5, December, 1935. 99 pp 1.00

Mental and Physical Development
  Vol. VI, No. 1, February, 1936. 152 pp 1.00

Pupil Personnel, Guidance, and Counseling
  Vol. VI, No. 2, April, 1936. 122 pp 1.00

Psychology of Learning, General Methods of Teaching, and Supervision
  Vol. VI, No. 3, June, 1936. 76 pp 1.00

OFFICIAL REPORTS

The Application of Research Findings to Current Educational Practises
  Official Report, 1935. 273 pp 1.50

Reconstructing Education Thru Research
  Official Report, 1936. 301 pp 1.50

Discount on Publications

Applicable only on orders for more than one copy of the same publication

2 to 9 copies — 10 percent
10 to 99 copies — 25 percent
100 or more copies — 33-1/3 percent

Orders should be accompanied by funds in payment of same. Make checks payable to the American Educational Research Association, 1201 Sixteenth Street, N. W., Washington, D. C.

REVIEW OF EDUCATIONAL RESEARCH

Official Publication of the American Educational Research Association, a department of the National Education Association.

The contents of the REVIEW are listed in the EDUCATION INDEX

Volume VI	October, 1936	Number 4

HISTORY OF EDUCATION AND COMPARATIVE EDUCATION

Prepared by the Committee on History of Education and Comparative Education: I. L. Kandel, Stuart G. Noble, Edward H. Reisner, Herman G. Richey, and Newton Edwards, *Chairman*; with the cooperation of R. Freeman Butts, Erich Hylla, Alina M. Lindegren, and D. S. Woods.

TABLE OF CONTENTS

Chapter	Page
Introduction	355

I. History of Education in the United States and Canada 357

   A. History of American Education during the Colonial Period .. 357
      EDWARD H. REISNER, *Teachers College, Columbia University, New York, New York*, and R. FREEMAN BUTTS.

   B. History of American Education since the Beginning of the National Period 363
      HERMAN G. RICHEY, *University of Chicago, Chicago, Illinois.*

   C. State Histories of Education 372
      STUART G. NOBLE, *Tulane University, New Orleans, Louisiana.*

   D. History of Education in Canada 377
      D. S. WOODS, *University of Manitoba, Winnipeg, Manitoba.*

II. History of Education in Europe 383

   A. History of Education in England 383
      NEWTON EDWARDS, *University of Chicago, Chicago, Illinois.*

   B. History of Education in France 387
      I. L. KANDEL, *Teachers College, Columbia University, New York, New York.*

   C. History of Education in Germany 389
      ERICH HYLLA, *Teachers College, Columbia University, New York, New York.*

Chapter	Page
D. History of Education in Italy	394

    I. L. KANDEL, *Teachers College, Columbia University, New York, New York.*

  E. History of Education in the Scandinavian Countries 396

    ALINA M. LINDEGREN, *United States Office of Education, Washington, D. C.*

III. Comparative Education 400

    I. L. KANDEL, *Teachers College, Columbia University, New York, New York.*

  Bibliography 417

Copyright, 1936
By National Education Association
Washington, D. C.

All Rights Reserved

INTRODUCTION

IN PREPARING THIS NUMBER of the *Review of Educational Research* it was necessary to choose between a general survey of the literature, regardless of date of publication, and a critical evaluation of relatively recent publications. The former alternative seemed the wiser at this time, although it necessitated the omission of some items which it would have been desirable to include. This choice also made it impossible to present a summary of the literature of all the countries of the world.

It should be pointed out, perhaps, that it is particularly difficult to summarize briefly the results of investigations in the history of education or in comparative education. About all that can be done in a summary of this kind is to provide workers in the field with a series of critical essays on the most valuable writings in the fields covered.

Each member of the committee and each collaborator was entirely free to present his summary in the form which seemed best adapted to the subjectmatter being summarized. This procedure resulted in lack of uniformity in the style of presentation, but it is hoped that it has not detracted from the usefulness of the monograph.

NEWTON EDWARDS, *Chairman*,
Committee on History of Education
and Comparative Education.

CHAPTER I
History of Education in the United States and Canada

A. HISTORY OF AMERICAN EDUCATION DURING THE COLONIAL PERIOD

WHILE MANY IMPORTANT AREAS remain to be treated, the literature of historical research in Colonial education is substantial in amount and much of it excellent in quality. In our listing there have been included not only monographs devoted to specific phases of Colonial education but also more comprehensive works which have good sections or chapters on education during the Colonial period. For convenience the titles have been grouped into the following categories:

1. Studies of education along statewide or sectional lines
2. Studies in the ecclesiastical control of education
3. Studies in the developing civil basis of education
4. Studies in elementary, secondary, and intermediate education
5. Studies in higher education.

Studies of Education along Statewide or Sectional Lines

Interest in histories of education along state lines was greatly stimulated at the time of the centennial celebration held in Philadelphia in 1876, when several states produced histories for that exhibit. Shortly thereafter a series of state histories of education was begun under the direction of Professor Herbert B. Adams and published in the Circulars of Information of the United States Bureau of Education from 1887 to 1903 (2). These histories were useful contributions at the time, but they were of extremely uneven quality. Some were quite inadequate according to standards of historical scholarship. The references to education during the Colonial period were usually scanty and showed little or no use of original documents. A considerable amount of early material on Colonial school systems is contained in Barnard's *American Journal of Education* (3).

New England colonies—In the nineties wide attention was called to Colonial schools when Martin (78) and Draper (34) carried on their lively controversy concerning whether Massachusetts or New York had contributed more to the development of the American public school system. In 1915 Jernegan (57) contributed a valuable and well-documented description of the important factors which influenced the beginnings of schools in the New England colonies. Butler (19) has made a recent study of Colonial schools in New England as revealed by early newspapers. For Maine, Chadbourne (22) gave a careful study of early schools in relation to their social and economic backgrounds. Bishop (6) and Carroll (20) produced two of the better state histories of education for New Hampshire and Rhode Island, respectively, but they included only a few pages on Colonial education.

Middle colonies—There are few examples of comprehensive colonywide studies of education for the middle colonies. In addition to Draper's study (34) of New York, early collections of source material concerning the beginning of education in that colony were made by Pratt (92) and Finegan (38). Wickersham's history (132) of the schools of Pennsylvania has been extremely valuable, in spite of some inadequacies. The best general record of Colonial education in Pennsylvania is that of Mulhern (86) made in 1933, with special reference to the conditions of secondary education.

Southern colonies—Although the Southern colonies may not have received as much early attention as some of the other colonies, numerous studies of recent years have greatly increased our knowledge of Colonial education in the South. Knight (68) and Jernegan (60) have written general accounts of the development of Colonial education in that section. Heatwole's study (49) of Virginia and Knight's study (69) of North Carolina were substantial studies, which, while written as textbooks, were based on authentic source material. Noble (87) has produced a more detailed and comprehensive history of education in North Carolina. Boogher (8) and Bowden (9) have done the same for early secondary education in Georgia. For South Carolina there is the history written by McCrady (73) in 1883, and a later work by Thomason (123).

Studies in the Ecclesiastical Control of Education

It is difficult to differentiate between civil and ecclesiastical control of education in most schools of the Colonial period. In the New England colonies the civil state and the Calvinist church were, except for Rhode Island, so indistinguishable that a study of New England town and district schools is virtually a study of Calvinist schools. The same close connection between church and state obtained in the Dutch colony of New Amsterdam, and in lesser degree in the Anglican colonies.

On the specifically religious side of schools in New England four studies may be mentioned here. From sermons, pamphlets, and children's books, Fleming (39) reconstructed the religious teaching of the New England church and home and the emotional responses of children to that system of indoctrination. Holtz (54) studied the religious and moral elements in American education up to 1800. Stewart (121) made a careful study of religious education and of the relation between church and school in Connecticut. Smith (119) did the same for Massachusetts.

The Dutch Reformed branch of the Calvinist faith has received considerable attention for its educational activities. Dunshee (35) made an early study of the Collegiate Reformed Dutch school in New York City, and his work has been supplemented and corrected by the important work of Kilpatrick (64, 65) who studied all of the Dutch schools in New Netherlands and Colonial New York. Hall (43) made a study of religious education in the schools of New York with a chapter on the Colonial period. Another important study is that of Livingood (71) who has written a careful story of the Reformed church schools in Pennsylvania in the eighteenth century. The part which the Quakers played in the education of Colonial Pennsylvania and New Jersey was thoroughly investigated by Woody (134, 137), and of New England and North Carolina, by Klain (66, 67).

The support of schools by the Anglican Church has been treated by Kemp (63) who studied the activities in New York of the Society for the Propagation of the Gospel in Foreign Parts, and by Brewer (10) who devoted several pages to the Colonial period in his history of religious education in the Episcopal church to 1835. Bell (5) studied religious education in Virginia, and Wells (131) prepared a thorough and judicial monograph on the parish schools of the same colony. The educational activities of the Lutherans in Colonial Pennsylvania are represented in the painstaking study by Maurer (79). The Colonial period of Mennonite educational activity is discussed in the first part of the study made by Hartzler (45) who relied for much of his description of Christopher Dock upon the study by Brumbaugh (16). The charity school movement as a whole in Colonial Pennsylvania was discussed in an earlier and briefer study by Weber (130).

The activities of the Catholic Church in American education antedated that of all other denominations if the schools of the friars in the South and Southwest are considered. That story is told at some length by Burns (17) in his general history of the Catholic school system in the United States, which relies almost entirely on secondary materials. More scholarly, but containing less on the Colonial period, is the study of McGucken (74) concerning the educational work of the Jesuits.

Studies in the Developing Civil Basis of Education

The story of the increasing authority of the civil government in the control and support of Colonial education has been told largely in studies of the development of the district system of control and of the laws requiring compulsory apprenticeship and schooling of poor and dependent children. One of the earliest compilations of Colonial legislation which referred especially to education was that by Hinsdale (51), but a much more thorough and complete collection of educational legislation passed by Colonial governments was made by Parsons (89). In addition to these works of compilation, considerable intensive study has been made of the growth of the district system and the extension of civil control over education in Massachusetts. Suzzallo (122), Updegraff (127), and Jackson (55) made competent studies which have contributed substantially to our knowledge of this phase of Colonial education. Also important and pertinent here is the work of S. W. Brown (15) which, while it deals mainly with the national period, gives considerable attention to the Colonial origins of state control of education.

The other phase of research which has thrown light upon the development of civil control of education has to do with laws concerning the compulsory education and apprenticeship of dependent children. Seybolt (104) made a contribution to this field in his study of apprenticeship and apprenticeship education in Colonial New England and New York. Jernegan (58, 59, 61) followed with periodical articles and more recently with a book in which he questioned some of Seybolt's conclusions and produced an important study of the origin and development of laboring and dependent classes in Colonial New England and the South with illustrations of the attendant social and economic problems, especially that of free education and apprenticeship for poor children. Douglas (33), in his general study of apprenticeship and industrial education, included two illuminating chapters on the Colonial period. Concentrating upon the colony of Virginia, Wells (131) showed the extent of public support of education in that colony. Maddox (76) also studied the free school idea in Virginia before the Civil War, but he included only a few pages on the Colonial period.

Studies in Elementary, Secondary, and Intermediate Education

Elementary schools, subjects, and textbooks—Considerable research has been directed to reproducing what actually went on inside the Colonial schools. Among the first in this field were the studies of early schools made by Small (116), Johnson (62), and Meriwether (81), all of which went into detail concerning the physical surroundings of Colonial schools, the life and spirit of pupils and teachers, the courses of study and the textbooks commonly used. Among the readily available studies which have been made of particular fields of Colonial subjectmatter are those by Monroe (82) on the development of arithmetic as a school subject, by Lyman (72) on the early teaching of English grammar, and by Simons (114) on the introduction of algebra into American schools in the eighteenth century.

Several detailed studies have been made of the various Colonial textbooks. A quite thorough history of the characteristics and influence of the horn-book in Europe and America was made by Tuer (125) in 1897. *The New England Primer* received extremely detailed treatment at the hands of Ford (40) and Heartman (48). Heartman (47) also published recently a bibliographical checklist of several different types of primers in use other than *The New England Primer*. Another important and quite rare book in this field is that of Littlefield (70), a famous Boston bookseller.

An interesting and yet often little noticed aspect of learning in Colonial educational activities is represented by the samplers which girls made in the dame schools. Bolton and Coe (7) made a large collection of such early samplers and devoted certain chapters in their book to the dame schools and schoolmistresses. The most valuable and thorough study of the education of Colonial girls is contained in the monumental study by Woody (136) who also provided an extensive bibliography on the education of women.

Secondary and intermediate schools—The New England Latin grammar schools have come in for a considerable amount of study. Early examples of such studies are those by Dillaway (32) who wrote about the free schools of Roxbury, and by Jenks (56) who studied in detail the Boston Public Latin School, the story of which has been brought down to the present by Holmes (53) in an able tercentenary history. Among the numerous general studies of the New England grammar schools, let it suffice to mention here the work of Small (117), Martin (77), and especially Seybolt (108) who has recently made a careful study of the public schools of Colonial Boston based upon extensive documentary evidence of varied sorts. Shipton (112) made a case for the position that the Puritans were not narrowly religious in their view of education but had broad secular and social ends in mind.

Although the older histories of education would lead us to believe that secondary education in the colonies was rather exclusively an affair of the Latin grammar schools, the work of Seybolt (105, 106, 107, 110) has been influential in dispelling that notion. His significant investigations of private and evening schools in Colonial America showed that an intermediate type of education which was more practical and more useful for commercial, business, and social life was widely available and utilized by Colonial boys and girls.

Schoolmasters and educators—The life and character of Colonial schoolmasters received considerable attention in some of the treatises mentioned above, but special reference may be made to other studies here. The early Dutch schoolmasters of New Amsterdam were studied by Van Vechten (128), and Seybolt (109) investigated and listed the schoolmasters of Colonial Boston. The most famous of all Colonial schoolmasters, Ezekiel Cheever, has had much written about him, the most valuable of which is perhaps the work by Gould (41) together with such references as were made to him in studies of the Boston Public Latin School (see above). Information regarding other early schoolmasters, such as Elijah Corlett and Edward Hopkins is given in Barnard's *American Journal of Education* (3).

A significant study was made by Brumbaugh (16) of the life and works of Christopher Dock, pioneer Mennonite schoolmaster and educational writer. The Irish Colonial schoolmasters have elicited considerable interest, especially in a series of articles by Purcell (93, 94, 95, 96, 97, 98, 99). Woody (135) helpfully edited the educational writings of Benjamin Franklin, and Curti (27) gave some attention to the Colonial period in his book on the social views of American educators.

Studies in Higher Education

In the past the histories of American institutions of higher learning have neglected or treated superficially the social and intellectual currents which have influenced the shaping of policies and curriculums of the colleges. They have been largely concerned with such external features of the colleges as the cataloging of faculties and students, detailed descriptions of outstanding personalities, personal reminiscences of professors, detailed accounts of fires, new buildings, financial resources, and enrolment of students. Of such nature were many of the earlier histories of individual universities and colleges as well as the state histories of higher education which appeared in the Circulars of Information of the United States Bureau of Education and the later series entitled *Universities and Their Sons* (24).

General studies—Despite the very considerable amount of research that has been expended upon American higher education, there has been written only one general history on the subject; that is the work of Thwing (124). Although valuable in its time, it is now inadequate in many respects. The definitive history of American higher education has yet to be written. Snow (120) set out to survey the development of the college curriculum, but his work was hardly more than preparatory to a comprehensive treatment of that theme.

Several studies have cast illumination on other aspects of higher education covering several institutions. Broome (12) studied the historical development of college admission requirements; Smallwood (118) investigated the examination and grading systems in early American colleges; Shores (113) brought together materials to illustrate the origins of college libraries; Elliott and Chambers (36) compiled the charters and basic laws of fifty-one universities, including six of the nine Colonial colleges; and Walsh (129) made a study of the dependence of the Colonial college curriculum upon medieval scholastic philosophy.

Studies dealing with individual institutions—Harvard has probably been the most studied of all the Colonial colleges. Among the early histories, that of Quincy (100) deserves special mention for its treatment of the development of the Harvard system of administration. All earlier studies of Harvard have now been superseded by the one which is being written by Morison. When all the volumes of the projected series have been completed, this work will probably be one of the most complete and significant histories of any American educational institution. Volume one (84) dealt with the founding of Harvard down to 1650, together with its medieval, renaissance, and reformation backgrounds. Volume two (85) continued the story during the seventeenth century from 1650 to 1708. Treating all aspects of Harvard's history, Morison has done an exhaustively thorough piece of work and has set a high standard of scholarship. Coupled with bright pictures of outstanding presidents and individuals, his work is at once humorous and revealing and will be a solid contribution to the intellectual and educational history of the United States. Rand (101), Seybolt (111), and Norton (88) have also aided in rounding out the growing picture of life and study at Colonial Harvard.

No other Colonial colleges have been the subject of such devoted study. Two early studies of the College of William and Mary were made by Tyler (126) and Adams (1), but both were little more than sketches. The most complete and helpful history of Colonial Yale has been contributed by Dexter (29, 30). Although no adequate history has been written of Princeton, MacLean's early study (75) and Collins' more recent book (26) are helpful, and the letters of William Paterson (90), a Princeton graduate in

1763, have been edited by Mills and provide interesting and illuminating sidelights on early college life and thought. Guild (42) contributed copiously on the early history of Brown, giving especial and not too critical attention to the work of the first president. Bronson (11) has written a scholarly history of Brown with considerable attention to the Colonial period. In 1904 the one hundred and fiftieth anniversary of Columbia College was celebrated by the publishing of a commemorative history (52) written by teaching and administrative staff members. It enlarged on the earlier sketches written by Moore and Van Amringe. The latter wrote the section on the undergraduate college for this volume and in it devoted considerable space to the Colonial period. The standard history of Dartmouth was written by Chase (25), the first volume of which dealt with the Colonial college. Richardson's recent history (103) of Dartmouth is a running account for the general reader. Montgomery (83) wrote a detailed and documentary history of the University of Pennsylvania from its foundation to 1770, with considerable material concerning the early history of Franklin's academy and college from which the university grew. A workmanlike history of Rutgers has been written by Demarest (28), a president of the college, in which is contained an extensive bibliography of titles relating to the history of the college.

B. HISTORY OF AMERICAN EDUCATION SINCE THE BEGINNING OF THE NATIONAL PERIOD

The decision to include in these brief summaries works on the history of education regardless of publication dates has made the task of preparing the section for the United States difficult. Of the many studies that have been made only a few could be included. The selection has been made on the basis of excellence as judged by the compiler, except that some inferior studies are listed when no others have been made on the topic or period treated, and some rather good studies have been omitted when others, judged to be more critical or more comprehensive, have covered much the same ground.

General References

Bibliographies—No thoroughgoing attempt has been made within recent years to compile a bibliography of the history of education. The several bibliographies prepared near the opening of the century contain few titles of current interest and are of historical value only. The best available bibliographies are those found in the two outstanding textbooks (174, 223). Historical studies published between 1906 and 1931 are listed in annual volumes of *Writings on American History* (201), a section of which is devoted to educational history. An index to these volumes covering the years up to and including 1930 is now being compiled.

Textbooks—An entirely adequate history of American education has not yet been written. Knight (223), in the preface to one of the two credible and somewhat satisfactory recent histories of American education, repeated a statement made in the earlier edition of the same work to the effect that a complete history cannot be written until more extensive study is made of the sources for every period from the Colonial to the present. The lack of such research is responsible, in the main, for the inadequacies of Cubberley's *Public Education in the United States* (174), the other relatively competent treatment of our educational history. The latter book is a revision of an earlier work which dominated college and university courses in the history of American education for more than a decade. Judged by modern standards of history writing, the texts of both authors may be criticized; however, there are no other treatments of the entire field of American education which equal them. A well-selected compilation (175) of source and illustrative materials accompanies Cubberley's revised work and supplements, to a certain extent, Knight's volume.

Other general histories of American education are those by Dexter (184) and Boone (156). The former is more than thirty years old but, for some purposes, is still useful. Boone's work, the first noteworthy attempt at a general history of education in the United States, is nearly fifty years old and is of little more than historical importance.

A number of works cover only a part of the entire period or only one section of the country. An example of the former is Thwing's account (285) of education since the Civil War. Illustrations of the latter are Knight's scholarly *Public Education in the South* (226) and numerous state histories of varying degrees of excellence.

Brief treatments of education in America are found in numerous general histories of education. Eby and Arrowood (188), Cubberley (173), Graves (200), Duggan (187), and others devoted several chapters or parts of chapters of their respective histories to tracing the origins and evolution of American education.

Encyclopedias and other general works—P. Monroe's *Cyclopedia of Education* (243), although published nearly a quarter of a century ago and in need of revision, is the most useful single work of reference. *The New Larned History for Ready Reference* (229) attempts to present a unified account of the history of American education by bringing together significant sections from standard works. Barnard's *American Journal of Education* (139), in thirty-two volumes (1855-82), supplemented by the *Analytical Index* (139), constitutes a virtual encyclopedia treating many aspects of the history of education during the first century of the national period.

From 1867 to the present, various publications of the United States Office of Education (called the Bureau of Education from 1869 to 1929) have presented administrative reports of the Office; lengthy monographs on educational subjects including state histories of education; reports on contemporary important movements in education; accounts of conventions; abstracts of legislation and books; and statistics on schools of all grades. There are useful indexes to the publications of the Office (288, 289, 290).

For more recent years the *Education Index* and the *Document Catalogue* are useful.

Considered collectively, the *Addresses and Proceedings of the National Education Association* (title varies) from 1857 to the present and the publications of its many departments constitute an important body of reference material. The volume of *Addresses and Proceedings* for 1906 serves as an index to all preceding volumes which consist for the most part of papers written by leading educators upon many problems in the field.

The Development of Educational Policy

Until recently educational policy was accepted as the contribution of theorists by historians who failed to recognize that these theorizing reformers lived and worked in a society in which the operation of numerous forces was constantly creating new educational problems.

Cubberley broke new ground in 1919 with his history of American education (174), in which a sustained effort was made to show the interrelationships between education and political, social, industrial, and other forces. Counts and others (172), in 1934, examined "the social background of American education from the beginnings of national organization and activity." Curti's recent study (179) shares with Counts' work "the recognition of tradition, accepted ideals and social habit as powerful forces in contemporary education," but where Counts attempted to discover these forces in the detailed development of the activities of American society, Curti "seeks to find them in the social ideas of leaders of American education." Reisner (269) traced the part nationalism has played in education in the United States and several other countries. These works and those by Knight (223, 226) recognize, as has never been recognized before, the bearing of various forces upon the development and history of our educational policy. They need to be supplemented, however, by numerous lesser studies which attempt to show the relation between education and other aspects of social policy.

Before the Civil War—The dominant ideas of the eighteenth century and our first attempts at educational planning were capably treated by Hansen (206). Several works dealing with Jefferson and his period indicated the influences of contemporary political and social forces. Arrowood (142) presented selections from Jefferson's writings on educational matters and appraised his services. This account should be supplemented by Honeywell's superior study (216), and by chapters from the works of Henderson (210), Heatwole (209), Maddox (233), and others.

The influence of the philanthropic movement upon the development of educational policy is treated in all standard manuals. However, a comprehensive history of the movement has not been written. Butler (165) devoted chapters to the Sunday schools, the infant school movement, and the Lancasterian schools. The work of the Public School Society of New York is authoritatively treated by Bourne (158). Fitzpatrick's study (194) on the educational influence of DeWitt Clinton contains some material on the work of the Society. Fitzpatrick and Bourne also discussed the monitorial system and supplemented Reigart's thesis (267) on Lancasterian schools in New York. Parker (257) and others provided additional material on the philanthropic movement.

The influences on education of the rise of the democratic state, the triumph of Jackson and his party, and the extension of suffrage are not treated adequately in histories of education. Carlton, in 1908, pioneered with his study (166) of the educational consequences of the growth of population and manufactures, the extension of suffrage, and the humanitarian and labor movements. Curoe's more intensive study (178) of the educational policies of organized labor attributes considerably less influence to labor in the development of our school system than does Carlton. These works should be supplemented by Fish's engaging and competent treatment (193) of the "great economic, humanitarian, and intellectual currents" of the period 1820-50 when schools were one of the institutions which "the commonfolk sought to subdue to their own purposes." References dealing with the educational implications of the waning of old religious influences and of the development of new religious problems are listed in a later section.

The influence of the ideas and works of Mann, Barnard, and other leaders of the "Awakening" has been admirably set forth in Curti's study (179). For Horace Mann, this work should be supplemented by Hinsdale's study (212), an article by Mayo (237), and the voluminous *Life and Works of Horace Mann* (235). For Barnard, Curti's work should be supplemented by biographies by Steiner (277), Mayo (236), and others. Extensive extracts from Barnard's work, selected to reveal his educational beliefs, are presented in *Henry Barnard on Education* (162). Weeks's article (294) on Calvin Wiley adds to the materials presented by Knight (226, 227), and Noble (253). Other leaders of the "Revival" are treated in special biographies, in standard texts, in Barnard's *American Educational Biography* (143), in P. Monroe's *Cyclopedia* (243), and in numerous journal articles.

Cubberley (174) discussed the importance of the lyceum, school conventions, and other organizations in shaping educational policy. The influence of Southern leaders is discussed by Dabney (180). Cubberley also indicated the importance of reports of early American travelers, of European ideas, and of educational journals. Other works that enlarge upon Cubberley's treatment of these various influences are Hayes's *The American Lyceum* (208), Hinsdale's article (213) on foreign influences upon education in the United States, and Davis' study (181) of educational journalism during the nineteenth century.

The influence of the economic and social revolution in the Southern states is ably treated by Knight (223, 224), Noble (253), and others. Dodd (186) pictured the political and economic background of the antebellum period, and Cole (170) set forth the "results of sectional clashes on educational efforts and intellectual life."

Since the Civil War—The effects of the Civil War and Reconstruction upon educational policy in the South are capably treated in the works of Knight (224, 226), and Noble (253); in Weeks's history (295) of education in Alabama and Cochran's study (169) of education in Florida; and by a number of lesser histories of education in Southern states. Fleming (195) provided additional background and materials.

For the period since the Civil War, historians have given much space to the influence of reformers on the development of educational policy. Curti's work (179) dealt at length with the ideas of Harris, Spalding, Hall, James, Thorndike, and Dewey. Textbooks of the history of education, particularly Parker's (257), have treated the contributions of Pestalozzi, Herbart, and Froebel to American education. The Pestalozzian movement in America was traced by Barnard (146) and Will S. Monroe (245). De Garmo (183) discussed the development of the Herbartian movement in Germany and the United States. Reisner (268) and others presented good accounts of Froebel's influence.

No history of education adequately interprets the educational implications of changes that have taken place in the social structure since the Civil War. Nevins (252) described economic and social life in all sections of the country immediately after the War. Schlesinger (271) pictured the movement toward the city; the increase in crime, vice, and graft; the growth of the slums; and the changes adversely affecting the lives of children. However, he also treated the city as a force making for a finer and broader civilization, promoting social reform, and providing more educational advantages and opportunities for leisure.

For the more recent period, Judd's monograph (218) and others prepared under the direction of the President's Research Committee on Social Trends are indispensable. These reports are presented in condensed form in *Recent Social Trends in the United States* (262). The works of Counts and others (172), Slosson (272), and Tugwell and Keyserling (287) set forth different social philosophies for the period.

The Development of State Systems of Education

The development of free public state systems of education is the principal theme of standard manuals. Many aspects of this movement are more fully discussed in Cubberley's *State School Administration* (176). Knight (226) treated all phases of the development of systems of education in Southern states. Mayo (291) described the development of common schools in all sections of the country in a series of often cited, but somewhat uncritical, articles. Butler (165), employing newspapers as sources, discussed common schools before 1850.

Educational histories of varying degrees of excellence trace the development of common schools in nearly all of the states. Among the superior ones are those by Knight (227), Noble (253), Cochran (169), and Weeks (295), already mentioned; and those by Bishop (149), Bolton and Bibb (154), Carroll (167), and E. A. Miller (241). In addition, state histories by Wickersham (296), Boone (157), Murray (251), Randall (264) and others are of some value. For others, the reader is referred to the section of this issue that deals with state histories of education.

School support—There is no comprehensive history of school support. The topic, however, is treated in all standard manuals. These are supplemented by Cubberley's *State School Administration* (176); Swift's old but authoritative history (281) of permanent school funds, as well as his more recent studies (280, 282); Mayo's article (238) on the establishment of school funds; Butler's chapter (165); and Barnard's article (144) on the Connecticut school funds; and other articles.

Mead (239) discussed taxation and the rate bill as found in the historical development of the school systems of Michigan and Connecticut. The struggles to provide tax support in the various states are described in appropriate state histories. Among these, Finegan's *Free Schools* (192) not previously mentioned, is good on the movement in New York. Burgess (164) studied the increase in school expenditures between 1840 and 1920, and Pitkin (260) dealt with the revival of education after the great depression in our history. However, serious gaps remain in the record of financing public education.

Public school administration—The best general histories of public administration are to be found in the standard texts, which present brief accounts of the decline in sectarian influences; the state's assumption of the educational function and the struggle to establish control over local districts; and the creation of administrative offices and development of the duties and powers of school officers. Cubberley's *State School Administration* (176) is a basic reference. Struggles to establish control in the various states are traced in works that deal with the educational labors of Mann (177, 212, 235, 237), Barnard (162, 236), and other leaders of the early movement for state schools. The reports of state educational officers, particularly those of Mann and Barnard, are important.

The centralization of state control is treated in numerous state histories of education and in special works, such as those by Fairlie (191), Orth (255), Rawles (265), Webster (293), and Strayer (279). *Modern School Administration* (138) dealt with progress in educational administration since the beginning of the century. The development of the city school superintendency was studied by Gilland (197), and the public school principalship by Pierce (259). Both studies are examples of needed research.

The secularization of education is well treated by Cubberley (174). S. W. Brown (161) competently discussed all aspects of the topic. Confrey (171) presented a brief statement on the subject from the Catholic point of view. A. J. Hall (204) and Bourne (158) treated all aspects of the movement to secularize the schools of New York. Bell's long and careful study (147) explains "present day attitudes toward the problem of religion in education, the relation of the church and state to that problem, from the point of view of historical development" in Virginia. The history of the movement in Massachusetts and Mann's part in the struggle was traced by S. M. Smith (275) and Culver (177). These latter should be supplemented by numerous pamphlets and journal articles.

Secondary Education

The history of secondary education receives appropriate emphasis in standard texts and state histories of education. More detailed accounts of the various types of secondary schools and the development of state systems of secondary education are to be found in E. E. Brown's *The Making of Our Middle Schools* (159), which, although nearly thirty-five years old, is still useful. The excellent chapter in Kandel's *History of Secondary Education* (219) should be expanded to book size. Mulhern's recent and important history (250) of secondary education in Pennsylvania sets a standard of excellence too seldom attained in historical research in education and represents a type of much needed research.

The academy movement—A comprehensive history of the academy movement has not been written. E. E. Brown (159) discussed many aspects of the movement in the United States. Knight (226) traced the origin and spread of academies in the South. G. F. Miller (242) provided a first-rate history of the academy movement in New York. Butler (165) devoted a chapter to the history of academies as revealed in New England newspapers. The growth and decline of manual labor institutions in America was treated by Anderson (141). Knight (225) traced the rise, spread, and abandonment of these institutions in the South.

Origin and development of the high school—Textbooks on the history of education, histories of secondary education, state histories, and special works in the field of secondary education are rich in materials on the origin, development, and present status of the high school. Inglis (217) treated the rise of the high school in Massachusetts. Hertzler (211) and O. B. Griffin (202) traced the origin and development of the high school in Connecticut. Gifford (196) studied the development of the New York state high-school system. Grizzell's important study (203) of the origin and development of the high school in New England is organized by periods and states. *The American Secondary School* by Koos (228) is a basic treatise on the modern secondary school. It should be supplemented by numerous journal articles and the publications of appropriate educational organizations.

Extension of secondary education—The recent reorganization and extension of secondary education is discussed briefly in current histories of education and in standard treatises on the junior high school and the junior college. Bunker (163) traced the junior high-school movement to its origin and described practices in 1916. Eells's book (190) is an excellent text on the work and history of the junior college. Additional materials on the newly organized secondary-school units are to be found in educational journals, reports of committees, and in publications of various educational societies.

Methods and Materials of Instruction

Except for brief treatments in texts, there are no general accounts of the development of methods of teaching or of the evolution of school curriculums.

History of methods—The development of methods in particular subjects is traced by a number of authors, among whom are the following: for arithmetic, Walter S. Monroe (244); for reading, Reeder (266); for geography, Phillips (258); for grammar before 1850, Lyman (230); and for history between 1825 and 1850, McManis (232).

The introduction of English-Pestalozzian methods, the influence of Herbart upon methods, and the contributions of later educators are traced in articles, monographs, and books on methodology.

Changes in the curriculum—The nearest approach to a general history of the curriculums of American schools is that by Rugg (270). Stout (278) traced the development of high-school curriculums in the North Central states from 1860 to 1890. Histories and other treatments of individual school subjects describe the modification of the old subjectmatter and the introduction and development of new studies. In addition to the works of Monroe, Reeder, Phillips, Lyman, and McManis previously cited, Powers' history (261) of the teaching of chemistry is of value. The development of manual training and various aspects of industrial and vocational education were traced by H. R. Smith (274), Anderson (140), Bennett (148), and Coates (168).

Numerous articles and longer studies trace the introduction and development of art, commercial subjects, home economics, and other additions to the course of study. The influence of the reports of the committees of the National Education Association and of other national committees is treated in Rugg's article (270), in textbooks in the history of education, in works on particular school subjects, and in numerous minor studies. Recent attempts to reconstruct the program of study are reported in special works on the curriculum, journal articles, and publications of societies organized for curriculum and other educational research.

History of the Training of Teachers

The history of the training of teachers in academies, normal schools, teachers colleges, and universities is traced in the standard texts. A more detailed account of the teacher-training movement before 1890 is presented by Gordy (199). Pangburn (256) traced the evolution of the teachers college and teacher training since 1890.

Barnard (145) presented several interesting documents, prepared by Carter, Stowe, Gallaudet, and others, on the origin and early development of normal schools. S. R. Hall's *Lectures on School-Keeping* (205), recently reprinted, throws light upon the nature of professional instruction during the early years of the movement. For the first state normal school, *The Journals of Cyrus Peirce and Mary Swift* (254) provides among other things, information concerning the program of studies, methods of teaching, proficiency of the scholars, and the accepted pedagogy. The Oswego movement was treated at length by Dearborn (182) and by Hollis (214).

The teacher-training movement in various states is traced in histories of individual institutions and in state histories of normal schools. Among the latter, two important works are Mangun's monograph (234) on the rise and development of the normal school in Massachusetts, and Meader's *Normal School Education in Connecticut* (240). One chapter of G. F. Miller's study (242), on the academy system of New York state dealt with the early attempts of academies to train teachers for the public schools. All aspects of the training of teachers in universities are discussed in numerous books and periodicals.

The History of Higher Education

A really good history of higher education is much needed. Thwing's history (286), until recently the only general account, is now supplemented by Wills's brief study (297) of the growth of American higher education. E. E. Brown (160) sketched the rise of a demand for state universities. The establishment of state and denominational colleges and universities before 1860 was traced by Tewksbury (284). Butler (165) devoted several chapters to newspaper accounts of Harvard, Yale, Dartmouth, Princeton, and other colleges before 1850.

A brief history of the land grant colleges was presented in the *Survey of Land-Grant Colleges and Universities* (222). Eckelberry (189) traced the history of the municipal universities.

Studies of particular aspects of higher education are numerous. Snow's study (276) on the curriculum, published in 1907, is still useful. Recent reforms in teaching, changes in the program of studies, and other changes are considered in various works. McGrath's study (231) of the evolution of administrative officers in institutions of higher learning is scheduled for publication. Blackmar's history (151) of federal and state aid to higher education and Bittner's work (150) on the university extension movement are useful but must be supplemented by more recent studies. Kirkpatrick's *The American College and Its Rulers* (221) is biased, but presents material not found elsewhere. Price's *The Financial Support of State Universities* (263), although limited to the old Northwest, is helpful.

All of the foregoing general and special accounts should be supplemented by catalogs, administrative reports, and surveys of individual institutions. Histories of separate colleges and universities, such as Morison's partly completed tercentenary history (246, 247, 248) of Harvard, and the biographies and autobiographies of great educators provide additional material on higher education.

The Education of Women

Woody's monumental history (299) of the education of women in the United States is thorough and comprehensive, and gives evidence of critical authorship. Certain aspects of the movement are treated in a number of lesser works. The social conditions which brought about education for women were discussed by Boas (153). Taylor (283) traced the early history of women's higher education. The history of the movement in the South prior to 1860 was treated by Blandin (152). Short biographical sketches of Catherine Beecher, Emma Willard, and Mary Lyon, and extracts from their works were presented in *Pioneers of Women's Education* (198). A more complete statement of the educational work of Mrs. Beecher is found in Harveson's excellent biography (207). Present problems in the education of women are treated at length in current educational literature.

History of Negro Education

The history of Negro education is traced briefly in the standard texts, state and sectional histories of education, and in many special studies of Negro life and problems. Woodson (298) discussed the education of the Negro prior to 1861, and Bond (155) presented a history of Negro education from 1860 to 1933. Dickerman (185) also dealt largely with the period since the Civil War. Additional materials are to be found in the reports of philanthropic agencies, the histories and catalogs of Negro colleges and universities, and in autobiographies and biographies of Booker T. Washington and other Southern educational leaders.

The Relation of the Federal Government to Education

A comprehensive history of the relation of the federal government to education has not been written. Keith and Bagley's argumentative book (220) outlined the subject to 1920. The recent report (292) of the National Advisory Committee on Education discussed the various aspects of the problem as it exists today. D. H. Smith (273) and Holt (215) traced the history, activities, and organization of the United States Office of Education and of the Federal Board for Vocational Education, respectively. Other aspects of the relationship of the national government to education were presented by Cubberley (174, 176), Blackmar (151), Swift (281, 282), in the publications of the National Education Association, the United States Office of Education, and in many educational periodicals.

C. STATE HISTORIES OF EDUCATION

There is a prodigious amount of literature relating to the development of state and local school systems. Besides the treatises that may be roughly classified as state histories of education, there are countless pamphlets, bulletins, and magazine articles dealing with the history of particular colleges, or with educational development restricted by title to certain aspects, levels, periods, or localities. In this class, fall histories of school legislation, accounts of the development of school supervision, and treatises on the growth of public high-school systems without reference to institutions of elementary or higher grade.

Within recent years, school history has furnished thesis topics to numerous candidates for advanced degrees. A few of the studies in this field are significant; many are mediocre; and some are positively crude. Seldom does a study appear that attempts a critical evaluation of methods, men, or movements in education. More often, the writers have been content with compiling source materials and laying them before the reader in intelligible English. Much that has been done fails to meet the requirements of modern research.

The National Society of College Teachers of Education recently became interested in this field of study. In 1929 its Committee on State Histories of Education, under the chairmanship of Stuart G. Noble, reported an evaluation of the historical data of forty-eight states (333). The Committee discovered sixty-two treatises that, for one reason or another, might be classified as state histories of education. In addition to these, the Committee examined and evaluated seventy-five printed documents relating to school history and an uncounted number of masters' theses in manuscript form. Its survey of the literature of the subject was practically complete. The present review of research studies need add little to the Committee's findings up to 1929. Nevertheless, in view of the fact that the report for the earlier period has not been widely circulated, it is desirable to include the chief items of the Committee's survey in this discussion.

Sporadic Attempts at History Writing

One of the earliest efforts, if not the first attempt, to present a comprehensive account of the development of a state school system appeared in Taylor's *A Manual of the Ohio School System* (346) published in Cincinnati in 1857. Sporadic attempts at writing the life stories of separate institutions and local school systems, however, have been found among the records of several of the older states. These efforts deserve to be mentioned only because of priority.

The Centennial Exposition, held in Philadelphia in 1876, furnished an impulse to the writing of the earliest state histories of education. It appears that the several states were invited to prepare for exhibition accounts of the development of their school systems. Indiana (337) and Ohio (323) prepared and published locally for this purpose, somewhat elaborate historical exhibits. Impelled, no doubt, by the same motive, Rhode Island (343), Wisconsin (352), and California (344, 345) during the same year printed state histories of education. With the exception of the history of California which was prepared in its entirety by the distinguished John Swett, all these accounts were the result of collaboration. The promoters of the history in each state enlisted for the task a group of prominent school officials, college presidents, and others having special knowledge of the subject. Each of these men contributed his account of the particular institution or phase of education which he knew best. This cooperative endeavor is an easy, but by no means effective, method of preparing a state history of education. The Committee on State Histories of Education, in making its appraisal of such works, condemned the collaborative method on the ground that the writers too frequently permitted local interest, personal bias, and institutional loyalty to interfere with an impartial presentation of the story.

The World's Columbian Exposition, held in Chicago in 1893, gave an added impulse to the same sort of composition. At least two states, Kansas (315) and Wisconsin (339) prepared educational exhibits on what had now become apparently the regulation pattern. The histories of this series, as well as that of 1876, though they may have in some degree served the purpose for which they were written, are far from being adequate when judged by modern standards.

The Circulars of Information, 1887-1903 [1]

During the administration of Commissioner Dawson, the United States Bureau of Education initiated in 1887 the policy of publishing as Circulars of Information the educational histories of the several states of the union. The policy was continued by Commissioner Harris until 1903. By the latter date, the histories, wholly or in part, of thirty-five states had been published. The remaining states not treated, were, in most instances, too young at that time to have any but brief histories.

Herbert B. Adams, professor of history in the Johns Hopkins University, was editor-in-chief of the series. For the writing of the histories, Dr. Adams enlisted talent wherever it could be found. To certain of his graduate students in Johns Hopkins University he assigned state histories as topics for their dissertations. The histories of North Carolina (338), Tennessee (328), and Louisiana (317), to mention only a few, were prepared as dissertations in partial fulfilment of the requirement for the Ph.D. degree. Upon several able assistants he relied for a part of the work. Bernard C. Steiner superintended the compilation of histories of Connecticut (340) and Maryland (341), and George G. Bush prepared works for Massachusetts (311), Vermont (310), New Hampshire (309), and Florida (308). For the histories of a number of the states, Dr. Adams secured as authors, prominent educators, better qualified by their long residence and intimate acquaintance with local institutions than by technical skill in writing history. Judge Edward Mayes of Mississippi and Dr. Willis G. Clark of Alabama were contributors of this type.

Nineteen volumes of this series appeared under the title "History of Education"; sixteen, under the title, "History of Higher Education." In general, there is little distinction to be made between the two, the chief emphasis in both instances being laid on secondary and higher institutions. The same method of preparation seems to have prevailed throughout the series. Following a brief introduction, which presented the political and social setting of early times, the author usually described the first schools, and proceeded next to outline the progress of educational legislation. He then described separately the development of each of the more important institutions of

---

[1] The bibliography of this series is too lengthy and too well known to students of education to be repeated in full, but the conspicuous state histories cited in this article are included here.

secondary and higher grade, apportioning the greater space (in some instances, nearly half the book) to the history of the state university or of the leading college. In many cases the author functioned mainly as a compiler of the histories of separate institutions, written by their respective presidents or specially chosen representatives.

The Committee on State Histories of Education in 1929 made an appraisal of all these Circulars of Information. Although the members of the Committee necessarily submitted the works to the test of more recently derived standards, they kept in mind the fact that the accounts were written thirty or forty years ago when the application of the scientific method either to education or to the writing of history was yet in its infancy. They remembered that the chroniclers of the eighties and nineties were pioneer historians of a pioneer period.

The Contributions of Stephen B. Weeks

After a lapse of a decade, the United States Bureau of Education resumed the responsibility for preparing state histories. Commissioner Claxton retained the services of Stephen B. Weeks as staff specialist in charge of this department. Weeks, a competent scholar, evidently recognized the need for rewriting some of the earlier publications of the Bureau when he prepared new histories for Arkansas in 1912 (350); Alabama in 1915 (348); Delaware in 1917 (351); and Arizona in 1918 (349). Taking the histories of Weeks as a whole, they set a standard somewhat in advance of the average of the Bureau's earlier series.

Histories of Education by School Officers

A number of state departments of education have published histories. The authors of such books, in most cases, have been superintendents. Among the states that may be mentioned are Kentucky (319), Maine (342), and Wisconsin (334). In addition to these, several other accounts have been published locally, but apparently not under the auspices of state departments. Included in this number should be mentioned Swett's two books on education in California (344, 345), Harris' series of articles for Louisiana (320), and Putnam's work on the Michigan school system (335). The list of such works can doubtless be considerably extended, but these references are sufficient to establish a classification for the type we have in mind. Speaking of these local products, the members of the Committee on State Histories of Education did not underestimate their value as treasuries of useful information of the kind best found in the personal memoir. Their authors having access, as was frequently the case, to documents no longer available, preserved data that would otherwise have been lost. The inexperience of the authors in the writing of history, however, cropped out repeatedly. The authenticity of their statements could not always be attested; their sense of proportion was sometimes warped by personal interest. Seldom did they get more than a narrow, legalistic view of the great national movement. This class of writings, therefore, failed to attain to the standards of excellence fixed by the Committee.

Eight Creditable State Histories of Education

The Committee found eight treatises that met the requirements of a readable narrative of convenient length covering the entire span of the history of the state, limited to public institutions and including a treatment of the social, economic, and political background. These are scholarly treatises written with due regard to the more recently derived standards of writing history. While these were reported subject to certain limitations, they approximately met the specifications designed by the Committee for such a treatise. Space does not permit more than the listing of these writers in this connection: Weeks (348), Cochran (314), Bishop (302), Carroll (312), Eby (316), E. W. Knight (324), Raymer (336), and Aurner (300).

In concluding its report in 1929 the Committee called attention to the fact that most of the histories which it had examined were out of date, out of print, incomplete, and unreliable. It cited the need for authoritative, historical treatises to be used by research specialists, writers of school surveys, curriculum makers, and other investigators of current school problems. Early in the next year, the Committee petitioned the United States Commissioner of Education, William John Cooper, to sponsor the publication of a new series of state histories of education. The Commissioner's assent was prompt and cordial and the Committee undertook to supply manuscripts for the purpose.

Some half a dozen manuscripts were collected, but upon examination by the Committee, only two were found to be suitable for the purpose in view. One of these has been published by the Office of Education; the other, submitted during the early years of the depression, could not be published because of shortage of revenues allotted to the Office. Several members of the Committee have begun to prepare manuscripts but no one, as yet, has completed his work. The ardor of the would-be historians has doubtless been dampened somewhat in recent years by the uncertainty of publication.

The number of the new series published so far is the *History of Education in Washington* by Bolton and Bibb (303). The Committee was fortunate in having a volume so well conceived and so judiciously executed appear as the first number of the series. This is a comprehensive survey of public educational institutions of all levels, including also a brief treatment of the history of private schools. The reader is led to see how the great national movement for education worked itself out in this Far-Western state. The space is well apportioned to legislation, school revenues, supervision, certification of teachers, etc. The authors have done more than merely set down facts; they have ventured to evaluate and make critical comments on the data. The book will serve as a good model for the treatment of a state with a brief history.

Since the publication of the Committee's report M. C. S. Noble (332) has published a history of the public schools in North Carolina. The account, which has been termed "an illuminating commentary on progress in a democracy," is based on old records, letters, and diaries and brings the story of education in that state down to 1900. It is an interesting and instructive volume.

Most recent studies are limited as to period covered or school level. Theses writers in institutions of higher learning since 1925 have turned in increasing numbers to the history of secondary education for titles of their dissertations. According to a bibliography of the United States Office of Education for the years 1927 to 1932, more than twenty writers prepared papers on the development of state high-school systems. Although some of these are creditable studies, very few have been published.

Two notable state histories of secondary education, however, should be mentioned in this connection. The first of these by Boogher (304) gives an account of the development of academies and high schools in Georgia from 1732 to 1858. For the period covered, the work has been well done. The second, by Mulhern (330), is more comprehensive. The author traced the history of secondary education in Pennsylvania from the settlement of the colony down to 1930. The extent of Mulhern's bibliography suggests the thoroughness of his inquiry. His list of sources alone requires seventy-three printed pages, of which fifteen pages are devoted exclusively to the titles of manuscripts used in the preparation of the volume. In no other state has the history of secondary education been so competently treated.

The history of elementary education has proved to be much less popular with theses writers. Brown (307) recently prepared a much-needed study of the public schools of Nevada on this level, but his work has not yet been published.

A few teachers of the history of education make extensive use of the state history in the course on public education in the United States; many more find it indispensable for reference. Writers of school surveys, curriculum makers, and research specialists find it essential in providing the background of their studies. But it is as a contribution to the history of education in the United States that the state history serves its chief purpose. A comprehensive treatise that does justice to every section of the country and to every aspect of education must wait upon the completion of the local chronicles.

The writing of up-to-date scholarly treatises in this field offers an inviting field to research students in history or education. Most of the states are without dependable histories and eight of the Western states have no printed accounts longer than encyclopedia articles. It is to be hoped that the United States Office of Education will continue to publish worthy manuscripts. It is more to be hoped that the men and women who enter this field will prepare manuscripts that meet modern standards of scholarship.

D. HISTORY OF EDUCATION IN CANADA

The British North America Act of 1867 established provincial autonomy in education, confirmed the principle of state control, and contributed to the centralization of school administration within each province. Section VI, subsection 93 provided, in part, that "In and for each Province the Legislature may exclusively make Laws in relation to education subject and according to the following provisions: (1) Nothing in any such Law shall prejudicially affect any Right or Privilege with respect to Denominational Schools which any class of Persons may have by Law in the Province at the Union." The provinces of Nova Scotia, New Brunswick, Quebec, and Ontario were confederated in 1867; Manitoba was organized as a province in 1870, British Columbia in 1871, Prince Edward Island in 1873, and Saskatchewan and Alberta in 1905.

The educational provisions of the British North America Act were the outcome of more than a century of conflict and compromise (358, 370, 374). Prior to 1763, beginnings under the direction of Roman Catholic Orders had been made in Quebec and Acadia, and under missionaries and lay teachers sent to Nova Scotia by the Society for the Propagation of the Gospel in Foreign Parts (356, 357, 372). After the conquest, the patriotic intent of the British government, acting in cooperation with the Anglican Church (370, 371), and the profound faith of the Scotch and New England settlers in the religious and social values of education (356, 370), made of the "school question" a permanent state issue. School systems reflecting the religious and racial traditions of Old France, of eighteenth and early nineteenth century England, of Calvinistic Scotland and New England, or representing a compromise of these traditions had taken definite form throughout Eastern Canada by 1867 (362, 370). The clash of religious and racial ideals in vigorous frontier settlements during a period of struggle for democratic institutions of government, produced two educational strains, the French Catholic and English speaking, the latter eventually to become largely non-sectarian. Moreover, the strength and singleness of leadership in matters of church and state, and the practical benefits to sparsely settled rural areas of governmental direction (357, 370) produced a tendency to safeguard, by law, established school practices, and to centralize school administration under state control. In every province of Canada, the duties and responsibilities delegated to administrative units and officials are specified in some detail and embodied in Public School Acts (364).

As the settlement of Western Canada, except for a few fur-traders, has occurred since 1867, the school systems of the West were patterned after those of the East (363, 370, 373). They have been modified to a greater extent by twentieth century trends in the middle and western parts of the United States. Although Canadians have clung with smug self-satisfaction to many traditional beginnings of pioneer days, they have not been able to evade the vigor of American educational research and experimentation (358, 365). This may be seen in Western Canadian cities where local initiative has had wider range, and in recent provincial regulations governing programs of study, textbooks, and provincial examinations (354, 364).

Educational Trends as Revealed by Provincial Legislation

Confederation, the growth of a Canadian spirit (370), economic development, the significant shift in population from rural to urban (359), and the persistent influence of trends in the United States, have so facilitated or promoted the interchange of educational thought that, although organized provincially, a Canadian pattern has evolved. We cannot remain provincial, even in Old Quebec (358). The truth of this may be seen by viewing Canadian school legislation prior to and following 1867.

Nova Scotia, New Brunswick, and Prince Edward Island—School legislation in Nova Scotia is representative of major trends in the three Maritime provinces. Educational beginnings were influenced by the Calvinistic and, to a lesser degree, by Roman Catholic and Anglican traditions (356, 370). The first government was formed in 1758 and in 1766 an act was passed providing for the state licensing of teachers in grammar and common schools (356). Important enactments following that date are summarized briefly as follows: 1780, financial provision for a school building and grammar schoolmaster in Halifax; 1794, annual grant to the Halifax grammar school and to other schools in the province; 1811, provision for the formation of school districts throughout the province, the encouragement of local assessment for school support; 1826, justices of the peace instructed to divide the counties into school districts; 1841, a provincial board of education; 1850, a provincial superintendent of education; 1854, a state normal school. The Free School Act of 1864 substituted a Council of Public Instruction for the board of education. This central body, composed of the Executive Council of the government in office, was made the supreme authority in education with power to license teachers, to prescribe programs of study and textbooks, to appoint inspectors and examiners, and to supervise the system in general (356). Ex-officio members have been added to the Council of Public Instruction in New Brunswick and Prince Edward Island. By the Act of 1864, Nova Scotia was divided into local school sections managed by an elective board of trustees in rural areas, and in towns and cities by a board appointed in part by the Council and in part by the governor-general-in-council. The Act of 1865 made elementary and secondary education free, the schools to be supported by local assessment and by county and provincial aid. The legislation of 1880 to 1885 organized the schools into a continuous system, Grades I to XII, and made secondary education preparatory to either normal school or university.

Quebec—Prior to 1763 little provision had been made for the habitant in rural parts (370, 375). The Act of 1801, providing for the organization of a national school in each parish or township, under the direction of trustees appointed by the government, did not meet with favor (366, 370). The Act of 1824, permitting local parishes to devote one-fourth of their income to school purposes, and that of 1829, providing for a school in each parish or township under the control of elected trustees were more successful (366, 370). Although the desire of the British government to use the school as an agent to foster the growth of British institutions among the

French population of Canada had failed it was successful in forcing cooperative action on behalf of the masses. The Act of 1841, supplemented by the Amending Acts of 1846 and 1849, established a system of common schools in each parish or township under an elected board of five commissioners and financed through local assessment and state aid. It also made provision whereby a religious minority might dissent, form a separate school under three elected trustees, and share the government grant with the commissioners' school (370). In 1856 normal schools were established under Catholic and Protestant supervision and supported by state funds. The Act of 1869 placed the school system under a Council of Public Instruction, composed of ex-officio and appointed members representative of the Catholic and Protestant elements of the population. The Act of 1875 constituted the Catholic and Protestant sections of the Council and gave to each the authority to function as a separate supervisory body with powers to prescribe curriculums and textbooks, to supervise examinations and teacher training, and to recommend teachers for certification. Until 1899 each section appointed inspectors for the schools under its supervision and still recommends to this position for appointment by the government (370).

Two school systems, subject to the instructions of the government but with lines of responsibility not clearly defined, supervise the activities of many overlapping school areas (361, 370). Religion is a fundamental subject in both Catholic and Protestant schools. The Protestant schools, although recognizing Grades I to VII as elementary and Grades VIII to XI as secondary, are organized under one board of trustees and have general as well as preparatory training as the educational aims of secondary education (360, 370).

Ontario—During the first half of the nineteenth century educational beginnings reflected the ideals of factions to the struggle for responsible government (370). It is difficult to determine the influence of religion or politics on school legislation during the period 1800 to 1840, as factional divisions did not completely correspond with the traditions of those who were parties to the struggle. The Grammar School Act of 1807 represented the wishes of the governing party and the Anglican Church, secondary education for the socially élite. It was not acceptable to the masses. The Common School Act of 1816 was championed by dissenters in both religion and politics. The determined support accorded either elementary or secondary education by political groups led to the definite organization of education at two levels, a condition still continued, in part, and one which influenced the organization of education in Saskatchewan at a later date. Moreover, the preparatory aim of secondary education has stubbornly maintained its place.

The Act of Union of 1840, Egertson Ryerson's appointment as superintendent in 1844, and his Report of 1846 mark the opening of a new era (362, 370). The Common Schools Act of 1850 framed by Ryerson provided for (a) the organization of "school sections" throughout the province, (b) permissive local assessment for school support, (c) government aid to schools, (d) a general board appointed by the Crown, (e) a superintendent appointed by and responsible to the governor, and (f) local inspectors appointed and paid by the county council. The superintendent's office became the education office for the province, the general board an advisory body (370). In 1871 elementary education was made free, supported by assessment and township and government grants. In 1875 the superintendency and general board were abolished and replaced by a department of education under a minister of the government. That has become the practice in the four Western provinces. The extreme centralization of authority in 1850 was contrary to the principles previously advocated by Ryerson and the Reform party. It was freely charged that Ryerson had become converted to the Prussian plan of centralization. The Act of 1875 was in a measure a return to liberal principles in that authority was vested in an elective ministry. The situation has not changed greatly; the practice of a quarter of a century under Ryerson during formative days has become a tradition (369).

In 1853 the supervision of secondary education was placed under the superintendent. Although this made for unity, a high-school district overlapping an elementary-school district and with a separate board of trustees appointed in part by the county council and in part elected, still constitutes the typical secondary-school unit in large towns and cities. Union districts having both elementary and secondary grades under the one elective board of trustees are common in smaller centers (355, 370).

Some General Characteristics of Canadian Education

The Dominion government supervises and finances Indian education; otherwise it stands in the same relation to provincial schools as does the federal government in the United States. The Agricultural Instruction Act of 1913 appropriated $1,000,000 a year for ten years in support of agricultural education. The Technical Education Act of 1919 made like provision for technical education. These grants were distributed on the basis of population. The Education Branch of the Dominion Bureau of Statistics, organized in 1921, issues an annual report and distributes information concerning education in all provinces. Beyond these provisions the central government has, so far, declined to assist provincial school systems.

Controls and finance—However constituted, the central authority acting through its committees and executive officers, either deputy ministers or superintendents, determines standards and directs the system (359). Authority delegated to local districts is rigidly defined and rather uniformly applied. The school district, of which there are approximately 23,000 in Canada, managed by elected trustees in rural areas or by boards constituted according to different methods in urban centers (361, 367), forms the local unit of administration except in Quebec and British Columbia. Almost 60 percent of the cost of all institutions of learning and 80 percent of the cost of publicly controlled schools is levied upon the real property in local districts (359). Approximately one-sixth of the cost of public schools is paid from provincial consolidated revenue. Consequently, there exists great divergence in the ability of school districts to provide leadership and funds to meet educational needs.

School enrolment, organization, and curriculum—Canada had an estimated population of 10,376,786 in 1933 and a school enrolment in all educational institutions of 2,527,358 of whom 2,237,188 were in the ordinary day and technical schools, 84,953 in privately controlled day schools, and 41,372 in standard university courses. The census of 1931 showed that 21.3 percent of rural boys, 30.2 percent of rural girls, 43.7 percent of urban boys, and 38.9 percent of urban girls, fifteen to nineteen years of age inclusive, were attending school (359). All provinces except Quebec have compulsory education. Separate school systems are provided for in Quebec, Ontario, Saskatchewan, and Alberta (370, 372).

The eighth-grade elementary school and a three- or four-year high school formed the typical organization during the nineteenth century, but in recent years there has been a tendency in the West to adopt the 6-3-3 plan (361, 370). The province of Quebec and two cities of Ontario have made seven years the elementary-school period.

There is marked uniformity in the curriculum of the elementary school throughout English speaking Canada. To the one-time three-R program have been added geography, history, civics, music, art, health, and in Grades VII and VIII, geometry, algebra, and science (354, 359). Despite progress made in establishing industrial arts and technical courses, the traditional academic subjects and preparatory aim still dominate secondary education (368). Except in the Catholic schools of Quebec, extended provision has been made for options beyond Grade IX, but Canadian secondary schools have been tardy in recognizing the claims of the élite in other than professional pursuits (360, 368, 369). This has been attributed to the influence of university admission requirements on state secondary-school examinations (361, 369). The formation of provincial examination boards representative of university and secondary-school interests, and the accrediting of well-equipped secondary schools in Western Canada, promise a greater degree of articulation between secondary and university education. However, much remains to be accomplished before the non-academic elements in the secondary curriculum will have received due recognition.

Teacher training—The desire for well-qualified teachers, expressed in the first piece of Canadian school legislation in 1766, has been voiced by leaders throughout our school history (369, 370). Normal schools, set apart from the system, were established as soon as a provincial organization began to take form. Periodically the training has been strengthened, and in recent years that for candidates holding degrees has been transferred to the universities. Provincial governments have always guarded the standards of training for and the certification of teachers. In all probability they will continue so to do long after other responsibilities have been delegated to local administrative units.

CHAPTER II
History of Education in Europe
A. HISTORY OF EDUCATION IN ENGLAND
General Historical Accounts

A COMPREHENSIVE, GENERAL HISTORY of education in England has not been written. Perhaps Adamson's *Short History of Education* (379) is the nearest approach to a comprehensive account of the development of English educational institutions. Relatively brief treatments of most phases of English educational history may be found in a number of general texts such as those of Cubberley (388), Reisner (433, 434), and Eby and Arrowood (391).

There are a number of authors whose works cover, in a general way, certain definite periods. For the period since 1789, a volume by Adamson (378) is indispensable. The author traced the development of the educational structure through legislative enactment and showed in considerable detail the effect of social change on educational policy. Practically all phases of education were considered. De Montmorency's treatment (389) of the history of the relation of the state to education from the earliest times to 1833 is old but still useful. It is particularly valuable for an understanding of the English common law relating to education and for the history of educational legislation. It should be supplemented by Balfour's excellent summary of educational legislation (382). Balfour's work also serves as a general account of the major lines of development in English education during the nineteenth century. For the whole of the eighteenth and the first half of the nineteenth century, Dobbs's scholarly treatment (390) of education as influenced by social movements is very valuable. Brebner (386) discussed briefly the development of English education since about 1800 with special emphasis on the educational implications of social change. Those who want a short, concise account of the history of English education since about 1860, with references to larger works, will find the two small volumes of Ward (439, 440) helpful. Two encyclopedias of education, one edited by Watson (442) and the other by Monroe (424), contain a great mass of information on various phases of English educational history. A volume edited by Wilson (445), although containing little strictly historical material, is mentioned here because of its value in giving one a general overview of the existing educational institutions of England.

History of Elementary Education

There are a number of histories of elementary education in England. The most recent and perhaps the most valuable of these is the volume by Smith (435). Birchenough (385) traced the evolution of the modern state system of elementary education, giving an account of changes in the curriculum and internal organization of the elementary schools, and treated in some detail the history of teacher education. Older and less valuable studies in the history of elementary education are those of Adams (376), Holman (407), Greenough (405), and Prideaux (431). Matthew Arnold's *Reports on Elementary Schools 1852-1882* (381) is an extremely useful source of information. Some interest attaches to Lochhead's discussion (415) of the background of present methods of teaching young children. The work and influence of Lancaster and of the British and Foreign School Society was interestingly treated by Binns (384). Jones's volume (409) on the training of teachers is valuable both for its historical treatment and for its analysis of current problems.

History of Secondary Education

Until about two decades ago, there was no reliable, systematic account of the history of the schools of Medieval England. In 1915 Leach (414) published the first comprehensive, scholarly history of English schools before the Reformation. It is not too much to say that Leach's investigation revolutionized the prevailing conception of education in England during the Middle Ages. He showed clearly that grammar schools were far more usual in that period than had commonly been supposed. Leach's work should be supplemented by Parry's more recent history of education in the Middle Ages (430). The two authors, it should be pointed out, are not in complete agreement. Leach's study (413) of education in the reigns of Henry VIII and Edward VI is indispensable for an understanding of the effects of the Reformation on the schools of England. Leach (412) has also compiled the salient documents illustrating the development and conduct of English educational institutions. The great majority of the documents relate to the period before 1550. The report of the Schools Inquiry Commission (404), prepared in 1868, contains a vast amount of information concerning the old grammar schools.

Shortly after the reign of Edward VI, there was a marked tendency to found new grammar schools to offset the losses occasioned by the policies of Henry and Edward. The movement to establish endowed secondary schools in the reign of Elizabeth was traced in detail by Stowe (436), who discussed the foundation and support of new schools and described their government, their teaching staffs, their curriculums, and the school life of their pupils. For an account of the curriculums and internal practices of the grammar schools in the sixteenth and seventeenth centuries, one should consult Watson's detailed and thorough study (443). The author of a more recent volume attempts to give "a comprehensive account, at once readable and accurate, of the conditions prevailing in the Grammar Schools, more particularly during the second half of the sixteenth century, with special emphasis on the human side" (387). Woodward's (449) and Mullinger's (425) discussions of secondary education in the sixteenth and seventeenth centuries are also valuable.

A recent volume by McLachlan (417) treated a neglected phase of the history of English education, namely, the work and influence of the dissenting academies. Attention was directed to the rise of the academies, their character, scholarship, curriculums, textbooks, and the like. Parker's older work (429) on the contribution of Puritanism to education should also be mentioned in this connection.

The most comprehensive and readable account of secondary education since the opening of the nineteenth century is that of Archer (380). He stressed the influence of intellectual and social movements in secondary education; appraised the work of individual endeavor as represented by such leaders as Matthew Arnold, Ruskin, and Kingsley; and traced the increasing participation of the state in the field of higher education. Norwood and Hope (428) treated briefly the history of secondary education. A considerable portion of Kandel's scholarly *History of Secondary Education* (411) was devoted to England and more particularly to the eighteenth and nineteenth centuries. Matthews (423) traced illuminatingly the history of the relation of the Board of Education to post-primary education as carried on in the elementary, secondary, and technical schools.

Higher Education

For the early history of Oxford and Cambridge, the general reader will find Rashdall's monumental study (432) the most valuable. Haskins' account (406) of the rise of the universities is not confined to English institutions but contains a good deal of material relating to them. It is a most fascinating description of the inner life of the early universities with emphasis on such matters as student activities, studies, and textbooks, methods of teaching, and examinations. Vaughn's treatment (437) of the origin and development of Oxford and Cambridge to the close of the thirteenth century is old but still of value. Irsay (408), in his excellent history of universities, devoted considerable attention to English institutions. Short but readable accounts of the history of the older universities may be found in various volumes of the *Cambridge History of English Literature* by Walker (438), Woodward (449), and Adamson (377). Mansbridge (421) has written a relatively short general history of the two older universities, showing in particular how they have made adjustments to the demands of national life through the admission of women and extra-mural teaching.

The first comprehensive and critical history of Oxford to appear was that by Lyte (416), published in 1886. It traced the development of Oxford through the first third of the sixteenth century. Mallet's three-volume history (419) of Oxford, which he began to publish in 1924 and which is now complete, is the most exhaustive and scholarly treatment of the subject. For some purposes the old work by Wood (448) is still valuable as is also the volume by Wells (444). The standard history of Cambridge is the three-volume work of Mullinger (427). A short volume by the same author is a good outline of the history of Cambridge to about 1885 (426).

Winstanley (446, 447) published two valuable books dealing with certain aspects of the history of Cambridge during the eighteenth century. Bellot's recent history (383) of University College, London, is excellent.

For the other universities one should consult the historical notices of the *Yearbook of the Universities of the Empire* (451). The histories of the individual colleges of the various universities are too numerous to be mentioned here.

Attention should be called to MacLean's treatment (418) of the tendencies in higher education in England during the closing years of the nineteenth and the early years of the present century. This work is of particular interest because of its emphasis on the rise and influence of the municipal universities. For an account of adult education, one should consult the studies by Mansbridge (420, 422).

Sources of the History of Education

The reports of the Board of Education (393) issued annually since 1899 are indispensable to the student of education in England. They contain statistical data and a record of events relating to practically all departments of public education. Not infrequently they contain more or less detailed studies of some particular phase of education. The report for 1908-09, for example, carries a summary of the history of secondary education down to 1902; the report for 1923-24 has a section on the recent development of secondary schools; and in the report for 1912-13 there is a detailed account of the history of the training of teachers. The Board also publishes a series of educational pamphlets which cover a great variety of topics. From time to time the Consultative Committee of the Board issues reports of paramount value. Two of these are indispensable for an understanding of recent developments of educational policy. The first of these is the report on *The Education of the Adolescent* (395), published in 1926; the second, *The Primary School* (396), is a complete report on the education of children from seven to eleven years of age. The *Special Reports on Educational Subjects* (394), initiated by Sir Michael Sadler in 1896-97, contain a storehouse of information which no serious student can overlook.

The richest body of source materials for the history of education in England is to be found in the numerous and voluminous reports of the various commissions appointed to investigate some aspect of the educational system. Among these reports the following are the most valuable: report of Her Majesty's Commissioners Appointed to Inquire into the Revenue and Management of Certain Colleges and Schools (392); report of the Commission to Inquire into the Present State of Popular Education in England (397); report from the Select Committee on Education (398); report from the Select Committee on the Education of the Lower Orders (399); report from the Select Committee on the Education of the Lower Orders in the Metropolis (400); a digest of parochial returns made to the Select Committee Appointed to Inquire into the Education of the Poor (401); reports of the Commissioners Appointed to Inquire into the Working of the Elementary Education Acts, England and Wales (402); report of the Royal Commission on Secondary Education (403); and the report of the Schools Inquiry Commission (404).

Finally, mention should be made of two other extremely valuable sources of information, one the annual *Year Book of Education* (450), issued under the editorship of Lord Eustace Percy, and the other the *Educational Yearbook of the International Institute of Teachers College, Columbia University* (410).

B. HISTORY OF EDUCATION IN FRANCE

Research in the history of education suffers in France from the disadvantage that the subject is not recognized as a university study and to the best of the writer's knowledge there is nowhere in French universities a chair in the subject. Only in the preparation of elementary-school teachers is the study of the history of education required; but at this level the courses are somewhat rudimentary. Despite this disadvantage, which means an absence of continuity and the persistence of undeveloped sections in the history of French education, important contributions had already been made in the nineteenth century and particularly since Gabriel Compayré published his notable works (462, 463, 464). Buisson's encyclopedia (460), of course, contains a mine of information on history of education. In 1906 a Swiss educator, François Guex (473) published a history of education definitely planned to fill certain omissions on French education in German texts and on German education in French texts, and to give more attention than was usually given to education in England and the United States.

But while the history of education has not been fully written up, materials for such history can be found in the codifications of laws and regulations for which Gréard (471, 472) laid the foundations in elementary education and Liard (482) in higher education. On these foundations other works of a similar kind have been developed by Dion (467) and Wissemans (488) in secondary education, and by Schwartz (485) and Soleil (486) in elementary education.

An extensive bibliography on French education which appears in an introduction to the very full and systematic account of French education prepared by the Commission Française pour l'Enquête Carnegie sur les Examens et Concours en France as a part of the International Examinations Inquiry, contains very few references to histories of education (461). Of the histories of elementary education, the majority were written before 1900 (452, 453, 454, 459); for the period up to 1906 the student will find a useful bibliography in Farrington's study (470); a history of elementary education in Paris appeared in 1911 (468); a work on the history of maternal schools was published in 1910 (480). In 1912 there was issued as a series of lectures and discussions on the social sciences of the Ecole des Hautes Etudes Sociales a volume on the educational conflict in the ninteenth century (458).

The literature on the history of secondary education is even briefer than that for elementary. Here too Farrington's work on secondary education (469) furnishes a good starting point up to 1910. The most important additions since this date are a study of the history of the *baccalauréat* (483) and a history of secondary education from 1802 to 1920 by Weill (487) in which a bibliography of histories of individual secondary schools will be found.

With the exception to be noted, little research has been done in the field of higher education. The standard work by Liard (482) has been supplemented by a detailed study of a brief period by Aulard (455).

The recent celebration of the fiftieth anniversary of the lay school was the occasion for the appearance of two new histories of elementary education. The first by Israël (476) presents a detailed study of the work of Jules Ferry and the conflicts around the proposed legislation for the free, compulsory, and lay school. The second is a monumental work in two volumes by Léaud and Glay (481), which is a complete history of elementary education in France from the dawn of history down to the present. As M. Herriot says in his preface to the two volumes, this work represents "an attempt to place education among the large achievements of history and the essential facts of philosophy which every educator and every cultivated man should possess." The scope of the work is indicated by the full title: *L'Ecole primaire en France: Ses origines—ses différents aspects au cours des siècles—ses luttes—ses victoires—sa mission dans la démocratie.* To this should be added the introductory half-title: *L'Ecole primaire en France: Histoire pittoresque, documentaire, anecdotique de l'école, des maîtres, des écoliers depuis les origines jusqu'à nos jours.* Apart from its contribution as a work of research this two-volume history is remarkable for its illustrations and as a sample of the best type of book production.

A work of great importance which has not received the attention which it merits is the *Histoire des Universités Françaises et Etrangères* (475). For the student of history this work which brings the history of higher education down to 1860 will prove invaluable not merely because of its catholicity but also because of the list of unpublished manuscripts (475:299-302) and an extensive bibliography of about four thousand titles (475:303-97). The analytical index in itself is an excellent guide to the extensive range of topics covered by the author.

A few studies on the history of French education have appeared in English. The outstanding works on the schools of Port Royal are the two volumes by Barnard (456, 457). The works by Reisner (484) and Kandel (477, 478, 479), while not devoted to the history of education in France, contain extensive material on various aspects of the subject. Two other American contributions to our knowledge of the history of education in France are translations with expository introductions by de la Fontanerie of the writings of La Chalotais, Turgot, Diderot, and Condorcet on national education (466) and of the conduct of schools of Jean Baptiste de la Salle (465). A brief history is included in a recent work on the maternal schools by Hawtrey (474).

C. HISTORY OF EDUCATION IN GERMANY

Scientific research in education has never been given as much scope in Germany as in the United States. There are no chairs of education in German universities; even the leading thinkers in German education—as far as they are university teachers—generally occupy chairs of philosophy and education, which indicates clearly that the theory of education is considered to be closely connected with, or even a part of, philosophy, and much less, if at all, as a "science" like physics or biology. The Hochschulen für Lehrerbildung (formerly Pedagogical Academies), being confined to a two-year course for prospective elementary teachers (and, starting this year, to a one-year course for students who want to prepare for secondary teaching), neither their professors of education nor their students find much time for research. Their main objective is teaching and learning, nor are the Academies equipped for large research enterprises. The examination essays of their elementary students are comparable to masters' theses; few of them venture into the field of research. The Zentralinstitut für Erziehung und Unterricht in Berlin sometimes undertook educational investigations, as did the Auskunftsstelle für Schulwesen; but the first always considered itself primarily as a clearing-house, and the latter never could go far beyond collecting facts and figures, and disseminating information on the present educational situation. Bureaus of research connected with offices of the public school administration are very rare, and whatever they possess in equipment and means they have to devote to the problems of the day and the locality with which they are associated. The reason for this situation, broadly speaking, is, that education always *has been* and recently consciously and intentionally *is*, considered to be an affair of the *will*; educational endeavors must be directed by *values* and not so much by logical reasoning.

During the last two years there has been a general complaint that the history of education was being neglected in the training of teachers. This may or may not have been true. Judging from the number of publications, however, the historical field seems relatively well cultivated compared with other parts of the science of education. If publications advocating some educational reorganization are excluded, or the giving of practical suggestions and helps for teaching, about four out of five educational books and articles deal with the history of education. Quite a number of them may be termed the result of research; this explains why the bibliography is rather extensive.

Owing to limitation of space a selection had to be made in the list which follows. A complete bibliography on the history of education is included in Hoffmann (556), and a rather extensive and very reliable selection of books, with good annotations to many of them, in Moog (598).

Since historical research in education appears for the first time within the frame of this review the writer has thought it advisable to include as part one the standard accounts of the history of education published in Germany. Cyclopedias of education, which, of course, contain a wealth of historical information, and similar reference books, however, are not discussed. Most of them (Schmid, Rein, Roloff, Clausnitzer, and Schwarz) are well known, even in this country.

Standard Works

Moog (598) is at present *the* German history of education. A library limited to one German book in the field, should certainly choose this, and would be relatively well provided with material about any problem for the period treated (modern times) and the region covered (German-speaking Europe). The book is based on original research to an unusual degree, is modern in the best sense of the word, since it deals with education in its connection with the general current of thought as well as with the changing state of civilization and society, and contains excellent bibliographies in general and for the single chapters. Unfortunately it has no chronological tables, and not even alphabetical indexes, which may, however, be added in a second edition. Still more unfortunately, owing to the death of the author, volume one, covering ancient times and the Middle Ages, is never likely to appear.

Eggersdorfer (526) is the standard work on Catholic education; Nohl (609) is liberal in attitude; a comparable recent book written from the Protestant point of view is not available. Krieck (574), the most prominent National-Socialist educator, stressed the type-forming institutions (not only the educational) and ways of life of the various ages and nations. Barth (496) indicated in his title the point of view of his book; Stein (656) and, in some way, Heubaum (554) are forerunners of Barth; the latter is a disciple of Dilthey and applies his method of "understanding" to the subject. Leser (583) conceived of the history of education as the development of ideas and ideals. Raumer (621), Schmid (634), and Schmidt (636) are "classics," somewhat primitive in their historical method (biographical, teleological, even theological), out of date in many respects, but still valuable as rich in material. Messer (593) is a handy compilation, standing on the borderline between this and the following group.

Handbooks, Textbooks, Outlines

Abb (489), Burckhardt (512), Hehlmann (550) Kynast (579), and Weimer (668) are outlines, useful for the reader who desires a short general survey of the field. Willmann (674), in his first volume, described the historic types of educational systems. Göttler (543), Schiller (633), and Ziegler (683) are handbooks for the university student of secondary education. Krieg (576), Sturm (658), and Wickert (673) are textbooks intended primarily for the former elementary teacher-training institutions (*Lehrer-*

seminare). Krieck (575) was written for the Hochschulen für Lehrerbildung (teachers colleges). Abb (489), Behn (499), Göttler (543), Krieg (576), and Willmann (674) presented the Catholic point of view. Behn (499) adopted a rather original scheme by distinguishing between the "classical," the "romantic," and the "modern" viewpoints with regard to each problem. Sturm (658) covered only the twentieth century.

Source Materials

The number of the single works contained in the series of editions referred to in this part being very large, it is impossible to enumerate them here; moreover those published before 1928 are included in the bibliography in Moog (598). More recent works of particular importance are included below. Special attention should be given to two publications really monumental in character, the *Monumenta* (597) and the great edition of Pestalozzi's complete works (615). The first contains, among others, the famous *Pestalozzi Bibliographie* by A. Israel (volumes 25, 29, 31; 1903-05); the latter is prepared with utmost scientific care by the best experts in the field, and has already contributed a wealth of new and reliable information on the life and work of the great Swiss *Praeceptor Mundi*.

Special Fields, Problems, and Individual Educators

In this part of the bibliography it was possible to include only important publications; this is especially true for books and articles published previous to about 1925.

A considerable number of investigations have been devoted to prominent educators of the past; obviously the biographic method still exercises a certain influence. Buchenau and others (511); Dejung (516); Delekat (517), which is an excellent monograph stressing the religious aspect of Pestalozzi's ideas and work; Feilchenfeld (529, 530); Haller (549), somewhat popular; Medicus (590); U. Pretzel (619); Schönebaum (640), who is one of the experts on Pestalozzi; Silber (649); Wernecke (671); Zander (681); and others (614) are devoted to the great Swiss educator. Some of these studies owe their publication to the Pestalozzi centenary in 1927.

Several studies on Wilhelm von Humboldt by Gloege (541), Grube (547), and Rüdiger (627) supplement the fundamental study by Spranger (653) and contribute to the historical side of the great problem—state, church, and education.

Among other educators, Froebel (548, 625) and Herder (500, 622) are represented twice; they arouse some present interest because of their romantic attitude, which appeals to some contemporary thinkers in education. Pauls (612) investigated Luther's educational ideas with a view to strengthening Protestant tendencies, endangered by modern political developments. Schröteler (643) was very active in defending the Catholic viewpoint. Lochmüller (586) gave an interesting biography of Hans Schemm.

(Compare remarks on page 394.) Bosshart (507) analyzed Spranger's ideas on education. Saupe's study (631) contained monographs on thirty-five more modern educators (W. Rein, O. Willmann, F. Meumann, H. Gaudig, H. Lietz, B. Otto, F. Paulsen, E. Spranger, G. Kerschensteiner, E. Krieck, P. Petersen, W. Stern, etc.). Andreesen (495), Fritzsch (537), Gerlach (539), Metzler (594), Seiler (647), and Sellmayr (648) studied individual educators of more or less general importance.

The relations of the state to education is an important topic with Vasconcellos (662) and Pokrandt (616), who dealt with the restoration of Prussia after 1807. J. F. Meyer (596) showed how the political reaction of 1840-70 damaged the elementary school, whereas Foerster (535) and Rosin (626) dealt with a happier period in Prussian educational history (after 1871). Kosler (573) is of particular interest, because he investigated Prussian educational policies in a bilingual region mainly of Catholic character (Upper Silesia), where the relations between the state and the church were somewhat tense. This relation itself is the main topic of Albrecht (490) Dackweiler (514), and Waag (665). Schemm and others (632), Seelhof (646), and Stark (655) viewed education from the National-Socialist point of view.

A large number of studies are devoted to specific periods. Of particular interest among them are the following: Eichler (527); Gleich (540); Götze (544), one of the very rare contributions to the history of adult education in Germany; Iven (559); and Knauth (572), mainly because of the relation of their topics to presentday problems. The latter is especially true for Keilhacker (568) and Wüllenweber (679), who investigated the field of old German education which was much neglected until recently. Jaeger's study (560) is a monumental work of high standing. Marx (589) and Stahl (654) throw some light on subjects on which very little was known heretofore.

As to the history of the educational developments since 1900 and in most recent times, special attention may be called to the general surveys by Hierl (555), Nohl (608), Riedel (624), Deiters (515), and Fischl (534); to Spranger's essays (650, 651); then to some studies on the socialist movement in education, by Breitenstein (508), Liedloff (584), Weise (669), and Wittenberg (677); and to an interesting effort of penetrating into a problem which was of paramount importance in the republican period of Germany, by Netzer (603). Careful and reliable surveys of the present developments are given by Wenke (670).

Not very numerous are studies of foreign education and international relations and their educational implications in Germany, like those by Eberhard (524), E. Lehmann (581), and Schröteler (642, 644).

The history of specific types of schools is dealt with by C. Müller (599); Heinemann (551); Wychgram (680), rather old but still important; Paulsen (613), one of the finest achievements of German scholarship in the field; and Rethwisch (623). University problems were treated by Nabakowsky (602) and Schmidhauser (635).

From the large number of historical studies on certain regions or single institutions only a few of the most typical ones are noted here: Bastian (497), Blinckmann (504), Clemenz (513), Krumbholz (577), Kuckhoff (578), G. Meyer (595), G. Müller (600), Wetzel (672), and Winkler (676).

Specific phases of the educational field were studied by Böhme (505), Kielhauser (569), and Neuendorff (606), a work of monumental character. In this connection Kehr and others (567) may be mentioned as somewhat unique in topic and thoroughness.

This brief survey cannot conclude without mentioning four books which deal with the history of the educational profession, namely Fischer (533), Mellmann (592), Murtfeld (601), and C. Pretzel (618), the latter being an excellent history of the German Elementary Teachers' Association (Deutscher Lehrerverein), which itself made history by being one of the first and certainly most successful teachers organizations of genuine professional character in the world.

Method of Historiography and Historical Research in Education and Bibliography

The method of historiography and consequently of historical research in education has undergone a far-reaching change during the last five or six decades. A brief account of its development was given by Thiele (660). Out of a history of systems, theories, methods, and personalities (until 1870) grew a history of "educational reality" (until 1914), the latter term being applied almost exclusively to schools and related institutions. Since the World War, however, education has been conceived more and more clearly to include a much wider field; and educational history since this time, is gradually broadening out into cultural history (Bildungsgeschichte), including all the influences molding the oncoming, and even the present, generation. Dolch (521) surveyed the field from a somewhat different point of view, distinguishing between the history of facts, doctrines, "heroes" (great educators), and "thinkers" in education. Hoffmann's study (556) contains a comprehensive bibliography, including all books and articles in German; those on history of education are organized into three groups: (a) general accounts, including bibliography and convention records; (b) history of single institutions or regions; and (c) single personalities (works, monographs). Scientific libraries should not dispense with this serial. Spranger (651) and Schneider (637, 638) discussed general problems of research in the history of cultural (geisteswissenschaftlich) subjects, the former's investigation being of a very immediate interest with regard to that present current of thought which denies to science the right to stipulate its own presuppositions.

For this section compare also Brunnengräber (510).

Periodicals

By far the most important periodical in this field is the *Zeitschrift* (682), published by the Gesellschaft für deutsche Erziehungs- und Schulgeschichte which edits the *Monumenta* (597), and contains a wealth of material, partly supplementary in character to the latter. Until about 1933 all the educational magazines devoted some of their space to history of education; under the pressure of the present situation, however, which calls the attention of the educational world in Germany to the needs of the day, historical topics have been pushed to the background; moreover a number of periodicals have been discontinued. For these reasons the list of periodicals is short. *Bildung und Erziehung* (503) is a Catholic publication. *Deutsches Bildungswesen* (519), founded by the late Hans Schemm, National-Socialist minister of education in Bavaria, and leader of the National-Socialist Teachers' League, is the League's official publication of a more scientific character; thus historical articles published in it have a specific interest so far as they apply the National-Socialist idea of "rewriting the history of the past" to the history of education. *Die Deutsche Schule* (518) was formerly the leading periodical of the Deutsche Lehrerverein; its older volumes contain many excellent historical studies. *Die Erziehung* (528) is a "free" periodical, since it has no connection with any league or association, and is of very high standing. Its character changed little after 1933. The articles of Wenke (670) furnish very valuable material for the historian of education. *Volk im Werden* (664), also independent of associations or groups, is the National-Socialist periodical of similar standing; while it does not definitely exclude historical studies, it devotes most of its space to present-day problems.

Publications in English

A history of German education written in English, to the writer's knowledge does not exist. Valuable historical material for the period from 1924 to the present day is to be found in Kandel (563). Kandel (562) also gives brief historical summaries on various problems for Germany as well as for the other countries covered. As to the other books, the titles speak for themselves (491, 492, 493, 498, 509, 545, 564, 565, 566, 588, 628).

D. HISTORY OF EDUCATION IN ITALY

As in France, the study of the history of education in Italy is confined in the main to the requirements for the preparation of teachers; there do not exist, as in Germany, centers for the promotion of research in this field. Hence the majority of the publications are in the form of textbooks with occasional research studies in special fields pursued by individual scholars. Adequate attention has not been given to the history of education in Italy which, particularly during the nineteenth century, represents a struggle toward a national philosophy of education finding its culmination in the work of Croce and Gentile. The history since the emergence of Fascism represents a further stage in this development with the domination of Fascist political ideology over the philosophic trend.

The contributions to the history of education may be divided into three groups. In the first are the textbooks for the use of students with the inclusion generally of sections on the history of education in Italy. The second group consists of research studies in Italian history of education. The third includes studies on special aspects of education.

The textbooks differ somewhat from those which have appeared in English to the extent that they draw more on research done in the field in England, France, Germany, and the United States, as well as Italy. A good example of this type of book is found in the two small volumes by Pietrosi (710). Some textbooks, like that of De Domenicis (696), include brief extracts from source materials. Since the books in this group in general present the type of content found in most textbooks it is unnecessary to do more than list them (684, 686, 688, 689, 695, 698, 706, 707, 708, 713, 714.).

The second group of books is devoted to research studies in general and special aspects of education in Italy. The volume *Pedagogia* in the *Enciclopedia delle Enciclopedie* (697) contains, outside of materials which would naturally be expected, important contributions to the history of education which might otherwise be overlooked. The history of the philosophy of education in Italy during the nineteenth century is presented in an article under the title "Pedagogia Spiritualista Italiana del Secolo XIX" (697:1250-88). A series of articles on educational thought in the literature of France, England, Italy, Spain, and Germany presents a novel and highly important approach to the study of educational thought (697:1288-1332). A long article is devoted also to the history of education in Italy during the eighteenth and nineteenth centuries (697:1586-1649).

Studies in the history of education in the Italian states have dealt with Piedmont (705), the Duchy of Este (700), the pontifical State (699), and Naples (717). A history of education in Italy in the second half of the nineteenth century has been developed in a work by Formiggini-Santamaria (701), and an account of the educational theorists of Italy up to 1900 has been presented by Gerini (702). A general history of elementary education by Angeli (685) appeared in 1908, and was followed ten years later by Castagnola's history of modern educational theory in Italy (690). The recent development of nursery schools in Italy is the subject of a brief study by Lombardo-Radice (703).

The progress of education under the Fascist régime was discussed by Spirito (712) in the *Educational Yearbook, 1924*. The philosophy underlying education in Italy was discussed in detail in the *Educational Yearbook, 1929* by Codignola (694). Codignola has contributed other articles to the *Educational Yearbook* on the expansion of secondary education in Italy (691), on the relation of the state to religious education in Italy (692), and on teachers associations in Italy (693). The *Educational Yearbook, 1931*, contains an article by Malvezzi de'Medici (704) on native education in the Italian colonies.

Among special topics which have been studied may be mentioned the following: the relations of the state to public education in the Roman Empire (687); public education in the French Revolution (716); and three studies on the history of physical education (709, 711, 715).

E. HISTORY OF EDUCATION IN THE SCANDINAVIAN COUNTRIES

Research in the history of education in the Scandinavian countries is a comparatively virgin field; in English particularly, very few publications have been issued. Several studies deal with some phase of education in each of the Scandinavian countries, but even in them gaps are numerous; the history of education is incidental and is generally discussed in a mere outline of the historical background of the particular phase. However, from time to time, brief general accounts of the contemporary status of education have been written for each country. In studies such as Abel's (718, 719), the student of the history of education will frequently find authoritative statements of a comparative nature giving the relative position on some educational problem of Scandinavia or of one of its parts, together with references to problems of other countries.

In its section on comparative education, the *Year Book of Education* for 1936 (724) gave excellent brief accounts of the historical background of education for each country. Pearson (723) and Thornton (725) presented material of historical interest representing the educational status of the time covered. Bibliographical material for each country is furnished by the International Bureau of Education (721) and Turosienski (726). Paludan (722) gave a comparative historical presentation in Danish of secondary education in Denmark and Sweden.

Denmark

Boje and others (730) presented a comprehensive view of Danish popular education and its development during the nineteenth and twentieth centuries. Besides elementary and secondary schools, there was included a discussion about agencies for adult education, associations for young people, libraries, broadcasting, etc. Knight (747) reported observations and impressions of various educational and cultural agencies from a visit in Denmark during 1925 and 1926.

Several brief general accounts of Danish education, many of which include some historical data and which are of value as indicating trends and movements prominent at the time they were written, have been published (727, 729, 737, 741, 744, 752, 757, 761). Of these, the works by Foght (737), Hegland (744), Rost (757), and Arnett and Smith (727), have sections devoted to historical development.

Most educational studies on Denmark deal with the folk high school. Good, comparatively recent studies are those of Begtrup and others (728), Cabot (731), Campbell (732), Davies (733), and Hart (743). Studies of a somewhat earlier date include those of Foght (736, 738), Friend (742), Hegland (744), and Marais (751). The reports by Foght (736) and Friend (742) were the result of studies made in Denmark during the winter and spring of 1913. The former is a comprehensive study of the folk high school and includes a chapter on its historical evolution; the latter is a description of the work and methods of the folk high school and includes a historical sketch. Among Danish works on the folk high school, that of L. C. Nielsen (754) gives the letters and lectures of one of the early pioneers of the movement; that of Rasmussen (756) information concerning the status of the folk high schools in 1896; while that of Schröder (758), published in 1905, is a contribution to the history of the folk high schools. Hollmann (746) presented a German view of the folk high school.

Foght's educational survey of Denmark (738) is the first of a series of reports on rural education in Denmark issued by the United States Office of Education in 1914-15. The other issues of the series are bulletins by Foght (735, 736) and Friend (742). The series, together with the bulletin by Hegland (744), gives a rather complete picture of the educational system of rural Denmark as it was at the time of its publication.

Chapter nine of De Gibon's work (734), which is written in French, adds to the picture by bringing the story to 1928, and furnishing for rural education a setting against a background of the main development and problems of the agricultural system of the country as a whole.

Studies by Forchhammer (739, 740) and Hart (743) dealt with special phases of education; that by J. Nielsen (753) was devoted to teachers associations, including their historical development; and that by Lindegren (750), after a brief statement about the organization of education in Denmark in preparation for admission to college, gave a factual account of the institutions of higher education in Denmark. To a student of educational hygiene, the work of Hertel (745), published in 1885, is of historical interest. Out of several monographs on the same subject, Hertel's was selected for re-publication in English because of the conviction on the part of those in charge that it was "an eminently careful and scientific treatise," placing "in a clear light the dangers and difficulties" which beset the educational enterprises of the day.

Among publications in Danish, two by Larsen (748, 749) definitely represent research in history of education. Part one of *Bidrag til den Danske Folkeskoles Historie, 1784-1898* (748) dealt with the history of the development of the elementary school in Denmark from 1784 to 1818; part two continued the story to 1898. *Den Danske Folkeskoles Historie* (749) is a history of the elementary school in Denmark prepared especially for teacher-training seminaries. The work of Thomassen (760), published in 1896, is a bibliography of Danish pedagogical literature.

Norway

A good idea of the organization, management, and operation of the educational system of Norway may be obtained from Anderson (764). Other accounts include those by French (772, 773), Gade (774), Knap (778), Sigmund (781), and Smith (782).

Special studies in secondary education include two by Anderssen (766, 767), one of which (766) is a discussion of the law of 1896; the other (767), a centennial publication in Danish covering the period 1814-1914;

and one by Loftfield (780), published in 1930, and which still remains the most complete and authoritative study in English on secondary education in Norway. Supplemental to this in the field of higher education is a bulletin by Lindegren (779).

Part two of Jensen's *The Rural Schools of Norway* (777) is an account of the historical evolution of the rural elementary school in Norway. The chapter in the *Educational Yearbook of the International Institute* by Askeland and others (769) is a study of the historical development of state regulations governing the various types of private education in Norway. Studies which discuss special phases of education are those by Anderssen (765), Askeland and others (769), Bjanes (770), and Helgesen (776).

Studies in Norwegian include one by Voss (783) which dealt with the educational struggle in Norway during the nineteenth century, with special references to the regulations of 1809, 1869, and 1896; and one by Feragen (771), a treatise on elementary education.

The appendix of Jensen's work (777:253-80) contains a bibliography of Norwegian pedagogical literature prepared by the staff of the Library of the University of Norway. Other valuable bibliographies in the studies listed are found in works by Anderson (764), Arent (768), French (773), Helgesen (776), Jensen (777), Lindegren (779), Loftfield (780), Smith (782), and Voss (783).

Sweden

Three good general accounts of recent date on education in Sweden have been published, two by Bergqvist (788, 789), formerly head of the Swedish Royal Board of Education, and one by Coles (792). The account by Lindström (803) is good for the period of 1913 in which it was written. It includes a bibliography and a brief historical account.

There are a number of studies on special phases of Swedish education which, when taken together, give a fairly good picture of the educational situation. Most of the accounts include some material on the historical development of the main theme. Among these studies are those by Bogoslovsky (790), which dealt with the national, political, and social background of Swedish education and which contain a brief historical survey of the movement for educational reform in Sweden; Borgeson (791), which dealt with elementary and secondary education previous to the reform of 1927; Coles (793), which is the best account in English of that reform; Peterson (805), a descriptive study of the training of elementary- and secondary-school teachers; Kilander (800), an interesting study on science education in the secondary schools; Lindegren (802), a study of institutions of higher education; and the Swedish Overseas Institute (821), which deals with higher professional education.

Special phases of education in Sweden, such as the folk high school, school hygiene, and teachers associations, have been studied by Jonsson (799), the Royal Swedish Committee for the Second International Congress on School Hygiene (807), and Malmborg (804). An official publication (787) gave an account of the reorganization of education in Sweden through the reforms of 1918 and 1927, and a work by Lagerstedt (801), also a Swedish publication, gave an account prepared in 1920 for the Eleventh Nordic School Meeting held in Christiania and covering the years 1910-20. The eleven official reports (807, 811 to 820 inclusive) represented the findings of committees appointed to investigate various phases and problems connected with education. Each committee was interested in the historical development of its problem and made some mention of this in its report. The committee on the elementary-school seminaries (812) devoted volume three of its four-volume report to a historical account of the development of the seminaries for the training of elementary teachers.

Among other studies in Swedish dealing with some period in the history of education, are those by Warne (822), which deals with the pre-history of the elementary school in Sweden; Westling (823), which is a treatise on the Swedish elementary school after 1842; and Rietz (806), which is a history of education in one of the well-known counties of Sweden.

CHAPTER III
Comparative Education

COMPARATIVE EDUCATION is a relatively recent arrival among the increasing number of branches which make up the professional study of education. Although it is a recent arrival as an organized branch, the study of what other nations have done in education is considerably older. One need only recall the influence in France and in the United States of Victor Cousin's *Report on Education in Prussia,* or of the reports of Calvin Stowe, Horace Mann, and others, on the development of education in this country, or the mine of information on foreign educational practices in Barnard's *American Journal of Education* and later in the reports and bulletins of the United States Bureau of Education, or finally, the reports of Matthew Arnold and the monumental *Special Reports*, initiated by Sir Michael Sadler and published by the Board of Education in England. The articles on educational systems of foreign countries throughout the world which appeared in Monroe's *Cyclopedia of Education* (934) just before the World War may be said to mark the culmination of an era.

The study of foreign school systems in the past twenty years may definitely be described as the natural outcome of two forces—first, the unrest in education caused by the upheaval of the World War, and second, the expansion and redefinition of the scope of the study of education. Immediately after the outbreak of the War the participating nations began to survey the strong and weak points of their own educational systems and to compare them with those of other nations. The result of the new demands placed upon education in the period of reorganization, already planned during the War, was a search for new philosophies and new methods of approach to the problems of education which confronted both educators and statesmen. There has thus developed a widespread interest and an extensive literature in comparative education.

From the point of view of this monograph, however, a discussion of research in comparative education is surrounded by a number of difficulties. As contrasted with educational psychology and its allied branches there is, first, no unanimity about the methods of research. In the main it may be said that the methods of comparative education are similar to those used in research in the fields of history and philosophy of education. Indeed, comparative education has for its field the study of contemporary history and philosophies, and the best preparation for research in comparative education is preparation in the methods of historical research and in philosophy in the broadest sense of the term. Secondly, there is no agreement or concerted drive on the topics to be studied; their selection depends upon the peculiar interest and equipment of the inquirer. Finally, the field is so broad and goes so deeply into the roots of national existence that few inquirers have the equipment which demands not merely an interest in and knowledge of all the phases of education but of all the social, political, and cultural backgrounds that give education its meaning, as well as a knowledge of foreign languages which will give access to these backgrounds. One thing is clear and that is that the mere study of educational practices or theories in isolation, of methods, of curriculums, of courses of study, of time schedules, of administration and organization, and of statistics has no meaning except in the light of such backgrounds, the possession of which is too often taken for granted even in the study of the educational system of one's own country. An excellent illustration of the thesis that no problem in education can be understood without going back to the roots from which it springs was provided in the discussions of the problem of examinations which were held at Eastbourne, England, in 1931. There were present at this conference representatives from England, Scotland, France, Germany, Switzerland, and the United States. The discussions of the examination problem inevitably led to a discussion of the type of education to be examined, and, although the discussions were not prepared in advance, the *Report of the Conference on Examinations* (870) which recorded the proceedings at Eastbourne, constitutes the best illustration of differences between national systems of education that can be found anywhere. It is because of failure to go into the fundamental bases that so many studies of education in foreign countries give but the skeletons of the systems without making that contribution which comparative education should furnish for a practical study of philosophy and principles of education. And this contribution is all the more possible because so many of the problems in education are today common to most countries; in their solution certain common principles or philosophies are involved; the practical outcomes may, however, differ because of differences in tradition, in social and political principles, and in cultural standards.

It is objected sometimes that all that can be secured from a comparative study of educational systems are subjective opinions, the personal judgments of the inquirer himself. There is some truth in this if what is done is to attempt to evaluate the quality of education. But this is not fundamentally the purpose of comparative education, although it may have its place under proper reservations; rather it is to discover what the problems in education are, to discuss how they are met, and to develop a philosophy or outlook on education. Another type of technic is beginning to be used and has possibilities of further development; this is the actual comparison of achievements in different subjects of the curriculums in different countries. Progress with this technic will depend, first, on the improvement of the scientific procedures of measurement, and, second, on a more widespread acceptance of such measures than exists at present.

Statistical comparisons in education are for the present worthless, partly because the methods of collecting data vary from country to country, and partly because of variety of terminology. Statistics of costs of expenditures again have little meaning because of the great divergences in purchasing power of the currencies used. It is not impossible that some scheme of uniform reporting and accounting may some day be developed and basic index numbers established which will make comparisons practicable. Comparisons are made, for example, between enrolments in high schools in the United States and in secondary schools abroad, ignoring the fact that such schools offer only academic courses in the main and excluding the vast array of other types of differentiated schools for adolescents which are found in most countries.

Despite language handicaps there is an increasing amount of material available in English for the student of comparative education. The specialist, however, can make but little progress without a command of at least two foreign languages. The difficulty is to discover boundaries for what is called the study of education. Books like those of Sieburg, *Who Are These French?* or of Renier, *The English, Are They Human?* or books in the political and social science fields, or current literature may at times be more important for throwing light on the meaning of education in a particular country than the educational system itself. It is from this point of view that the series on Civic Loyalty edited by Merriam and the two volumes by Tugwell and Keyserling (969) are written; education, in other words, is discussed in its proper setting of national aims and purposes which give meaning to those problems—administration, organization, curriculum, courses of study, methods of instruction, preparation and status of teachers, etc.—with which the professional educator is concerned.

The importance of this method of approach can best be illustrated by considering how educational systems in transition should be studied. There are today numerous examples of such systems—Mexico, China, Turkey, Iraq, Russia, Italy, and Germany, as well as many so-called backward countries which are beginning to plan the provision of educational facilities of a modern type. Merely to describe the present system of education in Italy, for example, or to study the administration of education, the organization of schools, the curriculum and courses of study, the preparation of teachers, and the examinations may be interesting but is meaningless without an intensive study of the political, economic, and cultural significance of Fascism, of the conflicting philosophies which dominated Italy before the advent of Fascism, the philosophy of the school of Croce and Gentile, the educational interpretations of such philosophy by Gentile, Lombardo-Radice, Codignola, and others, the recent history of Italian education which called for reform, the cultural tradition of Italy, the relation of state and church in Italy, and the more recent changes of Fascism itself with its emphasis on power politics, manifested in the educational emphasis on militarism in the schools.

Germany offers an excellent opportunity for the study of educational changes produced by two political revolutions in less than two decades. The educational system of the Republican period, 1918-33, must remain unintelligible without an understanding, first, of the type of education which it displaced and which had been based on a different political régime, and second, without a study of the Weimar Constitution with its social and political implications, of German character, and of the significance of doctrines of freedom for education. The great variety of experimentation which characterized German education during this period can be understood only in the light of a change in the philosophy governing the relation of the state to the individual. Such a study, including the impact on politics and education of the economic situation, gives the proper perspective for an understanding of the National Socialist Revolution, which in turn cannot be understood without going back further into the history in Germany of the conflicts in philosophy and politics between liberalism and totalitarianism. The triumph of the National Socialist Revolution means the restoration of the dominant rights of the state over the individual, which has set its mark on every aspect of education. But beyond this it is necessary to go back to the history of political theory and government in Germany from the days of Frederick the Great in order to appreciate the fact that National Socialist ideology, despite its professions of novelty, is but the culmination of more than a century of conflict between the totalitarian concept and liberal ideals. The study of education in Germany in the last two decades thus offers an excellent opportunity for appreciating the intimate relations between social, political, and general cultural traditions and theories on the one hand and educational theories and practices on the other. Without such a study the mere survey of the framework of the educational system must remain meaningless.

Soviet Russia offers another illustration of the same type. The ideological Revolution in Soviet Russia on which education has been concentrated can again be best understood in the light of Russian traditions and backgrounds which have left a certain impress on the Russian mind. Religious orthodoxy has been replaced by economic orthodoxy; the autocracy of the Czar has been supplanted by the autocracy of the Party; and for political and military nationalism there has been substituted a class consciousness whose influences are much the same. The history of Soviet education represents an attempt through free and uncontrolled experimentation to discover a type of education best suited to the present régime, culminating in recognition and admission of failure and a return to the pre-Revolutionary pattern with only a difference in the content of instruction and different methods of selection through the system.

The interest of the American student in change has been directed in the main to the educational systems of the revolutionary states and has not been devoted to education in those countries in which the tempo of progress is slower and less spectacular. And yet the same methods of research and inquiry are essential for a proper understanding of those countries which have built up strong traditions of culture with a resultant check on hasty changes in established institutions. Here the educational systems of France and England have as much to offer to philosophy of education as have those of the more revolutionary states. The student may well ask why a nation like France, which has set up the cult of reason as the supreme ideal of the human mind, is still content to have a system of education which apparently lags far behind the times. Here, too, the answer can be found only in a cultural history of over three centuries (to include only the modern period) and in the political history of a century and a half. From the one comes the tradition of *culture générale* and training in clarity and orderliness of ideas; from the other is derived that emphasis on *sécurité d'abord* which explains the desire through education to assure national solidarity. Cutting across both is the individualistic character of the Frenchman which education seeks to harness through its emphasis both on a common culture and on common objects of allegiance.

England, by contrast, appears on the surface to make no effort through education to impress either her traditions or national ideals on the rising generation. There the student finds an interplay between tradition and adaptation to new demands which is so subtle as to escape his attention. There the question is not preparation for an unknown future but, in the words of a president of the Board of Education, "Can we so adjust our system that, without dropping anything essential from our native inheritance, we can go forward confidently to meet the needs of a new world?" There one finds the reconciliation between a doctrine of laissez faire and a policy of developing a national system of articulated schools.

The same method of research, an analysis and interpretation of educational systems in the light of national traditions and the current political, social, and economic setting may be applied, not only to younger countries like the British Dominions and the South American nations, but also to the so-called backward peoples of the Near East and in colonial dependencies, often with a rich body of culture which needs to be reshaped to meet modern conditions. In the one group one finds centralized systems which were appropriate for sparsely populated countries; in the other there is beginning to spread the recognition that the imposition of foreign cultures has been a mistake and that the way of progress lies not through assimilation but through adaptation to indigenous cultures and folkways as well as local needs.

It is only as these methods are employed that the student can understand such questions as administration and organization of education, curriculum and methods, and the preparation of teachers. By such methods of research a student can come to a better understanding and appreciation of the meaning of education in his own country, which he is too often apt to take for granted and as a result to devote his attention to the mechanisms and technical aspects of education. Further, this method of approach stresses what is perhaps more important for the American student of education than anything else in face of the danger of too intense specialization—the enrichment of his cultural background and a fuller understanding of the significance of education in its national setting.

One thing comparative education cannot and should not attempt to undertake—i.e., to adopt directly and without the necessary safeguards of modification the theories and practices of other countries. There are today enough evidences of the failure of such attempts, which in most cases is not a criticism of the theories or practices but rather proof of the thesis which has been emphasized up to this point that educational systems reflect the ethos of their environment and that all that can be transported is the idea to be modified and applied to the ethos of the new environment. The history of the importation of foreign commissions to organize and administer systems of education in part or entirely in many South American countries is a history of failures. This was the burden of the report of the League of Nations' Mission of Educational Experts, entitled *The Reorganisation of Education in China* (925). The experts discovered that the transportation of the American system to China had failed, but went on to commit the same error in recommending that China look to the organization of school administration in the different European countries. The criticism of foreign influences in Persia (954) and in Egypt (832) run along the same lines, while authorities in charge of education in colonial dependencies (910) and those engaged in missionary education (916, 933) are also beginning to realize that education must be adapted to local traditions, culture, and needs. On the other hand the striking reform of education in Mexico shows what can be done by the adaptation of an educational theory to the ethos of a nation (874, 875, 912, 958).

The method of approach here outlined had already been discussed by Sir Michael Sadler, who, as editor of the English Board of Education's series of *Special Reports on Educational Subjects,* may be described as the modern founder of the study of comparative education. It is to be noted that this series was established not merely to promote the academic study of education but to assist the English authorities in deriving as much help as possible from as many sources as possible in the task of reorganizing the system of education. This practice has been continued down to the present, and, in addition to special issues devoted to the study of the educational system of a foreign country or of some special problem, the *Educational Pamphlets* series published by the Board of Education as well as the *Reports* issued from time to time by the Consultative Committee contain some account of foreign practices.

Discussing the value and methods of comparative education Sadler pointed out many years ago (955):

> In studying foreign systems of education we should not forget that the things outside the schools matter even more than the things inside the schools, and govern and interpret the things inside. We cannot wander at pleasure among the educational systems of the world, like a child strolling through a garden, and pick off a flower from one bush and some leaves from another, and then expect that if we stick what we have gathered into the soil at home, we shall have a living plant. A national system of education is a living thing, the outcome of forgotten struggles and difficulties and "of battles long ago." It has in it some of the secret workings of national life. It reflects, while seeking to remedy, the failings of national character. By instinct it often lays special emphasis on those parts of training which the national character particularly needs. Not less by instinct, it often shrinks from laying stress on points concerning which bitter dissensions have arisen in former periods of national history. But is it not likely that if we have endeavored, in a sympathetic spirit, to understand the real working of

a foreign system of education, we shall in turn find ourselves better able to enter into the spirit and tradition of our own national education, more sensitive to its unwritten ideals, quicker to catch the signs which mark its growing or fading influence, readier to mark the dangers which threaten it and the subtle workings of hurtful change? The practical value of studying in a right spirit and with scholarly accuracy the working of foreign systems of education is that it will result in our being better fitted to study and understand our own.

The same point of view was expressed by Thurber (967:2):

There are certain problems set for every people that undertake to deal with school organization. There have been various solutions worked out for these problems, chiefly in the nineteenth century, by different nations, each operating in its own historic spirit and environment. The answers obtained may or may not agree, but our view will be widened by seeing more than one solution. Moreover, such a study, dealing as it does with fundamental principles, should foster the acquisition of a philosophic attitude toward that wide field of interest covered by the term "organization of education". . . . Perhaps, too, we shall see more clearly that education, as a system, is a development, a product of the evolution of society, and that if the form we have seems not quite to fit our highest conceptions, the way to better it is not by bartering what we have for what someone else has, nor by building a lean-to against our present structure. Further study might well be given to the basal problem for each country: how has the existing condition and system or lack of it been developed out of the cooperation and antagonisms of universal principles and national peculiarities?

Thurber sounded a warning against holding up the foreign systems of education as models to be adopted and against that more or less fanatical chauvinism to which "we owe the other common class of allusion to foreign schools which are made for the purpose of showing how immeasurably inferior they are to the native product."

Meaning of Comparative Education

In what sense can such an approach to the study of the educational systems of foreign countries be called comparative? Does comparative education imply the existence of standards of measurement or of comparison? The first answer is that such standards do not yet exist. The second is that at present, at any rate, the purpose of comparative education, as of comparative law, comparative literature, or comparative anatomy, is to discover the differences in the forces and causes that produce differences in educational systems. This is all the more important today since most of the advanced nations are confronted with almost identical problems and yet the solutions are not universally identical. Thus the chief preoccupation in most countries is the problem of the education of the adolescent. All are interested in the American solution of this problem by the provision of equal and identical opportunities of education, but few are disposed to accept this solution in the form of a single comprehensive high school. On the other hand, there can be detected in the United States considerable dissatisfaction with what is called "the waste in secondary education." Other countries are looking for schemes for increasing and enriching the opportunities for the education of the adolescent, but fear that the American solution may militate against the retention of quality in education (908, 909, 914, 926, 958, 968).

More or less objective standards of comparison do exist at this point. Graduates from secondary schools in the leading European countries would be admitted to the junior year in an American college, provided they had an adequate command of English. Such standards are generally accepted, although there is not available any published statement on equivalents. The probability is that age for age the European student is accelerated by two years in advance of the American. This, of course, may point either to a longer secondary education and an earlier start or more careful selection, or it may impel one to inquire whether the American student derives some educational advantages which the European does not possess, and which are of a more practical and worldly rather than intellectualistic character (828, 867, 926, 930).

It is not altogether true, however, that objective comparisons cannot be made. For the present their scope is somewhat limited to the type of measurement that can be conducted through objective tests. Such comparisons have already been conducted. Thus Powers in 1927 administered American tests in chemistry to pupils in a few English secondary schools (949, 950). In 1929 the Educational Records Bureau of New York City tested English secondary-school pupils using American tests in English, French, and algebra (878). In 1931-33 an investigation was undertaken in the County of Fife, Scotland, "at the request of the Scottish Council for Research in Education, which was seeking evidence on two matters: first, the comparison of the standards of achievement in schools of Scotland and America; and second, the applicability of American achievement tests to Scottish pupils." The tests were conducted in reading, arithmetic-computation, arithmetic-reasoning, language usage, and spelling. The results showed that on the level of achievement, Fife "eleven-year-olds" were sixteen months ahead of American children of the same age; in reading they were five months ahead; in arithmetic-computation, twenty months; in arithmetic-reasoning, thirteen months; in language usage, twenty-four months; and in spelling, twenty-nine months. It was found that "group tests of intelligence devised in America are seriously misleading if the norms are not derived from the application of the tests derived in this country [Scotland]" (928).

The application of American tests has also been made elsewhere. They were used in the surveys conducted by the International Institute of Teachers College, Columbia University, under the direction of Monroe, in the Philippine Islands (937) and Puerto Rico (938). Sandiford used American tests as part of the survey of education in British Columbia (957). More recently Superintendent J. F. Cramer of The Dalles, Oregon, has followed up in Australia a comparative study of the achievement of American and Australian children which he had already begun in his own system a few years ago. The results have not yet been published.

The Modern Language Investigation, conducted under the direction of Fife of Columbia University, employed the same series of tests in modern languages in the United States, Canada, and England, which gave a basis of comparison of the strength and weakness of pupils as measured by a common standard (884).

This method of comparison lends itself to other uses. Thus H. R. Harper in 1931 conducted tests of international attitudes of students in Austria, Czechoslovakia, Denmark, England, France, Germany, Switzerland, and the United States (889). Hauck (892), in a study of American-Canadian relations, used an informational test in order to discover how much the children of one country knew about the other.

The use of objective tests for comparative purposes is promising but probably limited in its scope to the measurement of achievement of facts, knowledge, and information. It is not inconceivable, however, that the time may come when some central agency will be able to devise tests on the basis of courses of study and textbooks from a large number of countries in such forms that they will not be affected by translation into several languages. At the same time they may still remain inadequate because of the difficulty of devising international tests of intelligence against which to measure the results of the achievement tests.

Outside of the field of objective tests the Institute of Intellectual Coöperation of the League of Nations had a study of school texts prepared in the interest of eliminating or correcting references to foreign countries which militate against the development of international understanding (904). A similar study had already been made, but, in the opinion of the writer, rather prematurely, by Prudhommeaux under the auspices of the European branch of the Carnegie Endowment for International Peace (951). The Scandinavian countries through their international organization, Norden, have also agreed to examine textbooks in the interest of better understanding among the four nations—Denmark, Finland, Norway, and Sweden (971). Scott reversed the process and sought in his two studies, *The Menace of Nationalism* (961) and *Patriots in the Making* (962), to discover the cause of international antagonisms.

Another aspect of the same problem—the making of citizens—has been thoroughly treated from the social, political, and other points of view in the series on civic education edited by Merriam (836, 886, 890, 893, 906, 923, 932, 948, 959). This series, while not specifically devoted to education, is invaluable to students of comparative education as an illustration of the methodology appropriate to this field of study. Each volume furnishes an excellent example of the thesis developed earlier that the educational system of a nation cannot be understood fully except as an expression of everything that enters into the creation of that nation's mentality.

The progress of the study of comparative education has been essentially a post-War development due to two causes: The first has been the desire to obtain as broad a knowledge as possible of foreign school systems and theories as the basis for the educational reconstruction which has taken place everywhere. The second has been the increase in the number of international organizations interested in the exchange of educational ideas and in cooperative attack on some educational problems. The League of Nations, while at first remaining aloof from the consideration of education as the proper concern of each nation alone, has through some of its organizations undertaken the study of some common problems that affect all countries. Thus the International Labor Office has stimulated a revision of the laws of compulsory school attendance in many countries as a measure for the protection of children against economic exploitation. Another division, the Institute of Intellectual Coöperation, with its office in Paris, considered the careful analysis of school textbooks in the interest of peace by the avoidance of offensive statements against foreign nations (904). The Institute of Intellectual Coöperation was created "to deal with questions of intellectual coöperation" and, although the scope of its activities is in the main limited to questions of higher education, it stimulated the study of school textbooks through national committees, and publishes an *Educational Bulletin* and other information in the field of education, some of which will be mentioned later. Also under the League of Nations is the International Institute of Educational Cinematography with its headquarters in Rome.

Equally important for the student of comparative education is the emergence of international organizations of teachers and educators which at their annual or biennial meetings discuss reports on special subjects which have been prepared in advance. Thus the quarterly *Bulletin* of the Fédération Internationale des Associations d'Instituteurs has in the last few years contained discussions (in English, French, German, and Spanish) of such topics as practical means for the examination of the knowledge acquired in primary schools and the practical ways of selection to promote children from primary schools to different higher courses; the standstill of education for peace and the way out of the economical and political circumstances of our time; the training of teachers; the problem of young people's leisure; opportunities for organizing peace training in schools; and methods for the promotion of a continued cultural and professional education of teachers in service. On each topic reports from various countries prepared by teachers or their representatives and a summary of these are presented (882).

In the field of secondary education the Fédération Internationale des Fédérations Nationales des Members du Personnel de l'Enseignement Secondaire Officiel (International Federation of National Associations of Teachers in Public Secondary Schools) has issued a number of reports which have resulted from inquiries on a variety of topics. These reports have constituted the bases for discussion at the annual congresses held by the Fédération. The following subjects have been reported upon, discussed, and published in the *Bulletin International* (883), which appears quarterly: secondary education for girls; overpressure in secondary schools; the overcrowding of the time-table; the functions of the school doctor; out-of-school activities; the academic and professional preparation of the secondary-school teacher; the character, limit, and purpose of the educational task of the secondary teacher; the principles and conditions governing the admission to secondary schools. The reports are published in French, English, and German.

The New Education Fellowship, devoted to the promotion of progressive education, in addition to meetings of its constituent branches in each country, holds biennial international conferences, the proceedings of which are published (939, 941, 942, 943). In each country there is usually published an organ of the association (*Pour l'Ere Nouvelle* in France; *Das Werdende Zeitalter* in Germany until 1933; *The New Era in Home and School* in England).

The World Federation of Education Associations publishes proceedings of its biennial meetings which are devoted to the discussion of such topics as the following: character; moral and religious education; country youth and country school; health education; illiteracy; industrial education; international correspondence exchange; library service; adult education; behavior-problem children and adolescents; colleges and universities; preschool, nursery, and kindergarten handicapped children; elementary education; secondary education; parent and teacher—home and school; motion pictures; social adjustment; teachers associations; and preparation of teachers for international cooperation and goodwill. The Federation has recently begun to issue *World Education* as its official organ.

There are three important centers for study and research in problems of comparative education. The first of these, the Bureau International d'Education, is not a teaching institution but a clearing-house of information on education not only in those countries which are supporting members of the Bureau but throughout the world. The Bureau has published general descriptive accounts of education in fifty-three countries (855) which are brought up to date by an *Annuaire* (839). In addition to a number of reports on education for peace (842, 849, 856, 857), the Bureau has issued a large number of reports on special subjects, such as bilingualism (840), home and school (845), children's literature (846, 854), selection of books for school libraries (860), the married woman teacher (864), economies in education (847), compulsory education and its prolongation (862), admission to secondary schools (838), self-government in school (863), and group activities (865). Other reports have been devoted to the educational systems of different countries, e.g., Poland (848, 861), Egypt (852), Esthonia (853), and Roumania (858). The Bureau undertakes the preparation of reports on special issues at the request of its constituent members. Thus it has published a report on the preparation of elementary-school teachers (850), another on the preparation of secondary-school teachers (851), and a third on consultative committees in education (844). An annual report on the International Conference of the members on public education (843) has also been published. The special reports are in the main based on questionnaires addressed to and information received from ministries of education; in this sense they represent official views and interpretations rather than independent investigations.

The Institute of Education of the University of London was established as a center for the study of education for the British Empire. Its interest, however, is not limited to education in the British Empire. Through the publication of its *Studies and Reports* it is making available information on a variety of problems—education in the Far East and Near East, the education of backward peoples, etc. (829, 869, 873, 891, 894, 896, 917, 952). In connection with the Institute of Education there was begun in 1932 the *Year Book of Education* (946) under the editorship of Lord Eustace Percy until 1935 and subsequently of a joint editorial board. These yearbooks contain, in addition to a mine of information not otherwise generally available on education in Great Britain and Ireland, articles on education in the British Commonwealth of Nations and the leading countries of the world. Besides accounts of the educational systems, the yearbooks have contained articles on modern scientific aids to teaching, school architecture, ideals of religious education, the health services, universities in the British empire and the United States of America, education of the African native, education in the British colonies, and the League of Nations and intellectual cooperation; events in education in the English-speaking nations, survey of secondary education, creative education, the selection and supply of textbooks in the British Empire; events and special features in education in the English-speaking nations, the psychological aspects of child development, the testing of intelligence, outlines of medical education, other branches of professional education, education and the social crisis, the promotion of teachers in public elementary schools in the British Empire, and comparative study of native education in various dependencies; current events in education, problems of educational policy (with special reference to backward children), International Institute Examinations Inquiry, and juvenile delinquency in England and Wales.

Two of the purposes for which the International Institute of Teachers College, Columbia University, was established were "(a) to conduct investigations into educational conditions, movements and tendencies in foreign countries, and (b) to make the results of such investigations available to students of education in the United States and elsewhere in the hope that such pooling of information will help to promote and advance the cause of education." In fulfilment of these purposes the International Institute has published reports on the training of elementary teachers in Germany (826); on the attitudes of European students on international problems (889); on French elementary (913) and secondary education (918); on the teaching of modern languages abroad (929); on student homes in China (933); and on education in Iraq (905), Persia (954), Prussia (919), Hungary (922), Bulgaria (953), and Nazi Germany (915). The International Institute has conducted surveys and published reports on education in the Philippine Islands (937), Puerto Rico (938), and Iraq (936). Through its series of *Educational Yearbooks* (911), inaugurated in 1924 under the editorship of Dr. I. L. Kandel, the International Institute has made available information on education in practically all of the countries of Europe, in many of the Latin American countries, in India, China, Japan, Australia and New Zealand, and in South Africa. In addition special problems have been discussed such as method, the elementary-school curriculum, secondary education, teacher training, and vocational education. Topics dealt with in the five volumes for 1930-35 include the following: the expansion of secondary education; education in colonial dependencies of Belgium, France, pre-War Germany, Great Britain, Italy, and Japan; the relation of the state to religious education; missionary education and missionary activities; education in France and Russia; and teachers associations. The *Educational Yearbook* for 1929 was devoted to the philosophy underlying national systems of education and serves as an introduction to the methodology of comparative education. Beginning with the *Educational Yearbook* for 1936, surveys of education in the past ten years in the countries discussed in earlier volumes will be presented and will furnish an opportunity for comparing progress and discovering tendencies in education. Under the direction of members of the International Institute a number of Ph.D. research studies have been prepared and published on various aspects of education in different parts of the world (827, 832, 833, 880, 885, 889, 892, 905, 920, 921, 922, 924, 927, 931, 933, 945, 947, 954, 963).

Sources of Information

Perhaps the greatest difficulty which confronts the student of comparative education is that of securing information on the progress and tendencies in education. It is difficult enough to keep abreast of the rapidly growing literature on education in each country; it is still more difficult in view of language handicaps to discover what is going on in foreign countries. Fortunately the task is being simplified or brought within measurable control by such publications as were discussed in the preceding section, by the rise of centers of information, and by the appearance of valuable bibliographies. Another difficulty which presents itself is that there is not or perhaps there cannot be any concerted drive in different countries on the same problems at the same time. The concentration on particular problems through the Bureau International d'Education has already been mentioned (838 to 865, inclusive); to this may be added the publications of the International Institute of Educational Cinematography, or such reports as those issued by the International Institute of Intellectual Coöperation on broadcasting (901) and public libraries and leisure (900), or the series of *Entretiens* (902); here also belong the reports of proceedings of international associations already mentioned. Information on adult education throughout the world has been made available by the World Association for Adult Education (974, 975), on agricultural education by the Institut International d'Agriculture (897), on commercial education by the International Association for Commercial Education (898), and on technical education by the Bureau International de l'Enseignement Technique (866).

Cooperative study and research in the problem of examinations were initiated by the Carnegie Corporation through the International Institute of Teachers College, Columbia University, in 1931, when a conference was held on the subject in Eastbourne, England. The conference was attended by representatives from England, France, Germany, Scotland, Switzerland, and the United States, and resulted in the formation of national committees to undertake further research. Reports of these investigations have already begun to appear, and a report on a second conference held in Folkestone, England, in 1935, has recently been issued (871). A further extension of the investigation has been made possible by the appointment of committees in Sweden and Finland. The same problem has been studied and reported upon by the New Education Fellowship (940).

Although not the result of international cooperation the works of Swift of the University of California, which throw light on an aspect of educational administration (finance) in some European countries, not generally accessible, deserve to be mentioned (966).

Important guides to sources of information have been made available by the United States Office of Education in a bulletin on *National Ministries of Education* (825), and by the International Institute of Intellectual Coöperation in its *Handbook of National Centres of Educational Information* (903) which is a directory of the official, semiofficial, and private agencies for educational research and dissemination of information and which contains a list of principal educational reviews in each of the thirty-two countries concerned. To these should be added the list of educational yearbooks by Claparède (868), the *Education Index* (876), and the *Educational Abstracts* (877) which have recently begun to devote some attention to education in foreign countries.

The various yearbooks which have been mentioned will furnish a starting point for the student interested in the educational systems of foreign countries. Equally important for this purpose are the numerous encyclopedias of education which are now available, but, while no encyclopedia can be expected to be up to date, it can always be relied upon for useful information and references which will start the student on his way (837, 879, 881, 887, 907, 934, 944, 960, 965, 972, 973).

The task is beginning to be simplified by the appearance of bibliographies. In 1934 the United States Office of Education issued a bulletin on *Foreign and Comparative Education* (970), which contains references of a general character as well as special references on the educational systems of 103 countries—for the present the most comprehensive bibliography available from the point of view of the countries included. Another pamphlet published by the United States Office of Education presents a bibliography on the education of native and minority groups (872), and a mimeographed circular gives a list of references on higher education in foreign countries (824).

The International Institute of Intellectual Coöperation (899) has published a bibliography on education, prepared by national centers of information in twenty-two countries.

A remarkable and noteworthy, but unfortunately little known contribution to educational bibliography is the rich and comprehensive work of Blanco y Sánchez (831), formerly professor in the Escuela Superior del Magisterio in Madrid. The three-volume work is a bibliography of education throughout the world from 1900 to 1930. The first two volumes are arranged alphabetically by authors, the third by subjects, countries, and topics. The bibliography was supplemented for a few years by an annual (830) which unfortunately the author has been unable to continue.

Finally, the Bureau International d'Education maintains a bibliographical service, the results of which are published as a supplement to its quarterly *Bulletin* (841); the English edition contains lists of works in English only, the French edition, works in French and German. The bibliography, while useful, is by no means comprehensive since it is in the main restricted to the classification of educational news and reviews which appear in the *Bulletin*. The Bureau also communicates information on new departures in education to the educational press of all countries and maintains an exchange service of educational laws and decrees of special interest to school administrators.

Textbooks in Comparative Education

The scope of the field known as comparative education is so broad and has so many ramifications that it is no easy task to discuss textbooks in it. The field is in any case new and definitive works on the subject have not yet appeared. It is, furthermore, difficult to draw the line and say what book contributes to a knowledge and understanding of a nation's education. Phyllis Bentley's *Inheritance* for England or Sinclair Lewis' *Main Street* for the United States may furnish better material for a study of the respective educational systems of the two countries than any description of the schools. The approach may be made through a nation's literature and history, political and social theory, philosophy or anthropology, or through a combination of these, and produce a better picture and appreciation of its educational system than the dry bones of legislation, curriculums, and statistics. A good textbook in the history of education may well furnish the essential background for the study of comparative education.

The preparation of textbooks in comparative education as distinct from books on single systems of education labors definitely under the difficulties of defining the scope and the meaning of the term "comparative" itself. Since the point has already been stressed that any educational system is redolent of the traditions and culture of the people whom it serves, it is futile to expect that standards can ever be set up by which anything but the most technical aspects can be measured and these do not constitute the essentials. It is much more important, for instance, to study the interplay between political theories and practices and education than to compare statistical data; it is more fruitful to consider why a country like France adheres to methods which are regarded as obsolete, why the United States is only too ready to welcome innovations, and why England represents a blend between tradition and adaptations to changing demands. The fundamental contribution which comparative education can make is to furnish the student of education with a methodology against the background of which he can understand the essential problems of education and appreciate the bases of theory and practice.

The first modern textbook on comparative education, edited by Sandiford (956) of the University of Toronto, contains separate accounts of the educational systems of six countries knit together to some extent by a uniform scheme and a general introduction which discusses the basic approach to the subject. In 1931 there was published under the auspices of the teachers associations of Sweden, Norway, and Denmark a survey (964) of the educational systems in ten countries (United States, Denmark, England, Finland, France, Holland, Norway, Switzerland, Sweden, and Germany); the survey consisted of ten articles which followed a general plan (educational organization, elementary education, continuation schools, secondary education, and administration) but without any discussion of backgrounds.

In 1928 appeared the "Kritische Vergleichung des Schulwesens der anderen Kulturstaaten" by Hessen (895) which dealt with the educational practices of a number of countries under a number of topics, e.g., compulsory education, the state and education, the church and education, education and economic life, and the organization of education. Hans (888), in his *Principles of Educational Policy*, followed the same method but under a greater variety of topics—democracy and education, the state and the church, the state and the family, centralization and decentralization, national minorities, educational highway, exceptional children, vocational education, teachers, curriculum, textbooks and methods, universities, adult education, educational finances, and education and politics.

Following the same general principle but with a stronger emphasis on the relationship between cultural backgrounds and education and without any attempt to be comprehensive, the present author's *Comparative Education* (908) was intended to be a contribution to methodology, using six countries and the factual information arising out of them for illustrative purposes. The aim and plan of the book are indicated in the following prefatory statement:

> The comparison of the educational systems of several countries lends itself to a variety of methods of treatment, depending somewhat on its purpose. One method of approach might be statistical on the analogy of the method of comparing returns of exports and imports, size of armaments, and so on; from this point of view there would be compared the total national expenditures for education, the cost, size and character of school buildings, per capita costs for different items of expenditure in the educational systems, the enrollments, average attendance, and retention of pupils through

the different levels of the educational ladder. By another method it might be possible to institute a comparison between education and national welfare and progress as expressed in statistics of illiteracy, the volume of trade and commerce, per capita wealth, or incidence of crime and poverty. These methods are attractive and may some day be useful; at the present stage, as is indicated in the text, it is impossible to institute comparisons of such a character until the raw material, the statistics, becomes more uniform and comparable. Still another method would be to undertake comparative studies of the quality of education in different countries; this, too, may be possible in time, but not before the instruments of measurement have been made more perfect and reliable than they are at present or when aims of education in different countries are more nearly alike, or finally, when tests have been developed which can measure more accurately the results of education rather than of instruction in fundamentals of subject-matter.

In the present volume none of these methods have been followed. The task which has been undertaken is to discuss the meaning of general education, elementary and secondary, in the light of the forces—political, social, and cultural—which determine the character of national systems of education. The problems and purposes of education have in general become somewhat similar in most countries; the solutions are influenced by differences of tradition and culture peculiar to each. The present volume seeks accordingly to serve as a contribution to the philosophy of education in the light both of theory and practice in six of the leading educational laboratories of the world —England, France, Germany, Italy, Russia, and the United States.

Accordingly the volume deals with education and nationalism, education and national character, the state and education, the organization of national systems of education, administration of education, elementary education and the preparation of elementary-school teachers, and secondary education and secondary-school teachers. After a general discussion of the first two topics, the issues involved in each of the other topics are discussed before the characteristics of each country are taken up.

Other variations of these methods will no doubt be developed. The most important advance made so far is that the scope of methodology and research in comparative education is beginning to be defined and that the study is beginning to be raised above the purely pedantic preoccupation with details of facts and technics which have meaning only in the light of the backgrounds of their origin. This brief survey may well close with a quotation from Professor J. Dover Wilson's introduction to the work by Hans (888: viii):

> There is no reason why Comparative Education should not prove as interesting and fruitful a study as Comparative Politics. The time will come when men realize that the structure of a nation's educational system is as characteristic and almost as important as the form of its constitution. And when it does, we shall have our educational Montesquieus analysing educational institutions, and our Bryces classifying them.

BIBLIOGRAPHY ON HISTORY OF EDUCATION AND COMPARATIVE EDUCATION

Chapter I. History of Education in the United States and Canada

A. HISTORY OF AMERICAN EDUCATION DURING THE COLONIAL PERIOD

1. ADAMS, HERBERT B. *The College of William and Mary.* U. S. Dept. of the Interior, Bureau of Education, Circular of Information, 1887, No. 1. Washington, D. C.: Government Printing Office, 1887. 89 p.
2. ADAMS, HERBERT B., editor. *Contributions to American Educational History, Nos. 1-36.* U. S. Dept. of the Interior, Bureau of Education, Circulars of Information, 1887-1903. (See numbers dealing with the original thirteen colonies.)
3. *American Journal of Education.* (Edited by Henry Barnard.) 32 vols. August, 1855-1882. (Analytical index published by U. S. Bureau of Education in 1892.)
4. BATES, W. C. "Boston Writing Masters before the Revolution." *New England Magazine* 25: 403-18; December, 1898.
5. BELL, SADIE. *The Church, the State, and Education in Virginia.* New York: Science Press, 1930. 796 p. (Doctor's thesis, University of Pennsylvania, 1930.)
6. BISHOP, EUGENE ALFRED. *The Development of a State School System: New Hampshire.* Contributions to Education, No. 391. New York: Teachers College, Columbia University, 1930. 159 p.
7. BOLTON, ETHEL STANWOOD, and COE, EVA JOHNSTON. *American Samplers.* Boston: Massachusetts Society of the Colonial Dames of America, 1921. 416 p.
8. BOOGHER, ELBERT W. G. *Secondary Education in Georgia, 1732-1858.* Merchantville, N. J.: the Author, 1933. 452 p. (Doctor's thesis, University of Pennsylvania, 1932.)
9. BOWDEN, HAYGOOD S. *Two Hundred Years of Education; Bicentennial, 1733-1933, Savannah, Chatham County, Georgia.* Richmond, Va.: Dietz Printing Co., 1932. 381 p.
10. BREWER, CLIFTON HARTWELL. *A History of Religious Education in the Episcopal Church to 1835.* New Haven: Yale University Press, 1924. 362 p.
11. BRONSON, WALTER C. *The History of Brown University 1764-1914.* Providence: the University, 1914. 548 p.
12. BROOME, EDWIN C. *A Historical and Critical Discussion of College Admission Requirements.* Contributions to Philosophy, Psychology and Education, Vol. 11, Nos. 3-4. New York: Columbia University Press, 1902. 157 p.
13. BROWN, EDWIN H. "First Free School in Queen Anne's County." *New England Magazine* 6: 1-15; March, 1911.
14. BROWN, ELMER ELLSWORTH. *The Making of Our Middle Schools.* New York: Longmans, Green and Co., 1902. 547 p.
15. BROWN, SAMUEL WINDSOR. *The Secularization of American Education.* Contributions to Education, No. 49. New York: Teachers College, Columbia University, 1912. 160 p.
16. BRUMBAUGH, MARTIN G. *The Life and Works of Christopher Dock, America's Pioneer Writer on Education.* Philadelphia: J. B. Lippincott Co., 1908. 272 p.
17. BURNS, J. A. *The Catholic School System in the United States; Its Principles, Origin, and Establishment.* New York: Benziger Brothers, 1908. 415 p.
18. BUSH, GEORGE GARY. "The First Common Schools of New England." *Report of the Commissioner of Education for the Year 1896-97.* Washington, D. C.: Government Printing Office, 1898. Vol. 2, p. 1165-86.
19. BUTLER, VERA M. *Education as Revealed by New England Newspapers Prior to 1850.* Doctor's thesis, Temple University, 1935. 503 p.

20. CARROLL, CHARLES. *Public Education in Rhode Island.* Providence: E. L. Freeman Co., 1918. 500 p.
21. CASSIDY, FRANCIS PATRICK. *Catholic College Foundations and Development in the United States (1677-1850).* Washington, D. C.: Catholic University of America, 1924. 103 p.
22. CHADBOURNE, AVA H. *Beginnings of Education in Maine.* Contributions to Education, No. 336. New York: Teachers College, Columbia University, 1928. 135 p.
23. CHADBOURNE, AVA H., compiler. *Readings in the History of Education in Maine.* Bangor, Maine: Burr Printing Co., 1932. 104 p.
24. CHAMBERLAIN, JOSHUA L., chairman. *Universities and Their Sons.* (Harvard, Yale, Princeton, Columbia.) Boston: R. Herndon Co., 1898-1900. 5 vols.
25. CHASE, FREDERICK. *A History of Dartmouth College and the Town of Hanover, New Hampshire.* (Edited by John K. Lord). Vol. I. Cambridge, Mass.: J. Wilson and Son, 1891. 682 p.
26. COLLINS, VARNUM L. *Princeton.* New York: Oxford University Press, 1914. 416 p.
27. CURTI, MERLE. *The Social Ideas of American Educators.* Report of the Commission on the Social Studies, American Historical Association, Part X. New York: Charles Scribner's Sons, 1935. 613 p.
28. DEMAREST, WILLIAM H. S. *A History of Rutgers College, 1766-1924.* New Brunswick, N. J.: Rutgers College, 1924. 570 p.
29. DEXTER, FRANKLIN B. *Biographical Sketches of the Graduates of Yale College, with Annals of the College History: 1701-1815.* New Haven, Conn.: Yale University Press, 1885-1912. 6 vols.
30. DEXTER, FRANKLIN B., editor. *Documentary History of Yale University, under the Original Charter of the Collegiate School of Connecticut, 1701-1745.* New Haven, Conn.: Yale University Press, 1916. 382 p.
31. DEXTER, FRANKLIN B. "On Some Social Distinctions at Harvard and Yale before the Revolution." *Proceedings of the American Antiquarian Society* 9 (new series): 34-59; October, 1893.
32. DILLAWAY, CHARLES K. *A History of the Grammar School, or, "The Free School of 1645 in Roxburie."* Roxbury, Mass.: J. Backup, 1860. 202 p.
33. DOUGLAS, PAUL. *American Apprenticeship and Industrial Education.* New York: Columbia University Press, 1921. 348 p.
34. DRAPER, ANDREW S. "Public School Pioneering in New York and Massachusetts." *Educational Review* 3: 313-36; April, 1892. 4: 241-52; October, 1892. 5: 345-62; April, 1893.
35. DUNSHEE, HENRY W. *History of the School of the Collegiate Reformed Dutch Church in the City of New York, from 1633 to 1883.* 2d ed. rev. and enl. New York: Aldine Press, 1883. 284 p.
36. ELLIOTT, EDWARD C., and CHAMBERS, M. M., editors. *Charters and Basic Laws of Selected American Universities and Colleges.* New York: Carnegie Foundation for the Advancement of Teaching, 1934. 640 p.
37. ENSIGN, FOREST C. *Compulsory School Attendance and Child Labor.* Iowa City, Iowa: Athens Press, 1921. 263 p.
38. FINEGAN, THOMAS E. *Free Schools; a Documentary History of the Free School Movement in New York State.* Fifteenth Annual Report of the Education Department, Vol. I. Albany, N. Y.: State Education Department, 1921. 682 p.
39. FLEMING, SANDFORD. *Children and Puritanism.* New Haven: Yale University Press, 1933. 236 p.
40. FORD, PAUL LEICESTER, editor. *The New-England Primer.* New York: Dodd, Mead and Co., 1899. 78 p.
41. GOULD, ELIZABETH P. *Ezekiel Cheever, Schoolmaster.* Boston: Palmer Co., 1904. 94 p.
42. GUILD, REUBEN ALDRIDGE. *Early History of Brown University, including the Life, Times, and Correspondence of President Manning, 1756-1791.* Providence: Snow and Farnham, 1897. 631 p.
43. HALL, ARTHUR JACKSON. *Religious Education in the Public Schools of the State and City of New York.* Chicago: University of Chicago Press, 1914. 111 p.
44. HAMMOND, CHARLES. "New England Academies and Classical Schools." *Report of the Commissioner of Education, 1868.* Washington, D. C.: Government Printing Office, 1868. p. 403-29.
45. HARTZLER, J. E. *Education among the Mennonites of America.* Danvers, Ill.: Central Mennonite Publishing Board, 1925. 195 p.

46. *Harvard College Records.* Publications of the Colonial Society of Massachusetts. Vols. 15, 16, and 31. Boston: the Society, 1925-35. 3 vols.
47. HEARTMAN, CHARLES F., compiler. *American Primers, Indian Primers, Royal Primers, and Thirty-seven Other Types of Non-New England Primers Issued Prior to 1830.* Highland Park, N. J.: H. B. Weiss (19 N. 7th Ave.), 1935. 159 p.
48. HEARTMAN, CHARLES F., compiler. *The New England Primer, Issued Prior to 1830.* New York: R. R. Bowker Co., 1934. 148 p.
49. HEATWOLE, CORNELIUS J. *A History of Education in Virginia.* New York: Macmillan Co., 1916. 382 p.
50. HEILMAN, U. H. "Early Schools and Teachers among Our German Ancestors." *Lebanon County Historical Society Historical Papers and Addresses* 9: 291-307.
51. HINSDALE, B. A., compiler. "Documents Illustrative of American Educational History." *Report of the Commissioner of Education for the Year 1892-93.* Washington, D. C.: Government Printing Office, 1895. Vol. 2, p. 1220-1414.
52. *A History of Columbia University, 1754-1904.* New York: Columbia University Press, 1904. 493 p.
53. HOLMES, PAULINE. *A Tercentenary History of the Boston Public Latin School, 1635-1935.* Cambridge, Mass.: Harvard University Press, 1935. 541 p.
54. HOLTZ, ADRIAN A. *A Study of the Moral and Religious Elements in American Education up to 1800.* Menasha, Wis.: George Banta Publishing Co., 1917. 86 p. (Doctor's thesis, University of Chicago, 1914.)
55. JACKSON, GEORGE LEROY. *The Development of School Support in Colonial Massachusetts.* Contributions to Education, No. 25. New York: Teachers College, Columbia University, 1909. 95 p.
56. JENKS, HENRY F. *Catalogue of the Boston Public Latin School with an Historical Sketch.* Boston: Boston Latin School Association, 1886. 398 p.
57. JERNEGAN, MARCUS W. "The Beginnings of Public Education in New England." *School Review* 23: 319-30, 361-80; May and June, 1915.
58. JERNEGAN, MARCUS W. "Compulsory Education in the American Colonies." *School Review* 26: 731-49; December, 1918. 27: 24-43; January, 1919.
59. JERNEGAN, MARCUS W. "Compulsory Education in the Southern Colonies." *School Review* 27: 405-25; June, 1919.
60. JERNEGAN, MARCUS W. "The Educational Development of the Southern Colonies." *School Review* 27: 360-76; May, 1919.
61. JERNEGAN, MARCUS W. *Laboring and Dependent Classes in Colonial America, 1607-1783.* Chicago: University of Chicago Press, 1931. 256 p.
62. JOHNSON, CLIFTON. *Old-Time Schools and School-Books.* New York: Macmillan Co., 1904. 381 p. (Reprinted by P. Smith in 1935.)
63. KEMP, WILLIAM WEBB. *The Support of Schools in Colonial New York by the Society for the Propagation of the Gospel in Foreign Parts.* Contributions to Education, No. 56. New York: Teachers College, Columbia University, 1913. 279 p.
64. KILPATRICK, WILLIAM H. "The Date of the First School in New Netherland." *Educational Review* 33: 380-92; November, 1909.
65. KILPATRICK, WILLIAM H. *The Dutch Schools of New Netherlands and Colonial New York.* U. S. Dept. of the Interior, Bureau of Education, Bulletin, 1912, No. 12. Washington, D. C.: Government Printing Office, 1912. 239 p.
66. KLAIN, ZORA. *Educational Activities of New England Quakers.* Philadelphia: Westbrook Publishing Co., 1928. 228 p.
67. KLAIN, ZORA. *Quaker Contributions to Education in North Carolina.* Philadelphia: Westbrook Publishing Co., 1925. 351 p. (Doctor's thesis, University of Pennsylvania, 1924.)
68. KNIGHT, EDGAR W. *Public Education in the South.* Boston: Ginn and Co., 1922. 482 p.
69. KNIGHT, EDGAR W. *Public School Education in North Carolina.* Boston: Houghton Mifflin Co., 1916. 384 p.
70. LITTLEFIELD, GEORGE E. *Early Schools and School-Books of New England.* Boston: Club of Odd Volumes, 1904. 354 p.
71. LIVINGOOD, FREDERICK G. *Eighteenth Century Reformed Church Schools.* Norristown, Pa.: Norristown Press, 1930. 313 p. (Reprinted from Proceedings of the Pennsylvania German Society, Vol. 38.)

419

72. LYMAN, ROLLO LAVERNE. *English Grammar in American Schools before 1850.* U. S. Dept. of the Interior, Bureau of Education, Bulletin, 1921, No. 12. Washington, D. C.: Government Printing Office, 1921. 170 p.
73. MCCRADY, EDWARD. *Education in South Carolina Prior to and During the Revolution.* Charleston: News and Courier Book Presses, 1883. 54 p.
74. MCGUCKEN, WILLIAM JOSEPH. *The Jesuits and Education.* New York: Bruce Publishing Co., 1932. 352 p.
75. MACLEAN, JOHN. *History of the College of New Jersey, from Its Origin in 1746 to the Commencement of 1854.* Philadelphia: J. B. Lippincott and Co., 1877. 2 vols.
76. MADDOX, WILLIAM A. *The Free School Idea in Virginia before the Civil War.* Contributions to Education, No. 93. New York: Teachers College, Columbia University, 1918. 225 p.
77. MARTIN, GEORGE H. "Early Education in a Massachusetts Town." *Education* 15: 577-82; June, 1895.
78. MARTIN, GEORGE H. "Public School Pioneering." *Educational Review* 4: 34-46, June, 1892. 5: 232-42, March, 1893.
79. MAURER, CHARLES L. *Early Lutheran Education in Pennsylvania.* Philadelphia: Dorrance and Co., 1932. 294 p.
80. MAYO, A. D. "Public Schools during the Colonial and Revolutionary Period." *Report of the Commissioner of Education for the Year 1893-94.* Washington, D. C.: Government Printing Office, 1896. Part I, p. 639-738.
81. MERIWETHER, COLYER. *Our Colonial Curriculum, 1607-1776.* Washington, D. C.: Capital Publishing Co., 1907. 301 p.
82. MONROE, WALTER SCOTT. *Development of Arithmetic as a School Subject.* U. S. Dept. of the Interior, Bureau of Education, Bulletin, 1917, No. 10. Washington, D. C.: Government Printing Office, 1917. 170 p.
83. MONTGOMERY, THOMAS H. *A History of the University of Pennsylvania, from Its Foundation to A. D. 1770.* Philadelphia: G. W. Jacobs and Co., 1900. 566 p.
84. MORISON, SAMUEL ELIOT. *The Founding of Harvard College.* Cambridge, Mass.: Harvard University Press, 1935. 472 p.
85. MORISON, SAMUEL ELIOT. *Harvard College in the Seventeenth Century.* Cambridge, Mass.: Harvard University Press, 1936. 2 vols.
86. MULHERN, JAMES. *A History of Secondary Education in Pennsylvania.* New York: Science Press, 1933. 714 p.
87. NOBLE, M. C. S. *A History of the Public Schools of North Carolina.* Chapel Hill: University of North Carolina Press, 1930. 463 p.
88. NORTON, ARTHUR O. "Harvard Text-Books and Reference Books of the Seventeenth Century." *Transactions 1930-1933.* Publications of the Colonial Society of Massachusetts, Vol. 28. Boston: the Society, 1935. p. 361-438.
89. PARSONS, ELSIE CLEWS. *Educational Legislation and Administration of the Colonial Governments.* Columbia University Contributions to Philosophy, Psychology and Education, Vol. 6, No. 1-4. New York: Macmillan Co., 1899. 524 p.
90. PATERSON, WILLIAM. *Glimpses of Colonial Society and the Life at Princeton College, 1766-1773.* (Edited by W. Jay Mills.) Philadelphia: J. B. Lippincott Co., 1903. 182 p.
91. PEIRCE, BENJAMIN. *A History of Harvard University, from Its Foundation, in the Year 1636, to the Period of the American Revolution.* Cambridge, Mass.: Brown, Shattuck, and Co., 1833. 316 p.
92. PRATT, DANIEL J. *Annals of Public Education in the State of New York, from 1626 to 1746.* Rev. and enl. Albany, N. Y.: Argus Co., 1872. 152 p.
93. PURCELL, R. J. "Education and Irish Schoolmasters in Colonial Massachusetts." *Catholic Educational Review* 33: 467-79; October, 1935.
94. PURCELL, R. J. "Education and Irish Teachers in Colonial Maryland." *Catholic Educational Review* 32: 143-53; March, 1934.
95. PURCELL, R. J. "Maine: Early Schools and Irish Teachers." *Catholic Educational Review* 33: 211-25; April, 1935.
96. PURCELL, R. J. "Rhode Island's Early Schools and Irish Teachers." *Catholic Educational Review* 32: 402-15; September, 1934.
97. PURCELL, R. J. "Schools and Early Irish Teachers in New Hampshire." *Catholic Educational Review* 32: 606-18; December, 1934.
98. PURCELL, R. J. "Some Early Teachers in Connecticut." *Catholic Educational Review* 32: 332-38; June, 1934.

99. PURCELL, R. J. "Vermont: Schools and Early Irish Teachers." *Catholic Educational Review* 33: 277-81; May, 1935.
100. QUINCY, JOSIAH. *The History of Harvard University.* Boston: Crosby, Nichols, Lee, and Co., 1860. 2 vols.
101. RAND, EDWARD KENNARD. "Liberal Education in Seventeenth-Century Harvard." *New England Quarterly* 6: 525-51; September, 1933.
102. RAPER, CHARLES LEE. *The Church and Private Schools of North Carolina.* Greensboro, N. C.: J. J. Stone, 1898. 247 p.
103. RICHARDSON, LEON BURR. *History of Dartmouth College.* Vol. I. Hanover, N. H.: Dartmouth College Publications, 1932. 427 p.
104. SEYBOLT, ROBERT F. *Apprenticeship and Apprenticeship Education in Colonial New England and New York.* Contributions to Education, No. 85. New York: Teachers College, Columbia University, 1917. 121 p.
105. SEYBOLT, ROBERT F. *The Evening School in Colonial America.* Educational Research Bulletin, No. 24. Urbana, Ill.: University of Illinois, 1925. 68 p.
106. SEYBOLT, ROBERT F. "The Evening Schools of Colonial New York City." *Free Schools.* Fifteenth Annual Report of the Education Department, Vol. I. Albany, N. Y.: State Education Department, 1921. p. 630-52.
107. SEYBOLT, ROBERT F. *Private Schools of Colonial Boston.* Cambridge, Mass.: Harvard University Press, 1935. 106 p.
108. SEYBOLT, ROBERT F. *The Public Schools of Colonial Boston, 1635-1775.* Cambridge, Mass.: Harvard University Press, 1935. 101 p.
109. SEYBOLT, ROBERT F. "Schoolmasters of Colonial Boston." *Transactions 1927-1930.* Publications of the Colonial Society of Massachusetts, Vol. 27. Boston: the Society, 1932. p. 130-56.
110. SEYBOLT, ROBERT F. *Source Studies in American Colonial Education: The Private School.* Educational Research Bulletin, No. 28. Urbana, Ill.: University of Illinois, 1925. 109 p.
111. SEYBOLT, ROBERT F. "Student Libraries at Harvard, 1763-1764." *Transactions 1930-1933.* Publications of the Colonial Society of Massachusetts, Vol. 28. Boston: the Society, 1935. p. 449-61.
112. SHIPTON, CLIFFORD K. "Secondary Education in the Puritan Colonies." *New England Quarterly* 7: 646-61; December, 1934.
113. SHORES, LOUIS. *Origins of the American College Library, 1638-1800.* Contributions to Education, No. 134. Nashville, Tenn.: George Peabody College for Teachers, 1934. 290 p.
114. SIMONS, LAO GENEVRA. *Introduction of Algebra into American Schools in the Eighteenth Century.* U. S. Dept. of the Interior, Bureau of Education, Bulletin, 1924, No. 18. Washington, D. C.: Government Printing Office, 1924. 80 p.
115. SLAFTER, CARLOS. *A Record of Education: The Schools and Teachers of Dedham, Massachusetts, 1644-1904.* Dedham, Mass.: Transcript Press, 1905. 330 p.
116. SMALL, WALTER H. *Early New England Schools.* Boston: Ginn and Co., 1914. 401 p.
117. SMALL, WALTER H. "The New England Grammar School." *School Review* 10: 513-31; September, 1902. 14: 42-56; January, 1906.
118. SMALLWOOD, MARY L. *An Historical Study of Examinations and Grading Systems in Early American Universities.* Harvard Studies in Education, Vol. 24. Cambridge, Mass.: Harvard University Press, 1935. 132 p.
119. SMITH, SHERMAN M. *The Relation of the State to Religious Education in Massachusetts.* Syracuse, N. Y.: Syracuse University Book Store, 1926. 350 p. (Doctor's thesis, Clark University, 1925.)
120. SNOW, LOUIS F. *The College Curriculum in the United States.* Contributions to Education, No. 10. New York: Teachers College, Columbia University, 1907. 186 p.
121. STEWART, GEORGE. *A History of Religious Education in Connecticut to the Middle of the Nineteenth Century.* New Haven, Conn.: Yale University Press, 1924. 402 p.
122. SUZZALLO, HENRY. *The Rise of Local School Supervision in Massachusetts (the School Committee, 1635-1827).* Contributions to Education, No. 3. New York: Teachers College, Columbia University, 1906. 154 p.
123. THOMASON, JOHN FURMAN. *The Foundations of the Public Schools of South Carolina.* Columbia, S. C.: State Co., 1925. 237 p.
124. THWING, CHARLES FRANKLIN. *A History of Higher Education in America.* New York: D. Appleton and Co., 1906. 501 p.

125. TUER, ANDREW. *History of the Horn-Book.* New York: Charles Scribner's Sons, 1897. 486 p.
126. TYLER, LYON G. "A Few Facts from the Records of William and Mary College." *Papers of the American Historical Association* 4: 129-41; October, 1890. New York: G. P. Putnam's Sons.
127. UPDEGRAFF, HARLAN. *The Origin of the Moving School in Massachusetts.* Contributions to Education, No. 17. New York: Teachers College, Columbia University, 1908. 186 p.
128. VAN VECHTEN, EMMA. *Early Schools and School-Masters of New Amsterdam.* Half-Moon Series, Papers on Historic New York, 2d series, Vol. 2, No. 9. New York: G. P. Putnam's Sons, 1898. p. 319-44.
129. WALSH, JAMES J. *Education of the Founding Fathers of the Republic; Scholasticism in the Colonial Colleges.* New York: Fordham University Press, 1935. 377 p.
130. WEBER, S. E. *Charity School Movement in Colonial Pennsylvania.* Philadelphia: G. F. Lasher, 1905. 74 p. (Doctor's thesis, University of Pennsylvania.)
131. WELLS, GUY F. *Parish Education in Colonial Virginia.* Contributions to Education, No. 138. New York: Teachers College, Columbia University, 1923. 95 p.
132. WICKERSHAM, JAMES P. *A History of Education in Pennsylvania.* Lancaster, Pa.: Inquirer Publishing Co., 1886. 683 p.
133. WILLIAM AND MARY COLLEGE. *The History of the College of William and Mary from Its Foundation, 1660, to 1874.* Richmond: J. W. Randolph and English, 1874. 183 p.
134. WOODY, THOMAS. *Early Quaker Education in Pennsylvania.* Contributions to Education, No. 105. New York: Teachers College, Columbia University, 1920. 287 p.
135. WOODY, THOMAS, editor. *Educational Views of Benjamin Franklin.* New York: McGraw-Hill Book Co., 1931. 270 p.
136. WOODY, THOMAS. *A History of Women's Education in the United States.* New York: Science Press, 1929. 2 vols.
137. WOODY, THOMAS. *Quaker Education in the Colony and State of New Jersey.* Philadelphia: the Author, 1923. 408 p.

B. HISTORY OF AMERICAN EDUCATION SINCE THE BEGINNING OF THE NATIONAL PERIOD

138. ALMACK, JOHN C., editor. *Modern School Administration, Its Problems and Progress.* Boston: Houghton Mifflin Co., 1933. 382 p.
139. *American Journal of Education.* (Edited by Henry Barnard.) 32 vols. August, 1855-1882. (Analytical index published by U. S. Bureau of Education in 1892.)
140. ANDERSON, L. F. *History of Manual and Industrial School Education.* New York: D. Appleton and Co., 1926. 251 p.
141. ANDERSON, L. F. "The Manual Labor School Movement." *Educational Review* 46: 369-86; November, 1913.
142. ARROWOOD, CHARLES FLINN, editor. *Thomas Jefferson and Education in a Republic.* New York: McGraw-Hill Book Co., 1930. 184 p.
143. BARNARD, HENRY. *American Educational Biography: Memoirs of Teachers, Educators, and Promoters and Benefactors of Education, Science and Literature.* Syracuse, N. Y.: C. W. Bardeen, 1874. 526 p.
144. BARNARD, HENRY. "History of the School Fund of Connecticut." *American Journal of Education* 6: 367-425; June, 1859.
145. BARNARD, HENRY. *Normal Schools and other Institutions, Agencies, and Means Designed for the Professional Education of Teachers.* Part I, United States and British Provinces. Hartford: Case, Tiffany and Co., 1851. (Reprinted in 1929 by Colorado State Teachers College as Education Series No. 6.)
146. BARNARD, HENRY. *Pestalozzi and His Educational System.* Syracuse, N. Y.: C. W. Bardeen, 1906. 751 p.
147. BELL, SADIE. *The Church, the State, and Education in Virginia.* New York: Science Press, 1930. 796 p.
148. BENNETT, CHARLES ALPHEUS. *History of Manual and Industrial Education up to 1870.* Peoria, Ill.: Manual Arts Press, 1926. 461 p.
149. BISHOP, EUGENE A. *The Development of a State School System: New Hampshire.* Contributions to Education, No. 391. New York: Teachers College, Columbia University, 1930. 159 p.

150. BITTNER, W. S. *The University Extension Movement.* U. S. Dept. of the Interior, Bureau of Education, Bulletin, 1919, No. 84. Washington, D. C.: Government Printing Office, 1920. 124 p.
151. BLACKMAR, FRANK W. *History of Federal and State Aid to Higher Education in the United States.* U. S. Dept. of the Interior, Bureau of Education, Circular of Information, 1890, No. 1. Washington, D. C.: Government Printing Office, 1890. 343 p.
152. BLANDIN, I. M. E. *History of Higher Education of Women in the South Prior to 1860.* Washington, D. C.: Neale Publishing Co., 1909. 328 p.
153. BOAS, LOUISE SCHUTZ. *Woman's Education Begins: The Rise of the Women's Colleges.* Norton, Mass.: Wheaton College Press, 1935. 295 p.
154. BOLTON, FREDERICK E., and BIBB, THOMAS W. *History of Education in Washington.* U. S. Dept. of the Interior, Office of Education, Bulletin, 1934, No. 9. Washington, D. C.: Government Printing Office, 1935. 448 p.
155. BOND, HORACE MANN. *The Education of the Negro in the American Social Order.* New York: Prentice-Hall, 1934. 501 p.
156. BOONE, RICHARD G. *Education in the United States, Its History from the Earliest Settlements.* International Education Series, Vol. XI. New York: D. Appleton and Co., 1890. 402 p.
157. BOONE, RICHARD G. *A History of Education in Indiana.* New York: D. Appleton and Co., 1892. 454 p.
158. BOURNE, WILLIAM OLAND. *History of the Public School Society of the City of New York.* New York: W. Wood and Co., 1870. 768 p.
159. BROWN, ELMER ELLSWORTH. *The Making of Our Middle Schools.* Rev. ed. New York: Longmans, Green, and Co., 1905. 547 p.
160. BROWN, ELMER ELLSWORTH. *The Origin of American State Universities.* Publications in Education, Vol. 3, No. 1. Berkeley: University of California Press, 1903. 45 p.
161. BROWN, SAMUEL WINDSOR. *The Secularization of American Education.* Contributions to Education, No. 49. New York: Teachers College, Columbia University, 1912. 160 p.
162. BRUBACHER, JOHN S., editor. *Henry Barnard on Education.* New York: McGraw-Hill Book Co., 1931. 298 p.
163. BUNKER, FRANK FOREST. *Reorganization of the Public School System.* U. S. Dept. of the Interior, Bureau of Education, Bulletin, 1916, No. 8. Washington, D. C.: Government Printing Office, 1916. 186 p.
164. BURGESS, W. RANDOLPH. *Trends of School Costs.* New York: Department of Education, Russell Sage Foundation, 1920. 142 p.
165. BUTLER, VERA M. *Education as Revealed by New England Newspapers Prior to 1850.* Doctor's thesis, Temple University, 1935. 503 p.
166. CARLTON, FRANK TRACY. *Economic Influences upon Educational Progress in the United States, 1820-1850.* Economics and Political Science Series, Vol. 4, No. 1. Madison: University of Wisconsin, 1908. 135 p.
167. CARROLL, CHARLES. *Public Education in Rhode Island.* Providence: E. L. Freeman Co., 1918. 500 p.
168. COATES, CHARLES PENNY. *History of the Manual Training School of Washington University.* U. S. Dept. of the Interior, Bureau of Education, Bulletin, 1923, No. 3. Washington, D. C.: Government Printing Office, 1923. 86 p.
169. COCHRAN, THOMAS EVERETTE. *History of Public-School Education in Florida.* Lancaster, Pa.: New Era Printing Co., 1921. 270 p. (Doctor's thesis, University of Pennsylvania.)
170. COLE, ARTHUR CHARLES. *The Irrepressible Conflict, 1850-1865.* History of American Life, Vol. VII. New York: Macmillan Co., 1934. 468 p.
171. CONFREY, BURTON. *Secularism in American Education: Its History.* Educational Research Monographs, Vol. 6, No. 1. Washington, D. C.: Catholic University of America, 1931. 153 p.
172. COUNTS, GEORGE S., and OTHERS. *The Social Foundations of Education.* Report of the Commission on the Social Studies, American Historical Association, Part IX. New York: Charles Scribner's Sons, 1934. 579 p.
173. CUBBERLEY, ELLWOOD P. *The History of Education.* Boston: Houghton Mifflin Co., 1920. 849 p.
174. CUBBERLEY, ELLWOOD P. *Public Education in the United States.* Rev. and enl. ed. Boston: Houghton Mifflin Co., 1934. 782 p.

175. CUBBERLEY, ELLWOOD P., editor. *Readings in Public Education in the United States.* Boston: Houghton Mifflin Co., 1934. 534 p.
176. CUBBERLEY, ELLWOOD P. *State School Administration.* Boston: Houghton Mifflin Co., 1927. 773 p.
177. CULVER, RAYMOND B. *Horace Mann and Religion in the Massachusetts Public Schools.* New Haven, Conn.: Yale University Press, 1929. 301 p.
178. CUROE, PHILIP R. V. *Educational Attitudes and Policies of Organized Labor in the United States.* Contributions to Education, No. 201. New York: Teachers College, Columbia University, 1926. 201 p.
179. CURTI, MERLE. *The Social Ideas of American Educators.* Report of the Commission on the Social Studies, American Historical Association, Part X. New York: Charles Scribner's Sons, 1935. 613 p.
180. DABNEY, CHARLES WILLIAM. *Universal Education in the South.* Chapel Hill, University of North Carolina Press, 1936. 2 vols.
181. DAVIS, SHELDON EMMOR. *Educational Periodicals during the Nineteenth Century.* U. S. Dept. of the Interior, Bureau of Education, Bulletin, 1919, No. 28. Washington, D. C.: Government Printing Office, 1919. 125 p.
182. DEARBORN, NED HARLAND. *The Oswego Movement in American Education.* Contributions to Education, No. 183. New York: Teachers College, Columbia University, 1925. 189 p.
183. DE GARMO, CHARLES. *Herbart and the Herbartians.* New York: Charles Scribner's Sons, 1895. 268 p.
184. DEXTER, EDWIN GRANT. *A History of Education in the United States.* New York: Macmillan Co., 1904. 656 p.
185. DICKERMAN, GEORGE S. "History of Negro Education." *Negro Education, Vol. I.* U. S. Dept. of the Interior, Bureau of Education, Bulletin, 1916, No. 38. Washington, D. C.: Government Printing Office, 1917. p. 244-68.
186. DODD, WILLIAM E. *Expansion and Conflict.* 2d ed. Boston: Houghton Mifflin Co., 1919. 329 p.
187. DUGGAN, STEPHEN PIERCE. *A Student's Textbook in the History of Education.* Rev. ed. New York: D. Appleton and Co., 1927. 413 p.
188. EBY, FREDERICK, and ARROWOOD, CHARLES FLINN. *The Development of American Education in Theory, Organization, and Practice.* New York: Prentice-Hall, 1934. 922 p.
189. ECKELBERRY, R. H. *The History of the Municipal University in the United States.* U. S. Dept. of the Interior, Office of Education, Bulletin, 1932, No. 2. Washington, D. C.: Government Printing Office, 1932. 213 p.
190. EELLS, WALTER CROSBY. *The Junior College.* Boston: Houghton Mifflin Co., 1931. 833 p.
191. FAIRLIE, JOHN ARCHIBALD. *Centralization of Administration in New York State.* New York: Columbia University Press, 1898. 210 p.
192. FINEGAN, THOMAS E. *Free Schools; a Documentary History of the Free School Movement in New York State.* 15th Annual Report of the Education Department, Vol. I. Albany, N. Y.: State Education Department, 1921. 682 p.
193. FISH, CARL RUSSELL. *The Rise of the Common Man.* History of American Life, Vol. VI. New York: Macmillan Co., 1927. 391 p.
194. FITZPATRICK, EDWARD A. *The Educational Views and Influence of DeWitt Clinton.* Contributions to Education, No. 44. New York: Teachers College, Columbia University, 1911. 157 p.
195. FLEMING, WALTER LYNWOOD. *The Sequel of Appomattox; a Chronicle of the Reunion of the States.* Chronicles of America Series, Vol. 32. New Haven, Conn.: Yale University Press, 1919. 322 p.
196. GIFFORD, WALTER JOHN. *Historical Development of the New York State High School System.* Albany: J. B. Lyon Co., 1922. 203 p.
197. GILLAND, THOMAS MCDOWELL. *The Origin and Development of the Power and Duties of the City-School Superintendent.* Chicago: University of Chicago Press, 1935. 279 p.
198. GOODSELL, WILLYSTINE, editor. *Pioneers of Women's Education in the United States.* New York: McGraw-Hill Book Co., 1931. 311 p.
199. GORDY, J. P. *Rise and Growth of the Normal-School Idea in the United States.* U. S. Dept. of the Interior, Bureau of Education, Circular of Information, 1891, No. 8. Washington, D. C.: Government Printing Office, 1891. 145 p.

200. GRAVES, FRANK PIERREPONT. *A History of Education in Modern Times.* New York: Macmillan Co., 1913. 410 p.
201. GRIFFIN, GRACE GARDNER, compiler. *Writings on American History, 1906-date. A Bibliography of Books and Articles on United States and Canadian History with Some Memoranda on Other Portions of America.* (Imprint varies; since 1918 issued as supplementary volumes to Annual Report of the American Historical Association for the corresponding years.)
202. GRIFFIN, ORWIN BRADFORD. *The Evolution of the Connecticut State School System.* Contributions to Education, No. 293. New York: Teachers College, Columbia University, 1928. 261 p.
203. GRIZZELL, EMIT DUNCAN. *Origin and Development of the High School in New England before 1865.* New York: Macmillan Co., 1923. 428 p.
204. HALL, ARTHUR JACKSON. *Religious Education in the Public Schools of the State and City of New York.* Chicago: University of Chicago Press, 1914. 111 p.
205. HALL, SAMUEL R. *Lectures on School-Keeping.* Boston: Richardson, Lord and Holbrook, 1829. 135 p.
206. HANSEN, ALLEN OSCAR. *Liberalism and American Education in the Eighteenth Century.* New York: Macmillan Co., 1926. 317 p.
207. HARVESON, MAE ELIZABETH. *Catherine Esther Beecher, Pioneer Educator.* New York: Science Press, 1932. 295 p.
208. HAYES, CECIL B. *The American Lyceum.* U. S. Dept. of the Interior, Office of Education, Bulletin, 1932, No. 12. Washington, D. C.: Government Printing Office, 1932. 72 p.
209. HEATWOLE, CORNELIUS J. *A History of Education in Virginia.* New York: Macmillan Co., 1916. 382 p.
210. HENDERSON, JOHN C. *Thomas Jefferson's Views on Public Education.* New York: G. P. Putnam's Sons, 1890. 387 p.
211. HERTZLER, SILAS. *The Rise of the Public High School in Connecticut.* University Research Monographs, No. 10. Baltimore: Warwick and York, 1930. 258 p.
212. HINSDALE, B. A. *Horace Mann and the Common School Revival in the United States.* New York: Charles Scribner's Sons, 1898. 326 p.
213. HINSDALE, B. A. "Notes on the History of Foreign Influence upon Education in the United States." *Report of the Commissioner of Education for the Year 1897-98.* Washington, D. C.: Government Printing Office, 1899. Vol. 1, Chapter 13, p. 591-629.
214. HOLLIS, ANDREW PHILLIP. *The Contribution of the Oswego Normal School to Educational Progress in the United States.* Boston: D. C. Heath and Co., 1898. 160 p.
215. HOLT, W. STULL. *The Federal Board for Vocational Education.* Institute for Government Research. Service Monographs of the United States Government, No. 6. New York: D. Appleton and Co., 1922. 74 p.
216. HONEYWELL, ROY J. *The Educational Work of Thomas Jefferson.* Harvard Studies in Education, Vol. 16. Cambridge, Mass.: Harvard University Press, 1931. 295 p.
217. INGLIS, ALEXANDER JAMES. *The Rise of the High School in Massachusetts.* Contributions to Education, No. 45. New York: Teachers College, Columbia University, 1911. 166 p.
218. JUDD, CHARLES H. *Problems of Education in the United States.* New York: McGraw-Hill Book Co., 1933. 214 p.
219. KANDEL, I. L. *History of Secondary Education.* Boston: Houghton Mifflin Co., 1930. 577 p.
220. KEITH, JOHN A. H., and BAGLEY, WILLIAM C. *The Nation and the Schools.* New York: Macmillan Co., 1920. 364 p.
221. KIRKPATRICK, J. E. *The American College and Its Rulers.* New York: New Republic, Inc., 1926. 309 p.
222. KLEIN, ARTHUR J., director. *Survey of Land-Grant Colleges and Universities.* U. S. Dept. of the Interior, Office of Education, Bulletin, 1930, No. 9. Washington, D. C.: Government Printing Office, 1930. 2 vols.
223. KNIGHT, EDGAR W. *Education in the United States.* New ed. Boston: Ginn and Co., 1934. 613 p.
224. KNIGHT, EDGAR W. *The Influence of Reconstruction on Education in the South.* Contributions to Education, No. 60. New York: Teachers College, Columbia University, 1913. 100 p.

225. KNIGHT, EDGAR W. "Manual Labor Schools in the South." *South Atlantic Quarterly* 16: 209-22; July, 1917.
226. KNIGHT, EDGAR W. *Public Education in the South.* Boston: Ginn and Co., 1922. 482 p.
227. KNIGHT, EDGAR W. *Public School Education in North Carolina.* Boston: Houghton Mifflin Co., 1916. 384 p.
228. Koos, LEONARD V. *The American Secondary School.* Boston: Ginn and Co., 1927. 755 p.
229. LARNED, J. N., compiler. *The New Larned History for Ready Reference, Reading, and Research.* Rev. and enl. ed. Springfield, Mass.: C. A. Nichols Pub. Co., 1922-24. 12 vols.
230. LYMAN, ROLLO LAVERNE. *English Grammar in American Schools before 1850.* U. S. Dept. of the Interior, Bureau of Education, Bulletin, 1921, No. 12. Washington, D. C.: Government Printing Office, 1922. 170 p.
231. McGRATH, EARL JAMES. *The Evolution of Administrative Officers in Institutions of Higher Education in the United States from 1860 to 1933.* Unpublished doctor's thesis, University of Chicago, 1936. 208 p.
232. McMANIS, JOHN T. "History in the Elementary Schools, 1825-1850." *Educational Bi-Monthly* 6: 322-32; April, 1912.
233. MADDOX, WILLIAM ARTHUR. *The Free School Idea in Virginia before the Civil War.* Contributions to Education, No. 93. New York: Teachers College, Columbia University, 1918. 225 p.
234. MANGUN, VERNON LAMAR. *The American Normal School.* University Research Monographs, No. 3. Baltimore: Warwick and York, 1928. 443 p.
235. MANN, HORACE. *Life and Works of Horace Mann.* (Edited by Mary Mann and George C. Mann.) Boston: Lee and Shepard, 1891. 5 vols.
236. MAYO, A. D. "Henry Barnard." *Report of the Commissioner of Education for the Year 1896-97.* Washington, D. C.: Government Printing Office, 1898. Vol. 1, p. 769-810.
237. MAYO, A. D. "Horace Mann and the Great Revival of the American Common School, 1830-1850." *Report of the Commissioner of Education for the Year 1896-97.* Washington, D. C.: Government Printing Office, 1898. Vol. 1, p. 715-67.
238. MAYO, A. D. "Original Establishment of State School Funds." *Report of the Commissioner of Education for the Year 1894-95.* Washington, D. C.: Government Printing Office, 1896. Vol. 2, p. 1505-11.
239. MEAD, ARTHUR RAYMOND. *The Development of Free Schools in the United States as Illustrated by Connecticut and Michigan.* Contributions to Education, No. 91. New York: Teachers College, Columbia University, 1918. 236 p.
240. MEADER, J. L. *Normal School Education in Connecticut.* Contributions to Education, No. 307. New York: Teachers College, Columbia University, 1928. 96 p.
241. MILLER, EDWARD ALANSON. *The History of Educational Legislation in Ohio from 1803 to 1850.* Supplementary Educational Monographs, No. 13. Chicago: University of Chicago Press, 1920. 248 p.
242. MILLER, GEORGE FREDERICK. *The Academy System of the State of New York.* Albany: J. B. Lyon Co., 1922. 180 p.
243. MONROE, PAUL, editor. *A Cyclopedia of Education.* New York: Macmillan Co., 1911-13. 5 vols.
244. MONROE, WALTER SCOTT. *Development of Arithmetic as a School Subject.* U. S. Dept. of the Interior, Bureau of Education, Bulletin, 1917, No. 10. Washington, D. C.: Government Printing Office, 1917. 170 p.
245. MONROE, WILL S. *History of the Pestalozzian Movement in the United States.* Syracuse, N. Y.: C. W. Bardeen, 1907. 244 p.
246. MORISON, SAMUEL ELIOT, editor. *The Development of Harvard University since the Inauguration of President Eliot, 1869-1929.* Cambridge, Mass.: Harvard University Press, 1930, 660 p.
247. MORISON, SAMUEL ELIOT. *The Founding of Harvard College.* Cambridge, Mass.: Harvard University Press, 1935. 472 p.
248. MORISON, SAMUEL ELIOT. *Harvard College in the Seventeenth Century.* Cambridge, Mass.: Harvard University Press, 1936. 2 vols.
249. MORISON, SAMUEL ELIOT. *Three Centuries of Harvard, 1636-1936.* Cambridge, Mass.: Harvard University Press, 1936. 512 p.

250. MULHERN, JAMES. *A History of Secondary Education in Pennsylvania.* New York: Science Press, 1933. 714 p.
251. MURRAY, DAVID. *History of Education in New Jersey.* U. S. Dept. of the Interior, Bureau of Education, Circular of Information, 1899, No. 1. Washington, D. C.: Government Printing Office, 1899. 344 p.
252. NEVINS, ALLAN. *The Emergence of Modern America, 1865-1878.* History of American Life, Vol. VIII. New York: Macmillan Co., 1927. 446 p.
253. NOBLE, M. C. S. *A History of the Public Schools of North Carolina.* Chapel Hill: University of North Carolina Press, 1930. 463 p.
254. NORTON, ARTHUR O., editor. *The First State Normal School in America: The Journals of Cyrus Peirce and Mary Swift.* Harvard Documents in the History of Education, Vol. I. Cambridge, Mass.: Harvard University Press, 1926. 299 p.
255. ORTH, SAMUEL P. *Centralization of Administration in Ohio.* New York: Columbia University Press, 1903. 177 p.
256. PANGBURN, JESSIE M. *The Evolution of the American Teachers College.* Contributions to Education, No. 500. New York: Teachers College, Columbia University, 1932. 140 p.
257. PARKER, SAMUEL CHESTER. *A Textbook in the History of Modern Elementary Education.* Boston: Ginn and Co., 1912. 505 p.
258. PHILLIPS, C. A. "The Development of Methods in Teaching Modern Elementary Geography." *Elementary School Teacher* 10: 427-39; 501-15; May and June, 1910.
259. PIERCE, PAUL REVERE. *The Origin and Development of the Public School Principalship.* Chicago: University of Chicago Press, 1935. 223 p.
260. PITKIN, ROYCE STANLEY. *Public School Support in the United States during Periods of Economic Depression.* Brattleboro, Vt.: Stephen Daye Press, 1933. 143 p.
261. POWERS, SAMUEL RALPH. *A History of the Teaching of Chemistry in the Secondary Schools of the United States Previous to 1850.* Minneapolis: University of Minnesota Press, 1920. 68 p.
262. President's Research Committee on Social Trends. *Recent Social Trends in the United States.* New York: McGraw-Hill Book Co., 1933. 2 vols.
263. PRICE, RICHARD REES. *The Financial Support of State Universities.* Harvard Studies in Education, Vol. 6. Cambridge, Mass.: Harvard University Press, 1924. 205 p.
264. RANDALL, S. S. *History of the Common School System of the State of New York.* New York: Ivison, Blakeman, Taylor and Co., 1871. 477 p.
265. RAWLES, W. A. *Centralizing Tendencies in the Administration of Indiana.* New York: Columbia University Press, 1905. 336 p.
266. REEDER, RUDOLPH R. *The Historical Development of School Readers and Methods in Teaching Reading.* Columbia University Contributions to Philosophy, Psychology, and Education. Vol. 8, No. 2. New York: Macmillan Co., 1900. 93 p.
267. REIGART, JOHN FRANKLIN. *The Lancastrian System of Instruction in the Schools of New York City.* Contributions to Education, No. 81. New York: Teachers College, Columbia University, 1916. 105 p.
268. REISNER, EDWARD H. *The Evolution of the Common School.* New York: Macmillan Co., 1930. 590 p.
269. REISNER, EDWARD H. *Nationalism and Education since 1789.* New York: Macmillan Co., 1922. 575 p.
270. RUGG, HAROLD. "A Century of Curriculum-Construction in American Schools." *Curriculum-Making: Past and Present.* Twenty-Sixth Yearbook, Part I. National Society for the Study of Education. Bloomington, Ill.: Public School Publishing Co., 1926. p. 3-116.
271. SCHLESINGER, ARTHUR M. *The Rise of the City, 1878-1898.* History of American Life, Vol. X. New York: Macmillan Co., 1933. 494 p.
272. SLOSSON, PRESTON WILLIAM. *The Great Crusade and After, 1914-1928.* History of American Life, Vol. XII. New York: Macmillan Co., 1930. 486 p.
273. SMITH, DARRELL HEVENOR. *The Bureau of Education: Its History, Activities, and Organization.* Institute for Government Research, Service Monographs of the United States Government, No. 14. Baltimore: Johns Hopkins Press, 1923. 157 p.
274. SMITH, HAMILTON ROSS. *Development of Manual Training in the United States.* Lancaster, Pa.: Intelligencer Print, 1914. 90 p. (Doctor's thesis, University of Pennsylvania.)

275. SMITH, SHERMAN M. *The Relation of the State to Religious Education in Massachusetts.* Syracuse, N. Y.: Syracuse University Book Store, 1926. 350 p. (Doctor's thesis, Clark University, 1925.)
276. SNOW, LOUIS FRANKLIN. *The College Curriculum in the United States.* Contributions to Education, No. 10. New York: Teachers College, Columbia University, 1907. 186 p.
277. STEINER, BERNARD C. *Life of Henry Barnard.* U. S. Dept. of the Interior, Bureau of Education, Bulletin, 1919, No. 8. Washington, D. C.: Government Printing Office, 1919. 131 p.
278. STOUT, JOHN ELBERT. *The Development of High-School Curricula in the North Central States from 1860 to 1918.* Supplementary Educational Monographs, No. 15. Chicago: University of Chicago Press, 1921. 322 p.
279. STRAYER, GEORGE D., JR. *Centralizing Tendencies in the Administration of Public Education.* Contributions to Education, No. 618. New York: Teachers College, Columbia University, 1934. 123 p.
280. SWIFT, FLETCHER HARPER. *Federal and State Policies in Public School Finance in the United States.* Boston: Ginn and Co., 1931. 472 p.
281. SWIFT, FLETCHER HARPER. *A History of Public Permanent Common School Funds in the United States, 1795-1905.* New York: Henry Holt and Co., 1911. 493 p.
282. SWIFT, FLETCHER HARPER. "Public School Finance." *Twenty-Five Years of American Education.* (Edited by I. L. Kandel.) New York: Macmillan Co., 1924. Chapter 8, p. 197-224.
283. TAYLOR, JAMES MONROE, *Before Vassar Opened.* Boston: Houghton Mifflin Co., 1914. 287 p.
284. TEWKSBURY, DONALD G. *The Founding of American Colleges and Universities before the Civil War.* Contributions to Education, No. 543. New York: Teachers College, Columbia University, 1932. 254 p.
285. THWING, CHARLES FRANKLIN. *A History of Education in the United States since the Civil War.* Boston: Houghton Mifflin Co., 1910. 347 p.
286. THWING, CHARLES FRANKLIN. *A History of Higher Education in America.* New York: D. Appleton and Co., 1906. 501 p.
287. TUGWELL, REXFORD G., and KEYSERLING, LEON H., editors. *Redirecting Education.* Vol. I., The United States. New York: Columbia University Press, 1934. 273 p.
288. U. S. Department of the Interior, Bureau of Education. *Bulletins of the Bureau of Education, 1906 to 1927.* Bulletin, 1928, No. 17. Washington, D. C.: Government Printing Office, 1928. 65 p.
289. U. S. Department of the Interior, Bureau of Education. *Index to the Reports of the Commissioner of Education: 1867-1907.* Bulletin, 1909, No. 7. Washington, D. C.: Government Printing Office, 1909. 103 p.
290. U. S. Department of the Interior, Bureau of Education. *List of Publications of the United States Bureau of Education, 1867-1910.* Bulletin, 1910, No. 3. Washington, D. C.: Government Printing Office, 1910. 55 p.
291. U. S. Department of the Interior, Bureau of Education. *Reports of the Commissioner of Education for the Years 1894-95 to 1903-04.* Washington, D. C.: Government Printing Office, 1896-1906. (Contain articles by A. D. Mayo on the development of the common school system.)
292. U. S. National Advisory Committee on Education. *Federal Relations to Education.* Washington, D. C.: the Committee, 1931. 2 vols.
293. WEBSTER, WILLIAM CLARENCE. *Recent Centralizing Tendencies in State Educational Administration.* New York: Columbia University. 1897. 78 p.
294. WEEKS, STEPHEN B. "The Beginnings of the Common School System in the South; or, Calvin Henderson Wiley and the Organization of Common Schools in North Carolina." *Report of the Commissioner of Education for the Year 1896-97.* Washington, D. C.: Government Printing Office, 1898. Vol. 2, p. 1379-1474.
295. WEEKS, STEPHEN B. *History of Public-School Education in Alabama.* U. S. Dept. of the Interior, Bureau of Education, Bulletin, 1915, No. 12. Washington, D. C.: Government Printing Office, 1915. 209 p.
296. WICKERSHAM, JAMES P. *A History of Education in Pennsylvania.* Lancaster, Pa.: Inquirer Publishing Co., 1886. 683 p.
297. WILLS, ELBERT VAUGHAN. *The Growth of American Higher Education.* Philadelphia: Dorrance and Co., 1936. 225 p.
298. WOODSON, CARTER GODWIN. *The Education of the Negro Prior to 1861.* New York: G. P. Putnam's Sons, 1915. 454 p.

299. WOODY, THOMAS. *A History of Women's Education in the United States.* New York: Science Press, 1929. 2 vols.

C. STATE HISTORIES OF EDUCATION

Note: The Committee on State Histories of Education has compiled a bibliography of nearly two hundred titles which is too long to be reproduced here. The list here given consists chiefly of titles mentioned in the present survey.

300. AURNER, CLARENCE RAY. *History of Education in Iowa.* Iowa City: Iowa State Historical Society, 1914-20. 5 vols.
301. BELTING, P. E. *The Development of the Free Public High School in Illinois to 1860.* Springfield, Ill.: State Historical Journal, 1919.
302. BISHOP, EUGENE A. *The Development of a State School System: New Hampshire.* Contributions to Education, No. 391. New York: Teachers College, Columbia University, 1930. 159 p.
303. BOLTON, FREDERICK E., and BIBB, THOMAS W. *History of Education in Washington.* U. S. Dept. of the Interior, Office of Education, Bulletin, 1934, No. 9. Washington, D. C.: Government Printing Office, 1935. 448 p.
304. BOOCHER, ELBERT W. G. *Secondary Education in Georgia, 1732-1858.* Merchantville, N. J.: the Author, 1933. 452 p. (Doctor's thesis, University of Pennsylvania, 1932.)
305. BOONE, RICHARD G. *A History of Education in Indiana.* New York: D. Appleton and Co., 1892. 454 p.
306. BOSSING, WILSON L. *The History of Educational Legislation in Ohio from 1851 to 1925.* 296 p. (Unpublished manuscript in the Ohio Archaeological and Historical Society's Library.)
307. BROWN, HAROLD NICHOLAS. *A History of the Public Elementary School System of Nevada, 1861-1934.* Unpublished doctor's thesis, University of California, 1935. 375 p.
308. BUSH, GEORGE GARY. *History of Education in Florida.* U. S. Dept. of the Interior, Bureau of Education, Circular of Information, 1888, No. 7. Washington, D. C.: Government Printing Office, 1889. 54 p.
309. BUSH, GEORGE GARY. *History of Education in New Hampshire.* U. S. Dept. of the Interior, Bureau of Education, Circular of Information, 1898, No. 3. Washington, D. C.: Government Printing Office, 1898. 170 p.
310. BUSH, GEORGE GARY. *The History of Education in Vermont.* U. S. Dept. of the Interior, Bureau of Education, Circular of Information, 1900, No. 4. Washington, D. C.: Government Printing Office, 1900. 216 p.
311. BUSH, GEORGE GARY. *History of Higher Education in Massachusetts.* U. S. Dept. of the Interior, Bureau of Education, Circular of Information, 1891, No. 6. Washington, D. C.: Government Printing Office, 1891. 445 p.
312. CARROLL, CHARLES. *Public Education in Rhode Island.* Providence: E. L. Freeman Co., 1918. 500 p.
313. CHADBOURNE, AVA H. *Beginnings of Education in Maine.* Contributions to Education, No. 336. New York: Teachers College, Columbia University, 1928. 135 p.
314. COCHRAN, THOMAS EVERETTE. *History of Public-School Education in Florida.* Lancaster, Pa.: New Era Printing Co., 1921. 270 p.
315. *Columbian History of Education in Kansas.* Compiled by Kansas educators. Topeka: Hamilton Printing Co., 1893. 231 p.
316. EBY, FREDERICK. *The Development of Education in Texas.* New York: Macmillan Co., 1925. 354 p.
317. FAY, EDWIN WHITFIELD. *The History of Education in Louisiana.* U. S. Dept. of the Interior, Bureau of Education, Circular of Information, 1898, No. 1. Washington, D. C.: Government Printing Office, 1898. 264 p.
318. GREER, JOHN N. *The History of Education in Minnesota.* U. S. Dept. of the Interior, Bureau of Education, Circular of Information, 1902, No. 2. Washington, D. C.: Government Printing Office, 1902. 223 p.
319. HAMLETT, BARKSDALE. *History of Education in Kentucky.* Bulletin, Vol. 7, No. 14. Frankfort: Kentucky Department of Education, 1914. 330 p.
320. HARRIS, THOMAS H. *The Story of Public Education in Louisiana.* Baton Rouge: the Author, 1924. 118 p. (Also published in *Journal of the Louisiana Teachers Association* February to December, 1924.)

321. HASKINS, CHARLES H., and HULL, WILLIAM I. *A History of Higher Education in Pennsylvania.* U. S. Dept. of the Interior, Bureau of Education, Circular of Information, 1902, No. 4. Washington, D. C.: Government Printing Office, 1902. 272 p.
322. HEATWOLE, CORNELIUS J. *A History of Education in Virginia.* New York: Macmillan Co., 1916. 382 p.
323. *A History of Education in the State of Ohio; a Centennial Volume.* Published by Authority of the General Assembly. Columbus, 1876. 447 p.
324. KNIGHT, EDGAR W. *Public School Education in North Carolina.* Boston: Houghton Mifflin Co., 1916. 384 p.
325. KNIGHT, GEORGE W., and COMMONS, JOHN R. *The History of Higher Education in Ohio.* U. S. Dept. of the Interior, Bureau of Education, Circular of Information, 1891, No. 5. Washington, D. C.: Government Printing Office, 1891. 258 p.
326. LEWIS, ALVIN FAYETTE. *History of Higher Education in Kentucky.* U. S. Dept. of the Interior, Bureau of Education, Circular of Information, 1899, No. 3. Washington, D. C.: Government Printing Office, 1899. 350 p.
327. MCLAUGHLIN, ANDREW C. *History of Higher Education in Michigan.* U. S. Dept. of the Interior, Bureau of Education, Circular of Information, 1891, No. 4. Washington, D. C.: Government Printing Office, 1891. 179 p.
328. MERRIAM, LUCIUS S. *Higher Education in Tennessee.* U. S. Dept. of the Interior, Bureau of Education, Circular of Information, 1893, No. 5. Washington, D. C.: Government Printing Office, 1893. 287 p.
329. MILLER, EDWARD ALANSON. *The History of Educational Legislation in Ohio from 1803 to 1850.* Supplementary Educational Monographs, No. 13. Chicago: University of Chicago, 1920. 248 p. (First printed in *Ohio Archaeological and Historical Quarterly*, Vol. 27, Nos. 1 and 2.)
330. MULHERN, JAMES. *A History of Secondary Education in Pennsylvania.* New York: Science Press, 1933. 714 p.
331. MURRAY, DAVID. *History of Education in New Jersey.* U. S. Dept. of the Interior, Bureau of Education, Circular of Information, 1899, No. 1. Washington, D. C.: Government Printing Office, 1899. 344 p.
332. NOBLE, M. C. S. *A History of the Public Schools of North Carolina.* Chapel Hill: University of North Carolina Press, 1930. 463 p.
333. NOBLE, STUART G. "An Evaluation of State Histories of Education; the Report of the Committee on State Histories of Education, Appointed by the National Society of College Teachers of Education, 1928." *High School Journal (University of North Carolina)* 12: 197-206, 272-77; October and November, 1929.
334. PATZER, CONRAD E. *Public Education in Wisconsin.* Madison: State Department of Education, 1924. 511 p.
335. PUTNAM, DANIEL. *Development of Primary and Secondary Public Education in Michigan.* Ann Arbor, Mich.: George Wahr, 1904. 273 p.
336. RAYMER, ROBERT GEORGE. *A History of the Superintendency of Public Instruction in the State of Oregon, 1849-1925.* Doctor's thesis, University of Oregon.
337. SMART, J. H., editor. *Indiana Schools and the Men Who Have Worked in Them.* Cincinnati: Wilson Hinkle and Co., 1876. 239 p.
338. SMITH, CHARLES LEE. *The History of Education in North Carolina.* U. S. Dept. of the Interior, Bureau of Education, Circular of Information, 1888, No. 2. Washington, D. C.: Government Printing Office, 1888. 180 p.
339. STEARNS, J. W., editor. *The Columbian History of Education in Wisconsin.* Milwaukee: State Committee on Educational Exhibits for Wisconsin, 1893. 720 p.
340. STEINER, BERNARD C. *The History of Education in Connecticut.* U. S. Dept. of the Interior, Bureau of Education, Circular of Information, 1893, No. 2. Washington, D. C.: Government Printing Office, 1893. 300 p.
341. STEINER, BERNARD C. *History of Education in Maryland.* U. S. Dept. of the Interior, Bureau of Education, Circular of Information, 1894, No. 2. Washington, D. C.: Government Printing Office, 1894. 331 p.
342. STETSON, W. W. *A Study of the History of Education in Maine and the Evolution of Our Present School System.* Augusta: State Department of Education, 104 p.
343. STOCKWELL, THOMAS B. *A History of Public Education in Rhode Island.* Providence: Providence Press, 1876. 458 p.
344. SWETT, JOHN. *History of the Public School System of California.* San Francisco: A. L. Bancroft and Co., 1876. 246 p.

345. SWETT, JOHN. *Public Education in California.* New York: American Book Co., 1911. 320 p.
346. TAYLOR, JAMES W. *A Manual of the Ohio School System, Consisting of an Historical View of Its Progress and a Republication of the Schools Laws in Force.* Cincinnati: H. W. Derby and Co., 1857. 413 p.
347. WALSH, LOUISE G., and WALSH, MATTHEW J. *History and Organization of Education in Pennsylvania.* Indiana, Pa.: the Authors (State Teachers College), 1928. 412 p.
348. WEEKS, STEPHEN B. *History of Public-School Education in Alabama.* U. S. Dept. of the Interior, Bureau of Education, Bulletin, 1915, No. 12. Washington, D. C.: Government Printing Office, 1915. 209 p.
349. WEEKS, STEPHEN B. *History of Public School Education in Arizona.* U. S. Dept. of the Interior, Bureau of Education, Bulletin, 1918, No. 17. Washington, D. C.: Government Printing Office, 1918. 141 p.
350. WEEKS, STEPHEN B. *History of Public School Education in Arkansas.* U. S. Dept. of the Interior, Bureau of Education, Bulletin, 1912, No. 27. Washington, D. C.: Government Printing Office, 1912. 131 p.
351. WEEKS, STEPHEN B. *History of Public School Education in Delaware.* U. S. Dept. of the Interior, Bureau of Education, Bulletin, 1917, No. 18. Washington, D. C.: Government Printing Office, 1917. 181 p.
352. WHITFORD, W. C. *Historical Sketch of Education in Wisconsin.* Madison: Atwood and Culver, 1876. 127 p.
353. WICKERSHAM, JAMES P. *A History of Education in Pennsylvania.* Lancaster, Pa.: Inquirer Publishing Co., 1886. 683 p.

D. HISTORY OF EDUCATION IN CANADA

354. Annual Reports of Provincial Departments of Education, 1935.
355. BELL, WALTER N. *The Development of the Ontario High School.* Toronto: University of Toronto Press, 1918. 161 p. (Master's thesis.)
356. BINGAY, JAMES. *Public Education in Nova Scotia.* Kingston, Ontario: Jackson Press, 1919. 141 p.
357. BINNS, HENRY BRYAN. *A Century of Education; Being the Centenary History of the British and Foreign School Society, 1808-1908.* London: J. M. Dent and Co., 1908. 330 p.
358. BRACQ, JEAN C. *The Evolution of French Canada.* New York: Macmillan Co., 1924. 467 p.
359. Canada. Dominion Bureau of Statistics. *Annual Survey of Education in Canada, 1934.* Ottawa: the Bureau, 1936. 138 p.
360. CHARTIER, CANON EMILE. *The English and the French Systems of Secondary Education in Quebec.* Montreal: University of Montreal, 1934. 19 p.
361. DYDE, W. F. *Public Secondary Education in Canada.* Contributions to Education, No. 345. New York: Teachers College, Columbia University, 1929. 263 p.
362. HODGES, J. GEORGE. *Historical and Other Papers and Documents, Educational System of Ontario, 1792-1871.* Toronto: L. K. Cameron, 1912. Vols. I and II.
363. OLIVER, E. H. *The Canadian North-West, Its Early Development and Legislative Records.* Ottawa: Government Printing Bureau, 1915. Vol. 2, p. 689-1348.
364. Public School Acts and Regulations of Provincial Departments of Education, 1920-35.
365. RENNIE, HENRY LESLIE. *History of Education in the Eastern Townships.* Master's thesis, Bishop's University, 1930. 160 p.
366. REXFORD, ELSON I. *The Jewish Population and the Protestant Schools.* Montreal: Renouf Publishing Co., 1923. 50 p.
367. RICHARDSON, WILLIAM LEEDS. *The Administration of Schools in the Cities in the Dominion of Canada.* Toronto: J. M. Dent and Sons, 1922. 315 p.
368. ROBBINS, J. E. "Canadian Education Viewed in the Light of Social Needs." *Yearbook of Education, 1936.* London: Evans Brothers, 1936. p. 601-17.
369. SANDIFORD, PETER, editor. *Comparative Education.* New York: E. P. Dutton and Co., 1918. 500 p.
370. SHORTT, ADAM, and DOUGHTY, ARTHUR G., editors. *Canada and Its Provinces.* Toronto: Glasgow Brock and Co., 1914-17. Vols. 14, 16, 18, 20, and 22.
371. SHORTT, ADAM, and DOUGHTY, ARTHUR G. *Canadian Archives Documents Relating to the Constitutional History of Canada, 1759-1791.* Part I (2d ed.). Ottawa: King's Printer, 1918. 581 p.

372. SPRAGGE, GEORGE W. *Monitorial Schools in the Canadas, 1810-1845.* Doctor's thesis, University of Toronto, 1935. 318 p.
373. WAITE, WILLIAM HENRY. *The History of Elementary and Secondary Education in Saskatchewan.* Master's thesis, University of Manitoba, 1936. 184 p.
374. WEIR, GEORGE M. *The Separate School Question in Canada.* Toronto: Ryerson Press, 1934. 298 p.
375. WOODLEY, ELSIE CAROLINE. *The History of Education in the Province of Quebec.* Master's thesis, McGill University, 1932. 199 p.

Chapter II. History of Education in Europe

A. HISTORY OF EDUCATION IN ENGLAND

376. ADAMS, FRANCIS. *History of the Elementary School Contest in England.* London: Chapman and Hall, 1882. 349 p.
377. ADAMSON, JOHN WILLIAM. "Education." *Cambridge History of English Literature.* (Edited by A. W. Ward and A. R. Waller.) Cambridge, England: University Press, 1913. Vol. 9, p. 425-62.
378. ADAMSON, JOHN WILLIAM. *English Education, 1789-1902.* Cambridge, England: University Press, 1930. 519 p.
379. ADAMSON, JOHN WILLIAM. *A Short History of Education.* Cambridge, England: University Press, 1919. 371 p.
380. ARCHER, R. L. *Secondary Education in the Nineteenth Century.* Contributions to the History of Education, V. Cambridge, England: University Press, 1921. 363 p.
381. ARNOLD, MATTHEW. *Reports on Elementary Schools 1852-1882.* London: Macmillan and Co., 1889. 302 p.
382. BALFOUR, GRAHAM. *The Educational Systems of Great Britain and Ireland.* 2d ed. Oxford, England; Clarendon Press, 1903. 307 p.
383. BELLOT, H. HALE. *University College, London, 1826-1926.* London: University of London Press, 1929. 464 p.
384. BINNS, HENRY BRYAN. *A Century of Education.* London: J. M. Dent and Co., 1908. 330 p.
385. BIRCHENOUGH, CHARLES. *History of Elementary Education in England and Wales.* London: W. B. Clive, 1925. 514 p.
386. BREBNER, J. BARTLET. "Education in England." Redirecting Education. (Edited by Rexford G. Tugwell and Leon H. Keyserling.) New York: Columbia University Press, 1935. Vol. 2, p. 51-80.
387. BROWN, J. HOWARD. *Elizabethan Schooldays.* Oxford, England: Basil Blackwell and Mott, 1933. 173 p.
388. CUBBERLEY, ELLWOOD P. *The History of Education.* Boston: Houghton Mifflin Co., 1920. 849 p.
389. DE MONTMORENCY, J. E. G. *State Intervention in English Education.* Cambridge, England: University Press, 1902. 366 p.
390. DOBBS, A. E. *Education and Social Movements, 1700-1850.* London: Longmans, Green and Co., 1919. 257 p.
391. EBY, FREDERICK, and ARROWOOD, CHARLES FLINN. *The Development of Modern Education.* New York: Prentice-Hall, 1934. 922 p.
392. Great Britain. *Report of Her Majesty's Commissioners Appointed to Inquire into the Revenue and Management of Certain Colleges and Schools.* London: George E. Eyre and William Spottiswoode, 1864. 4 vols. in 2.
393. Great Britain. Board of Education. *Report, 1899-date.* London: H. M. Stationery Office, 1900-date.
394. Great Britain. Board of Education. *Special Reports on Educational Subjects.* (Edited by Sir Michael E. Sadler.) London: Wyman and Sons, 1897-1914. 28 vols.
395. Great Britain. Board of Education, Consultative Committee. *Report of the Consultative Committee on the Education of the Adolescent.* London: H. M. Stationery Office, 1926. 339 p.
396. Great Britain. Board of Education, Consultative Committee. *Report of the Consultative Committee on the Primary School.* London: H. M. Stationery Office, 1931. 290 p.

397. Great Britain. Commission to Inquire into the Present State of Popular Education in England. *Reports of the Assistant Commissioners.* London: George E. Eyre and William Spottiswoode, 1861. 6 vols.
398. Great Britain. Parliament. House of Commons, Select Committee on Education. *Report from the Select Committee on Education.* London, 1865-66. 2 vols.
399. Great Britain. Parliament. House of Commons, Select Committee on the Education of the Lower Orders. *Report.* London, 1816-18. 5 vols in 2.
400. Great Britain. Parliament. House of Commons, Select Committee on the Education of the Lower Orders. *Report from the Select Committee on the Education of the Lower Orders in the Metropolis.* London, 1816. 332 p.
401. Great Britain. Parliament. House of Commons, Select Committee on the Education of the Poor. *A Digest of Parochial Returns Made to the Select Committee Appointed to Inquire into the Education of the Poor: Session 1818.* London, 1819. 2 vols.
402. Great Britain. Royal Commission on Elementary Education Acts. *Reports of the Commissioners Appointed to Inquire into the Working of the Elementary Education Acts, England and Wales.* London: George E. Eyre and William Spottiswoode, 1886-88. 10 vols.
403. Great Britain. Royal Commission on Secondary Education. *Report of the Commissioners.* London: George E. Eyre and William Spottiswoode, 1895. 9 vols. in 7.
404. Great Britain. Schools Inquiry Commission. *Report of the Commissioners.* London: George E. Eyre and William Spottiswoode, 1868-69. 21 vols.
405. GREENOUGH, JAMES C. *The Evolution of the Elementary Schools of Great Britain.* New York: D. Appleton and Co., 1903. 265 p.
406. HASKINS, CHARLES HOMER. *The Rise of Universities.* New York: Henry Holt and Co., 1923. 134 p.
407. HOLMAN, H. *English National Education.* London: Blackie and Son, 1898. 256 p.
408. IRSAY, STEPHEN D'. *Histoire des Universités Françaises et Etrangères.* Tome I, Moyen Age et Renaissance. Paris: Auguste Picard, 1933. 372 p.
409. JONES, LANCE G. E. *The Training of Teachers in England and Wales.* London: Oxford University Press, 1924. 486 p.
410. KANDEL, I. L., editor. *Educational Yearbook of the International Institute. 1924-date.* New York: Teachers College, Columbia University, 1925-date. (Yearbooks for 1924-26 published by Macmillan Co.)
411. KANDEL, I. L. *History of Secondary Education.* Boston: Houghton Mifflin Co., 1930. 577 p.
412. LEACH, ARTHUR F. *Educational Charters and Documents 598 to 1909.* Cambridge, England: University Press, 1911. 582 p.
413. LEACH, ARTHUR F. *English Schools at the Reformation 1546-8.* Westminster: Archibald Constable and Co., 1896. 346 p.
414. LEACH, ARTHUR F. *The Schools of Medieval England.* New York: Macmillan Co., 1915. 349 p.
415. LOCHHEAD, JEWELL. *The Education of Young Children in England.* Contributions to Education, No. 521. New York: Teachers College, Columbia University, 1932. 226 p.
416. LYTE, H. C. MAXWELL. *A History of the University of Oxford.* London: Macmillan and Co., 1886. 504 p.
417. MCLACHLAN, H. *English Education under the Test Acts.* Manchester, England: University Press, 1931. 344 p.
418. MACLEAN, GEORGE EDWIN. *Studies in Higher Education in England and Scotland.* U. S. Dept. of the Interior, Bureau of Education, Bulletin, 1917, No. 16. Washington, D. C.: Government Printing Office, 1917. 279 p.
419. MALLET, CHARLES EDWARD. *A History of the University of Oxford.* London: Methuen and Co., 1924-27. 3 vols.
420. MANSBRIDGE, ALBERT. *An Adventure in Working-Class Education.* London: Longmans, Green and Co., 1920. 73 p.
421. MANSBRIDGE, ALBERT. *The Older Universities of England: Oxford & Cambridge.* London: Longmans, Green and Co., 1923. 296 p.
422. MANSBRIDGE, ALBERT. *University Tutorial Classes.* London: Longmans, Green and Co., 1913. 197 p.
423. MATTHEWS, RODERIC DONALD. *Post-Primary Education in England.* Philadelphia, 1932. 235 p. (Doctor's thesis, University of Pennsylvania, 1931.)

424. MONROE, PAUL, editor. *A Cyclopedia of Education.* New York: Macmillan Co., 1911-13. 5 vols.
425. MULLINGER, J. BASS. "English Grammar Schools." *Cambridge History of English Literature.* (Edited by A. W. Ward and A. R. Waller.) Cambridge, England: University Press, 1911. Vol. 7, p. 368-88.
426. MULLINGER, J. BASS. *A History of the University of Cambridge.* London: Longmans, Green and Co., 1888. 232 p.
427. MULLINGER, J. BASS. *The University of Cambridge.* Cambridge, England: University Press, 1873-1911. 3 vols.
428. NORWOOD, CYRIL, and HOPE, ARTHUR H. *The Higher Education of Boys in England.* London: John Murray, 1909. 568 p.
429. PARKER, IRENE. *Dissenting Academies in England.* Cambridge, England: University Press, 1914. 168 p.
430. PARRY, A. W. *Education in England in the Middle Ages.* London: W. B. Clive, 1920. 264 p.
431. PRIDEAUX, E. B. R. *A Survey of Elementary English Education.* London: Blackie and Son, 1914. 206 p.
432. RASHDALL, HASTINGS. *The Universities of Europe in the Middle Ages.* Vol. III, English Universities—Student Life. Oxford, England: Clarendon Press, 1936. 558 p.
433. REISNER, EDWARD H. *Historical Foundations of Modern Education.* New York: Macmillan Co., 1927. 513 p.
434. REISNER, EDWARD H. *Nationalism and Education since 1789.* New York: Macmillan Co., 1922. 575 p.
435. SMITH, FRANK. *A History of English Elementary Education, 1760-1902.* London: University of London Press, 1931. 360 p.
436. STOWE, A. MONROE. *English Grammar Schools in the Reign of Queen Elizabeth.* Contributions to Education, No. 22. New York: Teachers College, Columbia University, 1908. 200 p.
437. VAUGHN, EARNEST VANCOURT. *The Origin and Early Development of the English Universities to the Close of the Thirteenth Century.* University of Missouri Studies, Social Science Series, Vol. 2, No. 2. Columbia, Mo.: University of Missouri, 1908. 147 p.
438. WALKER, T. A. "English and Scottish Education. Universities and Public Schools to the Time of Colet." *Cambridge History of English Literature.* (Edited by A. W. Ward and A. R. Waller.) Cambridge, England: University Press, 1917. Vol. 2, p. 387-421.
439. WARD, HERBERT. *Notes for the Study of English Education from 1860 to 1902.* London: G. Bell and Sons, 1929. 64 p.
440. WARD, HERBERT. *Notes for the Study of English Education from 1900 to 1930.* London: G. Bell and Sons, 1931. 94 p.
441. WATSON, FOSTER. *The Beginnings of the Teaching of Modern Subjects in England.* London: Isaac Pitman and Sons, 1909. 554 p.
442. WATSON, FOSTER, editor. *The Encyclopedia and Dictionary of Education.* London: Isaac Pitman and Sons, 1921-22. 4 vols.
443. WATSON, FOSTER. *The English Grammar Schools to 1660: Their Curriculum and Practice.* Cambridge, England: University Press, 1908. 548 p.
444. WELLS, J., editor. *Oxford and Oxford Life.* London: Methuen and Co., 1899. 190 p.
445. WILSON, J. DOVER, editor. *The Schools of England: A Study in Renaissance.* London: Sidgwick and Jackson, 1928. 388 p.
446. WINSTANLEY, D. A. *The University of Cambridge in the Eighteenth Century.* Cambridge, England: University Press, 1922. 349 p.
447. WINSTANLEY, D. A. *Unreformed Cambridge.* Cambridge, England: University Press, 1935. 412 p.
448. WOOD, ANTHONY A. *Athenae Oxonienses.* London: F. C. and J. Rivington, 1813-20. 5 vols.
449. WOODWARD, W. H. "English Universities, Schools and Scholarship in the Sixteenth Century." *Cambridge History of English Literature.* (Edited by A. W. Ward and A. R. Waller.) Cambridge, England: University Press, 1909. Vol. 3, p. 475-98.
450. *The Year Book of Education, 1932-date.* (Edited by Lord Eustace Percy.) London: Evans Brothers, 1932-date.

451. *The Yearbook of the Universities of the Empire.* London: George Bell and Sons, 1914-date.

B. HISTORY OF EDUCATION IN FRANCE

452. ALLAIN, E. *Contribution à l'Histoire de l'Instruction Primaire dans la Gironde avant la Révolution.* Bordeaux, 1895.
453. ALLAIN, E. *L'Instruction Primaire en France avant la Révolution.* Paris, 1881.
454. ALLAIN, E. *L'Oeuvre scolaire de la Révolution 1789-1802.* Paris: F. Didot, 1891.
455. AULARD, A. *Napoléon et le Monopole Universitaire, Origine et Fonctionnement de l'Université Impériale.* Paris: A. Colin, 1911.
456. BARNARD, H. C. *The Little Schools of Port-Royal.* Cambridge, England: University Press, 1913. 263 p.
457. BARNARD, H. C. *The Port-Royalists on Education.* New York: Macmillan Co., 1918. 276 p.
458. Bibliothèque Générale des Sciences Sociales. *La Lutte scolaire en France au XIXe Siècle.* Paris: Alcan, 1912.
459. BROUARD, P. E. E. *Essai d'Histoire Critique de l'Instruction Primaire en France de 1789 jusqu'à nos Jours.* Paris: Hachette, 1901.
460. BUISSON, F. *Dictionnaire de Pédagogie et d'Instruction Primaire.* Paris: Hachette, 1911. 2 vols.
461. Commission Française pour l'Enquête Carnegie. *Atlas de l'Enseignement en France.* Paris, n. d. 183 p. Translated in *Educational Yearbook of the International Institute, 1934.* New York: Teachers College, Columbia University, 1934. p. 1-290.
462. COMPAYRÉ, GABRIEL. *Les Grands Educateurs.* Paris: P. Delaplane. (English translation of series published by T. Y. Crowell and Co. as "Pioneers in Education.")
463. COMPAYRÉ, GABRIEL. *Histoire Critique de l'Education en France.* Paris: Hachette, 1884. 2 vols.
464. COMPAYRÉ, GABRIEL. *Histoire Critique de la Pédagogie.* Paris: Delagrave, 1884.
465. DE LA FONTANERIE, FRANÇOIS. *The Conduct of the Schools of Jean Baptiste de La Salle.* New York: McGraw-Hill Book Co., 1935. 242 p.
466. DE LA FONTANERIE, FRANÇOIS, editor. *French Liberalism and Education in the Eighteenth Century.* New York: McGraw-Hill Book Co., 1932. 385 p.
467. DION, L., editor, *Recueil Complet de la Législation de l'Enseignement Secondaire (Réglements codifiés).* Paris: Papeterie Générale des Ecoles, 1935. 1148 p.
468. DROUARD, CH. *Histoire de l'Enseignement Primaire à Paris et dans le Departement de la Seine.* Paris, 1911.
469. FARRINGTON, F. E. *French Secondary Schools.* New York: Longmans, Green and Co., 1910. 450 p.
470. FARRINGTON, F. E. *The Public Primary School System of France.* Contributions to Education, No. 7. New York: Teachers College, Columbia University, 1906. 303 p.
471. GRÉARD, OCTAVE. *La Législation de l'Enseignement Primaire en France depuis 1789 jusqu'à nos Jours.* Paris: Délalain, 1890-1900. 6 vols.
472. GRÉARD, OCTAVE. *La Législation de l'Instruction Primaire depuis 1789 jusqu'à nos Jours (Recueil des lois, décrets, ordonnances, ets.).* Paris: Mourgues, 1874. 3 vols. in 4.
473. GUEX, FRANÇOIS. *Histoire de l'Instruction et de l'Education.* Lausanne: Alcan, 1906. 736 p.
474. HAWTREY, F. *French Nursery Schools.* London: J. M. Dent and Sons, 1935. 95 p
475. IRSAY, STEPHEN D', *Histoire des Universités Françaises et Etrangères.* Paris: Auguste Picard, 1933-35. 2 vols.
476. ISRAEL, A. *L'Ecole de la République, La Grande Oeuvre de Jules Ferry.* Paris: Hachette, 1931. 272 p.
477. KANDEL, I. L., translator. *French Elementary Schools: Official Courses of Study.* Studies of the International Institute, No. 3. New York: Teachers College, Columbia University, 1927. 270 p.
478. KANDEL, I. L. *History of Secondary Education.* Boston: Houghton Mifflin Co., 1930. 577 p.
479. KANDEL, I. L. *The Reform of Secondary Education in France.* Studies of the International Institute, No. 2. New York: Teachers College, Columbia University, 1924. 159 p.

480. KERGOMARD, MME. *Les Ecoles Maternelles de 1837 jusqu'en 1910.* Paris: Nathan, 1910.
481. LÉAUD, A., and GLAY, E. *L'Ecole Primaire en France.* Paris: La Cité Française, 1934. 2 vols.
482. LIARD, L. *L'Enseignement Supérieur en France, 1789-1893.* Paris: A. Colin, 1888-94. 2 vols.
483. MEURIOT, P. *Le Baccalauréat, son Evolution Historique et Statistique des Origines (1808) à nos Jours.* Nancy: Berger-Levrault, 1919. 54 p.
484. REISNER, E. H. *Nationalism and Education since 1789.* New York: Macmillan Co., 1922. 575 p.
485. SCHWARTZ, L. *Nouveau Code de l'Enseignement Primaire (Code Pichard).* Paris: Hachette, 1930. 601 p.
486. SOLEIL, J. *Le Livre des Instituteurs Traité Complet des Devoirs et des Droits des Membres de l'Enseignement Administration, Législation et Jurisprudence de l'Enseignement Primaire Public et Privé à Tous les Degrés.* Paris: H. Le Soudier, 1936. 350 p.
487. WEILL, G. *Histoire de l'Enseignement Secondaire en France, 1802-1920.* Paris: Payot, 1921. 253 p.
488. WISSEMANS, A. *Code d'Enseignement Secondaire.* Paris: Hachette, 1920. 668 p.

C. HISTORY OF EDUCATION IN GERMANY

489. ABB, E. *Kurze Geschichte der Pädagogik der neueren Zeit.* Ansbach, 1927.
490. ALBRECHT, H. *Die Stellung des politischen Katholizismus in Deutschland zu den Fragen des Unterrichtes und der Erziehung in den Jahren 1848-1850.* Liebertwolkwitz: Zeugner, 1933. 172 p.
491. ALEXANDER, THOMAS, and PARKER, BERYL. *The New Education in the German Republic.* New York: John Day Co., 1929. 387 p.
492. ALEXANDER, THOMAS. *Prussian Elementary Schools.* New York: Macmillan Co., 1918. 571 p.
493. ALEXANDER, THOMAS. *Training of Elementary Teachers in Germany.* Studies of the International Institute, No. 5. New York: Teachers College, Columbia University, 1929. 340 p.
494. ANDREAE, C. *Die Entwickelung der theoretischen Pädagogik.* Leipzig, 1911. 188 p.
495. ANDREESEN, A. *Hermann Lietz, der Schöpfer der Landerziehungsheime.* Munich: Lehmann, 1934. 224 p.
496. BARTH, P. *Die Geschichte der Erziehung in soziologischer und geistesgeschichtlicher Beleuchtung.* Leipzig, 1911. 800 p.
497. BASTIAN, OTTO. "Schnepfentaler Manuskripte." *Zeitschrift für Geschichte der Erziehung und des Unterrichts.* Vol. 17-19, p. 69-82. 1929.
498. BECKER, CARL H. *Secondary Education and Teacher Training in Germany.* Julius and Rosa Sachs Endowment Fund Lectures, No. 3. New York: Teachers College, Columbia University, 1931. 53 p.
499. BEHN, S. *Allgemeine Geschichte der Pädagogik in problementwickelnder Darstellung.* Paderborn: Ferdinand Schöningh, 1928. 2 vols.
500. BERGER, FR. *Menschenbild und Menschenbildung. Philosophisch-pädagogische Anthropologie J. G. Herders.* Stuttgart: Kohlhammer, 1933. 338 p.
501. *Bibliothek der Katholischen Pädagogik.* (Edited by Franz Xaver Kunz.) Freiburg i. Br.: Herder, 1888-date. (About 20 vols.)
502. *Bibliothek pädagogischer Klassiker, eine Sammlung der bedeutendsten pädagogischen Schriften älterer und neuerer Zeit.* (Edited by Friedrich Mann.) Beyer und Söhne: Langensalza, 1868-date. (About 50 vols.)
503. *Bildung und Erziehung* (Edited by Hans Brunnengräber and Joseph Schröteler.) Six issues annually. Münster-Verlag, Münster, 1936. (Replaces the former *Die katholische Privatschule, Pharus, Schule und Erziehung,* and *Vierteljahrsschrift für wissenschaftliche Pädagogik.*)
504. BLINCKMANN, TH. *Die öffentlichen Volksschulen Hamburgs in ihrer geschichtlichen Entwickelung.* Hamburg, 1930. 355 p.
505. BÖHME, HERMANN. "Die Entwickelung der Landwirtschaft zur selbständigen Wissenschaft und die Idee ihres Studiums an besonderen Instituten und Schulen." *Zeitschrift für Geschichte der Erziehung und des Unterrichts* 16: 24-50; 1928.
506. BORCH, R. *Bilderatlas zur Geschichte der Pädagogik.* Freiburg i. Br., 1920. 123 p.

507. BOSSHART, E. *Die systematischen Grundlagen der Pädagogik Eduard Sprangers.* Leipzig: Hirzel, 1935. 177 p.
508. BREITENSTEIN, D. *Die sozialistische Erziehungsbewegung.* Frieburg i. Br., 1930. 207 p.
509. BROWN, JOHN F. *The Training of Teachers for Secondary Schools in Germany and the United States.* New York: Macmillan Co., 1911. 335 p.
510. BRUNNENGRÄBER, HANS. "Geschichte der pädagogischen Ideen und Einrichtungen: ihre methodologische Grundlegung." *Handbuch der Erziehungswissenschaft.* (Edited by Eggersdorfer, F. X., and others.) Part V, Vol. 1, p. 1-21. 1934.
511. BUCHENAU, A.; SPRANGER, E.; and STETTBACHER, H. *Pestalozzi-Studien.* Berlin: de Gruyter, 1927 and 1932. 2 vols.
512. BURCKHARDT, G. *Geschichte des Kultur- und Bildungsproblemes nach den wichtigsten Dokumenten.* Leipzig, 1922. 167 p.
513. CLEMENZ, BRUNO. *Geschichte des schlesischen Bildungswesens im Mittelalter.* Leignitz, 1927. 206 p.
514. DACKWEILER, EDGAR WERNER. *Katholische Kirche und Schule. Eine Untersuchung über die historische und rechtliche stellung der katholisehen. Kirche zu erziehung und unterricht mit besonderer berücksichtigung der verhältnisse in Preussen.* Paderborn: Ferdinand Schöningh, 1933. 264 p.
515. DEITERS, H. *Die deutsche Schulreform nach dem Weltkriege. Beiträge zu ihrer Analyse.* Berlin: Kämmerer, 1935. 127 p.
516. DEJUNG, E. P. *Pestalozzi und die Züricherische Staatsreform, 1794-97.* Winterthur: Konkordia, 1929. 31 p.
517. DELEKAT, F. *Johann Heinrich Pestalozzi, der Mensch, der Philosoph, der Erzieher.* Leipzig: Quelle und Meyer, 1926. 314 p.
518. *Die Deutsche Schule.* (Edited by Kurt Higelke.) Twelve issues annually. Leipzig: Julius Klinkhard, 1896-date.
519. *Deutsches Bildungswesen.* (Founded by Hans Schemm.) Twelve issues annually. Bayreuth, 1933-date.
520. DOLCH, J. "Erziehung und Erziehungswissenschaft in Deutschland und Deutsch-österreich von 1900 bis 1930." *Handbuch der Erziehungswissenschaft.* (Edited by Eggersdorfer, F. X., and others.) Part V, Vol. 3, (Part 1). 66 p.
521. DOLCH, J. "Gegenstände und Formen der pädagogischen Geschichtschreibung." *Zeitschrift für Geschichte der Erziehung und des Unterrichts* 20: 275-300; 1930.
522. DÖRING, W. *Zur pädagogischen Problematik des Begriffes des Klassischen.* Langensalza: Beltz, 1934. 152 p.
523. DÜRR, L. *Das Erziehungswesen im Alten Testament und im antiken Orient.* Leipzig: Hinrichs, 1932. 154 p.
524. EBERHARD, O. *Welterziehungsbewegung, Kräfte und Gegenkräfte in der Völkerpädagogik.* Berlin: Furche, 1930. 253 p.
525. ECKLE, CH. *Der platonische Bildungsgedanke im 19. Jahrhundert. Beitrag zur Geschichte und Theorie seiner Interpretation.* Leipzig: Meiner, 1935. 120 p.
526. EGGERSDORFER, F. X., and OTHERS, editors. *Handbuch der Erziehungswissenschaft.* Ten volumes published to date. Munich: Kösel und Postet, 1930-date. Part V (Volumes 1-3) contains *Geschichte der Erziehung und der Theorie der Erziehung* by various authors.
527. EICHLER, A. *Die Landbewegung des 18. Jahrhunderts und ihre Pädagogik.* Langensalza: Beltz, 1933. 139 p.
528. *Die Erziehung.* (Edited by A. Fischer and others.) About twelve issues annually. Leipzig: Quelle und Meyer, 1925-date.
529. FEILCHENFELD, WALTER. "Aus unbekannten Schriften Joh. Heinrich Pestalozzis." *Zeitschrift für Geschichte der Erziehung und des Unterrichts* 23: 15-48; 1933.
530. FEILCHENFELD, WALTER. *Der Begriff der Wahrheit bei Pestalozzi.* Berlin: 1931. 30 p.
531. FELD, FRIEDRICH. "Sinn und Aufbau einer Geschichte der Berufserziehung." *Zeitschrift für Geschichte der Erziehung und des Unterrichts* 20: 120-43; 1930.
532. FELDER, H. *Geschichte der wissenschaftlichen Studien im Franziskanerorden um die Mitte des 13. Jahrhunderts.* Freiburg: Herder, 1904. 557 p.
533. FISCHER, K. *Geschichte des deutschen Volksschullehrerstandes.* 1892. 2 vols.
534. FISCHL, H. *Wesen und Werden der Schulreform in Österreich.* Wein, 1892, 291 p.
535. FOERSTER, E. *Leben und Wirken A. Falks als Preussischer Kultusminister, auf Grund des Nachlasses dargestellt.* Gotha, 1927. 712 p.

536. FREYTAG, WILLY. "Ein Bruderschaftsbund vor Jahrtausenden. Das pädagogisch-politische Problem der Pythagoräer." *Zeitschrift für Geschichte der Erziehung und des Unterrichts* 23: 83-112; 1933.
537. FRITZSCH, TH. *Waldemar Götze, der Vater der erziehenden Knabenhandarbeit.* Langensalza: Beltz, 1933. 103 p.
538. GANS, A. *Das ökonomische Motiv in der Pädagogik des 18. Jahrhunderts.* Halle, 1930. 160 p.
539. GERLACH, OTTO. *Die Idee des Nationalerziehung in der Geschichte der preussischen Volksschule. Band 1: Die Nationalerziehung im 18. Jahrhundert, dargestellt in ihrem Hauptvertreter Rochow.* Langensalza: Beltz, 1932. 132 p.
540. GLEICH, M. *Die Pädagogik des preussischen Konservativismus in der Epoche seiner Entstehung.* (About 1830-40.) Postberg: Bottrop, 1933. 81 p.
541. GLOEGE, C. W. v. *Humboldt und die Reformversuche der preussischen Unterrichtsverwaltung.* Bielefeld: Velhagen und Klasing, 1921. 169 p.
542. GLORIA, E. *Der Pietismus als Förderer der Volksbildung und sein Einflus auf die preussische Volksschule.* Osterwieck: Zickfeldt, 1933. 94 p.
543. GÖTTLER, JOS. *Geschichte der Pädagogik in Grundlinien.* 3d ed. Freiburg: Herder, 1935. 381 p.
544. GÖTZE, W. *Die Begründung der Volksbildung in der Aufklärungszeit.* Langensalza: Beltz, 1932. 134 p.
545. Great Britain, Board of Education. *Special Reports on Educational Subjects.* London: Wyman and Sons, 1898 and 1902. Vols. 3 and 9.
546. GRUBE, K. *Die Idee und Struktur einer reinmenschlichen Bildung. Beitrag zum Philanthropismus und Neuhumanismus.* Halle: Akad. Verlag, 1934. 273 p.
547. GRUBE, K. *Wilhelm v. Humboldts Bildungsphilosophie. Versuch einer Interpretation.* Halle: Akad. Verlag, 1935. 100 p.
548. HALFTER, FRITZ. "Der Weg Zu Fröbel. Eine bibliographische Umschau." *Zeitschrift für Geschichte der Erziehung und des Unterrichts* 22: 185-205; 1932.
549. HALLER, ADOLF. *Pestalozzi, eine Darstellung seines Lebens und Wirkens.* Frauenfeld, 1926. 225 p.
550. HEHLMANN, WILHELM. *Geschichte der Erziehungswissenschaft im Aufriss.* Berlin, 1933. 78 p.
551. HEINEMANN, KARL. *Geschichte der preussischen Mittelschule.* Halle: Karras u. Könnecke, 1931. 160 p.
552. HERMANN, H. *Die äusseren Formen der Schularbeit in den Schulklassen des 16. Jahrhunderts.* Munich, 1929. 93 p.
553. HESS-KRUG, E. *Die Kunde in der Pädagogik.* Langensalza: Beltz, 1934. 128 p.
554. HEUBAUM, A. *Geschichte des deutschen Bildungswesens seit der Mitte des 17. Jahrhunderts.* Berlin, 1905. 380 p.
555. HIERL, E. *Die Entstehung der neuen Schule. Geschichtliche Grundlagen der Pädagogik der Gegenwart.* Langensalza, Leipzig: Beltz, 1914. 211 p.
556. HOFFMANN, A., editor. *Die Erziehungswissenschaftliche Forschung. Pädagogische Gesamtbibliographie.* Erfurt: Stenger. Vol. 1, 1926, covering January-June, 1926; Vol. 29, 1936, covering July-December, 1935.
557. HOYLER, AUGUST. *Gentleman-Ideal und Gentleman-Erziehung, mit besonderer Berücksichtigung der Renaissance.* Leipzig: Meiner, 1933. 223 p.
558. *Das humanistische Gymnasium.* (Edited by Hermann Ostern and Hans Haas.) Six issues annually. Leipzig: Teubner, 1899-date.
559. IVEN, KURT. *Die Industriepädogogik des 18. Jahrhunderts.* Langensalza: Beltz, 1930. 128 p.
560. JAEGER, WERNER. *Paideia, die Formung des griechischen Menschen.* I, Von Homer bis Thukydides. Berlin, 1934. 513 p.
561. KAMMEL, J. *Geschichte des deutschen Schulwesens im Übergange vom Mittelalter zu Neuzeit.* 1882.
562. KANDEL, I. L. *Comparative Education.* Boston: Houghton Mifflin Co., 1933. 922 p.
563. KANDEL, I. L., editor. *Educational Yearbook of the International Institute, 1924-date.* New York: Teachers College, Columbia University, 1925-date. (Yearbooks for 1924-26 originally published by Macmillan Co.)
564. KANDEL, I. L. *History of Secondary Education.* Boston: Houghton Mifflin Co., 1930. 577 p.

565. KANDEL, I. L., and ALEXANDER, THOMAS, compilers and translators. *Reorganization of Education in Prussia, Based on Official Documents and Publications.* Studies of the International Institute, No. 4. New York: Teachers College, Columbia University. 1927. 647 p.
566. KANDEL, I. L. *The Training of Elementary School Teachers in Germany.* Contributions to Education, No. 31. New York: Teachers College, Columbia University, 1910. 137 p.
567. KEHR, C., and OTHERS. *Geschichte der Methodik des deutschen Volksschulunterrichtes.* 2d ed. Gotha, 1889. 6 vols.
568. KEILHACKER, M. "Altgermanische Erziehung." *Handbuch der Erziehungswissenschaft.* (Edited by F. X. Eggersdorfer and others.) Part V, Vol. I. 24 p.
569. KIELHAUSER, ERNST. *Geschichte des gewerblichen Bildungswesens im alten und neuen Österreich. Mit einer einleitenden Übersicht über die Geschichte der Pädagogik u. des österreichischen Schulwesens im allgemeinen.* Klagenfurt, 1931. 431 p.
570. *Die Klassiker der Pädagogik, eine Sammlung der hervorragendsten pädagogischen Werke älterer und neuerer Zeit.* (Edited by Fröhlich and Zimmer.) Langensalza: Gressler, 1887-date. About 40 vols.
571. KLUGE, OTTO. "Die griechischen Studien in Renaissance und Humanismus." *Zeitschrift für Geschichte der Erziehung und des Unterrichts* 24: 1-54; 1934.
572. KNAUTH, WOLFGANG. "Die spartanische Knabenerziehung im Lichte der Völkerkunde." *Zeitschrift für Geschichte der Erziehung und des Unterrichts* 23: 151-85; 1933.
573. KOSLER, A. M. *Die preussische Volksschulpolitik in Oberschlesien, 1742-1848.* Breslau, 1892. 386 p.
574. KRIECK, ERNST. *Bildungssysteme der Kulturvölker.* Leipzig: Quelle und Meyer, 1927. 387 p.
575. KRIECK, ERNST. "Geschichte der Bildung." *Handbuch der deutschen Lehrerbildung.* (Edited by Oskar Vogelhuber and others.) Vol. 1, Part 7. Leipzig, 1932. 81 p.
576. KRIEG, CORNELIUS. *Lehrbuch der Pädagogik.* 1. Teil: *Geschichte der Pädagogik,* Paderborn. 5. Aufl. 1923, bearb. von G. Grunwald.
577. KRUMBHOLZ, P. *Geschichte des Weimarischen Schulwesens.* Vol. 61 of *Monumenta.* Berlin: Weidmann, 1934. 290 p.
578. KUCKHOFF, JOSEPH. "Das Mädchenschulwesen in den Ländern am Rhein im 17. Jahrhundert." *Zeitschrift für Geschichte der Erziehung und des Unterrichts* 22: 1-60; 1923.
579. KYNAST, REINHARD. *Problemgeschichte der Pädagogik.* Berlin: Junder u. Dünnhaupt, 1932. 366 p.
580. LANGE, H. *Theorie und Praxis der Erziehungsstrafe im 18. Jahrhundert.* Osterwieck: Zickfeldt, 1932. 177 p.
581. LEHMANN, E. *Grundtvig.* Tübingen: Mohr, 1930. 280 p.
582. LEHMANN, R. "Prinzipien der Erziehungsgeschichte." *Die Geisteswissenschaften.* 1913. p. 89-117.
583. LESER, HERMANN. *Das pädagogische Problem in der Geistesgeschichte der Neuzeit.* Munich: Oldenbourg, 1925 and 1928. 2 vols.
584. LIEDLOFF, W. *Die Entwickelung des höheren Schulwesens in Thüringen von der marxistischen Revolution 1918 bis zur nationalsozialistischen Erhebung, 1933.* Borna: Noske, 1936. 182 p.
585. LIMMER, R. *Bildungszustände und Bildungsideen des 13. Jahrhunderts.* Munich, 1929. 263 p.
586. LOCHMÜLLER, R *Hans Schemm.* I, 1091-1919. Bayreuth: Deutscher volksverlag, 1935.
587. MAASSEN, J. *Drama und Theater der Humannistenschulen in Deutschland.* Augsburg, 1929. 130 p.
588. MCMURRY, RUTH E.; MÜLLER, MAX; and ALEXANDER, THOMAS. *Modern Foreign Languages in France and Germany; the Training of Teachers and Methods of Instruction.* Studies of the International Institute, No. 9. New York: Teachers College, Columbia University, 1930. 516 p.
589. MARX, HEINRICH. *Die Entstehung und die Anfänge der pädagogischen Presse im deutschen Sprachgebiet. Ein Beitrag zur Geschichtsschreibung des deutschen Erziehungswesens im 18. Jahrhundert.* Frankfurt: Diesterweg, 1929. 224 p.

590. MEDICUS, F. *Pestalozzis Leben.* Leipzig: Quelle und Meyer, 1927. 220 p.
591. MEISTER, R. *Über die Stellung der Erziehungs- und Schulgeschichte im System der Erziehungswissenschaft.* Österreichische Vierteljahrshefte für Erziehung Unterricht, Jahrgang 1931. p. 99-108.
592. MELLMANN, P. *Geschichte des deutschen Philologenverbandes.* Leipzig: Quelle und Meyer, 1929. 195 p.
593. MESSER, AUGUST. *Geschichte der Pädagogik.* I, *Altertum und Mittelalter;* II, *Beginn der Neuzeit bis Anfang des 18. Jahrhunderts;* III, *Anfang des 18. Jahrhunderts bis zur Gegenwart.* Breslau, 1925. 3 vols.
594. METZLER, JOHANNES. *Petrus Canisius als Erneuerer des Schul- und Erziehungswesens.* Düsseldorf, 1925.
595. MEYER, GERHARD. *Die Entwickelung der Strasburger Universität aus dem Gymnasium und der Akademie des Joh. Sturm.* Strassburg: Wiss. Institut für Elsass-Lothringen, 1926.
596. MEYER, J. F. *Reaktion und Volksschule. 30 Jahre preuss. Schulgeschichte, 1840-1870.* Leipzig, 1882. 188 p.
597. *Monumenta Germaniae Paedagogica. Schulordnungen, Schulbücher und pädagogische Miscellaneen aus den Landen deutscher Zunge.* (Edited by Karl Kehrbach.) Berlin: Weidmann, 1886-date. About 60 vols.
598. MOOG, WILLY. *Geschichte der Pädagogik.* Vol. 2, *Die Pädagogik der Neuzeit, von der Renaissance bis zum Ende des 17. Jahrhunderts;* Vol. 3, *Die Pädagogik der Neuzeit vom Ende des 17. Jahrhunderts bis zur Gegenwart.* Osterwieck: Zickfeldt, 1928-33; Vol. 2, 338 p.; Vol. 3, 540 p.
599. MÜLLER, C. *Grundriss der Geschichte des preussischen Volksschulwesens.* 6th ed. Osterwieck, 1914. 408 p. Supplementary volume: *Die preussische Volksschule im Volksstaate.* 1930. 200 p.
600. MÜLLER, G. *Die Kreuzschule in Dresden vom 13. Jahrhundert bis 1926.* Dresden: Ratsarchiv, 1926.
601. MURTFELD, O. *Der Weg der preussischen Lehrerschaft zum Dienst am Volke, 1805-1871.* Frankfurt: Diesterweg, 1934. 205 p.
602. NABAKOWSKY, J. *Die Pädagogik an der Universität Halle im 18. Jahrhundert.* Osterwieck: Zickfeldt, 1930. 76 p.
603. NETZER, J. *Das pädagogische Problem der Überparteilichkeit.* Langensalza: Beltz, 1933. 106 p.
604. *Neudrucke pädagogischer Schriften.* (Edited by Albert Richter.) Leipzig: Brandstetter, 1890-date. About 20 vols.
605. *Neue Jahrbücher (formerly Jahrbücher) für Wissenschaft und Jugendbildung.* (Edited by Ernst Wilmans.) Six issues annually. Leipzig: Teubner, 1924-date.
606. NEUENDORFF, E. *Geschichte der neueren deutschen Leibesübungen vom 18. Jahrhundert bis zur Gegenwart.* Dresden: Limpert, 1930-32. 3 vols.
607. NEUMANN, F. *Der Hofmeister. Ein Beitrag zur Geschichte der Erziehung im 18. Jahrhundert.* Osterwieck: 1930. 111 p.
608. NOHL, H. *Die pädagogische Bewegung in Deutschland und ihre Theorie.* Frankfurt: Schulte-Bulmke, 1935. 300 p.
609. NOHL, H., and PALLAT, L., editors. *Handbuch der Pädagogik.* Langensalza, 1933. 5 vols. (Vol. 1, Part 2, p. 81-464, contains *Die Geschichte der Bildung und ihrer Theorie* by various authors.)
610. *Pädagogische Bibliothek, eine Sammlung der wichtigsten pädagogischen Schriften älterer und neuerer Zeit.* (Edited by Karl Richter.) Leipzig: Siegesmund und Volkening, 1870-date. About 25 vols.
611. *Pädagogische Klassiker. Auswahl der besten pädagogischen Schriftsteller aller Zeiten und Völker.* (Edited by G. A. Lindner.) Wien: Pichler, 1877-date. About 20 vols.
612. PAULS, TH. *Erziehung und Unterricht in Luthers Theologie. Eine quellenmassige Studie als Beitrag zu einer lutherischen Grundlegung des Erziehungswerkes.* Berlin: Furche-Verlag, 1935. 134 p.
613. PAULSEN, FRIEDRICH. *Geschichte des gelehrten Unterrichtes auf den deutschen Schulen und Universitäten, vom ausgang des Mittelalters bis zur Gegenwart. Mit besonderer Rücksicht auf den klassischen Unterricht.* 3d ed. (by R. Lehmann). Leipzig: Veit and Co., 1919-21. 2 vols. (First edition, 1885.)
614. Pestalozzianum, und Zentralbibliothek, Zürich. *Pestalozzi und seine Zeit im Bilde.* Zürich, 1928. 83 p. 165 plates.

615. *Pestalozzis sämtliche Werke.* (Edited by A. Buchenau, E. Spranger, and H. Stettbacher.) Bd. 1-5, 8-11, 13, 16. Berlin, 1927-date.
616. POKRANDT, ALFRED. "Vaterland, Volk und Volkstum in der Pädagogik der preussischen Reformzeit." *Zeitschrift für Geschichte der Erziehung und des Unterrichts* 24: 81-100; 1934.
617. POLITSCH, G., and SCHWARZ, F. H. CH. *Der Begründer der pädagogischen Geschichtschreibung ein Beitrag zur Historiographie der Pädagogik im Zeitalter der Romantik.* Unpublished doctor's thesis, Giessen University, 1929.
618. PRETZEL, C. L. A. *Geschichte des deutschen Lehrervereins in den ersten fünfzig Jahren seines Bestehens. (Unter Benutzung von Robert Rissmanns "Geschichte des deutschen Lehrervereins,"* published in 1907). Leipzig: Klinkhardt, 1921. 375 p.
619. PRETZEL, U. "Pestalozzi und Snethlage." *Zeitschrift für Geschichte der Erziehung und des Unterrichts* 24: 100-52; 1935.
620. RAUHUT, K. *Die pädagogischen Theorien der französischen Revolution.* Halle: Akad. Verlag, 1934. 109 p.
621. RAUMER, KARL VON. *Geschichte der Pädagogik vom Wiederaufblühen klassischer Studien bis auf unsere Zeit.* Stuttgart, 1842-52. 4 vols. (Seventh edition, 1902.)
622. REDEKER, M. *Humanität, Volkstum und Christentum in der Erziehung. Ihr Wesen und gegenseitiges Verhältnis, an der Gedankenwelt des jungen Herder für die Gegenwart dargestellt.* Berlin: Junker und Dünnhaupt, 1934. 207 p.
623. RETHWISCH, C. *Deutschlands höheres Schulwesen im 19 Jahrhundert.* Leipzig, 1913.
624. RIEDEL, K. "Pädagogik als Wertwissenschaft. Ein Beitrag zur Geschichte der Bildungswissenschaft im 20. Jahrhundert." *Die Deutsche Schule.* No. 11, p. 505-12, and No. 12, p. 551-61.
625. RINKE, A. *Friedrich Fröbels philosophische Entwickelung unter dem Einfluss der Romantik.* Langensalza: Beyer und Söhne, 1935. 136 p.
626. ROSIN, H. *A. Falk, Der Erneuerer der preussischen Volksschule.* Magdeburg, 1927. 197 p.
627. RÜDIGER, H. "W. V. Humboldts Bildungsidee." *Neue Jahrbücher für Wissenschaft und Jugendbildung* 11: 193-214; 1935.
628. RUSSELL, JAMES E. *German Higher Schools.* New York: Longmans, Green and Co., 1913. 455 p.
629. *Sammlung der bedeutendsten pädagogischen Schriften aus alter und neuer Zeit.* (Edited by I. Gansen and others.) Paderborn, 1888-date. About 50 vols.
630. *Sammlung selten gewordener pädagogischer Schriften Früherer Zeiten.* (Edited by A. Israel and Joh. Müller.) Zschoupau i. Sa., 1879-date. About 15 vols.
631. SAUPE, E. *Deutsche Pädagogen der Neuzeit.* 8th ed. Osterwieck, 1929. 412 p.
632. SCHEMM, H., and OTHERS. *Deutsche Schule und deutsche Erziehung in Vergangenheit, Gegenwart und Zukunft.* Stuttgart: Pädag. Verlagsanstalt, 1934. 512 p.
633. SCHILLER, H. *Lehrbuch der Geschichte der Pädagogik.* 3d ed., 1894.
634. SCHMID, K. A. *Geschichte der Erziehung vom Anfang bis auf unsere Zeit.* 1884-1902. 10 parts in 5 vols.
635. SCHMIDHAUSER, JULIUS. *Der Kampf um das geistige Reich. Bau und Schicksal der Universität.* Hamburg, 1933. 390 p.
636. SCHMIDT, K. *Geschichte der Pädagogik, dargestellt in weltgeschichtlicher Entwickelung und im organischen Zusammenhange mit dem Kulturleben.* Cöthen, 1860-62. 4 vols. (4th edition, 1890, prepared by Dittes and Hannak.)
637. SCHNEIDER, P. *Kulturgeschichte und Bildungsgeschichte. Beitrag zur Strukturtheorie des historischen Gegenstandes.* Langensalza: Beyer und Söhne, 1930. 79 p.
638. SCHNEIDER, P. *Das Problem der Erziehungswissenschaft in der Kulturphilosophie der Gegenwart.* Leipzig, 1930. 168 p.
639. SCHÖNEBAUM, H. "Geschichte der Bildung und des Bildungswesens (a bibliography)." *Archiv für Kulturgeschichte* 22: 129-57.
640. SCHÖNEBAUM, H. *Der junge Pestalozzi, 1746-1782.* Leipzig: Reisland, 1927. 234 p.
641. *Schroedels Pädagogische Klassiker.* (Edited by E. Friedrich and H. Gehrig.) Halle, Schroedel, 1892-date. About 30 vols.
642. SCHRÖTELER, J. "Die internationalen Bildungsbestrebungen von 1900-1930." *Handbuch der Erziehungswissenschaft.* (Edited by F. X. Eggersdorfer and others.) Part V, Vol. 3 (Part 2). 46 p.
643. SCHRÖTELER, J. *Katholische Pädagogen. Beiträge zur Geschichte der Pädagogik.* 1929.

644. SCHRÖTELER, J., and OTHERS. "Die Pädagogik der Gegenwart in den grossen Kulturländern." *Handbuch der Erziehungswissenschaft.* (Edited by F. X. Eggersdorfer and others.) Part V, Vol. 3, Part 1, 282 p.; Part 2, 348 p.
645. SCHULZ, B. "Zur Geschichte der deutschen Schulgemeinden." *Die Erziehung* 1: 535 ff.; 1926.
646. SEELHOF, P. *Schule und Nation. Kulturgeschichte der deutschen Lehrers, mit einem Abriss der national-politischen Erziehung im neuen deutschen Reiche.* Dortmund: Nationalverlag Westfalia, 1934. 393 p.
647. SEILER, K. *Das pädagogische System Wolfgang Ratkes. Nach den handschriftlichen Quellen im Zusammenhange der europäischen Geistesgeschichte dargestellt.* Erlangen: Palm und Enke, 1931. 75 p.
648. SELLMAYR, JOSEPH. *Die Pädagogik des Jansenismus.* Donauwörth: Auer, 1932. 222 p.
649. SILBER, KATHE. *Anna Pestalozzi-Schulthess und der Frauenkreis um Pestalozzi.* Berlin: de Gruyter, 1932. 162 p.
650. SPRANGER, EDUARD. "Das deutsche Bildungsideal in geschichtlich-philosophischer Beleuchtung." *Die Erziehung* 1: 178-90, 473-92; 1926.
651. SPRANGER, EDUARD. *Der Sinn der Voraussetzungslosigkeit in den Geisteswissenschaften.* Berlin, 1929.
652. SPRANGER, EDUARD. *Volk, Staat, Erziehung.* Leipzig: Quelle und Meyer, 1932.
653. SPRANGER, EDUARD. *W. v. Humboldt und die Humanitätsidee.* 2d ed. Berlin, 1928. 506 p.
654. STAHL, E. L. *Die religiöse und die humanitäts-philosophische Bildungsidee und die Entstehung des deutschen Bildungsromans im 18. Jahrhundert.* Bern: Haupt, 1934. 175 p.
655. STARK, G. "Die Staatspädagogik der Griechen und Römer." *Deutsches Bildungswesen* 2: 330-38; 1934.
656. STEIN, L. v. *Das Bildungswesen.* Stuttgart, 1883-date. 3 vols.
657. STOECKERT, H. *Der Wandel der Bildungsidee von Plato bis in die neuzeitliche Schulreform.* Leipzig: Quelle und Meyer, 1928. 284 p.
658. STURM, K. F. *Von der pädagogischen Reformbewegung zur völkischen und politischen Erziehung.* 2d ed. Osterwieck-Harz: Zickfeldt, 1934. 212 p.
659. THALHOFER, H. *Unterricht und Bildung im Mittelalter.* Munich, 1928. 183 p.
660. THIELE, G. "Art und Umfang der Geschichtsschreibung der Erziehung." *Zeitschrift für Geschichte der Erziehung und des Unterrichts* 22: 110-24; 1932.
661. TRUNZ, ERICH. "Der deutsche Späthumanismus um 1600 als Standeskultur." *Zeitschrift für Geschichte der Erziehung und des Unterrichts* 21: 17-53; 1931.
662. VASCONCELLOS, M. MICHAELIS DE. *Nationalerziehung und Staatswille. Die Erziehungsidee in der preussischen Politik nach 1806.* Berlin: Junker und Dünnhaupt, 1934. 102 p.
663. VILSMEYER, F. *Die Wandlungen des Begriffs des Gesamtunterrichtes.* Langensalza: Beyer und Söhne, 1934. 91 p.
664. *Volk im Werden.* (Edited by Ernst Krieck.) Six issues annually. Frankfurt: Diesterweg, 1933-date.
665. WAAG, H. *Deutsche Lehrerschaft und deutsche Kirche im 19. Jahrhundert.* Leipzig: Meiner, 1928. 150 p.
666. WALLNER, NICO. "Bericht über die deutschen pädagogischen Schriften von 1926-1930." *Archiv für die Geschichte der Philosophie* 41: 250-81.
667. WEHRMANN, M. "Einiges zur Methode und zu den Aufgaben der schulgeschichtlichen Forschung." *Mitteilungen der Gesellschaft für deutsche Erziehungs- u. Schulgeschichte* (older form of *Zeitschrift für Geschichte der Erziehung und des Unterrichts*) 17: 1-17; 1907.
668. WEIMER, HERMANN. *Geschichte der Pädagogik.* 5th ed. Berlin. 1921. (Sammlung Göschen.)
669. WEISE, M. *Paul Östreich und die "Entschiedene Schulreform."* Leipzig: Dürr'sche Buchhandlung, 1928. 119 p.
670. WENKE, H. "Die pädagogische Lage in Deutschland." Summarizes reviews of current developments; published about six times annually in *Die Erziehung*, since 1933.
671. WERNECKE, F. *Pestalozzi und die Physiokraten.* Langensalza: Beyer und Söhne, 1927. 116 p.
672. WETZEL, E. *Geschichte des Königlichen Joachimthalschen Gymnasiums in Berlin, 1607-1907.* Halle, 1907. 417 p.

673. WICKERT, R. *Geshichte der Pädagogik.* Leipzig, 1916. 240 p.
674. WILLMANN, OTTO. *Didaktik als Bildungslehre.* Braunschweig, 1882. 2 vols. (Fourth edition, 1910.)
675. WINKELMANN, ELISABETH. "Schiller und Fichte." *Zeitschrift für Geschichte der Erziehung und des Unterrichts* 24: 177-248; 1934.
676. WINKLER, M. TH. *Maria Ward und das Institut der Englischen Fräulein in Bayern. Ein Beitrag zur Geschichte der Madchenbildung.* Munich, 1926. 203 p.
677. WITTENBERG, E. *Irrwege der marxistischen Bildungslehre. Kulturkritische Darstellung ihrer Grundlage.* Berlin: Puttkammer und Mühlbrecht, 1934. 306 p.
678. WOLFF, A. "Über Sinn und Wert der Erziehungsgeschichte." *Deutsche Schule* 33: 1-10, 65-73; 1929.
679. WÜLLENWEBER, FRITZ. *Altgermanische Erziehung dargestellt auf Grund der Islandsage und anderer Quellen.* Hamburg: Hanseatischer Verlag, 1935. 174 p.
680. WYCHGRAM, J. *Geschichte des höheren Mädchenschulwesens in Deutschland.* 1901.
681. ZANDER, A. *Leben und Erziehung in Pestalozzis Institut zu Iferten.* Aarau, 1932. 213 p.
682. *Zeitschrift für Geschichte der Erziehung und des Unterrichts.* (Edited by N. Wallner.) Quarterly. Berlin: Weidmann, about 1910-date. (Formerly *Mitteilungen der Gesellschaft für deutsche Erziehungsund Schulgeschichte.*)
683. ZIEGLER, THEOBALD. *Geschichte der Pädagogik mit besonderer Rücksicht auf das höhere Unterrichtswesen.* Munich, 1894. 320 p. (Fifth edition, 1923.)

D. HISTORY OF EDUCATION IN ITALY

684. ALIOTA, A. *Compendio di Storia della Pedagogia.* Naples, 1926.
685. ANGELI, A. *Storia delle Scuole Elementare e Populari d'Italia.* Florence, 1908.
686. ARRIGHI, G. I. *Storia della Scuola e delle Dottrina Pedagogica.* Milan, 1920.
687. BARBAGELLO, C. *Lo Stato e l'Istruzione pubblica nell'Impero Romano.* Catania, 1911.
688. BENVICENNI, I. *Storia dell'Educazione e della Pedagogia.* Livorno, 1923.
689. BETTACCHI, P. *Storia della Pedagogia.* Rome, 1930.
690. CASTAGNOLA, G. S. *Storia della Pedagogia Italiana Moderna.* Rome, 1918.
691. CODIGNOLA, ERNESTO. "Italy." *Educational Yearbook of the International Institute, 1930.* New York: Teachers College, Columbia University, 1930. p. 343-86.
692. CODIGNOLA, ERNESTO. "Italy." *Educational Yearbook of the International Institute, 1932.* New York: Teachers College, Columbia University, 1933. p. 295-314.
693. CODIGNOLA, ERNESTO. "Italy." *Educational Yearbook of the International Institute, 1935.* New York: Teachers College, Columbia University, 1935. p. 351-67.
694. CODIGNOLA, ERNESTO. "The Philosophy Underlying the National System of Education in Italy." *Educational Yearbook of the International Institute, 1929.* New York: Teachers College, Columbia University, 1930. p. 317-425.
695. CODIGNOLA, ERNESTO. *Il Problema Educativo. Breve Compendio de Storia dell'Educazione e della Pedagogia.* Vol. I, *Età Classica, Cristianesimo Medioevo*; Vol. II, *Dalla Crisi della Scolastica a Rousseau.* Florence: "La Nuova Italia" Editrice, 1936. 2 vols.
696. DOMENICIS, S. DE. *Linee di Pedagogia Elementare per le Scuole Normale e I Maestri.* Part 3, *Storia della Scuola e delle Instruzioni educativa. Cenni su l'odierna Legislazione comparata della Scuola Popolare. Antologia Storia della Pedagogia.* Milan, 1922.
697. *Enciclopedia delle Enciclopedie.* Volume entitled *Pedagogia.* Rome, n. d.
698. FERRERO, M. *Piccolo Dizionario di Pedagogia didattica e Storia della Pedagogia.* Milan, 1923.
699. FORMIGGINI-SANTAMARIA, E. *L'Istruzione Popolare nello Stato Pontifico, 1824-1870.* Modena, 1919.
700. FORMIGGINI-SANTAMARIA, E. *L'Istruzione Pubblica nel Ducato Estense.* Genoa, 1912.
701. FORMIGGINI-SANTAMARIA, E. *La Pedagogia Italiana nella Secunda Meta del Secolo XIX.* Rome, 1920.
702. GERINI, G. B. *Scrittori pedagogici Italiani del Secolo XIX.* Turin, 1900.
703. LOMBARDO-RADICE, GIUSEPPE. *Nursery Schools in Italy; the Problem of Infant Education.* (Translated by M. C. Glasgow.) London: Allen and Unwin, 1934. 196 p.

704. MALVEZZI DE'MEDICI, A. "Native Education in the Italian Colonies." *Educational Yearbook of the International Institute, 1931*. New York: Teachers College, Columbia University, 1932. p. 645-77.
705. MANTELLINO, G. *La Scuola Primaria e Secundaria in Piemonte*. Carmagnola, 1909.
706. MONROE, PAUL, and CODIGNOLA, ERNESTO. *Breve Corso di Storia dell'Educazione*. Florence: Valecchi, 1924. 2 vols. (Contains a translation of Monroe's *Brief Course in the History of Education* with the addition of two chapters on the history of education in Italy since the eighteenth century.)
707. MORGANA, A. *Storia della Pedagogia*. Milan, 1912.
708. NERETTI, L. *Storia della Pedagogia esposta in Forma di Sunti*. Milan, 1921.
709. PANNESE, G. *Storia della Ginnastica moderna negli Stati d'Europa in Rapporto con la Pedagogia scientifica*. Milan, 1912.
710. PIETROSI, E. *Piccolo Storia della Pedagogia*. Milan: Atyeno, 1928. 2 vols.
711. ROMANO, P. *Storia dell'Educazione fisica in Relazione coll'Educazione generale*. Turin, 1923-25.
712. SPIRITO, UGO. *Educational Yearbook of the International Institute, 1924*. New York: Macmillan Co., 1925. p. 329-52.
713. SUGLIA, G. *Brevi Cenni di Storia della Pedagogia moderna e contemporanea*. Lanciano, 1930.
714. TAROZZI, G. *L'Educazione e la Scuola. Cenni integrativi di Pedagogia Storia*. Bologna, 1921.
715. VALLETTI, F. *Storia della Ginnastica*. Milan, 1914.
716. VOLENTE, P. *La Scuola popolare nella Rivoluzione francese*. Turin, 1910.
717. ZAZO, A. *L'Istruzione Pubblica e Privata nel Napoletano*. Città di Castello, 1927.

E. HISTORY OF EDUCATION IN THE SCANDINAVIAN COUNTRIES

718. ABEL, JAMES F. *The Effects of the Economic Depression on Education in Other Countries*. U. S. Dept. of the Interior, Office of Education, Bulletin, 1933, No. 14. Washington, D. C.: Government Printing Office, 1933. 37 p.
719. ABEL, JAMES F. *National Ministries of Education*. U. S. Dept. of the Interior, Office of Education, Bulletin, 1930, No. 12. Washington, D. C.: Government Printing Office, 1930. 158 p.
720. HEDLEY, GERALD W., and MURRAY, GERALD W. *A Report on the Present Condition of Physical Education in Denmark and Sweden*. Great Britain Board of Education, Educational Pamphlets, No. 104. London: H. M. Stationery Office, 1935. 52 p.
721. INTERNATIONAL BUREAU OF EDUCATION. *L'Organisation de l'Instruction Publique dans 53 Pays*. Genève: the Bureau, 1932. 374 p.
722. PALUDAN, JULIUS. *Det Höiere Skolevaesen i Danmark, Norge og Sverig. En sammenlignende historisk Fremstilling, udarbeidet efter Opfordring af Bestyrelsen for det Letterstedtske Fond*. (The higher or secondary educational system of Denmark, Norway, and Sweden. A comparative historical presentation prepared at the request of the board of directors of the Letterstedt Fund.) Köbenhavn: Wilhelm Priors Hof-Boghandel, 1885. 809 p.
723. PEARCON, PETER H. *Schools of Scandinavia, Finland, and Holland*. U. S. Dept. of the Interior, Bureau of Education, Bulletin, 1919, No. 29. Washington, D. C.: Government Printing Office, 1919. 71 p.
724. PERCY, LORD EUSTACE, editor. *The Year Book of Education, 1936*. London: Evans Brothers, 1936. 1023 p.
725. THORNTON, JOSEPH SMITH. "Schools, Public and Private, in the North of Europe." *Special Reports on Educational Subjects*. Vol. 17. London: Printed for H. M. Stationery Office by Wyman and Sons, 1907. p. 36-65.
726. TUROSIENSKI, SEVERIN K. *Foreign and Comparative Education*. U. S. Dept. of the Interior, Office of Education, Bulletin, 1934, No. 10. Washington: Government Printing Office, 1934. 59 p.

Denmark

727. ARNETT, L. D., and SMITH, ANNA TOLMAN. "Education in Denmark." *A Cyclopedia of Education*. (Edited by Paul Monroe.) New York: Macmillan Co., 1911. Vol. 2, p. 295-302.
728. BEGTRUP, HOLGER; LUND, HANS; and MANNICHE, PETER. *The Folk High Schools of Denmark and the Development of a Farming Community*. Copenhagen: Nyt Nordisk Forlag, Arnold Busck, 1926. 168 p.

729. BJORNEBOE, OTTO. "Denmark." *Educational Yearbook of the International Institute, 1927.* New York: Teachers College, Columbia University, 1928. p. 49-64.
730. BOJE, ANDREAS, and OTHERS. *Education in Denmark.* Copenhagen: John Martin, 1932. 291 p.
731. CABOT, STEPHEN P. "The Folk High Schools of Denmark." *Secondary Education in Germany, France, England and Denmark.* Harvard Bulletins in Education, No. 15. Cambridge, Mass.: Harvard University Press, 1930. Part 4, p. 85-104.
732. CAMPBELL, OLIVE DAME. *The Danish Folk School; Its Influence in the Life of Denmark and the North.* New York: Macmillan Co., 1928. 359 p.
733. DAVIES, NOELLE. *Education for Life; a Danish Pioneer.* London: Williams and Norgate, 1931. 207 p.
734. DE GIBON, M. JEAN. "Aperçu Général sur l'Agriculture Danoise." *Annales de l'Institut National Agronomique.* Paris: J.-B. Baillière et Fils, 1928. p. 48-209.
735. FOGHT, HAROLD W. *Danish Elementary Rural Schools: With Some Reference to Seminaries for the Training of Rural Teachers.* U. S. Dept. of the Interior, Bureau of Education, Bulletin, 1914, No. 24. Washington, D. C.: Government Printing Office, 1914. 45 p.
736. FOGHT, HAROLD W. *The Danish Folk High Schools.* U. S. Dept. of the Interior, Bureau of Education, Bulletin, 1914, No. 22. Washington, D. C.: Government Printing Office, 1914. 93 p.
737. FOGHT, HAROLD W. "Education in Denmark." *Comparative Education; Studies of the Educational Systems of Six Modern Nations.* (Edited by Peter Sandiford.) New York: E. P. Dutton and Co., 1918. Chapter 6, p. 439-95.
738. FOGHT, HAROLD W. *The Educational System of Rural Denmark.* U. S. Dept. of the Interior, Bureau of Education, Bulletin, 1913, No. 58. Washington, D. C.: Government Printing Office, 1914. 46 p.
739. FORCHHAMMER, HENNI. "Moral Instruction and Training in Denmark." *Moral Instruction and Training in Schools.* (Edited by M. E. Sadler.) London: Longmans, Green and Co., 1908. Vol. 2, p. 137-79.
740. FORCHHAMMER, HENNI. "The Teaching of Domestic Science in Denmark." *Special Reports on Educational Subjects.* Vol. 16. London: Printed for H. M. Stationery Office by Wyman and Sons, 1906. p. 243-60.
741. FRENCH, FRANCES GRAHAM. "Educational System of Denmark." *Report of the Commissioner of Education for the Year 1889-90.* Washington, D. C.: Government Printing Office, 1893. Vol. I, p. 519-48.
742. FRIEND, L. L. *The Folk High Schools of Denmark.* U. S. Dept. of the Interior, Bureau of Education, Bulletin, 1914, No. 5. Washington, D. C.: Government Printing Office, 1914. 24 p.
743. HART, JOSEPH KINMONT. *Light from the North; the Danish Folk High Schools, Their Meanings for America.* New York: Henry Holt and Co., 1927. 159 p.
744. HEGLAND, MARTIN. *The Danish People's High School, Including a General Account of the Educational System of Denmark.* U. S. Dept. of the Interior, Bureau of Education, Bulletin, 1915, No. 45. Washington, D. C.: Government Printing Office, 1915. 182 p.
745. HERTEL, NIELS THEODORE AXEL. *Overpressure in High Schools in Denmark.* (Translated from the Danish by C. Godfrey Sörenson.) London: Macmillan and Co., 1885. 148 p.
746. HOLLMANN, A. H. *Die Dänische Volkshochschule und ihre Bedeutung für die Entwicklung einer völkischen Kultur in Dänemark.* (The Danish folk high school and its significance in the development of general culture in Denmark.) Berlin: Verlagsbuchhandlung Paul Parey, 1909. 130 p.
747. KNIGHT, EDGAR W. *Among the Danes.* Chapel Hill: University of North Carolina Press, 1927. 236 p.
748. LARSEN, JOAKIM. *Bidrag til den Danske Folkeskoles Historie, 1784-1898.* (Contributions to the history of the Danish elementary school, 1784-1898.) Köbenhavn: Forlagt af V. Thaning & Appel, 1893-99. Part I, 322 p.; Part II, 524 p.
749. LARSEN, JOAKIM. *Den Danske Folkeskoles Historie.* (History of the Danish elementary school.) Köbenhavn: A/S J. H. Schultz Forlagsboghandel, 1918. 141 p.
750. LINDEGREN, ALINA M. *Institutions of Higher Education in Denmark.* U. S. Dept. of the Interior, Office of Education, Bulletin, 1934, No. 13. Washington, D. C.: Government Printing Office, 1934. 126 p.

751. MARAIS, J. I. *Bishop Grundtvig and the People's High School in Denmark.* Report Furnished at the Instance of the Colonial Secretary of the late Cape Colony, and Published at the Instance of the Minister of Education of the Union of South Africa. Pretoria: Government Printing and Stationery Office, 1911. 38 p.
752. NIELSEN, JULIUS. "The Danish School System." *Danish Foreign Office Journal,* No. 175. Copenhagen: Danish Publishing Office, August, 1935. p. 107-13.
753. NIELSEN, JULIUS. "Denmark." *Educational Yearbook of the International Institute, 1935.* New York: Teachers College, Columbia University, 1935. p. 133-53.
754. NIELSEN, L. C. *En Dansk Höjskolemand. Breve og Foredrag af Forstande Chr. Nielsen.* Til Minde om Ham og Hindholm. Udgevne af L. C. Nielsen med en Biografi ved Höjskoleforstander H. Villumsen. (A Danish folk high school man. Letters and lectures by Chr. Nielsen. In memory of him and Hindholm. Edited by L. C. Nielsen with a biography by Folk High School Principal H. Villumsen.) Köbenhavn: Gyldendalske Boghandels Forlag, 1900. 225 p.
755. NOE-NYGARD. *Vinterskoleliv i Vestjylland.* (Winter school life in West Jutland.) Köbenhavn: Gyldendalske Boghandel-Nordisk Forlag, 1921. 221 p.
756. RASMUSSEN, S. (Koldt). *Hojskole Haandbogen.* (High school handbook.) Aarhus: Jydisk Forlags-Forretning, 1896. 85 p.
757. ROST, F. E. B. "Education in Denmark." *The Year Book of Education, 1933.* London: Evans Brothers, 1933. p. 801-21.
758. SCHRÖDER, LUDVIG. *Den Nordiske Folkehöjskole: Bidrag til dens historie.* (The Nordic folk high school. A contribution to its history.) Köbenhavn: G. E. C. Gad, 1905. 487 p.
759. SKIBSTED, H. V. *Almueskolevaesenet i de Danske Kjöbstaeder og Landdistricter.* (The public school system in the town and country districts of Denmark.) Köbenhavn: Forlagt af den Gyldendalske Boghandel, 1876. 419 p.
760. THOMASSEN, FREDERICK. *Fortegnelse over Dansk Paedagogisk Literatur.* Udgivet af Dansk Skolemuseum (A bibliography of Danish pedagogical literature. Prepared by the Danish School Museum.) Köbenhavn: N. C. Roms Bog- og Stentrykkeri, 1896. 130 p.
761. THORNTON, JOSEPH SMITH. "Recent Educational Progress in Denmark." *Special Reports on Educational Subjects.* Vol. 1. London: Printed for H. M. Stationery Office by Eyre and Spottiswoode, 1897. p. 587-614.
762. VIBÄK, MARIUS. "The Danish System of Commercial Education." *International Review for Commercial Education.* 2d Series, No. 8, p. 521-30. June, 1930. Zurich.
763. WEIS, ANDREAS PETER. *De Gaeldende Retsregler for det Höjere Skolevaesen i Danmark.* En systematisk og kronologisk Haandbog. Udgivet med understöttelse af Ministeriet for Kirke og Undervisningsvaesenet. (Legal regulations concerning secondary education in Denmark. A systematic and chronological handbook. Prepared at the instance of the Ministry of Education.) Köbenhavn: Graebes Bogtrykkeri, 1891. 368 p.

Norway

764. ANDERSON, DAVID ALLEN. *The School System of Norway.* Boston: Gorham Press, 1913. 232 p.
765. ANDERSSEN, OTTO. "Moral Instruction and Training in Norway." *Moral Instruction and Training in Schools.* (Edited by M. E. Sadler.) London: Longmans, Green and Co., 1908. Vol. 2, p. 180-95.
766. ANDERSSEN, OTTO. "The New Law for the Secondary Schools in Norway." *Special Reports on Educational Subjects.* Vol. 8. London: Printed for H. M. Stationery Office by Wyman and Sons, 1902. p. 1-68.
767. ANDERSSEN, OTTO. *Norges Höiere Skolevaesen 1814-1914.* En oversigt. Kirke- og Undervisningsdepartementets Jubileumsskrifter 1914. (Secondary education in Norway, 1814-1914. A survey. Jubilee publication 1914, of the Department of Church and Education.) Kristiania: J. M. Stenersens Forlag, 1914. 72 p.
768. ARENT, EMMA. *The Relation of the State to Private Education in Norway.* Contributions to Education, No. 235. New York: Teachers College, Columbia University, 1926. 94 p.
769. ASKELAND, O.; SETHNE, ANNA; and KOPPANG, K. "Norway." *Educational Yearbook of the International Institute, 1935.* New York: Teachers College, Columbia University, 1935. p. 383-403.

770. BJANES, O. T. "Agricultural Education in Norway." Reprint from *International Review of the Science and Practice of Agriculture*, Vol. 1, No. 1, January-March, 1923. Rome: International Institute of Agriculture, 1923. 12 p.
771. FERAGEN, A. M. *Tilbagesyn paa mit Liv med en Blik paa Folkeskolen för og nu.* Tillaegshefte til Norsk Skoletidende. (An autobiography with a comparison of the elementary school of the past with that of the present.) Hamar: Norsk Skoletidendes Bogtrykkeri, 1904. 122 p.
772. FRENCH, FRANCES GRAHAM. "Education in Norway." *Report of the Commissioner of Education for the Year 1896-97.* Washington, D. C.: Government Printing Office, 1898. Vol. 1, p. 103-23.
773. FRENCH, FRANCES GRAHAM. "The Educational System of Norway." *Report of the Commissioner of Education for the Year 1889-90.* Washington, D. C.: Government Printing Office, 1893. Vol. 1, p. 475-517.
774. GADE, GERHARD. *Report on the Educational System of Norway.* U. S. Dept. of the Interior, Bureau of Education, Circular of Information, July, 1871. Washington, D. C.: Government Printing Office, 1871. p. 29-47.
775. HEILBERG, J. V. "Education in Norway in the Year 1900." *Special Reports on Educational Subjects.* Vol. 8. London: Printed for H. M. Stationery Office by Wyman and Sons, 1902. p. 69-92.
776. HELGESEN, HELGA. "The Teaching of Domestic Economy in Norway." *Special Reports on Educational Subjects.* Vol. 16. London: Printed for H. M. Stationery Office by Wyman and Sons, 1906. p. 211-36.
777. JENSEN, ARNE SIGURD. *The Rural Schools of Norway.* Boston: Stratford Co., 1928. 280 p.
778. KNAP, CARL. "Education in Norway." *The Year Book of Education, 1935.* London: Evans Brothers, 1935. p. 876-97.
779. LINDEGREN, ALINA M. *Institutions of Higher Education in Norway.* U. S. Dept. of the Interior, Office of Education, Bulletin, 1934, No. 2. Washington, D. C.: Government Printing Office, 1934. 96 p.
780. LOFTFIELD, GABRIEL E. *Secondary Education in Norway.* U. S. Dept. of the Interior, Office of Education, Bulletin, 1930, No. 17. Washington, D. C.: Government Printing Office, 1930. 112 p.
781. SIGMUND, EINAR. "Norway." *Educational Yearbook of the International Institute, 1924.* New York: Macmillan Co., 1925. p. 353-83.
782. SMITH, ANNA TOLMAN. "Education in Norway." *A Cyclopedia of Education.* (Edited by Paul Monroe.) New York: Macmillan Co., 1913. Vol. 4, p. 496-504.
783. VOSS, P. *Kampen om Skolen i det Nittende Aarhundrede paa Norsk Grund.* Köbenhavn: Det Nordiske Forlag, Bogforlaget Ernst Bojesen, 1899. 94 p.

Sweden

784. ADAMS-RAY, EDWARD, and HIERTA-RETZIUS, A. "The Teaching of Domestic Economy in Sweden." *Special Reports on Educational Subjects.* Vol. 16. London: Printed for H. M. Stationery Office by Wyman and Sons, 1906. p. 151-210.
785. ANDREWS, C. C. *Report on the Educational System of Sweden.* U. S. Dept. of the Interior, Bureau of Education, Circular of Information, July, 1871. Washington, D. C.: Government Printing Office, 1871. p. 1-28.
786. BERGNAM, C. G. *Das Schwedische Unterrichtswesen.* Kurze übersicht für die Kunst- und Industrieausstellung in Stockholm, 1897. Ins Deutsch übertragen von Dr. Gust Elmquist. (The Swedish educational system. Survey for the Art and Industrial Exposition at Stockholm in 1897. Translated into German by Dr. Gust Elmquist.) Stockholm. Tidningsaktiebolaget Vårt Lands Trycheri, 1897. 170 p.
787. BERGQVIST, B. J:SON. *Sveriges Ungdomsskolor.* Till allmänhetens Kännedom Jämlikt K. Maj:ts beslut och på uppdrag av chefen för K. ecklesiastikdepartementet. (Sweden's schools for youth. For the information of the public in accordance with royal decree and at the instance of the chief of the Royal Ecclesiastical Department.) Kungl. Boktrycheriet, P. A. Nordstedt & Söner, 1931. 159 p.
788. BERGQVIST, B. J. "Sweden." *Educational Yearbook of the International Institute, 1926.* New York: Macmillan Co., 1927. p. 349-84.
789. BERGQVIST, B. J. "Sweden." *Educational Yearbook of the International Institute, 1930.* New York: Teachers College, Columbia University, 1931. p. 483-507.

790. BOGOSLOVSKY, CHRISTINA STAËL VON HOLSTEIN. *The Educational Crisis in Sweden in the Light of American Experience.* New York: Columbia University Press, 1932. 301 p.
791. BORGESON, FRITHIOF CARL. *The Administration of Elementary and Secondary Education in Sweden.* Contributions to Education, No. 278. New York: Teachers College, Columbia University, 1927. 231 p.
792. COLES, P. B. "Education in Sweden." *The Year Book of Education, 1932.* London: Evans Brothers, 1932. p. 903-16.
793. COLES, P. B. *Recent Educational Developments in Sweden.* Great Britain Board of Education Educational Pamphlets, No. 81. London: H. M. Stationery Office, 1930. 198 p.
794. FEVRELL, WALTER. *Bidrag till de Moderna Främmande Språkens Methodik med särskild hänsyn till de Svenska Läroverken jämte en inledande historik över språkundervisningens utveckling.* (Contribution to methods in modern foreign languages with special reference to secondary education in Sweden together with an introductory historical account of the development of language instruction.) Uppsala: Akademiska Boktryckeriet, 1909. 168 p.
795. GALLANDER, OTTO. "The Secondary Schools of Sweden." *Special Reports on Educational Subjects.* Vol. 3. London: Printed for H. M. Stationery Office by Wyman and Sons, 1898. p. 649-71.
796. Great Britain Board of Education. "Education in Sweden." *Special Reports on Educational Subjects.* Vol. 8. London: Printed for H. M. Stationery Office by Wyman and Sons, 1902. p. 95-140. (Summarized translation of the "Enseignement et Culture Intellectuelle en Suede," issued in connection with the Paris Exhibition of 1900 by the Swedish Government.)
797. HÖJER, NILS JAKOB. *Yttrande i Läroverksfrågan på uppdrag af Statsrådet och Chefen för Kungl. Ecklesiastikdepartementet.* Afgivet den 20 Juni 1899. (Report of June 20, 1899, made at the instance of the Council of State and the Chief of the Ecclesiastical Department on the question of secondary schools.) Stockholm: Ivar Haeggströms Boktryckeri, 1899. 213 p.; 40 tables.
798. HOLMQUIST, HJALMAR F. "De Svenska Domkapitlens Förvandling till Lärarekapitel 1571-1687. Ett bidrag till kyrkoorganisationens och kyrkolagstiftningens historia i Sverige." (The transformation of the Cathedral Chapters in Sweden to teaching chapters. A contribution to the history of church organization and church legislation in Sweden.) *Uppsala Universitäts Årsskrift, 1908.* (Annual Report of the University of Uppsala, 1908.) Uppsala: Akademiska Boktruckeriet, E. Berling, 1908. p. 1-174.
799. JONSSON, J. V. *The People's High Schools (Folkhögskolor) in Sweden.* (A short summary of their origin, organization, development, and aims.) Örebro: Örebro Dagblads Office, 1904. 19 p.
800. KILANDER, HOLGER FREDERICK. *Science Education in the Secondary Schools of Sweden; a Comparative Study of Sweden and the United States.* Contributions to Education, No. 463. New York: Teachers College, Columbia University, 1931. 166 p.
801. LAGERSTEDT, N. G. W. *Sveriges Undervisningsväsen, 1910-1920.* Kortfattad redogörelse utarbetad för 11: Nordiska Skolmötet i Kristiania, 1920. (The educational system of Sweden, 1910-1920. A brief account prepared for the 11th Nordic School Meeting at Christiania, 1920.) Stockholm: Otto Ahlströms Boktryckeri, 1920. 31 p.
802. LINDEGREN, ALINA M. *Institutions of Higher Education in Sweden.* U. S. Dept. of the Interior, Office of Education, Pamphlet No. 32. Washington, D. C.: Government Printing Office, 1932. 45 p.
803. LINDSTRÖM, P. E. "Education in Sweden." *A Cyclopedia of Education.* (Edited by Paul Monroe.) New York: Macmillan Co., 1913. Vol. 5, p. 477-82.
804. MALMBORG, NILS M. AF. "Sweden." *Educational Yearbook of the International Institute, 1935.* New York: Teachers College, Columbia University, 1935. p. 447-67.
805. PETERSON, AXEL GEORGE. *The Training of Elementary and Secondary Teachers in Sweden.* Contributions to Education, No. 575. New York: Teachers College, Columbia University, 1934. 110 p.
806. RIETZ, JOHN ERNST. *Skånska Skolvasendets Historia.* Utarbetad i synnerhet efter otryckta källor. (History of education in Scania. Prepared especially from unprinted sources.) Lund: Berlingska Boktruckeriet, 1848. 667 p.

807. Royal Swedish Committee for the Second International Congress on School Hygiene. *Some Features of Education in Sweden, with special reference to Hygienic Conditions.* Stockholm: Kungl. Boktryckeriet. P. A. Nordstedt and Söner. 1904. 63 p.
808. SANDBERG, K. L. E. *Folkskoleforfattningar.* Folkskolestadgan jämte andra författningar rörande folkundervisning och folkbildning från trycket utkomna intil den 6 November 1921. Sextonde upplagan. (Elementary school statutes. The elementary school statute and other laws concerning elementary instruction and popular education printed prior to November 6, 1921. 16th edition.) Stockholm: P. A. Nordstedt & Söners Förlag, 1921. 579 p.
809. SJÖFORS, OSCAR TH. *Kanslärsgillet och 1807 Års Skolordning.* (The Chancellery and the School Law of 1807.) Karlskrona: K. L. Svenssons Eftr:s Bokindustri -a -b, 1919. 218 p.
810. SUNDBERG, AXEL GUSTAV. "Education in Sweden." *Sweden, Its People and Its Industry.* Stockholm: Kungl. Boktryckeriet. P. A. Nordstedt and Söner, 1904. 69 p.
811. Sweden. Ecklesiastikdepartementet. *Betänkande och Förslag rörande Folkskolväsendet i de Finsktalande Delarna af Norrbottens Län.* Utarbetat av utav Statsrådet och Chefen för Kungl. Ecklesiastikdepartementet den 6 June 1919 tilkallade särskilda sakkunniga. (Report and recommendations concerning elementary education in the Finnish speaking sections of the County of Norrbotten. By the special experts summoned on June 6, 1919, by the Council of State and the Chief of the Royal Ecclesiastical Department.) Stockholm: Ivar Haeggströms Boktryckeri a. b., 1921. 423 p.
812. Sweden Folkundervisningskommitten, 1906. *Folkundervisningskommittens Betänkande i Folkskoleseminarierna.* (Report of the Committee on the Education of the People concerning the elementary school seminaries.) Stockholm: Kungl. Boktryckeriet. P. A. Nordstedt & Söner, 1911-12. 4 vols.
813. Sweden. K. Kommissionen för Sveriges deltagande i 1900 års verlds Utställning i Paris. *Catalogue de l'Exposition Suedoise de l'Enseignement Supérieur.* Etablissements d'Enseignement Supérieur et Savantes. Publications Savantes. (Royal Committee for Swedish participation in the Paris Exposition of 1900. Catalog of the Exposition, concerning higher education in Sweden. Establishments of higher education and learning. Learned publications.) Upsal: Edv. Berling, 1900. 103 p.
814. Sweden. Kommitte tillsatt att undersöka den Lägre Tekniska Undervisningen. *Underdånigt Utlåtande och Förslag till den Lägre Tekniska Undervisningens Ordnande afgivet af den Kungl. Maj:t den 4 Oktober 1907 tillsatta kommitten.* (Report and recommendations for the arrangement of lower technical instruction respectfully submitted by the Royal Committee appointed October 4, 1907.) Örebro: Örebro Länstidningens Tryckeri, 1911-12. 3 vols.
815. Sweden. Kommitte tillsatt till ordnandet af den Högre Tekniska Undervisningen. *Underdånigt Betänkande och Förslag till ordnandet af den Högre Tekniska Undervisningen i Riket.* Afgivet af den Kungl. Maj:t den 13 Juli 1906 för ändåmalet tillsatta Kommitte. (Reports and recommendations of the Royal Committee appointed July 13, 1906, for the arrangement of higher technical instruction in the kingdom.) Stockholm: K. L. Beckmans Boktryckeri, 1908. 2 vols.
816. Sweden. Kommitten för undersökning af Sveriges högre Flickskolor. *Underdånigt utlåtande afgivet den 19 Januari 1888 af utsedda komiterade.* (Report of January 19, 1888, of the committee appointed for the investigation of the secondary schools for girls.) Stockholm: Ivar Haeggströms Boktryckeri, 1888. 364 p.
817. Sweden. Läroverkskommitten. 1870. *Underdånigt betänkande och Förslag afgifna den 23 Juli 1872 af den för Revision af gällande Läroverksstadga och de särskilda, tid efter annan meddelade Föreskrifter rörande denna stadgas tillämpning i nåder förordnade Komite.* (Report and recommendations of July 23, 1872, of the committee for the revision of the present law concerning secondary education and amendments passed from time to time with reference to its operation.) Stockholm: Ivar Haeggströms Boktryckeri, 1872. (Various pagings.)

818. Sweden. Läroverkskommitten, 1882. *Läroverkskommitens Underdåniga Utlåtande och Förslag angående Organisationen af Rikets Allmänna Läroverk och dermed Sammanhängande Frågor.* Afgivet den 25 Augusti 1884. (Report and recommendations of the committee on secondary schools of the kingdom and the questions connected therewith, respectfully submitted on August 25, 1884.) Stockholm: Kongl. Boktryckeriet, P. A. Nordstedt & Söner, 1884. 516 p.
819. Sweden. Nykterhetsundervisningskommitten, 1914. *Förslag angående planmässig Nykterhetsundervisning såval inom som utom Skolan.* Avgivet den 16 Mars 1915 av tillkallade sakkunniga. (Recommendations concerning organized temperance instruction in and out of school. Offered March 16, 1915, by the committee of experts.) Stockholm: Ivar Haeggströms Boktryckeri Aktiebolag, 1915. 142 p.
820. Sweden. Skolrevisionen. *Berättelse af Revisionen öfver Rikets Elementar-Läroverk, i underdånighet afgifven den 13 December, 1843.* Med bilagor. (Accounts of December 13, 1843, of the revision of the elementary schools of the kingdom. With supplements.) Stockholm: P. A. Nordstedt & Söner, 1844. 202 p. Supplement, 134 p.
821. Swedish Overseas Institute. *Higher Professional Education in Sweden.* Stockholm: Ivar Haeggströms Boktryckeri Aktiebolag, 1932. 58 p.
822. WARNE, ALBIN. *Till Folkskolans Föhistoria i Sverige.* (The prehistory of the elementary school in Sweden.) Stockholm: Svenska Kyrkans Diakonistyrelses Bokförlag, 1929. 385 p.
823. WESTLING, GOTTFRID. *Svenska Folkskolan efter År 1842.* (The Swedish elementary school after 1842.) Stockholm: P. A. Nordstedt & Söners Förlag, 1911. 418 p.

Chapter III. Comparative Education

824. ABEL, JAMES F., compiler. *Higher Education in Foreign Countries, Its History and Present Status; a List of References.* Circular No. 77. Washington, D. C.: Office of Education, U. S. Dept. of the Interior, 1933. 30 p. (Mimeographed.)
825. ABEL, JAMES F. *National Ministries of Education.* U. S. Dept. of the Interior, Office of Education, Bulletin, 1930, No. 12. Washington, D. C.: Government Printing Office, 1930. 158 p.
826. ALEXANDER, THOMAS. *The Training of Elementary Teachers in Germany.* Studies of the International Institute, No. 5. New York: Teachers College, Columbia University, 1929. 340 p.
827. ARENT, EMMA. *The Relation of the State to Private Education in Norway.* Contributions to Education, No. 235. New York: Teachers College, Columbia University, 1926. 94 p.
828. BALL, SIDNEY. "Oxford's Opinion of the Rhodes Scholars." *American Oxonian* 1: 3-20; April, 1914.
829. BECKER, CARL H. *Educational Problems in the Far and Near East.* Studies and Reports of the Institute of Education, University of London, No. 1. London: Oxford University Press, 1933. 44 p.
830. BLANCO Y SÁNCHEZ, R. *Anuario de Bibliografía Pedagógica.* Madrid: Libreria y Casa Editorial de Hernando, 1933-date.
831. BLANCO Y SÁNCHEZ, R. *Bibliografía Pedagógica del Siglo XX, 1900-1930.* Madrid: Libreria y Casa Editorial de Hernando, 1932-33. 3 vols.
832. BOKTOR, AMIR. *School and Society in the Valley of the Nile.* Cairo: Elias' Modern Press, 1936. 299 p.
833. BORGESON, FRITHIOF CARL. *The Administration of Elementary and Secondary Education in Sweden.* Contributions to Education, No. 278. New York: Teachers College, Columbia University, 1927. 231 p.
834. BRIGGS, THOMAS H. *The Great Investment.* Inglis Lecture, 1930. Cambridge, Mass.: Harvard University Press, 1930. 143 p.
835. BRINKMANN, CARL. *Recent Theories of Citizenship in Its Relation to Government.* New Haven, Conn.: Yale University Press, 1927. 126 p.
836. BROOKS, ROBERT C. *Civic Training in Switzerland.* Studies in the Making of Citizens. Chicago: University of Chicago Press, 1930. 436 p.
837. BUISSON, F., editor. *Dictionnaire de Pédagogie.* Paris: Hachette et cie., 1911. 2 vols.
838. Bureau International d'Education. *L'Admission aux Ecoles Secondaires.* Publications No. 34. Geneva: the Bureau, 1934. 222 p.

839. Bureau International d'Education. *Annuaire Internationale de l'Education et de l'Enseignement.* Geneva: the Bureau, 1933-date.
840. Bureau International d'Education. *La Bilingualisme et l'Education.* Publications No. 4. Geneva: the Bureau, 1928. 184 p.
841. Bureau International d'Education. *Bullétin.* Quarterly. Geneva: the Bureau, 1932-date.
842. Bureau International d'Education. *Comment Faire Connaître la Société des Nations et Développer l'Esprit de Cooperation Internationale* Nos. 7-10. Geneva: the Bureau, 1929-32. 4 vols.
843. Bureau International d'Education. *Conference Internationale de l'Instruction Publique: Procès-verbaux et Rapports.* Publications No. 45. Geneva: the Bureau, 1934. 179 p.
844. Bureau International d'Education. *Les Conseils d'Instruction Publique.* Publications No. 41. Geneva: the Bureau, 1935. 180 p.
845. Bureau International d'Education. *The Cooperation of School and Home.* Publications No. 6. Geneva: the Bureau.
846. Bureau International d'Education. *La Coordination dans le Domaine de la Littérature Enfantine.* Publications No. 27. Geneva: the Bureau.
847. Bureau International d'Education. *Les Economies dans le Domaine de l'Instruction Publique.* Publications No. 32. Geneva: the Bureau, 1934. 128 p.
848. Bureau International d'Education. *L'Education en Pologne.* Publications No. 13. Geneva: the Bureau, 1931. 263 p.
849. Bureau International d'Education. *Education, Travail, et Paix.* Publications No. 3. Geneva: the Bureau.
850. Bureau International d'Education. *La Formation Professionnelle du Personnel Enseignant Primaire.* Publications No. 42. Geneva: the Bureau, 1935. 402 p.
851. Bureau International d'Education. *La Formation Professionnelle du Personnel Enseignant Secondaire.* Publications No. 40. Geneva: the Bureau, 1935. 206 p.
852. Bureau International d'Education. *L'Instruction Publique en Egypte.* Publications No. 25. Geneva: the Bureau, 1932. 25 p.
853. Bureau International d'Education. *L'Instruction Publique en Estonie.* Publications No. 26. Geneva: the Bureau, 1932. 15 p.
854. Bureau International d'Education. *Littérature Enfantine et Collaboration Internationale.* Publications No. 11. Geneva: the Bureau, 1932. 243 p.
855. Bureau International d'Education. *L'Organisation de l'Instruction Publique dans 53 Pays.* Geneva: the Bureau, 1931. 374 p.
856. Bureau International d'Education. *La Paix et l'Education.* Publications No. 23. Geneva: the Bureau, 1932. 22 p.
857. Bureau International d'Education. *La Paix par l'Ecole.* Publications No. 2. Geneva: the Bureau, 1927. 150 p. (Contains bibliography, *l'Education et la Paix,* p. i-xxx.)
858. Bureau International d'Education. *La Pédagogie et les Problèmes Internationaux d'après Guerre en Roumanie.* Publications No. 16. Geneva: the Bureau.
859. Bureau International d'Education. *Les Périodiques pour la Jeunesse.* Publications No. 46. Geneva: the Bureau.
860. Bureau International d'Education. *Quelques Méthodes pour la Choix des Livres de Bibliothèques Scolaires.* Publications No. 15. Geneva: the Bureau.
861. Bureau International d'Education. *La Réforme Scolaire Polonaise.* Publications No. 36. Geneva: the Bureau, 1934. 38 p.
862. Bureau International d'Education. *La Scolarité Obligatoire et sa Prolongation.* Publications No. 33. Geneva: the Bureau, 1934. 232 p.
863. Bureau International d'Education. *Le Self-Government à l'Ecole.* Publications No. 38. Geneva: the Bureau, 1934. 168 p.
864. Bureau International d'Education. *La Situation de la Femme Mariée dans l'Enseignement.* Publications No. 29. Geneva: the Bureau, 1933. 38 p.
865. Bureau International d'Education. *Le Travail par Equipés à l'Ecole.* Publications No. 39. Geneva: the Bureau, 1935. 229 p.
866. Bureau International de l'Enseignement Technique. *Congrès International de l'Enseignement Technique, 1932. Compte Rendu des Travaux.* Paris, 1933. 2 vols.
867. BURGESS, R. W. "The Record of the American Rhodes Scholars." *American Oxonian* 8: 1-36; January, 1921.

868. CLAPARÈDE, J. "Les Annuaires Pédagogiques Nationaux et Internationaux." *Internationale Zeitschrift für Erziehungswissenschaft,* No. 1, 1931.
869. CLARKE, FRED. *Quebec and South Africa; a Study in Cultural Adjustment.* Studies and Reports of the Institute of Education, University of London, No. 5. London: Oxford University Press, 1934. 29 p.
870. Conference on Examinations, Eastbourne, England. *Conference on Examinations.* New York: Teachers College, Columbia University, 1931. 316 p.
871. Conference on Examinations, Folkstone, England. *Conference on Examinations.* New York: Teachers College, Columbia University, 1936. 300 p.
872. COOK, KATHERINE M., and REYNOLDS, FLORENCE E., compilers. *The Education of Native and Minority Groups; a Bibliography, 1932-34.* U. S. Dept. of the Interior, Office of Education, Pamphlet No. 63. Washington, D. C.: Government Printing Office, 1935. 25 p.
873. DELLER, EDWIN. *Tendencies in University Education.* Studies and Reports of the Institute of Education, University of London, No. 3. London: Oxford University Press, 1933. 19 p.
874. DEWEY, JOHN. *Impressions of Soviet Russia and the Revolutionary World, Mexico—China—Turkey.* New York: New Republic, Inc., 1929. 270 p.
875. EBAUGH, CAMERON DUNCAN. *The National System of Education in Mexico.* Johns Hopkins University Studies in Education, No. 16. Baltimore: Johns Hopkins Press, 1931. 149 p.
876. *Education Index.* Nine monthly issues a year, cumulated frequently. New York: H. W. Wilson Co., 1929-date.
877. *Educational Abstracts.* Bi-monthly. New York (230 Fifth Ave.). Began publication in 1936.
878. Educational Records Bureau. *Testing School Achievement in England and America; Report of the Results of Intelligence and Achievement Tests Given in Four English Schools Compared with Records in Similar Tests of Students in American Independent Secondary Schools, May, 1929.* Educational Records Bulletin No. 5. New York: the Bureau, 1930. 58 p.
879. EGGERSDORFER, F. X., and OTHERS, editors. *Handbuch der Erziehungswissenschaft.* Munich: Verlag J. Kösel and F. Pustet, 1930-date. About twenty-eight volumes contemplated; ten published to date.
880. ELLIOTT, ARTHUR E. *Paraguay: Its Cultural Heritage, Social Conditions and Educational Problems.* Contributions to Education, No. 473. New York: Teachers College, Columbia University, 1931. 210 p.
881. *Enciclopedia delle Enciclopedie.* Volume entitled *Pedagogia.* Rome, n. d.
882. Fédération Internationale des Associations d'Instituteurs. *Bullétin Trimestriel.* Paris.
883. Fédération Internationale des Professeurs de l'Enseignement Secondaire Officiel. *Bullétin International.* Quarterly. Tongres, Belgium.
884. FIFE, R. H., editor. *The Modern Foreign Language Study.* Vols. 5-7. Vol. 5 published by Macmillan Co., 1929; Vols. 6 and 7 published by University of Toronto Press, 1928.
885. FISHER, JAMES EARNEST. *Democracy and Mission Education in Korea.* Contributbutions to Education, No. 306. New York: Teachers College, Columbia University, 1928. 187 p.
886. GAUS, J. M. *Great Britain; a Study of Civic Loyalty.* Studies in the Making of Citizens. Chicago: University of Chicago Press, 1929. 329 p.
887. GIOVANNI, M. *Dizionario delle Scienze Pedagogiche.* Milan: Società Editrice Libraria, 1929. 2 vols.
888. HANS, NICHOLAS A. *The Principles of Educational Policy.* London: P. S. King and Son, 1929. 190 p.
889. HARPER, H. R. *What European and American Students Think on International Problems.* Studies of the International Institute, No. 12. New York: Teachers College, Columbia University, 1931. 255 p.
890. HARPER, S. N. *Civic Training in Soviet Russia.* Studies in the Making of Citizens. Chicago: University of Chicago Press, 1929. 401 p.
891. HARTOG, SIR PHILIP. *Some Aspects of Indian Education, Present, Past and Future.* Studies and Reports of the Institute of Education, University of London.
892. HAUCK, A. A. *Some Educational Factors Affecting the Relations between Canada and the United States.* Easton, Pa.: the Author (Lafayette College), 1932. 100 p.

893. HAYES, C. J. H. *France; a Nation of Patriots.* Studies in the Making of Citizens. (Originally Included in the Columbia University Series of Social and Economic Studies of Post-War France.) New York: Columbia University Press, 1930. 487 p.
894. HECKEL, BENNO. *The Yao Tribe, Their Culture and Education.* Studies and Reports of the Institute of Education, University of London, No. 4. London: Oxford University Press, 1935. 53 p.
895. HESSEN, SERGIUS. "Kritische Vergleichung des Schulwesens der anderen Kulturstaaten." *Handbuch der Pädagogik.* (Edited by H. Nohl and L. Pallat.) Langensalza: Beltz.
896. HUSSEY, E. R. J.; SCOTT, H. S.; and WILLIS, J. J. *Some Aspects of Education in Tropical Africa.* Studies and Reports of the Institute of Education, University of London, No. 9. London: Oxford University Press, 1936. 66 p.
897. Institut International d'Agriculture. *Les Institutions de Génie Rural dans le Monde.* Rome: the Institute, 1932.
898. International Association for Commercial Education. *International Review of Commercial Education.* Zurich, 1927-date.
899. International Institute of Intellectual Cooperation. *Bibliographie Pédagogique Internationale.* Paris: the Institute, 1935. 142 p.
900. International Institute of Intellectual Cooperation. *Bibliothèques Populaires et Loisirs Ouvriers.* Paris: the Institute, 1933. 332 p.
901. International Institute of Intellectual Cooperation. *Educational Role of Broadcasting.* Paris: the Institute, 1935. 289 p.
902. International Institute of Intellectual Cooperation. *La Formation de l'Homme Moderne.* Paris: the Institute, 1935.
903. International Institute of Intellectual Cooperation. *Handbook of National Centres of Educational Information.* Paris: the Institute, 1934. 85 p. Supplement, 1935, 32 p.
904. International Institute of Intellectual Cooperation. *School Text-Book Revision and International Understanding.* Paris: the Institute, 1933. 192 p.
905. JAMALI, M. F. *The New Iraq: Its Problem of Bedouin Education.* Studies of the International Institute, No. 16. New York: Teachers College, Columbia University, 1934. 160 p.
906. JASZI, OSZKAR. *The Dissolution of the Hapsburg Monarchy.* Studies in the Making of Citizens. Chicago: University of Chicago Press, 1929. 488 p.
907. KALASHNIKOV, A. G., and EPSTEIN, M. C. *Pedagogischeskaia Enziklopedia.* Moscow: Rabotnik Prosveschenia, 1927-29. 3 vols.
908. KANDEL, I. L. *Comparative Education.* Boston: Houghton Mifflin Co., 1933. 922 p.
909. KANDEL, I. L. *The Dilemma of Democracy.* Inglis Lecture, 1934. Cambridge, Mass.: Harvard University Press, 1934. 79 p.
910. KANDEL, I. L., editor. *Education in Colonial Dependencies.* Educational Yearbook of the International Institute, 1931. New York: Teachers College, Columbia University, 1932. 721 p.
911. KANDEL, I. L., editor. *Educational Yearbook of the International Institute, 1924-date.* New York: Teachers College, Columbia University, 1925-date. (Yearbooks for 1924-26 published by Macmillan Co.)
912. KANDEL, I. L. *Essays in Comparative Education.* Studies of the International Institute, No. 11. New York: Teachers College, Columbia University, 1930. "Educational Reform in Mexico," p. 163-71.
913. KANDEL, I. L., translator. *French Elementary Schools: Official Courses of Study.* Studies of the International Institute, No. 3. New York: Teachers College, Columbia University, 1927. 270 p.
914. KANDEL, I. L. *History of Secondary Education.* Boston: Houghton Mifflin Co., 1930. 577 p.
915. KANDEL, I. L. *The Making of Nazis.* Studies of the International Institute, No. 17. New York: Teachers College, Columbia University, 1935. 143 p.
916. KANDEL, I. L., editor. *Missionary Education.* Educational Yearbook of the International Institute, 1933. New York: Teachers College, Columbia University, 1933. 642 p.
917. KANDEL, I. L. *The Outlook in Education.* Studies and Reports of the Institute of Education, University of London, No. 1. London: Oxford University Press, 1933. 18 p.

918. KANDEL, I. L. *The Reform of Secondary Education in France.* Studies of the International Institute, No. 2. New York: Teachers College, Columbia University, 1924. 159 p.
919. KANDEL, I. L., and ALEXANDER, THOMAS. *The Reorganization of Education in Prussia, Based on Official Documents and Publications.* Studies of the International Institute, No. 4. New York: Teachers College, Columbia University, 1927. 647 p.
920. KASUYA, YOSHI. *A Comparative Study of the Secondary Education of Girls in England, Germany, and the United States, with a Consideration of the Secondary Education of Girls in Japan.* Contributions to Education, No. 566. New York: Teachers College, Columbia University, 1933. 211 p.
921. KILANDER, HOLGER FREDERICK. *Science Education in the Secondary Schools of Sweden; a Comparative Study of Sweden and the United States.* Contributions to Education, No. 473. New York: Teachers College, Columbia University, 1931. 166 p.
922. KORNIS, JULIUS. *Education in Hungary.* Studies of the International Institute, No. 13. New York: Teachers College, Columbia University, 1932. 289 p.
923. KOSOK, P. *Modern Germany; a Study of Conflicting Loyalties.* Studies in the Making of Citizens. Chicago: University of Chicago Press, 1933. 348 p.
924. LANGFORD, HOWARD D. *Educational Service, Its Functions and Possibilities.* Contributions to Education, No. 509. New York: Teachers College, Columbia University, 1931. 212 p.
925. League of Nations' Mission of Educational Experts. *The Reorganisation of Education in China.* Paris: International Institute of Intellectual Cooperation, 1932. 200 p.
926. LEARNED, W. S. *The Quality of the Educational Process in the United States and Europe.* Bulletin No. 20. New York: Carnegie Foundation for the Advancement of Teaching, 1927. 133 p.
927. LOCHHEAD, JEWELL. *The Education of Young Children in England.* Contributions to Education, No. 521. New York: Teachers College, Columbia University, 1932. 226 p.
928. MACGREGOR, GREGOR. *Achievement Tests in the Primary School; a Comparative Study with American Tests in Fife.* Publications of the Scottish Council for Research in Education, Vol. I. London: University of London Press, 1934. 136 p.
929. MCMURRY, RUTH EMILY; MÜLLER, MAX; and ALEXANDER, THOMAS. *Modern Foreign Languages in France and Germany; the Training of Teachers and Methods of Instruction.* Studies of the International Institute, No. 9. New York: Teachers College, Columbia University, 1930. 516 p.
930. MACNEILLE, HOLBROOK M. "The Academic Records of American Rhodes Scholars, 1904-1928." *American Oxonian* 19: 215-27; July, 1932.
931. MEIER, LOIS. *Natural Science Education in the German Elementary Schools.* Contributions to Education, No. 445. New York: Teachers College, Columbia University, 1930. 158 p.
932. MERRIMAN, C. E. *The Making of Citizens; a Comparative Study of Methods of Civic Training.* Studies in the Making of Citizens. Chicago: University of Chicago Press, 1931. 371 p.
933. MILAM, AVA B. *A Study of the Student Homes of China.* Studies of the International Institute, No. 10. New York: Teachers College, Columbia University, 1930. 98 p.
934. MONROE, PAUL, editor. *A Cyclopedia of Education.* New York: Macmillan Co., 1911-13. 5 vols.
935. MONROE, PAUL. *Essays in Comparative Education.* Studies of the International Institute, Nos. 7 and 15. New York: Teachers College, Columbia University, 1927-32. 2 vols.
936. MONROE, PAUL, director. *Report of the Educational Inquiry Commission.* Baghdad: Government Press, 1932. 170 p. (Survey of Iraq.)
937. MONROE, PAUL, director. *A Survey of the Educational System of the Philippine Islands.* Studies of the International Institute, No. 6. Manila, P. I.: Bureau of Printing, 1925. 677 p.
938. MONROE, PAUL, director. *A Survey of the Public Education System of Porto Rico.* Studies of the International Institute, No. 8. New York: Teachers College, Columbia University, 1926. 453 p.

939. New Education Fellowship. *Education in a Changing Commonwealth.* London: the Fellowship, 1931. 275 p.
940. New Education Fellowship. *The Examination Tangle and the Way Out.* London: the Fellowship, 1935. 116 p.
941. New Education Fellowship. *Full Report of the Nice Conference.* London: the Fellowship, 1933. 634 p.
942. New Education Fellowship. *A New World in the Making; an International Survey of the New Education.* London: the Fellowship, 1933. 365 p.
943. New Education Fellowship. *Towards a New Education.* London: Alfred A. Knopf, 1930. 497 p.
944. NOHL, H., and PALLAT, L., editors. *Handbuch der Pädagogik.* Langensalza: Beltz, 1930. 5 vols.
945. PARKER, BERYL. *The Austrian Educational Institutes.* Vienna: Austrian Federal Publishers, 1931. 185 p.
946. PERCY, LORD EUSTACE, editor. *The Year Book of Education, 1932-date.* London: Evans Bros., 1932-date.
947. PETERSON, A. G. *The Training of Elementary and Secondary Teachers in Sweden.* Contributions to Education, No. 575. New York: Teachers College, Columbia University, 1934. 110 p.
948. PIERCE, BESSIE L. *Civic Attitudes in American School Textbooks.* Studies in the Making of Citizens. Chicago: University of Chicago Press, 1930. 297 p.
949. POWERS, SAMUEL R. "Chemistry in English and American Schools." *School Science Review* 8: 258-65; June, 1927.
950. POWERS, SAMUEL R. "Comparison of Content and Accomplishment of Students in English and American Schools." *Journal of Chemical Education* 4: 1505-14; December, 1927.
951. PRUDHOMMEAUX, J. *Enquête sur les Livres Scolaires d'Après Guerre.* Paris: Dotation Carnegie, 1923. 452 p.
952. QUICK, GRIFFITH. *Arts and Crafts in the Training of Bemba Youth.* Studies and Reports of the Institute of Education, University of London, No. 4. London: Oxford University Press, 1935.
953. RUSSELL, WILLIAM F. *Schools in Bulgaria, with Special Reference to the Influence of the Agrarian Party on Elementary and Secondary Education.* Studies of the International Institute, No. 1. New York: Teachers College, Columbia University, 1924. 101 p.
954. SADIQ, ISSA KHAN. *Modern Persia and Her Educational System.* Studies of the International Institute, No. 14. New York: Teachers College, Columbia University, 1931. 125 p.
955. SADLER, MICHAEL E. *How Far Can We Learn Anything of Practical Value from the Study of Foreign Systems of Education?* Guilford, England: 1900. 19 p.
956. SANDIFORD, PETER, editor. *Comparative Education; Studies of the Educational Systems of Six Modern Nations.* New York: E. P. Dutton and Co., 1918. 500 p.
957. SANDIFORD, PETER. "The Testing Programme." *Survey of the School System: Province of British Columbia.* (Directed by J. H. Putnam and G. M. Weir.) Victoria, B. C.: Charles F. Banfield, 1925. Appendix I, p. 436-509.
958. SAENZ, MOISÉS. "Mexico." *Educational Yearbook of the International Institute, 1927.* New York: Teachers College, Columbia University, 1928. p. 261-313.
959. SCHNEIDER, HERBERT W., and CLOUGH, SHEPARD B. *Making Fascists.* Studies in the Making of Citizens. Chicago: University of Chicago Press, 1929. 211 p.
960. SCHWARZ, H., editor. *Pädagogisches Lexikon.* Leipzig: Velhagen und Klafing, 1928-31. 4 vols.
961. SCOTT, JONATHAN F. *The Menace of Nationalism in Education.* London: G. Allen and Unwin, 1926. 223 p.
962. SCOTT, JONATHAN F. *Patriots in the Making; What America Can Learn from France and Germany.* New York: D. Appleton and Co., 1916. 262 p.
963. SIEGL, MAY HOLLIS. *Reform of Elementary Education in Austria.* New York: the Author, 1933. 145 p. (Doctor's thesis, Teachers College, Columbia University, 1932.)
964. *Skolväsendet i Tio Länder. En Översikt.* Stockholm: Svensk Lararetidnings Förlagsaktiebolag.
965. SPIELER, J., editor. *Lexikon der Pädagogik der Gegenwart.* Freiburg in Breisgau: Herder and Co., 1930-32. 2 vols.

966. SWIFT, FLETCHER HARPER. *European Policies of Financing Public Educational Institutions.* Publications in Education, Vol. 8, Nos. 1-3. Berkeley, Calif.: University of California Press, 1933-34. 3 vols. (France, Czechoslovakia, and Austria.)
967. THURBER, CHARLES H. *Principles of School Organization; a Comparative Study, Chiefly Based on the Systems of the United States, England, Germany and France.* Worcester, Mass.: Oliver B. Wood, 1899. 72 p. (Doctor's thesis, Clark University.)
968. TILDSLEY, JOHN L. *The Mounting Waste of the American Secondary School.* Inglis Lecture, 1936. Cambridge, Mass.: Harvard University Press, 1936. 91 p.
969. TUGWELL, REXFORD G., and KEYSERLING, LEON H., editors. *Redirecting Education.* New York: Columbia University Press, 1934-35. 2 vols.
970. TUROSIENSKI, SEVERIN K., compiler. *Foreign and Comparative Education; a List of References.* U. S. Dept. of the Interior, Office of Education, Bulletin, 1934, No. 10. Washington, D. C.: Government Printing Office, 1934. 59 p.
971. VIGANDER, HAAKON. "Historieundervisningen og det Nordiske Samarheid." *Nordisk Tidskrift* 9: 525-39; 1933. Stockholm.
972. VORBRODT, W., and HERMANN, K., editors. *Handwörterbuch des preussischen Volksschulrechts.* Leipzig: 1930.
973. WATSON, FOSTER, editor. *Encyclopedia and Dictionary of Education.* London: Sir Isaac Pitman and Sons, 1921-22. 4 vols.
974. World Association for Adult Education. *Bulletins.* London.
975. World Association for Adult Education. *International Handbook of Adult Education.* London: the Association, 1929. 476 p.

REVIEW OF EDUCATIONAL RESEARCH

Official Publication of the American Educational Research Association, a department of the National Education Association.

The contents of the REVIEW are listed in the EDUCATION INDEX

Volume VI	December, 1936	Number 5

MENTAL HYGIENE AND ADJUSTMENT
(Literature reviewed to approximately January 1, 1936)

Prepared by the Committee on Mental Hygiene: Willard C. Olson, S. L. Pressey, Percival M. Symonds, J. Harold Williams, and Harry J. Baker, *Chairman;* with the cooperation of John P. Anderson, John J. B. Morgan, and George S. Stevenson.

TABLE OF CONTENTS

Chapter	Page
Introduction	459
I. Historical Development and Modern Trends	461
GEORGE S. STEVENSON, *National Committee for Mental Hygiene, New York, New York.*	
II. School Influences	471
S. L. PRESSEY, *Ohio State University, Columbus, Ohio.*	
III. Community Influences	478
JOHN J. B. MORGAN, *Northwestern University, Evanston, Illinois.*	
IV. The Normal Child	490
PERCIVAL M. SYMONDS, *Teachers College, Columbia University, New York, New York,* and JOHN P. ANDERSON.	
V. Behavior Problems and Delinquency	499
J. HAROLD WILLIAMS, *University of California at Los Angeles, Los Angeles, California.*	

VI. Physically and Mentally Exceptional Children............ 514
  Harry J. Baker, *Detroit Public Schools, Detroit, Michigan.*

VII. Technics and Instruments of Mental Hygiene............... 524
  Willard C. Olson, *University of Michigan, Ann Arbor, Michigan.*

Bibliography 537

Membership List.. 564

Copyright, 1937
By National Education Association
Washington, D. C.

———

All Rights Reserved

INTRODUCTION

ALTHOUGH PRACTICALLY ALL TOPICS or fields of education have been covered twice in cycles of the *Review of Educational Research,* this is the first number devoted to mental hygiene. As a former member of the editorial board, the chairman pointed out the possibility of mental hygiene as a topic for review, and somewhat true to form in such matters he was assigned to a committee to prepare it.

Mental hygiene has a wider scope than many of the traditional activities of education. It extends beyond the limits of subjectmatter into the whole life of the child. Many of these non-school influences are apparently as important as school in molding the lives of children, although education has been only vaguely aware of their true significance. This *Review* is dedicated to a better understanding of these factors and of their influence upon children, and to the goal that education may develop a broader base so as to better capitalize them.

George S. Stevenson, M. D., of the National Committee for Mental Hygiene, and John J. B. Morgan, of Northwestern University, have kindly prepared sections of this report for our committee. Special acknowledgment is hereby given them for this service.

HARRY J. BAKER, *Chairman,*
Committee on Mental Hygiene and Adjustment.

CHAPTER I
Historical Development and Modern Trends

TODAY the term, "mental hygiene," is familiar in the idiom of teacher, doctor, judge, social worker, nurse, and even minister. There is probably no other special tool of speech that is used as much in common by these groups. There is, therefore, none more promising to use as a bridge to span the gaps between their fields. The concepts underlying the term "mental hygiene," to be sure, are not entirely agreed on, but there is enough uniformity to allow it to serve as a vehicle of intercommunication.

This is rather a remarkable fact when one considers that at the opening of the century, the term was unknown. The knowledge which mental hygiene has come to include was then found in the frontiers of several isolated professional fields working almost independently to advance their scientific borders. These fields—education, medicine, theology, social work, etc.— were isolated from each other because they started from what seem to be discrete human problems—ignorance, illness, bewilderment, and poverty, whose full relationship to each other is not obvious. The activities that mental hygiene has now come to represent were earlier the unrationalized and intuitive expressions of genius rather than scientific formulations. They are such things as Burnham discussed in his *Great Teachers and Mental Health* (6). But the trend of every live profession is to rationalize its intuitions through scientific method. The different scientific forefronts and the variously worded principles laid down by different professional leaders had so much in common in their fundamentals that a single term "mental hygiene" reflecting the needs for happy, productive living, of the whole person, not just the condition of his heart, lungs, etc., was seized upon readily. Since then the interchanges of these various fields have been much more striking and there is no one of them but finds itself progressing faster because it is enriched by facts and ideas that it has taken over from the others.

Another influence must be recognized as setting the stage for the acceptance of the pervading concept of mental hygiene. At the same time that mutual interests were being discovered in the professional fields, the professional people were being forced farther and farther apart by the growing bulk of scientific fact and the need for specialization and division of labor to retain control of this fact. There was need for a unifying device to compensate for the insufficiency of human scholarship. The term "mental hygiene," helped counteract this dispersion because it described the common objective toward which each was working.

Most important of all is the fact that the concept, mental hygiene, helps the scientist to retain the lay and the primitive perspective and appreciation of the person as a unified creature. Professions are interested in the behavior of man's parts or his organs chiefly as these parts influence man's dealing with life's demands. Narrower scientific perspectives have often blinded us. We are forcing ourselves to get over the idea that a child can be a purely health consideration on Thursday, a learner on Friday, a player on Saturday, and a prayer on Sunday, or that he grows from birth to five, learns from five to twenty, and works from then on. We discount the idea that a teacher's life from 4 p. m. to 8 a. m. is her own private concern apart from her teaching. We have found that all these functions go on inseparably at all times, in complete mutual dependence, and that we have effected these divisions artificially in order to simplify a complexity that is life itself.

Receptivity to mental hygiene has thus been aided by these three circumstances: (a) the overlapping of fields through scientific growth; (b) the demand for a unifying instrument in the face of specialization and division of labor; and (c) the need for a broadened scientific perspective on human integration. It will perhaps be of value to inspect briefly the early life and parentage of mental hygiene in more detail because an understanding of its genesis will clarify its meaning.

Milestones in the Evolution of Mental Hygiene

In its overt form mental hygiene was first concerned with the care of the mentally ill. It came to include certain facts and practical standards that could be used to combat obvious defects in the treatment of these unfortunates, such as overcrowding, antiquated methods of treatment, physical restraint, insufficient staff, fatalistic attitudes, and harmful methods of legal commitment.

This interest in the institutionalized psychotic naturally led, as a second step, to the closely related needs of the mentally defective and drew into mental hygiene such information as would influence both institutional and community control of those so handicapped. It was at this point that the first overt connections with the field of education took place, for community control was to a large degree dependent on preparation for community living. The special class in the public school was designed to provide a large part of this preparation.

The relation of mental deficiency and psychopathology to crime made it imperative that mental hygiene should embody pertinent fact in the field of criminology, at first looking toward a better understanding of the individual criminal, later toward treatment and prevention. Preventive mental hygiene has been expressed, for the most part, as the individual approach as contrasted to the public health approach. It has been conceived of, however, as a complement rather than an alternative to the mass attack. The individual study and treatment of the delinquent were at first applied at the beginning of his law breaking, but these efforts soon revealed the greater strategy of attacking before the overt stage. The attack thus became a non-specific approach through treating the disorders of behavior and personality of children, rather than through overt infractions of the law. One could not tell in many cases whether or how much one might be dealing with a developing criminal or psychotic or both. The development of the child guidance clinic was a direct response to this demand for a preventive approach to delinquency by careful individual study at the earlier stage.

The individual study of cases, furthermore, gave unprecedented evidence of the mass social defects that produce individual deviation, and supported the principle that prevention must be communitywide (4). While there is a tendency to draw into mental hygiene these broader sociological elements and certain elements of classroom organization give promise in this direction, little progress has been made to date beyond the individual approach. This communitywide concept of prevention leads logically to the viewpoint that mental hygiene is achieveable only through the success of many community agencies. Only so far as schools, social agencies, health agencies, courts, and recreational centers, including industry, succeed in developing human potentialities and refine their scientific foundations and technical methods, can mental hygiene progress.

Mental hygiene has become enmeshed with education at several points. The early interest in the mental defective led directly to the special class and the whole testing movement. The child guidance clinic was jointly sponsored with the visiting teacher movement by the Commonwealth Fund and found its most consistent sponsors among school men. Mental hygiene services to college students and studies of mental health implications in the training and selection of teachers do not by any means complete the list.

The serious shortage of personnel created by these applications of new and borrowed fact, and the new functions added to old professions have had much to do with changes in professional education: social work, psychiatry, nursing, theology, law, have all become more dynamic and more therapeutic. More recently, in line with the whole community concept, general medicine and public health have tended to accept their responsibilities for influencing mental health (2). Meanwhile, steady progress in teacher-training institutions has been made through absorbing these accumulations of other fields routed through the channel of mental hygiene (11).

While the popularization of new scientific developments, concepts, and technics as they pass from one field to another has often savored of a vogue, the general tendency of mental hygiene has been a critical scientific eclecticism and a diminution in the identification of mental hygiene with any one of the disciplines. Psychiatry is tending to see its own ambitions realized only as other professional fields assume quasi-psychiatric functions (10). This has encouraged a greater openness on the part of professions toward the acceptance of facts bearing on mental health regardless of their source.

Cultural Relationships of Social Problems Demanding Mental Hygiene

The needs to which mental hygiene is a response are found primarily in the field of criminology, psychiatry, social service, and education. Delinquency, mental disease, dependency, and school failure may in part be conceived of as the waste products of our existing unstable social structure and processes. This instability is not in itself a curse, but a very necessary requisite for progress. Any progressive achievement presupposes a degree of instability, that is, readiness to change. At the same time, the change may not always be for the better and if we want this capacity to progress, we must take the risks of instability; these social problems are in part the price. An extremely stable and adjusted society is static and does not progress.

> The social consequences of the caste system have proved to be extremely unfortunate. In a static society regulated by a strict caste system, the place of each individual is fixed from the moment he is born and that place cannot be changed under any circumstance in this world and in this birth. This is a total negation of the dignity of man, as a man, and the democratic principle of individuality. It entails terrible loss for the society in every direction. It runs counter to the principle of selection which reigns supreme in nature. It gives a sort of stability to society provided the habit of "no questions asked" is inculcated. For that reason it kills all initiative and men lose their faith in effort and the pernicious doctrine of fatalism rules supreme (3).

A parallel to unstable productive social structure is seen in plant breeding where instability brought about through crossing results in a few valuable new hybrids, but only at the cost of many that are useless (cf. delinquency, mental disease, school failure, poverty) which must pass into the discard. Accordingly we are at present attempting to transform social waste products into innoxious debris (cf. custody) where conversion into valuable by-products (cf. social rehabilitation) is unattainable.

There always have been differences in the way these social problems have been met, differences due to arbitrary or empirical principles, but during the past two centuries scientific progress has affected the very foundations of these arts and induced some generally accepted procedures. The evolution of mental hygiene cannot be understood without some appreciation of these advances. In the central position are those sciences of human behavior: physiology which is concerned with the behavior of tissues, organs, and system of organs; psychology, taking up the sequence there and concerning itself with these systems combined into what we call a person; then sociology, dealing with the behavior of persons integrated into society; and finally culture carrying the sequence into the limbo of science. These sciences go by four names, but actually they are one continuous science of human function. Hand in hand with them the arts of pedagogy, medicine, criminology, and social work have made a parallel progress. While it is obviously impossible to discuss the advances made in each of these fields in detail, certain highlights can be selected as representing the primordium of mental hygiene.

Advances in the Sciences Contributing to Mental Hygiene

In physiology, scientific discoveries have thrown special light on human integration. The integrative value of the central nervous system has been further elucidated by new technical processes of microscopy and experimentation and it appears to be less the autocrat than had once been supposed. Tradition that the different traits of character are controlled by different parts of the brain has been shattered by careful research and study of cases of brain disease and injury. What remains of brain localization is concerned largely with specialized sensory and motor functions such as vision and not directly with derived, complex, or symbolic functions of character traits as Gall and the phrenologists would have had us believe. On the other hand, more generalized brain disorders, such as result from violence, defective growth, or infection are seen to disrupt or limit behavior in a more general way (1), and while specific motor and sensory functions may remain intact, the derived functions suffer. This has led, on the one hand, to the discovery of brain disorders previously unrecognized and, on the other, to mild mental states accompanying less serious anatomical lesions. The fiction that brain clot or pressure explains crime, mental defect, or insanity has been reduced physiologically to extremely narrow proportions compared to popular belief. Meanwhile, other integrating mechanisms of human conduct have become more evident. Our knowledge of the importance of metabolism and nutrition in affecting behavior has expanded. The glands of internal secretion have proved at times to be none too subservient vassals of the cerebro-spinal overlord, at other times too responsive. Here, also, the idea that this gland or that rules over a certain function has given way somewhat as the interrelationship between glands appeared. The definite response of cretinism (absence of thyroid gland) to thyroid feeding did much to stimulate study in this field and we are led to a better understanding of these glands of internal secretion and their effects on physical and personality development. Of importance to mental health also was the better understanding of the relationship between one's feelings and emotions and one's vegatative nervous system and behavior of one's organs (7, 14). It showed that we have to know about the affective life of the person with a stomach complaint and also about the stomach of the person with a grouch. Our norms of health and disease have been quite confused by these antics of organs in the face of difficult life situations. On the abnormal side, toxic and infectious conditions, fatigue and malnutrition have proved to be important for their upsetting effect on behavior generally as well as for their interference with the work of some particular organ. To put several of these advances on a practical basis, simple laboratory technics for measurement and diagnosis have been developed. Less and less can it be confidently stated that the disturbance of any particular organ, heart, lungs, eyes, stomach, leg, is separable from the total life situation of the person, both as to its causes and as to its effects (8). The gap between physiology and psychology has thus been closed and the separation relegated to the artificial.

Psychological advancement naturally was not separable from that in physiology; as it concerned the problems of delinquency, dependency and mental disease, and interferences with education, it came chiefly from the abnormal field. In all these there was built up a mass of fact showing how the later or adult behavior is genetically connected with earlier behavior or experience. These advances depended on the development of new methods. One method (psycholanalysis) rests largely on the memory of the subject (released from repression) and the interpretive capacity of the examiner. Psychoanalysis started out with mentation as an unexplained fact to be taken at face value. In general, it attempted to make little connection with underlying physiological functions excepting in such efforts as those of Alfred Adler who pointed out the psychic meaning of bodily defects. Even then, the psychological mechanism did not join hands with the physiological. Contrasted to this, though not conflicting seriously with it, was objective psychology which rejected the postulation of the mind and sought an understanding of behavior through simpler and related reactions and circumstances. Thorndike and Pavlov striking independently from distant beginnings opened points of identity of two fields, psychology and physiology. William James and his pupil, G. Stanley Hall, instilled a fluidity into current thinking and by encouraging practical applications forged permanent links between psychology and education.

Contrasted to this dyamic psychology, which was concerned chiefly with changing emotional responses, was the progress in measuring intellectual and later other mental capacities. This greatly facilitated the acceptance of individual differences as a prime fundamental to planning for healthy mental development. Impetus for this was provided by Binet, of course preceded by the spade work of others. Analytical and experimental work in the field of education gave an appreciation of the learning process that was needed in order to use our knowledge of these differences. The classification of soldiers during the war not only gave publicity to testing methods, but offered an opportunity for their refinement and evaluation. It also prepared personnel for the coming demands of the clinical field. The contrast of the dynamic and appraisal psychology today again is breaking down on all sides, the interests and technics of one being carried over abundantly to the procedures of the other. The institution for mental defectives is finding more and more of its cases understandable only in terms of a dynamic psychopathology and in the light of a better appreciation of dementia praecox.

None of these biological fields is well delineated. In consequence of this we constantly find the workers of one contributing to the other. Much of the advance of sociology is attributable to this proximity to other sciences. Sociologists have organized and refined material thus acquired besides adding to it out of their own store of fact and procedures. Studies of the theory and genesis of law and mores are basic to a consideration of the needs of the violator and the one protected. The improvement of technics of social examination in line with revelations of biological functions of family and community, broadened the perspective on the individual to a point where he could be rationally treated. The indirect attack on social problems would have been blind without such a guide, and prevention through community organization would have been inconceivable.

Technical Advances Contributing to Mental Hygiene

Advances in the technical fields have resulted from progress both in the sciences basic to human function and in empirical technics and refinements of technical organization. In every case the movement was from the mass, toward the individual approach and often back again toward mass application of things discovered by individual approaches. It was from the developed situation to the full-blown problem to the incipient one, from the mere detection of problems (diagnosis) to their correction (treatment) and their anticipation (prevention). Progress has also been from indirect, manipulatory, environmental approaches to direct utilization of the individual's capacity to progress on a more voluntary basis. In all fields there is more or less of a tendency today to be moved not merely by people who are sick or in trouble or who are irritating society, but by well people whose resources have been allowed to go to waste. Pedagogy, psychiatry, criminology, and social work have all had a part to play in this more positive effort. But criminology, psychiatry, and social work are bound to be largely occupied with custody, treatment, and prevention. Pedagogy, pediatrics, and public health are coming to be recognized as the fields par excellence for the positive conservational effort. The genetic studies of social problems has led invariably to this conclusion.

The diagnostic, remedial, and preventive aspects of schoolwork have contributed much to the evolution of mental hygiene. The consideration of sensory and motor handicaps in relation to learning has provided experience that bears on the determination of human behavior generally. Special educational programs to provide segregation for the protection of the majority or better to meet special defects and needs of those segregated has brought forth general principles of individualization that proved to be generally applicable not only to other school children but to other fields. Identical principles have been elicited in other fields in a way that has given further support to the concept of oneness in the person. Some of these principles: spontaneity, the opportunity for the individual to grow along lines constructed by himself; directive supervision in which the direction is laid out for him to follow; imposed experience providing, in addition, the initiative from without, and securing of perspective through verbalization, call it confession if you will, have found their places in all these fields, often under differing names. Frequently, the preoccupation with one or the other of these methods has produced a one-sided approach, although the emphasis so effected has had value.

In all these fields and again particularly in the school, the rightness and wrongness of method has been accepted as relative (e. g., as to the time and place). The ideal Negro school in the South or the secondary school of 1900, are not accepted as appropriate for New York or 1936.

Similarly in psychiatry, the efforts of Beers (5) in the twentieth century were relatively more influential in the care of the insane than those of Dix in the nineteenth or Pinel in the eighteenth; because they were tuned to a period of social receivability, the world was ready for them. Also, the psychiatric classification of Kraepelin, which in the nineteenth century constituted an immense forward step in bringing order out of chaos, became the twentieth century strait-jacket of the institutional psychiatrist and has slowed up his progress in the direction of a genetic and dynamic concept of mental disorder, in the subordination of diagnosis to treatment and the inclusion of the community in his thinking about patients, and in mental disease as a social problem. Classification has given a false feeling of definiteness and has clouded the fact that each person is an experiment of nature that is never repeated. For each person nature has set up a different combination of circumstances of which the person and his behavior is the resultant. These circumstances include heredity, past experience, health, physical make-up, and all present life experiences and activities. They tell us what a reconstructive, preventive or even a positive approach must touch in order to effect growth; they force us to a very broad scope for mental hygiene. The development of the psychopathic hospital was an effort to get away from some of the constraints of previous forms of psychiatric organization; the development of the community (child guidance) clinic represented another. Pressure for improvement of the more backward state programs and for the certification of psychiatrists served more to relieve the field of a drag than to enhance the forefront. On the other hand, the steps to advance the teaching of psychiatry in medical schools buttressed the frontier of the field whose progress cannot proceed any faster than its provision of well-equipped personnel.

While the recording of certain factual data in connection with service to individual cases has long been routine, the conception of this "history" at its best, as in reality an examination of the patient through his past experiences, social situations and their reflections of him, was necessitated by the genetic concept. The utilization of this historical part of the examination as a method of treatment in itself grows very logically out of the concept that all experience is dynamic. The verbal review of the past and of the setting is such an experience that many have treatment value. This has become a milestone in the progress of social case work. At the same time, it is not characteristic of any one endeavor.

These scientific and technical changes that have been so intermingled in the various fields that they cannot be identified with any one have become the body and spirit of mental hygiene.

One cannot consider the development of mental hygiene during the past twenty years without appreciating the very important role of psychiatric social work. On the one hand, this new activity grew out of several pressing needs; on the other, it later related itself to phases of community service which contributed little to its origin. Out of the queries of psychiatry as to what happens to patients discharged from mental hospitals, and what environment and circumstances have contributed to their breakdown, out of the field investigations of those interested in the heredity of mental disease, out of the shortage of psychiatrists during the World War and the need to conserve their efforts through technically trained assistants, out of the inevitable yearning of social work to understand its clients, out of all these things and more came that combination of functions known as psychiatric social work. Several schools, notably Smith College and the New York School of Social Work, early established full training courses for psychiatric social work and thus gave it a professional definiteness that has afforded it security and courage to forge ahead. Once established, this training proved an unparalleled preparation in mental hygiene and opened a demand for those so trained as aids in other than the medical and social work field. As visiting teachers, probation officers, consultants in nursing agencies, in fact in practically every professional field using or working toward an individualized approach, the psychiatric social worker has been called on as a mental hygiene aid, and in this way the experiences and viewpoints of one field were made available to others. It then became evident that what appeared to be a specific preparation for a definite field was not so specific after all. The essentials of psychiatric social work representing the dynamics of human relationships were specific of nothing short of all professions dealing with people in need or in trouble. Today, therefore, several professional fields that formerly thought their foundations to be pretty distinctive are trying to clarify their boundaries. The presenting symptoms that used to distinguish them—poverty, illness, antisocial behavior, ignorance—are so often traceable to the same cause that the symptom cannot act alone as the distinguishing feature. The differences between the professions seem to lie more in the grasp of such specific things as degrees of disorder, laws, methods of organization, customs, and technical devices than in varying appreciations of human behavior.

Closely related to this development in social work is the viewpoint that the material or personal service contributed by the professional worker—the health formulas of the nurse, the treatment plan of the doctor, the lesson of the teacher, the financial or planning help of the social worker, and the protection of the juvenile court—require a technical approach that is in itself a very personal thing. This case work is needed both to make the formal contribution more effective and at the same time to preserve to the recipient the highest potentialities for growth and self-realization that he may be neither materially nor spiritually pauperized. This requires a fluidity in the professional organization which is not always an asset. It has to be tuned to the stage of social progress of the community in order that it may not merely result in advantage for uninspired political opportunists. The juvenile court has suffered from this political interference and such procedures as commitment, individual study and classification, indeterminate sentence, parole, probation, and vocational training, all inherently sound, have so often worked in the wrong way because the right hands were not there to direct them.

All of these measures that call for flexibility and allow for the salvaging of special potentialities, person by person, require a high degree of security and general mental health on the part of those administering them, and to a degree of the community as a whole. In the absence of this security, the community becomes alarmed. It protests against the coddling of prisoners, the boondoggling of the unemployed, and the spoiling of children by progressive education.

The viewpoints and principles that have become identified with mental hygiene have found expression in the child guidance clinic. It was organized on the principle that the fields dealing with people in need or in trouble are not clearly separable. It thus combined in one staff the psychiatrist, psychologist, and social worker. It set up a mechanism, the case conference, whereby the examinations of these specialists were seen as merely parts of one large examining procedure, and out of which one plan of treatment emerged. It set up the same principle in relation to other community agencies, administratively separate from it, and called the principle "cooperative case work." Under this principle, the staff of two or more agencies dealing with the same case meet as one unit and plan together. It adhered to a high standard of professional training and its cooperative case work has tended to foster high standards elsewhere. It acted not only to help the case, but to give community leadership in mental hygiene generally—a public health leadership in the mental field. It has tended to insist on the assumption of mental hygiene responsibilities by other community agencies rather than to deal with all cases itself. As one clinic put it: "In so far as we are successful, the demands for our case services by other agencies will grow less and less." It is undoubtedly true that the period of greatest opportunity is not when the child has become a patient in need of clinic service, but while he is just a child in a family and a pupil in a school.

CHAPTER II
School Influences[1]

THE REVIEWER saw something of the mental hygiene movement fifteen and more years ago. The present review naturally leads to comparison of that era and the present. Two changes seem notable: the development of research and even experimentation in the field, and the growing emphasis on the importance of the school in any adequate mental hygiene program. The research approach will be evident throughout this review, and the amount of material bearing on mental hygiene in the school will be evidence of the second point. Certain material, such as on motivation, may seem outside the field of mental hygiene, but seemed best included because of important relationships.

Mental Hygiene and Teacher Training

Ways in which the teacher's personal problems of unhappiness or insecurity and differences in social attitudes of teachers and pupils influence pupil-teacher relationships were discussed by Meredith (53). The author felt that the achievement of an objective point of view should be the teacher's goal. A plea for preventing the temperamentally unqualified from entering training schools for teachers was made by Townsend (76), who reported investigations indicating clearly the prevalence of emotionally unstable, neurotic, and even psychopathic personalities in public school teaching positions. "Studies have disclosed that the chances are almost 7 to 1 that in the course of 12 years of public school education a child will encounter at least 2 such maladjusted persons in the teacher's position." An elaborate study of characteristics by W. S. Phillips (64) included emphasis upon the importance of emotional adjustment and lack of neuroticism in selecting teachers.

Causes of teacher maladjustment were drawn from correspondence over a ten-year period with young teachers in four different training schools by an English writer, M. Phillips (63). These causes were grouped under nine heads:

1. Personal difficulties of a kind to be intensified rather than relieved by the strains and stresses of vocational training, and subsequently of professional life
2. Unsuitable placing of young teachers in their first posts
3. Unfavorable conditions of work such as inadequate buildings and equipment
4. The management of large classes and treatment of difficult individuals
5. The attitude of head teachers and older members of the staff toward young teachers

---

[1] The author wishes to acknowledge the assistance of Ruth Vendig, graduate student at the Ohio State University, in the preparation of this chapter.

6. Divergence of educational outlook and practice between generations
7. Social conditions in the school area
8. Insufficient leisure during the first two or three years of teaching life
9. Financial difficulties.

Items 4, 5, and 6 appeared to the author to be most important. Case studies illustrating each type were included.

An attempt to discover the relation between teacher and pupil stability was made by Boynton, Dugger, and Turner (18). Seventy-three fifth- and sixth-grade teachers, and 1,095 of their students selected at random, filled out the Woodworth-Mathews personal data sheet to which had been added twenty-five similar questions. In terms of this inventory, the pupils of the teachers who had the best mental health were more stable on the average than were the pupils of the most unstable teachers, although the student-teacher relationships had existed only about two to two and a half months prior to the study.

An outline of possible psychiatric contributions to teacher training, involving suggested courses of study and the set-up of an organization for promoting the mental health of students and staff, was furnished by Patry (61). Five pages of selected references are included. Suggestions as to how the teacher may aid in pupil adjustment by "an awareness of the significance of certain behavior tendencies in the young child" were made by C. W. Flemming (30). A case study is included. A course in personnel work was presented by Strang (72), from the standpoint of (a) the teacher's role in personnel work, (b) methods and information useful in the identification and solution of problems of students, and (c) technics which enable teachers to make effective contacts with students and to cooperate with specialists. From the psychoanalytic school, Homburger (38) claimed that knowledge of psychoanalytic concepts is a necessity for the teacher in understanding his pupils. Only thus (the contention is) can the teacher really understand what is back of the questions and acts of the pupils.

It has frequently been noted that the teacher who is uninformed in matters of mental hygiene is apt to emphasize as a problem case the child who is disobedient and difficult to control, while ignoring the quiet, withdrawn child who in reality may present a more serious problem from the mental hygiene point of view. Laycock (46) found this to be true of a group of Canadian teachers. He asked them to list items of undesirable behavior and to rate the seriousness of these acts; the ratings correlated —.125 with ratings of mental hygienists. However, Peck (62) found that the majority of the characteristics which teachers in his classes considered important in the selection of maladjusted pupils were really undesirable personality traits.

In short, the importance of the teacher as the outstanding factor in the mental hygiene situation in the school, and of both selection and training of teachers in the light of this fact, is becoming increasingly evident.

School Procedures and Mental Hygiene

There has been much desirable emphasis on the extent to which the routines of the school involve consequences in the field of mental hygiene. Four contributions from abroad are to be noted. From Switzerland has come a volume by Schohaus (67) on "the dark places of education" based upon replies written to the editor of a Swiss educational paper in answer to the question, "From what did you suffer most at school?" The results were more than interesting, stressing children's suffering from contempt and sarcasm, excessive demands, and corporal punishment. Valentiner (80) discussed the conflict arising as a result of the uniform demands of the school, the very different individualities of the pupils, and the possibilities of a therapeutic pedagogy. Heller (35) pointed out the adjustment problem in going from school to vocation, the numerous mental hygiene problems arising in school, and the need that the teachers should educate the public in mental, as they have in physical, hygiene. That the teacher may by such simple and natural acts as praise and recognition of good work (the praise, however, causing jealousy and antagonism on the part of the other pupils) cause life-long maladjustment of individual pupils is illustrated in a case study by Mey (54).

Myers (56) discussed practices found in schools, with an analysis of their desirability or undesirability from a mental hygiene point of view. Wile (84) stressed the importance of failure in school as leading to truancy and delinquency and presented the "challenge of childhood" to society, asking the educator and psychiatrist what is being planned that children may develop into adults who are not only physically sound but active intellectually, emotionally mature, and socially adequate. Washburne (83) supplied the educator's response to this "challenge of childhood" with a description of the progressive school's efforts to give the child a sense of security, outlets for energy, and opportunities for group participation and adequate personality development. Curiously, a summary of the work of the Winnetka schools is included.

C. W. Flemming (29) furnished an account of the guiding principles and technics employed in student adjustment at the Horace Mann School. The author considered such topics as functions of a division of psychological service and pupil adjustment, classification of pupils, problems of adjustment for individual children, integration of interests and activities of school staff for constructive effort toward pupil adjustment, the school's responsibility for superior children, and dynamic individual pupil records and reports.

The activity program of the Newark schools was reported by Trolan (78). The use of group projects in the first two grades has given the teacher time to study the child's individual problems, guide early school adjustment, and adjust work to ability so as to develop confidence and a feeling of security. Possible contributions of physical education to mental hygiene were emphasized by J. E. Davis (27).

Problems of evaluation of pupils' achievement are in great need of consideration by the mental hygienist with regard to their bearing on individual adjustment and motivation. A digest of the literature on marks and marking systems was made by Crooks (26) with consideration of such topics as purposes of marking, reliability of marks, ability grouping, and absolute standards. A bibliography of eighty titles is included. Hill (37) reported an analysis of the report card in present practice:

> Variation in practice seems to be the distinguishing feature of the 443 report forms analyzed. . . . In general, the reports of the kindergarten, primary, and elementary grades are less formal and represent a more progressive educational outlook than the reports of the secondary schools. . . . The lower grade cards are more frequently informal in appearance and in the letter to the parents, more often unconventional in their marking systems, more concerned with character and health outcomes.

Three studies show interest abroad in these problems. Muchow (55) discussed the revision of scholastic reports in Germany, with consideration of the value of "psychological portraits" rather than formal marks. Two French investigators, Laugier and Weinberg (45), found French professors highly unreliable in examination grading. In addition to the usual findings of disagreement between graders they added this delightful bit, that a person totally ignorant of a subject could, after reading a few papers, turn in as reliable grades as professors of that subject. An investigation into the fears connected with examinations, which according to the above evidence might well be warranted, was made by Redl (66). The causes of such fear were classified, with stress upon such factors as the attitude of teachers and of parents, and "pathological fear." Such topics were discussed as the teacher's attitude toward such fears, means of preventing them, and underlying causes.

A discussion of school discipline from the developmental rather than the repressive point of view was offered by Huang (39). He stressed psychological causes and treatment with reference to characterological outcomes. The problem of school discipline in India as made particularly difficult due to the influence of political agitators, was discussed by Maiti (50), and a psychological viewpoint stressed.

The honor system, a device used in school administration, is of some interest from a mental hygiene point of view. Wahlquist (81) reported a survey of eighty-one major colleges and universities in the United States regarding their use of and attitudes towards the honor system. He found that the honor system is more often employed in private colleges than in public universities; that more institutions have used and abandoned this system than are now using it; that the most frequent cause of failure with this system is lack of student cooperation; and that it appears to be most apt to succeed in small professional schools and private colleges where it is supported by tradition.

Mathews (52) investigated the attitudes of students and faculty members of Ohio Wesleyan University toward academic honesty, by means of a personal opinion blank. The author found rationalizations employed to justify almost any form of academic dishonesty in this university, where the honor system has been employed for twenty-five years, and interpreted his results as indicating that honor systems are ineffective.

Organization of Mental Hygiene Work

A detailed questionnaire study on the organization, personnel, training, practices, etc., in thirty-four psychoeducational clinics in colleges and universities was presented by Witty and Theman (86), who found that "very few institutions of higher education offer a curriculum and provide opportunity for clinical work which appear adequate to prepare individuals for mental hygiene and psychoclinical work." Cattell (23) reported the relations between psychologist, teacher, and physician, and the organization of the psychological clinic in British cities. Ide (40) discussed the organization of the Division of Special Education of the public school system of Philadelphia, with an account of the different types of problem children with which the division deals. Snedden (68) outlined the work of a psychoeducational and mental hygiene clinic. Newell (57) emphasized the importance of cooperation between home and school in the prevention of maladjustment.

McBee (49) stressed the need for a mental hygiene clinic in every high school. He attempted to evaluate the behavior problems, the methods of study, and the results, in connection with 328 normal adolescents in a Chicago high school dealt with in a demonstration mental hygiene clinic. Improvement occurred in 70 percent of those presenting scholarship problems, 83 percent of those presenting personality problems, and 100 percent of the delinquents. A plan for a mental hygiene unit in the high school was presented. The importance of a coordinated mental hygiene program in secondary schools was also emphasized by Zachry (87).

Williamson and Paterson (85) described counseling at the University of Minnesota where certain members of the faculty are appointed as advisers for problems of speech disorders, mental hygiene, social relationships, finances, and employment. Each adviser who gives this "out of routine" advice to students reports to a faculty-student contact desk in order to coordinate this work and prevent duplication in case a student should contact another adviser. The paper includes an analysis of 3,970 problems discovered and discussed by 287 faculty members in one week. The set-up of a college mental hygiene unit was outlined by Patry (60).

Motivation

An important summary of forty-two experimental studies dealing with the problem of incentives has been prepared by R. A. Davis and Ballard (28). The authors found that "investigation in this field was hardly known before 1920, when there is a marked increase in the amount of research which has been produced." Important conclusions may be summarized as follows:

When pupils are informed concerning the quantity and quality of their performance of tasks, effort and attitude are improved. Praise is more effective than reproof as an incentive, although any comment is better than a neutral attitude. . . . The presence of a co-working group has the effect of increasing the number of ideas and speed of the individual, but the quality of the thought processes is usually superior when the performer is working alone. . . . Individuals tend to improve to a greater extent when they are working for self than when working for the group of which they are members.

A study of the effects of a continued story, a game, reproof, praise, an Easter party, and delayed play upon drill in arithmetic in the fourth grade was reported by Warden and Cohen (82). The authors concluded that "these commonly used incentives are not as effective as might be supposed, at least insofar as the type of task investigated is concerned, when applied under schoolroom conditions. . . . The incentives used were mainly effective in inducing accuracy, and in many cases at the expense of speed."

A study of the effect of competitive motivation versus no given incentive upon addition and number comparison tests administered to 217 pupils in the sixth, seventh, and eighth grades has been made by Zubin (88). The author reported measurable improvement produced by the incentive. The effect of knowledge of results upon the performance in arithmetic drill of 138 children in Grades V A and VII A was reported by Brown (19), who found that practice with knowledge produced more continuous gains than practice without knowledge.

Forlano (32) compared the effects of individual competition and work for the group upon cancelation tests given thirty-four eleven-year-old children. The average child was found more highly motivated by the possibility of personal gain than by the incentive of helping his class or team score.

Mental Hygiene and Academic Progress

It has long been recognized that various factors besides ability affect schoolwork and make inaccurate prediction of school marks from intelligence tests alone. Stagner (69) reported correlations of some eight personality tests with academic grades and intelligence test scores, using college students as subjects. He concluded that personality factors have a definite influence on academic achievement. A bibliography of forty-five titles is included. E. G. Flemming (31) outlined a method of prediction of academic grades by a combination of intelligence test score, score on certain tests of emotionality and personality, and an estimate of emotional steadiness. Harris (33), in an analysis of results from 800 men entering the College of the City of New York, found that such factors as non-conformity in religious and other fields and extroversion were associated with school achievement lower than might be expected from intelligence test scores. An analysis of the relation of school success to introversion-extroversion in 120 primary-school pupils was made by Hendrickson and Huskey (36), who concluded that "it probably argues better for school success in intermediate grades to be ambiverted than to be either introverted or extroverted." A case study analysis of thirty-one students who had failed in secondary school was reported by Karlan (42). The author concluded that emotional problems caused failure in students with high intelligence ratings. Counseling met with good success in these cases.

Character Education Methods

Several experimenters have attempted to investigate the formation of student attitudes. Kroll (43) administered Harper's scale for measuring conservatism-liberalism-radicalism to the boys in six twelfth-grade classes in history and English at the beginning and end of a semester. Three of these classes were being taught by teachers who were rated as conservative and the other three classes were being taught by teachers rated as radical. From data so gathered, the author concluded that "there is little foundation for the statement that conservative teachers indoctrinate conservatism. There seems to be some basis for the opinion that radical teachers are probably teaching the pupils to question the status quo."

Lichtenstein (48), using as subjects 900 children in the intermediate grades, attempted to determine the effects of stressing for a year in the teaching, two attitudes: (a) appreciation of outdoors, specifically in preference to moving picture shows; and (b) the so-called "scientific attitude." It was found that superstitions were reduced by the experimental procedure, but scientific attitudes and the preference for movies over outdoors, were not affected. Chen (25) attempted to measure the effect a single propaganda lecture produced on attitudes of college students. He found decided shifts of attitudes for or against the Japanese Manchurian policy.

A program of sex teaching developed by the Cincinnati Social Hygiene Society in cooperation with the Cincinnati schools, was discussed by Strain (71). Lectures on the physical and social aspects of maturation and reproduction are given to seventh- and eighth-grade children, and a more extensive course which includes talks on marriage and sex education of young children is provided for girls in senior home economics classes. Butler (22) investigated, by means of tests, the needs of 1,586 high-school students in understanding of child development and family relationships. A program was then set up involving the use by the students of observations of life situations, as well as reading materials, lantern slides, motion pictures, and photographs. Comparison of pupils given the program with control groups indicated significant gains not only in knowledge but also in self-reliance as measured by an attitude scale.

CHAPTER III
Community Influences

THE EFFECTS OF COMMUNITY INFLUENCES upon the mental health of any individual depend upon the mental stamina of that person. Thom (214) says: "There are, at any given moment, a vast number of individuals who are carrying on with apparent success, but who are just on the verge of an incapacitating illness. . . . There is probably for each and every individual a limit to the physical strain and the mental stress that he is capable of withstanding without reaching the breaking point."

Latham (150) went further and stated that the determining factor in personality development is not the influence of the environment but the attitude of the individual toward the environment. That these attitudes are, nevertheless, the result of interaction with environmental influences was pointed out by Künkel (149) and Levy (152).

The relative emphasis given to the attitudes of the individual and to environmental influences varies with writers. C. M. Campbell (100) and Blatz (94) stressed the significance of the child's attitude, while Lewin (154) stressed the environment in his analysis of some of the forces which operate in child behavior and development.

Family Influences

It has come to be fairly agreed that the most significant forces in mental health are those which operate early in childhood and that family influences rank first in importance. The present researches in this connection are devoted chiefly to isolating the significant forces in the family environment and in determining the manner of their operation.

In reporting upon the White House Conference on Child Health and Protection, Burgess (97) pointed out that the externals of home life are not nearly so significant as personal relationships in their influence upon personality development of children, that the good home is not to be measured in terms of economic conditions, neatness, parental status, or parental control, but in terms of human responses.

These pronouncements seem to be substantiated by extensive studies made by Francis and Fillmore (124, 125). They reported a statistical investigation in which one group of thirty families from a wealthy area and another group of thirty families from a middle-class area were analyzed. They computed biserial correlations to discover any possible relationship between good and bad environmental factors and the personality adjustment of the children in the families studied. The environmental factors having apparently little or no statistical significance as to their influence on personality were nativity of parents, esthetic standards of the home, hygienic conditions of the home, economic status of the home, broken homes, and unsupervised play space. Those environmental influences having significance were recreational clubs and the health of parents.

They found that the following parental attitudes had a statistical significance in relation to the child's personality: the parents' knowledge of schoolmates; the parents' knowledge of the child's games at school; the parents' attitudes toward the mixing of the sexes, toward discipline, toward the child's health, and toward education; the entertainments favored by parents; and employment of the parents.

Those attitudes of the parents which had little or no statistical significance as to their influence on the child's personality development were the parents' attitudes toward recreational facilities in the home, control of spending money, sex instruction, and the time spent with the children.

In other words, physical environment by itself was shown to be of comparatively little importance, whereas a number of the parental attitudes appeared to be significantly influential. Thus, the factors originally thought to be important, namely, poor economic conditions, broken homes, foreign-born parents, and physical sickness, had little effect on their own account. They found a tendency for harmful attitudes of parents to produce maladjustments in their children and for helpful attitudes to do the reverse. They concluded: "In each succeeding generation the importance of parental attitudes upon the child is paramount, and the influence of the social environment is felt through this channel rather than directly. Further, emotional swings are handed on from generation to generation in the same fashion, thereby forming a heritage to the child upon which the social environment can have little effect directly."

Most of the statements that can be found in current literature concerning the specific effect of various parental attitudes on the child are generalizations from case histories or general clinical observations. Stone and Hart (212) made a study of the first 100 mental cases at the maternal health center in Newark and found that at least half included anxiety neurosis in the wife, most of which resulted from a fear of pregnancy. They advocated a wider dissemination of contraceptive information to avoid this condition.

A study of the home conditions of 40 manic-depressive and of 68 dementia praecox patients revealed that a large proportion of the homes had unwholesome emotional conditions of one type or another (220).

A variety of suggestions are offered as to the type of home situations which are harmful and as to what should be done to improve them. Some of these offer speculative hypotheses which could well be tested. Most of these speculations are derived from psychoanalytic interpretations and not from experimental, statistical, or case history technics (123, 185). Some of these speculations are very pessimistic. For example, Crichton-Miller (109) asserted that the only solution is for teachers to be able to educate out of the child the mistakes made by the mother and father in the first five years.

Since the assumption is made that maladjustments in parents are influential in the personality development of children, the research of Johnson and Terman (144) in connection with the personality characteristics of happily married, unhappily married, and divorced persons is very timely. Outstanding traits of the happily married are emotional stability, social adaptability, conservatism, and tolerance. The unhappily married give evidence of neurotic and introvertive tendencies. Divorced women are self-reliant, independent, tolerant, and manifest initiative and vigor. Divorced persons, both men and women, have more intellectual interests than married persons.

These findings suggest that the most unfortunate home situation, so far as the mental health of the child is concerned, would be a home which, although externally intact, is filled with emotional discord.

In this same connection, Silverman (206) examined 138 children who were placed by a child-placing agency because their homes had been broken. It was found that there was no significant relationship between the homes broken through delinquency and incompatibility of the parents, and the behavior of the children. Where problem behavior occurred it was related more to the subtle emotional relationships than to the overt delinquencies of the parents.

Clinicians are agreed that treatment of a problem child without the cooperation of the parents is likely to prove fruitless (91, 157, 169, 221, 227), and that it is often more necessary to treat the parents than it is to treat the child.

Changing parental attitudes—To what extent can parents' attitudes be changed? As a preliminary to the answering of this question, it is important to develop a reliable and valid scale for measuring attitudes. Peterson and Thurstone (182, 183, 184) have contributed to the technic for measuring attitudes, although their work was not done in connection with the attitudes of parents toward the care of children. A number of investigators have constructed attitude scales for parents (89, 90, 91, 140, 211), but Stogdill (211) seems to have done the most elaborate study of the significance of such a scale. He used an attitude scale consisting of sixty items, having each item rated on a ten-point scatter, according to how seriously or unfavorably the rater believed the behavior of the parent to affect the child. Child guidance specialists (fifty in number) regarded as relatively more harmful those forms of activity on the part of parents that tend to cause the child to lose confidence in human beings and to feel a lack of security in his environment, such as scolding the child for asking questions about sex, telling the child that God sees everything he does, praising him for being such a quiet child, expressing passionate love toward the child, and telling the child the stork brought him. Parents, on the other hand, regarded as relatively more harmful those forms of parental activity which allow the child a certain degree of aggressiveness, independence, and freedom from moral repression, such as using profane language in the child's presence, finding fault with accepted conventions, allowing him to make his own mistakes, answering his questions about sex with the facts, finding fault with food in the child's presence, walking in on the child in the bathroom, and making the child angry.

Ojemann (176) and Fitz-Simons (120) made similar studies. Ojemann used 319 statements or generalizations relating to child development and had them rated by competent judges on the basis of the importance of each generalization for parents of preschool children, elementary-school children, and high-school students.

These studies all stressed the importance of parental attitudes and indicated some of the attitudes which should be changed, but the method that is best suited for changing parental attitudes has still to be discovered. A teaching program based on the findings of experimental studies was proposed by Hedrick (140) and class study with parents was tried by Cushing (110). A number of books for parents have been published which attempt to put in popular style the opinions of mental hygienists (136, 170, 172, 178, 190, 194, 222).

The child's attitude toward his parents—While the attitudes of parents toward their children and the emotional adjustments of parents are considered important, it has also been recognized that the attitudes of the children toward their parents may have significance. Indeed, the more important for the child's mental health is, in the last analysis, his attitude toward his parents rather than their opinions on child training. Simpson (207) studied the preferences of young children for mother or father. She used several technics, such as asking questions, getting responses to a set of pictures, reactions to stories, and the narration of dreams. She found that, in the main, the mother was preferred.

Stagner and Drought (209) developed an affection-aversion scale, using the Thurstone technic, and gave it to a number of college students, comparing their scores on this scale with self-ratings and biographical data. They found no reliable differences between the attitudes of men and women toward their fathers and mothers and suggested that these results are evidence against the validity of the Freudian theory of the Oedipus complex. They qualified this conclusion, nevertheless, by saying that the contradiction is more apparent than real. Taken together these two investigations suggest that the attitude of the child is the result of the type of treatment he has received at the hands of his parents rather than any fixed relationship due to sex.

Meltzer (168) developed a free association technic for use with young children to determine their real attitudes toward their parents as contrasted with the conventional attitudes which the children are likely to manifest. His method consisted of giving a child instructions to "think aloud" on different ideas, the idea of mother and father being included in the list of topics. Valid and reliable estimates of the child's parental attitudes were obtained by a technic for evaluating the child's responses which Meltzer described.

Feelings of security and independence—A number of studies point out the importance of feelings of security in the home and, at the same time, others indicate that this security must not lead to overdependence. Rosenheim (198) gave five cases to support the theory that attitudes of overprotection and rejection play important roles in child maladjustments. Myers (173), by means of a questionnaire of 114 items, evaluated the various factors of the home environment of high-school pupils. She found that unquestioning obedience demanded by parents was associated with good adjustments of younger children but with poor adjustments of older children. Fitz-Simons (120) constructed a guide which may be used clinically to determine the degree of attachment of the parent for the child.

While most clinicians agree that the child should be taught to gain freedom from excessive parental supervision as he matures, there is some feeling that too much freedom is dangerous. Several studies have attempted to throw light upon this question.

Ford and Balen (122) made a statistical study to determine whether the lack of supervision of boys would affect delinquency rates. For three months all the boys studied were under supervision during recreational play. After the initial three-month period, some of the boys were continued under supervision while the remainder were unsupervised. A comparison of the two groups showed no evident effect upon the delinquency rate of the unsupervised group.

In a social and medical study of thirty hyperactive children, Childers (105) found that the feeling of insecurity plays an important part in producing disturbances in children. It is urged that the hyperactive child be given as much security as possible, that he be placed in a régime of curtailed activities, that regularity be stressed, and that suppression be avoided.

Size of family—Levy (153) made a study to test the thesis that size of family and ordinal position within the family are factors in determining behavior deviations among children. He found that behavior difficulties were independent of the size of the family. He found also that an only boy in the family and the second child seemed to be more likely to become involved in delinquencies in rich, small communities. Hence, the ordinal position seems to function only when it obtains in connection with other factors. Maller (162) found that the size of the family correlates negatively with intelligence, moral knowledge, cultural background, and honest behavior. The relation was curvilinear and not linear, the only child not being superior to others.

An excellent review of the literature on the personality adjustments of only children was given by A. A. Campbell (98). He pointed out that the armchair theories continue to stress the importance of the only-child constellation as a personality determiner at the same time that research, both clinical and non-clinical, has given increasingly little support to this importance.

Witty (224) found, in a statistical study of 153 only children of five years of age in Kansas City, that the only child shows himself superior to other children in health, physical development, intelligence, and character traits. In later studies, Witty (223, 225) made numerous comparisons of only children with other children and found that, in social and emotional adjustments, there were no significant differences.

Foster parents—What effect have stepmothers on the mental health of children? Neumann (174) had 489 eighth-grade pupils write essays upon the subject of stepmothers. Thirty of the children were stepchildren. He found that half of the latter, 16 boys and 14 girls, indicated an unfavorable attitude toward their stepmothers. The stepmother, he pointed out, is in an unfortunate position and such antagonism is the result of preconceived notions rather than in any inherent characteristic of the stepmother situation.

When the child is adopted into a foster home the situation is likely to be more favorable. Dudley (114) and Leahy (151) studied the characteristics of foster homes and of foster parents, but their analyses throw little light upon whether foster homes are favorable or inimical to the mental health of the adopted child. Dudley contended that the difference between a good and a poor foster home lies in the degree of security which the home gives to the child.

Rogers (197) tried an experiment to see whether boys who had become delinquent, presumably because of faulty home structure, could be trained to become normal personalities. He took ten bad boys and, by seeing that they gained security and personal recognition in selected foster homes, made them into normal, law-abiding boys.

Inspired by the work of Mrs. Walrath of the Cradle Society, in Evanston, Illinois, Gallagher (127) presented in book form the various aspects of child adoption. Its aim seems to be to create in the lay individual a different attitude toward foster children. Doubtless, the mental health of the adopted child depends upon the attitudes of the adoptive parents and the others whom he contacts during his life.

Play and Recreation

More research needs to be done to determine the exact significance of play and recreation for mental health. Emery (117) gave a typical discussion of the value of recreation for hospital patients, asserting that dancing is one of the best socializing influences. He gave no evidence to prove that recreation is better than occupational therapy in the form of serious work for patients. Reeves (191) reported an attempt to promote street play in twenty cities. He stated that, in 1929, 36 cities closed 165 streets for play under leadership. Attendance at 105 of these streets was reported to be over 720,000. Kaplan (146) found that the organization of street play reduced delinquency. Pendry and Hartshorne (179) described 49 presentday organizations which devote their energies to providing recreation and leisure-time activities for young people.

We may conclude from the emphasis given in the above studies that play is valuable for patients in hospitals and that it keeps idle persons occupied and thus diminishes delinquency; but we may also ask whether there is any evidence that recreation plays an important role in the mental health of the normal, employed man.

Thisted (213) attempted to answer the question as to whether participation in college athletics had any deleterious effects. He obtained replies from 500 alumni to a questionnaire and attitude scale and concluded that athletes were as successful as non-athletes in their vocations, and that college athletics had been of personal value to the athletes.

Hardy (135) studied the relationship between out-of-school activities and the personality adjustments of children. She obtained her estimate of adjustment from teachers' ratings, observations, pupil interviews, and parents' reports. She found that attendance at movies, organized recreational and educational activities, the size of play units, and the types of play were not related to personal adjustments. She made the rather sweeping generalization that "what children of elementary school age do with their after-school hours is not an important conditioning factor in their personal adjustments."

Economic Depression

Gaudet and Curry (128) presented graphs (no correlations were computed) to show the relation between business conditions and first admissions to the New Jersey State Hospital at Greystone Park, New Jersey, for the years 1895 to 1930, inclusive. During every period of prosperity (with minor exceptions) there is a decrease in the number of first admissions, and, in every period of depression, there is a corresponding increase in the first admissions. They contended that their graphs support the claims of hospital superintendents and clinicians that, during business depressions, a greater amount of mental illness appears than during business prosperity.

Other studies indicate that this relationship is not so apparent. A questionnaire was sent to hospital superintendents during 1933 and 1934 by the National Committee for Mental Hygiene to determine in what way the economic crisis had affected these institutions and to learn how they were functioning under depression conditions (141, 148). Most state hospitals reported that there was an increased number of first admissions and re-admissions from 1929 to 1932, and the inference was drawn that the depression was a precipitating or contributing factor to this increase.

Pollock (187) compared the populations of mental hospitals in New York state from 1929 to 1934 with the populations from 1924 to 1929. The rate of first admissions has been rising since 1924. The populations of hospitals increased more rapidly from 1929 to 1934 than from 1924 to 1929. This increase was greatest in 1933. The trend in the manic-depressive group has been slightly upward with a marked increase in 1933. A significant increase in the rate of dementia praecox admissions has occurred since 1927, the rate being exceedingly high in 1932 and 1933. Pollock pointed out that the increase in the year 1933 may be due to the cumulative effect of the depression. Taking his figures as a whole, he concluded that the economic crisis does not seem to be the dominant factor in the increase of first admissions in any one diagnostic group; it is, however, a precipitating factor of importance in all groups.

It would seem that the increase in state hospitals, if these studies are representative, is partly due to the fact that fewer persons are able to afford the luxury of private sanitariums and partly due to the fact that hospitals provide a refuge for those on the borderline of a breakdown when economic stresses become acute. This interpretation is supported by the reports of superintendents that there was an increase in senile cases during the depression (presumably because their relatives could no longer support them) and that it was more difficult to parole patients. In other words, the state hospitals provided an economic haven and changes in hospital populations should not be interpreted to indicate that the economic depression caused mental diseases.

Statistics dealing with the type of cases applying for admissions to New York institutions, presented by Malzberg (163), indicate that they are more influenced by social and other environmental factors than by the degree of mental health or disease of the community.

The effects of economic depression upon the psychoneurotics is not discernable through statistical studies and all the writings bearing upon this point are expressions of opinion or generalizations from clinical evidence. It is contended that the psychic life of a people contracts with a narrowing of economic scope (201); that there is a decrease in family solidarity with a lowering of the economic level (92); that poverty builds in children feelings of insecurity which result in vagrancy and delinquency (201); and that revolutionists and psychopathic personalities are the natural outcome of the conflicts that grow from the breaking down of family ties, homelessness, and economic hazards (201).

A brief statement, summarizing the above studies dealing with economic depressions and their effect on mental health, might be in order. We have no positive evidence that economic depressions cause an increase in the numbers of persons who develop psychoses. The increase in population of state hospitals in depression years is greater than the normal expectancy, but this increase may be accounted for by the inability of relatives to care for the mentally ill either in private institutions or at home. New behavior patterns and new attitudes are evidences as a probable result of economic depressions, but these are in the direction of detrimental and disrupting behavior only in mature persons. In students, adolescents, and children such detrimental changes are not found. Since unemployment fosters feelings of insecurity, anxiety, and bewilderment, it is possible that economic depressions affect more those individuals already subject to such neurotic behavior than normal adults or immature children. More research is needed in order to discover the specific effects of economic depressions upon the psychoneurotic individual.

Motion Pictures

The strongest impetus given to research relating to the effect of motion pictures upon personality development was provided by the Payne Fund. Under the chairmanship of W. W. Charters (103, 104), committees were appointed to study various aspects of motion picture influence and, as a result of the research thus accomplished, twelve studies have been published. These studies cover practically every aspect of the motion picture influence, but it is hard to glean from them just what influence motion pictures may have upon the mental health of the community.

Freeman and Hoefer (126) tried an experiment to test the degree to which motion pictures may influence behavior. They gave instructions as to the care of the teeth to two groups of students. One group, in addition to the oral instruction, was given supplementary instruction by the use of models and diagrams, and by two pictures depicting social situations involving care of the teeth. The film group did worse on an information test than did the control group. In reported care of the teeth both groups were equal. In improvement of the condition of the teeth, the film group excelled slightly.

From a questionnaire study of 888 Los Angeles students, Seagoe (202) concluded that the primary appeal of the movie appears to be emotional rather than intellectual, and that any influence upon the child's conduct must be through the mediation of his emotions.

Peterson and Thurstone (184) showed pictures whose dominant theme dealt with such subjects as nationality, race, crime, war, capital punishment, prohibition, and penology. Their general plan was to measure the attitudes of a group of children by means of an attitude scale or a paired comparison schedule; to show the children a motion picture which had been judged by others to have some value on the issue in question; and then to measure the attitudes of the children again after the picture had been shown.

The most striking change in attitude which they found was the change in sentiment toward the Negro as a result of seeing the picture "The Birth of a Nation." The film "Son of the Gods" showed a definite change in attitudes favorable to the Chinese, and "Four Sons" made the children more favorable toward the Germans. "The Criminal Code" made a group more lenient in their attitude toward the punishment of criminals. The pictures "Big House" and "Numbered Men" in combination had a similar effect.

A group of high-school children were less favorable toward war after seeing "All Quiet on the Western Front." One group who saw "Journey's End" showed no change in attitude toward war; a second group showed a small change in the direction of pacifism. A group of high-school children were more severe in their judgment of gambling after seeing the picture "Street of Chance." The motion pictures used to study changes in attitude toward capital punishment and prohibition showed no effect on the children's attitudes.

It seems evident that pictures which have an adequate emotional appeal can change the attitudes of children. Furthermore, Peterson and Thurstone demonstrated that the change is a specific effect for each picture. It is foolish to generalize and to state that motion pictures have a definite effect in changing attitudes. It depends very largely upon the specific picture.

Holaday and Stoddard (142) measured the degree to which children are able to retain what they see in movies. They exhibited seventeen pictures in all and tested the children who witnessed them by means of true-false tests, four response multiple-choice tests, and ten-minute essays. They gave one-third of the observers the tests one day after seeing the picture; one-third of the observers they tested one month to six weeks after the showing; and the other one-third they tested two to three months after the showing. The general information of children and adults increased to a considerable extent by correctly shown information through the medium of motion pictures. General information presented incorrectly by the pictures was frequently accepted as valid unless the incongruity was quite apparent. Retention of specific incidents of motion pictures was high. The second-third grade group retained, on the average, nearly 60 percent as much as the group of superior adults. Action was remembered best when it concerned activities such as sports, general action, crime, and fighting; when it had a high emotional appeal; and when it occurred in a familiar type of surrounding, such as home, school, or tenement. The percents of retention found by these investigators surpassed to a large degree the percents previously obtained in learning experiments.

Dysinger and Ruckmick (115) studied, by means of psychogalvanic and pulse records, and by verbal reports, the emotional effects produced by motion pictures in children and in adults. While they reported definite emotional effects which vary with individuals, they were able to draw no conclusions as to the possibility that such emotional reactions were pernicious or beneficial in their effects upon the mental health of those who witnessed the pictures.

Renshaw, Miller, and Marquis (192) made an extensive study of the effects of motion pictures upon the sleep of children. Their experiments were very carefully done and provide a valuable contribution to the psychology of sleep, even apart from any light that they throw on the significance of motion pictures for mental health or ill-health. They found that some films do induce a disturbance of sleep in children which may be as great as, or greater than, the effect of ingesting from 4 to 6 grains of caffein between the hours of 6 and 9 p. m. They give evidence to refute the theory that restlessness in sleep following exposure to motion pictures is due to the effects of the flicker of the picture. It seems to be the emotional effect which is operative, but no inference can be made as to which is the best type of picture for children to see. They suggest that the best hygienic regulations should limit attendance at certain types of films.

The experimental evidence seems to be very strong that motion pictures can affect children's attitudes, that they can be well retained, that they have an emotional effect, and that the excitement aroused by the picture may persist as would a drug stimulant. When it comes to evaluating the effect of pictures on the mental health of the child who witnesses them, not so much can be said.

Dale (112) made an analysis of the content of motion pictures. He found that three out of four pictures deal with crime, sex, or love. Love-making of an intense sort is seen in 70 percent of the pictures. Murder is the crime most often pictured. Vulgarity and drinking occur in two out of three pictures. The tone of the writer makes the reader feel that Dale believes the content has a bad influence, but he gives no evidence, except his opinion, that motion pictures are harmful to the mental health or welfare of those who view them.

Dale (111) also made a study of the attendance of children at motion picture performances. He found that more than one-third of the motion picture audience is under twenty-one years of age and that two-thirds of the attendance of children is in the evening. On the average, boys attend 1.10 times a week, and girls .88 times. Judging by the frequency with which the audience reviews the program, the comedy is the most popular part of the program, the main picture is second in popularity, and the newsreel, the third.

Blumer (95) made a study of the effect of the movies on the conduct of college and grade-school students. He collected his evidence from written narratives of motion picture experiences, from questionnaires, personal interviews, direct observation, and studies of conversations on movie subjects. He interpreted his results to indicate that imitation of movie situations, ideals, mannerisms, and modes of conduct is frequent and that attitudes, and notions of rights and privileges, may be implanted by witnessing motion pictures.

Blumer and Hauser (96) attempted to study the effect of motion pictures on the production of delinquency and crime. They conducted personal interviews and studied the autobiographies of young delinquents, ex-convicts, grade-school and high-school students. While they presented results to indicate that the motion pictures were an important factor in the delinquent careers of 10 percent of the males and 25 percent of the females, it would seem that these results should be accepted with great reservations. When a person is asked whether certain specific influences operated in leading him into misconduct, he is being tempted to evade responsibility, and the answer should be discredited.

Peters (180) made an elaborate attempt to measure the degree to which pictures conformed to or departed from the mores of the community. He devised scales for measuring the mores by having adults arrange described bits of conduct in hierarchical order according to "goodness" or "badness." These scales were then used to measure the "goodness" or "badness" of the movies. Movies were found to oppose the present values regarding aggressiveness of girls in love-making; they parallel life from the standpoint of both approval and practices in respect to kissing; they surpass the mores in respect to democratic attitudes and practices; and, finally, they challenge admiration in respect to their treatment of children by parents. They found a negative correlation between the success of the films and their degree of offense against the mores.

Throughout the Payne studies one detects a militant tone. Presumably unbiased, the authors seem (with some exceptions) to be on the hunt for evidence with which to condemn the movies. The meager proof against the movies is evident when all the studies are related. There is no evidence that motion pictures are undermining the mental health of the community. The appeal of motion pictures is emotional, but that is no condemnation of them. They are intended to appeal to the emotions of the audience. They may effect changes in attitudes which are enduring. Such an instrument can, of course, be used unwisely; but the evidence seems to be that, in the main, the effects are not pernicious. The producers must conform fairly closely to the moral attitudes of the community or suffer the penalty of losses at the box office. It would seem more nearly correct to say that the content and tone of pictures reflect the mental life of the community instead of assuming that their influence is to arouse mental conflicts and to produce neuroses in the individuals who witness them.

Radio

Because no philanthropist has been generous enough to donate funds to promote research in connection with the radio, studies in this field are not numerous.

Robinson (196) tested the effect upon the opinions of the listeners of listening to four radio speeches on the subject of unemployment. He found that those ideas spread most rapidly which were already well established in the group, the changes being largely in the direction of strengthening the favorable judgments and decreasing the frequency of doubt.

Kirkpatrick (147) suggested that there is more responsiveness to radio programs among the lower occupational groups and those not so well educated, and possibly those of lower degrees of intelligence. The evidence for this opinion is not very conclusive.

Most of the research in connection with radio is in the direction of ascertaining the size of the radio audience and in analyzing the type of program to which people listen, as well as their reaction to programs of various kinds (101, 160).

Psychologists could well make use of the results of the investigations made by commercial organizations in order to carry out a program designed to tell us more about the effect of the radio on the mental health of the listener.

CHAPTER IV
The Normal Child

ALTHOUGH MUCH HAS BEEN WRITTEN about the mental hygiene of the normal, little of it can be termed research in the strict sense of the word. This chapter will indicate some of the more important discussions of positive mental hygiene as well as the few research studies which bear on positive mental health.

The first treatise on mental health from the positive point of view was Burnham's book, *The Normal Mind* (240). Burnham indicated his debt to James's *Talks to Teachers,* particularly the last three chapters on life's ideals. Burnham's book was the first of a series relating to mental hygiene which have come out with increasing frequency in recent years. It is impossible to mention them all. Shaffer (315), Symonds (332), Morgan (295), Kirkpartrick (285), Woodworth (345), Wallin (334), and Patey and Stevenson (300) have written on mental hygiene as psychologists. Sherman (316), Howard and Patry (278), Menninger (294), and Crawford and Menninger (247) have written as psychiatrists and Groves (267) has written as a sociologist. Jastrow (279) and Seabury (314) have written similar books in a more popular style for the general reader.

Shaffer (315) has the most extended treatise on the psychology of adjustment from the viewpoint of objective psychology, maintaining that behavior and adjustment may be explained by hypotheses familiar to experimental psychology. Symonds (332) discussed the mental hygiene of the school child and applied the principles of mental hygiene to the situation. Wallin (334), Sherman (316), and Patey and Stevenson (300) wrote with the needs of educators in mind. These books include a number of helpful case studies. Books by Morgan (295) and Kirkpatrick (285) are designed primarily for students in college classes. Howard and Patry (278) and Menninger (294) wrote books on mental hygiene from the point of view of the physician and indicated the psychiatrist's point of view with respect to understanding of problems of adjustment. It may be added that the books written by those with different professional backgrounds are not clearly distinguishable in terminology or point of view. All apparently borrowed from certain commonly accepted principles which originally were associated with the psychoanalysis developed by Freud, conditioned response developed by Pavlov, the insight into problems of adjustment contributed by orthodox psychiatry, etc. Most of these books, however, found it easier to describe various types of maladjustment than adjustment and none hewed to the line of describing the normal mind better than those by Burnham (240, 241).

Mental Hygiene of the Young Child

The mental hygiene of the growing child has been discussed in chapters devoted to the topic in various treatises on child psychology and child development, among the more recent of which may be mentioned those by Goodenough (263), Gesell and others (261), Jersild (280), Stoddard and Wellman (320), Bühler (239), E. Dewey (250), J. E. Anderson (228), Hazlitt (275), Groves and Groves (268), Johnson (283), Norsworthy and Whitley (297), and Bott (236).

The books by J. E. Anderson (228), Foster (258), and Stuart (329) presented discussions of physical growth, the development and guidance of children and youth, and guidance through play and activity. Material for these books was gathered for the White House Conference on Child Health and Protection. The book by Norsworthy and Whitley (297) is a revision of an earlier book of the same title. The book by Stoddard and Wellman (320) kept to the line of research findings as closely as any. Goodenough (263) presented a clear picture for various levels or periods of development. Jersild (280) gave a psychological interpretation of the process of development. Gesell and others (261) wrote primarily of the development of the infant, basing his work on the exact development studies made in his laboratory at Yale.

Experimental studies of the development of emotional habits in young children have been largely devoted in the last few years to studies of the incidence of various types of behavior. Goodenough's study (262) of anger in young children summarized what was known in this field to the date in which she wrote. Subsequent studies on anger have been made by Ricketts (309). Caille (242) studied the incidence and development of resistant behavior. Jersild and associates (281, 282) and Hagman (269) made studies of the development of fears in young children. Jersild's studies are of particular importance because of their thoroughness and comprehensiveness. Jersild and Holmes (281) studied fears in children through observations in daily life by parents, the reports given by children themselves, the fears recalled from childhood by adults, and certain experimental and statistical studies of the origin and incidence of fear. These various methods of collecting data with regard to fear show a high degree of consistency. In this monograph a helpful summary is included in a final chapter giving practical suggestions on origin, utility, and prevention of fear. Heering (276) studied the incidence of thumbsucking. Levy (288) experimented with a litter of new-born dogs, feeding some with bottles having nipples with fine holes and others with nipples having larger holes. Keeping the amount of food constant, he found that there was more tendency to suck between feedings on the part of the dogs who had the small-holed nipples, indicating that thumbsucking may be due to defects in the normal process of obtaining food.

The mental hygiene problems of the normal child are reflected in the attitudes which parents and teachers have toward children's problems.

These have been revealed in a number of studies. Laws (287) and Wickman (342) indicated attitudes that parents and teachers have toward children's problems. More recently Bain (233), MacClenathan (291), and Yourman (346) provided supplementary data as to the attitude of teachers toward problems of children. Fitz-Simons (257), Koch and others (286), Ojemann (298), and R. M. Stogdill (322, 323, 325) studied the attitudes of parents toward their children's problems. These studies, according to a review by R. M. Stogdill (324), indicate that parents and teachers are highly conservative in their attitude toward children, approving behavior that makes for the smooth running of home and school, and showing little regard for wholesome personality development. Psychologists, on the other hand, find that active and extrovert behavior is better adapted to the social adjustment of children regardless of annoyance to teachers and parents. Psychologists, in general, emphasize freedom, while parents and teachers put more stress on submission and discipline.

Mental Hygiene of Adolescence

The mental hygiene of adolescence is discussed in a number of recent books on the psychology of adolescence, the more outstanding of which are those by Garrison (260), Garland (259), McCarthy (290), Conklin (245), Cole (244), Averill (232), Arlitt (231), Richmond (308), and Sadler and Sadler (312). Cole (244) and Averill (232) devoted much attention to adolescent adjustments, illustrated with numerous case studies. Conklin's book (245) is more scientific in character with frequent references to the experimental literature on adolescent development. Garland (259) wrote from the point of view of the pediatrician. The book by the Sadlers (312) is very popularly written.

The period from 1932 to 1935 was characterized by the use of the questionnaire method in studying adolescent adjustments. Pintner and others (304), R. B. Smith (318), Maller (293), Washburne (335, 336), Symonds and Jackson (331), and Pressey and Pressey (306) made such studies. Pintner and others (304) devoted their work primarily to the elementary and junior high-school pupil. R. B. Smith (318) made a special study of inferiority feelings of high-school pupils and developed a scale for their measurement. Maller (293) specialized on the development of various types of instruments for measuring adolescent adjustment, including adaptations of the free association test, a test of persistence, a test of moral judgment, a test of honesty, and a psychoneurotic inventory. Recently he brought together the best items from all of these different tests into a battery which he calls the Case Inventory. Washburne's approach (335, 336) perhaps involves the greatest psychological insight of any of these studies of adolescent adjustments. He developed a questionnaire which measures such factors as impulse, self-control, rapport-alienation, sympathy, and happiness. Symonds and Jackson (331) reported an Adjustment Questionnaire which samples pupils' attitudes toward various phases of their environment and used it in conjunction with behavior ratings for a study of adolescent adjustments. The Presseys (306) revised their X-O test and published a new test of emotional maturity which they call the Interest Attitudes Test to be used with junior and senior high-school pupils.

These investigators and others used these instruments for studying adolescent adjustments as related to school adjustment and to the problems of delinquency. Myers (296) investigated the relation between the school adjustments and various factors of the home environment. For the study of the home environment he developed a special inventory on intrafamily relationships. In general he found that there was a distinct relationship between school adjustment and intrafamily relations. A subcommittee of the White House Conference on Child Health and Protection (340) made a significant questionnaire study of the factors in the family situation which condition the adjustment of the adolescent. Whitlow (341), by a questionnaire study, investigated the moral attitudes of high-school students and found that stealing, drinking, and lying are the cardinal offenses, although swearing, disobedience, and lying were most frequently admitted.

Mental Hygiene of Early Adulthood

On the college and early adult level a number of significant studies of the nature of normal adjustment have been made, beginning with G. Watson's study (337) of happiness among graduate students of education. Watson's procedure was repeated by Sailer (313), working with Y. M. C. A. members. Using a questionnaire with 300 opportunities for response, replies were received from approximately 500 young men. The reports indicated that those men who considered themselves happy also considered themselves above the average of the general population in happiness. The unhappy group considered dancing and card-playing as unimportant for happiness; they also considered religious worship and activities unnecessary. Physical handicaps appeared to be of more importance in causing unhappiness than nervous habits. It was noted that "only" children showed a greater tendency toward sociability than others. No relation between intelligence and happiness was reported, as very few of the intelligence tests sent out were returned. Hartmann (271, 272), in two studies at Pennsylvania State College, surveyed the adjustment problems among college students and the personality traits associated with variations in happiness. In the first study (271), one hundred sophomores submitted lists of not less than five and not more than ten major life problems. Vocation and personality development were high in all of the three methods of classification which Hartmann used. Sexual questions dropped to a low place in the importance index, while feelings of inferiority ranked high. Esthetic problems were largely absent from the list. In the other study (272) Hartmann attempted to find the personality traits associated with variations in happiness in a college population. With the possible exception of finding that unhappy people were mildly inclined to be neurotic, most of the contributions were negative. However, several interesting relationships were tentatively suggested, although the correlations were low. Among these were: emotional health was the most *important* factor associated with happiness, but not the *sole* producer; the dominant person has a slightly greater chance of being happy than the submissive; the nature of ideals was an irrelevant matter; and no relation existed between interest in future career and happiness. Seventy-five percent of the group rated themselves as possessing happiness equaling or exceeding that of the average, which may be explained by the relatively sheltered existence of the college undergraduate. There was a disconcertingly low correlation between the self-rating of happiness and the ratings of associates, indicating disparity between attributed and experienced felicity.

Reinhardt (307) reported the problems most often mentioned in a questionnaire submitted to 147 women and 73 men students in a college freshman class. The difficulties listed in order of their importance indicated that nearly one-half of the students worried about certain matters not connected with school work. The need for a mental hygiene expert was indicated.

J. G. Patrick (301), by means of personal interviews and questionnaires, attempted to study the role of intimate groups in the personality development of college men. The subjects studied were exclusively male, white, native Americans, who had graduated previous to 1920. The intimate groups were divided into two types: (a) small groups such as the family and childhood play groups; and (b) larger groups such as the church, social group, and club. Some of the important findings were:

1. Intimate groups stand not only as symbols, but as major instrumentalities through which personality is attained.
2. The reactions to a small group of male friends persist as an enduring pattern resulting in a strong basis for predictability in the carry-over of these patterns from one to succeeding developmental periods.
3. There was indication of a desire to reconstruct intimate groups previously found satisfying, and where this was not possible a feeling of frustration usually appeared.
4. Students in small colleges as contrasted with those in large colleges spread their activities over a greater range of activities and a larger number of intimate groups, the social distance between students and faculty was less, the church was a more important element, and the students exhibited a more critical evaluation of their respective institutions. While the larger college offered greater intellectual opportunities the small college was more favorable to social development.

Stratton (327) studied the personal problems reported by 1,000 students in a graduate school of education. Major problems in order of their importance: (a) finance, (b) leisure and recreation, (c) part-time work, (d) placement, (e) social relationships, and (f) academic problems. The study indicated that students sought aid from college officials more frequently for academic problems than any other. Problems of leisure time and recreation were harder to solve than any others, while problems of finance, part-time work, and placement were being solved by 40 to 50 percent of the students.

From a survey of case records in a college psychological consultation service for a ten-year period, E. L. Stogdill (321) concluded that the problem as stated by the student is not always the problem needing clinical analysis, but indicates the student's insight into the difficulty. Four problems, personality defects, poor home adjustments, physical and social strain, were found to be closely connected as a group in a great many cases, regardless of the student's statement of his difficulty.

After studying the vocational fitness of 888 college students who had chosen vocations, Sparling (319) concluded that there was a great need for vocational guidance in college. While the group was not typical in vocational choices of college students in general, since a great majority had foreign-born parents and 95 percent desired to enter the four overcrowded professions of law, medicine, teaching, and dentistry, the data indicated that a majority of the students expected to enter a vocation in which they would have an intelligence handicap. There was little evidence of accurate information about the profession chosen, and 80 percent thought they would earn more than average salary in the field chosen.

A number of writers (230, 246, 256, 289, 299, 310, 311, 338, 344) have discussed the need and opportunities in college for mental hygiene, both remedial and preventive. V. V. Anderson and Kennedy (230), from their experience in a large commercial organization, estimated that 85 percent of the students in college showed some need for help in integrating their emotional life, while 10 to 15 percent were in danger of mental breakdown. Ruggles (311) and V. V. Anderson and Kennedy (230) pointed out that college mental hygiene programs should emphasize the possibilities to be achieved with every student in increasing happiness and efficiency, and not merely the treatment of the abnormal. The treatment of maladjusted students by deans and other college officers on the symptom level has led to general agreement that there is a great need for trained leadership in this field. Williams (344) pointed out that theoretical training for a college psychiatrist is not sufficient but must include clinical experience with normal individuals.

There is disagreement as to the place mental hygiene should occupy in the college organization. Livingood (289) and V. V. Anderson and Kennedy (230) asserted that the mental hygiene program should be located in the personnel department as an educational agency rather than in the health department as a health agency. This would have the added advantage of combining the counseling and advisory facilities of the college, not only for academic issues but for all life adjustment problems of the individual. However, Ruggles (310) pointed out that the psychiatrist should be located in the health department in order to get the close cooperation of the college physician. All records should be kept confidential and the mental hygienist should not attempt to be an educator.

Although no college is equipped to give individual guidance to all the students that may need some help in their adjustment problems, a great many difficulties may be cleared up through the giving of mental hygiene or orientation courses (255, 292, 303). McKinney (292) drew an analogy between facts of mental hygiene and physical vaccination. By encouraging self-analysis and autosuggestion, the student was encouraged to understand that personality defects were not permanent but had causes and these causes could be removed.

Burnham (240, 241) and Morgan (295) have written books in non-technical language on the preservation of mental health, suitable for texts in a college mental hygiene course. Bennett (234) wrote a text to be used as the basis of a freshman orientation course. In addition to mental hygiene, such problems as wise distribution of time, efficiency in study, vocational planning, and love and marriage were discussed.

Strang (326) summarized the results of investigations relating to personnel work in a book intended for specialists and teachers.

Mental Hygiene of Middle Age and Senescence

The mental hygiene of middle age has not shared the experimental interest of recent years in the development of the infant and adolescent. Elliott (254) criticized modern education in its emphasis on individual development. While these goals may be useful criteria for adulthood, they prove themselves inadequate to the needs of middle life when waning physical energy and diminishing opportunity for active participation quite often lead to a feeling of frustration and defeat. Our presentday society has overlooked the contributions that older people may make in emphasizing the development of initiative and responsibility in young people at the expense of ideals of service. Education must have its aims remade to the purpose of helping the individual realize the other-than-ego values of self. "Satisfaction in later life involves, also, the individual's having developed goals of endeavor and found patterns of life sufficiently inclusive and dynamic to carry him through the whole of life." Jung (284), probably more than any other psychologist, has been interested in the problems and mental health of middle age. He has concluded that many problems of middle age are brought on by the inability of the person to reject the role of youth and cultivate his capacities for achievement at higher levels of satisfaction. The first half of life is concerned with the making of a living and establishing social contacts, an identification with the outer world. With middle age must come a liberation from this identification and an adjustment to internal realities, an "assimilation of the unconscious into the conscious self." This takes the form of realizing and developing individual traits and aspects of personality hitherto undeveloped and neglected. Jung also emphasized the importance of a religious point of view in realizing what life should mean.

Pitkin (305), in a popular book on the value of life after forty, pointed out that to live effectively after middle age one must have learned how to live earlier, that the period before forty should not be considered the most important part of life, but merely the preparation for the fuller and more varied existence that opens with the coming of middle age.

Sex Adjustments

Antedating the three-year period to be covered by this review, the three main pieces of research which have provided us with information concerning sex life of normal people are those by Davis (248), Hamilton (270), and Dickinson and Beam (251). There seems to have been little recent investigation or discussion of sex adjustments especially of the period from six years to adolescense. The trend in recent literature has been to point out the need for sane and wholesome sex education at all levels of development.

Dillon (252) studied the attitudes of children toward their own bodies and those of other children. The study was based on the observation of 38 children ranging in age from twenty-seven months to sixty-two months in a nursery school. The author concluded that the little sex play that was evidenced was motivated largely by curiosity. Manipulation of genitals appeared, but no sensory satisfaction was shown except in the case of one girl. Differences in sex structure were noted by the children but seemed to carry no sex significance. The older children appeared to have a more definite awareness and interest in their bodies, but in none of the children was there a sense of shame in appearing undressed before either adults or other children.

Groves (265) pointed out the serious sex maladjustments that may arise among college students due to the deliberate postponement of marriage. He concluded that colleges have the greatest need and best opportunity to distribute recent scientific sex information. E. S. Smith (317) undertook to ascertain the factors that were responsible for the unconventional behavior in twenty-five unmarried adolescent mothers. These data were collected by means of questionnaires and interviews and comparable material was gathered from 100 Girl Reserves. Both groups showed disappointment at the failure of the school in giving them sex information. The author stressed the duty of the school in giving special attention to a program of sex education which should include great concern and guidance in boy-girl relationships and adequate preparation of both students and parents for parenthood.

Several recent discussions have emphasized the importance of informed and well-adjusted parents and teachers in building healthy sex attitudes in children (235, 243, 249, 253, 266, 273, 343). Edson (253) warned parents that child and adult wants in sex are entirely different. Those training children must constantly put themselves in the child's place, to determine what his needs are, how he got them, and how they can best be satisfied. Groves and Groves (266) emphasized the importance of realizing that sex does not wait until puberty to become a force in life, but appears at birth and is the most influential factor in the formation of character. Hattendorf (273), from an analysis of problems presented by mothers in a study group in sex education, concluded that first questions about sex come in greatest numbers at four or five years of age, while the greatest interest in sex is shown by children between five and nine years of age. The earliest interest is shown in organs of the body and in physical sex differences, then follows interest in babies and the process of reproduction. De Schweinitz (249) warned against the oversimplification of sex instruction, since information in itself has not been a solution. Too often sex instruction has been harmful because the parent approached the whole subject aggressively with varying degrees of tension, and overlooked the emotional implications involved. Sex should not be considered an isolated phenomenon, but as inextricably tied up in the conditions of the home. The author's formula was "Love them, set them a good example, and let them alone." Bigelow (235) concluded that the greatest good from sex education has come not from the content of courses, as much as the elimination of taboos and inhibitions formerly surrounding the whole field of sex.

Mental Hygiene in Industry

There has been in recent years a striking lack of research and investigation into the conditions that influence the mental health of workers. V. V. Anderson (229), from his experience in a large industrial organization, pointed out that the mental hygienist may be of very practical importance to industry by saving money and raising morale through reducing turnover and increasing production. Soviet Russia has been aware of the importance of the worker's mental health to efficiency and quality of production. Zacharoff (347) reported the two main avenues by which the Soviet Union has attacked this problem: first, by prophylactic psychiatry which aims to correct the mental and nervous complaints arising from industry; second, by vocational guidance which is primarily medical guidance. Granniss (264) estimated that 85 percent of all industrial accidents are caused by workers' mental attitudes. A person trained in mental hygiene in the personnel department of industrial organizations could uncover the causes of unhealthy mental attitudes and help to remove them. Hersey (277) compared groups of American and German workers. He found that happiness of the workers increased output 2 percent above normal while unhappiness resulted in a drop of 7 percent below normal. He further estimated that only half of the time were all workers in a healthy frame of mind. The author listed three conditions indispensable to mental health: having a goal; making progress toward the goal; and feeling that one is accomplishing something worthwhile. The enthusiasm of Russian and German workers exceeded that of American workers due to the former's greater feeling of worthwhile accomplishment. The author emphasized the employer's responsibility in providing medical and psychiatric service for his employees.

CHAPTER V
Behavior Problems and Delinquency

INVESTIGATIONS OF BEHAVIOR PROBLEMS, as related to the field of educational research, deal primarily with observation of behavior, the mental, physical and emotional characteristics of maladjustment, and methods of treatment, with special reference to prevention. Most of the earlier researches were confined to the problem of juvenile delinquency, in the belief that a knowledge of causes, with deflection of emphasis from criminal to educational implications, might lead to the elimination of much antisocial conduct. More recently the interest has shifted somewhat toward the study of behavior as an aspect of child development in general, with the result that delinquency as such is less often mentioned.

It is not known whether misbehavior in children is increasing or decreasing. Statistics of juvenile arrests and probation activities throw little light on this problem, because changing procedures and unstandardized terminology have rendered difficult the comparison of data for different localities, or even for different years in the same locality. While it is not unlikely that the increasing complexities of life have contributed to delinquency by giving rise to more varied opportunities for unsocial behavior, there has been increased diligence on the part of all agencies concerned with treatment and prevention.

The literature of this subject is vast, and many valuable contributions, of both extensive and intensive character, are available. Enough is known about problem children to serve as a basis for intelligent treatment. Some of the programs for prevention, based upon research findings, are obtaining promising results.

All general works on juvenile delinquency deal with mental hygiene aspects of the problem. Among the writers may be mentioned Healy (406), Burt (371), Fenton and others (390), Goddard (399), Reckless and Smith (437), Van Waters (464), Aichhorn (353), and the White House Conference committee (469).

Symptoms of Maladjustment

Types of misconduct—Until recently it has been the practice, in cases of juvenile arrest or detention, to designate the specific offense which led to the action. If more than one offense was charged in a given case, the principal offense was used for statistical purposes. The types of misconduct were described largely in terms of criminal behavior, and in many instances the same terminology was applied. A typical classification is that used by Healy and Bronner (404). In a summary (471) of 1,250 cases studied by the California Bureau of Juvenile Research from 1915 to 1923, the offenses, 14 in number, were classified in three groups, with frequencies as follows:

property, 47.8 percent; persons, 6.9 percent; peace and order, 43.5 percent. The individual offenses of incorrigibility, stealing, and truancy were most frequent, while those involving personal injury or damage to property were relatively infrequent.

During the progress of the study just referred to, Clark (378) devised a scale for grading juvenile offenses, through the use of which the seriousness of a given child's conduct was indicated by the "delinquency index." The offenses appeared in the scale, in order of seriousness, as follows: truancy, incorrigibility, vagrancy, malicious mischief, drunkenness, stealing, burglary, larceny, forgery, assault, sex immorality, arson, highway robbery, murder. Each offense was judged on a scale of ten points, the composite score being the delinquency index. For the California boys measured by the scale, Clark found indexes ranging from 0 to 39 points, with a median of 14 points. He considered an index of less than 10 to be of little consequence; indexes of 10 to 20, characterizing about 55 percent of the cases studied, were considered "typical cases of juvenile delinquency"; while an index greater than 20 was interpreted as representing serious misconduct. A revision of the scale was offered by Mursell (425).

A more recent study (397) of 983 Boston juvenile court boys gave the following classification and (overlapping) frequencies: truancy 64.1 percent; stealing, 51.4 percent; "bunking out," 48.9 percent; sex delinquency, 13.4 percent; excessive and frequent lying, 12.5 percent; while 7.3 percent "were known to have indulged in various forms of misbehavior such as repeated disobedience, drinking, marked cruelty, and the like."

Fenton and others (390) found twenty-nine separate offenses in the case histories of 400 delinquent boys in California, various forms of stealing and truancy being most frequent. He found that 35 percent of the boys had been involved in the theft of automobiles. His classification includes several items which are not usually listed as offenses of delinquents: school problem, destruction, inadequate home, cruelty, excessive smoking, fighting, failure in foster home, bad companions, fits of temper, nuisance, and excessive movie-going.

In the case of delinquent girls, sex offenses lead in frequency. Where other offenses occur, they are likely in some way to be associated with sex conduct.

Studies of problem children who are not considered delinquent tend to use similar, but less specific, classification of misconduct. Paynter and Blanchard (435) found the predominating behavior difficulties in child guidance clinic cases to be stealing, truancy, sex experience, and disobedience. They also included as behavior difficulties speech defects, bullying, and temper tantrums. In behavior cases occuring in the same family, Weill (467) found that disobedience, temper tantrums, food capriciousness, enuresis, destructiveness, restless sleep, and masturbation are most frequent. Weill's list included thirty-five forms of misconduct, with stealing and truancy relatively low in frequency.

Ackerson (348) made a comprehensive study of the behavior difficulties of 5,000 children, from which a group of 154 cases were selected for intensive study of personality and conduct. The traits were considered in relation to age, mental level, personality-conduct-total, and their predictive value.

Wickman (470) had lists of behavior symptoms rated by teachers and mental hygienists, finding much disagreement as to the relative importance of some traits. Studies by Haggerty (402) were based upon extensive samplings of school children. Olson (433) offered a method of measuring problem tendencies, and later (430) described their clinical use.

Valuable descriptions of individual forms of misbehavior, considered in the light of related factors, are to be found in case studies, among the first of which were those reported by Healy (406). The Joint Committee on Methods of Preventing Delinquency (410), in one of the early reports from the child guidance clinics, told the story of three problem children, including detailed descriptions of behavior. Baker and Traphagen (360) reported seven illustrative case studies, each rated on the behavior scale.

Haggerty, Olson, and Wickman (401) devised behavior rating schedules, especially applicable to young children, in which the occurrence or nonoccurrence of each of a series of behavior characteristics is checked by the rater. Norms, based on more than 2,000 children, were made available.

An elaborate study of delinquent behavior symptoms, with an attempt to predict outcomes, was made by Casselberry (374). The study resulted in the adoption of a battery of tests for the prediction of reform, designed for the use of courts and institutions. The sequence of juvenile offenses was investigated by Burkey (370), who found that normal children are most likely to begin their deliquencies by running away.

Armstrong (357) investigated the cases of 660 runaway school boys between seven and sixteen years of age. The chief motive was escape from some emotional conflict with family or school or from some excessive burden of responsibility.

Emotional and mental characteristics—Healy (406), who pioneered in the laboratory study of delinquents, denied having "the slightest inclination to place delinquents as such in the list of abnormal individuals." However, his investigations revealed that certain mental and emotional abnormalities are closely linked with misbehavior, and his case studies, together with his general conclusions, stimulated much of the early research along this line. In a later study Healy and Bronner (404) pointed out that "the mentally abnormal among delinquents constitute a much greater proportion than is found in the general population." Of the 4,000 cases studied they found 72.5 percent to be "definitely normal."

Glueck and Glueck (397) found their delinquent children of considerably lower mentality than a comparative group of public school children, with an "excess of dull, borderline and defective individuals." Their further analysis of the mental condition of this fairly typical group of approximately 1,000 delinquents revealed "a question of mental abnormality" in 47 cases; 3 were definitely psychotic; 39 constitutionally inferior; 19 psychopathic personalities (e.g., egocentrics); 13 were designated as "peculiar" personalities; 10 showed epileptic characteristics; 5 were diagnosed as psychoneurotics; 70 showed marked adolescent instability; and 350 manifested an abnormal degree of various deviant personality characteristics such as impulsiveness, oversuggestibility, marked sensitiveness, etc. They further stated that none of the foregoing characteristics or traits was found in 44.3 percent of the 1,000 cases. Their general conclusion is that three-fifths of the children had "marked emotional and personality defects."

Ackerson (349) found personality and conduct traits closely interwoven, although each of the two types of problems has its own peculiar patterns. Paynter and Blanchard (435) emphasized the importance of observable personality characteristics on the ground that they are as likely to lead to vocational and social maladjustments in maturity as are the overt behavior disorders which are forced upon the attention of teachers.

Many recent writers take the psychoanalytic view that delinquent behavior is closely bound up with restriction and renunciation of instinct. Alexander (354) contended that criminal behavior is acquired when these conflicts are unresolved. Personality, as expressed in social participation, is associated with delinquency, according to the findings of Atwood (359), who scored matched groups of 100 delinquent and 100 non-delinquent boys twelve to sixteen years of age in this respect. At every age except twelve the delinquents scored higher (meaning more participation) than the non-delinquents.

Boynton and McGaw (367) submitted a list of some forty traits which, in the opinion of teachers, are most likely to cause children in the fifth and sixth grades to be considered problem cases. The average number of undesirable traits for a child was 7.23. Among these are many personality traits, such as inattention, carelessness, sullenness, lack of interest, overactivity, quarrelsomeness, "cuteness," stubbornness, shyness, and suggestibility. The conclusion was reached that subtle personality disturbances are more symptomatic of potential delinquency than are infractions of school discipline; but that teachers are concerned disproportionately with behavior related to classroom disturbance.

Courthial (380) used a series of tests to study the emotional reactions of delinquent girls, with the finding that they are less well adjusted socially, and suffer more feelings of physical discomfort, than do non-delinquent girls of matched age, intelligence, and environment. Laslett and Manning (415), after applying the Laslett test of delinquent tendencies and the Murray psychoneurotic inventory to 332 high-school pupils, found no significant relationship between delinquent tendencies and emotional maladjustment. Moore (424), in a comparative study of 150 problem boys and normal children, found the former to be less stable emotionally, with indications that certain antisocial deeds of apparent bravery are merely compensatory reactions for an underlying fear.

The personal attitudes of delinquent boys were investigated by Reusser (440) who found them more critical than the average boy and less critical of themselves than were non-delinquent boys of similar age, grade, intelligence, and socio-economic status. Mental conflicts in behavior cases were described clinically by Healy (407).

Methods of observation—Prior to the development of clinical technics there were no reliable methods for observing the characteristics of behavior problem children. Reports of parents, teachers, and police officers were often inaccurate and prejudiced. The clinical method, introduced into the Chicago juvenile court by Healy (406), was soon accepted as a regular procedure by courts and institutions. Among the early reports of these technics are those of Bronner (369), Fernald (393), Kuhlmann (412), Weidensall (466), and Williams (473). More recent examples are those of Adler (351) and Fenton and others (390).

Methods of observation include (a) personal interviews; (b) testing; (c) studies of family and environmental conditions; (d) evaluation of school and home behavior; and (e) observations of parole or after-success.

A general discussion of methods and procedure used in the Harvard Crime Survey was offered by Glueck and Glueck (397). Casselberry (374) developed an objective method for the analysis of delinquents, based on tests and other forms of investigation. Ackerson (349) described a special technic for studying children's behavior problems. Anderson and others (355) set forth the procedures used in a typical child guidance clinic. Baker and Traphagen (360) prepared a detailed description of a new technic embodied in the Detroit Behavior Scale, with directions for its use. Olson (431) worked out a diagnostic method especially applicable to the study of problem children. Selling (445) and Doll (386) prepared handbooks for use in the examination of offenders.

Many studies are available in which intelligence and achievement tests serve as the basis for the investigation of delinquency. The current tendency is to utilize tests of non-intellectual traits, especially those related to emotional stability and attitudes. Fenton and Wallace (392) surveyed the use of tests in twenty-eight child guidance clinics. Haggerty, Olson, and Wickman (401) developed two schedules for the study of problem tendencies in children, with special reference to factors entering into maladjustment.

The test series of Raubenheimer (436) was planned to detect problem tendencies in the potentially delinquent. A new test of delinquency was described by Laslett and Manning (415) who showed its application to high-school pupils. An inventory of interests, especially applicable to child guidance clinics, was described by Wallace (465).

Most studies of problem children, even when based largely upon psychological tests, make use of case histories and other supplementary methods for the exploration of environmental factors. An excellent outline of case procedure is found in Glueck and Glueck (397). Williams (472) devised a method of grading home conditions, used for the study of the social backgrounds of delinquents, and the use of a similar scale for grading neighborhoods was reported by Clark and Williams (377). Records of after-success of delinquents were reported by Fenton and others (390). A report on the adjustment of clinic cases under a child guidance program was given by Davidson (382).

Prediction of delinquency—Attempts to predict delinquency are based largely upon studies of behavior symptoms in children who have not yet become delinquent, in the light of the early behavior of children who become delinquent. Ackerson (349) made a comprehensive study on the feasibility of inventorying children's behavior traits with special reference to the analysis of commonly recognized gross behavior patterns, most of which represent forms of maladjustment common to delinquent careers. Boynton and McGaw (367) found, in a checklist of forty traits in problem children, certain ones (inattention, carelessness, lack of interest in work, unwillingness to study, tendency to disturb classes) to be of such relative frequency as to suggest the further development of maladjustment. Burkey (370) found a predictive sequence of offenses; e. g., normal children who begin with truancy and incorrigibility take readily to stealing. Dickson (384) believed that teachers can be trained to recognize early symptoms of maladjustment, a view evidently shared by E. T. Glueck (396). The method proposed by Olson (432) is in a sense a prediction of further maladjustment. Speer (454) found the Bernreuter Personality Inventory to be of no aid in prediction of problem tendencies.

Causes of Behavior Difficulties

It is generally agreed that behavior difficulties cannot be attributed to any single cause or pattern of causes. Neither can such maladjustment be said to be solely hereditary or environmental. The patterns of causes, or, more properly, related factors, involve both constitutional and environmental conditions.

Constitutional factors—The situation with respect to heredity in delinquency has changed little since the early summary by Healy (406) in which he said: "The whole problem of human conduct is so complicated by environment and other genetic factors, that only now and then do we get satisfactory evidence of the part that heredity plays in the background." Investigations in California based upon extensive family history case work, revealed no evidence that delinquency, as such, is inherited (471). These studies and others of more recent date, however, show the relationship of behavior maladjustment to certain traits more definitely traceable to hereditary origin, feeble-mindedness, epilepsy, emotional instability, and nomadism. Healy reported cases of inherited excess energy, irritable temper, hypersexual tendencies, and certain physical characteristics, all of which appeared to be major factors in maladjustment. Fenton and others (390) implied doubt that heredity is an important factor, although pointing out that delinquents, on the whole, are of lower intelligence than unselected children, and that certain races contribute more than their proportion to the institutionalized delinquent population. Glueck and Glueck (397) offered no direct evidence of hereditary causation.

Environmental factors—Most investigators agree that environmental factors are potent in the causation of behavior maladjustment, although the precise connection is difficult to establish. Francis and Fillmore (394) reported an extensive study of the influence of environment upon the personality of children. Sheldon (449) computed indexes for male delinquency and five variable social factors. Inter-tract correlations ranged from .51 to .75, with a multiple of .84. A small proportion of families contributed a large proportion of offenses. Healy and Bronner (404) included a large number of factors, chiefly environmental, in their summary of causation: bad companions, adolescent instability, early sex experiences, mental conflicts, social suggestibility, love of adventure, motion pictures, school dissatisfaction, poor recreations, street life, vocational dissatisfaction, and sudden impulse. Glueck and Glueck (397) and Fenton and others (390) also emphasized complex environmental patterns.

Physical conditions have not been found important; delinquents on the whole, are within normal limits physically. Healy and Bronner (404) found physical conditions of all sorts to be causally related to delinquency in only 5.6 percent of the cases. Christie (376) found little evidence of causal relation of physical defects. Molitch and Adams (422) found significant frequency of hearing defects among delinquent boys. Molitch and Eccles (423) found no significant deviation of delinquents in calcium metabolism. On the other hand, Timme (460) found a slightly higher incidence of physical defects among problem than among non-problem children. Tobias (461) found indications of syphilis in 14.2 percent of a group of delinquents, but made no attempt to show a causal relationship. Armstrong (356) found evidence that primogeniture is related to delinquency, in cases in which the offense is against the home, while Parsley (434) found nothing significant in the ordinal position of delinquent girls, or in the size of the family. Sletto (452) found no greater tendency to delinquency on the part of the only child and no significant relationship to ordinal position.

School conditions appear to be related to behavior maladjustment in numerous ways. Delinquent boys and girls are often retarded in school. Glueck and Glueck (397) found their cases considerably more retarded than the general school population of the same area, even when allowances were made for mobility of the families. Fenton and others (390) found that 47.5 percent of 400 delinquent boys were retarded by age-grade status, while only 2.5 percent were accelerated. The New York State Crime Commission (428) reported that truants, as a rule, disliked academic subjects and tended to fail, while they enjoyed and pursued successfully the shop subjects. Boynton, Dugger, and Turner (368) submitted evidence that the emotional stability of teachers is reflected in the behavior of pupils. Healy and Bronner (405) found school conditions often directly contributory to delinquency.

Home conditions of delinquent children have been extensively studied. Using the Whittier scales for grading homes and neighborhoods, Williams (472) found lower indexes for delinquents than for non-delinquents, but pointed out that delinquents sometimes came from apparently good homes, and that even the bad homes contributed relatively few delinquents, considering the number of children in the family. Hodgkiss (409) found that 67 percent of a group of delinquent girls came from broken homes, while only 45 percent of a matched control group came from such homes. Glueck and Glueck (397) found the home broken by death of one or both parents in 26.7 percent, and by desertion, separation, or divorce in 18.8 percent of their cases. Fenton and others (390) found 59 percent of broken homes, against a normal expectation of 25 percent. Keogh (411) found relatively more broken homes in cases of runaway boys than in a control group. Maller (419) reported that of New York City delinquents, 39 percent of the boys and 55 percent of the girls came from broken homes. Approximately 50 percent of the families of a selected group of Wisconsin delinquents are receiving incomes below the health and decency living level established by Paul Douglas (372). The analysis indicated a direct influence of economic factors in the causation of delinquency. Gilmore (395) reported a study of five generations of a begging family, revealing a transmitted social pattern of behavior. Seagoe (444) found that presentday transient pupils commit more social acts than do other school pupils. Sullenger (457) found a relationship between economic status and delinquency, and an especially high delinquency rate among newsboys.

Reinhardt and Harper (439) compared the environmental factors of delinquent and non-delinquent boys, and found that the former had fewer club affiliations; came from larger families, from families of male dominance, and from mobile families; had fewer tools of culture (books, etc.); attended church less regularly; had older fathers, and greater disparity in parental ages.

Studies of delinquency areas reveal significant concentrations of behavior problems in different communities. The exhaustive investigation by Shaw and others (448) included maps showing such areas in Chicago, the ratio of delinquency varying inversely with the distance of the area from the business center of the city. He assumed that "delinquent behavior is very closely related to certain community situations which arise in the process of city growth." Maller (418) reported delinquency areas for New York City, Wilson (474), and Adler, Cahn, and Stuart (350), for communities in California.

Mental Aspects of Behavior Maladjustment

Results of intelligence tests—The use of intelligence tests with groups of problem children has resulted in extensive discussion and controversy. Originally a method of exploring what were believed to be basic factors in conduct, namely, intellectual concepts as related to moral judgment, such tests are now regularly applied wherever problem children are under observation. In his early studies Healy (406) used tests of his own devising together with other tests which were in process of standardization. Later studies were based largely upon Binet tests. A summary of these early tests, with results of testing at Whittier State School, was presented by Williams

(473). A summary including more recent work was given by Lane and Witty (414). Most of these investigations found delinquents to be of lower intelligence than non-delinquents, and the percents of mental deficiency were often large.

McClure (417) reported, for a group of Toledo juvenile court cases, a Stanford-Binet I. Q. range of 40 to 118, with a mean I. Q. of 79.34. Girls tested slightly higher than boys, and colored children slightly lower than whites. About 1 percent of the whole group classified as superior; 27.14 percent as borderline; and 24.92 percent as clearly feeble-minded.

Growden and Calhoon (400) found, in 1,104 admissions to the Ohio Boys' Industrial School, feeble-minded, 6.8 percent; defective delinquents, 14.3 percent; psychotic, 0.3 percent. Of 313 girls, 17.5 percent were classified as feeble-minded; 4.7 as defective delinquents; and 1.2 percent as psychotic. Rogers and Austin (441) showed a distribution of the intelligence quotients of 3,584 children from the juvenile court of Toronto, Canada. A normal frequency curve was indicated, with a mean I. Q. of 82.2. Correlations of first tests with retests ranged from .63 to 82, the highest correlation being obtained between tests given five years apart. Their classification was: superior, 1.96 percent; normal, 24.52 percent; subnormal, 59.72 percent; deficient, 13.9 percent. Selling (446), in a study of juvenile automobile thieves, found a median I. Q. of 83 with a range of 57 to 112. Snyder (453) used Stanford-Binet tests with 100 consecutive admissions of boys and 100 consecutive admissions of girls to the Pennsylvania State Training School. The average I. Q.'s were: boys, 71.25; girls, 71.46. The classification for boys was: normal, 8 percent; dull-normal, 14 percent; borderline, 28 percent; high moron, 35 percent; low moron, 15 percent. The classification for girls was: normal, 7 percent; dull-normal, 17 percent; borderline 31 percent; high moron, 33 percent; low moron, 12 percent. Lane and Witty (414) found 700 delinquent boys in the St. Charles (Illinois) School for Boys, by the Otis Group Test, to range in I. Q. from about 50 to about 129, the mean I. Q. being 87.96, the median 88.25. More than 80 percent were rated as being below average mental ability, and 10 percent as feeble-minded. Correlation of Otis and Binet tests of 145 cases was .84. The mean I. Q. of children from delinquency areas was somewhat lower than those from districts where delinquency is infrequent. In studies of behavior problems in high schools, Laslett and Manning (415) found a mean I. Q. of 105.8. Fenton and others (390) found Stanford-Binet tests to give a mean I. Q. of 91.7 and a median I. Q. of 90.4 for 393 delinquent boys at Whittier State School in California. It was pointed out, however, that subnormals have been largely eliminated or refused admission. His classification was as follows: feeble-minded, 4 percent; borderline, 15 percent; dull-normal, 29 percent; normal, 41 percent; superior normal, 8 percent; superior, 3 percent.

That the distribution of intelligence among the inmates of institutions for delinquents varies greatly with the institution policy concerning the admission and retention of cases was shown by Sullivan (458) in a comparative chart of the intellectual composition of Whittier State School in 1918 and 1926. During that time the mean I. Q. changed from about 82 to 91, the percent of feeble-minded from 29.9 to 2.2, and the percent of superior cases from 5.5 to 10.9.

Glueck and Glueck (397), in their study of 1,000 delinquents, classified 41.6 percent as normal or supernormal; 28.2 percent as dull; 17.1 percent as borderline; and 13.1 percent as feeble-minded. The relation of intelligence to specific types of misconduct was analyzed by White and Fenton (468) who found forgery to be the only offense significantly associated with high mental ability. Slawson (451) concluded that the deficiency of delinquents is mostly manifested in verbal intelligence and that in nonverbal intelligence such boys are on a par with non-delinquents. Doll (387), reviewing and discussing investigations in this field, concluded that apart from large incidence of feeble-mindedness, criminal intelligence is not inferior to that of the non-criminal population.

Results of achievement and aptitude tests—The educational retardation of delinquents as indicated by age-grade status is usually substantiated by achievement tests, although in individual cases the achievement is higher than would be indicated by rate of promotion in school. Sullivan (458) applied Stanford Achievement tests to 304 delinquent boys at Whittier State School, with the result that the group showed marked retardation in educational age and in all subject ages. The average retardation in educational age was two years, five months from chronological age, and one year, one month from mental age. There was less retardation in reading than in other subjects. In some cases Sullivan concluded that educational retardation was the main cause of the maladjustment. In the same institution, five years later, Chase (375) found mean achievement ratios to range from 80.9 (arithmetic computation) to 101.4 (paragraph meaning). Achievement in reading was consistently higher than in other subjects. Lane and Witty (413), in a study of delinquent boys, found their subjects more seriously retarded in educational growth than in mental development.

Paynter and Blanchard (435), using Stanford Achievement Tests and the Otis Classification Test, found problem children admitted to child guidance clinics to have educational quotients varying from 37.4 to 102, but concluded that there is no consistent tendency for such children to be of low achievement when all factors are taken into consideration.

In a study of mechanical aptitude reported by the New York State Crime Commission (429), delinquent boys were compared with their non-delinquent brothers. Although the former were of lower intelligence, they were superior to their brothers in mechanical aptitude, and even slightly superior in this respect to unselected children. Moore (424), however, found problem boys inferior in mechanical aptitude.

Mental disorders in behavior problems—Evidences of mental disorder, apart from mental deficiency, are recognized by many investigators, although varying methods of classification and diagnosis make comparison of groups difficult. Healy and Bronner (404), in analyzing 4,000 cases studied in Chicago and Boston juvenile courts, found definite psychoses in 5.6 percent of the Chicago cases, and in 1 percent of the Boston cases. The lesser frequency for Boston was attributed to the better local facilities for the study of psychoses. Psychopathic personality, enumerated only for Boston, occurred in 2.8 percent of the cases. The frequency of epilepsy was 5.5 percent in Chicago and 1.6 percent in Boston. Glueck and Glueck (397) found, in 1,000 delinquents, "certain identical complexes of an emotionally-toned, obsessive, recurring nature," but none of these "mental mechanisms" in 86.3 percent of the cases.

Treatment of Behavior Problems

Provisions in regular schools—Educational facilities for problem children are surveyed in a *Research Bulletin* of the National Education Association (427), wherein it is suggested that such facilities "appear to be meager." The aspects of the problem stressed are, first, the making of special provisions for the potentially delinquent child, and second, the rehabilitation of children who have been dealt with by the courts.

E. T. Glueck (396) takes the position that inasmuch as the control of antisocial behavior involves the concentration of social forces and agencies, the elementary school should assume the responsibility for the early recognition of delinquency and participation in a treatment program. This view is shared by Dickson (384) who believed that teachers can and should be taught to recognize the symptoms of behavior maladjustment. Durling and Powell (389) advocated the more extensive use of special classes in the schools as a less expensive alternative for institution treatment, and more care in regular school classification on the ground that behavior difficulties are not so likely to occur in children whose work is of a difficulty commensurate with their ability. Sayles (442) gave examples of methods used in dealing with problem children in the school. A committee of the National Education Association (426) developed a plan for training teachers in this field. A relatively new and promising educational contribution is that of the visiting teacher (381). An investigation conducted in ten Minneapolis schools undertook to discover ways of improving the behavior of kindergarten children by observing types of activity and recording teachers' remarks about them (383).

Special schools—The segregation of problem children is effected in city school systems by the establishment of special institutions of the parental school type. These differ from most state correctional schools in that they are under the control of educational authorities, and are financed with school funds. State laws provide for twenty-four hour parental schools in Illinois, Pennsylvania, and California. In some instances such schools are maintained under private auspices. They are usually small and emphasize manual and prevocational work.

Examples of institutions maintained by city school systems, cited in a report of the National Education Association (427), include the Thomas A.

Edison School in Cleveland, enrolling about 1,500 boys who are educationally maladjusted elsewhere, and the Montefiore Special School in Chicago. The functioning and accomplishments of the latter school were described by Dolton (388).

The junior republic type of school, based on self-government, appears to have been successful in certain cases, although some doubt has been expressed as to the effectiveness of the plan. Thomas and Thomas (459) believed that self-government is a convenient device, but questioned its use in the treatment of delinquency, inasmuch as it allows children to depend on "a form of group approval which may have little extra-institutional force."

The work of state institutions for delinquent boys was described in a survey by Bowler and Bloodgood (365) who reported intensively on five institutions: Whittier State School, Whittier, California; Boys' Vocational School, Lansing, Michigan; State Home for Boys, Jamesburg, New Jersey; State Agricultural and Industrial School, Industry, New York; and Boys' Industrial School, Lancaster, Ohio. The work of institutions for girls was described by Reeves (438).

Fenton and others (390) reported on some of the recent developments at Whittier State School, in which the school program in all its aspects is correlated with the diagnostic work of the Bureau of Juvenile Research. Included was a stenographic report of a guidance conference in which various members of the staff participated and formulated recommendations for treatment. Semans (447) made a special study of the recreational program for younger boys at an institution for delinquents, and developed a plan for the improvement of this phase of institution work. Evaluations of the training programs of institutions were offered by Asher (358), Dobbs (385), and Caldwell (373).

Aichhorn (353), a Viennese, and a disciple of Freud, organized a school for problem children some of whom were especially difficult cases. His approach was that of psychoanalysis and his results were described largely in terms of changes in attitude and personality in individual cases. Adler (352) predicted that institutions will tend to specialize in the training of the more difficult cases.

Special segregation problems—One of the perplexing problems of schools for problem children is the proper care of the mentally deficient. While some of these can be transferred to institutions for the feeble-minded, the difficulties in the way of such transfers are great. Since the discovery that large numbers of delinquents are mentally deficient, there have been efforts on the part of most correctional schools to reject such cases, with the result that the percent of feeble-minded in correctional schools has steadily declined. Merrill (420) recommended special institutions for defective delinquents, to have the characteristics of schools with the security of prisons. Commitment should be indeterminate, with careful diagnosis and treatment and gradual adjustment to social situations of increasing complexity. It has been shown that subnormal offenders, despite difficulties of training, can be so treated as to become reasonably well adjusted (450).

Foster homes—In a study of several hundred children placed in foster homes (408) it was found that the ratio of success with such treatment is high, especially attributed to the factor of removal from the disturbing sphere of influence. However, the success varies with mentality and personality, and it is recommended that foster-home placement be made only upon expert advice. Glueck and Glueck (397) found that 225 of their 1,000 delinquents had lived in foster homes, and agreed with the contention that such placement should be handled with great care, and in the light of diagnostic data.

Relationship to Courts and Society

Extent and distribution of delinquency—It is estimated that the number of children brought before the juvenile courts in the United States annually approximates 200,000, the number of boys exceeding the number of girls in a ratio of five to one (427). It is evident, however, that court cases constitute no index of the actual number of problem children for whom no reliable estimate is obtainable. Data from the Children's Bureau (463) showed that, in 1930 eighty-eight juvenile courts in the United States handled 50,000 cases, including 40,000 white and 10,000 colored children.

Juvenile court procedures—Referred to by Healy and Bronner (405) as "that notably American institution," the juvenile court has greatly extended its work and importance in recent years. An account of its scope and procedure was given by Lou (416), including history, organization, and special technic. Scott (443), viewing the problems of the juvenile court from the judge's bench, recommended that the work of the court should be based on consideration of the total individual in his setting. The function of the court is becoming increasingly preventive, although it must continue to deal with cases of advanced deliquency. It has been shown that although the juvenile court cannot fairly be held responsible for the failure of many of its cases, changes in the present set-up are probably necessary and research is needed to that end (403). In the field of probation S. Glueck (398) contended that we are in the wasteful stage of "extensive agriculture"; the equipment is inadequate, the personnel insufficiently trained, and both supervision and record-keeping are in need of radical improvement. Scientific methods alone offer a solution. Beard (361) gave data based on records of 500 children studied at the Judge Baker Foundation and later placed on probation by the Boston Juvenile Court. Success is measured in terms of preprobation conditions. Beckham (362), reviewing the range of jurisdiction of juvenile courts in the United States, concluded that the range of cases and authority of the court could well be extended.

Prevention of delinquency—It is generally agreed that delinquency is preventable, and that prevention requires the use of more research and guidance methods, and appropriate coordinated efforts of home, school, and community. A few years ago it seemed that a solution would be afforded by the twenty-four-hour school, and some states have enacted legislation authorizing the establishment of such schools. At present the most promising lines of approach are the child guidance clinic and the coordinating council.

The child guidance clinic, established specifically as an agency for the prevention of delinquency, has grown rapidly in extent and influence. Stevenson and Smith (455), reviewing a quarter century of child guidance work, said:

> Clinical service for child guidance gives effect, on a limited scale, to the best current thinking about the way to prevent delinquency and mental disease. While its failure to develop conclusive methods for measuring results makes it impossible to say definitely that it does prevent delinquency or mental disease, evidence of a subjective and personal sort, impressive in the mass, indicates that it can and does relieve specific tensions in children, free them from crippling demands, add to their happiness, smooth their way.

The work of a typical child guidance clinic was described by Anderson and others (355) who reported on the accomplishments of six years' work in Los Angeles. The working policy is summed up as follows:

> The Child Guidance Clinic is a team. By pooling the knowledge, experience, and "conditioned reflexes" of trained workers in the fields of social case work, psychology, medicine, and psychiatry, it is possible to bring to the study and treatment of an individual child a combined intelligence which, when backed by enthusiasm and supplemented by the common garden variety of "horse sense" and aimed directly at finding an answer to the question "What can be done about it all?" should, theoretically at least, prove a powerful agent in solving the perplexing problems that are the daily grist of the child guidance mill.

The need for coordinated efforts was emphasized by Truitt (462), in an address to a group of psychiatrists:

> Prevention of behavior problems is no monopoly of the psychiatric group, and the isolated efforts of this group involve a struggle against all sorts of undercurrents in the fields of industry, law, education, public health, housing, politics, etc. Psychiatry will operate in a vacuum until it can join forces with preventive work in other fields and evolve with them common methods of preventing difficulties which contribute to undermine public health—mental and physical. Our methods for preventing delinquency will be only partially effective so long as allied groups fail to understand our purpose and to see how our work may reinforce theirs.

Bowman (366) showed how community recreational projects, especially during the summer months, may be effective in the prevention of delinquency. He believed the problem is essentially an educational one, and that all social agencies in the community should coordinate their efforts to make the recreation program effective. "The home, where values normally group themselves about the effort to make life whole, should be an intimate part of the scheme."

The coordinating council was described by Fenton (391) as "the voice of the community expressing in action its ideals and aspirations, its hopes for the progress of human society." The movement in California originated in the city of Berkeley and in 1931 had extended to eighty-one communities in that state. The coordinating council consists of a group of persons representing various educational and social agencies in the community which assumes responsibility for the diagnosis, guidance, and treatment of problem children. There is some evidence that delinquency is appreciably reduced in communities in which these organizations have been formed. Cooperative community efforts in an Indiana city are reported to have increased school attendance by 7.5 percent, and for eight months no new cases of delinquency were brought from that area to the juvenile court (379).

Other social problems found to be related to the prevention of delinquency are unemployment insurance (475), the economic depression (364), and race attitudes (363). Beard (361) recommended measures of the following order as being most promising for communities wishing to prevent delinquency: parental education, adequate family income, periodic medical examinations for all children and free treatment when necessary, adequate recreation facilities, flexible school curriculum and cooperating clinics, vocational guidance for all children with an adequate follow-up system, enlarged court facilities, better trained probation officers, and better contact between the court and child guidance clinics.

Summary

Behavior maladjustment in children is widespread, and varies from slight misbehavior to serious delinquency. Misbehavior in school usually begins with minor infractions of school regulations, such behavior being often overrated in importance by teachers, who are apparently more concerned with orderly school procedure than with pupil development. Behavior of this sort, however, is often the forerunner of a career of juvenile delinquency, and it appears possible in some cases to predict outcomes. The causes are probably both constitutional and environmental, but there is no evidence that delinquency as such is inherited. Much relationship is found between delinquency and environmental factors, although direct causes are seldom established. Behavior problem children are usually below average in mental development, the percent of mental deficiency among them being greater than in the general school population. Special mental conditions and emotional disturbances are of relatively high frequency, and are generally considered as having a causal relationship. The machinery for treatment includes special classes, special schools of the parental-school type, and institutions, usually maintained by the state, receiving cases through the juvenile courts. There are also private special schools, including those of the junior republic type. The placement of problem children in foster homes is used as an alternative to institution commitment. The juvenile court is extending its sphere of influence, especially through probation procedures. The child guidance clinics are helpful in individual cases, and have contributed much to the understanding of the problem child. These clinics reach relatively few cases, however, and their influence on the prevention of delinquency is as yet unmeasured. The newest development is the coordinating council, wherein various agencies in the community work together for prevention of delinquency.

CHAPTER VI
Physically and Mentally Exceptional Children

SINCE BEHAVIOR PROBLEMS AND DELINQUENCY were reviewed in the preceding chapter, this discussion of exceptional children is limited to those showing two general types of variations: (a) physical and sensory defects and (b) intellectual deviations, ranging from feeble-mindedness to genius as well as special talents and defects. There is no scarcity of experimental and research material at hand dealing with these types of cases. From over 3,000 studies and reports our selection is limited to scarcely over 100.

Physical and Sensory Handicaps

The effects of physical and sensory handicaps extend over a wider range than the loss of educational efficiency. They include social maladjustment with its feelings of inferiority and a struggle to overcome the deleterious effects of one-sided competition, which may extend into the classroom. Such frustrations carry the feeling of inferiority into a search for other avenues of compensation which cannot always be achieved. The types of emotional strains arising from such conflict and how they operate in various types of handicaps will be the general theme of this chapter.

General health and vitality—Good health and vitality usually tend to generate hopeful outlooks while poor health is conducive to less hopeful trends. Kanner and Lachman (537) showed that illness frequently develops unjustified apprehensions and undesirable parental attitudes which must be changed. Nilson (558) prepared an age-grade study of 1,500 physically disabled children in the Minnesota public schools and declared that this status was "fairly comparable" to that of regular pupils. A sense of comedy and jollity was powerful in the recovery and restoration of sick children in an institution according to Schmidt-Lamberg (571). Pfleger (563) described the frenzied tyranny exercised over four different girls by a girl with heavily disfiguring features, in an attempt to compensate for her unattractive appearance. Residual assets as well as defect liabilities, according to Crothers (502), must be discovered if children with sensory-motor defects are to be happily educated.

Visual defects—Defects of vision range from slight incapacity to total blindness. All degrees of vision impairment offer problems of adjustment, differing in nature according to the severity of the handicap. Hathaway (526) stated that there are 50,000 partially seeing children in need of special sight-saving education with only 10 percent of them getting such training. Many of these partially seeing children constitute a problem of mental hygiene according to Flanigan (517) who showed that the nervous tension attendant upon unusual eyestrains reflects itself in difficult behavior patterns. The sight-saving teacher faces the double task of instructing in unusual ways accommodated to the visual defects and of restoring and maintaining a better mental and social balance of her pupils.

Various studies show that the unusual powers often attributed to the blind in the use of other sensations are contrary to fact. Koch and Ufkess (542) found that blind subjects tend to be less successful on the average in a stylus maze-learning test than seeing persons. Bechtold (481) discovered that the blind surpassed the seeing in the immediate retention of meaningless material, but were inferior in meaningful material. In the former case the concentration through the ear assisted the blind, but in the latter they lacked the ability to retain the image of the ideas. Persons who became blind after the first five years of life progressively deteriorate in the visual images in dreams as reported by Bolli (488). Dumas (513) found that the blind are incapable of mimicry of the emotions of delight, joy, anger, and fear, and he concluded that such traits are of visual and social origin.

Dry and Cooper (512) surveyed a school for the blind and found many of the inmates also feeble-minded, others pseudo-feeble-minded, stubborn, reluctant to assume responsibility, and extremely inattentive. Other studies of the feeble-minded blind were summarized by Burritt (498) and in two anonymous bibliographies (487, 574). Two blind individuals, Villey-Desmeserets (578) and Cutsforth (503), have written extensive treatises on the limitations and abilities of the blind.

Auditory defects—Combinations of visual and auditory defects were described extensively by Helen Keller (538) and Laura Bridgman (567). Goodenough (522) studied a blind-deaf child and concluded that the primary forms of expressive behavior are determined by native factors. The major problem of the deaf is the extreme social and psychological isolation which the defect produces, and to break down this seclusion is among the most difficult teaching processes. According to Haines (525), deafness is characterized by an isolation from much of reality, a childish curiosity to break down the wall of separation, becoming self-centered and often morose, mistaking other people's actions, distorted vocal expression, and often a feeling of inferiority. The deafened person may pretend he is not deaf.

Bieri (485) and Brauckmann (490) showed that the performance of the deaf rises rapidly with the acquisition of speech, although it never reaches that of the normal child. Brauckmann disclosed that speech of the deaf is acquired through exercise of the mechanism of the vocal and speech movements when they are ready to function which is the same principle in the learning of the hearing child.

In his mental survey of the deaf, Pintner (565) found that the deaf child from twelve to fifteen years of age achieves what the hearing child of eight or nine years does, with little difference between the oral and manual methods of instruction. Long (548) found that the deaf and hearing persons are not widely different in motor abilities with deaf boys superior to hearing boys and hearing girls superior to deaf girls. In a balance test Long found the deaf significantly inferior. Mann (555), in an article on "The Seventh Sense," discussed the great importance of the vestibular sense in aviation, and outlined tests for prospective aviators along these lines.

Pintner (564) and Welles (580) used the Bernreuter Inventory on hard-of-hearing individuals living in small towns and compared them with hearing persons paired in age, education, and social background. The hard of hearing were found to be more neurotic, introverted, and submissive, with no relationship to age at loss of hearing. Those who were clearly maladjusted had a high neurotic score, but the readjustment of many cases was worthy of attention. Lyon (552) reported that 30 percent of deaf high-school boys and girls, tested on the Thurstone Personality Schedule, are either emotionally maladjusted or should have psychiatric advice, but raised doubt as to the suitability of the test to the group.

Orthopedic defects—In addition to the basic unsocial pattern, feelings of helplessness and inferiority, crippled children suffer disturbances of the sympathetic nervous system from distortion of the viscera and various vital organs. Von Baeyer (579) classified three mental distortions of the crippled: (a) the basic disease permanently or temporarily damages the biological substratum of mental life; (b) the condition of being a cripple threatens the free development of the mental capacities; and (c) the emotional tension caused by the experience of being a cripple may manifest itself in neurotic phenomena.

Studies of the intelligence of crippled children have given the impression that they are quite backward mentally, but in more recent years surveys of schools for the crippled, such as those in Detroit, show an encouraging improvement in the I. Q. levels to about 90 rather than ten to fifteen points lower. This result is thought to be due to a better understanding of the functions of these schools with the consequent enrolment of better classes of children mentally. Witty and Smith (584) reported an average I. Q. of 84.5 on 1,480 crippled children. Lee (546) reported the I. Q.'s of 148 patients in the Seattle Orthopedic Hospital appreciably below that of normal children. Winkler (583) found 100 crippled children only slightly retarded with greatest handicap in imaginational activity or in powers of observation.

Williamson and Christian (582) examined disabled students at the University of Minnesota as to mechanical, artistic, clerical ability, space relations, dexterity, etc., with necessary reorientation of some who had previously been given too much encouragement as to their possibilities, motivating those with poor morale, discovering mental disorders of which the students were often unaware. Since there are at least 10,000 crippled children in the United States and only one-tenth are receiving any special attention, Ingram (532) stresses the purpose, adaptations, and values of special orthopedic schools.

Cardiac disorders—There are many thousands of cases of cardiac impairment which do not present obvious external symptoms, although the fatal effects operate in sudden and unexpected places. Bronk and Ferguson (494) conducted physiological investigations which showed that the vagal branches going to the heart carry a large number of sympathetic fibers which conduct impulses concerned with cardiac acceleration. That the heart is very persistent in its reactions was shown in experiments on cats by Britton, Hinson, and Hall (493). They proved that after one and a half minutes of excitement the heart rate is approximately 50 percent over that of the normal, and that animals who were subjected to emotional stimulation every second day over a period of eight weeks showed no diminution on cardiac response. Lombard and Cope (547) discovered that the systolic phase of the heart is longer and the heart rate faster in women than in men. Fulstow (520) found that the weight of the hearts of schizophrenics underwent the same changes as in normals, but with a weight somewhat less than for normals.

Children and adults may use their physical cardiac handicap as an excuse for abandoning any competitive behavior according to Foster (518). Thus they uncover features of their personality which had otherwise been concealed and dormant. Emotional states may produce physiological states which are interpreted as cardiac abnormalities. Sigel (572) also found restriction of activities with a very high correlation between the presence of cardiac difficulty and mental hygiene problems. The majority of cardiac patients do not complain of subjective symptoms, whereas those who do complain usually have emotional problems.

Epileptic disorders—Eyrich (514) distinguished three typical syndromes of epilepsy: (a) slowing of all psychic functions with loss of spontaneous activity; (b) explosive irritability with egocentric oversensitiveness to slights of interests and vanity; and (c) hyperkinesis with elemental compulsive restlessness, increased suggestibility, and poverty of feeling. Bartemeier (480) emphasized the study of actual social situations in which convulsions took place, organization of the family constellation, and sometimes removal to a different environment. Epileptoid reactions in children are classified by Branham (489) into two groups: (a) the latent type of epilepsy with attacks usually at night with the following day characterized by pallor, confusion, and dullness; and (b) the *petit mal* type with headache, nausea, dizziness, flashes of color, unusual pallor, and dilation of the pupils without apparent cause. His stress on mental retardation was confirmed by Patterson and Fonner (562), Bridge (492), and R. R. Brown (497). Grossmann (523) interpreted their frequent criminal trends as an attempt to conquer death in themselves which always seems imminent, and annihilation is paid back with annihilation. In religiosity they hope for liberation from the fear of death.

Dr. O. P. Kimball has recently done experimental work in Cleveland and Detroit with medication for epileptics which attempts to control changes in the chemical composition of the brain of epileptics. He modestly claims reduction in seizures in more than one-half of the children under his care.

In Detroit a first public school for epileptic children has been established, with the theoretical increase of seizures due to exposure and suggestion failing to materialize.

Endocrine phenomena—The ductless glands or the endocrines have been investigated with regard to disturbances in physical growth, mental development, and disturbances of character, personality, and behavior. "Toledo's strong boy" had a sexual and anatomical development of an adolescent when only four or five years of age, resulting from a suspected tumor of the pineal gland according to McClure and Goldberg (553). Fassbender (515) reported on a similar condition in a seven-year-old girl with premature development of genitalia. Rockwell (568) reviewed over 200 publications on effects of the thyroid gland with voluminous evidence of disturbances of physical growth associated with malfunctioning of the thyroid. Joll's monumental volume (535) dealt exhaustively with diseases and disturbances resulting from the thyroid gland. Studies by Fox (519) and by Kimball and Marinus (539) disproved popular beliefs that sensational changes in intelligence result from glandular therapy. They found among the feeble-minded that treatment tends to check the fall of intelligence quotient and to lend greater stability to general nervous control. Hayward and Woods (527) pointed out the misleading impressions of mental deficiency resulting from hypothyroidism. Lurie (551) reported that of 500 children studied at the Psychopathic Institute of the Jewish Hospital at Cincinnati, fully 10 percent had marked endocrine disorders and 60 percent had some types of internal disorder. In a similar study Rowe (569) found about one-third of behavior cases definitely linked with glandular disturbance. Berman (482) concluded that endocrine disturbances were from two to three times as frequent among criminals as among control groups. All of these studies and many others suggest the great importance of more intensive and general study of the endocrine among backward and maladjusted children.

Manual and motor development—Motor skill and manual dexterity vary among individuals and with reflections in emotional strains and social adjustments. Langdon (545) showed that while there is a central or common factor to manual dexterity among the various activities of any individual there are also specific skills, and the excellence in one phase is not a sure guarantee of similar trends in others. Landauer (544) emphasized the role of motor forces in behavior, with grace and rhythm in the infantile stage, a latent period of awkwardness, followed by adult habits evolving from puberty. These adult motor reactions resolve into a personal tempo for each individual, according to Braun (491), which are not susceptible to any extreme change. Hicks (528) reached a similar conclusion in studying the acquisition of motor skill among young children which seemed to be derived from structural maturation and general practice rather than from specific practice.

Handedness—The determination of preferential handedness in children from two to six years of age was developed by Updegraff (577) on controlled observations and by tests. Preference was usually found throughout all activities, and in 36 out of 40 cases tests and observations agreed. A study of 25 unchanged left-handed and 43 changed left-handed children in handwriting only by Haefner (524), comparing them with 68 pure right-handed children matched as to chronological age, sex, and school grade, showed no significant differences in intelligence, school achievement, height, general interest, or worries. Pyle and Drouin (566) examined the 7 percent of children in three Detroit elementary schools who wrote left-handed, but found a slightly lower level of intelligence and school achievement which they believed to be due to handicaps arising from an environment designed for right-handed subjects. Many cases of letter reversals, inaccuracies, and confusions leading to special disabilities were attributed to handedness by Dearborn (505). Downey (510) noted relapses to the preferred handedness in novel tasks, in curious experiences involving vision, in orientation, and in changes in organic tension. Dominance of function is known to concern eyes and feet as well as hands. The relations of these dominances to each other in individuals is a matter of conflicting evidence.

Nervous and encephalitic children—Since in the preceding chapter on behavior problems and delinquency, physical and nervous causes were considered, only incidental mention will be made here. Chadwick (499) classified children's neuroses under four heads: (a) infantile impulses seeking gratification in conflict with repressions; (b) the child in conflict with infantile impulses; (c) the child's ego in alliance with infantile impulses in open conflict with parents, society, and environment; and (d) the child in conflict with reality.

The cases of post-encephalitis offer some extremely baffling problems related to nervousness. Often the parents and the school are not aware of the presence of this disease and attribute behavior and mental manifestations to deliberate intention of maladjustment. Dawson and Conn (504) presented definite statistical evidence of mental deterioration with cases of encephalitic lethargica. Berrien (484) discussed the similarity of encephalitic and psychopathic children in temper tantrums, uncontrolled emotional outbursts, lying, truancy, petty thieving, lack of foresight, impulsiveness, and sex offenses, but with a dissimilarity that the encephalitic children rate uniformly below their chronological age on all mental tests. The same author (483) found that *only* encephalitic children tend to reverse sex characteristics in drawing the human figure.

Gibbs (521) found that emotional disturbances were the most constant clinical factor in encephalitic cases. Hill (529) noted that following encephalitis there is a loss of inhibition over the primary emotions, with impulsiveness, restlessness, lack of self-control, lack of concentration, disobedience, and defiance. While the number of cases is quite limited, their severe maladjustments constitute a serious school problem.

Speech disorders—Many investigators have noted the close relationship between the changing of handedness and speech disorders, although the exact nature of this phenomenon has never been established. Oates (559) observed that while sinistrality is not correlated with either superiority or inferiority of intellect, marked departure from unilateral functioning is definitely related to complications in the nervous organization. Kistler (541) discovered that individuals who remain left-handed are generally retarded in motor development and that this same delay in motor development brings about functional disturbances in speech.

Low intelligence is a symptom rather than a cause of speech defects, according to Barnard (479), who also declared that personality traits are more enlightening than intelligence in the study of speech defects, since they point to emotional difficulties as the source of stuttering and kindred speech defects. Smirnova (573) explained that speech, being the most subtle of movements, is the most delicate of them, and hence disorders of speech often arise from general maladjustments. Stutterers are featured by shyness, anxiety, depression, and nervous instability with increasing burden in the face of increasing age and greater social and vocational responsibilities, according to the experiences and observation of W. Johnson (534). Dorsey (509) emphasized that stutterers should be made to act more and think less since this is a disorder of the person, and F. W. Brown (496) suggested personality integration as the essential factor in curing stuttering permanently.

Intellectual Deviations

In this group are children ranging from the lowest level of institutional feeble-mindedness to mental genius. While mental ability has long been recognized as an important factor in success or failure in school, in this report consideration will also be given to effects on personality and social adjustment arising from intelligence and its influence upon school success.

Institutional feeble-mindedness—Many of these cases enter the public schools and sometimes they are allowed to remain unrecognized except as backward children, deriving a minimum of benefit and often causing unnecessary worry and concern to teachers. A common subtype of this group are Mongolian idiots who bear some resemblance to Oriental races with slanting eyes, dark coarse hair, and highly flushed cheeks. They are generally recognized as arising from some debility or unusual condition of the mother during pregnancy. Ordahl (560) found that they are usually among the later-born of families, while Kuenzel (543) gave additional notations on tongues long, thick, and broad often protruding from the mouth, with thick lips, hands dry and chapped, and a shambling gait. They are pleasant and agreeable in contrast to opposite trends in many other low-grade feeble-minded.

Mental growth studies of the feeble-minded by Chipman (501), Moore (556), and Woodall (586), showed a tendency for a slight fall in I. Q. upon repeated tests, Chipman noting that in 79 percent of his cases there was no significant change. Doll (507) estimated that fully 10 percent of the feeble-minded are characterized by birth injury, which is also attended by handicaps of speech and movement. These, however, tend to lessen later in life. Lowrey (550) is one of several who reported universally that contrary to popular opinion the feeble-minded do not constitute the criminal and delinquent class since they are usually guarded and protected either in or outside of institutions. DeBeer (506) noted a decreased degree of concentration of attention, lack of foresight, and enhanced suggestibility as characteristics of the feeble-minded. In contrast to the American system, the feeble-minded in Belgium are cared for in homes rather than institutions, which affords a possibility of better social adjustment, as reported by Doll (508).

Borderline and subnormal cases—A common practice is to provide special class training in public schools for cases ranging in I. Q. from 50 to 75, but to dispatch the socially unstable of this group to institutions. E. H. Johnson (533), Ide (531), and Kinder and Rutherford (540) emphasized that social adjustment is the critical factor of success or failure within the special class type of children. Kinder and Rutherford found only 14 out of 68 in a five-year follow-up study who were adjusting satisfactorily, and that these 14 were from good social environments, whereas the remainder were universally from undesirable situations. Lord (549) investigated over 400 cases in Massachusetts special classes with a surprisingly large number making satisfactory adjustments, and three-fourths of the homes being also effective. The most extensive follow-up study was conducted by the United States Children's Bureau (500), in which approximately 2,000 cases were followed over a five-year period in several large cities. Approximately 80 percent of the group of 400 cases from the Detroit group of this study were gainfully employed at the time of the investigation. From these studies it may be concluded that the mentally subnormal may succeed when socially stable, and that a mild amount of supervision and placement aid yield surprisingly good returns.

The intellectually inferior and superior—These two groups represent distinct and separate classes of children each with approximately one-fourth of the school population slightly below and above the average, respectively. The inferior group presents some characteristics allied to the mentally subnormal, and the superior, allied to the gifted which is considered next. The most comprehensive discussion of these groups was presented, with Coxe as chairman, by a committee of the National Society for the Study of Education (557) in which the characteristics, the social implications, and problems of instruction and curriculum adaptations were described. McElwee (554) used a checklist of fourteen characteristics, such as school work, good effort, quietness, obedience, and stubbornness, on inferior and superior groups, and while there was an encouraging presence of desirable traits in all levels they were much more predominant in the superior. Baker (477) summarized the opinions of 500 Detroit elementary teachers on differences between these groups. Differences were noted in social and mental traits more marked than in those of educational achievement, chiefly in the dull being unsocial, selfish, self-centered, lacking in initiative, and honeycombed with all manner of educational disabilities, while the superior were characterized positively in all of these respects. Cohen and Coryell (476) recently prepared a new study on educating superior students at the high-school level, reporting investigations in New York City schools.

The intellectually gifted—The most exhaustive studies of genius have been produced under the direction of Terman (575). The reports, particularly in volume one, show overwhelmingly that the gifted are superior in all types of social and personality traits as well as in intelligence. Finch and Carroll (516) found significant superiority as high-school leaders in 66 gifted matched against an equal number of superior and of average pupils. Jones (536) reported physiological condition and home environment superior in 120 superior children. Great versatility of interests was shown in 300 eminent men reported in the Stanford studies as investigated by White (581), with scientific and literary interests being the most predominant and scholastic and administrative less predominant. Terman (576) reported that satisfactory progress has been made in 40 cities in which special classes for the gifted have been established.

Witty and Lehman (585) characterized the genius as a highly delicate mechanism which is prone to develop nervous instability whenever problems of adjustment arise. They designated him as unstable, often neurotic, and almost invariably eccentric. Hollingworth (530) discussed a gifted girl with respect to lack of conformity in social adjustment. Since the gifted represent a small but very important element of the population, education needs to give more care to problems of their education.

Special talents and defects—This topic has always been marked by spectacular interest, and its results and frequencies grossly overestimated. The cases are probably less marked than supposed, but memory of the rare case of feeble-mindedness with the special ability approaching the average, or the disability of the infrequent gifted serves as an excuse for making less effort to provide for the great majority who run true to form. Baker (478) investigated 900 children nine years of age and discovered approximately 7 percent who offered problems of educational disability. These cases were also suffering from personality and social maladjustments in 53 of 60 cases, which were probably generated in part from failure in one school subject. A. W. Brown (495) studied the unevenness of the abilities of dull and bright children on the Stenquist Mechanical Tests, and Mechanical Assembly, Haggerty Intelligence Examination, Delta 2, and Pintner Non-Language Mental Test and concluded that dull and bright show nearly equal unevenness. Billings (486) reported on a case of inverted writing and drawing but with marked improvement upon special coaching. Cases of specific reading disability were described by Orton (561) who has given special attention to reversals which he ascribes to lack of dominance in cerebral hemispheres. Instruction including directional kinesthetic training is effective in remedial teaching. Mathematical prodigies were described by Sándor (570) who found Finkelstein superior to Diamandi and Inaudi, but inferior to Ruckle. Requisites for such performances are power of concentration, rapid orientation among figures, interest in and a sentiment for mathematical combinations, knowledge of number theory, sensing of abstract relations discovered empirically, a ready-made stock of partial sums, and auxiliary images. These unusual cases serve as a fine laboratory for educational research.

Summary

There is a wide variety and diversity of types of physically and mentally handicapped children who offer challenges to education. Most of these cases afford problems of psychological and educational disability. They also tend to show evidence of emotional and social deviations which further complicate their educational and vocational success. In order to be successful the schools must make special provisions, and also be able and willing to cooperate with the social, medical, and all other agencies in the community. The education of handicapped children opens avenues for a wider conception of all educational programs.

CHAPTER VII
Technics and Instruments of Mental Hygiene

MENTAL HYGIENE CONCEPTS are synthetic in character and rest on a vast body of case materials and quantitative researches which come through special organizations of knowledge from such fields as psychoanalysis, psychiatry, psychology, sociology, religion, eugenics, and education. The task of the present chapter is primarily to survey the systematic formulations, the technics employed in diagnosis and treatment, illustrative case procedures, and the appraisals of the effects of treatment. To bring the material into the confines of the space allotted and to meet the interests of the majority of readers of the *Review of Educational Research,* preference has been given to systematic treatments, articles with a research orientation, environmental and mental therapies, and work with children. Mental hospital, adult, neurological, and operative studies have been excluded for the most part.

SYSTEMATIC FORMULATIONS

Psychoanalysis

The technics and principles of psychoanalysis have been largely derived from work with adult patients. Adult analyses, however, immediately assign a major role to the patient's childhood experiences. The extensive and early work of Freud, Jung, and Adler is too familiar to require special citations. A résumé of the history and principles of psychoanalysis may be found in books by Healy and others (633) and Hendrick (637). The ramifications of psychoanalytic concepts in many fields were presented in a series of essays edited by Lorand (665).

In recent years direct analytic work with children has become more extensive. The January, 1935, number of the *Psychoanalytic Quarterly* was devoted exclusively to child analysis.

Interested readers may well consult the work of Anna Freud (617, 618, 619), daughter of Sigmund Freud, for orientation. Her emphasis is that every hysteria or compulsion neurosis can be traced to early childhood. Klein (653) has given an exposition of methods used in child analysis. She stressed the role of early anxiety situations in the development of the child. The facts in her presentation are made to bear an elaborate speculative superstructure.

Psychoanalysis has supplied or organized a large technical vocabulary pertaining to the facts and principles of mental life—normal and abnormal. The importance for mental hygiene of concepts such as are illustrated in the following terms is obvious: unconscious, repression, rationalization, conversion symptoms, abreactions, catharsis, free association, displacement, identification, transference, projection, complex, pleasure principle, repetition compulsion, libido, ego, id, superego, narcissism, identification, anxiety, inhibition, symbolism, resistance, and interpretation.

Child Psychiatry

Kanner's book (650) was written primarily for pediatricians and has a psychobiological emphasis. A brief section on general principles is followed by a discussion of examination, diagnosis, and case records. Separate chapters are devoted to complaints, age, physical health, intelligence, emotion, sex, constitutional and environmental factors. Treatment is discussed in relation to work with the child, family, and community. Four chapters are devoted to personality difficulties directly traceable to pathological alterations of nervous tissue. Eight chapters are devoted to disorders of functioning which cannot be traced to organic lesions. Tics, disturbances in digestion, respiration, perception, etc., are placed in this category. The last thirteen chapters are devoted to problems involving the personality as a whole. Richards' account (692) was based on the clinical work in Johns Hopkins Hospital. The rationale of psychotherapy with children was well stated by Potter (684).

Child Development

Research in child development has been a particularly productive source of accurate descriptions of the physical, mental, emotional, and social growth of normal children and of experimental studies of the conditions under which behavior may be modified. Investigations have been reported in the February, 1936, *Review of Educational Research* (703) devoted to mental and physical development and in other special issues devoted to learning and the use of tests. Texts in child psychology give special attention to social and personal problems such as those by Curti (609), Goodenough (625), Jersild (642), B. J. Johnson (645), and Stoddard and Wellman (702). Russian pedology has placed similar emphasis upon integrated research (688).

Sociology

Reckless and Smith (691) surveyed the field of juvenile delinquency and summarized some of the outstanding problems and methods of work. The book reports statistical analyses, discussions of physical and mental traits, social background, juvenile courts, and institutional care. Some chapters are also devoted to school maladjustment and readjustment by clinics and placement bureaus. Chapters are devoted to preventive programs and the results of treatment. Glueck and Glueck (623) edited a symposium on crime prevention programs grouped under the large divisions of community, school policy, intramural and extramural guidance, and boys clubs and recreation.

Mental Hygiene

A number of books have been written which relate the principles of mental hygiene directly to education, the community, and the family. Earlier works by Blanton and Blanton (594), Burnham (601), Groves and Blanchard (628), Kirkpatrick (652), Morgan (673), Sherman (701), Symonds (707), and Zachry (725) can be noted only by name. The point of view of psychiatric social work is represented by Bassett (591) and by Lee and others (658). Books first published in 1935 and 1936 are given special mention here. The chief contribution of Wallin (714) lies in the extensive retrospective reports dealing with early difficulties of adjustment on the part of normal persons. Even granting the reservations one must maintain with respect to accounts of this type, the vast number of problems of mental hygiene significance occurring in the family and in home and school situations can hardly be questioned. Mechanisms and modes of adjustment are discussed in connection with the case material. The book by Howard and Patry (639) is concerned with the detection and prevention of unwholesome mental patterns, the hygiene of emotion, child training, and family relationships. The teacher audience has been kept in mind by Rivlin (693) in a book which gives a brief overview of the contributions of various schools of psychology to problems of behavior and to the mental hygiene of the classroom. Shaffer (697) illustrated the possibility of a conception of adjustment which can be stated in objective terms. He avoided the use of psychoanalysis and pointed out the equal acceptibility of principles and procedures which are the outgrowth of objective psychology.

Critiques

Mental hygiene concepts have been attacked and defended vigorously from both the scientific and professional points of view. The discussions by research workers have been more concerned with the nature of evidence which is acceptable to support theoretical formulations and with the need for the verification of claims made by exponents of particular schools. On the other hand, professional discussions have been centered upon the unique contributions and competence of workers concerned with children from such fields as education, neurology, psychiatry, psychology, pediatrics, sociology, religion, speech, and general medicine. In practice, clinical organizations usually recognize the desirability of a multidiscipline approach. Increased research and the growth of eclecticism are evidences of the coming of age of a science of human relations.

DIAGNOSIS AND TREATMENT

Diagnosis in the sense of classification has a relatively small place in the mental hygiene literature, most of the attention being devoted to securing types of evidence significant for a solution of a particular problem. Frequently diagnostic procedures are an intrinsic part of a continuing plan which also involves treatment. Systematic discussions of problems in diagnosis and treatment were prepared by Symonds (706) and Olson (677). The comparison of delinquents and their siblings offers a new technic for the determination of etiologic factors (631).

The Interview

The interview continues to be the basic method for securing data to determine causative factors, diagnosis, and treatment. The most comprehensive systematic account of the interview is that of Bingham and Moore (593). They described an interview as a conversation with a purpose. Unreliability may be due to the interviewer, the interviewee, or their relationship. It was suggested that an interviewer utilize some interest of the interviewee as the point of departure. A large number of recommendations were given concerned with the establishment of rapport and the method of securing data. The employment, social case, educational, mental clinic, and journalistic interview were described. Problems of testimony involved in court examination and cross examination were discussed and research studies quoted. A bibliography of 338 titles is a useful adjunct.

Young (724) treated briefly of general interview methods but dwelt particularly upon the types involved in diagnosis and treatment in social case work. The diagnostic interview is usually intended to define the situation and the problem, and the subject's motives, attitudes, and aspirations. The value of collective interviewing, as for example that with the family of a delinquent in bringing out conflicts and relationships, was noted.

In the chapter on the technic of the interview she stressed the value of a period of preparatory thinking, but at the same time advised leaving the situation flexible for new developments. Approach, rapport, and physical setting were discussed. The interviewee should know the relationship of the interviewer to the situation. Such details as manner of greeting, facial expression, and personal appearance were regarded as important. The establishment of common purposes, the observance of convention, and "face-saving" are as essential in the interview as in social life in general. Other problems discussed were concerned with dishonesty, the closing of the interview, and the test of its success.

The ethics of the interview situation were considered, and numerous outlines were presented indicating their factual content for various purposes. The conscious use of technics on the part of the interviewer was well described and the interactive process was analyzed. The last three chapters of the book are specifically devoted to a discussion of the dynamics of social therapy. Sympathetic insight, identification, mental catharsis, definition of the problem, the conditioning and reconditioning of attitudes, the supplying of motivation, mutual planning, and satisfaction of wishes are paragraph headings which indicate content. Both mental and social therapy are involved. A bibliography of 242 titles adds to the value of the work.

Promising beginnings on the objective study of the interview were made by Lasswell (657). Specific practical suggestions were made by Allen

(588), Burlingham (600), Moore (672), Sheehan-Dare (700), Symmes (705), and Whitley (719).

Free Association

Free association, especially stressed in psychoanalysis, constitutes an important method of securing data concerning a particular condition which is disturbing the child or adult patient. There is an extensive psychological literature on free association in which a stimulus word is given and the response analyzed either for its logical or emotional relationship. The common analytic practice would be to establish rapport with the patient and then ask him to report freely whatever thoughts came to his mind. The analyst may at times sense the significance of a specific portion of the material and ask for further associations. In this manner emotionally linked material is gradually brought to the fore. Such an association may never have been fully comprehended by the patient or may have been largely forgotten. Patients frequently report dreams in their free associations. The process in itself may be regarded as therapeutic (passive therapy), or the analyst may interpret the material (active therapy) so as to give the patient insight into the problem. Both systematic work and clinical accounts mentioned elsewhere in this chapter give special attention to association methods. Many workers feel that there are limitations in the direct use of these methods with children and they may implement the situation so as to secure associations with toys, child products, or in imaginative play. These methods are reviewed in later parts of the chapter.

Diagnostic Aids

Family and personal history—Most of the systematic accounts mentioned in earlier sections of this chapter contain outlines designed to secure data of importance for treatment. Clinics usually have prepared forms or suggestions. A form usually contains routine identifying data concerning the child, hereditary factors, special abilities and disabilities, educational and health history and status, and some account of the personalities and relationships in the family. The "complaint" with a redefinition of the problem and predisposing and precipitating factors usually finds a place.

Observations of "natural" behavior—The superior validity and reliability of observations made and recorded at the time the specific behavior occurs in its natural setting is coming to be recognized. The value of cumulative records of incidents in behavior journals has been noted by Blatz and Bott (596), Charters (606), Lämmermann (656), Moldovan (671), Olson (676), Randall (690), Winkler (721), Wood (723), and others (686). Such observations may be employed as part of a routine or may be used as a basis for the study of particular children. Methods of using direct observation for measurement purposes were reviewed by Olson and Cunningham (680).

Questionnaires, rating scales, and tests—Summaries of measurement technics of significance for research and programs in mental hygiene were prepared by Horsch and Davis (638), Maller (668), Olson (678), G. Watson (716), and Symonds (708). Three extensive recent researches should receive special mention. Baker and Traphagen (590) devised a method of scoring 66 diagnostic items having to do with a variety of environmental, historical, and present status material about children. The items and total score were related to the diagnosis of delinquency. A ten-year investigation of sex differences in interests, attitudes, and thought trends was recently reported by Terman and Cox (710). The masculinity-femininity scores were given a quantitative analysis and related to clinical material. Doll (612) elaborated the concept of growth in independence in a social maturity scale now available with a manual of directions and preliminary norms.

Autobiography, biography, composition, diary, poetry—The value of the autobiography as a technic in case work has been best discussed by Selling (696). From some persons a written autobiography is more readily obtainable than the same facts through direct examination. Kamaryt (649) secured some of the earliest memories of seventh-grade pupils. He discovered that many of the recollections thus obtained were accompanied by a strong emotional tone, both pleasant and unpleasant. The amount of recall of the unpleasant tends to question Freudian theories of repression. Dudycha and Dudycha (614) had college students report their preschool experiences and again found such emotional coloring of fear and joy. Bühler (599) indicated the research possibilities of diaries by the analysis of 93 diaries written by boys and girls born between 1830 and 1915. Tramer (713) published the diary of a psychotic child. Analyses based upon samples of poetry composed by the subject have received but slight attention (674). Popovic (683) suggested that the writing of self reports has therapeutic value. He observed two groups of adolescents for several years, one which had practice in writing self reports and the other which had little or no practice. The reports were written as school exercises in composition and dealt with the pupils' intimate lives. The claim is that practiced pupils control their instinctive and emotional life better than the unpracticed. The problem should be subjected to quantitative study.

Dreams—The important role ascribed to dreams in early Freudian literature has continued to find a place in recent studies. Most readers will be content with the summary prepared by Kimmins (651) in *The Handbook of Child Psychology*. He pointed out that healthy children enjoy dreams and the telling or recording of them. He classified dreams as wish fulfilment and fear dreams; kinesthetic dreams; references to fairy stories; compensation dreams; dreams of bravery and adventure, school activities, motion pictures, exciting books, and death incidents; and dreams with conversation, and the presence of other witnesses than the dreamer. The compensatory function of the dream is shown in children in certain types of schools. Fear dreams are common among the deaf and the blind. A child blind before the age of five never sees in dreams. There has been some success with dream control, but no definite conclusions have so far been reached. The dreams of problem children have been related to the defensive character of their acts by Seidler (695). Willoughby (720) analyzed a simple dream to reveal and realign the motives involved. An extensive analysis of children's dreams was prepared by Jersild and others (644). Cason's study (604) of the nightmare dream includes an extensive bibliography on mechanisms and treatment.

Play and child products—As was previously stated, toys and manipulative materials have been used extensively to implement the interview situation, both for diagnostic and treatment purposes. For example, D. M. Levy (661) used dolls representing the mother, the baby, and a younger sister or brother to bring out the child's reactions of jealousy and sibling rivalry. Liss (664) used puppets and drawings. Ramos (689) and Fries (620) used toys. Lowenfeld (666) utilized free play in a pleasant room as a means of treating psychoneuroses in childhood. Clark (607) took the point of view that we can begin to recognize tendencies in infancy and childhood which may lead to later mental disorders. In the use of play technics, the child may dramatize his conflicts and reveal mechanisms. The materials produced in drawing, poster painting, finger painting, and plastic work have served as a basis for data collection and interpretation among various investigators (663, 699).

Treatment Procedures

A widely used formula in the mental hygiene approach to problems of behavior is to modify the child, the environment, or both in order to secure adjustment. The distinction between procedures is usually one of emphasis, since there is constant interaction between the child and his environment. General problems of treatment are surveyed in opening sections of the present chapter, and it has been noted that when personal relationships are involved in data collection and diagnosis, treatment may also be in progress. The nature of some of the more specific attempts at environmental or child adjustments will be noted in the following pages. Methods of treatment which involve adding or subtracting stimuli from the child's environment are considered to be environmental adjustments. Such adjustments would include measures aimed at the modification of the parents, home, school, or by transfer to a special institution.

Parent education, family relationships, and the home—The frequency with which the problems of children can be directly related to some undesirable situation in the home has often led to the conclusion that the parent rather than the child should be the focus of a treatment program. A study of means has resulted in an enormous amount of literature on parent education from many points of view. Special literature on research and problems may be secured from the National Council of Parent Education, the National Congress of Parents and Teachers, the Child Study Association of America, or from any of the child research centers. The literature of social work is replete with studies of methods of handling economic and physical factors and problems of family relationships. The importance of the parent-child relationship and of the desirability of leading the parents to an understanding of their problems was brought out in the discussion of social treatment prepared by Heath (634). When the home cannot be made suitable for the child, foster home placement is a frequent method of adjustment (632).

Educational adjustment—Conflicts between the adjustment ability of the child and the requirements of the school situation have received considerable attention in the literature of mental hygiene. One possible solution suggests a preliminary study of the child to place him at that point in the educational organization which offers the greatest assurance of his success. This method is represented in the report of Noetzel and Hildreth (675). A more definite attempt to modify schools to the nature of children is also apparent in progressive practices everywhere. Avoidance of pressure, competitive comparisons, and discouragement was advocated by Plank-Spira (682) in connection with the adjustment of children having emotional problems. The manipulation of physical features of the environment is receiving attention (646). The effect of special school provisions on the conduct of problem children was described by Stullken (704) in connection with the Montefiore School. A number of private schools have been organized so as to take the child from the complex life of the large city to the simplified environment of country life in a supervised setting.

Institutional treatment—When a child is continually getting into trouble in his natural environment, a frequent recourse has been to place him under supervision in a correctional institution with a simplified environment. The institutional literature is omitted here. The amount of recidivism among graduates of schools of this type has led to considerable pessimism concerning their efficacy. Institutions that have held the correctional and educational function as paramount to that of punishment have done better than others. Institutional placement often appears to be the last resort when family and local community resources fail. Mental hospitals are making more adequate provisions for the care of children. Fenton and others (615) recently prepared an account of the delinquent boy and the correctional school.

Child management, training, and instruction—A series of books describing the technics for situational analysis and physical and verbal control of children was prepared by Waring and Wilker (715). Environmental and child management constitute the content of books by Blatz and Bott (595) and Thom (711). Palmborg (681) has written a popular discourse on methods of work with problem children. Suggestions for the classroom teacher were given in accounts by Pullias (687) and Campbell (602). Combinations of medical and educational services, as in the Austrian "Heilpedagogik," are of interest in this connection (670). Literature on the conditioning of children's emotions was reviewed by Jones (648). Specific suggestions for a combined manual and verbal technic for the elimination of thumb sucking were described by Hazzard (630). Studies of the oral insufficiency theory by D. M. Levy (659, 660) are highly suggestive. The relationship between mental hygiene and the habit formations of children was discussed by Held (635). Investigations of tics by Blatz and Ringland (597) and of fears by Jersild and Holmes (643) contained suggestions which are useful in treatment. Language that is directive, unhurried, and approving showed superior efficiency in behavior control in the studies by M. W. Johnson (647). Character education methods concerned with attitudes, problems of group living, and the requirements of citizenship commonly aim at the influence of behavior by direct and indirect instructional technics. Character education may be defined so as to be all-inclusive of mental hygiene or it may be restricted in definition so as to constitute one of the special types of treatment employed. Previous issues of the *Review of Educational Research* are concerned with the research in this area. The relation of special disabilities in school subjects and remedial teaching to mental hygiene has received consideration in other numbers of the *Review* devoted to the psychology of the school subjects. Bradley and Bosquet (598) recommended books for their psychotherapeutic value.

Physical treatment—There are very few disorders commonly deemed nonmental which fail to present mental or behavioral symptoms. In some instances it is not clear whether the physical or mental factor is antecedent. Fritz (621) reviewed 669 references related to the general field of psychodietetics. Studies are surveyed on the relation of nutrition and behavior in such problems as nervousness, anemia, allergy, epilepsy, and hypertension. Investigations by Laird, Levitan, and Wilson (655) and Goodenough (624) are suggestive for behavior control. Addition of glucose to the diet has been reported as partially successful for the treatment of night terrors, car sickness, vomiting, insomnia, sleep walking, and nocturnal enuresis. This work is described in scattered clinical literature and in the systematic text of Henderson and Gillespie (636). The mental hygiene effect of hydrotherapy, diathermy, etc., are discussed from time to time in the *Physiotherapy Review*. The old prescription of rest and relaxation has come in for renewed attention through the researches of Jacobson (640) on progressive relaxation.

Occupational therapy—Occupational therapy has an extended range of treatment possibilities in both institutional and individual work. For practices in the field, readers should consult the *Journal of Occupational Therapy and Rehabilitation*. In this journal J. B. Gordon (627) described presentday methods of treating the mentally sick through occupational therapy which diverts attention and prevents further introversion. In the same journal Cooper (608) described the possibilities of occupational therapy in a child guidance clinic. The Pittsburgh Child Guidance Center used a workshop as an aid (654). The situation is used as a basis for observation, the development of rapport, and treatment. The therapeutic value of labor was emphasized by Chalisov (605). Values of recreational therapy were noted by Davis (611). Systematic treatments stress the importance of a satisfying occupation as a factor in therapy. (See also section on play.)

ILLUSTRATIVE CASE STUDIES

The field of mental hygiene places much dependence upon case material for data and for the development of both explanatory concepts and treatment procedures. *Child Guidance Cases,* edited by Sayles (694) and released for limited circulation among professional workers by the Commonwealth Fund, offers excellent examples of coordinated study and treatment. These cases were presented in detail with the data of the social history, physical examination, psychological examination, psychiatric examination, and the initial interviews with mother or child. Detailed notes were given on treatment conferences among the workers concerned, treatment plans, and summaries of progress. The above book was preceded by more abbreviated and popular accounts of typical children in home and school situations published under the same auspices.

The mental as contrasted to the social approach to criminality receives added support from the report of psychoanalysis of adult prisoners by Alexander and Healy (587). The child's own story was used with unusual success in the various accounts of the delinquency problem by C. R. Shaw (698). With the use of representative cases, Dollard (613) analyzed criteria for the life history.

Through the use of two extended records of work with children, Taft (709) defined a concept of "relationship therapy." Primarily aimed at individual treatment, the relationship is emotional and social rather than intellectual and technical. Her discussion perhaps differs from many of those concerned with mental therapy in a greater unwillingness to speculate on the forces and factors involved in treatment where one person takes a friendly interest in another. M. E. Watson (717) utilized a series of cases to illustrate history taking, interpretation, and technics of treatment.

Practically all of the general texts mentioned in preceding pages contain illustrative cases as do many of the non-quantitative articles concerned with diagnostic and therapeutic methods. It has appeared to be impractical to include many references to the voluminous literature of case studies. Such material may be examined by consulting practically any issue of such journals as the following:

American Journal of Orthopsychiatry
American Journal of Psychiatry
International Journal of Individual Psychology
International Journal of Psychoanalysis
Internationale Zeitschrift für Individual-psychologie
Internationale Zeitschrift für Psychoanalyse
Journal of Abnormal and Social Psychology
Journal of Juvenile Research
Mental Hygiene
Psychoanalytic Review
Psychiatric Quarterly
Psychological Clinic
Zeitschrift für Kinder Psychiatrie
Zeitschrift für psychoanalytische Pädagogik

A more extensive list of publications of significance to mental hygiene has been prepared by Jenkins (641).

APPRAISAL OF THE EFFECTS OF TREATMENT

It is reassuring that as mental hygiene has established a field and method of work, a literature on appraisal of outcome has gradually grown to meet the many inquiries concerning the effectiveness of treatment work in the areas of social and emotional maladjustment.

Practically unique in its use of both experimental and quantitative methods in this field is a study by Martens and Russ (669). Using a modification of the Haggerty-Olson-Wickman technic, they secured a quantitative appraisal of behavior before and after child guidance clinic treatment extending over a period of two years. A control group assisted in the interpretation of the findings. Granting the difficulties involved in the measurement of change by these technics, it is of interest to note that while the treated group did not show much absolute improvement on the scale, the non-treated group showed marked deterioration.

The most common procedure in appraisal study is to follow up cases after the lapse of a period of years and secure some judgment on their adjustmental status. Even such an appraisal must be conceded to be a large improvement over no attempt to question or appraise results. Controls are urgently needed, although obviously difficult to secure in programs aimed primarily at service. Olson (679) outlined what he considered to be a type of experimental approach to this problem.

Witmer (722) summarized the investigations of a number of persons on the success of treatment in various clinics. A scale from A to E has been used to describe the success of adjustment and percents are reported in terms of types of cases, clinics, and other characteristics of children. The material is difficult to express in brief space because of variations in treatment contacts, length of treatment, variations in intelligence, personality, type of behavior disorders, and parent attitudes. In the average situation apparently about 25 percent of the children show no improvement or deterioration, while something over 40 percent show definite improvement or complete disappearance of the problem.

A statistical study has been made of the success of foster home and reformatory school placement of neglected and delinquent children in Oslo, Norway (589). A number of selective factors appear to affect any practical deduction as to the optimum time for removing a child from his home or the relative efficacy of foster home versus institution placement. The test of success was the number of children convicted after being discharged. About one-third of the boys and only 5 percent of the girls had later convictions during the period of the study. Children removed earlier had fewer convictions than those removed later. Only about one-fifth of the boys who had been placed in families had later offenses as compared with one-half of the boys who were placed in reform school. As might be expected, the figures are dependent upon the seriousness of the case before the period of treatment.

The success of clinic treatment is dependent upon the recommendations made and the extent to which they are carried out. In a follow-up study

Growden (629) concluded that the ratio of success to failure is 7 to 3 if the recommendations are followed, 4 to 5 if partially followed, and only 2 to 8 if not followed. This internal analysis of the evidence is added weight for its acceptance as indicating beneficial results, even though selective factors are undoubtedly operative in the matter of carrying out recommendations.

The Child Guidance Institute in Bucharest reported complete cures for 17 percent of its cases, improvement for 50 percent, continued treatment for 30 percent, no improvement for 14 percent, and 24 percent discontinued (718).

Thom (712) reported improvement in 65 percent of the cases of preschool children treated in a habit clinic. About the same amount of improvement was noted immediately after discharge among adult patients from the Institute of Medical Psychology, London, with a drop to 55 percent after three years (667). States of anxiety and sexual difficulties were most responsive, and success seemed independent of the number of interviews.

The Bureau of Children's Guidance secured appraisals of treatment from parents and on the basis of staff judgment (658:40). The parental estimate was: success, 55 percent; partial success, 34 percent; and failure, 11 percent. Corresponding staff judgments were 48 percent, 31 percent, and 21 percent. An appreciable correlation existed between judgments on individuals by staff and parents.

Carberry (603) included a study of the consistency of judgment regarding the adjustment status in her follow-up of children examined by the California Bureau of Juvenile Research. The parents, teacher, local workers, and Bureau workers were asked to rate the present status of each child. A four-point scale of adjusted, partially adjusted, unimproved, and worse was utilized. Detailed figures on percent agreements were given. Differences in rating tendency indicate the desirability of using judges representing different areas of child contact. On the whole, about 20 percent of the children were regarded as adjusted, about double this number as partially adjusted, and the balance as unimproved or worse.

According to Davidson (610), the prospects of improvement through clinical guidance are improved when the child is young, bright, and in a school grade corresponding to his mental age.

Berk, Lane, and Tandy (592) reported that problems are reduced by about 50 percent in a follow-up of habit clinic children. Improvement is most obvious when the children are normal and superior in intelligence and when the home and agency are cooperative in carrying out recommendations.

The most comprehensive follow-up study of problem children treated through placement in foster families was made in connection with the work of Healy and others (632) of the Judge Baker Foundation. Their figures indicated 80 to 90 percent success in the cases of delinquent children or children with personality and habit problems when they are of normal mentality. These figures were reduced to 50 percent for the small group of defectives and children with abnormal personalities. Considerable controversy has been caused by the report of the Gluecks (622) on the high percent of recidivism of juvenile court cases, even among those who had been referred to the Judge Baker Clinic. It has been pointed out in this connection, however, that the Clinic was primarily performing a diagnostic service for the court. The court was not equipped for a comprehensive treatment program. Clinically treated cases should be used as a test of the possibilities of the method.

A study by Foster and Anderson (616), in which 100 children were traced after a period of four years, showed that the disappearance of behavior problems is much more likely to occur in home situations which would be described as good.

J. Levy (662) made a year's study of thirty-six children referred to a clinic by schools. The clinic made recommendations concerning academic programs and the social work included parents as well as patients and teachers. Schools were cooperative and it is estimated that the cases treated showed 50 percent improvement.

It is of interest to note the regularity with which improvement is noted in from one-half to two-thirds of the children given intensive treatment. Improvement is particularly marked when the child is good human material, comes from a good home, and when treatment agencies secure cooperation. The picture is perhaps too hopeful for the skeptical scientist. Martens and Russ' study (669) is the only research contacted which has attempted to appraise the progress in a control group. To what extent do children show a reduction in problems with age irrespective of treatment? For what percent of a group of problem children referred on a complaint basis will improvement be noted without treatment when the precipitating circumstances concerned with referral have disappeared? The evidence from clinical judgment must be accepted as establishing a high probability that improvement over and above maturation occurs when treatment programs are instituted. In spite of the scientific difficulties involved in securing comparable controls and valid appraisal instruments, the effort should be made. At least two current programs are attempting such controls.

SUMMARY

Mental hygiene utilizes the generalizations from all fields dealing with human behavior in planning programs that will lead to a maximum of personal integration and social adjustment. It seeks positive mental health as well as the avoidance of overt failures of personal and social breakdown as manifested in mental illness or infractions of law. Mental hygiene is concerned with a field of unquestioned importance. Studies of methods, principles, and results increase in impressiveness. The obligation of the research worker is to seek to refine methods of investigation and to add to the body of verified conclusions. The evidence to date justifies the applied worker in areas of human relationship in adding some information and skill in mental hygiene to his professional armament.

BIBLIOGRAPHY ON MENTAL HYGIENE AND ADJUSTMENT

Chapter I. Historical Development and Modern Trends

1. ACKERLY, SPAFFORD. "Instinctive Emotional and Mental Changes Following Prefontal Lobe Extirpation." *American Journal of Psychiatry* 92: 717-28; November, 1935.
2. ADAMSON, ELIZABETH I. "A Community Program for Prevention of Mental Disease." *American Journal of Public Health* 26: 480-86; May, 1936.
3. ALTEKAR, M. D. "Caste System and Its Relation to Social and Economic Life." *Annals of the American Academy of Political and Social Science* 115 (Part 2): 183-87; September, 1929.
4. BASSETT, CLARA. *Mental Hygiene in the Community.* New York: Macmillan Co., 1934. 394 p.
5. BEERS, CLIFFORD W. *A Mind that Found Itself.* Garden City, N. Y.: Doubleday, Doran and Co., 1935. 434 p.
6. BURNHAM, WILLIAM H. *Great Teachers and Mental Health.* New York: D. Appleton and Co., 1926. 351 p.
7. CANNON, WALTER BRADFORD. *Bodily Changes in Pain, Hunger, Fear and Rage.* 2d ed. New York: D. Appleton and Co., 1929. 404 p.
8. DUNBAR, HELEN FLANDERS. *Emotions and Bodily Changes.* New York: Columbia University Press, 1935. 595 p.
9. FLEMING, GRANT. *Mental Hygiene in the Provincial Health Service.* Paper presented at annual meeting of American Public Health Association, Milwaukee, Wis., 1935.
10. HEATH, ESTHER. *The Approach to the Parent.* New York: Commonwealth Fund, 1933. 163 p.
11. "A Mental Hygiene Study of the Selection and Training of Teachers." *Mental Hygiene* 19: 152-54; January, 1935.
12. NATIONAL COMMITTEE FOR MENTAL HYGIENE. *Twenty Years of Mental Hygiene, 1909-1929.* New York: American Foundation for Mental Hygiene, 1930. 259 p.
13. PATRY, FREDERICK L. "Integrating Mental Hygiene from the Point of View of the Public Health Officer and School Physician." *American Journal of Public Health* 26: 471-79; May, 1936.
14. TODD, T. WINGATE, and ROWLANDS, MARGARET E. "Studies in the Alimentary Canal of Man: VI. Emotional Interference in Gastric Behavior Patterns." *Journal of Comparative Psychology* 10:167-88; April, 1930.
15. TREADWAY, W. L. *The Place of Mental Hygiene in a Federal Health Program.* Paper presented at annual meeting of American Public Health Association, Milwaukee, Wis., 1935.
16. WEISENBURG, THEODORE H., and MCBRIDE, K. E. *Aphasia; A Clinical and Psychological Study.* New York: Commonwealth Fund, 1935. 634 p.

Chapter II. School Influences

17. BOSE, R. G. "Character Guidance for College Students." *Religious Education* 27: 223-24; March, 1932.
18. BOYNTON, P. L.; DUGGER, HARRIET; and TURNER, MASAL. "The Emotional Stability of Teachers and Pupils." *Journal of Juvenile Research* 18: 223-32; October, 1934.
19. BROWN, F. J. "Knowledge of Results as an Incentive in School Room Practice." *Journal of Educational Psychology* 23: 532-52; October, 1932.
20. BURLING, T. "Integrating Psychiatry with the Winnetka (Illinois) Public School System." *American Journal of Orthopsychiatry* 5: 132-40; 1935.
21. BUSEMANN, A. "Interesse an geistigen Gegenständen als Unterrichtswirkung höherer Schulen. (Intellectual interests as a result of instruction in higher schools.)" *Archiv für die gesamte Psychologie* 83: 325-56; August, 1932.

22. BUTLER, E. I. "A Study of the Needs of High School Students and the Effectiveness of a Program of Learning in Selected Phases of Child Development and Family Relationships." *Researches in Parent Education III.* Studies in Child Welfare, Vol. 10. Iowa City: University of Iowa, 1934. p. 169-248.
23. CATTELL, R. B. "The Practising Psychologist in the Educational System." *Human Factor* 9: 54-62; 1935.
24. CHASE, LUCILE. *Motivation of Young Children.* Studies in Child Welfare, Vol. 5, No. 3. Iowa City: University of Iowa, 1932. 119 p.
25. CHEN, W. K.-C. *The Influence of Oral Propaganda Material Upon Students' Attitudes.* New York: Columbia University, 1933. 43 p.
26. CROOKS, A. D. "Marks and Marking Systems: A Digest." *Journal of Educational Research* 27: 259-72; December, 1933.
27. DAVIS, JOHN E. "What Can Physical Education Contribute to Mental Hygiene?" *Mental Hygiene* 17: 235-45; April, 1933.
28. DAVIS, ROBERT A., and BALLARD, C. R. "The Effectiveness of Various Types of Classroom Incentives." *Educational Method* 12: 134-45; March, 1932.
29. FLEMMING, CECILE W. *Pupil Adjustment in the Modern School.* New York: Teachers College, Columbia University, 1934. 94 p.
30. FLEMMING, CECILE W. "The Rôle of the Teacher in Pupil Adjustment." *Teachers College Record* 34: 560-68; April, 1933.
31. FLEMMING, E. G. "College Achievement, Intelligence, Personality, and Emotion." *Journal of Applied Psychology* 16: 668-74; December, 1932.
32. FORLANO, GEORGE. "An Experiment in Coöperation." *Journal of Educational Research* 25: 128-31; February, 1932.
33. HARRIS, DANIEL. *The Relation to College Grades of Some Factors Other Than Intelligence.* New York: Columbia University, 1931. 55 p.
34. HAUFF, W. V. *Der Lehrer als Seelsorger (The Teacher as Spiritual Guide.)* Schwerin: Schweitzer, 1931. 48 p.
35. HELLER, T. "Psychische Hygiene und Lehrberuf. (Mental hygiene and the teaching profession.)" *Zeitschrift für psychische Hygiene* 6: 40-48; 1933.
36. HENDRICKSON, GORDON, and HUSKEY, J. F. "Extroversion as a Factor Conditioning Achievement in the Fifth and Sixth Grades of an Elementary School." *Journal of Educational Research* 25: 6-13; January, 1932.
37. HILL, GEORGE E. "The Report Card In Present Practice." *Educational Trends (Northwestern University)* 3: 6-14; February, 1934.
38. HOMBURGER, E. "Psychoanalysis and the Future of Education." *Psychoanalytic Quarterly* 4: 50-68; 1935.
39. HUANG, I. "Reform of School Discipline." *Chung Hua Educational Review (Chinese)* 21: 115-27; 1934.
40. IDE, G. G. "The Public School and the Problem Child." *Psychological Clinic* 22: 53-60; March, 1933.
41. JONES, EDWARD S. "The Grade-Test Correlation as an Index of Motivation." *School and Society* 36: 478-80; October 8, 1932.
42. KARLAN, S. C. "Failure in Secondary School as a Mental-Hygiene Problem." *Mental Hygiene* 18: 611-20; October, 1934.
43. KROLL, ABRAHAM. "The Teacher's Influence upon the Social Attitude of Boys in the Twelfth Grade." *Journal of Educational Psychology* 25: 274-80; April, 1934.
44. LÄMMERMANN, H. *Typologie und Aetiologie der Schulbegabung. (Typology and etiology of scholastic ability.)* Leipzig: Voske, 1931.
45. LAUGIER, H., and WEINBERG, D. "Le Facteur subjectif dans les notes d'examen. (The subjective factor in examination grades.)" *Année Psychologique* 31: 229-441; 1930.
46. LAYCOCK, S. R. "Teachers' Reactions to Maladjustments of School Children." *British Journal of Educational Psychology* 4: 11-29; February, 1934.
47. LEHRER, L. "The Psychology of the Teacher's Personality." *Yivobleter* 4: 97-119; 1932.
48. LICHTENSTEIN, ARTHUR. *Can Attitudes Be Taught?* Johns Hopkins University Studies in Education No. 21. Baltimore: Johns Hopkins Press, 1934. 89 p.
49. MCBEE, MARIAN. "A Mental-Hygiene Clinic in a High School." *Mental Hygiene* 19: 238-80; April, 1935.
50. MAITI, H. P. "The Problem of Discipline from the Psychological Standpoint." *Indian Journal of Psychology* 6: 71-81; 1931.

51. MANEY, C. A. "Sex-Bias in College Marking." *Journal of Higher Education* 4: 29-31; January, 1933.
52. MATHEWS, C. O. "The Honor System." *Journal of Higher Education* 3: 411-15; November, 1932.
53. MEREDITH, L. A. "Teachers' Personalities and the Problems of Children." *Journal of Educational Sociology* 7: 387-96; February, 1934.
54. MEY, W. "Durch den Lehrer zum Aussenseiter geworden. (An outsider through a teacher's influence.)" *Viertel jahrsschrift für Jugendkunde* 1: 274-77; 1931.
55. MUCHOW, M. "Zum Problem der Zeugnisreform. (On the problem of reform in scholastic reports.)" *Zeitschrift für paedagogische Psychologie* 31: 222-33; 1930.
56. MYERS, G. C. *Developing Personality in the Child at School.* New York: Greenberg, 1931. 375 p.
57. NEWELL, H. W. "The Methods of Child Guidance Adapted to a Public-School Program." *Mental Hygiene* 18: 362-72; July, 1934.
58. PATRY, FREDERICK L. "A Formulation of Possible Psychiatric Contributions to Teacher Colleges and Normal Schools." *Journal of Abnormal and Social Psychology* 28: 419-34; January-March, 1934.
59. PATRY, FREDERICK L. "A Glimpse into the Modern Progressive Psychiatric Storehouse for the Best Functioning of the Educator." *Psychiatric Quarterly* 5: 492-98; 1931.
60. PATRY, FREDERICK L. "The Place of the Psychiatrist in a State Education Department or School System." *Mental Hygiene* 15: 757-60; October, 1931.
61. PATRY, FREDERICK L. "Some Suggestions on a Mental-Hygiene Program for Schools and Colleges." *Mental Hygiene* 18: 621-28; October, 1934.
62. PECK, LEIGH. "Teachers' Reports of the Problems of Unadjusted School Children." *Journal of Educational Psychology* 26: 123-38; February, 1935.
63. PHILLIPS, MARGARET. "Some Problems of Adjustment in the Early Years of a Teacher's Life." *British Journal of Educational Psychology* 2: 237-56; November, 1932.
64. PHILLIPS, WENDELL S. *An Analysis of Certain Characteristics of Active and Prospective Teachers.* Contributions to Education, No. 161. Nashville, Tenn.: George Peabody College for Teachers, 1935. 51 p.
65. PRINGLE, R. W. *The Psychology of High-School Discipline.* New York: D. C. Heath and Co., 1931. 362 p.
66. REDL, F. "Wir Lehrer und die Prüfungsangst. (We teachers and the fear of examinations.)" *Zeitschrift für psychoanalytische Pädagogik* 7: 378-400; 1933.
67. SCHOHAUS, WILLI. *The Dark Places of Education.* (Translated by M. Chadwick.) New York: Henry Holt and Co., 1932. 351 p.
68. SNEDDEN, DONALD S. "The Work of a Psycho-Educational and Mental-Hygiene Clinic." *Journal of Educational Sociology* 6: 516-24; May, 1933.
69. STAGNER, ROSS. "The Relation of Personality to Academic Aptitude and Achievement." *Journal of Educational Research* 26: 648-60; May, 1933.
70. STEPHENS, J. M. *The Influence of the School on the Individual.* Ann Arbor, Mich.: Edward Brothers, 1933. 106 p.
71. STRAIN, F. B. "New Patterns in High-School Sex Teaching." *Journal of Educational Sociology* 8: 342-52; February, 1935.
72. STRANG, RUTH. *The Rôle of the Teacher in Personnel Work.* Rev. ed. New York: Teachers College, Columbia University, 1935. 417 p.
73. SULEA-FIRU, I. "Consideratii asupra psihologiei profesorului. (Considerations in regard to the psychology of the teacher.)" *An. Psihol.* 1: 108-13; 1934.
74. SWARD, KEITH. "Temperament and Direction of Achievement." *Journal of Social Psychology* 4: 406-29; November, 1933.
75. TALLMADGE, MARGARET, and DOUGLASS, HARL R. "What College Students Believe They Think About Certain Types of Examinations." *School and Society* 39: 349-52; March 17, 1934.
76. TOWNSEND, M. ERNEST. "The Implication to the Psychologist of Public School Pupil Personnel." *Training School Bulletin (Vineland, N. J.)* 29: 185-91; February, 1933.
77. TOWNSEND, M. ERNEST. "Mental Hygiene and Teacher Recruiting." *Mental Hygiene* 17: 598-604; October, 1933.
78. TROLAN, HELEN. "The Activity Program in the Newark Schools from a Mental-Hygiene Point of View." *Journal of Educational Sociology* 7: 379-86; February, 1934.

79. Tudoranu, D. "Temperamentul si viata scolara. (Temperament and school life.)" *Satul si Scoala* 2: 11-15; 1932.
80. Valentiner, T. "Seelische Dynamik in Schülerleben. (Psychic dynamics in school life.)" *Internationale zeitschrift für Individual-psychologie* 9: 207-13; 1931.
81. Wahlquist, J. T. "The Honor System in American Colleges and Universities." *School and Society* 37: 757-60; June 10, 1933.
82. Warden, C. J. and Cohen, A. "A Study of Certain Incentives Applied under Schoolroom Conditions." *Pedagogical Seminary and Journal of Genetic Psychology* 39: 320-27; September, 1931.
83. Washburne, Carleton. "The Challenge of Childhood: The Educator's Response." *Mental Hygiene* 19: 47-58; January, 1935.
84. Wile, Ira S. "The Challenge of Childhood: The Challenge." *Mental Hygiene* 19: 38-46; January, 1935.
85. Williamson, E. G., and Paterson, D. G. "Co-ordinating Counseling Procedures." *Journal of Higher Education* 5 :75-78; February, 1934.
86. Witty, P. A. and Theman, Viola. "The Psycho-Educational Clinic." *Journal of Applied Psychology* 18: 369-92; June, 1934.
87. Zachry, Caroline B. "Mental Hygiene Programs in Secondary Schools." *Occupations* 13: 134-39; November, 1934.
88. Zubin, Joseph. *Some Effects of Incentives.* Contributions to Education, No. 532. New York: Teachers College, Columbia University, 1932. 60 p.

Chapter III. Community Influences

89. Ackerley, Lois. "The Information and Attitude of Elementary School Children." *Researches in Parent Education III.* Studies in Child Welfare, Vol. 10. Iowa City: University of Iowa, 1934. p. 113-67.
90. Ackerley, Lois. "The Knowledge and Attitudes Possessed by Parents of Elementary School Children." *Proceedings of the Iowa Academy of Sciences for 1933.* Des Moines: State of Iowa, 1933. p. 202-3.
91. Anderson, J. E. "Child Behavior and Parental Attitudes." *Mental Health Observer* 3: 3; June, 1934.
92. Angell, R. C. "The Influence of Severe and Apparently Lasting Decrease in Income Upon Family Life." *Publications of the American Sociological Society* 28: 85-89; 1934.
93. Barker, R. H. "The Effect of an Unsatisfactory Relationship of Brother to Brother on the Development of Personality." *Social Forces* 9: 85-91; October, 1930.
94. Blatz, W. E. "The Significance of Early Environmental Factors in Personality Development." *Toward Understanding Children II.* Extension Bulletin No. 283. Iowa City: University of Iowa, 1932. p. 49-55.
95. Blumer, Herbert. *Movies and Conduct.* New York: Macmillan Co., 1933. 257 p.
96. Blumer, Herbert, and Hauser, P. M. *Movies, Delinquency, and Crime.* New York: Macmillan Co., 1933. 233 p.
97. Burgess, E. W. "Implications for Parents of the White House Conference on Child Health and Protection." *Toward Understanding Children* II. Extension Bulletin No. 283. Iowa City: University of Iowa, 1932. p. 30-48.
98. Campbell, Albert A. "The Personality Adjustments of Only Children." *Psychological Bulletin* 31: 193-203; March, 1934.
99. Campbell, Albert A. "A Study of the Personality Adjustments of Only and Intermediate Children." *Pedagogical Seminary and Journal of Genetic Psychology* 43: 197-206; September, 1933.
100. Campbell, C. M. *Human Personality and the Environment.* New York: Macmillan Co., 1934. 252 p.
101. Cantril, Hadley, and Allport, G. W. *The Psychology of Radio.* New York: Harper and Brothers, 1935. 276 p.
102. Cavan, Ruth Shonle. "The Relation of Home Background and Social Relations to Personality Adjustment." *American Journal of Sociology* 40: 143-54; September, 1934.
103. Charters, W. W. *Motion Pictures and Youth: A Summary.* New York: Macmillan Co., 1933. 66 p.
104. Charters, W. W. "A Technique for Studying a Social Problem." *Journal of Educational Sociology* 6: 196-203; December, 1932.

105. CHILDERS, A. T. "Hyper-Activity in Children Having Behavior Disorders." *American Journal of Orthopsychiatry* 5: 227-43; July, 1935.
106. COLE, LUELLA W. *Psychology of Adolescence*. New York: Farrar and Rinehart, 1936. Chapters 12-14.
107. CRESSEY, P. G. "The Motion Picture as Informal Education." *Journal of Educational Sociology* 7: 504-15: April, 1934.
108. CRESSEY, P. G. "The Social Rôle of Motion Pictures in an Interstitial Area." *Journal of Educational Sociology* 6: 238-43; December, 1932. Also in *Publications of the American Sociological Society* 28: 90-94; 1934.
109. CRICHTON-MILLER, HUGH. "The Home Background of the Pupil." *Mental Hygiene* 16: 23-25; January, 1932.
110. CUSHING, H. M. "Parent Education as a Mode in Mental Hygiene." *Mental Hygiene* 17: 635-41; October, 1933.
111. DALE, EDGAR. *Children's Attendance at Motion Pictures*. New York: Macmillan Co., 1935. 81 p. (Published with his *Content of Motion Pictures*.)
112. DALE, EDGAR. *The Content of Motion Pictures*. New York: Macmillan Co., 1935. 234 p.
113. DALE, EDGAR. "Methods for Analyzing the Content of Motion Pictures." *Journal of Educational Sociology* 6: 244-50; December, 1932.
114. DUDLEY, VIRGINIA. "Foster Mothers: Successful and Unsuccessful." *Smith College Studies in Social Work* 3: 151-82; December, 1932.
115. DYSINGER, W. S., and RUCKMICK, C. A. *The Emotional Responses of Children to the Motion Picture Situation*. New York: Macmillan Co., 1933. 122 p.
116. ECKSTEIN, L. "Die erzieherischen Kräfte der Familie." *Zeitschrift für Pädagogische Psychologie* 35: 312-18; September, 1934.
117. EMERY, M. "Recreation for Mental Patients." *Occupational Therapy and Rehabilitation* 11: 91-100; April, 1932.
118. EMME, E. E. Significant Counseling Relationships on the College Campus." *Religious Education* 27: 145-50; February, 1932.
119. FISCHER, M. L. "Character Education in Magazines for Parents." *Religious Education* 27: 785-92; December, 1932.
120. FITZ-SIMONS, M. J. *Some Parent-Child Relationships As Shown in Clinical Case Studies*. Contributions to Education, No. 643. New York: Teachers College, Columbia University, 1935. 162 p.
121. FOLSOM, J. K. *The Family: Its Sociology and Social Psychiatry*. New York: John Wiley and Sons, 1934. 604 p.
122. FORD, C. A., and BALEN, HERMAN. "The Effect of Stopping Supervision of Certain Department of Recreation Play Areas Upon the Delinquency Rates of Older Boys." *Psychological Bulletin* 31: 639-40; October, 1934.
123. FOWLER, BURTON P. "The Child as Affected by the Family." *Mental Hygiene* 18: 431-41; July, 1934.
124. FRANCIS, K. V., and FILLMORE, E. A. *The Influence of Environment upon the Personality of Children*. Studies in Child Welfare, Vol. 9, No. 2. Iowa City: University of Iowa, 1934. 71 p.
125. FRANCIS, K. V. "A Study of the Means of Influence of Socio-economic Factors upon the Personality of Children." *Journal of Juvenile Research* 17: 70-77; April, 1933.
126. FREEMAN, F. N., and HOEFER, CAROLYN. "An Experimental Study of the Influence of Motion Picture Films on Behavior." *Journal of Educational Psychology* 22: 411-25; September, 1931.
127. GALLAGHER, ELEANOR G., *The Adopted Child*. New York: Reynal and Hitchcock, 1936. 291 p.
128. GAUDET, F. J., and CURRY, M. A. "The Effects of Business Conditions upon the Sanity of a Population." *Journal of Applied Psychology* 17: 130-35; April, 1933.
129. GINSBURG, E. L. "The Relation of Parental Attitudes to Variations in Hyperactivity." *Smith College Studies in Social Work* 4: 27-54; 1933.
130. GROVES, E. R. "Adaptation of Family Life." *American Journal of Sociology* 40: 772-79; May, 1935.
131. GROVES, E. R., and BROOKS, L. M., editors. *Readings in the Family*. Philadelphia: J. B. Lippincott Co., 1934. 526 p.
132. GRUENBERG, S. M., and GRUENBERG, B. C. *Parents, Children and Money*. New York: Viking Press, 1933. 212 p.

133. HALL, O. M. "Attitudes of Unemployed and Employed Engineers." *Personnel Journal* 12: 222-28; December, 1933.
134. HAMILTON, A. E. "Good Heredity—Bad Environment." *Eugenical News* 20: 31-32; January-February, 1935.
135. HARDY, M. C. "The Out-of-School Activities of Well-Adjusted and Poorly Adjusted Elementary School Pupils." *Journal of Educational Psychology* 26: 455-67; September, 1935.
136. HART, H. N., and HART, E. B. *Personality and the Family.* New York: D. C. Heath and Co., 1935. 381 p.
137. HARTWELL, SAMUEL W. "Adult Adjustments and Non-Adjustments in Relation to Their Effects upon Children." *Mental Hygiene* 16: 598-609; October, 1932.
138. HAUSER, P. M. "How Do Motion Pictures Affect the Conduct of Children?" *Journal of Educational Sociology* 6: 231-37; December, 1932.
139. HAYWARD, R. S. *The Child's Report of Psychological Factors in the Family.* Archives of Psychology, No. 189. New York: Columbia University, 1935. 75 p.
140. HEDRICK, BLANCHE E. "The Effectiveness of a Program of Learning Designed to Change Parental Attitudes Toward Self-Reliance." *Researches in Parent Education III.* Studies in Child Welfare, Vol. 10. Iowa City: University of Iowa, 1934. p. 249-68.
141. HINCKS, C. M. "Mental Hospitals in the Depression." *Mental Health Observer* 3: 1; June, 1935.
142. HOLADAY, PERRY W., and STODDARD, GEORGE D. *Getting Ideas from the Movies.* New York: Macmillan Co., 1933. 102 p. (Bound with W. W. Charters' *Motion Pictures and Youth: A Summary.*)
143. ISAACS, SUSAN. "The Experimental Construction of Environment Optimal for Mental Growth." *A Handbook of Child Psychology.* (Edited by Carl Murchison.) Worcester, Mass.: Clark University Press, 1931. p. 128-57.
144. JOHNSON, WINIFRED BENT, and TERMAN, LEWIS M. "Personality Characteristics of Happily Married, Unhappily Married, and Divorced Persons." *Character and Personality* 3: 290-311; June, 1935.
145. JONES, HAROLD E., and HSAIO-HUNG, HSAIO. "Pregnancy Order and Early Development." *Child Development* 4: 140-47; June, 1933.
146. KAPLAN, F. "Experiments in Informal Education. I. Block Recreation Project." *Journal of Educational Sociology* 7: 516-20; April, 1934.
147. KIRKPATRICK, CLIFFORD. "Intelligence and the Radio." *Sociology and Social Research* 19: 203-9; January-February, 1935.
148. KOMORA, PAUL O., and CLARK, MARY AUGUSTA. "Mental Disease in the Crisis." *Mental Hygiene* 19: 289-301; April, 1935.
149. KÜNKEL, F. *Charakter, Wachstum und Erziehung.* Leipzig: Hirzel, 1931. 223 p.
150. LATHAM, H. L., translator. "Social Consciousness." *Journal of Abnormal and Social Psychology* 29: 287-92; October-December, 1934.
151. LEAHY, A. M. "Some Characteristics of Adoptive Parents." *American Journal of Sociology* 38: 548-63; January, 1933.
152. LEVY, JOHN. "The Impact of Cultural Forms upon Children's Behavior." *Mental Hygiene* 16: 208-20; April, 1932.
153. LEVY, JOHN. "A Quantitative Study of Behavior Problems in Relation to Family Constellation." *American Journal of Psychiatry* 87: 637-54; January, 1931.
154. LEWIN, KURT. "Environmental Forces in Child Behavior and Development." *A Handbook of Child Psychology.* (Edited by Carl Murchison.) Worcester, Mass.: Clark University Press, 1931. p. 94-127.
155. LIEDERMAN, JOSHUA. *Creative Camping.* New York: Association Press, 1931. 251 p.
156. LINDQUIST, RUTH. *The Family in the Present Social Order.* Chapel Hill: University of North Carolina Press, 1931. 241 p.
157. LOTZ, E. R. "Emotional Status of the Parents of Problem and Psychopathic Children." *School and Society* 42: 239-40; August 17, 1935.
158. LOUTTIT, C. M. "Family Harmony and the Child." *Some Practical Efforts to Teach Good Will.* Bulletin, School of Education, Vol. 11, No. 4. Bloomington: Indiana University, 1935. p. 126-30.
159. LOWREY, LAWSON G. "The Family as a Builder of Personality." *American Journal of Orthopsychiatry* 6: 117-24; January, 1936.

160. LUMLEY, F. H. *Measurement in Radio.* Columbus: Ohio State University, 1934. 318 p.
161. MALLER, J. B. "Conflicting Ideals and Their Bearing upon Character Education." *Journal of Educational Research* 25: 161-67; March, 1932.
162. MALLER, J. B. "Size of Family and Personality of Offspring." *Journal of Social Psychology* 2: 3-25; February, 1931.
163. MALZBERG, BENJAMIN. "Mental Disease in New York State According to Nativity and Parentage." *Mental Hygiene* 19: 635-60; October, 1935.
164. MALZBERG, BENJAMIN. "A Statistical Study of Age in Relation to Mental Disease." *Mental Hygiene* 19: 449-76; July, 1935.
165. MATHEWS, J. "Personality and the Parent-Child Relationship." *Family* 12: 208-13; November, 1931.
166. MATHEWS, SELMA M. "The Development of Children's Attitudes Concerning Mothers' Out-of-Home Employment." *Journal of Educational Sociology* 6: 259-71; January, 1933.
167. MATHEWS, SELMA M. "The Effect of Mothers' Out-of-Home Employment upon Children's Ideas and Attitudes." *Journal of Applied Psychology* 18: 116-36; February, 1934.
168. MELTZER, H. "Children's Attitudes to Parents." *American Journal of Orthopsychiatry* 5: 244-65; July, 1935.
169. MILLER, F., and RICHARDS, L. "Parental Behaviour as an Index to the Probable Outcome of Treatment in a Child Guidance Clinic." *Smith College Studies in Social Work* 4: 139-50; 1933.
170. MONASH, LOUIS. *Know Your Child.* New York: McGraw-Hill Book Co., 1931. 246 p.
171. MORGAN, C. L., and REMMERS, H. H. "Liberalism and Conservatism of College Students as Affected by the Depression." *School and Society* 41: 780-84; June 8, 1935.
172. MOWRER, HARRIET R. *Personality Adjustment and Domestic Discord.* New York: American Book Co., 1935. 290 p.
173. MYERS, T. R. *Intra-Family Relationships and Pupil Adjustment.* Contributions to Education, No. 651. New York: Teachers College, Columbia University, 1935. 115 p.
174. NEUMANN, G. "Untersuchungen über das Verhältnis zwischen Stiefmutter und Stiefkind." *Zeitschrift für Pädagogische Psychologie* 34: 358-67; October, 1933.
175. NIMKOFF, M. F. *Parent-Child Relationships.* School of Research Studies, No. 11. Los Angeles: University of Southern California, 1935. 39 p.
176. OJEMANN, RALPH H. "Generalizations Relating to Child Development Involved in Intelligent Parental Guidance." *Researches in Parent Education III.* Studies in Child Welfare, Vol. 10. Iowa City: University of Iowa, 1934. p. 29-99.
177. OLSON, W. C. "Birthplace and Occupation of Father as Factors in Nervous Habits in Children." *Pedagogical Seminary and Journal of Genetic Psychology* 40: 214-19; March, 1932.
178. PAYNE, A. F. *My Parents: Friends or Enemies?* New York: Brewer, Warren and Putnam, 1932. 278 p.
179. PENDRY, ELIZABETH R., and HARTSHORNE, HUGH. *Organizations for Youth.* New York: McGraw-Hill Book Co., 1935. 359 p.
180. PETERS, CHARLES C. *Motion Pictures and Standards of Morality.* New York: Macmillan Co., 1933. 285 p. (Published with W. S. Dysinger and C. A. Ruckmick's *Emotional Responses of Children to the Motion Picture Situation.*)
181. PETERS, CHARLES C. "The Relation of Motion Pictures to Standards of Morality." *Journal of Educational Sociology* 6: 251-55; December, 1932. Also in *School and Society* 39: 414-15; March 31, 1934.
182. PETERSON, RUTH C., and THURSTONE, L. L. "The Effect of a Motion Picture Film on Children's Attitudes toward Germans." *Journal of Educational Psychology* 23: 241-46; April, 1932.
183. PETERSON, RUTH C., and THURSTONE, L. L. *The Effect of Motion Pictures on the Social Attitudes of High School Children.* Chicago: University of Chicago Bookstore, 1933. 113 p.
184. PETERSON, RUTH C., and THURSTONE, L. L. *Motion Pictures and the Social Attitudes of Children.* New York: Macmillan Co., 1933. 75 p.
185. PLANT, JAMES S. "The Child as a Member of the Family." *Annals of the American Academy of Political and Social Science* 160: 66-74; March, 1932.

186. PLANT, JAMES S. "Mental Hygiene Aspects of the Family." *Family* 13: 39-45, 90-99, 118-26; April-June, 1932.
187. POLLOCK, HORATIO M. "The Depression and Mental Disease in New York State." *American Journal of Psychiatry* 91: 763-71; January, 1935.
188. PRESSEY, L. C. "Some Serious Family Maladjustments Among College Students." *Social Forces* 10: 236-42; December, 1931.
189. PRITCHETT, H. L. "The Adjustment of College Students' Family Problems." *Social Forces* 10: 84-89; October, 1931.
190. PRUETTE, L. *The Parent and the Happy Child.* New York: Henry Holt and Co., 1932. 290 p.
191. REEVES, W. R. "Report of the Committee on Street Play." *Journal of Educational Sociology* 4: 607-18; June, 1931.
192. RENSHAW, SAMUEL; MILLER, V. L.; and MARQUIS, D. P. *Children's Sleep.* New York: Macmillan Co., 1933. 242 p.
193. RENSHAW, SAMUEL. "Sleep Motility as an Index of Motion-Picture Influence." *Journal of Educational Sociology* 6: 226-30; December, 1932.
194. RENZ, CARL, and RENZ, M. P. *Big Problems on Little Shoulders.* New York: Macmillan Co., 1934. 129 p.
195. RIGGS, A. F. *Play: Recreation in a Balanced Life.* Garden City, N. Y.: Doubleday, Doran and Co., 1935. 239 p.
196. ROBINSON, EDWARD S. "Are Radio Fans Influenced?" *Survey* 68: 546-47, 567, 569-70; November 1, 1932.
197. ROGERS, CARL R. "A Good Foster Home; Its Achievements and Limitations." *Mental Hygiene* 17: 21-40; January, 1933.
198. ROSENHEIM, FREDERICK. "Parental Attitudes as Observed in Child Guidance Clinics." *Psychiatric Quarterly* 9: 279-86; April, 1935.
199. RUCKMICK, C. A. "How Do Motion Pictures Affect the Attitudes and Emotions of Children?" *Journal of Educational Sociology* 6: 210-16; December, 1932.
200. SCHMEING, K. "Das 'einzige Kind' und der Pubeszent." *Zeitschrift für Pädagogische Psychologie* 32: 449-54; October, 1931.
201. SCHUMACHER, H. C. "The Depression and Its Effect on the Mental Health of the Child." *American Journal of Public Health* 24: 367-71; April, 1934.
202. SEAGOE, M. V. "The Child's Reaction to the Movies." *Journal of Juvenile Research* 15: 169-80; July, 1931.
203. SHAFFER, L. F. *The Psychology of Adjustment.* Boston: Houghton Mifflin Co., 1936. 600 p.
204. SHORT, W. H. "The Effect of Motion Pictures on the Social Attitudes of High-School Children." *Journal of Educational Sociology* 6: 220-26; December, 1932.
205. SHUTTLEWORTH, F. K. "Measuring the Influence of Motion-Picture Attendance on Conduct and Attitudes." *Journal of Educational Sociology* 6: 216-19; December, 1932.
206. SILVERMAN, BARUCH. "The Behavior of Children from Broken Homes." *American Journal of Orthopsychiatry* 5: 11-18; January, 1935.
207. SIMPSON, MARGARETE. *Parent Preferences of Young Children.* Contributions to Education, No. 652. New York: Teachers College, Columbia University, 1935. 85 p.
208. STAGNER, ROSS. "Economic Status and Personality." *School and Society* 42: 551-52; October 19, 1935.
209. STAGNER, ROSS, and DROUGHT, NEAL. "Measuring Children's Attitudes toward Their Parents." *Journal of Educational Psychology* 26: 169-76; March, 1935.
210. STODDARD, GEORGE D. "Measuring the Effect of Motion Pictures on the Intellectual Content of Children." *Journal of Educational Sociology* 6: 204-9; December, 1932.
211. STOGDILL, R. M. "Attitudes of Parents toward Parental Behavior." *Journal of Abnormal and Social Psychology* 29: 293-97; October-December, 1934.
212. STONE, HANNAH M., and HART, HENRIETTE. "Contraception and Mental Hygiene." *Mental Hygiene* 17: 417-23; July, 1933.
213. THISTED, MOSES N. "Participation in College Athletics and Vocational Success." *Doctoral Theses in Education I.* Studies in Education, Vol. 9, No. 1. Iowa City: University of Iowa, 1934. p. 131-49.
214. THOM, DOUGLAS A. "Mental Hygiene and the Depression." *Mental Hygiene* 16: 564-76; October, 1932.

215. THUROW, MILDRED B. "A Study of Selected Factors in Family Life as Described in Life History Material." *Social Forces* 12: 562-69; May, 1934.
216. WALLIN, J. E. W. *Personality Maladjustments and Mental Hygiene.* New York: McGraw-Hill Book Co., 1935. 511 p.
217. WANG, C. K. A. "The Significance of Early Personal History for Certain Personality Traits." *American Journal of Psychology* 44: 768-74; October, 1932.
218. WARD, ANNE. "The Only Child; a Study of One Hundred Only Children Living at Home with Both Parents, Referred to a Child Guidance Clinic." *Smith College Studies in Social Work* 1: 41-65; September, 1930.
219. WHITE HOUSE CONFERENCE ON CHILD HEALTH AND PROTECTION. *The Adolescent in the Family.* New York: D. Appleton-Century Co., 1934. 473 p.
220. WITMER, HELEN LELAND, and OTHERS. "The Childhood Personality and Parent-Child Relationships of Dementia Praecox and Manic-Depressive Patients." *Smith College Studies in Social Work* 4: 289-377; 1934.
221. WITMER, HELEN LELAND. "Parental Behavior as an Index to the Probable Outcome of Treatment in a Child Guidance Clinic." *American Journal of Orthopsychiatry* 3: 431-44; October, 1933.
222. WITTELS, F. *Set the Children Free.* (Translated by E. and C. Paul.) London: George Allen & Unwin, 1932. 242 p.
223. WITTY, PAUL A. "'Only' and 'Intermediate' Children of High School Ages." *Psychological Bulletin* 31: 734; November, 1934.
224. WITTY, PAUL A. "The Only Child of Age Five." *Psychological Clinic* 22: 73-87; June-August, 1933.
225. WITTY, PAUL A. "The Physical, Mental, and Social Growth and Development of Three Hundred 'Only' Children of Chronological Age Five." *Psychological Bulletin* 30: 694; November, 1933.
226. WÜLKER, L. "Das einzige Kind." *Zeitschrift für Pädagogische Psychologie* 35: 324-26; September, 1934.
227. ZILBOORG, GREGORY. "Sidelights on Parent-Child Antagonism." *American Journal of Orthopsychiatry* 2: 35-43; January, 1932.

Chapter IV. The Normal Child

228. ANDERSON, JOHN E. *Happy Childhood.* New York: D. Appleton-Century Co., 1933. 321 p.
229. ANDERSON, V. V. "The Contribution of Mental Hygiene to Industry." *Proceedings of the First International Congress on Mental Hygiene.* New York: the Congress, 1932. Vol. 1, p. 696-718.
230. ANDERSON, V. V., and KENNEDY, WILLIE-MAUDE. "Psychiatry in College; a Discussion of a Model Personnel Program." *Mental Hygiene* 16: 353-83; July, 1932.
231. ARLITT, ADA H. *Adolescent Psychology.* New York: American Book Co., 1933. 250 p.
232. AVERILL, LAWRENCE A. *Adolescence.* Boston: Houghton Mifflin Co., 1936. 496 p.
233. BAIN, WINIFRED E. "A Study of the Attitudes of Teachers Toward Behavior Problems." *Child Development* 5: 19-35; March, 1934.
234. BENNETT, MARGARET E. *College and Life.* New York: McGraw-Hill Book Co., 1933. 456 p.
235. BIGELOW, M. A. "Sex Education and Sex Ethics." *Encyclopaedia of the Social Sciences* 14: 8-13. New York: Macmillan Co., 1934.
236. BOTT, HELEN. *Personality Development in Young Children.* Toronto: University of Toronto Press, 1934. 139 p.
237. BRIDGMAN, RALPH P. *The Quest for Emotional Honesty.* Child Welfare Pamphlets, No. 22. Iowa City: University of Iowa, 1933. 12 p.
238. BÜHLER, CHARLOTTE. "The Child and Its Activity With Practical Material." *British Journal of Educational Psychology* 3: 27-41; February, 1933.
239. BÜHLER, CHARLOTTE. *From Birth to Maturity.* London: George Routledge and Sons, 1935. 237 p.
240. BURNHAM, WILLIAM H. *The Normal Mind.* New York: D. Appleton Co., 1924. 702 p.
241. BURNHAM, WILLIAM H. *The Wholesome Personality.* New York: D. Appleton and Co., 1932. 713 p.

242. CAILLE, RUTH K. *Resistant Behaviour of Preschool Children.* Child Development Monographs, No. 11. New York: Teachers College, Columbia University, 1933. 142 p.
243. CLARK, JUDITH. "Education at the College Level for Marriage, Parenthood and Family Life." *Journal of the American Association of University Women* 24: 132-35; April, 1931.
244. COLE, LUELLA. *Psychology of Adolescence.* New York: Farrar and Rinehart, 1936. 503 p.
245. CONKLIN, EDMUND S. *Principles of Adolescent Psychology.* New York: Henry Holt & Co., 1935. 437 p.
246. COWDERY, KARL M. "The Guidance of Youth in the Colleges." *Occupations* 12: 14-20; December, 1933.
247. CRAWFORD, NELSON ANTRIM, and MENNINGER, KARL A., editors. *The Healthy-Minded Child.* New York: Coward-McCann, 1930. 198 p.
248. DAVIS, KATHARINE B. *Factors in the Sex Life of 2200 Women.* New York: Harper and Brothers, 1929. 430 p.
249. DE SCHWEINITZ, KARL. "The Dangers and Advantages of Sex Instruction for Children." *Mental Hygiene* 15: 561-69; July, 1931.
250. DEWEY, EVELYN. *Behaviour Development in Infants.* New York: Columbia University Press, 1935. 321 p.
251. DICKINSON, ROBERT L., and BEAM, LURA. *A Thousand Marriages.* Baltimore: Williams and Wilkins Co., 1931. 482 p.
252. DILLON, MIRIAM S. "Attitudes of Children Toward Their Own Bodies and Those of Other Children." *Child Development* 5: 165-76; June, 1934.
253. EDSON, NEWELL W. *Sex Conduct.* Child Welfare Pamphlets, No. 21. Iowa City: University of Iowa, 1933. 10 p.
254. ELLIOTT, GRACE LOUCKS. *Women After Forty.* New York: Henry Holt and Co., 1936. 213 p.
255. EMERY, E. V. N. "The Content and Method of Instructing College Students in Mental Hygiene." *Mental Hygiene* 17: 590-97; October, 1933.
256. FAVILL, JOHN, and SENIOR, ROSE D. "A Report of the First Year's Work in Mental Hygiene in the Student Health Service of the University of Chicago." *Journal of Nervous and Mental Disease* 73: 627-34; June, 1931.
257. FITZ-SIMONS, MARION J. "Some Parent-Child Relationships as Shown in Clinical Case Studies." *Journal of Experimental Education* 2: 170-96; December, 1933.
258. FOSTER, JOSEPHINE C. *Busy Childhood.* New York: D. Appleton-Century Co., 1933. 303 p.
259. GARLAND, JOSEPH. *The Road to Adolescence.* Cambridge, Mass.: Harvard University Press, 1934. 293 p.
260. GARRISON, KARL C. *The Psychology of Adolescence.* New York: Prentice-Hall Publishing Co., 1934. 337 p.
261. GESELL, ARNOLD S., and OTHERS. *Infant Behavior.* New York: McGraw-Hill Book Co., 1934. 343 p.
262. GOODENOUGH, FLORENCE L. *Anger in Young Children.* Minneapolis: University of Minnesota Press, 1931. 278 p.
263. GOODENOUGH, FLORENCE L. *Developmental Psychology.* New York: D. Appleton-Century Co., 1934. 619 p.
264. GRANNISS, EDWARD R. "Mental Hygiene as Applied to Industrial-Accident Prevention." *Mental Hygiene* 19: 398-404; July, 1935.
265. GROVES, ERNEST R. "Sex Adjustment of College Men and Women." *Journal of Educational Sociology* 8: 353-60; February, 1935.
266. GROVES, ERNEST R., and GROVES, GLADYS H. *Sex in Childhood.* New York: Macaulay, 1933. 247 p.
267. GROVES, ERNEST R. *Understanding Yourself.* New York: Greenberg, 1935. 278 p.
268. GROVES, ERNEST R., and GROVES, GLADYS H. *Wholesome Childhood.* New ed. Boston: Houghton Mifflin Co., 1931. 201 p.
269. HAGMAN, ELMER R. "A Study of Fears in Children of Pre-School Age." *Journal of Experimental Education* 1: 110-30; December, 1932.
270. HAMILTON, G. V. *A Research in Marriage.* New York: Albert and Charles Boni, 1929. 570 p.
271. HARTMANN, GEORGE W. "The Classification of Adjustment Problems among College Students." *Journal of Abnormal and Social Psychology* 28: 64-69; April-June, 1933.

272. HARTMANN, GEORGE W. "Personality Traits Associated with Variations in Happiness." *Journal of Abnormal and Social Psychology* 29: 202-12; July-September, 1934.
273. HATTENDORF, KATHARINE W. "A Home Program for Mothers in Sex Education." *Researches in Parent Education I.* Studies in Child Welfare, Vol. 6. Iowa City: University of Iowa, 1932. p. 11-92, 211-88.
274. HAZLITT, VICTORIA. "Modern Trends in Infant Psychology." *British Journal of Educational Psychology* 1: 119-29; June, 1931.
275. HAZLITT, VICTORIA. *The Psychology of Infancy.* New York: E. P. Dutton and Co., 1933. 149 p.
276. HEERING, GERTRUDE A. "A Study of Thumbsucking in Infants from Two to Seventeen Weeks of Age." *Child Development* 3: 273-77; September, 1932.
277. HERSEY, R. B. "The Mental Health of Workers." *Mental Hygiene* 18: 462-68; July, 1934.
278. HOWARD, FRANK E., and PATRY, FREDERICK L. *Mental Health.* New York: Harper and Brothers, 1935. 551 p.
279. JASTROW, JOSEPH. *Piloting Your Life.* New York: Greenberg, 1930. 372 p.
280. JERSILD, ARTHUR T. *Child Psychology.* New York: Prentice-Hall, 1933. 462 p.
281. JERSILD, ARTHUR T., and HOLMES, FRANCES B. *Children's Fears.* New York: Teachers College, Columbia University, 1935. 356 p.
282. JERSILD, ARTHUR T., and OTHERS. *Children's Fears, Dreams, Wishes, Daydreams, Likes, Dislikes, Pleasant and Unpleasant Memories.* Child Development Monographs No. 12. New York: Teachers College, Columbia University, 1933. 172 p.
283. JOHNSON, BUFORD J. *Child Psychology.* Springfield, Ill.: C. C. Thomas, 1932. 439 p.
284. JUNG, CARL G. *Modern Man in Search of a Soul.* New York: Harcourt, Brace and Co., 1933. 282 p.
285. KIRKPATRICK, EDWIN A. *Mental Hygiene for Effective Living.* New York: D. Appleton-Century Co., 1934. 387 p.
286. KOCH, HELEN LOIS, and OTHERS. "A Scale for Measuring Attitude Toward the Question of Children's Freedom." *Child Development* 5: 253-67; September, 1934.
287. LAWS, GERTRUDE. *Parent-Child Relationships.* Contributions to Education, No. 283. New York: Teachers College, Columbia University, 1927. 57 p.
288. LEVY, DAVID M. "Experiments on the Sucking Reflex and Social Behavior of Dogs." *American Journal of Orthopsychiatry* 4: 203-24; April, 1934.
289. LIVINGOOD, F. G. "Mental Hygiene and the Small College." *Mental Hygiene* 18: 245-53; April, 1934.
290. McCARTHY, RAPHAEL C. *Training the Adolescent.* New York: Bruce Publishing Co., 1934. 298 p.
291. MACCLENATHAN, RUTH H. "Teachers and Parents Study Children's Behaviors." *Journal of Educational Sociology* 7: 325-33; January, 1934.
292. McKINNEY, FRED B. "An Outline of a Series of Lectures on Mental Hygiene for College Freshmen." *Journal of Abnormal and Social Psychology* 29: 276-86; October-December, 1934.
293. MALLER, JULIUS B. *The Case Inventory; Controlled Association Test; Character Sketches; Ethical Judgment Test.* New York: Teachers College, Columbia University.
294. MENNINGER, KARL A. *The Human Mind.* New York: Alfred A. Knopf, 1930. 447 p.
295. MORGAN, JOHN J. B. *Keeping a Sound Mind.* New York: Macmillan Co., 1934. 440 p.
296. MYERS, THEODORE R. *Intra-Family Relationships and Pupil Adjustment.* Contributions to Education, No. 651. New York: Teachers College, Columbia University, 1935. 115 p.
297. NORSWORTHY, NAOMI, and WHITLEY, MARY T. *The Psychology of Childhood.* New York: Macmillan Co., 1933. 515 p.
298. OJEMANN, RALPH H. "The Measurement of Attitude Toward Self-Reliance." *Researches in Parent Education III.* Studies in Child Welfare, Vol. 10. Iowa City: University of Iowa, 1935. p. 101-11.
299. PALMER, HAROLD D. "Mental-Hygiene Problems in a University." *Mental Hygiene* 18: 233-44; April, 1934.

300. PATEY, HENRY C., and STEVENSON, GEORGE S. "The Mental Health Emphasis in Education." *American Journal of Orthopsychiatry* 3: 241-65, July; 464-94, October, 1933. 4: 138-77; January, 1934. (Republished as a separate bulletin by National Committee for Mental Hygiene, New York.)
301. PATRICK, JAMES G. *The Role of Intimate Groups in the Personality Development of Selected College Men.* School of Research Studies, No. 6. Los Angeles: University of Southern California, 1935. 43 p.
302. PATRICK, JAMES R., and SIMS, V. M. "Personality Differences Between Negro and White College Students, North and South." *Journal of Abnormal and Social Psychology* 29: 181-201; July-September, 1934.
303. PATRY, FREDERICK L. "What the College Student Should Know About Present-Day Mental Hygiene." *Journal of Abnormal and Social Psychology* 30: 4-16; April-June, 1935.
304. PINTNER, RUDOLF, and OTHERS. "The Measurement of Pupil Adjustment." *Journal of Educational Research* 28: 334-46; January, 1935.
305. PITKIN, WALTER B. *Life Begins at Forty.* New York: McGraw-Hill Book Co., 1932. 175 p.
306. PRESSEY, SIDNEY L., and PRESSEY, LUELLA C. "Development of the Interest-Attitude Test." *Journal of Applied Psychology* 17: 1-16; February, 1933.
307. REINHARDT, EMMA. "Freshman Difficulties." *Journal of Higher Education* 4: 307-9; June, 1933.
308. RICHMOND, WINIFRED V. *The Adolescent Boy.* New York: Farrar and Rinehart, 1933. 233 p.
309. RICKETTS, AGNES F. "A Study of the Behavior of Young Children in Anger." *Behavior of the Preschool Child.* Studies in Child Welfare, Vol. 9, No. 3. Iowa City: University of Iowa, 1934. p. 159-71.
310. RUGGLES, ARTHUR H. "Mental Hygiene in Colleges." *Occupations* 13: 140-45; November, 1934.
311. RUGGLES, ARTHUR H. "Mental Hygiene of the College Student." *Proceedings of the First International Congress on Mental Hygiene.* New York: the Congress, 1932. Vol. 2, p. 70-84.
312. SADLER, WILLIAM S., and SADLER, LENA. *Piloting Modern Youth.* New York: Funk and Wagnalls, 1931. 370 p.
313. SAILER, RANDOLPH C. *Happiness Self-Estimates of Young Men.* Contributions to Education, No. 467. New York: Teachers College, Columbia University, 1931. 116 p.
314. SEABURY, DAVID. *Growing Into Life.* New York: Boni and Liveright, 1928. 715 p.
315. SHAFFER, LAURANCE F. *The Psychology of Adjustment.* Boston: Houghton Mifflin Co., 1936. 600 p.
316. SHERMAN, MANDEL. *Mental Hygiene and Education.* New York: Longmans, Green and Co., 1934. 295 p.
317. SMITH, ENID S. *A Study of Twenty-five Adolescent Unmarried Mothers in New York City.* New York: Salvation Army Women's Home and Hospital (314 E. 15th St.), 1935. 97 p.
318. SMITH, RANDOLPH B. *The Development of an Inventory for the Measurement of Inferiority Feelings at the High School Level.* Archives of Psychology, No. 144. New York: Columbia University, 1932. 118 p.
319. SPARLING, EDWARD J. *Do College Students Choose Vocations Wisely?* Contributions to Education, No. 561. New York: Teachers College, Columbia University, 1933. 110 p.
320. STODDARD, GEORGE D., and WELLMAN, BETH L. *Child Psychology.* New York: Macmillan Co., 1934. 419 p.
321. STOGDILL, EMILY L. "A Survey of the Case Records of a Student Psychological Consultation Service Over a Ten-Year Period." *Psychological Exchange* 3: 129-33; November-December, 1934.
322. STOGDILL, RALPH M. "Attitudes of Parents, Students, and Mental Hygienists Toward Children's Behavior." *Journal of Social Psychology* 4: 486-89; November, 1933.
323. STOGDILL, RALPH M. "Attitudes of Parents Toward Parental Behavior." *Journal of Abnormal and Social Psychology* 29: 293-97; October-December, 1934.
324. STOGDILL, RALPH M. "Experiments in the Measurement of Attitudes Toward Children, 1899-1935." *Child Development* 7: 31-36; March, 1936.

325. STOGDILL, RALPH M. "Parental Attitudes and Mental Hygiene Standards." *Mental Hygiene* 15: 813-27; October, 1931.
326. STRANG, RUTH M. *Personal Development and Guidance in College and Secondary School.* New York: Harper and Brothers, 1934. 341 p.
327. STRATTON, DOROTHY C. *Problems of Students in a Graduate School of Education.* Contributions to Education, No. 550. New York: Teachers College, Columbia University, 1933. 167 p.
328. STRECKER, EDWARD A. "Everyday Psychology of the Normal Child." *Mental Hygiene* 17: 65-81; January, 1933.
329. STUART, HAROLD C. *Healthy Childhood.* New York: D. Appleton-Century Co., 1933. 393 p.
330. SULLIVAN, ELLEN B. "Emotional Disturbances Among Children." *Journal of Juvenile Research* 16: 56-65; January, 1932.
331. SYMONDS, PERCIVAL M., and JACKSON, CLAUDE E. *Measurement of the Personality Adjustments of High School Pupils.* New York: Teachers College, Columbia University, 1935. 110 p.
332. SYMONDS, PERCIVAL M. *Mental Hygiene of the School Child.* New York: Macmillan Co., 1934. 321 p.
333. THOM, DOUGLAS A. *Normal Youth and Its Everyday Problems.* New York: D. Appleton and Co., 1932. 368 p.
334. WALLIN, JOHN E. W. *Personality Maladjustments and Mental Hygiene.* New York: McGraw-Hill Book Co., 1935. 511 p.
335. WASHBURNE, JOHN N. "The Impulsions of Adolescents as Revealed by Their Written Wishes." *Journal of Juvenile Research* 16: 193-212; July, 1932.
336. WASHBURNE, JOHN N. "A Test of Social Adjustment." *Journal of Applied Psychology* 19: 125-44; April, 1935.
337. WATSON, GOODWIN. "Happiness Among Adult Students of Education." *Journal of Educational Psychology* 21: 79-109; February, 1930.
338. WATSON, MAUD E. "Mental-Hygiene Implications of Student Relationships With the Dean of Women." *Mental Hygiene* 18: 83-91; January, 1934.
339. WEGROCKI, H. J. "The Effect of Prestige Suggestibility on Emotional Attitudes." *Journal of Social Psychology* 5: 384-94; August, 1934.
340. WHITE HOUSE CONFERENCE ON CHILD HEALTH AND PROTECTION. *The Adolescent in the Family.* New York: D. Appleton-Century Co., 1934. 473 p.
341. WHITLOW, C. M. "Attitudes and Behavior of High-School Students." *American Journal of Sociology* 40: 489-94; January, 1935.
342. WICKMAN, E. K. *Children's Behavior and Teachers' Attitudes.* New York: Commonwealth Fund, 1928. 247 p.
343. WILE, IRA S. "Sex Education in Relation to Mental and Social Hygiene." *Mental Hygiene* 18: 40-50; January, 1934.
344. WILLIAMS, FRANKWOOD E. "Mental Hygiene and the College; Levels of Mental-Hygiene Work." *Mental Hygiene* 15: 532-41; July, 1931.
345. WOODWORTH, ROBERT S. *Adjustment and Mastery.* Baltimore: Williams and Wilkins Co., 1933. 137 p.
346. YOURMAN, JULIUS. "Children Identified by Their Teachers as Problems." *Journal of Educational Sociology* 5: 334-43; February, 1932.
347. ZACHAROFF, L. "Mental Hygiene in Soviet Industry." *Mental Hygiene* 15: 522-26; July, 1931.

Chapter V. Behavior Problems and Delinquency

348. ACKERSON, LUTON. *Children's Behavior Problems I. Incidence, Genetic and Intellectual Factors.* Chicago: University of Chicago Press, 1931. 268 p.
349. ACKERSON, LUTON. "On the Feasibility of Inventorying Children's Behavior Traits." *Journal of Juvenile Research* 16: 32-39; January, 1932.
350. ADLER, HERMAN M.; CAHN, FRANCES; and STUART, JOHANNES. *The Incidence of Delinquency in Berkeley, 1928-1932.* Berkeley: University of California Press, 1934. 102 p.
351. ADLER, HERMAN M. *Twelfth Annual Report of the Criminologist (July 1, 1928 to June 30, 1929).* Springfield: Illinois Department of Public Welfare, 1930. 104 p.
352. ADLER, HERMAN M. "The Work of Institutions in the Prevention of Delinquency." *Journal of Juvenile Research* 15: 18-27; January, 1931.

353. AICHHORN, AUGUST. *Wayward Youth.* New York: Viking Press, 1935. 236 p.
354. ALEXANDER, FRANZ. "Mental Hygiene and Criminology." *Mental Hygiene* 14: 853-82; October, 1930.
355. ANDERSON, FORREST N., and OTHERS. "Six Years of Child Guidance." *Journal of Juvenile Research* 15: 73-96; April, 1931.
356. ARMSTRONG, CLAIRETTE P. "Delinquency and Primogeniture." *Psychological Clinic* 22: 48-52; March, 1933.
357. ARMSTRONG, CLAIRETTE P. *Six Hundred Runaway Boys; Why Boys Desert Their Homes.* Boston: Richard G. Badger, 1932. 208 p.
358. ASHER, E. J. "The Training Needs of Reform School Boys Experimentally Determined." *Journal of Delinquency* 11: 151-58; September, 1927.
359. ATWOOD, BARTLETT S. "Social Participation and Juvenile Delinquency." *Indiana Bulletin of Charities and Correction* 210: 208-11; September, 1933.
360. BAKER, HARRY J., and TRAPHAGEN, VIRGINIA. *The Diagnosis and Treatment of Behavior-Problem Children.* New York: Macmillan Co., 1935. 393 p.
361. BEARD, BELLE B. *Juvenile Probation.* New York: American Book Co., 1934. 219 p.
362. BECKHAM, A. S. "Juvenile Crime." *Journal of Juvenile Research* 16: 66-76; January, 1932.
363. BECKHAM, A. S. "A Study of Race Attitudes in Negro Children of Adolescent Age." *Journal of Abnormal and Social Psychology* 29: 18-29; April-June, 1934.
364. BENJAMIN, PAUL L. "The Family Society and the Depression." *Annals of the American Academy of Political and Social Science* 160: 135-43; March, 1932.
365. BOWLER, ALIDA C., and BLOODGOOD, RUTH S. *Institutional Treatment of Delinquent Boys.* U. S. Dept. of Labor, Children's Bureau Publication No. 228. Washington, D. C.: Government Printing Office, 1935. 324 p.
366. BOWMAN, LEROY E. *Community Programs for Summer Play Schools.* New York: Child Study Association of America, 1935. 48 p.
367. BOYNTON, PAUL L., and McGAW, BONNIE H. "The Characteristics of Problem Children." *Journal of Juvenile Research* 18: 215-22; October, 1934.
368. BOYNTON, PAUL L.; DUGGER, HARRIET; and TURNER, MASAL. "The Emotional Stability of Teachers and Pupils." *Journal of Juvenile Research* 18: 223-32; October, 1934.
369. BRONNER, AUGUSTA. *A Comparative Study of the Intelligence of Delinquent Girls.* Contributions to Education, No. 68. New York: Teachers College, Columbia University, 1914. 95 p.
370. BURKEY, RUTH E. "A Statistical Study of the Sequence of Successive Delinquencies." *Journal of Juvenile Research* 16: 133-44; April, 1932.
371. BURT, CYRIL. *The Young Delinquent.* New York: D. Appleton and Co., 1925. 619 p.
372. CALDWELL, MORRIS GILMORE. "The Economic Status of Families of Delinquent Boys in Wisconsin." *American Journal of Sociology* 37: 231-39; September, 1931.
373. CALDWELL, MORRIS GILMORE. "Is the Reformatory Reforming the Prisoner?" *Journal of Juvenile Research* 18: 90-102; April, 1934.
374. CASSELBERRY, WILLIAM S. "Analysis and Prediction of Delinquency." *Journal of Juvenile Research* 16: 1-31; January, 1932.
375. CHASE, VERA A. "Educational Achievement of Delinquent Boys." *Journal of Juvenile Research* 16: 189-92; July, 1932.
376. CHRISTIE, AMOS U. "Physical Defects in Delinquent Boys." *Journal of Juvenile Research* 18: 13-22; January, 1934.
377. CLARK, WILLIS W., and WILLIAMS, J. HAROLD. *A Scale for Grading Neighborhood Conditions.* Bulletin No. 3. Whittier, Calif.: California Bureau of Juvenile Research, Whittier State School, 1916. 25 p.
378. CLARK, WILLIS W. *Whittier Scale for Grading Juvenile Offenses.* Bulletin No. 11. Whittier, Calif.: California Bureau of Juvenile Research, Whittier State School, 1922. 8 p.
379. CORREVONT, ANN M., and CORREVONT, H. EARL. "Prevention of Delinquency from the Community Approach." *Journal of Juvenile Research* 17: 54-61; January, 1933.
380. COURTHIAL, A. *Emotional Differences of Delinquent and Non-Delinquent Girls of Normal Intelligence.* Archives of Psychology, No. 133. New York: Columbia University, 1931. 102 p.
381. CULBERT, JANE F. *The Visiting Teacher at Work.* New York: Commonwealth Fund, 1929. 235 p.

382. DAVIDSON, MARION. "The Relationship of Adjustment Status of Child Guidance Clinic Cases to Age, Mental Capacity, and School Placement." *Journal of Juvenile Research* 19: 160-70; July, 1935.
383. DAWE, HELEN C. "Raising Standards of Behavior in the Kindergarten." *Elementary School Journal* 35: 267-80; December, 1934.
384. DICKSON, VIRGIL E. "Behavior Difficulties That Baffle Teachers." *Journal of Juvenile Research* 16: 93-101; April, 1932.
385. DOBBS, HARRISON A. "Institutional Care of Delinquent Children: A New Appraisal." *Annals of the American Academy of Political and Social Science* 151: 173-79; September, 1930.
386. DOLL, EDGAR A., editor. *Handbook of Casework and Classification Methods for Offenders.* Vineland, N. J.: The Author (Training School), 1934. 29 p. (Publication of the Committee on Casework, Methods and Treatment for Prisoners of the American Prison Association.)
387. DOLL, EDGAR A. "The Relation of Intelligence to Criminality." *Journal of Social Psychology* 1: 527-31; November, 1930.
388. DOLTON, ISABELLA A. "The Montefiore School; an Experiment in Adjustment." *Journal of Educational Sociology* 6: 482-90; April, 1933.
389. DURLING, DOROTHY, and POWELL, WEBSTER. "Improper School Placement as a Factor in Juvenile Delinquency." *Journal of Applied Psychology* 16: 519-24; October, 1932.
390. FENTON, NORMAN, and OTHERS. *The Delinquent Boy and the Correctional School.* Claremont, Calif.: Claremont Colleges Guidance Center, 1935. 182 p.
391. FENTON, NORMAN. "Purposes and Accomplishments of the Coordinating Councils." *Journal of Juvenile Research* 19: 98-103; April, 1935.
392. FENTON, NORMAN, and WALLACE, RAMONA. "Use of Tests in Twenty-eight Child Guidance Clinic Centers in the United States." *Journal of Juvenile Research* 18: 115-18; April, 1934.
393. FERNALD, GRACE M. "Report of the Psychological Work in the California School for Girls." *Journal of Delinquency* 1: 22-32; March, 1916.
394. FRANCIS, KENNETH V., and FILLMORE, E. A. *The Influence of Environment Upon the Personality of Children.* Studies in Child Welfare, Vol. 9, No. 2. Iowa City: University of Iowa, 1934. 71 p.
395. GILMORE, HARLAN W. "Five Generations of a Begging Family." *American Journal of Sociology* 37: 768-74; March, 1932.
396. GLUECK, ELEANOR T. "The Family, the School, and Crime." *Harvard Teachers Record* 5: 71-81; April, 1935.
397. GLUECK, SHELDON, and GLUECK, ELEANOR T. *One Thousand Juvenile Delinquents.* Cambridge, Mass.: Harvard University Press, 1934. 341 p.
398. GLUECK, SHELDON. "The Status of Probation." *Mental Hygiene* 15: 290-98; April, 1931.
399. GODDARD, HENRY H. *Juvenile Delinquency.* New York: Dodd, Mead and Co., 1921. 120 p.
400. GROWDEN, C. H., and CALHOON, C. H. "An Analysis of Cases Admitted to the Boys' Industrial School and the Girls' Industrial School During the Year 1931." *Ohio Welfare Bulletin* 10: 6-14; 1933.
401. HAGGERTY, M. E.; OLSON, W. C.; and WICKMAN, E. K. *Behavior Rating Schedules.* Yonkers-on-Hudson, N. Y.: World Book Co., 1930.
402. HAGGERTY, M. E. "The Incidence of Undesirable Behavior in Public-School Children." *Journal of Educational Research* 12: 102-22; September, 1925.
403. HEALY, WILLIAM; BRONNER, AUGUSTA F.; and SHIMBERG, M. E. "The Close of Another Chapter in Criminology." *Mental Hygiene* 19: 208-22; April, 1935.
404. HEALY, WILLIAM, and BRONNER, AUGUSTA F. *Delinquents and Criminals; Their Making and Unmaking.* New York: Macmillan Co., 1926. 317 p.
405. HEALY, WILLIAM, and BRONNER, AUGUSTA F. "How Does the School Produce or Prevent Delinquency?" *Journal of Educational Sociology* 6: 450-70; April, 1933.
406. HEALY, WILLIAM. *The Individual Delinquent.* Boston: Little, Brown and Co., 1915. 839 p.
407. HEALY, WILLIAM. *Mental Conflicts and Misconduct.* Boston: Little, Brown and Co., 1917. 330 p.
408. HEALY, WILLIAM, and OTHERS. *Reconstructing Behavior in Youth.* New York: Alfred A. Knopf, 1929. 325 p.

409. HODGKISS, MARGARET. "The Delinquent Girl in Chicago: II. The Influence of Broken Homes and Working Mothers." *Smith College Studies in Social Work* 3: 259-74; March, 1933.
410. JOINT COMMITTEE ON METHODS OF PREVENTING DELINQUENCY. *Three Problem Children.* New York: The Committee (50 E. 42d St.), 1924. 146 p.
411. KEOGH, CORNELIA R. "A Study of Runaways at a State Correctional School for Boys." *Journal of Juvenile Research* 19: 45-61; April, 1935.
412. KUHLMANN, FRED. "The Mental Examination of Reformatory Cases." *Journal of Criminal Law and Criminology* 5: 666-74; January, 1915.
413. LANE, HOWARD A., and WITTY, PAUL A. "The Educational Attainment of Delinquent Boys." *Journal of Educational Psychology* 25: 695-702; December, 1934.
414. LANE, HOWARD A., and WITTY, PAUL A. "The Mental Ability of Delinquent Boys." *Journal of Juvenile Research* 19: 1-12; January, 1935.
415. LASLETT, H. R., and MANNING, JUANITA. "A Delinquency Survey of a Medium-Size High School." *Journal of Juvenile Research* 18: 71-78; April, 1934.
416. LOU, HERBERT H. *Juvenile Courts in the United States.* Chapel Hill: University of North Carolina Press, 1927. 277 p.
417. MCCLURE, W. E. "Intelligence of 600 Juvenile Delinquents." *Journal of Juvenile Research* 17: 35-43; January, 1933.
418. MALLER, J. B. "Delinquency Areas in New York City." *Psychological Bulletin* 31: 640-41; October, 1934.
419. MALLER, J. B. "The Trend of Juvenile Delinquency in New York City." *Journal of Juvenile Research* 17: 10-18; January, 1933.
420. MERRILL, MAUDE A. "The Care of the Psychopathic or Defective Delinquent." *Journal of Juvenile Research* 14: 165-70; July, 1930.
421. MITCHELL, ALICE M. *Children and the Movies.* Chicago: University of Chicago Press, 1929. 181 p.
422. MOLITCH, MATTHEW, and ADAMS, EDGAR M. "Hearing Defects in Behavior Problems." *Journal of Juvenile Research* 20: 15-19; January, 1936.
423. MOLITCH, MATTHEW, and ECCLES, AUGUST K. "Serum Calcium in Juvenile Delinquents." *American Journal of Orthopsychiatry* 4: 73-78; January, 1934.
424. MOORE, H. K. "Is the Problem Boy a Weakling?" *Journal of Juvenile Research* 18: 79-89; April, 1934.
425. MURSELL, GEORGE REX. "A Revision of the Whittier Scale for Grading Juvenile Offenses." *Journal of Juvenile Research* 16: 246-50; July, 1932.
426. NATIONAL EDUCATION ASSOCIATION, COMMITTEE ON BEHAVIOR PROBLEMS. *The Preparation of Teachers for Dealing with Behavior Problem Children.* Washington, D. C.: the Association, 1928. 11 p.
427. NATIONAL EDUCATION ASSOCIATION, RESEARCH DIVISION. "Crime Prevention Through Education." *Research Bulletin* 10: 133-201; September, 1932. Washington, D. C.: the Association.
428. NEW YORK STATE CRIME COMMISSION. *From Truancy to Crime; a Study of 251 Adolescents.* Albany: the Commission, 1928. 139 p.
429. NEW YORK STATE CRIME COMMISSION. *A Study of Problem Boys and Their Brothers.* Albany: the Commission, 1929. 408 p.
430. OLSON, WILLARD C. "The Clinical Use of Behavior Rating Schedules." *Journal of Juvenile Research* 15: 237-45; October, 1931.
431. OLSON, WILLARD C. "The Diagnosis and Treatment of Behavior Disorders of Children." *Educational Diagnosis.* Thirty-Fourth Yearbook, National Society for the Study of Education. Bloomington, Ill.: Public School Publishing Co., 1935. Chapter 18, p. 363-97.
432. OLSON, WILLARD C. "The Location of Problem Children by a Nomination Method." *Journal of Juvenile Research* 19: 193-200; October, 1935.
433. OLSON, WILLARD C. *Problem Tendencies in Children: A Method for their Measurement and Description.* Minneapolis: University of Minnesota Press, 1930. 92 p.
434. PARSLEY, MANNIE. "The Delinquent Girl in Chicago: III. The Influence of Ordinal Position and Size of Family." *Smith College Studies in Social Work* 3: 274-83; March, 1933.
435. PAYNTER, RICHARD H., and BLANCHARD, PHYLLIS. *A Study of Educational Achievement of Problem Children.* New York: Commonwealth Fund, 1929. 72 p.
436. RAUBENHEIMER, ALBERT SYDNEY. *An Experimental Study of Some Behavior Traits of the Potentially Delinquent Boy.* Psychological Monographs, Vol. 34, No. 6. Whole No. 159. Princeton, N. J.: Psychological Review Co., 1925. 107 p.

437. RECKLESS, WALTER C., and SMITH, MAPHEUS. *Juvenile Delinquency.* New York: McGraw-Hill Book Co., 1932. 412 p.
438. REEVES, MARGARET. *Training Schools for Delinquent Girls.* New York: Russell Sage Foundation, 1929. 455 p.
439. REINHARDT, JAMES M., and HARPER, FOWLER VINCENT. "Comparison of Environmental Factors of Delinquent and Non-Delinquent Boys." *Journal of Juvenile Research* 15: 271-77; October, 1931.
440. REUSSER, JOHN L. "Personal Attitudes of Delinquent Boys." *Journal of Juvenile Research* 17: 19-34; January, 1933.
441. ROGERS, K. H., and AUSTIN, O. L. "Intelligence Quotients of Juvenile Delinquents." *Journal of Juvenile Research* 18: 103-6; April, 1934.
442. SAYLES, MARY B. *The Problem Child in School.* New York: Joint Committee on Methods of Preventing Delinquency (50 E. 42d St.), 1925. 288 p.
443. SCOTT, ROBERT H. "Modern Science and the Juvenile Court." *Journal of Juvenile Research* 14: 77-86; April, 1930.
444. SEAGOE, MAY V. "The Transient Child." *Journal of Juvenile Research* 16: 251-57; July, 1932.
445. SELLING, LOWELL S. *Diagnostic Criminology.* Ann Arbor, Mich.: Edwards Brothers, 1935. 176 p.
446. SELLING, LOWELL S. "Psychopathology without Functional Change as Shown in a Delinquent Group." *Journal of Juvenile Research* 17: 153-62; July-October, 1933.
447. SEMANS, HUBERT H. "Non-Athletic Phases of the Recreational Program in Children's Institutions." *Journal of Juvenile Research* 16: 40-55; January, 1932.
448. SHAW, CLIFFORD R., and OTHERS. *Delinquency Areas: A Study of the Geographic Distribution of School Truants, Juvenile Delinquents, and Adult Offenders in Chicago.* Chicago: University of Chicago Press, 1929. 214 p.
449. SHELDON, H. D. "Problems in the Statistical Study of Juvenile Delinquency." *Metron* 12: 201-23; 1934.
450. SHIMBERG, MYRA E., and REICHENBERG, WALLY. "The Success and Failure of Subnormal Problem Children in the Community." *Mental Hygiene* 17: 451-65; July, 1933.
451. SLAWSON, JOHN. *The Delinquent Boy: A Socio-Psychological Study.* Boston: Richard G. Badger, 1926. 477 p.
452. SLETTO, RAYMOND F. "Sibling Position and Juvenile Delinquency." *American Journal of Sociology* 39: 657-69; March, 1934.
453. SNYDER, MARGARET A. "A Comparison of Mental Traits and Attitudes of Delinquent Boys and Girls." *Journal of Juvenile Research* 15: 181-91; July, 1931.
454. SPEER, GEORGE S. "The Use of the Bernreuter Personality Inventory as an Aid in the Prediction of Behavior Problems." *Journal of Juvenile Research* 20: 65-69; April, 1936.
455. STEVENSON, GEORGE S., and SMITH, G. *Child Guidance Clinics: A Quarter Century of Development.* New York: Commonwealth Fund, 1934. 186 p.
456. SULLENGER, T. EARL. "Economic Status as a Factor in Juvenile Delinquency." *Journal of Juvenile Research* 18: 233-45; October, 1934.
457. SULLENGER, T. EARL. "The Newsboy as a Juvenile Delinquent." *Journal of Juvenile Research* 15: 215-19; July, 1931.
458. SULLIVAN, ELLEN B. "Age, Intelligence, and Educational Achievement of Boys Entering Whittier State School." *Journal of Delinquency* 11: 23-38; March, 1927.
459. THOMAS, WILLIAM I., and THOMAS, DOROTHY S. *The Child in America.* New York: Alfred A. Knopf, 1928. 583 p.
460. TIMME, ARTHUR R. "The Role of Physical Conditions in Behavior Problems." *Mental Hygiene* 15: 468-79; July, 1931.
461. TOBIAS, NORMAN. "A Study of Syphilis Among One Thousand Cases of Juvenile Delinquency." *Journal of Delinquency* 12: 188-92; June, 1928.
462. TRUITT, RALPH P. *Team-Work in the Prevention of Crime.* New York: Joint Committee on Methods of Preventing Delinquency (50 E. 42d St.), 1926. 18 p.
463. UNITED STATES DEPARTMENT OF LABOR, CHILDREN'S BUREAU. *Juvenile-Court Statistics 1930.* Publication No. 212. Washington, D. C.: Government Printing Office, 1932. 69 p.
464. VAN WATERS, MIRIAM. *Youth in Conflict.* New York: New Republic, 1925. 293 p.
465. WALLACE, RAMONA. "An Interest Inventory for Use in the Child Guidance Clinic." *Journal of Juvenile Research* 17: 147-52; July-October, 1933.

466. WEIDENSALL, C. JEAN. *The Mentality of the Criminal Woman.* Baltimore: Warwick and York, 1916. 332 p.
467. WEILL, BLANCHE C. *The Behavior of Young Children of the Same Family.* Cambridge, Mass.: Harvard University Press, 1928. 220 p.
468. WHITE, RALPH, and FENTON, NORMAN. "Aspects of Delinquency and Superior Mentality." *Journal of Juvenile Research* 15: 101-7; April, 1931.
469. WHITE HOUSE CONFERENCE ON CHILD HEALTH AND PROTECTION. *The Delinquent Child.* New York: Century Co., 1932. 499 p.
470. WICKMAN, E. K. *Children's Behavior and Teachers' Attitudes.* New York: Commonwealth Fund, 1928. 247 p.
471. WILLLIAMS, J. HAROLD. "Early History of the California Bureau of Juvenile Research." *Journal of Juvenile Research* 18: 187-214; October, 1934.
472. WILLIAMS, J. HAROLD. *A Guide to the Grading of Homes.* Bulletin No. 7. Whittier, Calif.: California Bureau of Juvenile Research, Whittier State School, 1918. 21 p.
473. WILLIAMS, J. HAROLD. *The Intelligence of the Delinquent Boy.* Journal of Delinquency Monograph No. 1. Whittier, Calif.: Whittier State School, 1919. 198 p.
474. WILSON, RUTH T. "Delinquency Areas in San Jose." *Psychological Bulletin* 31: 588-89; July, 1934.
475. YODER, DALE. "Some Probable Effects of Unemployment Insurance Upon Delinquency." *Journal of Juvenile Research* 15: 260-67; October, 1931.

Chapter VI. Physically and Mentally Exceptional Children

476. ASSOCIATION OF FIRST ASSISTANTS IN THE HIGH SCHOOL OF THE CITY OF NEW YORK. *Educating Superior Students.* (Edited by Helen L. Cohen and Nancy G. Coryell.) New York: American Book Co., 1935. 340 p.
477. BAKER, HARRY J. *Characteristic Differences in Bright and Dull Pupils.* Bloomington, Ill.: Public School Publishing Co., 1927. 118 p.
478. BAKER, HARRY J. *Educational Disability and Case Studies in Remedial Teaching.* Bloomington, Ill.: Public School Publishing Co., 1929. 172 p.
479. BARNARD, RAYMOND H. "The Relation of Intelligence and Personality to Speech Defects." *Elementary School Journal* 30: 604-20; April, 1930.
480. BARTEMEIER, LEO H. "Some Observations of Convulsive Disorders in Children." *American Journal of Orthopsychiatry* 2: 260-67; July, 1932.
481. BECHTOLD, E. "Ueber das unmittelbare Behalten bei blinden und sehenden Schulkindern. (On Immediate Retention in Blind and Seeing School Children.)" *Zeitschrift für Kinderforschung* 30: 161-71; 1925.
482. BERMAN, LOUIS. "Crime and the Endocrine Glands." *American Journal of Psychiatry* 89: 215-38; September, 1932.
483. BERRIEN, F. K. "Psychological Differences in Psychopathic and Post-Encephalitic Children." *Journal of Applied Psychology* 18: 536-49; August, 1934.
484. BERRIEN, F. K. "A Study of the Drawings of Abnormal Children." *Journal of Educational Psychology* 26: 143-50; February, 1935.
485. BIERI, E. *Ein Beitrag zur Kenntnis der geistigen Entwicklung des taubstummen Schulkindes. (A Contribution to the Understanding of the Mental Development of the Deaf and Dumb Child.)* Zurich: Leeman, 1931. 86 p.
486. BILLINGS, MARION LEROY. "A Report of a Case of Inverted Writing and Drawing." *Child Development* 6: 161-63; June, 1935.
487. "The Blind Feeble-Minded [A Bibliography]." *Teachers Forum for Instructors of Blind Children* 2: 14-16; January, 1930.
488. BOLLI, L. "Le Reve et les Aveugles. II. De la survivance des Images Visuelles. (The Dream and the Blind, II. The Survival of Visual Images.)" *Journal de psychologie normale et pathologique* 29: 258-309; January to April, 1932.
489. BRANHAM, V. C. "Epileptoid Reactions in Children." *American Journal of Psychiatry* 82: 423-29; January, 1926.
490. BRAUCKMANN, K. *Das gehörleidende Kind: wie kann es hineinwachsen in unsere Sprache und geistige Gemeinschaft? (The Deaf Child: How Can It Grow Into Our Speech and Common Mental Life?)* Jena: Fischer, 1931. 160 p.
491. BRAUN, F. "Untersuchungen über das personliche Tempo. (Studies on the Personal Tempo.)" *Archiv für die gesamte Psychologie* 60: 317-60; 1927.

492. BRIDGE, E. M. "Mental State of the Epileptic Patient." *Archives of Neurology and Psychiatry* 32: 723-36; October, 1934.
493. BRITTON, S. W.; HINSON, A.; and HALL, W. H. "Neural and Hormonal Influences on Bodily Activity." *American Journal of Physiology* 93: 473-79; June, 1930.
494. BRONK, D. W., and FERGUSON, L. K. "Impulses in Cardiac Sympathetic Nerves." *Proceedings of the Society for Experimental Biology and Medicine* 30: 339-40; December, 1932.
495. BROWN, ANDREW W. *The Unevenness of the Abilities of Dull and Bright Children.* Contributions to Education, No. 220. New York: Teachers College, Columbia University, 1926. 112 p.
496. BROWN, FREDERICK W. "Personality Integration as the Essential Factor in the Permanent Cure of Stuttering." *Mental Hygiene* 17: 266-77; April, 1933.
497. BROWN, R. R. "A Study of the Mental and Physical Traits of the Relatives of Epileptics." *Journal of Applied Psychology* 14: 620-36; December, 1930.
498. BURRITT, O. H. "The Visually Handicapped Feeble-Minded." *Teachers Forum for Instructors of Blind Children* 3: 9-12; March, 1931.
499. CHADWICK, MARY. "The Neurotic Child." *Proceedings of the First International Congress on Mental Hygiene.* New York: the Congress, 1932. Vol. 2, p. 447-65.
500. CHANNING, ALICE. *Employment of Mentally Deficient Boys and Girls.* U. S. Dept. of Labor, Children's Bureau Publication No. 210. Washington, D. C.: Government Printing Office, 1932. 107 p.
501. CHIPMAN, CATHERINE E. "The Constancy of the Intelligence Quotient of Mental Defectives." *Psychological Clinic* 18: 103-11; May, 1929.
502. CROTHERS, BRONSON. "Mental-Hygiene Problems of Children with Sensory-Motor Defects." *Proceedings of the First International Congress on Mental Hygiene.* New York: the Congress, 1932, Vol. 2, p. 475-87.
503. CUTSFORTH, THOMAS D. *The Blind in School and Society.* New York: D. Appleton-Century Co., 1933. 263 p.
504. DAWSON, S., and CONN, J. C. M. "Effect of Encephalitis Lethargica on the Intelligence of Children." *Archives of Disease in Childhood* 357-58; December, 1926.
505. DEARBORN, WALTER F. "The Nature of Special Abilities and Disabilities." *School and Society* 31: 632-36; May 10, 1930.
506. DE BEER, P. "Karakter en omgangsfeuten van Zwaksinningen. (Character-Faults and Faults in Sociability of the Feeble-minded.)" *Jeugd en Beroep* 1: 188-92; 1928.
507. DOLL, EDGAR A. "Psychological Aspects of the Birth-Injured Mentally Deficient." *Proceedings and Addresses, 1932.* Godfrey, Ill.: American Association for the Study of the Feebleminded (Groves B. Smith, sec., Beverly Farm), 1932. p. 304-11.
508. DOLL, EDGAR A. "Social Adjustment of the Mentally Subnormal." *Journal of Educational Research* 28: 36-43; September, 1934.
509. DORSEY, JOHN M. "The Treatment of a Person Who Stutters." *Mental Hygiene* 18: 409-30; July, 1934.
510. DOWNEY, JUNE E. "Some Curious Problems Suggested by Case-Studies of Handedness." *Journal of Abnormal and Social Psychology* 27: 152-58; July, 1932.
511. DOWNEY, JUNE E. "Types of Dextrality and Their Implications." *American Journal of Psychology* 38: 317-67; July, 1927.
512. DRY, WALTER R., and COOPER, ELIZABETH C. "The Psychological Study of Blind Children." *Psychological Clinic* 20: 184-91; November, 1931.
513. DUMAS, G. "La Mimique des Aveugles. (Mimicry of the Blind.)" *Bulletin de l'Academie de Medicine* 107: 607-10; May 3, 1932.
514. EYRICH, M. "Ueber Charakter und Charakterveränderung bei Kindlichen und jugenlichen Epileptikern. (Character and Character Alteration in Epileptic Children and Adolescents.)" *Zeitschrift für die gesamte Neurologie und Psychiatrie* 141: 640-44; 1932.
515. FASSBENDER, F. "Über einen Fall von Praecositas somo-psychogenitalis bei einem 7½ jahre alter Mädchen. (A Case of Prascositas Somo-Psycho-Genitalis in a 7½-year-old girl.)" *Zeitschrift für Kinderheilkunde* 54: 642-56; 1933.
516. FINCH, F. H., and CARROLL, H. A. "Gifted Children as High-School Leaders." *Pedagogical Seminary and Journal of Genetic Psychology* 41: 476-81; December, 1932.

517. FLANIGAN, CATHARINE A. *The Sight-Saving Class as a Mental Hygiene Measure.* Publication No. 153. New York: National Society for the Prevention of Blindness. 12 p.
518. FOSTER, NELLIS B. "Psychic Factors in the Course of Cardiac Disease." *Journal of the American Medical Association* 89: 1017-18; September 24, 1927.
519. FOX, EDNA J. "An Investigation of the Effect of Glandular Therapy on the Intelligence Quotient." *Mental Hygiene* 12: 90-102; January, 1928.
520. FULSTOW, M. "The Weight of the Heart in Schizophrenia and in Other Mental Disorders." *Archives of Neurology and Psychiatry* 16: 620-28; November, 1926.
521. GIBBS, CHARLES E. "Behavior Disorders in Chronic Epidemic Encephalitis." *American Journal of Psychiatry* 86: 619-36; January, 1930.
522. GOODENOUGH, FLORENCE L. "Expression of the Emotions in a Blind-Deaf Child." *Journal of Abnormal and Social Psychology* 27: 328-33; October, 1932.
523. GROSSMANN, I. "Theorie des Epileptischen Charakters. (Theory of the Epileptic Character.)" *Zeitschrift für die gesamte Neurologie und Psychiatrie* 117: 12-18; 1928.
524. HAEFNER, RALPH. *The Educational Significance of Left-Handedness.* Contributions to Education, No. 360. New York: Teachers College, Columbia University, 1929. 84 p.
525. HAINES, CORA M. "The Effects of Defective Hearing upon the Individual as a Member of the Social Order." *Journal of Abnormal and Social Psychology* 22: 151-56; July-September, 1927.
526. HATHAWAY, WINIFRED. "Educational Opportunities in the United States for Partially Seeing Children." *Journal of Educational Sociology* 6: 331-38; February, 1933.
527. HAYWARD, EMELINE P., and WOODS, ANDREW H. "Mental Derangements in Hypothyroidism." *Journal of the American Medical Association* 97: 164-65; July 18, 1931.
528. HICKS, J. A. "The Acquisition of Motor Skill in Young Children." *Child Development* 1: 90-105; June, 1930.
529. HILL, T. R. "Juvenile Behavior Disorders in Epidemic Encephalitis." *Lancet* 216: 968-71; May 11, 1929.
530. HOLLINGWORTH, LETA S. "The Child of Very Superior Intelligence as a Special Problem in Social Adjustment." *Annals of the American Academy of Political and Social Science* 149 (Part 3): 151-59; May, 1930.
531. IDE, GLADYS. "Aspects of Special Education for the Handicapped Child." *Proceedings and Addresses, 1932.* Godfrey, Ill.: American Association for the Study of the Feeble-Minded (Groves B. Smith, sec., Beverly Farm), 1932. p. 412-16.
532. INGRAM, MARGUERITE L. "Trends in Education of Crippled Children." *Journal of Educational Sociology* 6: 339-47; February, 1933.
533. JOHNSON, ELEANOR H. "School Maladjustment and Behavior." *Mental Hygiene* 11: 558-69; July, 1927.
534. JOHNSON, WENDELL. *The Influence of Stuttering on the Personality.* Studies in Child Welfare, Vol. 5, No. 5. Iowa City: University of Iowa, 1932. 140 p.
535. JOLL, CECIL A. *Diseases of the Thyroid Gland.* London: William Heineman, 1932. 682 p.
536. JONES, ALICE M. "An Analytical Study of One Hundred Twenty Superior Children." *Psychological Clinic* 16: 19-76; January, 1925.
537. KANNER, LEO, and LACHMAN, SANDER E. "The Contribution of Physical Illness to the Development of Behavior Disorders in Children." *Mental Hygiene* 17: 605-17; October, 1933.
538. KELLER, HELEN A. *A Story of My Life.* Garden City, N. Y.: Doubleday, Page and Co., 1905. 441 p.
539. KIMBALL, O. P., and MARINUS, C. J. "The Relation of Endemic Goitre to Mental Deficiency." *Annals Internal Medicine* 4: 569-77; December, 1930.
540. KINDER, ELAINE F., and RUTHERFORD, ELIZABETH J. "Social Adjustment of Retarded Children." *Mental Hygiene* 11: 811-33; October, 1927.
541. KISTLER, K. "Linkshändigkeit und Sprachstörungen. (Left-Handedness and Speech Disturbances.)" *Schweizerische Medizinische Wochenschrift* 60: 32-34; January 11, 1930.
542. KOCH, HELEN L., and UFKESS, JENNETTE. "A Comparative Study of Stylus Maze Learning by Blind and Seeing Subjects." *Journal of Experimental Psychology* 9: 118-31; April, 1926.

543. KUENZEL, MYRA W. "A Survey of Mongolian Traits." *Training School Bulletin (Vineland, N. J.)* 26: 49-58; June, 1929.
544. LANDAUER, K. "Infantile Motor Unrest." *International Zeitschrift für Psychoanalyse* Vol. 12, No. 3, 1930.
545. LANGDON, J. N. *An Experimental Study of Certain Forms of Manual Dexterity.* Industrial Health Reserve Board Report No. 66. London: H. M. Stationery Office, 1932. 64 p.
546. LEE, MARY V. "The Children's Orthopedic Hospital: A Survey of the Intelligence of Crippled Children." *Journal of Educational Research* 23: 164-66; February, 1931.
547. LOMBARD, W. P., and COPE, O. M. "Sex Differences in Heart Action." *American Journal of Physiology* 83: 37-46; December, 1927.
548. LONG, JOHN A. *Motor Abilities of Deaf Children.* Contributions to Education, No. 514. New York: Teachers College, Columbia University, 1932. 67 p.
549. LORD, ARTHUR B. "A Survey of Four Hundred Forty-Nine Special Class Pupils." *Journal of Educational Research* 27: 108-14; October, 1933.
550. LOWREY, LAWSON G. "The Relationship of Feeblemindedness to Behavior Disorders." *Proceedings and Addresses, 1928.* Godfrey, Ill.: American Association for the Study of the Feeble-Minded (Groves B. Smith, sec., Beverly Farm), 1928. p. 96-100.
551. LURIE, LOUIS A. "The Relation of Endocrinopathic States to Conduct Disorders of Children." *American Journal of Psychiatry* 86: 285-305; September, 1929.
552. LYON, VERNE W. "The Use of Vocational and Personality Tests with the Deaf." *Journal of Applied Psychology* 18: 224-30; April, 1934.
553. McCLURE, W. E. and GOLDBERG, BRONETT. "A Clinical Study of 'Toledo's Strong Boy'." *Journal of Abnormal and Social Psychology* 27: 159-67; July-September, 1932.
554. McELWEE, EDNA WILLIS. "A Comparison of the Personality Traits of 300 Accelerated, Normal, and Retarded Children." *Journal of Educational Research* 26: 31-34; September, 1932.
555. MANN, W. L. "The Seventh Sense (Vestibular or Balance Sense) in Aviation." *Military Surgeon* 65: 1-23; July, 1929.
556. MOORE, LUCILE. "Mental Growth of Low Grade Feeble-Minded." *Training School Bulletin (Vineland, N. J.)* 26: 88-95; October, 1929.
557. NATIONAL SOCIETY FOR THE STUDY OF EDUCATION. *The Grouping of Pupils.* Thirty-Fifth Yearbook, Part I. Bloomington, Ill.: Public School Publishing Co., 1936. 319 p.
558. NILSON, KENNETH. "An Age-Grade Study of Physically Disabled Pupils in Minnesota Public Schools." *Elementary School Journal* 33: 122-29; October, 1932.
559. OATES, DAVID W. "Left-Handedness in Relation to Speech Defects, Intelligence and Achievement." *Forum of Education* 7: 91-105 June, 1929.
560. ORDAHL, GEORGE. "Birth Rank of Mongolians." *Journal of Heredity* 18: 429-31; October, 1927.
561. ORTON, SAMUEL T. "Specific Reading Disability—Strephosymbolia." *Journal of the American Medical Association* 90: 1095-99; April 7, 1928.
562. PATTERSON, HAROLD A., and FONNER, DELMA. "Some Observations on the Intelligence Quotient in Epileptics." *Psychiatric Quarterly* 3: 542-48; October, 1928.
563. PFLEGER, E. "Soziale Verhaltensweisen einer körperlich entstellten Halbwaisen. (Social Behavior in a Physically Ill-Favored Half-Orphan.)" *Zeitschrift für Jugendkeit* 4: 129-32; 1934.
564. PINTNER, RUDOLF. "Emotional Stability of the Hard of Hearing." *Pedagogical Seminary and Journal of Genetic Psychology* 43: 293-311; December, 1933.
565. PINTNER, RUDOLF. "A Mental Survey of the Deaf." *Journal of Educational Psychology* 19: 145-51; March, 1928.
566. PYLE, W. H., and DROUIN, ALICE. "Left-Handedness: An Experimental and Statistical Study." *School and Society* 36: 253-56; August 20, 1932.
567. RICHARDS, LAURA E. *Laura Bridgman: The Story of an Opened Door.* New York: D. Appleton and Co., 1928. 154 p.
568. ROCKWELL, JOHN G. "The Thyroid Gland." *Psychological Bulletin* 25: 341-60; June, 1928.
569. ROWE, ALLAN W. "A Possible Endocrine Factor in the Behavior Problem of the Young." *American Journal of Orthopsychiatry* 1: 451-75; October, 1931.

557

570. Sándor, Béla. "The Functioning of Memory and the Methods of Mathematical Prodigies." *Character and Personality* 1: 70-74; September, 1932.
571. Schmidt-Lamberg, H. "Die Erziehung des kranken Kindes in der Anstalt. (The Education of the Sick Child in the Institution.)" *Psychologie und Medizin* 4: 331-35; 1932.
572. Sigel, Evelyn. "The Mental Hygiene Problems of Cardiac Patients." *Smith College Studies in Social Work* 2: 336-57; June, 1932.
573. Smirnova, A. M. "Pathogenesis, Treatment and Prophylaxis of Stuttering in Children of School Age." *Sovetsk Nevropatol* 3: 74-94; 1934.
574. "Supplementary Bibliography on the Blind Feeble-Minded." *Teachers Forum for Instructors of Blind Children* 3: 12; March, 1931.
575. Terman, Lewis M., editor. *Genetic Studies of Genius*. Stanford University, Calif.: Stanford University Press, 1925-30. 3 Vols.
576. Terman, Lewis M. "The Gifted Child." *Handbook of Child Psychology*. (Edited by Carl Murchison.) Worcester, Mass.: Clark University Press, 1931. p. 568-84.
577. Updegraff, Ruth. "Preferential Handedness in Young Children." *Journal of Experimental Education* 1: 134-39; December, 1932.
578. Villey-Desmeserets, P. *The World of the Blind: A Psychological Study*. New York: Macmillan Co., 1930. 403 p.
579. Von Baeyer, W. "Zur Psychologie verkrüpelter Kinder und Jugendlicher. Ein Beitrag zur Erkenntniss ihrer geistigen und seelischen Entwicklungsweisen. (The Psychology of Crippled Children and Youths. A Contribution to the Understanding of their Intellectual and Emotional Modes of Development.)" *Zeitschrift für Kinderforschung* 34: 229-92; 1928.
580. Welles, Henry H. *The Measurement of Certain Aspects of Personality Among Hard of Hearing Adults*. Contributions to Education, No. 545. New York: Teachers College, Columbia University, 1932. 77 p.
581. White, Ralph K. "The Versatility of Genius." *Journal of Social Psychology* 2: 460-89; November, 1931.
582. Williamson, Edmund G., and Christian, A. M. "Vocational Advisement of Disabled College Students." *Occupational Therapy and Rehabilitation* 13: 179-84; 1934.
583. Winkler, H. "Psychische Entwicklung und Krüppeltum. (Mental Development and Deformity.)" *Deutsche Kruppelhilfe, Erganzungsheit des Zeitschrifts für Krüppelfursorge*. 1931, No. 8. 122 p.
584. Witty, Paul A., and Smith, Muriel B. "The Mental Status of 1480 Crippled Children." *Educational Trends (Northwestern University)* 1: 21-24; January, 1932.
585. Witty, Paul A., and Lehman, Harvey C. "Nervous Instability and Genius: Some Conflicting Opinions." *Journal of Abnormal and Social Psychology* 24: 486-97; January-March, 1930.
586. Woodall, C. S. "Analysis of the I. Q. Variability." *Proceedings and Addresses, 1931*. Godfrey, Ill.: American Association for the Study of the Feeble-Minded (Groves B. Smith, sec., Beverly Farm), 1931. p. 247-62.

Chapter VII. Technics and Instruments of Mental Hygiene

587. Alexander, Franz, and Healy, William. *Roots of Crime; Psychoanalytic Studies*. New York: Alfred A. Knopf, 1935. 305 p.
588. Allen, Frederick H. "Therapeutic Work With Children." *American Journal of Orthopsychiatry* 4: 193-202; April, 1934.
589. Arctander, Signy, and Dahlström, Sigurd. *What Becomes of the Children Removed from Home by the Oslo Child Welfare Board?* Albany: New York State Department of Social Welfare, 1932. 138 p.
590. Baker, Henry J., and Traphagen, Virginia. *Diagnosis and Treatment of Behavior-Problem Children*. New York: Macmillan Co., 1935. 393 p.
591. Bassett, Clara. *Mental Hygiene in the Community*. New York: Macmillan Co., 1934. 394 p.

592. BERK, A.; LANE, L.; and TANDY, M. C. "Follow-Up Study of Thirty Habit Clinic Children Who Manifested Delinquency Problems Before the Age of Ten Years." *Bulletin of the Massachusetts Department of Mental Diseases* 17: 61-81; April, 1933.
593. BINGHAM, W. V., and MOORE, B. V. *How to Interview*. New York: Harper and Brothers, 1934. 308 p.
594. BLANTON, SMILEY, and BLANTON, MARGARET GRAY. *Child Guidance*. New York: Century Co., 1927. 301 p.
595. BLATZ, W. E., and BOTT, HELEN. *The Management of Young Children*. New York: William Morrow and Co., 1930. 354 p.
596. BLATZ, W. E., and BOTT, E. A. "Studies in Mental Hygiene of Children: I. Behavior of Public School Children—A Description of Method." *Pedagogical Seminary and Journal of Genetic Psychology* 34: 552-82; December, 1927.
597. BLATZ, W. E. and RINGLAND, M. C. *The Study of Tics in Pre-School Children*. Child Development Series No. 3. Toronto: University of Toronto Press, 1935. 58 p.
598. BRADLEY, CHARLES, and BOSQUET, ELIZABETH S. "Uses of Books for Psychotherapy with Children." *American Journal of Orthopsychiatry* 6: 23-31; January, 1936.
599. BÜHLER, C. *Drei Generationen im Jugendtagebuch. (Three Generations of Youth as Seen in Their Diaries.)* Jena: Fischer, 1934. 184 p.
600. BURLINGHAM, D. T. "Child Analysis and the Mother." *Psychoanalytic Quarterly* 4: 69-92; January, 1935.
601. BURNHAM, WILLIAM H. *The Wholesome Personality*. New York: D. Appleton and Co., 1932. 713 p.
602. CAMPBELL, N. M. *The Elementary School Teacher's Treatment of Classroom Behavior Problems*. Contributions to Education, No. 668. New York: Teachers College, Columbia University, 1935. 71 p.
603. CARBERRY, MABEL A. "An Attempt to Determine the Consistency of Judgments Regarding the Adjustment Status of Children Examined by a Child Guidance Clinic." *Journal of Juvenile Research* 19: 75-92; April, 1935.
604. CASON, HULSEY. *The Nightmare Dream*. Psychological Monographs, Vol. 46, No. 5. Whole No. 209. Princeton, N. J.: Psychological Review Co., 1935. 51 p.
605. CHALISOV, M. A. "O psikhohigienicheskoi rabote sredi bolnikh kliniki nevrozov. (Mental-Hygiene Work Among the Patients of the Clinic of Neuroses.)" *Sovetskaia psikhonevrologiia* 2: 132-37; 1934.
606. CHARTERS, W. W. "A Character Development Study." *Personnel Journal* 12: 119-23; August, 1933.
607. CLARK, L. PIERCE. "Can Child Analysis Prevent Neuroses and Psychoses in Later Life?" *Psychoanalytic Review* 19: 46-55; January, 1931.
608. COOPER, O. A. "Possibilities of Occupational Therapy in a Child Guidance Clinic." *Occupational Therapy and Rehabilitation* 12: 293-98; 1933.
609. CURTI, MARGARET WOOSTER. *Child Psychology*. New York: Longmans, Green and Co., 1930. 527 p.
610. DAVIDSON, MARION. "The Relationship of Adjustment Status of Child Guidance Clinic Cases to Age, Mental Capacity and School Placement." *Journal of Juvenile Research* 19: 160-70; July, 1935.
611. DAVIS, J. E. "Some Social Aspects of Mental Re-education." *Occupational Therapy and Rehabilitation* 11: 129-34; April, 1932.
612. DOLL, EDGAR A. *Vineland Social Maturity Scale*. Vineland, N. J.: Extension Department, Training School, 1936. (Manual of Directions and Scale.)
613. DOLLARD, JOHN. *Criteria for the Life History*. New Haven, Conn.: Yale University Press, 1935. 288 p.
614. DUDYCHA, G. J., and DUDYCHA, M. M. "Adolescents' Memories of Pre-School Experiences." *Pedagogical Seminary and Journal of Genetic Psychology* 42: 468-80; June, 1933.
615. FENTON, NORMAN, and OTHERS. *The Delinquent Boy and the Correctional School*. Claremont, Calif.: Claremont College Guidance Center, 1935. 182 p.
616. FOSTER, JOSEPHINE, and ANDERSON, JOHN E. *The Young Child and His Parents*. Minneapolis: University of Minnesota Press, 1930. 247 p.
617. FREUD, ANNA. *Introduction to the Technic of Child Analysis*. Washington, D. C.: Nervous and Mental Disease Publishing Co., 1928. 59 p.
618. FREUD, ANNA. *Psycho-Analysis for Teachers and Parents*. New York: Emerson Books, 1935. 117 p.

619. FREUD, ANNA. "Psychoanalysis of the Child." *A Handbook of Child Psychology.* (Edited by Carl Murchison.) Worcester, Mass.: Clark University Press, 1931. p. 555-67.
620. FRIES, M. "Beispiele der Spieltechnik in der Analyse des Kleinkindes. (Examples of the Play Technique in the Analysis of the Small Child.)" *Zeitschrift für psychoanalytische Pädagogik* 7: 301-10; 1933.
621. FRITZ, MARTIN F. *A Classified Bibliography on Psychodietetics.* Psychological Monographs, Vol. 46, No. 2. Whole No. 206. Princeton, N. J.: Psychological Review Co., 1934. 53 p.
622. GLUECK, SHELDON, and GLUECK, ELEANOR. *One Thousand Juvenile Delinquents, Their Treatment by Court and Clinic.* Cambridge, Mass.: Harvard University Press, 1934. 341 p.
623. GLUECK, SHELDON, and GLUECK, ELEANOR, editors. *Preventing Crime.* New York: McGraw-Hill Book Co., 1936. 509 p.
624. GOODENOUGH, FLORENCE L. *Anger in Young Children.* Minneapolis: University of Minnesota Press, 1931. 278 p.
625. GOODENOUGH, FLORENCE L. *Developmental Psychology.* New York: D. Appleton-Century Co., 1934. 619 p.
626. GORDON, ALFRED. "Some Undesirable Habits in Children and Their Management." *Child Development* 4: 259-64; September, 1933.
627. GORDON, J. B. "Present-Day Methods of Treating the Mentally Sick." *Occupational Therapy* 13: 299-306; October, 1934.
628. GROVES, ERNEST R., and BLANCHARD, PHYLLIS. *Introduction to Mental Hygiene.* New York: Henry Holt and Co., 1930. 467 p.
629. GROWDEN, C. H. "Preliminary Study of the Effectiveness of a State-Wide Behavior Clinic." *Quarterly Bulletin of Mgng. Off. Assoc. (Ohio Department of Public Welfare)* 12: 6-12; 1935.
630. HAZZARD, FLORENCE W. "A Thumb Sucking Cure." *Child Development* 3: 80-81; March, 1932.
631. HEALY, WILLIAM, and BRONNER, AUGUSTA F. *New Light on Delinquency and Its Treatment.* New Haven, Conn.: Yale University Press, 1936. 226 p.
632. HEALY, WILLIAM, and OTHERS. *Reconstructing Behavior in Youth.* New York: Alfred A. Knopf, 1929. 325 p.
633. HEALY, WILLIAM, and OTHERS. *The Structure and Meaning of Psychoanalysis.* New York: Alfred A. Knopf, 1930. 482 p.
634. HEATH, ESTHER. *The Approach to the Parent.* New York: Commonwealth Fund, 1933. 163 p.
635. HELD, OMAR C. "Habit Formation and Hygiene." *Child Development* 4: 346-57; December, 1933.
636. HENDERSON, D. K., and GILLESPIE, R. D. *A Textbook of Psychiatry.* London: Oxford University Press, 1932. Chapter 16, "The Psychiatry of Childhood," p. 488-536.
637. HENDRICK, IVES. *Facts and Theories of Psychoanalysis.* New York: Alfred A. Knopf, 1934. 308 p.
638. HORSCH, A. C., and DAVIS, R. A. "Mental Hygiene and Personality Tests." *American Journal of Sociology* 40: 646-58; March, 1935.
639. HOWARD, F. E., and PATRY, F. L. *Mental Health.* New York: Harper and Brothers, 1935. 551 p.
640. JACOBSON, EDMUND. *Progressive Relaxation.* Chicago: University of Chicago Press, 1929. 428 p.
641. JENKINS, R. L. "Periodicals for Child-Guidance Clinics." *Mental Hygiene* 16: 624-30; October, 1932.
642. JERSILD, ARTHUR T. *Child Psychology.* New York: Prentice-Hall, 1933. 462 p.
643. JERSILD, ARTHUR T., and HOLMES, FRANCES B. *Children's Fears.* New York: Teachers College, Columbia University, 1935. 356 p.
644. JERSILD, ARTHUR T., and OTHERS. *Children's Fears, Dreams, Wishes, Daydreams, Likes, Dislikes, Pleasant and Unpleasant Memories.* Child Development Monographs, No. 12. New York: Teachers College, Columbia University, 1933. 172 p.
645. JOHNSON, BUFORD J. *Child Psychology.* Springfield, Ill.: Charles C. Thomas, 1932. 439 p.
646. JOHNSON, MARGUERITE WILKER. "The Effect on Behavior of Variation in the Amount of Play Equipment." *Child Development* 6: 56-68; March, 1935.

647. JOHNSON, MARGUERITE WILKER. "The Influence of Verbal Directions on Behavior." *Child Development* 6: 196-204; September, 1935.
648. JONES, MARY COVER. "Emotional Development." *A Handbook of Child Psychology.* (Edited by Carl Murchison.) 2d ed. rev. Worcester, Mass.: Clark University Press, 1933. p. 271-302.
649. KAMARYT, S. "Die frühesten Erinnerungen der Septimaner. (The Earliest Memories of Seventh-Grade Pupils.)" 4 *Versamml. f. Kinderforsch.*, Bratislava, 256-62; 1932.
650. KANNER, LEO. *Child Psychiatry.* Springfield, Ill.: Charles C. Thomas, 1935. 527 p.
651. KIMMINS, C. W. "Children's Dreams." *A Handbook of Child Psychology.* (Edited by Carl Murchison.) Worcester, Mass.: Clark University Press, 1931. p. 527-54.
652. KIRKPATRICK, E. A. *Mental Hygiene for Effective Living.* New York: D. Appleton-Century Co., 1934. 387 p.
653. KLEIN, MELANIE. *The Psychoanalysis of Children.* New York: W. W. Norton and Co., 1932. 393 p.
654. KNAPP, ISABEL. "An Evaluation of a Work-Shop as an Aid in Child Guidance Treatment." *Smith College Studies in Social Work* 5: 352-73; June, 1935.
655. LAIRD, DONALD A.; LEVITAN, MICHAEL; and WILSON, VIRGINIA A. "Nervousness in School Children as Related to Hunger and Diet." *Medical Journal and Record* 134: 494-99; November 18, 1931.
656. LÄMMERMANN, H. *Anleitung zur Psychologischen Beobachtung und Beurteilung der Schüler. (Guide for the Psychological Observation and Judgment of Pupils.)* Mannheim: Haas, 1931. 12 p.
657. LASSWELL, HAROLD D. "Certain Prognostic Changes During Trial (Psychoanalytic) Interviews." *Psychoanalytic Review* 33: 241-47; July, 1936.
658. LEE, PORTER R., and OTHERS. *Mental Hygiene and Social Work.* New York: Commonwealth Fund, 1929. 309 p.
659. LEVY, DAVID M. "Experiments on the Sucking Reflex and Social Behavior of Dogs." *American Journal of Orthopsychiatry* 4: 203-24; April, 1934.
660. LEVY, DAVID M. "Fingersucking and Accessory Movements in Early Infancy." *American Journal of Psychiatry* 84: 881-918; May, 1928.
661. LEVY, DAVID M. "Use of Play Technic as Experimental Procedure." *American Journal of Orthopsychiatry* 3: 266-77; July, 1933.
662. LEVY, JOHN. "A Clinical Study of the Application of Mental Hygiene to the Treatment of Children's School Problems." *Pedagogical Seminary and Journal of Genetic Psychology* 41: 439-61; December, 1932.
663. LEVY, JOHN. "The Use of Art Techniques in Treatment of Children's Behavior Problems." *Proceedings and Addresses, 1934.* Godfrey, Ill.: American Association on Mental Deficiency (Groves B. Smith, sec., Beverly Farm), 1934. p. 258-60.
664. LISS, EDWARD. "Play Techniques in Child Analysis." *American Journal of Orthopsychiatry* 6: 17-22; January, 1936.
665. LORAND, A. S., editor. *Psycho-Analysis Today: Its Scope and Function.* New York: Covici Friede, 1933. 370 p.
666. LOWENFELD, MARGARET F. "A New Approach to the Problem of Psychoneurosis in Childhood." *British Journal of Medical Psychology* 11: 194-227; November, 1931.
667. LUFF, MARY C., and GARROD, MARJORIE. "The After-Results of Psychotherapy in 500 Adult Cases." *British Medical Journal* 2: 54-69; July 13, 1935.
668. MALLER, J. B. "Character and Personality Tests." *Psychological Bulletin* 32: 500-23; July, 1935.
669. MARTENS, ELISE H., and RUSS, HELEN. *Adjustment of Behavior Problems of School Children.* U. S. Dept. of the Interior, Office of Education, Bulletin, 1932, No. 10. Washington, D. C.: Government Printing Office, 1932. 78 p.
670. MICHAELS, JOSEPH J. "The Heilpedogogical Station of the Children's Clinic at the University of Vienna." *American Journal of Orthopsychiatry* 5: 266-75; July, 1935.
671. MOLDOVAN, M. "Studiul Individualitastii Copilului pe Baza Observatiei. (The Study of the Individuality of the School Child, Based on Observation.)" *Rev. de psihol.* 1: 23-35; 1931.
672. MOORE, KATHARINE. "A Specialized Method in the Treatment of Parents in a Child Guidance Clinic." *Psychoanalytic Review* 21: 415-24; October, 1934.

673. MORGAN, JOHN J. B. *The Psychology of the Unadjusted School Child.* Rev. ed. New York: Macmillan Co., 1936. 339 p.
674. NIEMER, G. "Selbstbekenntnisse höherer Schüler in dichterischer Form. (Self-Revelation of High-School Students in Poetical Form.)" *Vierteljahrsschrift für jugendkunde* 2: 154-71; 1932.
675. NOETZEL, ELINOR S., and HILDRETH, HAROLD M. "A Survey of the Mental Hygiene Needs of 250 School Children." *Psychiatric Quarterly* 9: 525-37; October, 1935.
676. OLSON, WILLARD C. *The Behavior Journal.* Manual of Directions and Form (Revised). Ann Arbor, Mich.: University Elementary School, University of Michigan, 1935.
677. OLSON, WILLARD C. "The Diagnosis and Treatment of Behavior Disorders of Children." *Educational Diagnosis.* Thirty-Fourth Yearbook, National Society for the Study of Education. Bloomington, Ill.: Public School Publishing Co., 1935. Chapter 18, p. 363-97.
678. OLSON, WILLARD C. "Measures of Character and Personality through Conduct and Information." *Review of Educational Research* 5: 273-90, 325-31; June, 1935.
679. OLSON, WILLARD C. "Needed Research in the Prevention of Delinquency." *Elementary School Journal* 36: 9-11; September, 1935.
680. OLSON, WILLARD C., and CUNNINGHAM, ELIZABETH MECHEM. "Time-Sampling Techniques." *Child Development* 5: 41-58; March, 1934.
681. PALMBORG, STINA. *Svorhanterliga Barn.* Stockholm: Bokforlaget Natur Och Kultur, 1935. 181 p.
682. PLANK-SPIRA, E. "Affektive Förderung und Hemmung des Lernens. (Affective Facilitation and Inhibition of Learning.)" *Zeitschrift für psychoanalytische, Pädagogik* 7: 122-28; 1933.
683. POPOVIC, S. *Samoiskazi kao sredstva za vezbanje mladezi u samoposmatranju. (Self-Reports as Means of Exercising the Introspection of Adolescents.)* Beograd, 1933. 146 p.
684. POTTER, HOWARD W. "Psychotherapy in Children." *Psychiatric Quarterly* 9: 335-48; July, 1935.
685. POTTER, HOWARD W. "The Treatment of Problem Children in a Psychiatric Hospital." *Proceedings and Addresses, 1934.* Godfrey, Ill.; American Association on Mental Deficiency (Groves B. Smith, sec., Beverly Farm), 1934. p. 261-72.
686. PROGRESSIVE EDUCATION ASSOCIATION. *Anecdotal Records.* Evaluation in the Eight Year Study, Bulletin No. 1. Columbus: Ohio State University, September, 1935. (Mimeographed.)
687. PULLIAS, EARL V. "How Do You Behave When the Children Misbehave?" *Childhood Education* 10: 230-37; February, 1934.
688. RADIN, E., and KAZENELSON, C., editors. *Methodika Pedologicheskovo Obsledovania Rebyonka. (Methods of Pedological Investigation of the Child.)* Moscow: State Institute for the Protection of Children and Adolescents, 1930. 260 p.
689. RAMOS, A. "A Technica da Psychanalyse Infantil. (Technique of Infantile Psychoanalysis.)" *Arch. brasil. Hyg. Ment.* 6: 195-205; 1933.
690. RANDALL, JOHN A. "The Anecdotal Behavior Journal." *Progressive Education* 13: 21-26; January, 1936.
691. RECKLESS, WALTER C., and SMITH, MAPHEUS. *Juvenile Delinquency.* New York: McGraw-Hill Book Co., 1932. 412 p.
692. RICHARDS, ESTHER L. *Behavior Aspects of Child Conduct.* New York: Macmillan Co., 1932. 299 p.
693. RIVLIN, HARRY N. *Educating for Adjustment.* New York: D. Appleton-Century Co., 1936. 419 p.
694. SAYLES, MARY B., editor. *Child Guidance Cases.* New York: Commonwealth Fund, 1932. 584 p.
695. SEIDLER, R. "Kinderträume. (Children's Dreams.)" *International Zeitschrift für Individual-Psychologie* 11: 450-59; 1933.
696. SELLING, LOWELL S. "The Autobiography as a Psychiatric Technique." *American Journal of Orthopsychiatry* 2: 162-71; April, 1932.
697. SHAFFER, LAURANCE F. *The Psychology of Adjustment.* Boston: Houghton Mifflin Co., 1936. 600 p.
698. SHAW, CLIFFORD R., editor. *The Jack-Roller.* Chicago: University of Chicago Press, 1930. 205 p.
699. SHAW, RUTH FAISON. *Finger Painting.* Boston: Little, Brown and Co., 1934. 232 p.

700. SHEEHAN-DARE, HELEN. "On Making Contact with the Child Patient." *International Journal of Psycho-Analysis* 15: 435-39; October, 1934.
701. SHERMAN, MANDEL. *Mental Hygiene and Education.* New York: Longmans, Green and Co., 1934. 295 p.
702. STODDARD, GEORGE D., and WELLMAN, BETH L. *Child Psychology.* New York: Macmillan Co., 1934. 419 p.
703. STODDARD, GEORGE D., chairman. "Mental and Physical Development." *Review of Educational Research* 6: 1-152; February, 1936.
704. STULLKEN, EDWARD H. "How the Montefiore School Prevents Crime." *Journal of Criminal Law and Criminology* 26: 228-34; July, 1935.
705. SYMMES, EDITH F. "Some Techniques in Securing Rapport with Pre-School Children." *American Journal of Orthopsychiatry* 3: 181-90; April, 1933.
706. SYMONDS, PERCIVAL M. *Diagnosing Personality and Conduct.* New York: Century Co., 1931. 602 p.
707. SYMONDS, PERCIVAL M. *Mental Hygiene of the School Child.* New York: Macmillan Co., 1934. 321 p.
708. SYMONDS, PERCIVAL M. *Psychological Diagnosis in Social Adjustment.* New York: American Book Co., 1934. 362 p.
709. TAFT, J. *The Dynamics of Therapy in a Controlled Relationship.* New York: Macmillan Co., 1933. 296 p.
710. TERMAN, LEWIS M., and COX, CATHARINE M. *Sex and Personality.* New York: McGraw-Hill Book Co., 1936. 600 p.
711. THOM, DOUGLAS A. *Normal Youth and Its Everyday Problems.* New York: D. Appleton and Co., 1932. 368 p.
712. THOM, DOUGLAS A. "Treatment of Special Problems in the Pre-School Period." *Proceedings of the First International Congress on Mental Hygiene.* New York: the Congress, 1932. Vol. 2, p. 752-66.
713. TRAMER, M. "Tagebuch über ein Geisteskrankes Kind. (Diary on a Psychopathic Child.)" *Z. Kinderpsychiat.* 2: 17-28; February, 1935.
714. WALLIN, JOHN E. W. *Personality Maladjustments and Mental Hygiene.* New York: McGraw-Hill Book Co., 1935. 511 p.
715. WARING, ETHEL B., and WILKER, MARGUERITE. *The Behavior of Young Children.* New York: Charles Scribner's Sons, 1929-32. 3 vols.
716. WATSON, GOODWIN. "Mental Hygiene and Emotional Adjustment." *Review of Educational Research* 5: 245-58, 315-20; June, 1935.
717. WATSON, MAUD E. *Children and Their Parents.* New York: F. S. Crofts and Co., 1932. 362 p.
718. WEIGL, E. "Behandlung von Psychischen Störungen bei Kindern und Jugendlichen. (Treatment of Psychic Disturbances of Children and Adolescents.)" *Ned. Tijdschr. Psychol.* 3: 179-206; 1935.
719. WHITLEY, ROBERT L. "Interviewing the Problem Boy." *Journal of Educational Sociology* 5: 89-100, 140-51; October and November, 1931.
720. WILLOUGHBY, R. R. "A Note on a Child's Dream." *Pedagogical Seminary and Journal of Genetic Psychology* 42: 224-28; March, 1933.
721. WINKLER, H. *Richtlinien zur Beobachtung und Beurteilung der Drei- bis Sechsjährigen im Kindergarten. (Principles for the Observation and Judgment of Three- to Six-Year Olds in the Kindergarten.)* 2d ed. Munich: Reinhardt, 1931. 15 p.
722. WITMER, HELEN LELAND. "A Comparison of Treatment Results in Various Types of Child Guidance Clinics." *American Journal of Orthopsychiatry* 5: 351-60; October, 1935.
723. WOOD, BEN D. "Information for Guidance; the Anecdotal Method of Personal Analysis." *Occupations* 13: 795-803; June, 1935.
724. YOUNG, PAULINE V. *Interviewing in Social Work.* New York: McGraw-Hill Book Co., 1935. 432 p.
725. ZACHRY, CAROLINE B. *Personality Adjustments of School Children.* New York: Charles Scribner's Sons, 1929. 306 p.

AMERICAN EDUCATIONAL RESEARCH ASSOCIATION

Membership[1]

HONORARY AND LIFE

Ayres, Leonard P., Vice President, Cleveland Trust Co., Cleveland, Ohio.
Buckingham, B. R., Directing Editor, Elementary School Books, Ginn and Co., Boston, Massachusetts.
Cattell, J. McKeen, Editor of *Science* and *School and Society*, Garrison, New York.
Coffman, L. D., President, University of Minnesota, Minneapolis, Minnesota.
Hanus, Paul H., Professor of Education Emeritus, Harvard University, Cambridge, Massachusetts. (3 Channing Circle, Cambridge, Massachusetts.)
Judd, Charles H., Head of Department of Education, University of Chicago, Chicago, Illinois.
Russell, James E., Dean Emeritus, Teachers College, Columbia University, New York, New York. (R. F. D. 4, Trenton, New Jersey.)
Russell, William F., Dean, Teachers College, Columbia University, New York, New York.
Terman, Lewis M., Professor of Psychology, Stanford University, California.
Thorndike, E. L., Professor of Education, Columbia University, New York, New York.
Wissler, Clark, Professor of Anthropology, Institute of Human Relations, Yale University, New Haven, Connecticut.
Zook, George F., President, American Council on Education, Washington, D. C.

ACTIVE

Ade, Lester Kelly, State Superintendent of Public Instruction, Harrisburg, Pennsylvania.
Alexander, Carter, Library Professor, Teachers College, Columbia University, New York, New York.
Allen, Ira M., Superintendent of Schools, Highland Park, Michigan.
Alschuler, Rose H., Director, Winnetka Public School Nursery Unit, Skokie School, Winnetka, Illinois.
Alves, H. F., Senior Specialist in State School Administration, United States Office of Education, Washington, D. C.
Anderson, Earl W., Professor of Education, Bureau of Educational Research, Ohio State University, Columbus, Ohio.
Andrus, Ruth, Chief of Child Development and Parent Education Bureau, State Department of Education, Albany, New York.
Arnold, William E., Assistant Professor of Education, University of Pennsylvania, Philadelphia, Pennsylvania.
Ashbaugh, E. J., Dean, School of Education, Miami University, Oxford, Ohio.
Averill, William A., Instructor in Education, Lesley Normal School, Cambridge, Massachusetts.
Ayer, Fred C., Professor of Educational Administration, University of Texas, Austin, Texas.
Baer, Joseph A., Assistant Supervisor in Office of Research and Finance, State Department of Education, Hartford, Connecticut.
Baker, Harry J., Director, Psychological Clinic, Detroit Public Schools, Detroit, Michigan.
Bamberger, Florence E., Professor of Education, Johns Hopkins University, Baltimore, Maryland.
Barr, A. S., Professor of Education, University of Wisconsin, Madison, Wisconsin.
Barthelmess, Harriet M., Special Assistant to Director, Division of Educational Research, Board of Education, Philadelphia, Pennsylvania.

---

[1] Corrected up to December 1, 1936. Errors should be reported to the Secretary-Treasurer immediately.

Barton, W. A., Jr., Head, Department of Education, Psychology, and Philosophy, Coker College, Hartsville, South Carolina.
Beeby, C. E., Chief Executive Officer, New Zealand Council for Educational Research, Southern Cross Building, Wellington, C. 1, New Zealand.
Benjamin, Harold, Director, Center for Continuation Study, University of Minnesota, Minneapolis, Minnesota.
Benz, H. E., Professor of Education, Ohio University, Athens, Ohio.
Bergman, W. G., Department of Research, Detroit Public Schools, Detroit, Michigan.
Betts, Emmett Albert, Director of Teacher Education, State Normal School, Oswego, New York.
Betts, Gilbert L., Director, Curriculum Department, West Allis Public Schools, West Allis, Wisconsin.
Billett, Roy O., Professor of Education, Boston University, Boston, Massachusetts.
Bixler, Harold H., Director of Research and Guidance, Board of Education, City Hall, Atlanta, Georgia.
Boardman, Charles W., Professor of Education, University of Minnesota, Minneapolis, Minnesota.
Booker, Ivan A., Assistant Director, Research Division, National Education Association, Washington, D. C.
Bowyer, Vernon, Principal, Skinner School, Chicago, Illinois.
Boyer, Philip A., Director, Division of Educational Research, Administration Building, Philadelphia, Pennsylvania.
Brainerd, Mrs. Margaret, 1101 Walnut Street, Martins Ferry, Ohio.
Branson, Ernest P., Counselor, Polytechnic High School, Long Beach, California.
Breed, Frederick S., Associate Professor of Education, University of Chicago, Chicago, Illinois.
Brewton, John E., Director of Research, Board of Education, Louisville, Kentucky.
Bright, Ira J., Superintendent of Schools, Leavenworth, Kansas.
Bristow, William H., General Secretary, National Congress of Parents and Teachers, Washington, D. C.
Broening, Angela M., Assistant Director of Research, Public Schools, Baltimore, Maryland.
Brooks, Fowler D., Head, Departments of Education and Psychology, De Pauw University, Greencastle, Indiana.
Brown, Clara M., Associate Professor of Home Economics Education, University Farm, St. Paul, Minnesota.
Brown, Edwin J., Director, Graduate Division, Kansas State Teachers College, Emporia, Kansas.
Brownell, S. M., Superintendent of Schools, Grosse Pointe Farms, Michigan.
Brownell, W. A., Professor of Educational Psychology, Duke University, Durham, North Carolina.
Brueckner, Leo J., Professor of Elementary Education, University of Minnesota, Minneapolis, Minnesota.
Brumbaugh, A. J., Acting Dean of the College of Education, University of Chicago, Chicago, Illinois.
Brunner, Edmund deS., Professor of Education, Teachers College, Columbia University, New York, New York.
Buckner, C. A., Professor of Education, University of Pittsburgh, Pittsburgh, Pennsylvania.
Buros, Oscar K., Assistant Professor of Education, Rutgers University, New Brunswick, New Jersey.
Burr, Samuel Engle, Superintendent of Schools, New Castle, Delaware.
Bursch, James F., Assistant Superintendent and Director of Research, Sacramento City Schools, Sacramento, California.
Buswell, G. T., Professor of Educational Psychology, University of Chicago, Chicago, Illinois.
Butsch, R. L. C., Associate Professor of Education, Marquette University, Milwaukee, Wisconsin.
Butterworth, Julian E., Director, Graduate School of Education, Cornell University, Ithaca, New York.
Caldwell, Otis W., General Secretary, American Association for the Advancement of Science, Boyce Thompson Institute, Yonkers, New York.
Cammack, James W., Jr., Member, Public Service Commission, Frankfort, Kentucky,

Campbell, Doak S., Professor of Education, Division of Surveys and Field Studies, George Peabody College for Teachers, Nashville, Tennessee.
Carr, William G., Director, Research Division, National Education Association, Washington, D. C.
Carroll, Herbert A., South Berwick, Maine.
Caswell, Hollis L., Professor of Education, Division of Surveys and Field Studies, George Peabody College for Teachers, Nashville, Tennessee.
Cattell, Psyche, Research Fellow, Department of School Hygiene, School of Public Health, Harvard University, Cambridge, Massachusetts.
Cavins, L. V., Director of Research, State Department of Education, Charleston, West Virginia.
Chambers, M. M., Staff Member, American Youth Commission, American Council on Education, Washington, D. C.
Chapman, Harold B., Assistant Director, Bureau of Educational Research, Public Schools, Baltimore, Maryland.
Charters, W. W., Director, Bureau of Educational Research, Ohio State University, Columbus, Ohio.
Chase, Vernon Emory, Director, Bureau of Research and Adjustment, Public Schools, Dearborn, Michigan.
Chisholm, Leslie L., Associate Professor of Education, State College of Washington, Pullman, Washington.
Christofferson, H. C., Director of Secondary Education, Miami University, Oxford, Ohio.
Clapp, Frank L., Professor of Education, University of Wisconsin, Madison, Wisconsin.
Clark, Harold F., Professor of Education, Teachers College, Columbia University, New York, New York.
Clark, Zenas R., Director of Research, Wilmington Public Schools, Wilmington, Delaware.
Clem, Orlie M., Superintendent of Schools, Owego, Tioga County, New York.
Cobb, Margaret V., National Youth Administration, Manchester, New Hampshire.
Cocking, Walter D., State Commissioner of Education, Nashville, Tennessee.
Coffey, Wilford L., Research Student, Teachers College, Columbia University, New York, New York.
Connor, William L., Chief, Bureau of Educational Research, Board of Education, Cleveland, Ohio.
Conrad, Herbert S., Assistant Professor of Education, University of California, Berkeley, California.
Cooke, Dennis H., Professor of School Administration, George Peabody College for Teachers, Nashville, Tennessee.
Coon, Beulah I., Agent for Studies and Research in Home Economics Education, United States Office of Education, Washington, D. C.
Cooper, Lewis B., Director of Research, Texas State Teachers Association, Fort Worth, Texas.
Cornell, Ethel L., Research Associate, Educational Research Division, State Department of Education, Albany, New York.
Counts, George S., Professor of Education, Teachers College, Columbia University, New York, New York.
Courtis. S. A., Professor of Education, University of Michigan, Ann Arbor, Michigan.
Coxe, W. W., Director, Educational Research Division, State Department of Education, Albany, New York.
Coy, Genevieve L., Psychologist, Dalton School, New York, New York.
Craig, Gerald S., Associate Professor, Natural Sciences, Teachers College, Columbia University, New York, New York.
Crawford, C. C., Professor of Education, University of Southern California, Los Angeles, California.
Cureton, Edward E., Associate Professor of Education, Alabama Polytechnic Institute, Auburn, Alabama.
Cutright, Prudence, Assistant Superintendent, Minneapolis Public Schools, Minneapolis, Minnesota.
Cutts, Norma E., Supervisor, Department of Exceptional Children, Board of Education, New Haven, Connecticut.

Dale, Edgar, Associate Professor, College of Education, Ohio State University, Columbus, Ohio.
Davis, Hazel, Assistant Director, Research Division, National Education Association, Washington, D. C.
Davis, Mary Dabney, Senior Specialist, Nursery-Kindergarten-Primary Education, United States Office of Education, Washington, D. C.
Dearborn, Ned H., Dean, Division of General Education, New York University, New York, New York.
Deffenbaugh, Walter S., Chief, American School Systems Division, United States Office of Education, Washington, D. C.
DeVoss, J. C., Dean, Upper Division, San Jose State College, San Jose, California.
Dickson, Virgil E., Superintendent of Schools, Berkeley, California.
Dolch, E. W., Assistant Professor of Education, University of Illinois, Urbana, Illinois.
Douglass, Harl R., Professor of Secondary Education, University of Minnesota, Minneapolis, Minnesota.
Downing, Elliot R., Associate Professor Emeritus, the Teaching of Science, University of Chicago, Chicago, Illinois. (P. O. Box 147, Williams Bay, Wisconsin.)
Downs, Martha, Director of Research, New Jersey State Normal School, Newark, New Jersey.
Dunlap, Jack W., Associate Professor, Graduate School, Fordham University, New York, New York.
Durost, Walter N., Test Editor, World Book Company, Yonkers, New York.
Durrell, Donald D., Professor of Education, Boston University, Boston, Massachusetts.
Eads, Laura Krieger, Research Associate, Erpi Picture Consultants, Inc., New York, New York.
Easley, Howard, Assistant Professor of Educational Psychology, Duke University, Durham, North Carolina.
Edmiston, Robert Wentz, Director of Extension, Miami University, Oxford, Ohio.
Edmonson, James B., Dean, School of Education, University of Michigan, Ann Arbor, Michigan.
Edwards, Newton, Professor of Education, University of Chicago, Chicago, Illinois.
Eells, Walter C., Coordinator, Cooperative Study of Secondary School Standards, 744 Jackson Place, N. W., Washington, D. C.
Ellingson, Mark, President, Rochester Athenaeum and Mechanical Institute, Rochester, New York.
Elliott, Charles H., Commissioner of Education for New Jersey, Trenton, New Jersey.
Elliott, Eugene B., State Superintendent of Public Instruction, Lansing, Michigan.
Elsbree, Willard S., Associate Professor of Education, Teachers College, Columbia University, New York, New York.
Engelhardt, N. L., Professor of Education, Teachers College, Columbia University, New York, New York.
Eurich, Alvin C., Assistant Dean, College of Education, University of Minnesota, Minneapolis, Minnesota.
Evenden, Edward S., Professor of Education, Teachers College, Columbia University, New York, New York.
Feder, Daniel D., Associate, Psychology and Personnel, University of Iowa, Iowa City, Iowa.
Ferriss, Emery N., Professor of Education, Rural Educational Department, Cornell University, Ithaca, New York.
Flanagan, John C., Statistician, Cooperative Test Service of the American Council on Education, New York, New York. (500 West 116th Street.)
Flemming, Mrs. Cecile White, Director of Individual Development and Guidance, Teachers College, Columbia University, New York, New York.
Foote, John M., Director, Reference and Service, State Department of Education, Baton Rouge, Louisiana.
Foster, Richard R., Assistant Director, Research Division, National Education Association, Washington, D. C.
Fowlkes, John G., Professor of Education, University of Wisconsin, Madison, Wisconsin.
Fox, Guy, Assistant Director, Research and Curriculum, Denver Public Schools, Denver, Colorado.

Franklin, E. E., Associate in Education, Johns Hopkins University, Baltimore, Maryland.
Frederick, Orie I., Associate Professor of Secondary Education, University of Mississippi, University, Mississippi.
Freeman, Frank N., Professor of Educational Psychology, Department of Education, University of Chicago, Chicago, Illinois.
Fritz, Ralph A., Professor of Education, Kansas State Teachers College, Pittsburg, Kansas.
Frostic, Fred W., Superintendent of Schools, Wyandotte, Michigan.
Frutchey, Fred P., Assistant Professor, Bureau of Educational Research, Ohio State University, Columbus, Ohio.
Fulk, Joseph Richard, Professor of Public School Administration, College of Education, University of Florida, Gainesville, Florida.
Gambrill, Bessie L., Associate Professor, Elementary Education, Yale University, New Haven, Connecticut.
Ganders, Harry S., Dean, School of Education, Syracuse University, Syracuse, New York.
Gans, Roma, Associate in Elementary Education, Teachers College, Columbia University, New York, New York.
Garrison, K. C., Professor of Psychology, University of North Carolina, Raleigh, North Carolina.
Garrison, S. C., Professor of Educational Psychology and Dean of the Graduate School, George Peabody College for Teachers, Nashville, Tennessee.
Garver, F. M., Professor of Elementary Education, University of Pennsylvania, Philadephia, Pennsylvania.
Gates, Arthur I., Professor of Education, Teachers College, Columbia University, New York, New York.
Gerberich, J. R., Associate Director, Project in Research in Universities, United States Office of Education, Washington, D. C.
Geyer, Denton L., Head of Department of Education, Chicago Normal College, Chicago, Illinois.
Gifford, C. W., Chairman, Department of Psychology, Wright City Junior College, Chicago, Illinois.
Gillet, Harry O., Principal, Elementary School, University of Chicago, Chicago, Illinois.
Gilmore, Charles H., Director of Research, State Department of Education, Nashville, Tennessee.
Glenn, Earl R., Head of Science Department, New Jersey State Teachers College, Montclair, New Jersey.
Goldthorpe, J. Harold, Professor of Education, University of Rochester, Rochester, New York.
Good, Carter V., Professor of Education, Teachers College, University of Cincinnati, Cincinnati, Ohio.
Goodrich, T. V., Director of Research, Public Schools, Lincoln, Nebraska.
Goodykoontz, Bess, Assistant Commissioner of Education, United States Office of Education, Washington, D. C.
Gordon, Hans C., Special Assistant to the Director of Educational Research, Board of Education, Philadelphia, Pennsylvania.
Gray, C. T., Professor of Educational Psychology, University of Texas, Austin, Texas.
Gray, Howard A., Research Associate, Erpi Picture Consultants, Inc., New York, New York.
Gray, Robert Floyd, Director, Bureau of Research, Evening Schools, and Adult Education, Board of Education, San Francisco, California.
Gray, William S., Professor of Education and Secretary, Committee on the Preparation of Teachers, Department of Education, University of Chicago, Chicago, Illinois.
Greenberg, Benjamin B., Assistant Superintendent of Schools, New York, New York.
Greene, Crawford, Director, Information and Service, State Department of Education, Little Rock, Arkansas.
Greene, H. A., Director, Bureau of Educational Research, Extension Division, University of Iowa, Iowa City, Iowa.
Gregory, Marshall, Director, Division of Finance and Research, State Department of Public Instruction, Oklahoma City, Oklahoma.

Grossnickle, Foster E., Professor of Mathematics, State Teachers College, Jersey City, New Jersey.
Grover, Elbridge C., Superintendent of Schools, Euclid, Ohio.
Guiler, Walter S., Professor of Education and Director of Remedial Instruction, Miami University, Oxford, Ohio.
Haggerty, M. E., Dean, College of Education, University of Minnesota, Minneapolis, Minnesota.
Hanna, Paul R., Associate Professor, Stanford University, California.
Hanson, Whittier L., Professor of Education, School of Education, Boston University, Boston, Massachusetts.
Harap, Henry, Professor of Education, Bureau of Educational Research, Ohio State University, Columbus, Ohio.
Harrington, H. L., Supervising Director of Intermediate Schools, Detroit Public Schools, Detroit, Michigan.
Harry, David P., Jr., Associate Professor of Education, Graduate School, Western Reserve University, Cleveland, Ohio.
Hartmann, George W., Associate Professor of Education, Teachers College, Columbia University, New York, New York.
Heaton, Kenneth L., Director, Division of Curriculum Research, State Department of Public Instruction, Lansing, Michigan.
Heck, Arch O., Professor of Education, Ohio State University, Columbus, Ohio.
Heilman, J. D., Director of Personnel Department and Professor of Educational Psychology, Colorado State Teachers College, Greeley, Colorado.
Henmon, V. A. C., Professor of Psychology, University of Wisconsin, Madison, Wisconsin.
Henry, Nelson B., Associate Professor of Education, School of Education, University of Chicago, Chicago, Illinois.
Hertzberg, Oscar Edward, Head, Department of Psychology and Director of Research, State Teachers College, Buffalo, New York.
Hertzler, Silas, Director of Teacher Training, Goshen College, Goshen, Indiana.
Hicks, J. Allan, Professor of Education, New York State College for Teachers, Albany, New York.
Hildreth, Gertrude, Psychologist, Lincoln School of Teachers College, Columbia University, New York, New York.
Hockett, John A., Department of Education, University of California, Berkeley, California.
Hoke, K. J., Dean, College of Education, College of William and Mary, Williamsburg, Virginia.
Hollingworth, Leta S., Professor of Education, Teachers College, Columbia University, New York, New York.
Holy, T. C., Bureau of Educational Research, Ohio State University, Columbus, Ohio.
Hopkins, L. Thomas, Associate Professor of Education, Teachers College, Columbia University, New York, New York.
Horan, Ellamay, Professor of Education, De Paul University, Chicago, Illinois.
Horn, Ernest, Professor of Education, State University of Iowa, Iowa City, Iowa.
Hubbard, Frank W., Associate Director, Research Division, National Education Association, Washington, D. C.
Hughes, W. Hardin, Research Consultant in Education, Pasadena Junior College, Pasadena, California.
Hurd, A. W., Associate Professor of Education, Northern Montana College, Havre, Montana.
Hyde, Richard E., Acting Director of Research, State Department of Education, Charleston, West Virginia.
Irby, Nolen M., State Supervisor of Colored Schools, State Department of Education, Little Rock, Arkansas.
Irwin, Manley E., Director, Department of Instruction, Detroit Public Schools, Detroit, Michigan.
Jacobs, Clara M., Director of Educational Research, Centennial High School Building, Pueblo, Colorado.
Jensen, Kai, Associate Professor of Education, University of Wisconsin, Madison, Wisconsin.
Jersild, Arthur T., Associate Professor of Education, Teachers College, Columbia University, New York, New York.

Jessen, Carl A., Senior Specialist in Secondary Education, United States Office of Education, Washington, D. C.
Job, Leonard B., President, Ithaca College, Ithaca, New York.
Johnson, George R., Director, Division of Tests and Measurements, Board of Education, St. Louis, Missouri.
Johnson, J. T., Head, Department of Mathematics, Chicago Normal College, Chicago, Illinois.
Johnson, Loaz W., Graduate Student, University of California, Berkeley, California.
Johnson, Palmer O., Associate Professor of Education, College of Education, University of Minnesota, Minneapolis, Minnesota.
Johnston, Edgar Grant, Principal, University High School, University of Michigan, Ann Arbor, Michigan.
Jones, Arthur J., Professor of Secondary Education, University of Pennsylvania, Philadelphia, Pennsylvania.
Jones, Harold E., Professor of Psychology, and Director, Institute of Child Welfare, University of California, Berkeley, California.
Jordan, A. M., Professor of Educational Psychology, School of Education, University of North Carolina, Chapel Hill, North Carolina.
Jorensen, A. N., President, Connecticut State College, Storrs, Connecticut.
Kawin, Ethel, Psychologist, Laboratory Schools, University of Chicago, Chicago, Illinois.
Kearney, Leo I., Assistant Director, Reference, Research, and Statistics, Board of Education, New York, New York.
Keeler, Louis Ward, Associate Professor of Educational Psychology, University of Michigan, Ann Arbor, Michigan.
Keener, E. E., Principal, John Hay School, Chicago, Illinois.
Kelley, Truman L., Professor of Education, Graduate School of Education, Lawrence Hall, Harvard University, Cambridge, Massachusetts.
Kelley, Victor H., Assistant Director of Research and Guidance, Phoenix Union High School, Phoenix, Arizona.
Kelly, Fred J., Chief, Division of Higher Education, United States Office of Education, Washington, D. C.
Kemmerer, W. W., Director of Child Accounting and Curriculum, Independent School District, Houston, Texas.
Keys, Noel, Associate Professor of Education, University of California, Berkeley, California.
Kingsley, John H., Director, Division of Research, Board of Education, Albany, New York.
Kirby, T. J., Professor of Education, College of Education, State University of Iowa, Iowa City, Iowa.
Knight, F. B., Professor of Education and Psychology, University of Iowa, Iowa City, Iowa.
Knudsen, C. W., Lecturer in Secondary Education, Graduate School of Education, Lawrence Hall, Harvard University, Cambridge, Massachusetts.
Koch, Harlan C., Assistant Director, Bureau of Cooperation, University of Michigan, Ann Arbor, Michigan.
Koopman, G. Robert, Associate Director, Division of Curriculum Research, State Department of Public Instruction, Lansing, Michigan.
Koos, L. V., Professor of Secondary Education, University of Chicago, Chicago, Illinois.
Kramer, Grace A., Baltimore Public Schools, Baltimore, Maryland.
Kyte, George C., Professor of Education, University of California, Berkeley, California.
Larson, Emil L., Professor of Education, University of Arizona, Tucson, Arizona.
LaSalle, Jessie, Assistant Superintendent in Charge of Educational Research, D. C. Public Schools, Washington, D. C.
Latham, O. R., President, Iowa State Teachers College, Cedar Falls, Iowa.
Lee, J. Murray, Director of Curriculum and Research, Burbank City Schools, Burbank, California.
Lehman, Harvey C., Professor of Psychology, Ohio University, Athens, Ohio.
Lentz, Theodore F., Director, Character Research Institute, Washington University, St. Louis, Missouri.

Leonard J. Paul, Professor of Education, College of William and Mary, Williamsburg, Virginia.
Lide, Edwin S., Sullivan High School, Chicago, Illinois.
Lincoln, Edward A., Consulting Psychologist, Harvard Graduate School of Education, Harvard University, Cambridge, Massachusetts.
Lindquist, E. F., Associate Professor of Education, State University of Iowa, Iowa City, Iowa.
Linn, Henry H., Business Manager, Board of Education, Muskegon, Michigan.
Loomis, Arthur K., Superintendent of Schools, Shaker Heights, Ohio.
Lovejoy, Philip, First Assistant Secretary, Rotary International, Chicago, Illinois.
MacLatchy, Josephine, Bureau of Educational Research, Ohio State University, Columbus, Ohio.
Madsen, I. N., Director, Department of Tests and Measurements, Lewiston State Normal School, Lewiston, Idaho.
Maller, Julius B., Research Associate, Teachers College, Columbia University, New York, New York.
Mallory, Clara, Professor of Education, Lamar Junior College, Beaumont, Texas.
Malmberg, C. F., Acting Head, Department of Psychology, Illinois State Normal University, Normal, Illinois.
Mann, Carleton H., Lecturer in Education, University of Southern California, Los Angeles, California.
Manuel, H. T., Professor of Educational Psychology, University of Texas, Austin, Texas.
Masters, Harry V., Dean, College of Education, Drake Universiy, Des Moines, Iowa.
Mathews, C. O., Professor of Education, Ohio Wesleyan University, Delaware, Ohio.
McCall, William A., Professor of Education, Teachers College, Columbia University, New York, New York.
McClure, Worth, Superintendent of Schools, Seattle, Washington.
McDowell, Elizabeth D., Associate Professor of Speech, Teachers College, Columbia University, New York, New York.
McLaughlin, Katherine L., Associate Professor of Education, University of California at Los Angeles, Los Angeles, California.
McLure, John R., Professor of Educational Administration, University of Alabama, University, Alabama.
Mead, A. R., Director of Educational Research, University of Florida, Gainesville, Florida.
Meek, Lois Hayden, Director, Child Development Institute, Teachers College, Columbia University, New York, New York.
Melby, Ernest O., Dean, School of Education, Northwestern University, Evanston, Illinois.
Melcher, George, Superintendent of Schools, Kansas City, Missouri.
Mendenhall, James E., Research Associate, Lincoln School of Teachers College, Columbia University, New York, New York.
Meriam, Junius L., Professor of Education, University of California, Los Angeles, California.
Merriman, Curtis, Registrar, University of Wisconsin, Madison, Wisconsin.
Miller, Chester F., Superintendent of Schools, Saginaw, Michigan.
Miller, W. S., Professor of Educational Psychology, University of Minnesota, Minneapolis, Minnesota.
Moehlman, Arthur B., Professor of School Administration and Supervision, University of Michigan, Ann Arbor, Michigan.
Monroe, W. S., Director, Bureau of Educational Research, University of Illinois, Urbana, Illinois.
Moore, Clyde B., Professor in the Graduate School of Education, Cornell University, Ithaca, New York.
Morgan, Walter E., Assistant Superintendent of Public Instruction and Chief, Division of Research and Statistics, State Department of Education, Sacramento, California.
Morphet, Edgar L., Associate Director, Local School Units Project, United States Office of Education, Washington, D. C.
Morphett, Mabel Vogel, Director of Research, Skokie School, Winnetka, Illinois.

Morrison, J. Cayce, Assistant Commissioner for Elementary Education, State Department of Education, Albany, New York.
Mort, Paul R., Director of the Advanced School of Education, Teachers College, Columbia University, New York, New York.
Morton, R. L., Professor of Education, Ohio University, Athens, Ohio.
Mosher, Raymond M., Professor of Psychology, State College, San Jose, California.
Munson, Saron E., Director of Research, School District of Lancaster, Lancaster, Pennsylvania.
Myers, Anna G., Assistant Director of Research, Public Schools, Kansas City, Missouri.
Myers, Charles Everett, Supervisor, Research and Finance, Board of Education, Richmond, Virginia.
Myers, Garry C., Head, Department of Parent Education, Cleveland College, Western Reserve University, Cleveland, Ohio.
Nelson, M. J., Dean of the Faculty, Iowa State Teachers College, Cedar Falls, Iowa.
Nelson, Milton G., Dean, New York State College for Teachers, Albany, New York.
Newkirk, Louis V., Director, Industrial Arts, Board of Education, Chicago, Illinois.
Newland, T. Ernest, Assistant Professor of Education, Bucknell University, Lewisburg, Pennsylvania.
Nifenecker, Eugene A., Director, Bureau of Reference, Research, and Statistics, Board of Education, New York, New York.
Noble, Stuart G., Professor of Education, Tulane University, New Orleans, Louisiana.
Norton, John K., Professor of Education, Teachers College, Columbia University, New York, New York.
Norton, Mrs. John K., 464 Riverside Drive, Apt. 91, New York, New York.
Obrien, F. P., Director, Bureau of School Service and Research, University of Kansas, Lawrence, Kansas.
Odell, C. W., Associate Professor of Education, University of Illinois, Urbana, Illinois.
Ogan, R. W., Professor of Education, Muskingum College, New Concord, Ohio.
Ojemann, R. H., Assistant Professor, Iowa Child Welfare Research Station, State University of Iowa, Iowa City, Iowa.
Olson, W. C., Director of Research in Child Development and Professor of Education, School of Education, University of Michigan, Ann Arbor, Michigan.
Oppenheimer, J. J., Dean of College of Liberal Arts, University of Louisville, Louisville, Kentucky.
O'Rear, F. B., Associate Professor of Education, Teachers College, Columbia University, New York, New York.
Orleans, Jacob S., Associate Professor of Education, College of the City of New York, New York.
O'Rourke, L. J., Director of Research in Personnel Administration, United States Civil Service Commission, Washington, D. C.
Osburn, W. J., Professor of Education, University of Washington, Seattle, Washington.
Otis, Arthur S., Editorial Consultant, World Book Company, Yonkers, New York.
Otto, Henry J., Consultant in Education, W. K. Kellogg Foundation, Battle Creek, Michigan.
Parsons, Rhey Boyd, Associate Professor of Education, Florida State College for Women, Tallahassee, Florida.
Paul, Joseph B., Director of Research, Iowa State Teachers College, Cedar Falls, Iowa.
Peik, W. E., Professor of Education, University of Minnesota, Minneapolis, Minnesota.
Perry, Winona M., Professor of Educational Psychology and Measurements, University of Nebraska, Lincoln, Nebraska.
Peters, Charles C., Director of Educational Research, Pennsylvania State College, State College, Pennsylvania.
Peterson, Elmer T., Professor of Education, College of Education, University of Iowa, Iowa City, Iowa.
Phillips, Albert J., Executive Secretary, Michigan Education Association, Lansing, Michigan.
Potter, Mary A., Supervisor of Mathematics, Washington Park High School, Racine, Wisconsin.

Potthoff, Edward F., Assistant Professor of Education, University of Illinois, Urbana, Illinois.
Powers, S. R., Professor of Natural Sciences, Teachers College, Columbia University, New York, New York.
Prall, Charles E., Dean, School of Education, University of Pittsburgh, Pittsburgh, Pennsylvania.
Prescott, D. A., Professor of Education, Rutgers University, New Brunswick, New Jersey.
Pressey, S. L., Professor of Educational Psychology, College of Education, Ohio State University, Columbus, Ohio.
Price, Malcolm P., Chairman, Personnel Committee, Detroit Public Schools, Detroit, Michigan.
Proffitt, Maris M., Educational Consultant and Specialist in Guidance and Industrial Education, United States Office of Education, Washington, D. C.
Rankin, Paul T., Supervising Director, Curriculum and Research, Public Schools, Detroit, Michigan.
Reavis, W. C., Professor of Education, University of Chicago, Chicago, Illinois.
Reed, H. B., Professor of Psychology, Fort Hays Kansas State College, Hays, Kansas.
Reeder, Ward G., Professor of School Administration, Ohio State University, Columbus, Ohio.
Reeves, Floyd W., Professor of Education, University of Chicago, Chicago, Illinois.
Remmers, H. H., Professor of Education and Psychology, Purdue University, Lafayette, Indiana.
Remmlein, Madaline Kinter, Research Assistant, National Education Association, Washington, D. C.
Reusser, Walter C., Professor of Education, University of Wyoming, Laramie, Wyoming.
Richey, Herman G., Assistant Professor of Education, University of Chicago, Chicago, Illinois.
Rinsland, H. D., Professor of School Measurements, University of Oklahoma, Norman, Oklahoma.
Rogers, Don C., Director, Bureau of Research and Building Survey, Board of Education, Chicago, Illinois.
Rosenlof, George W., Professor of Secondary Education, University of Nebraska, Lincoln, Nebraska.
Rothney, John W. M., Research Associate, Psycho-Educational Clinic, Harvard University, Cambridge, Massachusetts.
Rowland, W. T., Jr., Assistant Superintendent in Charge of Secondary Education, Louisville Public Schools, Louisville, Kentucky.
Royer, Elmer B., Technical Assistant in Mathematics, Research Department, The Proctor and Gamble Company, Ivorydale, Ohio.
Ruch, G. M., Scott, Foresman and Company, Chicago, Illinois.
Rugg, Earle U., Head, Division of Education, Colorado State College of Education, Greeley, Colorado.
Rugg, Harold, Professor of Education, Teachers College, Columbia University, New York, New York.
Rulon, Phillip J., Assistant Professor of Education, Harvard University, Cambridge, Massachusetts.
Russell, John Dale, Associate Professor of Education, University of Chicago, Chicago, Illinois.
Sackett, Everett B., Research Associate, Regents' Inquiry, Albany, New York.
Sanchez, George I., Educational Consultant, Julius Rosenwald Fund, Chicago, Illinois.
Sangren, Paul V., President, Western State Teachers College, Kalamazoo, Michigan.
Sawyer, Guy E., Chadds Ford, Pennsylvania.
Scates, Douglas E., Director of School Research, Cincinnati Public Schools, Cincinnati, Ohio.
Schorling, Raleigh, Professor of Education and Director of Instruction, University High School, University of Michigan, Ann Arbor, Michigan.
Schrammel, H. E., Director, Bureau of Educational Measurements, Kansas State Teachers College, Emporia, Kansas.
Sears, Jesse B., Professor of Education, Stanford University, California.

Segel, David, Specialist, Tests and Measurements, United States Office of Education, Washington, D. C.
Senour, A. C., Assistant Superintendent, Public Schools, East Chicago, Indiana.
Shea, James T., Director, Curriculum and Research, Board of Education, San Antonio, Texas.
Simpson, Alfred D., Assistant Commissioner of Education for Finance, State Department of Education, Albany, New York.
Simpson, B. R., Professor of Educational Psychology, Western Reserve University, Cleveland, Ohio.
Sims, Verner M., Associate Professor of Psychology, College of Education, University of Alabama, University, Alabama.
Singleton, Gordon G., Dean of Education, Mercer University, Macon, Georgia.
Smith, Dora V., Associate Professor in Education, College of Education, University of Minnesota, Minneapolis, Minnesota.
Smith, H. L., Dean, School of Education, Indiana University, Bloomington, Indiana.
Smith, Harry P., Professor of Education, Syracuse University, Syracuse, New York.
Snyder, Agnes, Assistant Professor of Education, New College, Teachers College, Columbia University, New York, New York.
Soper, Wayne W., Research Associate, State Department of Education, Albany, New York.
Spaulding, Francis T., Associate Professor of Education, Harvard University, Cambridge, Massachusetts.
Spencer, Peter L., Professor of Education, Claremont Colleges, Claremont, California.
Starbuck, Edwin D., Director of the Institute of Character Research, University of Southern California, Los Angeles, California.
Stenquist, John L., Director, Bureau of Educational Research, Baltimore Public Schools, Baltimore, Maryland.
Stern, Bessie C., Statistician, State Department of Education, Baltimore, Maryland.
Stoddard, George D., Dean, Graduate College, University of Iowa, Iowa City, Iowa.
Stoke, Stuart M., Chairman of Education Department, Mount Holyoke College, South Hadley, Massachusetts.
Stokes, C. Newton, Chairman of Mathematics Department, Temple University, Philadelphia, Pennsylvania.
Strachan, Lexie, Psychologist, Public Schools, Kansas City, Missouri.
Strang, Ruth M., Associate Professor of Education, Teachers College, Columbia University, New York, New York.
Stratemeyer, Florence B., Associate Professor of Education, Teachers College, Columbia University, New York, New York.
Strayer, George D., Professor of Education, Teachers College, Columbia University, New York, New York.
Strayer, George D., Jr., Professor of Education, George Peabody College for Teachers, Nashville, Tennessee.
Streitz, Ruth, Professor of Education, University of Cincinnati, Cincinnati, Ohio.
Sumstine, David R., Director, Department of Curriculum Study and Research, Public Schools, Pittsburgh, Pennsylvania.
Sutton, D. H., Director, Division of School Finance, State Department of Education, Columbus, Ohio.
Swift, Fletcher Harper, Professor of Education, University of California, Berkeley, California.
Symonds, Percival M., Professor of Education, Teachers College, Columbia University, New York, New York.
Terry, Paul W., Professor of Educational Psychology, University of Alabama, University, Alabama.
Theisen, W. W., Assistant Superintendent of Schools, Milwaukee, Wisconsin.
Thurber, Clarence Howe, President, University of Redlands, Redlands, California.
Tidwell, Robert E., Director of Extension and Professor of Education, University of Alabama, University, Alabama.
Tiegs, Ernest W., Dean, University College, University of Southern California, Los Angeles, California.
Tilton, J. Warren, Associate Professor of Educational Psychology, Department of Education, Yale University, New Haven, Connecticut.
Tink, Edmund L., Superintendent of Schools, Kearny, New Jersey.

Toops, Herbert A., Professor of Psychology, Department of Psychology, Ohio State University, Columbus, Ohio.
Torgerson, T. L., Associate Professor of Education, University of Wisconsin, Madison, Wisconsin.
Tormey, T. J., President, Arizona State Teachers College, Flagstaff, Arizona.
Townsend, M. Ernest, President, State Normal School, Newark, New Jersey.
Trabue, M. R., Director, Division of Education, University of North Carolina, Chapel Hill, North Carolina.
Trow, William Clark, Professor of Educational Psychology, University of Michigan, Ann Arbor, Michigan.
Turney, Austin Henry, Associate Professor of Education, University of Kansas, Lawrence, Kansas.
Tyler, Ralph W., Professor of Education, Bureau of Educational Research, Ohio State University, Columbus, Ohio.
Tyler, Tracy Ferris, Room 308, One Madison Ave., New York, New York.
Uhl, Willis L., Professor of Education and Dean, School of Education, University of Washington, Seattle, Washington.
Umstattd, J. G., Associate Professor of Education and Supervisor in Secondary Education, Wayne University, Detroit, Michigan.
Updegraff, Harlan, American Youth Commission, American Council on Education, Washington, D. C.
Upshall, Charles Cecil, Director, Bureau of Research, State Normal School, Bellingham, Washington.
Van Wagenen, M. J., Assistant Professor of Educational Psychology, University of Minnesota, Minneapolis, Minnesota.
Vreeland, Wendell, Director, Division of University Research and Finance, Wayne University, Detroit, Michigan.
Walker, Helen M., Associate Professor of Education, Teachers College, Columbia University, New York, New York.
Waples, Douglas, Professor of Educational Method, Graduate Library School, University of Chicago, Chicago, Illinois.
Washburne, Carleton W., Superintendent of Schools, Winnetka, Illinois.
Washburne, John N., Associate Professor of Educational Psychology, Syracuse University, Syracuse, New York.
Waterman, Ivan R., Chief, Division of Textbooks and Publications, California State Department of Education, Sacramento, California.
Watkins, Ralph K., Professor of Education, University of Missouri, Columbia, Missouri.
Watson, Goodwin, Associate Professor of Education, Teachers College, Columbia University, New York, New York.
Webb, Paul E., Director of Research, Los Angeles City Schools, Los Angeles, California.
Weidemann, Charles C., Associate Professor of Education, Ohio State University, Columbus, Ohio.
Welles, J. B., Principal, State Normal School, Geneseo, New York.
West, Paul V., Professor of Education, New York University, New York, New York.
Wheat, Harry G., Professor of Education, West Virginia University, Morgantown, West Virginia.
Williams, J. Harold, Professor of Education and Dean of Summer Session, University of California at Los Angeles, Los Angeles, California.
Willing, M. H., Professor of Education, University of Wisconsin, Madison, Wisconsin.
Wilson, Guy M., Professor of Education, Boston University, Boston, Massachusetts.
Wilson, W. K., Assistant, School Building and Grounds Division, State Department of Education, Albany, New York.
Witham, Ernest C., Associate Professor of Education, Rutgers University, New Brunswick, New Jersey.
Witty, Paul A., Professor of Education, Northwestern University, Evanston, Illinois.
Wood, Ben D., Associate Professor of Collegiate Research, Columbia University, New York, New York.
Wood, E. R., Associate Professor of Psychology, New York University, New York, New York.

Woods, Elizabeth L., Supervisor, Educational Research and Guidance Section, Chamber of Commerce, Los Angeles, California.
Woods, Roy C., Professor of Education, Marshall College, Huntington, West Virginia.
Woody, Clifford, Director, Bureau of Educational Reference and Research, University of Michigan, Ann Arbor, Michigan.
Worcester, D. A., Head, Department of Educational Psychology and Measurements, University of Nebraska, Lincoln, Nebraska.
Wray, Robert P., Instructor in Mathematics, Crafton School, Crafton, Pennsylvania.
Wrenn, C. Gilbert, Assistant Director of the General College and Associate Professor of Education, University of Minnesota, Minneapolis, Minnesota.
Wright, Wendell W., Professor of Education, Indiana University, Bloomington, Indiana.
Wrightstone, J. Wayne, Research Associate, Teachers College, Columbia University, New York, New York.
Yates, Mrs. Dorothy H., Associate Professor of Psychology, San Jose State College, San Jose, California.
Yeager, William A., Professor of Administration, University of Pittsburgh, Pittsburgh, Pennsylvania.
Young, William E., Assistant Professor, School of Education, Syracuse University, Syracuse, New York.
Zirbes, Laura, Professor of Education, Ohio State University, Columbus, Ohio.